Why Visual Basic? Why the Beginner's Guide?

Visual Basic revolutionized the world of program development for Windows. Now version 4.0 is doing the same for Windows 95 and NT. What used to take hours using C and other languages, now takes minutes. A friendly and intuitive interface doesn't lessen the power and flexibility that Visual Basic offers through its extensive event-driven language, its object-based structure, and its support for OLE.

Visual Basic has a lot to offer, so there's a lot to explain; The Beginner's Guide to Visual Basic 4.0 rises to that challenge. Using a relaxed and visual style, the book takes you quickly and painlessly to outstanding results. Motivating and entertaining at every stage, it's the book that Visual Basic deserves.

What is Wrox Press?

Wrox Press is a computer book publisher which promotes a brand new concept - clear, jargon-free programming and database titles that fulfill your real demands. We publish for everyone, from the novice through to the experienced programmer. To ensure our books meet your needs, we carry out continuous research on all our titles. Through our dialog with you we can craft the book you really need.

We welcome suggestions and take all of them to heart - your input is paramount in creating the next great Wrox title. Use the reply card inside this book or mail us at:

feedback@wrox.demon.co.uk
or
Compuserve 100063, 2152

Wrox Press Ltd.   Tel: (312) 465 3559
2710 W. Touhy   Fax: (312) 465 4063
Chicago
IL 60645
USA

The Beginner's Guide to Visual Basic 4.0

Peter Wright

Wrox Press Ltd.®

The Beginner's Guide to Visual Basic 4.0

Published by Wrox Press Ltd. Unit 16, 20 James Road, Tyseley, Birmingham, B11 2BA
Printed in the USA
Library of Congress Catalog no. 95-61105

ISBN 1-874416-55-9

Trademark Acknowledgements

Wrox has endeavored to provide trademark information about all the companies and products mentioned in this book by the appropriate use of capitals. However, Wrox cannot guarantee the accuracy of this information.

Credits

Author
Peter Wright

Technical Editors
David Maclean
Alex Stockton

Series Editor
Gina Mance

Technical Reviewers
David Niemann

Managing Editor
John Franklin

Production Manager
Deb Somers

Design/Layout
Eddie Fisher
Greg Powell
Neil Gallagher
Graham Butler

Proof Readers
Melanie Orgee
Pam Brand
Emma Duncombe

Cover Design
Third Wave

For more information on Third Wave, contact Ross Alderson on 44-121 236 6616
Cover photo supplied by The Image Bank

About the Author

Peter Wright is the managing director and lead developer at Psynet Interactive Ltd, a multimedia software house specializing in the development of applications for Windows 95. To date, Psynet have been responsible for Hamster, a leading Internet front end, as well as numerous commercial multimedia Windows projects.

This book is one in a series from Peter, including *The Beginner's Guide To Visual Basic 3*, as well as a small contribution to *Instant VB3*. Due soon is *The Revolutionary Guide To Multimedia Programming in Visual Basic*, place your orders now.

Peter can be contacted by e-mail by a variety of methods, but peter@gendev.demon.co.uk is probably the safest bet. Contact Psynet Interactive at admin@gendev.demon.co.uk or psynet@msn.com.

Acknowledgements

It's a Friday night, it's very late, Aerosmith are keeping me company courtesy of the Windows 95 CD Player and the writing of the book you now have in your hands is drawing to a close. It has been a long hard slog, full of good times and bad. There were times when I wanted to simply stop and move to Barbados. There were other times when the thrill of working on products at the very leading edge of Windows technology (Windows 95, VB4 and Office 95) really drove me to press on and learn more.

Throughout it all though, there has been one source of constant encouragement - YOU. The e-mail I received after the first edition was released, the letters, the occasional phone call and the thrill of seeing someone at a show caught up in the wonder of having just learnt VB, were more instrumental in driving the writing process forward than anything else. This book was written for you, driven by you and to a great extent influenced by you. I thank you, from the bottom of my heart.

There were other people of course, some whose faces I have never seen, but who, through the wonders of e-mail, have become quite dear to me. First, my colleagues: Simon, Kees, Eric, and Richard. Your encouragement, unceasing faith in what I can accomplish, and ability to bring me down to earth every time I get mail from a reader, are invaluable. Thanks guys!

Out of sight, but never out of mind, there is, of course, Wrox. In particular my thanks to Gina for turning plain text into a work of art, and to Alex for usually provocative, but always informative, input into the technical content of the early chapters of the book. Above all though, my thanks to Dave Maclean. Through slipped deadlines, temper tantrums, late nights and early mornings you have always provided a never ending stream of support and encouragement. This book is as much a reflection of this man's vision as it is of my technical skills.

At Microsoft, my thanks to Andrew King for the information he provided at the start of the project on a new MS project called VB4, to the Microsoft Team and the WPG Beta group for providing a great product, and supporting a stream of normally distressed beta questions in the online beta forums. My thanks also to Text 100 for providing shipping copies of the products used to create the code and content in this book.

There are of course a lot of other people who helped in this book in some way, either in its content, or in shaping the way I view the world and my work. To Simon Bandy for teaching me how to catch that first wave and in turn for showing me how small we all are. To Terry and Pat, for their support, encouragement and baby-sitting services. To my father, John, for buying me that first computer, and to my late mother, Jean, for encouraging me to want to learn and explore.

As always though, and above everyone else on this list, my love and gratitude to my wife and children. To Sharon, for her patience, love and tactful withdrawals during the difficult moments. To my nine year old son Chris - more than anything else I am proud of the hard work you did so that you can read this page yourself. And finally to my three year old daughter Eloise, the true head of this household!

Read on, surf's up, I'm gone!

Peter Wright.

BEGINNER'S
VB4

Summary of Contents

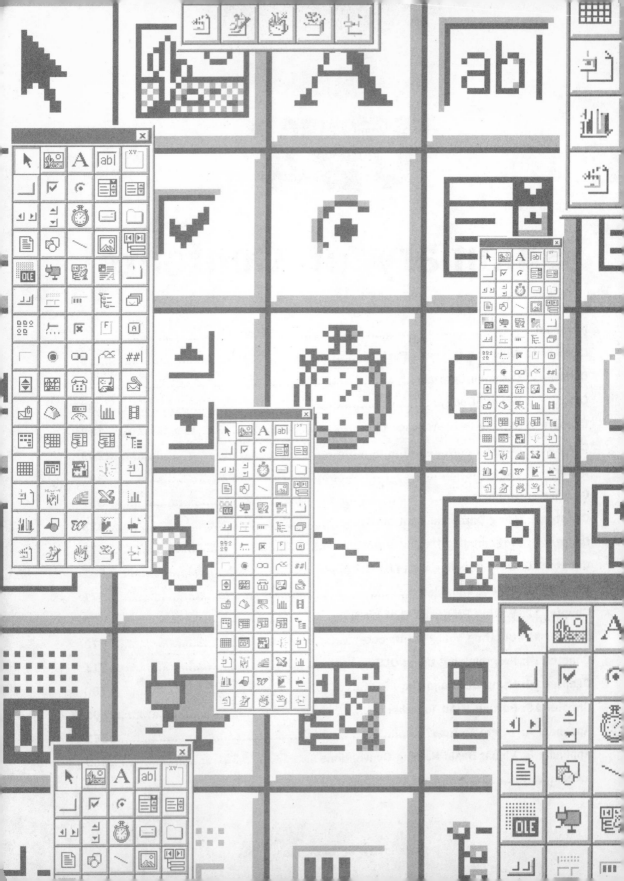

BEGINNER'S
VB4

Contents

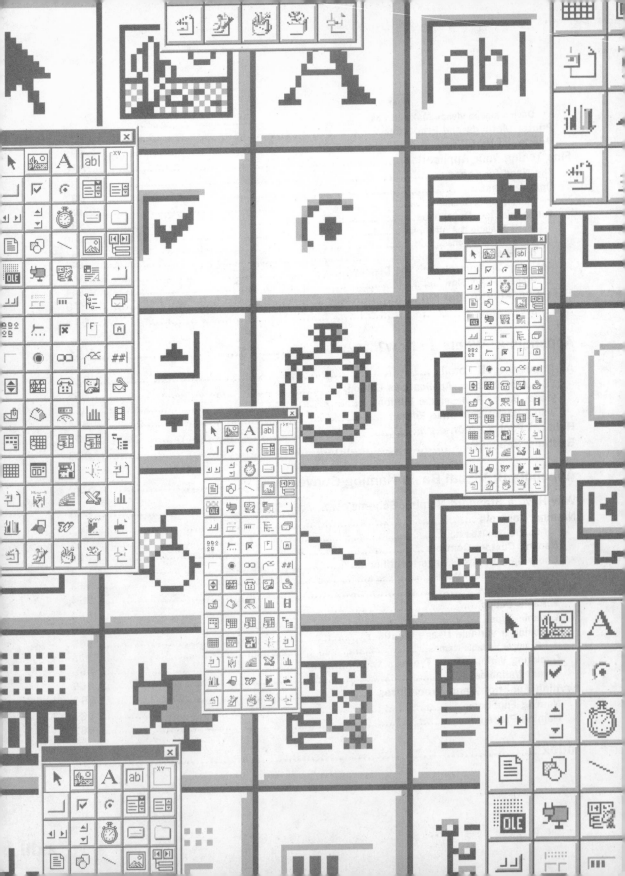

BEGINNER'S
VB4

Introduction

Who's This Book For?

This book is designed to teach you how to write useful programs in Visual Basic 4 as quickly and as easily as possible. There are two kinds of beginners for whom this is the ideal book:

- You're a **beginner to programming** and you've chosen Visual Basic as the place to start. Great choice! Visual Basic is easy, it's fun and it's also powerful. This book will hold your hand throughout.

- You can program in another language but you're a **beginner to Windows programming**. Again, great choice! Come in from the cold world of C or whatever language you use and enjoy. This book will teach you how Visual Basic does things in terms you'll understand. Along the way, I'll give you all the background information you need on Windows programming to help you to develop really professional applications.

At the risk of contradicting myself, there is also a third type of reader. If you are familiar with Visual Basic 3 and need to get up to speed on VB4, then this book can also help, though you may also want to have a look at Wrox's Instant VB4.

What's Covered in This Book

This book is about the **Standard Edition** of Visual Basic. Newcomers with the Professional and Enterprise editions can also learn a great deal, but an explanation of the features specific to these two great packages is a little beyond the scope of a beginner's book.

Visual Basic is a big baby. Take a look at the Language Reference Manual that comes in the box. That's a 500+ page manual that just lists every word in the Visual Basic lexicon, without even telling you how or when to use it. We're not going to try and look into every nook and cranny of Visual Basic. What we *are* going to do is cut a wide path through the undergrowth to a suitable clearing where we can write our own programs.

Think of this book as a tour guide to Visual Basic country. You're only here for a short period, and it's never long enough (just like a real vacation). What you *don't* want is to go down every street in town. What you *do* want is the big picture, together with enough local understanding to enable you to find your own way around without getting into tricky situations. Sure, we'll look at some of the local highlights together, but these can only ever be a taster.

So what's in the tour? There are some things you have to know, like how Visual Basic programs fit together, and what the main components are. All these fundamental building blocks are covered in detail. We then take a look at what you can actually do with Visual Basic. Just because something appears in Visual Basic doesn't mean it's in the book - we've only included those things that you can be useful to you. This book gets you where you want to go.

What's Not Covered in This Book

The things omitted from the book you can live without at this stage in your Visual Basic career. I've tried to cover all the main features of the Standard Edition, but I have avoided features unique to the Professional and Enterprise editions. On occasions, this means we have to do a little workaround to achieve something that would be easy in the more expensive versions of the product, but I've pointed these out where appropriate. Whilst the features of the bigger versions are incredibly powerful and useful, they aren't necessary for everyone. In the words of a famous Vulcan, "The needs of the many outweigh the needs of the few".

By committing ourselves to the Standard Edition, we are ignoring the 16-bit version of VB. All the code in this book is for the 32-bit version.

What's also left out of this book are a lot of formal definitions and exhaustive lists of options. Visual Basic is a rich language, and each command has a welter of options. I'm just going to tell you what you need to know at the time. There are lots of good references, like the Visual Basic Manuals and Help Screens, that can give you all the minute detail. Alternatively, take a look at Appendix A which points you in the direction of some very useful Internet newsgroups, national user groups and other great sources of help and information.

I'm also not going to tell you how to actually use Windows 95. If you haven't already installed Windows 95 and learnt about the incredible power it has to offer, then now is the time to do so. Throughout the course of the book, I assume you already know the basics of using a Windows program, such as how to select a menu option, or how to double-click something, and so on.

As Visual Basic 4 is designed to be run on a 32-bit operating system, like Windows 95 or Windows NT, all the screen shots in the book are based around Windows 95. It's a great new addition to the Windows family and if you haven't got it yet, then the price of an upgrade is really quite small, compared to the features that you get.

What You Need to Use This Book

Apart from a willingness to learn, you'll need access to a PC running Windows 95 and the Standard Edition of Visual Basic 4. Although many of the examples in the book will work under Visual Basic 3, Visual Basic 4 has a great many features that make life as a developer much easier.

In order to install and use the samples on the disk included with this book, you'll need a hard drive with at least 3 megabytes of space. It's also important that you *do* install the samples from the disk as they form an integral part of the book's tutorial style.

To install the examples disk, place the disk in your A: drive and select Run... from the Start menu. In the box type A:\Setup and click OK. From there the installation program takes over.

Conventions

We have used a number of different styles of text and layout in the book to help differentiate between the different kinds of information. Here are examples of the styles we use and an explanation of what they mean:

Try It Outs - How do They Work?

1 Each step has a number.

2 Follow the steps through.

3 Then read How It Works to find out what's going on.

▶ **Important Words** are in a bold type font.

▶ Words that appear on the screen in menus like the <u>F</u>ile or <u>W</u>indow menu are in a similar font to what you see on screen.

▶ Keys that you press on the keyboard, like *Ctrl* and *Enter*, are in italics.

▶ All filenames are in capitals, like **CONTROL.VBP**.

FYI

Advice, hints, or background information comes in boxes like this.

▶ Visual Basic code has two fonts. If it's a word that were talking about in the text, for example, when discussing the **For...Next** loop, it's in a bold font. If it's a block of code that you can type in as a program and run, then it's also in a gray box:

```
Private Sub cmdQuit_Click()
    End
End Sub
```

▶ When a line of code has been split onto two lines because of space considerations, the continuation is marked with a ↘. When typing the code in Visual Basic, you should put any lines marked like this at the end of the code on the line above.

Note that VB4 does have its own line continuation character. It's a space followed by an underscore (_). I don't think this is very clear in print, so we've stuck with the bendy arrow.

These are all designed to make sure that you know what it is you're looking at. I hope they make life easier.

How to Get the Most Out of This Book

This book is designed as a hands-on tutorial. That means you have to get your hands on the keyboard as often as possible. Throughout the book there are Try It Outs! which is where you'll find step by step instructions for creating and running a Visual Basic program. This program illustrates the concept that's currently being explained. Some of the larger Try It Outs! use code that I've already prepared for you on the companion disk.

I also use the Try It Outs! to teach you new concepts when it's better to see them in action first, rather than bury them in text. After each Try It Out! there is a How It Works section that explains what's going on. As the programs get longer, later in the book, some of the How It Works sections themselves get quite large. Please read them through, though. It's all part of the plan.

There are a lot of what technical writers call forward references in this book. These are where I say 'Don't worry about this difficult concept here. I'll explain it in Chapter *whatever*'. This kind of reckless behavior will preclude me from ever entering the Logical Writers Hall Of Fame, but frankly I don't care. What I do really care about is that you have exciting and interesting programs to play with as early as possible in the book, and to do that, I sometimes have to ask to you to take things on trust. Where I do use language elements that we haven't covered properly yet, I'll tell you. And believe me, they are all there later on, as promised.

At the end of each chapter is a list of my suggestions for ways to put the concepts you've just learnt into practice. I've found that the best way to learn is to tinker about on your own, extending current projects and creating new ones. These suggestions are just that - suggestions - so use them if you want.

When you've finished the book, the one thing you can be sure of is that you'll be hungry for more. You'll have an excellent grounding in Visual Basic, but that's only the beginning. The whole world of Visual Basic development will be at your feet. To help you decide what to do next, I've put some unashamedly personal and opinionated advice into Appendix A - Where Do We Go From Here?

Tell Us What You Think

We have tried to make this book accurate, enjoyable and honest. But what really matters is what it does for you. Please let us know your views by either returning the reply card in the back of the book, or by contacting us at Wrox Press. The easiest way is to use email:

feedback@wrox.com
http:\\www.wrox.com\
Compuserve: 100063,2152

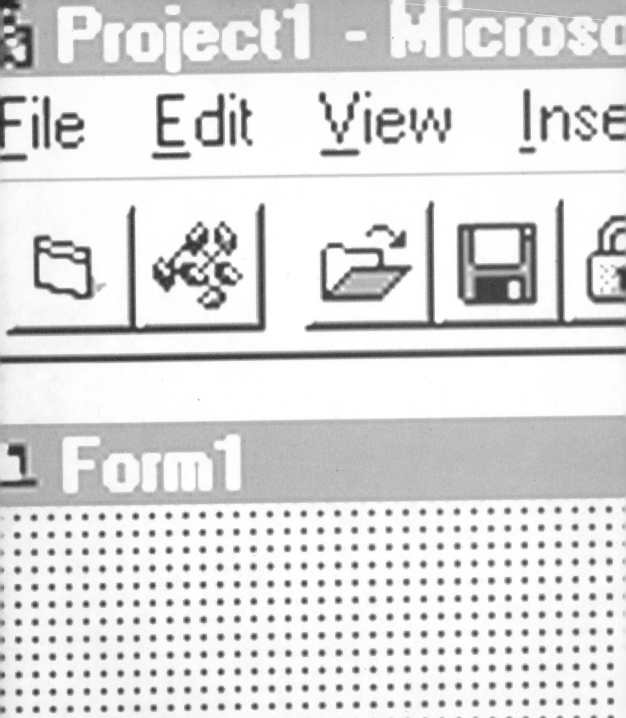

1

Welcome to Visual Basic

As you will hear time and time again in this book and other journals, the best way to learn about something as interactive as Visual Basic is to actually sit down at a computer and try things out. In this chapter you will do just that.

You will learn about:

▶ The Visual Basic desktop.

▶ What makes up a Visual Basic program.

▶ Event-driven programming, and how it works in Visual Basic.

▶ How to write actual code in Visual Basic, and where to put it.

▶ How to design, create, install and run a complete Visual Basic application.

A Quick Tour of Visual Basic

We'll kick off by getting comfortable with the Visual Basic environment, before having a go at creating a complete Visual Basic application from start to finish. The program we'll create will hardly be a program at all, but in experimenting with it you will get an all-round feel for what Visual Basic has to offer.

After a brief tour of the Visual Basic desktop, we will take a good look at **forms**, the mainstay of any Visual Basic program. We'll experiment with properties and even write a small amount of code. Once you have created a real Windows application, you will learn how to save all the components of your program as a Visual Basic project. Finally, you will create an executable program that can be run outside of Visual Basic. Along the way we will look at some of the unique design features that make Visual Basic such an exciting programming tool.

Fasten your seatbelt, we are going on a lightning tour of Visual Basic!

The Opening Visual Basic Screen

When you click on the Visual Basic icon to load and run Visual Basic, a confusing array of windows, icons and scroll bars appears, overlaying the Windows 95 desktop.

Title bar

Menu bar

Menu Toolbar

Project Window

Properties Window

Toolbox

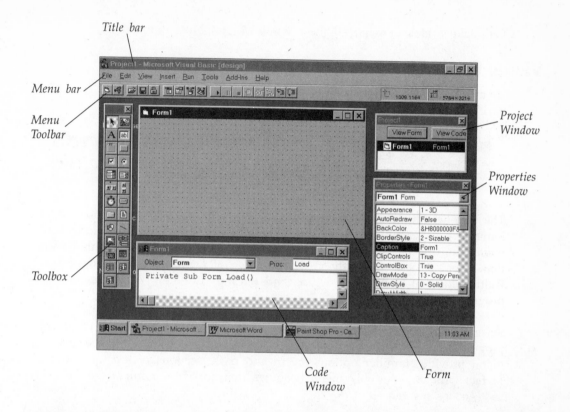

Code Window

Form

FYI

Don't panic if your screen appears different to the one pictured here. Visual Basic remembers how the windows and toolbars were arranged on the screen the last time it was used, and automatically sets itself up in the same way each time you run it. To be honest, the way that Visual Basic overlays any other program you may have hiding in the background is distracting if not downright annoying. Many Visual Basic developers prefer to minimize all other Windows applications that might be running in order to keep the screen as uncluttered as possible.

Let's take a look at what all these windows and buttons mean.

Visual Basic Menus

At the top of the screen, just as with any other Windows program, you have the title bar and menus.

The title bar shows you that you are currently in Microsoft Visual Basic, and reminds you exactly what you are doing. On my screen, and hopefully on yours, the title bar reads Project 1 - Microsoft Visual Basic [design]. This means that Visual Basic is currently in design mode of a project called Project 1, waiting for you to begin designing and writing your new Windows program.

Since it was written by Microsoft, Visual Basic is a truly standard Windows program. The File menu allows you to load and save your work, the Edit menu provides familiar options to cut and paste sections of text, and so on. In fact, probably the only menu headings that appear unfamiliar are the Run and Add-Ins menus.

We will cover all of the menu headings in detail later on in the book. However, the Add-Ins item is particularly interesting since it illustrates the power of Visual Basic. If you have used Microsoft Access before then you will already have come across the concept of an add-in: it's a plug-in program which is able to take control of some aspect of the program you are using. In our case an add-in is a program which bolts on to Visual Basic and extends the way in which it works. The important point here is that not only is Visual Basic a powerful, extensible development tool, but that the add-ins that ship with Visual Basic were actually written in Visual Basic themselves. There is no better advertisement for its power than the fact that certain parts of Visual Basic were themselves written in Visual Basic.

All of the menus work just as they would in any other Windows program. If you point at the File menu, for example, and click the left mouse button once, a list of options for dealing with files appears:

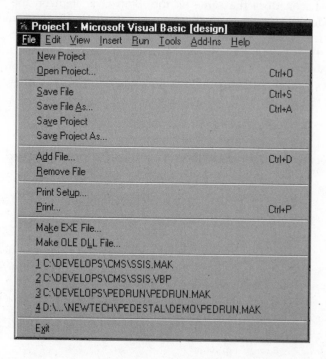

Don't worry too much at the moment about what all the menu headings and options mean - the easiest way to learn Visual Basic is by trying it out. And that's exactly what we are going to do.

The Toolbar

Underneath the menu headings is a rather complex-looking toolbar.

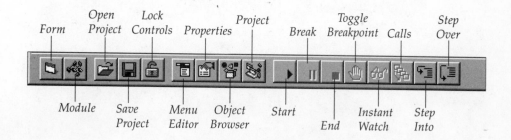

The icons on the toolbar provide an easy way for you to perform common operations without having to plow through the menus. For example, the leftmost icon does the same as the Form item on the Insert menu, and the rightmost icon does the same as the Step Over item on the Run menu.
Again, don't worry too much about what all the buttons mean at this stage; you'll pick them up with ease when we write a simple program later on.
For the time being, though, you can get a simple explanation of each button by simply leaving the cursor over a button for a few seconds; a standard Windows tooltip pops up telling you what the button does.

Forms

In the center of the screen there is a blank window entitled Form1.

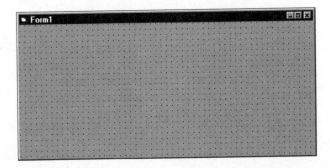

Forms are central to everything you do in Visual Basic. When your program is running, the user sees the forms as normal windows. In these windows the user selects menu options, clicks icons that you have drawn, or enters data into text boxes you have arranged.

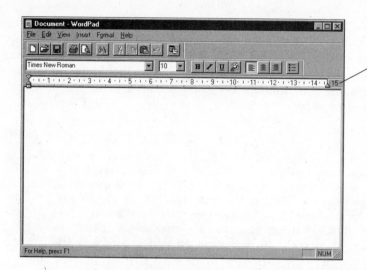

The window in which this typical application operates is derived from a form. It's your job as a programmer to get to such a point from the blank form you see on your screen.

We can compare the process of writing a Visual Basic program to the job of an artist. The artist starts with a blank piece of canvas. In our case, this would be the form. The artist, equipped with a palette of different colors and brushes, then begins to lay down images on his canvas. In the same way, Visual Basic programmers lay down **controls**, such as command buttons, text boxes and so on, onto their 'canvas' - the form. When the work is complete, the artist exhibits his masterpiece to a waiting public who see not a canvas sheet, but a painting. When the Visual Basic programs are complete, they are shipped to the user who sees the elements of a Windows application and not empty and confusing Visual Basic forms.

Visual Basic Program Code

There are two sides to forms: what appears in the Form Window and what does not appear. Your user sees and interacts with the visible aspect. The invisible aspect is the form **code**. This is program text which you enter to tell the computer exactly what you want the program to do.

If you have never written a computer program before, code is the collection of English-like commands which tell the computer what to do step-by-step. In the past, programmers spent hours keying in page after page of program code before seeing anything actually work on screen. Thankfully, times have changed and the amount of traditional coding required in writing a Visual Basic program is very small.

FYI

If you have already come across other programming languages, such as C, Pascal or even the original BASIC, then you are in for an easy ride. The Visual Basic language is really a hybrid of these languages incorporating many of their best features, as well as features from older languages such as Algol and Fortran. However, the strongest influence in Visual Basic is, as its name suggests, the BASIC programming language. If you have already come across BASIC, the structure of the programs we'll write later on will appear very familiar, even if the commands themselves look somewhat alien.

Viewing the Code Window

Try It Out!

It is likely that the window missing from your screen at the moment is the Code Window. This doesn't normally appear immediately when you start Visual Basic, so let's make it appear.

▶ Move the mouse over the form on your screen, and double-click the left mouse button.

The Code Window will appear for whatever control or form you select, in this case your form labeled Form1.

You type in code here.

Close the window by clicking the Close button in the top right corner of the window, or by pressing Alt-F4.

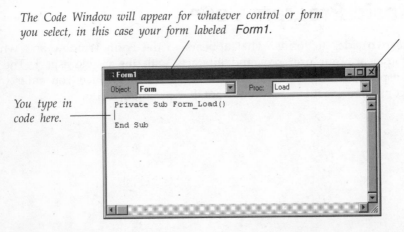

```
Private Sub Form_Load()
|
End Sub
```

You can also use function keys to open the Code Window.

▶ Move the mouse to the control or form whose Code Window you want to look at, and click the left mouse button once to select it, then press *F7*.

You can even use the Project Window to bring up the Code Window:

▶ If the Project Window isn't visible, select Project from the View menu. When it appears, click on the name of your form once, and then click on the View Code command button. Once again, the Code Window pops into view.

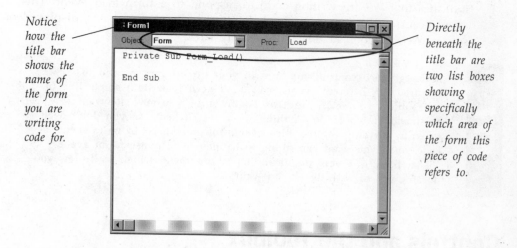

Notice how the title bar shows the name of the form you are writing code for.

Directly beneath the title bar are two list boxes showing specifically which area of the form this piece of code refers to.

Objects and Events

In Visual Basic the majority of the code you write deals with a combination of two things: objects and their events.

▶ **Objects** are the elements that make up your program's user interface. Forms and controls (such as command boxes and radio buttons) are all classed as objects.

▶ **Events** are the actions which are performed on a particular object, usually as a result of the user doing something. For example, if a user clicks a command button in your program, Visual Basic translates this action into a **click** event, and runs the code you have written to handle this event.

Event Handlers

The two list boxes at the top of the Code Window simply give you additional information on what exactly you are writing code for. The list box on the left, labeled Object:, shows that we are writing code for the form object itself. The list box on the right, labeled Proc: (for **procedure**), indicates that we are writing code to respond to a form load event. This event occurs when a form is loaded into memory before being displayed on screen. We will look at this more closely later.

FYI

Although each control and form in your project can respond to hundreds of different events, you don't need to write a single line of code unless you really want to. For instance, you may not want a command button to do anything when it's clicked - so you don't need to write anything for the click event. You only need to write event code when you want something to happen in response to an event. Visual Basic is a very undemanding environment, which really lets you do as much or as little as you want.

Controls and the Toolbox

The next stop on our whirlwind tour of the Visual Basic environment is the toolbox.

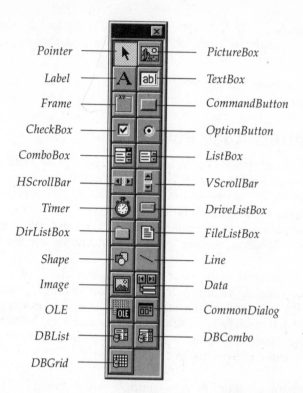

The toolbox contains icons for each control you can draw on your form. Controls put the Visual into Visual Basic. You use controls in Windows all the time: typing into text boxes, clicking option buttons and so on. In fact, almost every functional element of a Windows program is a control.

Each control, such as text boxes or command buttons, has three aspects to it:

> ▶ A graphical representation that you see when you click on an icon in the toolbox and then place the control onto your form.

19

▶ Properties which govern the way it looks and behaves, determining for example its color, shape, size, the text that appears as a caption, and so on.

▶ Event codes which are Visual Basic commands you enter to tell a control what to do when it is clicked, moved or dragged over.

Adding Controls Adds Power

If you are using either the Professional or Enterprise Editions of Visual Basic, you will find that there are a great many more icons in your tool palette than in the above screen shot. Enhanced 3D versions of many of the standard controls will be included, as will be controls for drawing graphs, playing sampled sounds, communicating over modems, animating icons and many more. However, we are going to concentrate on the Standard Edition.

One of the strongest features of Visual Basic is the way in which you can heighten its capabilities through the addition of more powerful controls. Controls that you add to the standard toolbox are known as **custom controls**, and they may be **OCXs (OLE controls)** or **VBXs (Visual Basic eXtensions)**. These are actually files on your hard disk which usually have these three letter extensions to their file name.

Many companies supply custom controls which greatly enhance Visual Basic. Adding these controls to your project makes additional icons appear in the toolbox. The range of controls available is staggering, with companies supplying OCXs and VBXs to do everything from providing enhanced database support, to printing bar-codes, or displaying the latest type of graphics file. Take a look at the toolbox below. This has a number of controls which aren't included with either the standard or professional editions of Visual Basic.

You won't recognize these controls as they are custom controls that I have added to my toolbox.

So what's the difference between an OCX and a VBX? Essentially they represent two different Microsoft standards for component-based software development. The VBX standard is the older and less flexible of the two. VBX controls work well in 16-bit operating systems like Windows 3.1, but not too well in a 32-bit environment such as Windows 95 or Windows NT.

Although Visual Basic can support all formats of VBX, they are tough to incorporate into other development environments.

OCXs, on the other hand, can be plugged into any development environment that makes use of the OLE 2 standard. Microsoft is also encouraging developers to provide both 16-bit and 32-bit versions of their controls. This means that software developers can work with OCXs safe in the knowledge that, should the need arise, the tools they use can be transferred to other development environments as well as to other operating systems.

The moral of the story is simple. If you are going to develop applications that you want to run on both Windows 95 and Windows 3.1, then go for OCX. If you are certain that the apps you are going to write will only need to work on 16-bit Windows platforms, then use whatever is available to you, be it OCX or VBX. Throughout the rest of this book, though, we will be concentrating on OCX.

We will see how to incorporate add-in components into your applications a little later.

The Project Window

To understand how useful the **Project Window** is, you need to understand what makes up a project in Visual Basic.

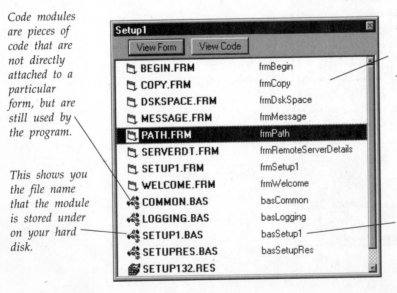

Code modules are pieces of code that are not directly attached to a particular form, but are still used by the program.

This shows you the file name that the module is stored under on your hard disk.

Forms include all the code that is directly attached to that form and the controls placed on it, provided that these controls are standard parts of Visual Basic.

This is the name that you use to refer to your module in code.

A project is a collection of forms, code modules and class modules. We've loosely covered what forms and code modules are, but classes?? Sounds ugly...

FYI

Actually, classes are a bit tricky. I can't lie to you about this. They are one of the new features that Microsoft have introduced in this version of Visual Basic that just get more powerful the more you understand about them, so getting to grips with them is worth the effort. We will take a close look at them in Chapter 13, but if it helps now, think of a class module as a template for an object. It's sort of like a mold. You can create class modules and then in the rest of your code use the objects created from this mold just as you would any other object in your program, such as a form or component. You don't use the class module itself directly, but you do use it to create useful objects. Anyway, don't worry. It can be part of a project and that's that for now.

Each form, code module or class module is stored on the hard disk as a separate file with its own file name. In addition, each module, class and form can have a different name which you use to refer to it in code. You can see this in our screen shot of the Project Window: the highlighted line shows a form with a filename of **PATH.FRM**, but you would refer to it in code as **frmPath**.

The Project Window simply shows you a list of all the files in your project. By double-clicking the name of a form in the Project Window, the form appears on screen. By highlighting a form in the Project Window and hitting the View Code button, the form's code appears on screen.

In keeping with the Windows 95 standard, you can also select a file in the Project Window and press the right mouse button to bring up a menu with a range of options, allowing you to choose what you want to see, whether or not you want to save the file, remove it from the project and so on. Try it here and on other areas of the Visual Basic environment to see what I mean.

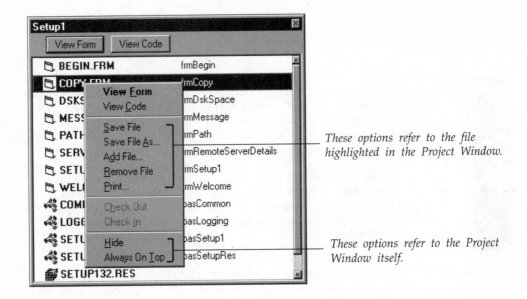

These options refer to the file highlighted in the Project Window.

These options refer to the Project Window itself.

The Project VBP File

The Project Window is really a viewer for a file on your hard disk with the extension **VBP**. This is the Visual Basic Project file and tells Visual Basic which forms, modules and so on, are used in your project. The project's file name can be anything you want, but it normally ends in the letters .**VBP**. It still works OK if you call it something else, but that seems a great way to sow the seeds of total confusion to me.

The file itself is a straight text file that contains the settings for all the environment variables and file names for the complete project. It doesn't contain the actual project files in the way that, say, an Access **MDB** file does. You can open up a **VBP** file in Notepad and take a look. However, if you play with the settings and crash the system then that's your own fault.

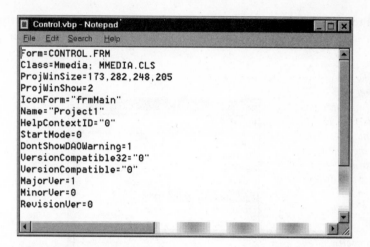

```
Control.vbp - Notepad
File   Edit   Search   Help
Form=CONTROL.FRM
Class=Mmedia; MMEDIA.CLS
ProjWinSize=173,282,248,205
ProjWinShow=2
IconForm="frmMain"
Name="Project1"
HelpContextID="0"
StartMode=0
DontShowDAOWarning=1
VersionCompatible32="0"
VersionCompatible="0"
MajorVer=1
MinorVer=0
RevisionVer=0
```

The Properties Window

Every form and control has properties. Even some objects that you can't manipulate at all at design-time, such as the screen and the printer, have properties. Properties control the appearance and behavior of the objects in Visual Basic. These are some of the ways that forms can be customized using their properties.

This text is set by the Caption property.

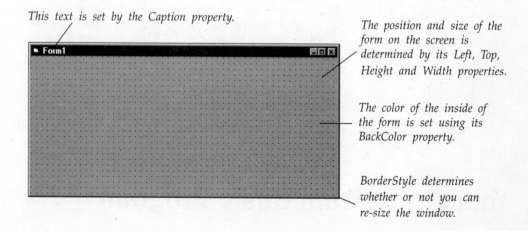

The position and size of the form on the screen is determined by its Left, Top, Height and Width properties.

The color of the inside of the form is set using its BackColor property.

BorderStyle determines whether or not you can re-size the window.

The **Properties Window** allows you to set and view the properties of your forms and controls at design-time (before you actually run your program).

The object box tells you which control or form you are referring to. You can get a list of all the objects on your form by clicking the little arrow at the side.

This property is highlighted, ready for editing.

Each property has a standard name. You can change properties in here manually at design-time, or with your code at run-time.

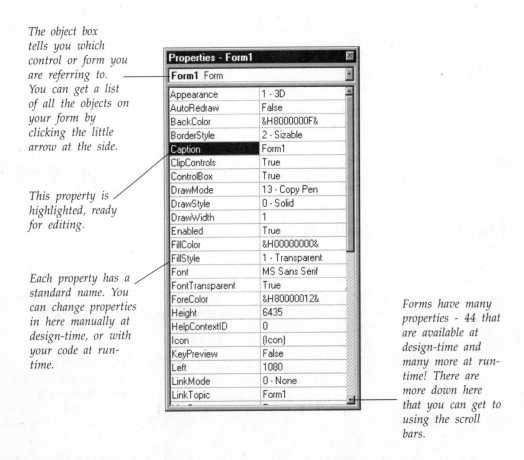

Forms have many properties - 44 that are available at design-time and many more at run-time! There are more down here that you can get to using the scroll bars.

By far the best way to get to grips with properties is to use them. We will do this in the next section.

Your First Visual Basic Program

Having had a quick look around, it's time to see just how easy it is to produce Windows programs using Visual Basic. The program we will write is extremely simple, but it will serve to illustrate all the major steps we are going to take in subsequent chapters when we write real Visual Basic programs.

Filling Out the Forms

Forms are not the passive background canvas that our painting analogy suggests. With a multitude of different properties that can be manipulated, and a host of events to respond to, they are the foundation of your program. In this section, we'll get a glimpse of what forms can do.

Customizing Your Forms

1 If you don't currently have Visual Basic running, then run it by selecting it from the Windows 95 Start Menu. (If you intend to work a lot with Visual Basic then it may be a good idea to make a shortcut to it on the Windows 95 desktop - consult the Windows 95 manuals or on-line help for information on how to do this.)

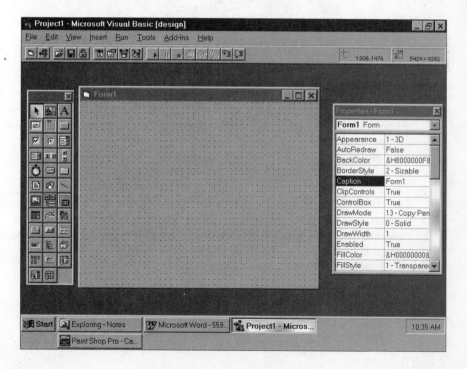

2 Although the form you work with in Visual Basic at design-time is supposed to closely resemble the form in the final program, the reality is somewhat different. To see this, run the current project by doing one of the following:

▶ Hit *F5*

▶ Or click on the Start button on the toolbar

▶ Or select <u>S</u>tart from the <u>R</u>un menu.

After a short pause the program will run and the main form will be displayed.

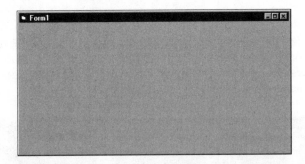

At this stage you will notice three things. First of all the window looks almost identical to the way the form looks when you are in design mode, except the pattern of dots normally displayed over the form in design mode has vanished. Secondly, the title bar of Visual Basic has now changed to show Microsoft Visual Basic [run] to indicate that the program is now running.

The third difference is a little more subtle. Even though we have not written any code, or placed anything functional on the form, the program still has a surprising amount of functionality. You can move and re-size the form just as you would a window in any other program.

You can also click the minimize and maximize buttons in the top right corner of the form to dramatically increase its size or turn it into an icon on the Windows 95 taskbar. Also, clicking the control box in the top left corner once brings up the standard Windows control menu, allowing you to quit the application, or again change the size of the window.

To write an equivalent program in a language such as C would require in excess of 150 lines of code. That's about the same number of pages on a printout as you have so far covered in this chapter!

3 To stop the program running, either:

▶ Click the End icon in the Visual Basic toolbar

▶ Close the window by clicking the close button in the top right corner.

▶ Press *Alt-F4*.

▶ Or select End from the Run menu.

Programming Using Properties

Once the program has stopped running and Visual Basic has reverted to design mode, we can take a look at the properties of our new form. If the Properties Window isn't visible, you can display it by:

▶ Clicking once on the form to select it as the current object and then pressing *F4* to display the Properties Window with the properties for the current form. (You can tell when a particular window is selected as its title bar is highlighted.)

▶ Selecting Properties from the View menu.

▶ Or by right-clicking the form to bring up a pop-up menu, and selecting Properties from the bottom of it.

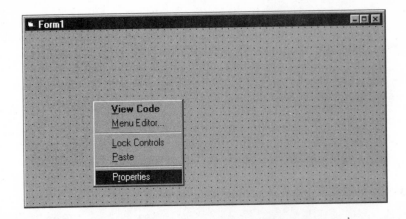

Changing a Property

1 Click on the form to select it and then press *F4* to display the Properties Window. Then move to the ControlBox property either by using the scroll bar on the right of the Properties Window or by pressing *Shift+Ctrl+C*. Pressing this key combination will move you to the first property in the list beginning with the letter C - if you keep on pressing *Shift+Ctrl+C*, the highlight will move again and soon fall on the ControlBox property. This property defines whether a control box (the icon in the top left corner of the window that allows you to re-size and close it) will be placed on the form at run-time.

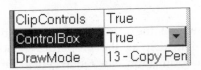

2 To the right of the words Control Box you will see the word True. This means that there is a control box attached to the form at present. Change this to False by double-clicking the word True, by clicking the arrow to the right of the property and selecting a value from the drop-down list, or by typing the word directly into the box.

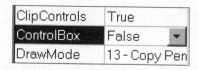

3 Did you notice that nothing actually changed on the form on screen? Now run the program again, either by pressing *F5* or by clicking the Start button. See how different the form looks now?

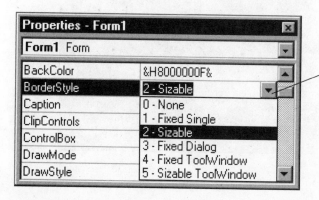

*There is no way to close the form now, other than by clicking the **End** icon on the Visual Basic toolbar. The maximize and minimize buttons are also gone, although you can still maximize it and normalize it by double-clicking on its title bar.*

You can still drag the form around the screen and re-size it by dragging the borders.

4 Stop the program. Now find the property called BorderStyle. The text to the right of the property name should say 2 - Sizable.

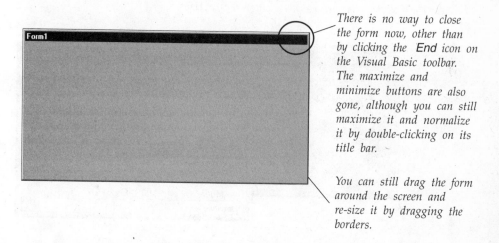

You can see all the alternatives for the property by clicking the arrow at the side to drop down the list box.

5 Keep double-clicking the BorderStyle field until it says 1 - Fixed Single, or click on the arrow and select this option. Nothing appears to have changed on the form at the moment.

6 Now find the Caption property. Click on the text that says Form1 and press *BkSp* to delete the current caption.

This time your form does change in design mode.
The title bar changes as you change the caption.

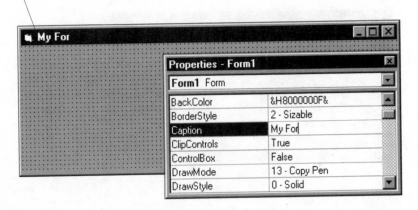

7 The rest of our form doesn't seem so different at design-time. Press *F5* to run your application to see what it looks like at run-time.

The result should be a plain box with a single line border round the outside. There is no way to move this window, re-size it, or close it. Since you deleted the form's caption, Visual Basic automatically decides not to give the form a title bar. To stop the program click on the Visual Basic End icon again.

Changing Properties Interactively

Certain properties of your form can be changed without you even noticing it. For example, with Visual Basic in design mode, dragging the form to a new position, or changing its size will cause the Width, Height, Top and Left properties to change. This is an important point to remember. By simply moving the form around in design mode you are actually programming Visual Basic by telling it to display the form in a different position. If you re-size the form, the new size will be adopted by the window in the running program; if you move the form, the window the user sees will appear in the same position on their screen as the form does on yours.

Of course, simply being able to change the caption or border type of a form doesn't really make for a best-selling Windows program. Real functionality can be added to your programs by adding code to handle the form's **events**.

Event-Driven Programming

Events are what sets Visual Basic apart from other versions of the BASIC programming language, or languages such as C and Pascal. When a traditional BASIC or C program is run, the computer trots through the program code line by line, starting at the top and following a specific route, defined by the programmer, to the end. In Visual Basic, the program starts by displaying a form or by executing a small fragment of code. However, from that point onwards, it's the user who determines which parts of the program code are run next.

A New Way of Thinking

Think about making a cup of coffee. In a traditional programming language you could write a program to make a cup of coffee as follows:

1 Fill kettle with water.

2 Put kettle on.

3 Place coffee in cup.

4 Place milk in cup.

5 Wait until kettle has boiled.

6 Pour water into cup.

This is pretty simple stuff to follow. A good way to think of the same task in Visual Basic is:

1 Show coffee, kettle, water, milk and cup to user.

2 Let user make the coffee.

The user can use each of the components shown, in whatever sequence he or she wants, in order to make the coffee. As a programmer in this situation, you would just provide small fragments of code to handle specific events. For example, when the user turns the kettle on, Visual Basic will run the code you have written to deal with that particular event, which would probably involve heating up the water, and such like. The actual order of events required to end up with a cup of coffee is left to the user to decide, not forced on them by the programmer.

Object-Oriented Programming

In addition to event-driven programming, Visual Basic 4 is one of the first Windows development systems to support OOP - object-oriented programming.

If you are regular reader of serious computer magazines, then you will have already come across the term OOP many times. But what does it mean?

Well, traditionally, programmers would write programs that were called **structured** programs. The program would be designed to solve one big problem, but the programmers would break the problem down into smaller, more manageable problems and write small sections of code to solve each one.

OOP is the natural successor to this way of programming. Instead of simply breaking the problem down into smaller problems, OO programmers break the problem down into objects, each with a life of their own. For example, a Space Invaders game would typically have an **Alien** object. Just like an object in real life, this **Alien** object would have certain characteristics (properties) and certain functions that it is able to perform (methods). The programmer would then have to figure out what properties an object needs to function, and the methods necessary to bring it to life.

In the case of our **Alien**, the properties might include **x** and **y** coordinate properties to define its position on the screen, along with **Move**, **Fire** and **Die** methods. Visual Basic lets you define templates for objects in the form of class modules. You can then turn these templates into real objects.

Defining the class is rather like talking to an alien and saying "A human looks like this, can do such and such" and so on. Turning the class into a particular object (known as **instantiation** or creating an **instance** of an object) is like saying "...hey, and there goes one now!".

We take a look at object-oriented programming in greater detail a little later in the book.

Making the Transition to Event-Driven Programming

You can write code with Visual Basic in the traditional way, but it serves no purpose. Users will be using your Visual Basic program because they like the flexibility of Windows. They enjoy the freedom to do what they want, when they want. Besides, writing a traditional (let's just call it old-fashioned) program in Visual Basic actually requires a great deal more effort than writing an event-driven one. The net result of all your extra effort is a program that users hate and refuse to use!

Comparing DOS and Windows Applications

1 When you install the sample programs from the disk, a program called **AGE.EXE** is installed along with the Visual Basic stuff (see the **Introduction** for details of how to install the programs). Open a DOS window by clicking the MS-DOS Prompt icon.

2 Change to the directory where you installed the samples (by using the DOS **cd** command like in the screenshot below) and type AGE. Then press *Enter*.

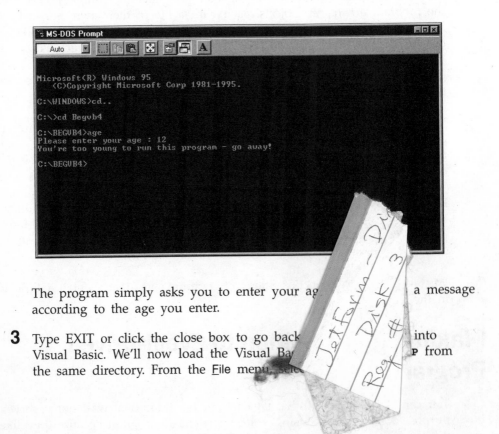

The program simply asks you to enter your ag_____ a message according to the age you enter.

3 Type EXIT or click the close box to go back_____ into Visual Basic. We'll now load the Visual Ba_____ P from the same directory. From the File menu_____

4 Since we have made changes to the form's properties, Visual Basic will check with you whether or not you want to save your work on disk.

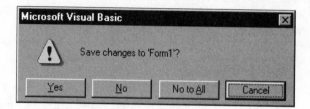

Click on the No button when asked if you want to save the form.

5 In the Open Project dialog box, use the list boxes to select the **AGE.VBP** project from the same directory as before and load it.

6 When you have loaded the project, run it in the normal way.

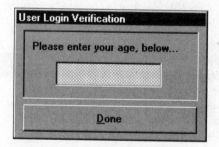

See the difference!

Where Code Fits in Visual Basic

This diagram illustrates exactly how the user, your form and your form's event code all fit together in Windows.

All controls in a Visual Basic program (such as text boxes, command buttons and forms) have a set of pre-defined events which you can add code to. With forms, for example, there is a `Load` event that is triggered the first time the form is loaded up and displayed. You can add code to this event to do various jobs at set-up time, like positioning the form automatically, or displaying some standard values on the form, and so on. There is also an `Unload` event that is triggered when the form is closed down. Each code fragment is called an **event handler**.

Your First Visual Basic Event Handler

Time to write some code I think! As we have just mentioned, each form has certain events associated with it, one of the most important of which is the `Load` event. The `Load` event is triggered whenever a form is first loaded and just before it is displayed. A common use for this event is to center the form - this is done by placing code in the `Load` event which uses the form's `Top` and `Left` properties to update the form's position in relation to the screen. We will use this feature to create a simple program which places today's date in the center of the screen.

Writing an Event Handler

Try It Out!

1 If Visual Basic is not running, then load it up now. If you have followed the examples so far, then start afresh by selecting New Project from the File menu.

2 Click on the No button when asked if you want to save the form and again when asked if you want to save the project.

3 After a short pause you will end up with a new project complete with a clean, new form.

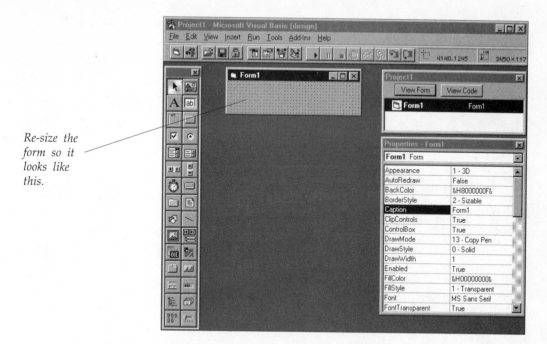

Re-size the form so it looks like this.

4 Next, we need somewhere to display the date. The easiest way to do this in Visual Basic is to place a label control onto your form, and then put the value of today's date into it.

FYI

A control in Visual Basic is an object that sits on your form. They have particular functions. This sounds a bit general, but that's just what controls are - general. They range from buttons, to lists, to more specialized controls that access databases. Adding a control to your form allows you to use the facilities of that control in your program. We want to show some text on the form, so the label control will allow us to do that. Chapter 2 gives you a proper introduction to controls, but for now, just take it step by step, and we'll cover the bigger picture later.

To add the label control to your form, click on its icon in the toolbox.

5 Now use the cross-hair cursor to draw a box on the form which is the shape and size you want for the label, holding down your mouse button all the time as you draw. In this case, make it about this size.

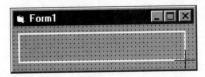

6 When it's the right size, release the mouse button and the label appears.

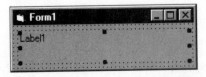

Visual Basic has named the control Label1, the default name for a label control. We'll use this name to address the control in our code.

7 Let's run the program now for the hell of it and see what it looks like. Press *F5* or hit the Start button on the tool bar.

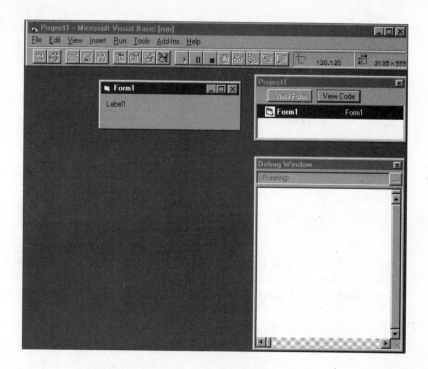

8 Stop the program by clicking the End button on the toolbar. We now need to add some code to the project to center the form, and to place today's date into the label. When you want to add code to a form or other object, the easiest way to display the Code Window is to simply double-click the object itself. A Code Window will appear with the top of the window showing the object that you double-clicked and a default event which you can write code for.

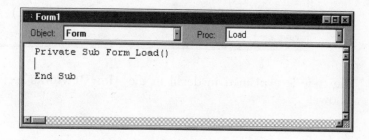

9 Clicking the down arrow to the right of the word Load will show a list of all the events that can happen to a form.

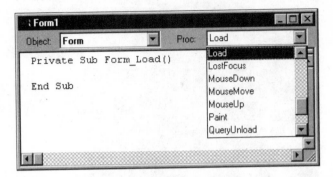

For now though, just keep Load selected. The main area of the Code Window shows the code that makes up this event's subprocedure. A subprocedure is a piece of code that performs a specific operation.

10 Click in the Code Window and type in code so that the subprocedure looks like this.

```
Private Sub Form_Load()

    Form1.Left = (Screen.Width - Form1.Width) \ 2
    Form1.Top = (Screen.Height - Form1.Height) \ 2

    Label1.Caption = "Today is " & Date

End Sub
```

The code is explained in detail in the **How It Works** section that follows.

In future, I may not show you a screenshot of exactly how the Code Window should look. Use the Object and Proc list boxes to find the object and event you need to write code for - you will find it all too easy to just bring up a Code Window, type a couple of screens full of code and then find you have put it in the wrong event. Always check where you are, and where you should be!

11 Try running the program now by pressing *F5* or clicking the Start icon (from now on I will assume that you can remember how to run a program). The form will appear on screen as in the other examples, except now it will always appear dead center of the screen. In it is today's date.

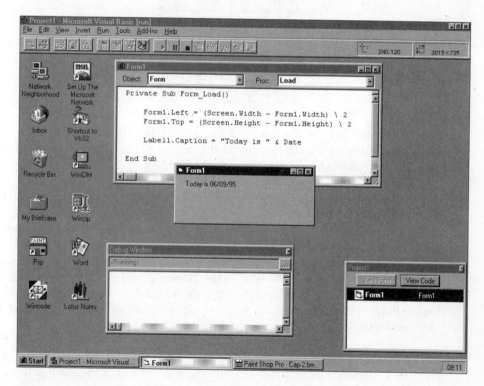

Stop the program running by clicking the form's close box.

Typing In Code

Newcomers often get concerned about the way their code looks in the Code Window.

As far as Visual Basic is concerned, though, as long as you spell the commands correctly, and put spaces between each command, then it doesn't really care how you go about arranging your code. If you type something incorrectly, Visual Basic will tell you straight away. For example, try changing the minus signs (-) to the word "minus". When you move to the next line, you should see the following:

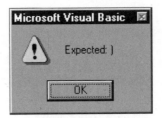

If you now hit the OK button on this dialog box, Visual Basic returns you to the Code Window and highlights the offending lines. Change the lines back to how they should be.

As a rule, indenting using the *Tab* key makes blocks of your code stand out clearly. This is a real help when it comes to debugging. Visual Basic gets upset if you treat the Code Window like a wordprocessor. Single commands, such as those in the example above, must be kept on the same line. If you reach the right-hand edge of the code window when you are typing, don't panic and don't press *Enter*! The Code Window will scroll to keep up with your typing. Often, if you do hit *Enter* in the middle of a line of code, Visual Basic will wake you up with an error message complaining that it can't understand what you are trying to say.

Visual Basic also helps you by doing its best to format all your lines of code in a standard way. It spaces out your code and adds capital letters to words it recognizes. This makes for neater and safer code.

The other important issue when writing event code is not to delete the first or last lines of code - that is, the line beginning with **Private Sub** and the line that says **End Sub**. If you do delete them, Visual Basic won't know where your code starts and ends, so you'll have to re-type them again yourself.

How It Works

Let's take a look at the `Form_Load()` event line by line.

```
Private Sub Form_Load()

  Form1.Left =(Screen.Width - Form1.Width) \ 2
  Form1.Top =(Screen.Height - Form1.Height) \ 2

  Label1.Caption = "Today is " & Date

End Sub
```

The first line, `Private Sub Form_Load()`, tells Visual Basic where the code for the load event actually starts. The `Sub` command tells Visual Basic that the code is a **subprocedure.** There is another kind of code block in Visual Basic known as a **function.** We will cover this in Chapter 12. `Private` means that this piece of code is only visible to other bits of code attached to the same form or module. This is important and we'll cover it later when we talk about the big picture of what goes where in a project. For now, just ignore it.

The `Form_Load` bit is the name of the subprocedure. Visual Basic automatically names any event code you write to indicate the object it deals with and the event that will trigger its execution: in this case `form` and `load.`

The two brackets `()` are used to hold something called **parameters.** These are values that are passed to a procedure to allow it to do its job, such as two numbers to be added together. In this case no parameters are needed. Don't worry about this now, it will all become clear later in the book.

The next line sets the Left property of the object called `Form1`.

```
Form1.Left =(Screen.Width - Form1.Width) \ 2
```

`Left` is one of the properties of a form that you can select and change with the Properties Window. In general, if you can change a property at design-time, you can also change it at run-time through your code (the reverse isn't always true, however - you'll see that there are some properties available at run-time that don't appear in the Properties Window).

This particular line of code sets the `Left` property of the form by subtracting its width, `Form1.Width`, from the screen's width, `Screen.Width`. The result is then divided by two to give the position of the left edge. If that all seems a little weird, don't panic! As long as you understand that you can both read and write properties through code, that's the important point. The math is not really crucial to Visual Basic; in fact this particular piece of code is one of hundreds of standard routines you'll probably come across in magazines, books, bulletin boards and so on.

This calculation causes the form's horizontal position to be dead center of the screen. `Form1` is the default name given to our form. We could change it, but for now it's OK as it is. Notice the periods in the middle of `Form1.Left` and `Screen.Width`. When dealing with properties in code, Visual Basic must know both the name of the object whose properties you wish to change and the property itself. The two are separated by a period. In the example here, we are dealing with two objects, one called `Form1`, which is our form, the other called `Screen`, which is what Visual Basic calls the screen (surprise, surprise!). The `Left` property is a number which tells Visual Basic where the left edge of the control should appear.

The screen is actually arranged like a piece of graph paper with each tiny dot on the screen being numbered from 0 to whatever across the screen from the left, and from 0 to whatever down the screen from the top. I say 'whatever' because the maximum value across or down the screen can change depending on the way you have Windows set up on your machine and on which coordinate system you are using. Coordinate systems are covered much later in the chapter on graphics. For now, let Visual Basic handle the details in the background.

The next line of code does roughly the same as the previous one, although this time it positions the top edge of the form so that the form is now centered vertically as well as horizontally.

The line of code that inserts today's date into the label looks like this:

```
Label1.Caption = "Today is " & Date
```

There's a lot of things going on here, not all of which it makes sense to explain at the moment. Put simply, the Caption property of `Label1` is set to hold a phrase (or **string** as it's officially known) that is made up of the words `Today is` and today's date, represented in our code as `Date`. The word `Date` is actually a built-in function of Visual Basic that goes and gets the date from the system clock inside your machine, and tacks it onto the end of the string. The Caption property of the text box holds the characters that are displayed on the form at run-time. These replace the word `Label1` which was the default value of the property we saw on the label at design-time. As I said, there's a lot going on here, but I wanted to throw you in at the deep end and show you how Visual Basic can make a little code go a long way.

Finally, the line `End Sub` marks the end of the subprocedure.

Adding Code to the Form_Unload Event

Now let's add some code to make the form say "goodbye" when it's closed down. First of all, you need to get to the right routine in the Code Window.

1 If the program is still running, then stop it. Double-click on the form to bring up the Code Window. Click on the downward arrow to the right of the word Load, at the top of the Code Window. The event list will appear as before.

Try It Out!

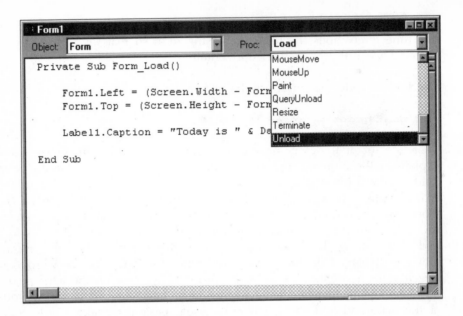

2 Use the scrollbars to find the word Unload, and select it. For the Unload event, the code should read:

```
Private Sub Form_Unload(Cancel As Integer)
    Msgbox "Goodbye!"
End Sub
```

The **MsgBox** line simply displays a message box with the word **Goodbye** inside. We'll cover message boxes in full later in the book. Basically, though, a message box is simply a ready-made form for displaying messages to the user which they must respond to before carrying on. This is great for error messages and the ubiquitous "You just formatted your hard disk" style of message.

3 Try running your program now. As before the form appears centered on the screen.

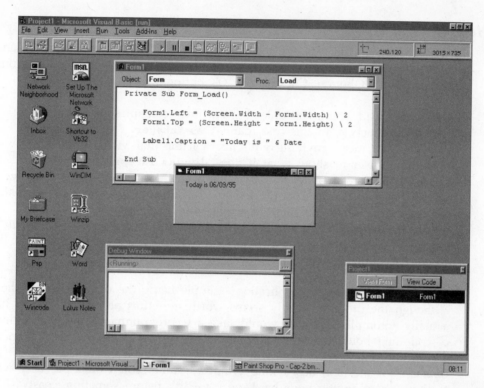

4 If you stop the program by double-clicking the control box on the form or using its close button, another window appears, (this time a message box), telling you "goodbye".

How It Works

You can change the way the message box looks and behaves from within your program, but our box is the plain vanilla version which contains only text and an OK button. Clicking the OK button will end the program.

Unlike the load event, the unload event does contain some parameters within the brackets, in this case `Cancel As Integer`. The word `Cancel` doesn't really mean anything - it's just a name that Visual Basic has given to the parameter to show what it does. The `As Integer` tells you that `Cancel` is an integer. Integers and other weird names are covered in the section on variables in Chapter 4. For now, all you need to know is that integer means whole number. By setting `Cancel` to a number, you can cancel the unload event. For instance, your code may not want the form to unload in a real program if the user needed to save some data first. If this all seems confusing then don't worry, it will become clear later.

That's it for our simple application - simple being the operative word here. Although the program hardly seems worth the effort at this stage, you have actually accomplished what would take a C programmer hundreds of lines of code and hours of leafing through extremely technical documentation to accomplish. However, if this was a big project, say a customer order database, or the next best-selling Windows game, you would probably want to think about saving your hard work to disk before something nasty happens and you lose the lot. Let's see how you can do this...

Saving Your Work

We have already looked at projects and seen how they contain the names of the files and modules that make up your application. How do these forms and modules get given file names, and how does your project get a file name?

Saving Your Project

As with most other Windows programs, Visual Basic has a File menu which contains the menu items to let you load and save. In addition, there is a Save Project button on the toolbar.

This allows you to save your work quickly at any point without having to fumble about with the menus. Take a look at Visual Basic's File menu.

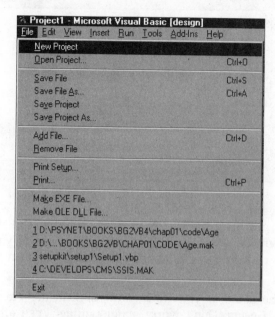

Notice how many options there are to load, open or save something. Normally you would just use the Save Project menu item to save all your forms, including the properties such as position, size, color and so on, along with all your program code.

Saving Your Project

We'll now save the above Date program so that we can use it later. If you haven't followed the examples so far, just load up Visual Basic and save the default project it creates.

1 Click on the Save Project menu item and a file dialog box will appear asking you to give your form a file name.

Try It Out!

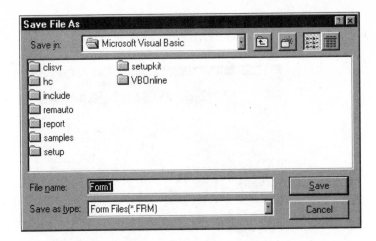

If you have more than one form or code module in a project, Visual Basic will put up a file dialog box for each one and display a name it thinks might be suitable for the form or module. If you want to change the name, click in the File name text box and type in an alternative.

2 Change the name of your form now. Click in the File name text box and enter Firstfrm. Don't worry about putting .FRM after the name as Visual Basic will do that for you if you don't provide a file extension yourself.

3 When you are happy with the file name for your form and the directory it will be stored in, click on the Save button. Visual Basic will now display a file dialog box for your project. This allows you to give a name to the project as a whole.

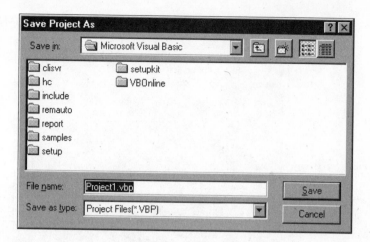

4 Visual Basic links the file names of your forms into your project, so that when you load up a project it automatically knows what all your forms and modules are called and where they are stored on your computer. Once a project has been set up, you can load and save all the components of your program in one go. For now just type in FirstPrg as the name of the project.

As with the form, Visual Basic will automatically tack a **.VBP** bit to the name. When you are happy, click on the Save button to go ahead and save the project.

5 Take a look at your File menu again. At the bottom of the menu you will now see the name of your project. This makes it very quick and easy to re-load your work whenever you come into Visual Basic - Visual Basic automatically remembers the names of the last 4 projects that you worked on.

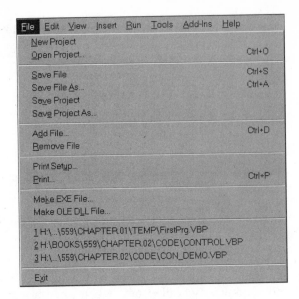

Once you have named all the forms and code modules in your project, saving your work becomes a much simpler task.

6 Try moving the form somewhere else on the screen and then re-select the Save Project menu item. You should notice the disk light come on for a short period of time, but this time Visual Basic won't show you any file dialog boxes. The reason for this is simple: as far as Visual Basic is concerned you have already named your constituent files, so it can just go away and re-save them all with the names you set previously.

The next item on the menu is the **Save Project As...** item. If you have previously saved your project, this item enables you to re-name it. Be careful though - all you are re-naming is the project itself (the `.VBP` file Visual Basic loads which contains a list of all your forms and code modules). You aren't re-naming the forms or code modules themselves. Personally, I've never found a realistic use for this particular menu item, but no doubt somebody amongst us will need it.

Working with Individual Project Files

The File menu also enables you to work with individual files within the project.

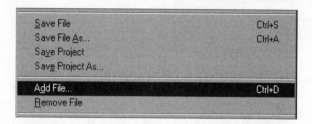

Save File	Ctrl+S
Save File As...	Ctrl+A
Save Project	
Save Project As...	
Add File...	Ctrl+D
Remove File	

You may have a form somewhere in a different project which handles UserIDs and passwords for example. Rather than re-invent the wheel, the Add File... item could be used to add this file to your project. We'll cover this in Chapter 4.

Equally, you may have a form in the project which is no longer needed. Selecting the Remove File menu item would remove it from your project. If you remove the first form in your project however, you will find that Visual Basic is no longer able to run your project. You can get round this by telling Visual Basic to look somewhere else for your initial form. This is done in the options dialog box, as you will see later in this chapter.

Removing Files

Adding a file is easy - simply select the Add File... item and a file dialog will appear asking you to select the file you wish to add. The Remove File item, however, is a little more problematic. Selecting this option will remove the currently selected form or module.

FYI

A module is a piece of code that isn't attached to a form as an event handler and just floats about on its own, waiting to be called by name. More on this in Chapter 3 - Writing Code.

For example, if you were working with Form1, meaning it is on screen and is currently selected, then hitting the Remove File option will remove that form from the project.

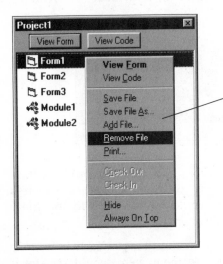

Another way of indicating which file to remove is to bring up the Project Window and select a file in the list shown. Right-clicking on the window will bring up a list of options, including some for adding and removing files.

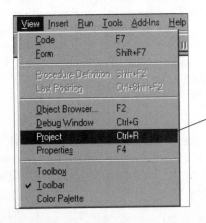

*You can display the Project Window at any time by selecting the **Project** item from the **View** menu on the Visual Basic menu bar.*

Saving Files

The Save File and Save File As... items let you save individual files in your project. You can use these to save work you have done to a form before removing it from your project. As with the Remove File item, these both work with the currently selected form or module. When you save a form, what actually gets written to the disk is a snapshot of the form's properties along with the event handler code attached to that form. This is stored on the disk in the form of a text file like the one shown below. It's interesting to see how Visual Basic describes forms in terms of raw text, but it isn't something that needs to worry a Visual Basic programmer as it's all handled behind the scenes.

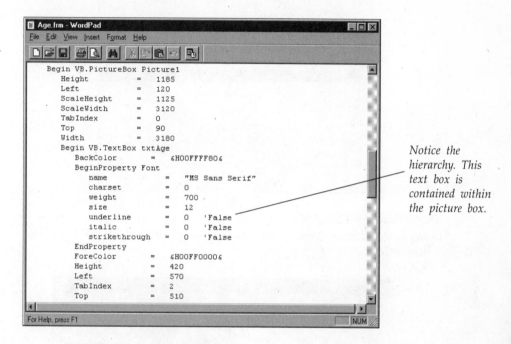

Notice the hierarchy. This text box is contained within the picture box.

Printing Out a Project

Earlier on we looked at what was actually inside the VBP file and saw that is was just a text file with all the settings and file names for the project. It is possible to view all the components in a Visual Basic project as text configuration files. This lets you create the equivalent of a hard copy code listing.

Printing Out a Project Listing

1 Make sure you still have the date project open, then select Print... from the File menu.

Try It Out!

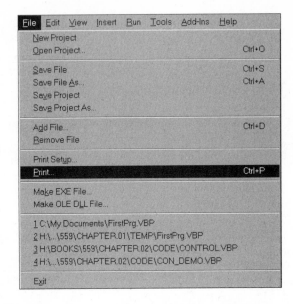

2 The following dialog box appears, inviting you to select a number of options. As this is only a little project, select Project to print out the whole thing.

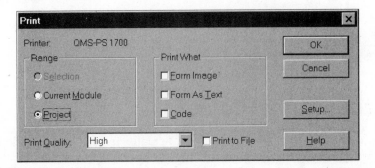

3 The Print What box gives you the choice between seeing the form printed out as a graphic image, or as a listing of all properties that define how the form looks. It also lets you choose to print out the code. On this occasion, chose Form As Text and hit OK.

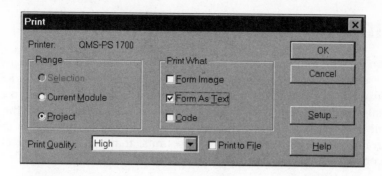

4 This is what you get:

```
Form1 - 1
VERSION 4.00
Begin VB.Form Form1
   Caption      =    "Form1"
   ClientHeight  =    828
   ClientLeft   =    2208
   ClientTop    =    1824
   ClientWidth   =    2724
   Height       =    1212
   Left       =    2160
   LinkTopic     =    "Form1"
   ScaleHeight   =    828
   ScaleWidth    =    2724
   Top        =    1488
   Width       =    2820
   Begin VB.Label Label1
      Caption      =    "Label1"
      Height       =    612
      Left       =    120
      TabIndex     =    0
      Top        =    120
      Width       =    2412
   End
End
```

Making an Executable File

So far the program we have written has been run from within the Visual Basic environment by clicking on the Start icon or by pressing *F5*. Visual Basic wouldn't get far as a tool for serious developers if each user of a Visual Basic program had to go into Visual Basic itself to use the application. Visual Basic therefore provides a way to turn your finished programs into, effectively, stand-alone units, that can be run by clicking the appropriate icon, just like other programs.

When your program is complete and ready to go to the users, a long way off yet I know, then it's time to make it an **.EXE**, or **executable file**. Turning your work of art into an **.EXE** is very easy.

Visual Basic follows a slightly unorthodox route to produce code that can be executed by the PC. It lies some way between a compiler and an interpreter. Let me explain.

Compilers and Interpreters

In most of its forms, BASIC has been an **interpreted** language. This means that to run a BASIC program you need to have the BASIC system as well. The BASIC interpreter then chugs through each line of your code, telling the PC what to do, as and when required. It's rather like you talking to a Martian through an interpreter. Every time the Martian says something, you must wait for the interpreter to translate it into something you can understand.

A compiler works as though the Martian has written down his document, which is in turn translated (compiled) into an English document. Reading the document for yourself is quicker than waiting for the interpreter to translate.

Strictly speaking, Visual Basic is compiled (cue flood of letters from Visual Basic gurus!). The compiler translates all of your code into an executable file which the PC can work through without any need to ask Visual Basic what it thinks you want to do. In reality, though, it's more like giving the PC most of your code already translated, along with a phrase book for those bits that aren't. The **.EXE** file which Visual Basic produces tells your PC to look up those parts of the program which can't easily be translated in a file called **VB40032.DLL**.

FYI

The compiler or interpreter issue is regularly fought over in magazines and electronic mail services. To my mind, Visual Basic is only *almost* a compiler. More often than not, though, you will hear it called an interpreted language, with most users aching for the day Microsoft produce a true Visual Basic compiler. The resultant **.EXE** files should run much faster than they do now, as they do, I regret to say, with Borland's Delphi.

Creating an EXE File

Try It Out!

1 When writing a program you may need to tell Visual Basic which part of your program to run first. To do this, select Options... from the Tools menu. A tabbed dialog appears which allows you to customize specific parts of Visual Basic and the current project. Click on the Project tab now to bring up the project options.

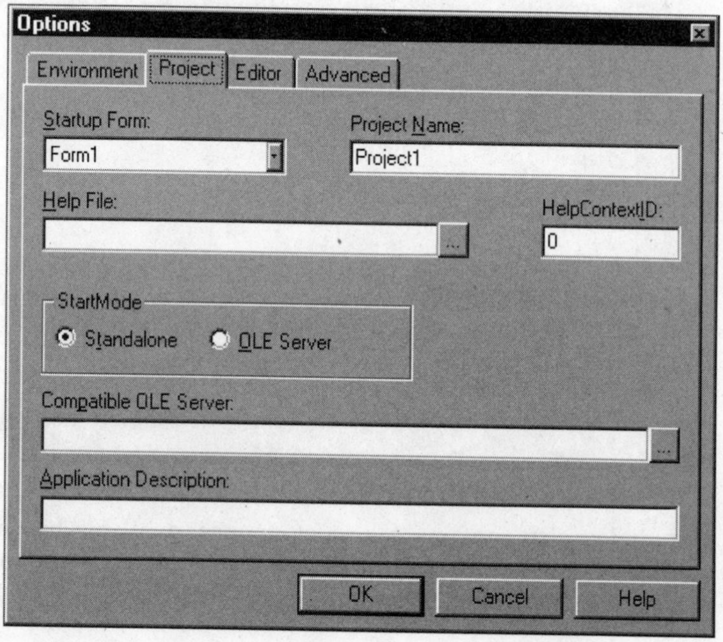

One of the first options on the project options dialog is Startup Form. By clicking the arrow to the right of the text box and selecting the name of a form in your project from the list provided, you can tell Visual Basic exactly where to start the program when you finally compile it. You'll notice that in addition to the forms in your project, there is also an option Sub Main. This allows you to start the execution of your application with code contained in a module rather than a form. Don't worry about this or the other options available for now, just get rid of the dialog by clicking on Cancel.

2 Now go to the File menu and select the Make EXE File... option. A dialog box appears, asking you to enter a file name for your finished program, such as **MYAPP.EXE** or **WROXWRITE.EXE** and allowing you to determine where your file will be saved. In the file box that appears, type in Test as the program name. Visual Basic will automatically add a **.EXE** to the end of the name to produce an executable program called **TEST.EXE**.

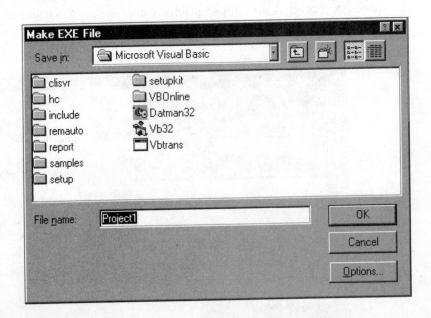

3 This dialog also contains a host of options, available by clicking on the Options... button. Click this now and give your program an **application name** by typing something into the Title box. This is the name of the program that will appear when it's running and you try to switch between it and other applications. It isn't necessarily the same as its file name. Let's call this program Today.

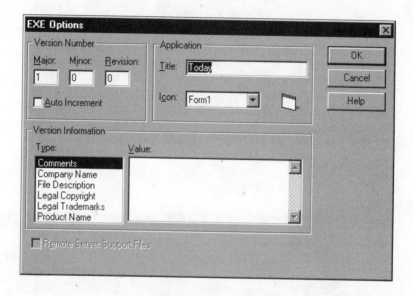

As you can now see from this dialog, there is a lot more to an **EXE** file than meets the eye. The EXE Options dialog lets you embed information into the final executable, such as who wrote it, the version number, copyright information and so on. In these days of rife software piracy, this can be a godsend if ever you need to prove that a program you wrote belongs to you.

4   Finally, hit OK in the EXE Options dialog and again in the Make EXE File dialog. Providing there are no obvious bugs in your code, Visual Basic will produce an **EXE** file which you can then run.

Setting Up Your Program on the Desktop

1   Now go to your desktop and right-click on it to bring up an options menu and select New and then Shortcut.

Try It Out!

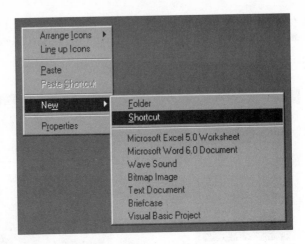

2 The following dialog appears:

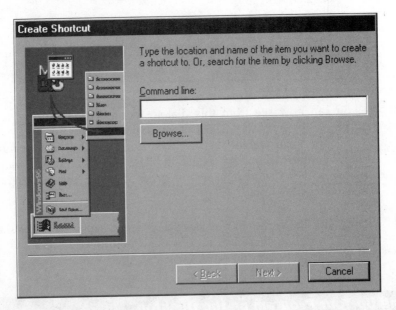

3 Next enter the full name of your `.EXE` program into the Command Line
text box. The easiest way to do this is to hit Browse..., select the **EXE** file
we have just placed into the Visual Basic directory, and then click on
Open.

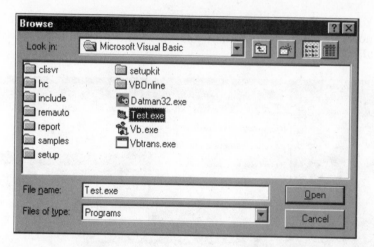

4 Once you have selected your file, hit the Next > button to take you to a screen which lets you give a name to your shortcut. Once you have chosen an appropriate name for your shortcut (Windows 95 uses the file name as a default), click the Finish button and an icon will be created on your desktop. Note that it uses the icon that you associated with your program automatically.

5 You can double-click the icon displayed to run the program anytime now, without having to run up Visual Basic first. Let's do it now, after all this work.

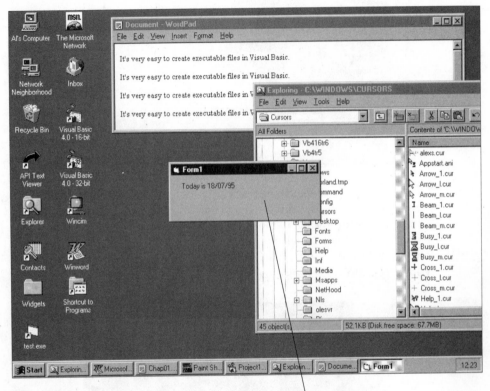

There it is. Great!

Changing the Program Icon

The program icon is a property of one of the forms in the project. By default it is the same as the first form to be displayed, but it can be changed to the icon of one of the other forms in the EXE Options dialog. The form's Icon property holds the name of an icon file which will be displayed if the program is minimized, or when the program is placed within a Program Manager group or in the Windows 95 Start menu, as it will be when you send out the finished application.

You can set the icon yourself, rather than taking the default one as we just did, by bringing up the Properties Window of a form, moving to the Icon property and double-clicking it.

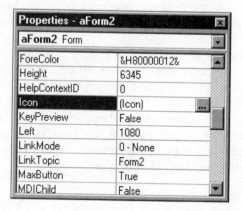

A dialog box will appear asking you to select the name of an icon file. These usually end in .ICO.

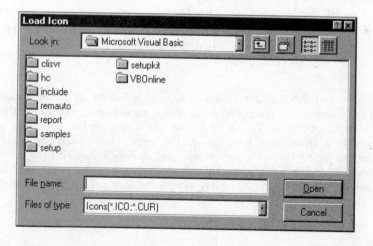

If you installed all the clip art and sample programs that came with Visual Basic, you would find a vast number of icons waiting for you in the ICONS folder. Typically this will be C:\VB\ICONS.

After that, just go through the same steps as before for creating an EXE file and setting it up on your desktop, and voilà! The icon of your choice!

The Set-up Wizard

When you actually send your program out to your users, you will need to make the installation process as simple as possible. Visual Basic supplies a program called **Application Set-up Wizard** to help you do this.

Set-up Wizard creates an installation program for you which can lead your users through the process step by step. It also makes sure that you don't forget to give them any files, sets up your program icons properly, and makes the whole thing look a lot more polished than if you simply gave your users a scrap of paper telling them what to do. Set-up Wizard is covered in detail later in this book when your projects become larger, and frankly, more suitable for mass distribution. Today is a good start, but I wouldn't give up your day job just yet.

Getting Help

Visual Basic is a complex package. Not only must you master writing programs in the Visual Basic language, but you also need to master the Visual Basic environment, as well as reading the sometimes cryptic messages it can send you. Thankfully Microsoft have supplied one of the best help systems of any development tool.

You might think it a bit strange for an author to be recommending that you use the Help system as much as you can. You bought the book to teach you Visual Basic and you don't expect to be told to go and look it up on a help screen. However, what you really want from me is the best way to get results, and that is a combination of this book (to teach you the techniques and give you the overview), and the help screens (for the itsy-bitsy references that are impossible to remember).

Context-Sensitive Help

At any point while using Visual Basic you can hit *F1*, your panic button. This will activate the Microsoft Visual Basic Help system where you can obtain help and advice, as well as example program code for anything you come across whilst using Visual Basic.

Try this out now. Bring up the form's Properties Window, find the Name property and click on it. Now press *F1*. Visual Basic will display a page of text describing what exactly the name property is and what it does.

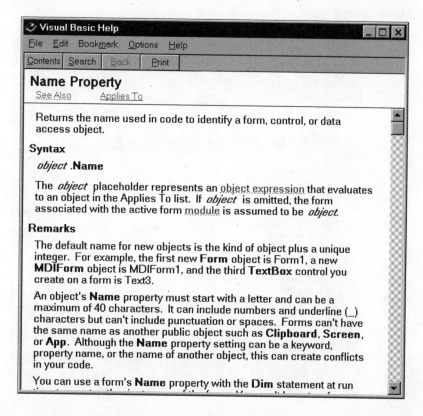

If you are a regular Windows user you have probably come across context-sensitive help before. Visual Basic also provides two other routes to help. Open up the Help menu on the Visual Basic menu bar and select Contents. The Visual Basic help contents page appears, enabling you to choose to read complete documents on various aspects of Visual Basic.

Have a play with the help system for a while to get used to how it works. You may notice as you progress through the system that text in green appears. These items of text represent further topics that you can call up help on. If you click them, Visual Basic will whisk you away to another page of the help file to supply further reading, which itself may have green text enabling you to cross reference even further.

Searching for Help

By far the most common way to access help is via the Search button. Try clicking Search now.

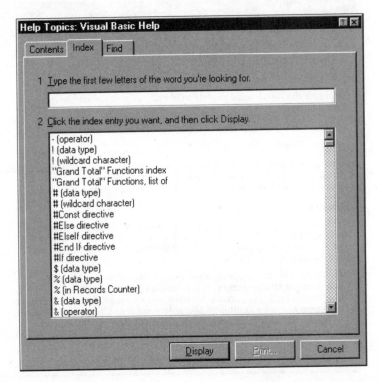

The dialog that appears lets you find a specific topic based on a keyword you enter. You'll notice that it's split into two tabbed pages: Index and Find. The first of these searches according to an index set up by the creators of the help file and the second searches for text anywhere in the body of the help file. Because the first method is faster and more focused than the second, you'll probably find yourself using the Index page most of the time, but if you can't find what you're looking for there, then try the Find page for a more extensive search.

We'll just look at a search by index for the moment. Type FORM into the text box. Notice that the list scrolls to the relevant point as you type each letter. Press *Enter* or click on the Display button now and a new window containing relevant topics will be shown. Double-click on an interesting topic (or highlight it then click Display) to view the help text itself. A page of help of some relevance to Forms will appear with green text across the top allowing you to jump to specific help on form events, properties, some example code or other related topics.

Summary

We have covered a lot of ground very quickly in this first chapter, so let's just recap on what we've done. Over the course of this chapter you have:

▶ Explored the layout of the Visual Basic environment.

▶ Learnt how to create a new project by starting Visual Basic.

▶ Discovered what a form is and what properties can do.

▶ Run and stopped a Visual Basic program.

▶ Added code to a form to respond to events affecting that form.

▶ Loaded and saved your work on your hard disk.

▶ Created an executable program (**.EXE**) that can be run without Visual Basic.

▶ Learnt how to use the Visual Basic help system.

At various points in this chapter you've got a taste of what you're going to learn in future chapters. First on the list are controls and what you can do with them. This is the subject of Chapter 2.

Why Not Try.......

1 Change the date project to place the form at different locations on the screen. Do this by altering the number values in the `Form1.Left` and `Form1.Top` properties.

2 Make the form and the label really big in the date project, and then choose a large font to display the date. Use the Font property in the label's Property Window.

3 Play around with the colors and sizes of your editor fonts in the Options part of the Tools menu.

4 Put a welcome message box into the form load event of the date project.

5 Add more labels to the date form to show other information, such as your name.

6 Open up the `AGE` project and change the cut off age for being old enough to run the program to 21. This is tricky as there's a lot of code we haven't covered. See if you can do it.

7 In the `AGE` project, make the button beep when it's pressed.

Common Controls

Although forms are the mainstay of any Visual Basic application, they are not much use without controls. Controls are the text boxes, list boxes, command buttons and so on that give your user something to interact with. They are also the means by which your program obtains and displays its data.

In this chapter we'll look at a complete application that contains some of the most common controls. We will see how controls work, and how they fit into a Visual Basic program. In this chapter you will learn about:

- How to select controls and place them on your form.

- What controls really do.

- How the command button is used.

- Why controls have properties.

- Using other common controls such as text boxes, labels, option buttons, image controls and picture boxes.

Working with Controls

In this chapter, we'll start with the general techniques for selecting and placing the different controls on your form. We'll then look at how the appearance and behavior of controls can be programmed using properties, much as we did with forms in Chapter 1.

We will use the command button as an example of a frequently-used control, but also run through some of the other common controls that you will use, such as **option buttons**, **check boxes**, **text boxes** and **image controls**. We will also look at some of the problems these controls bring with them, and how to overcome them.

Before we go any further, let's take a look at an example program from the disk supplied with the book that illustrates some of the key points about controls. If you have not already installed these programs onto your hard disk, then now is the time to do so. Instructions for this are contained in the Introduction.

Controls in Action

Try It Out!

1 Using the Open Project item on the File menu, load the project called **CON_DEMO.VBP**. When you have loaded it, run it by pressing *F5* or by clicking the Start icon in the toolbar.

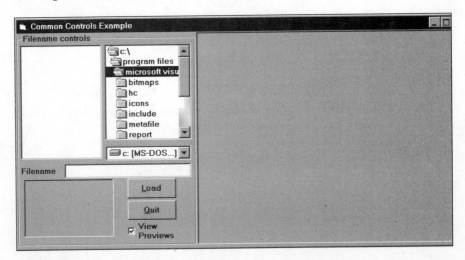

This simple image file viewer is cobbled together from the most common Visual Basic controls, with a few small bits of code thrown in to make it work. Let's take a closer look.

2 The three list boxes on the left of the form enable you to navigate your hard disk in search of image files. One good place to start looking is in your **VB\ICONS** directory.

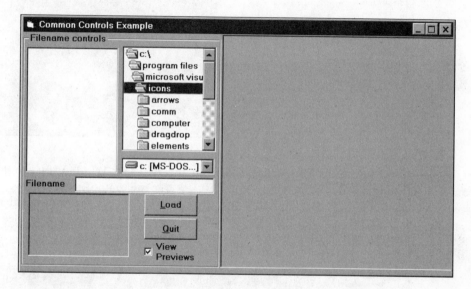

3 Once you have located the right drive and directory, you'll see a list of the files you can load in.

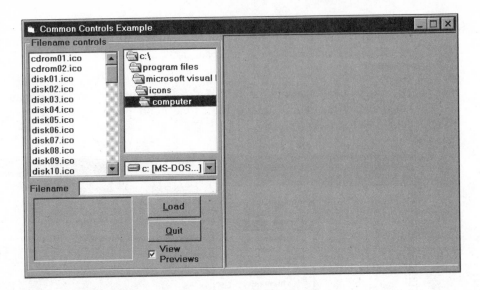

4 If you now select an image file from the File List Window by single-clicking on it, the text box will display the full name of that file, including the drive and directory that it lives in. At that point, an event is triggered which loads the image file into memory. You'll then see a preview of it in the bottom left-hand corner of the form.

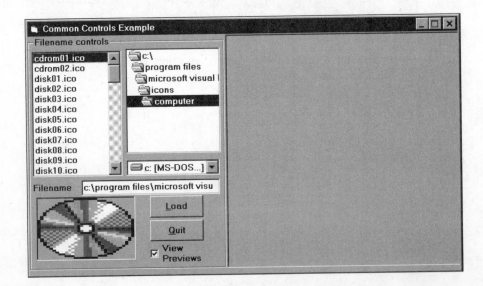

5 To actually load the file into the main viewing area, you can either double-click on it, or hit the Load button.

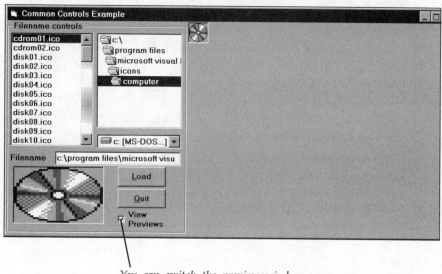

You can switch the preview window on or off using the check box at the bottom.

Play around with the program for a while and you should soon find yourself coming up with some questions:

- How does the text box know what the three list boxes are doing?

- How does the program check to see whether or not a file exists?

- Why is the image stretched in the preview window, but normal sized in the main window?

The best way to answer these and other questions is to take a good look at how CON_DEMO.VBP is put together from its constituent components.

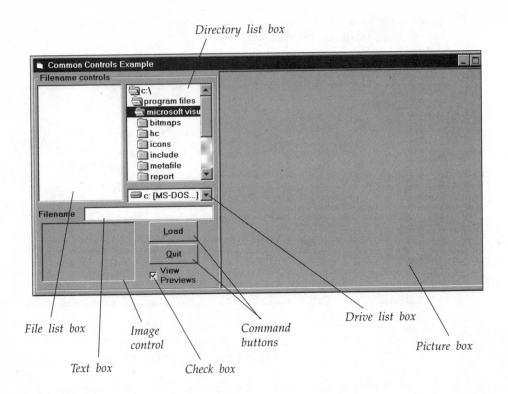

Directory list box

File list box

Image control

Command buttons

Drive list box

Picture box

Text box

Check box

To do this, we need to take a look at the most common controls in the toolbox.

The Toolbox

Just as with other aspects of Visual Basic, placing a control such as a command button or a text box onto a form is merely a question of pointing and clicking with the mouse. As we saw in Chapter 1, all of your controls are kept in the toolbox, waiting for you to put them onto your form.

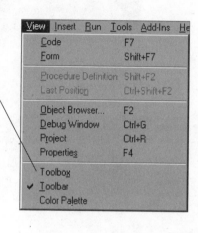

The toolbox can be displayed by selecting Toolbox from the View menu.

Once displayed, you can move the toolbox around the screen by dragging its title bar, just like any other window. You close it by clicking the close button in the top right corner of the toolbox window.

Placing Controls onto Your Form

In Chapter 1, we placed a simple label control onto a form to display today's date. Let's do it again, this time with a command button.

Placing Controls

1 Start a new project by selecting New Project from the File menu.

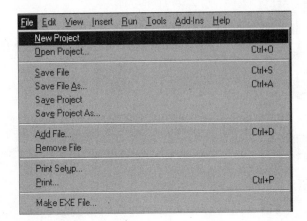

2 Select the control you want by clicking on its icon in the toolbox. Here we want the command button. Don't forget that, if you get lost, you can simply move the mouse pointer over the icons in the toolbox to have a pop-up tip appear, telling you what you are pointing at.

3 Move the cursor to the place on the form where you want the control to go, and draw the control by holding the left mouse button down and dragging the mouse. A rectangle will appear on the form representing the size of the control.

When you are happy with the size, just release the mouse button and the control will be drawn onto the form in full.

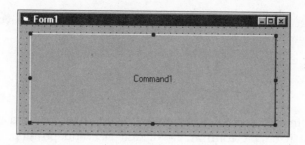

4 You can now click on the control itself and drag it around until you are happy with its position.

Alternatively, if you need to move a control around the form a pixel (dot on the screen) at a time, you can do so by holding down the *Ctrl* key and using the cursor keys on the keyboard. Each press of an arrow on the keyboard translates to a movement of just one dot on the screen in the indicated direction.

Re-sizing Controls

Even after a number of controls have been added to the form, it's still possible to move them around or re-size them.

Re-sizing Controls

1 Clicking on a control you have already drawn selects that control and displays the control **re-size handles**. These are small black boxes on each edge and each corner of the control.

Clicking on these buttons and dragging the mouse around causes the control to change size.

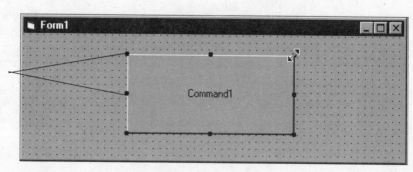

Try It Out!

FYI Some controls cannot be changed in size, while others have pre-set minimum heights or widths below which you can't go.

2 Sometimes it's faster to double-click on a control and allow Visual Basic to put it on the form at the default size and position. You can then re-size and move it around. Visual Basic lays each control one on top of the other in the default position, so they can be a little hard to find if you don't move each one as you place it.

FYI Just as with moving controls, you can also re-size a selected control on a pixel by pixel level. Instead of holding down *Ctrl* and pressing the arrow keys though, hold down *Shift* and press the arrow keys. Each click of a cursor key results in a small change in the size of the selected control.

The Alignment Grid

To help you position the controls neatly, Visual Basic provides an **alignment grid**. This is the grid of small black dots that covers your form. The grid can be changed in size or removed completely using the Environment tab on the Options dialog (you may remember from Chapter 1 that you can bring up the options dialog by selecting Options from the Tools menu).

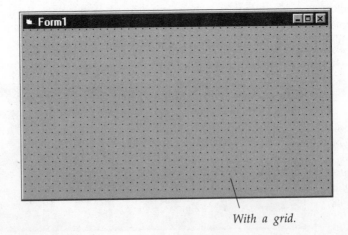

With a grid.

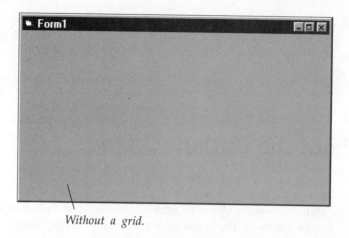

Without a grid.

The Alignment Grid

1 Select the Environment tab from the Options dialog.

The first four options on this box allow you to set up the size of the grid, decide whether or not you want the grid shown, and whether or not Visual Basic should force you to place controls on grid points (snap to grid). You can change all these options to suit your requirements.

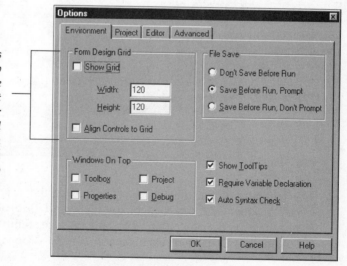

Try It Out!

I tend to use quite a fine grid (height and width both 150). This allows me a great deal of flexibility when moving my controls around, yet still lets me line the controls up neatly on the form rather than in a cluttered mess. Some people don't like using the grid at all and turn it off at the first possible instance. Do whatever you feel happy with!

More About the Options Dialog

We have already had a brief look at some of the facilities the Options dialog provides. Now would be a good time to look at some of these features in a little more detail, in particular the editor options. The editor options box lets you change the way the code editor in Visual Basic works and how it looks.

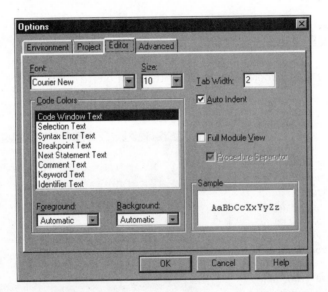

The left part of the dialog lets you change the way text is displayed in the Code Window. The top two boxes (Font and Size) let you change the actual appearance of the text (the font) and its size. Simply click on the arrows on the right hand edges of each combo box to drop down a list of options.

Underneath these boxes are the various different types of code that Visual Basic can recognize. By selecting any of these, and then changing the foreground or background color in the bottom combo boxes, you can change the colors that Visual Basic uses to display the bits of code that it recognizes.

The top two items on the right hand side of the dialog let you change the way tab works. When you write code in Visual Basic, it's a good idea to get on first name terms with the tab key, since strategic use of tabs can make your code much more readable.

The first option, Tab Width, is where you tell Visual Basic how many spaces make up a tab on screen. If you like big tabs, then try changing this number to something like 9 or 10. I prefer, though, to work with the default value of 4, and that is how the code examples here are laid out.

The Auto Indent checkbox lets you tell Visual Basic to automatically continue with any tabs you start, effectively auto-indenting each new line of code you type.

Normally, when you work in Visual Basic, the Code Window only shows you the event, procedure or function you are working on. However, by checking the Full Module View checkbox, you can tell Visual Basic to display all the code in a form or module, in addition to the code you are working on at this moment. I find this particular feature a godsend, since it makes getting a big picture view of your code a real snip.

One of the problems with working in this mode for a beginner, though, is seeing at a glance where one procedure ends and another starts. Checking the Procedure Separator checkbox makes Visual Basic draw a solid line across the screen between each block of code.

Control Locking

Once you get your form festooned with controls, it becomes very easy to drag them out of alignment by accident. Fortunately, the Visual Basic environment provides a control locking feature that freezes all your controls on a form into place.

Control Locking

1 Load up **CON_DEMO.VBP** in design mode and make sure the form is displayed. You can move any control you like around.

2 Hit the padlock icon on the toolbar to lock the controls.

3 Now try and move the controls around. You get the little re-sizing handles, but they are white and won't let you move anything.

What is a Control?

If controls were merely nice looking graphics on your form, then Visual Basic would be little better than a fancy painting program with a programming language attached (quiet at the back there!). The real power of Visual Basic comes as a result of the functionality that is built into each control. But what does this really mean?

Controls are Windows

A control is really a window that has a program running inside it. This is no different to what you are used to with your own Windows Desktop. To run a new application, you open a new window. This application will take control of that window and invest it with its own appearance and functionality. A Visual Basic control takes control of a window in a rather more extreme fashion than an application, but it's essentially the same.

A control is, therefore, a lump of pre-written code inside a window which can be dropped into your own program. It incorporates into your own project the functions which that code provides. The software industry has been eagerly awaiting these kind of standard components for many years, in order to speed up the process of writing software.

Before Visual Basic introduced custom controls, each programmer would write almost every line of code in an application from the ground up. This meant that there was a large amount of repetition of coding which had no doubt been done by other programmers in other projects. Although we consider Visual Basic to be truly revolutionary, it is only a result of what has happened in every other industry. Your PC is made up of components from dozens of different manufacturers, each specializing in producing one particular part. What makes Visual Basic controls special is not the idea of re-useable software components alone - these have existed in different incarnations for many years. Rather, it is the elegance with which each control can be customized to, and integrated with, your particular application.

Properties and Events

You interact with a control by using two types of hook: properties and events.

▶ **Properties** are a collection of parameters that you can set to control the way a control looks and behaves. If controls were people, properties would be characteristics like height, weight, fitness and programming skills.

▶ **Events** are the things you can do to a control that it will recognize and be able to respond to. Each control has a set of events it understands. You will be relieved to hear that controls respond to a far narrower range of events than people do. You also don't have to persuade or encourage controls to do anything - you just click on them with the mouse.

Each control has its own set of properties and events that make it useful for particular purposes. To make this a bit clearer, let's take a look at probably the most common control of all, the **command button**.

Command Buttons

Second only in popularity to the text box, and unsurpassed for its sheer simplicity and lack of charisma, is the command button. I talk in terms of simplicity, because although command buttons are incredibly useful and enormously widespread throughout the world of Windows, they can only really do one thing - click. You point at them with the mouse, click the left mouse button and voilà, a **click** event occurs.

Events

Of course there are other events that a command button can respond to, but the majority of them all center around whether or not the button is being clicked. Events such as **MouseDown** and **KeyDown** are useful in detecting exactly what the user is trying do to the command button, and with which weapon. Essentially, however, it's all a question of clicking.

Properties

Once you start to think about controls as windows, it becomes easy to see why they have properties in common with forms:

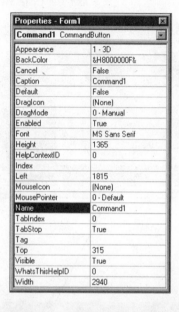

Command Buttons

1 Create a new Visual Basic project by selecting <u>N</u>ew Project from the <u>F</u>ile menu. Once the project has been created, select the command button icon from the toolbox and draw a command button on the form.

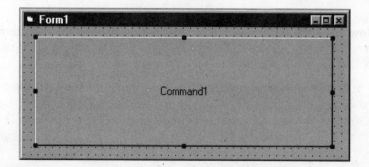

91

2 Let's actually make the command button do something; this time we'll make it beep whenever it's clicked. To do this we need to display the Code Window and type in some code.

Double-click on your new command button and the Code Window will pop up.

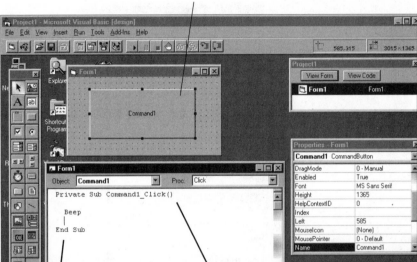

Type in code so that the Code Window looks like this:

Notice that the text inside the Code Window says **Private Sub Command1_Click()**. *This means that we are looking at the code that will occur whenever the command button,* Command1, *is clicked. We cover code in a lot more detail a little later in the book, so don't fret if you can't understand the strange words and symbols. All you need to know is that we are going to be writing code which Visual Basic will run whenever this command button is clicked.*

3 Now try running the program by either pressing *F5*, selecting Start from the Run menu, or by clicking the Start icon on the main Visual Basic toolbar.

If you now click the command button you will find it beeps, because the code you typed into the command button's click event tells it to. When you have had enough of the program, you can stop it by pressing *Alt* and *F4* together or by clicking the End icon on the toolbar.

Returning to the Property Market

Before we go any further, it's worth talking a little more about properties, especially some of the more common ones.

In order to make Visual Basic as easy to learn as possible, Microsoft were kind enough to give most of the controls in Visual Basic similar properties. For instance, all controls have an Enabled property, most also have a Visible property and so on. This makes it worth speaking generally about properties and controls before delving into specific instances.

The Name Property

One extremely common property you will come across is the Name property. This is used in order to write code which will differentiate between each of your Visual Basic controls. In other words, each control is given a name.

Whenever you create a new control or form in Visual Basic, a default name is automatically given. For example, when you start up a new project in Visual Basic, the default form is called Form1. When you draw the first command button onto that form it will be called Command1, the next Command2, and so on.

Standard Names

There are some common standards for giving a name to your controls. Text boxes, for example, are nearly always prefixed with **txt**, forms begin with **frm**, option buttons with **opt**, and so on.

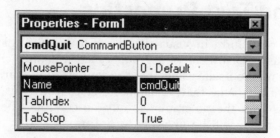

A full list of these is in Appendix B, but you will come across many of them as we cover the example program in this chapter. At first, the names may seem a little strange, but the end result is that they do make your code a lot easier to read and understand.

For example, if you see a line like

```
optDrive.text = "D:"
```

Visual Basic seems to dislike it. It's easy to see why, since the name of the control indicates that it's an option button, and option buttons don't have a Text property.

Of course, if you wanted to name a drive control `optDrive`, then that's entirely up to you. Visual Basic only complains if you try to use properties that don't belong to certain controls, such as a Text property with an option button. If this happens, Visual Basic gives you an error message and lets you go away and fix the error.

FYI In the final analysis, Visual Basic doesn't really care what you call your controls - it's quite happy for you to name them all A, B, C, D etc. However, that doesn't really make your life as a programmer very easy. Sticking to a standard way of naming your controls can make your life as a programmer a lot more hassle-free, especially when you have to come back to the code in a few months time to maintain it or fix a bug. By that time you probably won't have a clue what the code does. The last thing you need at that stage is to waste time trying to figure out what the control and variable names mean.

Caption and Text Properties

Each control on a form in Visual Basic has to have a unique name, unless you deliberately place them in a group called a control array. You can assign the name yourself, using the standard naming convention, or you just accept the default name that Visual Basic gives you. This is really a private name between you the programmer, and the control. When you run the program, the name will be invisible to the user.

There are, however, two other text labels that can be assigned to certain controls and which will display that text on screen. These are the Caption and Text properties.

The Caption Property

Captions are usually found on objects such as forms, frames and command buttons. A caption is simply a piece of text that is displayed on screen to give the object some kind of header or title.

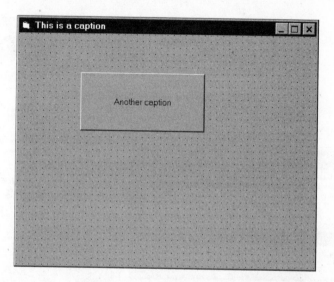

In the case of the command button, the text is actually displayed in the center of the command button itself.

The Text Property

The Text property is somewhat different. This is normally found on controls that can accept data entry from the user, such as a **text box** or **combo box**. By setting the Text property, you are actually telling Visual Basic what to display on screen in the text entry area. The following line of code is from `CON_DEMO.VBP` - it makes the file name appear in the file name text box by assigning it to the **Text** property of the text box.

```
txtFileName.Text = filFileNames.Path & "\" & filFileNames.filename
```

We'll see how this works in detail when we look at the label and text box controls later in the chapter.

Shortcut Keys

There is another interesting feature of the Caption property, which in fact applies to any control which can have a caption. Look closely at the wording of the caption on the Quit button.

*Notice how the letter Q is underlined. This is called a **hot key**, and it means that by pressing Alt-Q when the program is running, you can trigger the Quit button click event without having to move the mouse to point and click.*

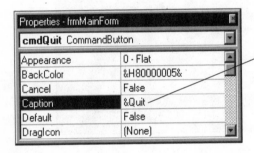

Hot keys can be set up on any control that can have a caption by simply placing an & sign in front of the letter you want underlined.

From a user's point of view, this makes your programs much easier to use.

Text Boxes

Text boxes are one of the most common controls found in any Windows program. They provide an area on screen into which the user can enter information and where you can also display information to the user.

The area inside these controls behaves like a DOS text screen of old. Like many of the other controls in Visual Basic, much of the hard work with text boxes is done for you. In a great many cases, all you need to do is simply place a text box onto a form before your users start entering data. Visual Basic and Windows automatically handle all the complex stuff such as displaying the characters which the user types, inserting and deleting characters, scrolling the data in the text box, selecting text, cutting and pasting text, and so on.

It's so easy, in fact, there's nothing stopping us trying it out!

Text boxes

1 Start a new project in Visual Basic by selecting <u>N</u>ew Project from the <u>F</u>ile menu. Select the text box control from the toolbox.

2 Draw a text box on the default form.

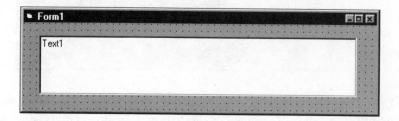

3 You can radically change the way a text box looks by using its Font property. This handy little property lets you change absolutely everything you could ever want to change about the style of the text in the text box.

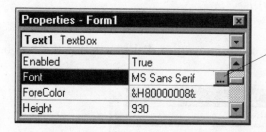

Click on the command button with the little dots to the right of the font property and a font dialog box will miraculously appear.

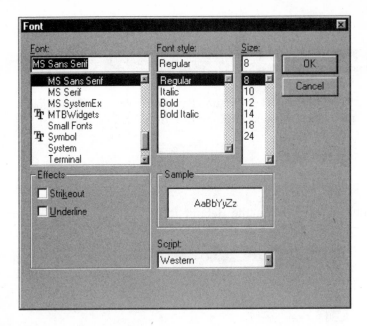

Using this one dialog, you can change the font name, its style (whether or not it is bold, underlined, italicized, and so on) and its size, all by doing nothing but pointing and clicking. The only stuff you can't do with this dialog is set up the font colors.

Colors... there is more than one? Sure, you can change the background color of the text (the color behind the writing), and the foreground color (the color of the actual text). To accomplish this you use the background and foreground color properties.

4 Find the BackColor property in the properties dialog box, for the text box

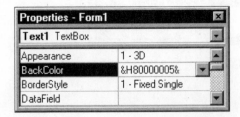

5 Don't worry about the complicated value shown - just click on the down arrow to the right of the property and a color dialog will appear showing you all the colors that are available. To select one, just point and click - try it!

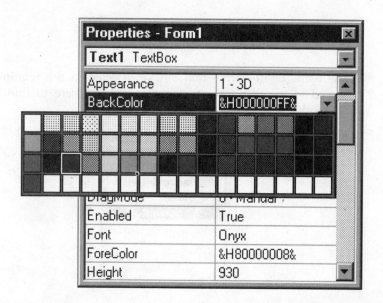

That's really all there is to it. We'll take a look at fonts and colors in more detail in Chapter 7 - Graphics. For now, though, let's move on to some of the other more common properties of the great text box.

Text Box Properties

The most important property of a text box is the Text property. In the example above we changed this at design-time. At any point your program can examine the Text property to see exactly what is in the text box on screen, or to change that text on the fly.

Earlier on we saw how the **CON_DEMO.VBP** program places the name of the selected file into the Text property of the **txtFileName** text box. Before we look at how we deal with this, we need to understand where the file name itself is coming from.

This text box sits at the end of a long chain of file controls:

▶ The drives drop-down list box shows a list of the local and network drives that are available.

▶ The name of the drive that you've selected in the window is then passed to the directories list box to tell it where to find the directories to display.

When I say passes, what actually happens is that some code attached to the directories list box inserts what's called a path into the Path property of the filename list box. A path is just everything that comes before the actual file name to tell you where it is, like `C:\MYPROG\VB\`. When you click on the file you want in the file name box, it runs its own bit of code.

This is the code that runs when you click a file name.

```
Private Sub filFilenames_Click()

    txtFileName.Text = filFileNames.Path & "\" & FilFileNames.filename
    imgPicture.picture = LoadPicture(txtFileName.Text)

End Sub
```

What this code does is to feed the name of the selected file and its path into the text box. There are two properties in which the full name of the file is stored in the file control: `Path` and `Filename`. The Path property is the full path of a file. For example, if you select a file in `C:\TEST`, then the Path property will read `C:\TEST`.

The line where this is joined onto the actual file name is:

```
txtFileName.Text = filFileNames.Path & "\" & filFileNames.filename
```

This sets the Text property of the text box to the **Path** and **Filename**, combined, but separated by a backslash. The **&** sign tells Visual Basic to join more than one piece of text together.

After that, we load this picture into the image control. We cover image controls later in the chapter, so not long to wait.

```
imgPicture.picture = LoadPicture(txtFileName.Text)
```

This is not an easy thing to understand at this point in your career. The good news is that you will rarely use the file controls at all. Windows supplies you with a built-in dialog box called a custom dialog that you can use to work with files. We will cover these in Chapter 6 - Dialogs.

Checking User Input

Really the only thing text boxes can't do without your help is check the data that the user enters. Problems occur because a text box allows the user to key in more information than can be displayed, and to enter alphabetic data when your program only really wants numeric information, and so on.

By default, the text box allows you to type in data that is larger than its width. When this happens, the text box scrolls to show you the next section. You can also scroll it yourself by placing the cursor inside the text box and using the arrow keys to move left and right. This can be great when you need such a feature, but it can make your interface look badly planned.

Visual Basic provides a property to help us get round this. Setting the MaxLength property to anything other than 0 limits the amount of data that can be keyed in. Try it. Set the MaxLength property to something silly like 5 and run the program. Now when you select a file name, only the first 5 characters of it will be displayed in the text box and the program no longer works reliably. Stop it, and change it back to zero.

Text Box Events

I keep on saying **displays data** and **enters data** for the text box when really it would be more logical to say that a text box holds and displays **text**. Well, despite the somewhat misleading name, text boxes don't only hold text. They can hold punctuation marks, numbers, arithmetic symbols - in fact anything you can produce by pressing a key, the text box can display. This can become a little bit of a problem if, for example, you needed the user to enter a number, and only a number.

Checking Input to a Text Box

Let's look at a program that does check what is entered into a text box. Load up the **DETAILS.VBP** example project and run it.

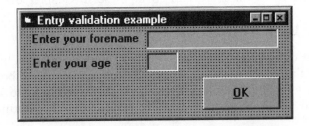

This program has just the problem we were discussing. It prompts for your forename and your age, but it doesn't prevent you from entering numbers in your forename or letters in your age.

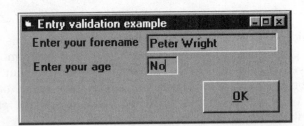

We're going to fix that now. We also need to check that when the user hits the OK button they have actually entered data in both the name and age text boxes.

Adding Code to the KeyPress Event

The best way to check data as it's entered is using the **KeyPress** event. This is triggered for a text box whenever the user presses a key that's displayed in the text box and tells us the **ASCII** code for the key pressed.

> **FYI**
>
> Each character on your keyboard has a specific unique number, called the ASCII (pronounced as-key) code. Using this we can check that the right keys have been pressed, and we can also tell the KeyPress event to ignore certain keys. Convenient, huh?
>
> To help you, Visual Basic also has a complete list of these ASCII codes built in. Select Search from the Help menu and enter the word ASCII. Visual Basic will search its help topics and display the results. The result, called the ASCII character set, shows you a complete list of all the characters and their associated codes.

To enter code in the **txtForeName_KeyPress()** event, first stop the program running.

1 View the form and double-click the Forename text box to bring up the Code Window. When it appears, click on the arrow next to the word Change. Select KeyPress from the list shown. The Code Window should now look like this:

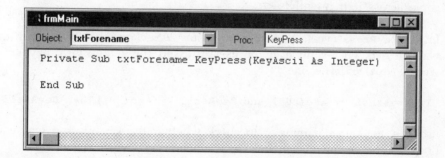

```
frmMain                                          _ □ ✕

Object:  txtForename      ▼    Proc:  KeyPress          ▼

   Private Sub txtForename_KeyPress(KeyAscii As Integer)

   End Sub
```

Try It Out!

2 The first line of code

```
Private Sub txtForename_KeyPress(KeyAscii As Integer)
```

marks the start of the event code. It tells us, and Visual Basic, where the code for dealing with the **KeyPress** event starts, and also lets us know the name of the control whose **KeyPress** event we are writing code for. The **KeyAscii** bit in brackets is called a **parameter**, but let's take one thing at a time!

Conveniently, the ASCII codes for the numbers 0 to 9 all run in sequence, so our event code to catch them is fairly simple. Let's add a line to the event to check which key was pressed and deal with it. Change the event code so that it now looks like this:

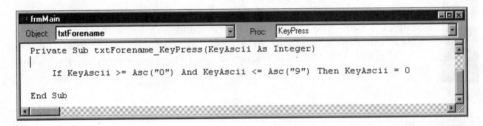

How KeyPress Works

The first line of the **KeyPress** event has the phrase **KeyAscii As Integer** in it. **KeyAscii** is called a parameter - it's a way for Visual Basic to give your code a value which it can use to figure out what's going on - you'll come across it frequently!

In the **KeyPress** event, **KeyAscii** holds the ASCII number of the key that was pressed. For example, if the user pressed the A key, then **KeyAscii** would equal 65. The line

```
If keyAscii >= Asc("0") and KeyAscii <= Asc("9") Then KeyAscii = 0
```

uses the **KeyAscii** parameter to check whether the key pressed was valid. It does this using the Visual Basic **Asc** function.

A function is a piece of code, in this case built into Visual Basic, that takes something from your code, processes it away on its own, then returns a new value. The Asc function allows us to get at the ASCII value for a symbol. So saying Asc("0") will give our code the ASCII code for 0.

We can then compare whatever is held in **KeyAscii** against the value returned by **Asc** to determine whether or not the key pressed was numeric or not.

Finally the **>=** symbol means *is greater than or equal to* and the **<=** symbol means *is less than or equal to*. Armed with this knowledge, the line of code actually reads:

If the parameter **KeyAscii** *is greater than or equal to the ASCII code of '0', and less than or equal to the ASCII code of '9, then set* **KeyAscii** *to 0.*

Setting **KeyAscii** to 0 in the **KeyPress** event has the effect of canceling the key just pressed. If you run the program now, and try typing numbers into the forename text box, you will find that they are simply ignored. All the other characters work fine, though.

Verifying Input into the Age Field

We can use a similar technique for the age text box. In this case, we only need to keep the numbers and ignore everything else. The code goes into the **txtAge_KeyPress()** event.

1 Stop the program running.

2 Double-click the age text box.

3 When the Code Window appears, select the **KeyPress** event.

4 Key in the event handler code:

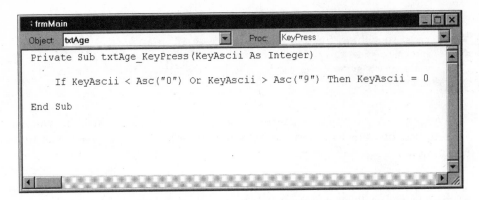

Now, if you run the program, you will find that the age text box only accepts numbers, and ignores spaces, letters or any other character you decide to hit. In addition, because the MaxLength property has already been set to 2, you will not be able to enter an age of more than 2 digits in length - the chances of a 100+ year old reading this book and using Visual Basic is pretty remote, so I'm confident I can get away with this.

Checking for an Empty Text Box

Now all we need to do is check that the user has actually entered something in the text boxes when the OK button is hit. We have already seen that the Text property lets us see what is in a text box, so if the Text property equals "", then obviously the user has entered nothing. In Visual Basic, "" is how you would check to see if a piece of text actually contains nothing. This is commonly called an empty string.

Checking for an Empty Text Box

Try It Out!

1 If the program is running, stop it and double-click the command button to bring up its click event code.

2 A few lines of code, and the program is complete.

```
Private Sub cmdOK_Click()

  If txtAge.Text = "" Then
    Msgbox "You must enter your age"
    Exit Sub
  End If
```

```
    If txtForename.Text = "" Then
      Msgbox "Enter your name please"
      Exit Sub
    End If

    End

End Sub
```

The code checks the value of each text box to see if anything was entered. In either case, if nothing was entered, a message box is put on screen with an error message in it. Then the `Exit Sub` line exits the event code. Event code like this is normally called a **subprocedure**. We cover what subprocedure really means later in the book.

In actual fact, in our case, we never get that far, and the `End` statement terminates the program once we've got it right.

We can make the program even better by using a command called `SetFocus` to move the cursor to the offending text box. Focus is a tricky subject best discussed in a separate section, so I'll leave it to the end of the chapter.

Label Control

The **Label** control is the perfect complement to the text box. The text box is one of the few controls that doesn't have a caption of its own, so a label is used to place some text on the form near to the text box to show exactly what it represents.

Label Properties

Just as with the text box, the style of the label font can be changed with the Font property. You can even add a border around a label to make it appear, to all intents and purposes, the same as a text box. This is done by changing the BorderStyle property in the same way as you did with the form in the last chapter.

Label Events

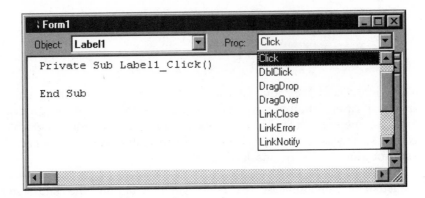

Labels are **lightweight** controls - they use less system resources, such as memory, and they need less processor power to manage them. This is simply because Visual Basic doesn't have to worry too much about the user entering data in them, re-sizing them, and so on. However, while they may be lightweight from a Windows management point of view, they are up there with the best of them when it comes to event handling.

Labels can respond to a full set of events, with the obvious exception of events such as change, since the data in the label caption wouldn't normally need to be changed. One of the most common events coded for labels is the click event. For example, in a banking application you may have a client's personal details, such as their address, on the screen. Adding code to the click event of the label that says Address could be used to bring up another form showing the other addresses that the customer may have lived at over the years.

Other programs tend to use label click events as backdoors - ways into a program if all else fails. I recently came across one such program, which, if you double-clicked the **Password** label on a particular form, allowed you to change or re-set the password - very convenient for forgetful users!

Check Boxes

Check boxes allow you to present on/off, true/false options to users. Think back to school - remember the old multiple choice questions? Well, a check box is similar to the squares that you ticked to indicate your answers.

Check Boxes

1 Create a new Visual Basic project. When the default form appears, select the check box from the toolbox.

2 Double-click the check box icon to draw a check box on the form at the default size and position.

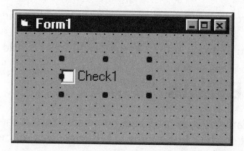

3 By default, the caption of a check box appears to the right of the box. You can change this by changing the Alignment property. Bring up the properties window and find the Alignment property. By default, it is set to 0 - Left Justify, meaning that the box, not the text, is on the left. Double-click this property to change it to 1 - Right Justify. The text moves automatically.

Try It Out!

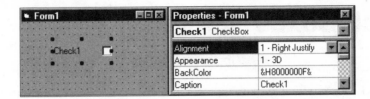

4 Add a couple more check boxes to the form, so that the form now looks like this. Don't forget to change the Alignment property of each.

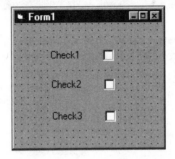

5 Now try running the program. You can select any of the check boxes independently of the others.

Check boxes are independent of each other, which means that checking one does not affect any of the others on the form. This is very different to the way that option buttons work, as you will see a little later.

Check Box Events

There aren't many events that can be used with a check box, and by far the most important is the **click** event. This triggers both when the user points and clicks on the check box and when the user presses the hot-key combination. You can add code to the click event to do something based on the status of the check box at that time. However, you can't just insert the action you want performed into the click event directly, as the clicking action could either **select** or **de-select** the option, depending on what state the check box was in beforehand.

To really make use of check boxes, you have to use the Value property.

The Check Box Value Property

The current status of a check box can be examined using its Value property.

Value Property	Status of Check Box
0	Unchecked
1	Checked
2	Grayed out

Let's write a small program to look at the Value property of a check box while the program is running.

Checking the Check Box

1 Create a new Visual Basic project and draw a check box onto the default form. Add a caption, as shown.

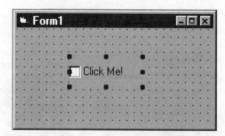

2 Still in design mode, double-click the check box to bring up the Code Window. Type in a message box line so that the Code Window looks like this.

```
Private Sub Check1_Click()

  MsgBox "The value is now " & Check1.Value

End Sub
```

Try It Out!

3 Now try running the program.

Each time you click on the check box a message box will appear showing you what is in the Value property of the check box. If the check box is checked, then Value will be 1. If it is not checked, then Value is 0. The only value you won't see here is 2, which you get when the check box is grayed.

Check Boxes in CON_DEMO

I used a check box as a toggle switch in CON_DEMO to enable or disable the preview image box.

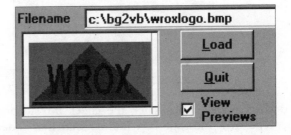

If you take a look at the click event for this control, you can see what's going on.

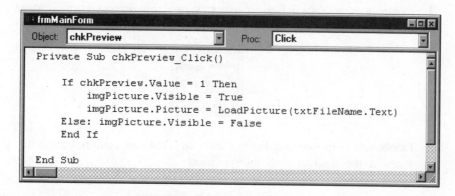

```
frmMainForm                                                    _ □ ×
Object:  chkPreview          ▼     Proc:  Click            ▼

Private Sub chkPreview_Click()

    If chkPreview.Value = 1 Then
        imgPicture.Visible = True
        imgPicture.Picture = LoadPicture(txtFileName.Text)
    Else: imgPicture.Visible = False
    End If

End Sub
```

When the click event happens, the check box's value will change. We first test to see if it has been selected, and if it has, we enable the image control. If it is not selected, we disable the image control.

Option Buttons

Option buttons are a close cousin of the check box. They are also an on/off switch for various options. The difference is that option buttons are **mutually exclusive**. Because they are essentially on/off switches, they are ideal for this. They are very useful in database type applications to let the user quickly choose one from a number of options in a list.

> **FYI**
>
> All the option buttons on a form or in a frame (more on these later) work together: clicking one option button clears all the others. It's like the station selector on a radio, where pressing the button for a new station makes the old one pop out. In fact, they are also known as radio buttons.

Option Buttons

1 Create a new Visual Basic project. When the default form appears, select the option button from the toolbox.

2 Double-click the option button icon to draw an option button on the form at the default size and position.

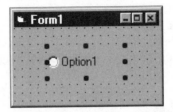

3 Like the check boxes we saw earlier, the caption of an option button always appears, by default, to the right of the button. Just as with the check box, this can be changed, using the option button Alignment property. Bring up the Properties Window and find the Alignment property. Double-click this property to change it to 1 - Right Justify.

4 Add a couple more option buttons to the form so that it now looks like this.

5 Now try running the program.

Any option buttons placed directly onto a form or into the same frame cancel each other out. If you select one, all the others are de-selected. Try it out - with the program running, try clicking on each of the buttons in turn and you'll see the result.

Other than that, the option buttons work in the same way as check boxes, the only exception being the way the Value property works. Instead of having 3 possible values (0, 1 or 2), option buttons only have 2: true or false. If the option button value is set to true, then the button is set, otherwise it is not.

Picture and Image Controls

Visual Basic provides two controls specifically for displaying graphic images: the **Picture** control and the **Image** control. These controls are both very powerful and each has advantages and disadvantages over the other. In this section you will get an overview of both, how they work and what they can be used for. Later, in Chapter 7, we will go into each of them in much more detail. For now, however, it's just a brief glimpse.

Using the Picture and Image Controls

The most important property of both the picture box and the image control is the Picture property, which determines the image file that is loaded into the control. By displaying the Properties Window and double-clicking the Picture property, Visual Basic will display a file requester and ask you to select a file which you want displayed in the control.

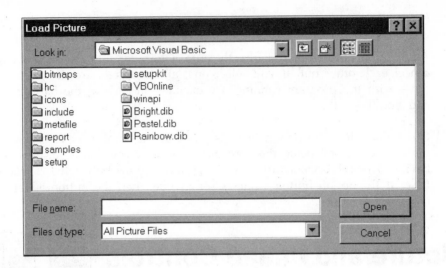

Image File Formats

You can load a number of different kinds of graphics files into the picture and image controls.

Image File Type	File Extension	Description
Bitmap	*.BMP	The traditional Windows format for graphics. Windows Paint is the usual source of these images, which can be used for everything from clip art to icon symbols.
Windows Metafile	*.WMF	Normally a graphic file drawn with a structured drawing package, such as Microsoft Draw. Good for clip art in a program since metafiles take a lot less memory than any other format.
Icon	*.ICO	Small icon graphic, such as those found on toolbars.

Changing the Image

You can load a picture into an image or picture control either at run-time or at design-time. In CON_DEMO as it stands, the controls are empty at the start. Let's change it so the picture control is loaded on startup.

1 Load up CON_DEMO in design mode, view the form and click on the picture box. If it's not visible, bring up the Properties Window by pressing *F4*.

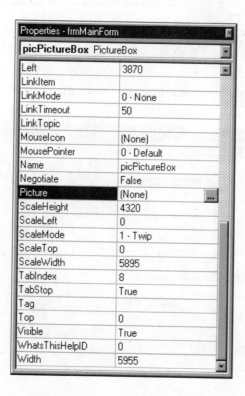

2 Double-click on the Picture property to display the file selector box. Load in one of the sample images supplied with Visual Basic (look in the \VB\ICONS directory).

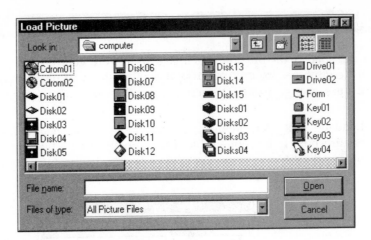

3 You will see the image load up instantly, even at design-time.

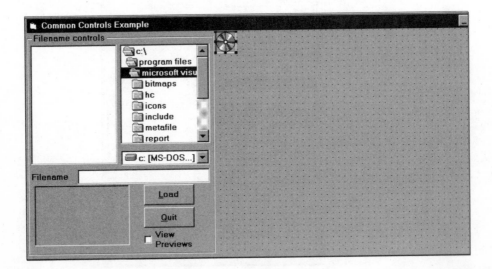

4 You will have noticed that the picture displayed in the picture box is normal sized, whereas when you display an image in the preview window it appeared stretched. In design mode, bring up the Properties Window for the image control and find the Stretch property. This is set to true. Double click the property to change it to false and run the program again - this time the image appears normal sized.

From the point of view of loading in an image, the image and picture controls work the same. However, there are some significant differences between the two.

Picture and Image Controls Compared

An image control is one of a collection of controls known as **lightweight** controls, some of the others being the line control, shape control, and label. In a nutshell, lightweight controls require less system resources (such as computer time and memory) to manage them than other controls do, for example, the picture box, the command button or the heaviest of them all, the grid. The reasons for this are fairly complex, but from our point of view it is the limitations of the image control compared to the picture control that are of interest.

▶ **Images** cannot be placed on top of other controls, unless they are first placed inside a container object, such as a frame or picture box. Also, they cannot receive focus at run-time. We cover focus a little later.

▶ **Picture Boxes** are much more functional than image controls. They can be drawn anywhere and they can receive the focus, which makes them very useful for creating your own graphical toolbars. They can also act as container controls, which means you can place other controls inside them, almost like a form within a form.

In Chapter 7 - Graphics, you will learn how to really put these two controls to work.

More Common Properties

Many of the controls presented in this chapter have properties in common. We looked at some of the simpler ones at the start. However, having gained some more knowledge about specific controls, we can now get a better understanding of more advanced properties such as Enabled.

The Enabled Property

As we have said, check boxes can have three states from the user's point of view. These are **selected**, **de-selected** or **grayed**. A check box, like most other Visual Basic controls, has an Enabled property to control whether it's able to be selected on the form at run-time. The Enabled property can only ever be one of two values, as far as Visual Basic is concerned - true (meaning on), or false (meaning off).

If you have programmed in C or Assembler before, then you will be used to the words True and False. For the rest of us, this may seem awkward - why not simply use the words Yes and No? This is, unfortunately, one of the many areas of programming where jargon has crept in from the bad old days of binary and machine code programming. It stems from something called Boolean logic. We will look at this in more detail much later in the book, but for now I'm afraid you're just going to have to get used to it.

Setting Properties at Run-Time

We've seen in this and the last chapter how to set properties at design-time by using the Properties Window. It's also possible to set them up from within your program code. In fact this is one of the easiest ways to make your programs come alive.

Design-time is the time when your program is not running and you are placing controls onto your form and writing code. *Run-time* is when you have clicked the **Start** button and your forms and controls respond to events by running the relevant procedures.

Disabling Controls

Imagine the user has just entered some text, the result of which is that you want to disable two command buttons, named Command1 and Command2. In your code you would simply write:

```
Command1.Enabled = False
Command2.Enabled = False
```

Visual Basic would then gray out the command buttons to indicate that they no longer work, and your user would be unable to click them.

Enabled   *Disabled*

Disabling a Command Button

It would be useful to disable the <u>L</u>oad button on the CON_DEMO project until the user has selected a file.

1 If CON_DEMO.VBP isn't already loaded, load it up. Call up the Code Window and enter this code into the form load event.

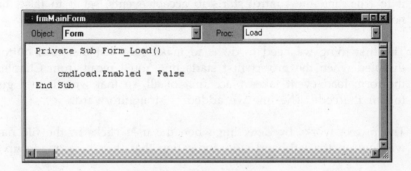

2 Now we need to enter the code that will turn the load button back on again. This should happen when a file is selected, so open up the `filFileNames_Click` event.

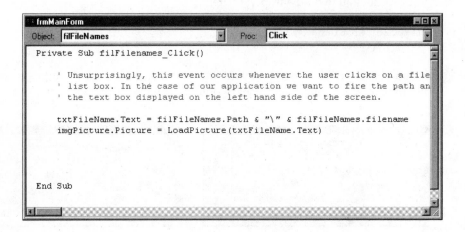

3 Add this line of code:

```
txtFileName.TEXT = filFileNames.Path & "\" & filFileNames.filename
imgPicture.picture = LoadPicture(txtFileName.TEXT)
cmdLoad.Enabled = True
```

4 Now run it and see what happens. At the start the button is disabled. Select a file, and it's enabled.

How It Works

The Enabled property can only ever be one of two values: true or false. Set it to true, and the control starts to accept events, set it to false, and it does not. It's basically an on/off switch.

The first thing we need to do is to make sure that the Load button is disabled when the project first starts up. You'll recall from Chapter 1 that the form load event takes place first of all, so that would be a good place to put the code. The line we added is straightforward.

The project works by detecting when the user clicks in the file names window on the left-hand side, indicating that they have made up their mind which file to choose. The `filFileNames_Click` event responds to the action of the user making their selection. In the original project, this procedure copies the name of the chosen file into the file name text box. The line of code we added follows this by enabling the Load button, thus allowing the user to go ahead and load the file they have chosen.

We'll have another look at the **Enabled** property later in the chapter when we see how out it operates with some other controls.

If you want to reverse the current condition of a control without having to keep track of its current state, then the **Not** operator simply flips backwards and forwards from true to false. If, for example, a command button had been previously enabled, then you can reverse its condition using:

```
Not cmdLoad.Enabled
```

Visual Basic knows that the effect we are after is *whatever the load button is not*. The only other alternative is true, so Visual Basic sets it to that.

Enabling Different Controls

When the Enabled property is used to turn an object off, the effect is visible on screen. Text boxes, command buttons, list boxes and menu items all tend to appear grayed out, indicating to the user that they no longer function.

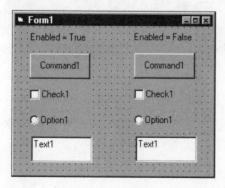 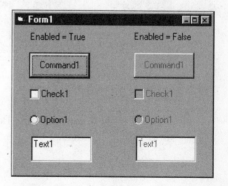

Enabling Controls

You can see this in the example program **CON_DEMO.VBP**. Most of the controls on this form are grouped into what are known as **frames**. These are container controls that can have other controls inside them, and cause these interior controls to effectively inherit some of the properties of the frame in which they reside. We will cover frames in more detail when we discuss container objects in Chapter 7 - Graphics.

At run-time, the left-hand frame and the controls in it are enabled, meaning that you are able to access the file controls on the form. Let's take a look at the frame.

1 Load up **CON_DEMO.VBP** and show the main form. Click on the left-hand frame.

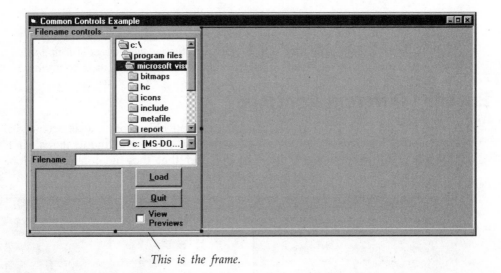

This is the frame.

2 Press *F4* to bring up the Properties Window. Find the Enabled property and set it to false.

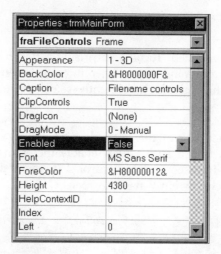

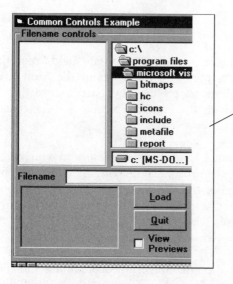

Run the program to see the effect of the frame grayed out. Try and use one of the controls inside the disabled frame - it doesn't work! Although the directory list box will appear enabled, you won't be able to select anything. The same applies for the other two list boxes.

Another common property which operates in a similar way to Enabled is Visible. Setting this property to false has the effect of removing the control from the screen. In the case of a container object such as a form or frame, all controls within it would also disappear when the program is run.

Focus

Earlier on we mentioned **focus** - surprisingly this has nothing to do with karma or the summoning of an inner force to accomplish a goal! In Windows, focus tells us which control is currently selected when the program is running.

To see it in practice, run the example program, **CON_DEMO.VBP**, and press *Tab* a few times (make sure you re-enable the frame). You will see the highlight move from control to control. Wherever the highlight lands, that is the control which currently has the focus.

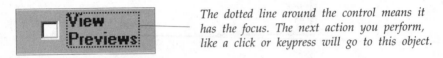

The dotted line around the control means it has the focus. The next action you perform, like a click or keypress will go to this object.

The TabIndex Property

Focus is really useful on a form that has a lot of separate fields requiring data entry. Many experienced typists prefer to move about the form using the *Tab* key, rather than taking their hand off the keyboard to use the mouse. You control the order in which the controls receive the focus using the TabIndex property.

When the **CON_DEMO** project is running, keep pressing *Tab* and you will see the highlight move from control to control starting with the directory list box, then moving to the drive combo, the file list box, filename text box, load button and so on. If you stop the program running and bring up the Properties Window for those controls, you will see the TabIndex starts at 1 for the directory list box, 2 for the drive list box and so on.

1 is not the true first index value, though. The frame containing the file controls is actually the first with an index of 0. Since you can't actually select a frame at run-time, the frame will transfer the focus to the next control in sequence within it, in this case the directory list box.

Whenever you change a TabIndex property, Visual Basic automatically re-orders the rest. Again, you can see this if you bring up the Properties Window for the Quit command button. Set the TabIndex of this to 0 and re-run the program. This time the Quit button gets the focus first, then the directory list box, drive combo, and so on.

Using Focus at Run-Time

You can also move the focus from within your program code. For example, if the user enters some bad data, you can move the focus back to the offending control by using the **SetFocus** command.

Controlling Focus

You can track whether or not a control has focus through the **GotFocus** and **LostFocus** events. Now, this is where the problems start to creep in.

1 Load up the project called **FOCUS.VBP** and view the form.

2 The program has two text boxes, one for a Userid, the other for a Password. There is event code attached to Userid for the **LostFocus** event.

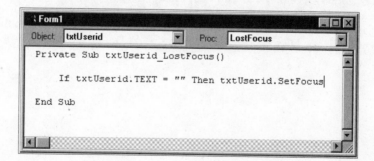

3 If the control loses focus, meaning the command button was clicked or the user moved to the Password box without entering any data, then the **LostFocus** code sets the focus back onto itself.

Run the program and try moving off the Userid box without entering anything. You will see the cursor snap straight back into the Userid box, forcing you to enter something - no problems there!

Now imagine we want to do the same to the Password box.

4 Back in design mode, double-click the Password box to bring up the Code Window and select the **LostFocus** event. Now change the code so that it looks like this:

```
Private Sub txtPassword_LostFocus()
    If txtPassword.Text = "" then txtPassword.Setfocus
End Sub
```

Now we have a problem. For one control to lose focus, another has to gain it. If you run the program now and try moving off the Userid box, the program will hang up; it will lock itself into a loop which you can only stop by pressing *Ctrl-Break*.

What happens here is that as Userid loses focus, so Password gains it. The Userid box then says "Hang on...you didn't enter anything", and grabs the focus back, causing the Password box to lose focus itself. The Password box then does exactly the same as the Userid box just did.

For this reason many programmers do not use the **LostFocus** or **GotFocus** events at all, and especially not for text box validation. The preferred route is to use the **KeyPress** or **Change** events. However, if you must use **LostFocus** then there are ways around the problems, as you will see later.

For My Last Trick...Ole!

We have covered a lot of ground in this chapter - taking you hopefully from the position of someone who knows nothing about Visual Basic to someone who is at least able to draw a user interface, and even add a little code to bring it to life. Now it's time to have some fun with a funky thing called OLE.

In a nutshell, what OLE lets you do is embed entire applications and their data within your own. For example, if you have Microsoft Word 6 or later, then you can actually cut and paste an entire document from it into a Visual Basic application with no code. At run-time, the user is then able to fully edit and interact with the text they see in the application, just as they would as if it were in Word itself.

It sounds too good to be true.

OLE

1 Create a new project. When the new form appears, select the OLE control from the toolbox

2 Draw it onto your form just as if it were any other control.

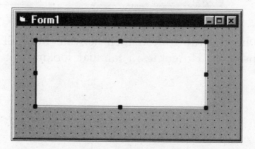

3 After a short pause, a dialog will appear asking you what kind of OLE object you intend to play with. The dialog will list all the OLE applications that your version of Windows knows about. Choose Microsoft Word Document and click OK.

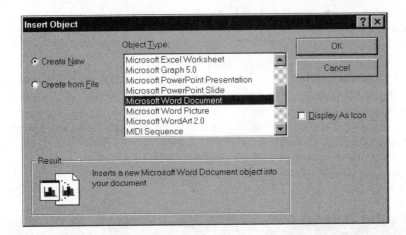

4 After some bumping and grinding (I never said OLE was fast), your form doesn't look all that different.

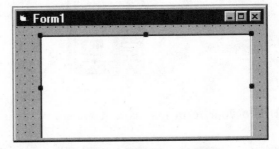

5 However, hit the run button then activate the OLE document by double clicking inside it. Up comes a familiar looking set of toolbars!

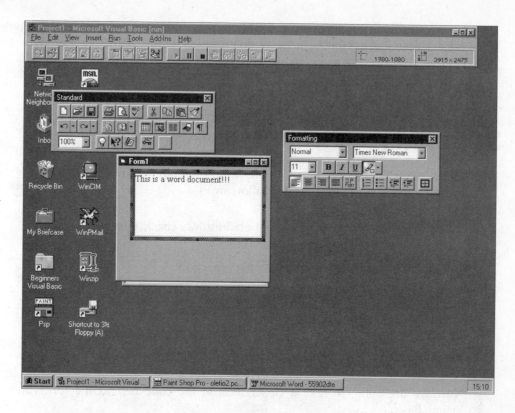

You can now type away and format as though you have a mini version of Word running.

How It Works

In actual fact, you do have a mini version of Word running! What OLE does is load in the parts of MS Word that you need to support the feature set that the control gives us, and then runs this alongside your Visual Basic program. Windows 95 sits between the two applications and makes sure they work together happily.

You don't need much imagination to see how powerful this can be. Microsoft themselves see Visual Basic as "glue" to stick OLE components together with custom applications. Any application that is OLE-compliant can be plundered for functionality.

We go into a lot more detail on OLE later in the book. However, the whole subject does have a bit of a nasty smell about it for many programmers since it is supposed to be so hard to use from a programming point of view. As you can see, Visual Basic 4 changes all that.

Summary

In this chapter, you learnt about the more common controls and how to apply them. You also learnt the following:

- How to use text boxes, option buttons, check boxes, command buttons, picture and image controls.

- How to change properties in your code.

- How to validate a text box.

- The problems that come with text boxes, option buttons and control focus.

- A little about the mysterious world of OLE.

Now we are going to take a closer look at the code behind the forms in Visual Basic.

Why Not Try.......

1 Add a text box to **CON_DEMO** that will show a list of previously opened image files. Make it big enough to accept, say, the last 5 files. The secret is to keep adding the last file name to the existing Text property whenever the file is loaded. Make sure that you set the MultiLine property of the text box to true to make the text wrap around. Try putting a **Chr$(10)** and a **Chr$(13)** at the end of each name to start a new line in the box.

2 Create a program that cycles through colors on a form. Create a blank form and add code to the click event that changes the **BackColor** property to various increasing values. Change the amount you add to **BackColor** each time to see what happens.

3 Use the keypress event on a text box to copy all the keys pressed, except the vowels, to another text box. To do this, you'll have to use an **If** statement that excludes the characters with the ASCII codes of the 5 vowels. Then put a check box on the form to switch this "feature" on and off.

4 Add a text box to the **DETAILS** form that calculates how many seconds you have been alive.

5 If you are feeling really ambitious, try adding a grid of image controls on the right-hand side of **CON_DEMO** instead of the single large picture control. Then add a **LoadPicture** statement to the click event for each box that loads the currently selected image into the box. You can then assemble a custom grid of images.

```
Click
SelectFile_Click()

ne error handling - wh
ger a run time error,
To Dialog_Error

ommon dialog control's
 the Cancel button the
.CancelError = True

e common dialog's titl
.DialogTitle = "Select
```

Writing Code

It's now time to bring your programs to life and make them think for themselves. Designing forms and adding controls isn't enough. Among other things, your programs need to be able to make decisions and run different bits of code depending on what the user does.

In this chapter, we'll look at some of the building blocks of Visual Basic programming. If you've programmed in BASIC, C or Pascal before, then most of this will be familiar.

You will learn:

▶ How to make choices using `If...Then`.

▶ How to select from various options.

▶ How to loop using `For...Next` and `Do...While`.

▶ How to combine all these language features into working Visual Basic programs.

Writing Code in Visual Basic

In the first two chapters you gained an understanding of the main components of a Visual Basic program:

▶ **Forms** are the framework on which you build your interface.

▶ **Controls** are the building blocks from which you construct that interface.

▶ **Event procedures** are the glue that binds these components together and makes it into a system that achieves what you want.

One of our objectives in this book is to try and get you up and running fast, with practical and interesting programs. To do this, we've thrown you in at the deep end. You saw your first lines of code in Chapter 1, using the `Form_UnLoad` event to display a message box wishing you good-bye. In Chapter 2, you saw even more code in the `CON_DEMO.VBP` project. We explained some of this as we went along; the rest we've kept under wraps for the moment.

Now, I'm afraid, the party's over and it's time to get down to some serious programming. The next two chapters are about the techniques you need to write effective event handlers.

▶ In this chapter, we'll explain how to structure your program code so you can make choices and respond to different events and conditions.

▶ In Chapter 4, you'll find out how to represent data in your code, and what you can do to that data to get your required results.

These two subjects are fundamental building blocks for programming in Visual Basic. You will learn all sorts of other things along the way, including the rich set of built-in functions that Visual Basic offers. We'll throw all of these in as and when appropriate. For now though, if you are going to get to grips with writing code in Visual Basic, you need to understand its structure and the data within it. So, let's make a start!

Making Choices in Programs

Two of the most important parts of any programming language are its decision making and branching capabilities. These terms need some explanation.

Decision Making

In an event procedure, your code will normally start to run at the first line of code and proceed down through the rest until it meets either an **Exit Sub** or an **End Sub** statement. The word **Sub** is short for **subprocedure**, which is the name Visual Basic gives to a single block of code. For example, many applications include a Quit command button. When this button is clicked, the application shuts down. The simplest event code you would find for this command button being clicked is:

```
Private Sub cmdQuit_Click()
    End
End Sub
```

The word **Private** tells Visual Basic that this particular block of code can only be called from within the same form or module; don't put **Private** in front of a procedure that you plan to run from all over your program.

Decision making takes place when the program code decides to perform a particular action *providing* that a certain condition is met. As a programmer, you first of all have to test the condition, then write the code that needs to be executed in response.

Think about the Quit command button again. Although the event code does the job just fine, it could make a safer exit. What would happen if the user hit the Quit button by accident? The application would close down and, if they had forgotten to save their work, your poor user would lose the lot. Decision making can get around this problem:

```
Private Sub cmdQuit_Click()

    If WorkSaved = False Then
        MsgBox "Save your work first!"
    Else
        End
    End If

End Sub
```

With just a few extra lines of decision making code, your users become happy bunnies. When they hit the Quit button, the code checks to see if their work is saved. It does this by checking the value of a variable called **WorkSaved**. If the work has not been saved, then our old friend the **MsgBox** is used to display a message to that effect. Otherwise, the application ends as before.

If you want to run this fragment of code yourself, then add the line WorkSaved = False directly before the If statement. It's really intended to work as part of a larger program where the value of WorkSaved would have been set elsewhere.

Branching

Branching occurs when the program code takes control of itself and decides that the next line to run is in fact ten lines back, or a hundred lines further on.

Decision making and branching are closely related. The code won't normally branch to a different line unless a decision has been made saying that it should do so. Think about a trip to the beach. Given that everything goes to plan you:

1 Drive to the beach.

2 Find a pleasant spot.

3 Relax for the rest of the day.

4 Pack up your stuff.

5 Drive home.

Decision making comes into play if you live in a country like England, which has no roof! In that case you:

1 Drive to the beach.

2 **If** the weather is rotten, **Go to** step 6.

3 Find a pleasant spot.

4 Relax for the rest of the day.

5 Pack up your stuff.

6 Drive Home.

The same techniques apply with Visual Basic. You lay out your code in the order you want things to happen. You then use condition statements like **If** to check things are OK. If they aren't, then **Goto**, **GoSub** or **Call** statements can be used to branch to another part of the code.

Over the course of this chapter, you will learn everything you need to know about **If** statements, **Goto**, **Gosub**, and **Call** - so don't panic if it isn't all completely crystal clear straight away.

It is possible to branch off to another part of the program without having tested any condition. However, this is regarded as bad programming practice and I'll explain why in the course of this chapter.

Decision Making

There are various ways to make choices and selections in code though they all come back to the same basic action - testing whether or not something is true. As you will see over the next few pages, you will sometimes be glad of a way of handling a decision making process that is more elegant than a long and complicated line of **If** statements. This is where methods such as **Select Case**, which we will be looking at later, come into play.

Testing for Conditions with If

The simplest way to make a decision in a program is using the `If` statement. You may remember that we have already used this in some of the examples in the book. Hopefully, everything that you've seen already will now begin to fall into place. Let's try out some code to see how the `If` statement works.

The Basic If Statement

Many business applications have some form of security built in to prevent unwanted users from playing around with information they shouldn't have access to. Normally, you use the `If` statement to check the user's name and password before letting them go any further.

Let's see how to do this.

1 Start a new Visual Basic project.

2 Bring up the Properties Window for the default form by pressing *F4*. Change the Caption property to Please enter your password.

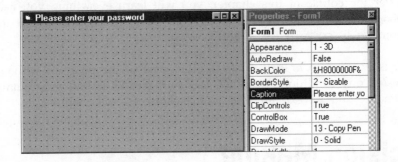

3 Draw one text box and one command button on the form. Re-size the form and move the new controls around so that your form looks something like this:

4 Select the text box and bring up its Properties Window. Find the PasswordChar property and set it to *. See how the text box caption is replaced by *****.

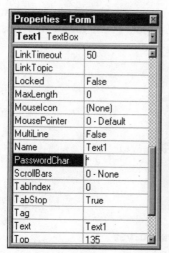 

5 Then, find the Text property and blank it out: select the property by clicking on it, then press the *BkSp* key on your keyboard, followed by *Enter*. This removes the ***** from the box.

6 Select the command button, bring up its Properties Window and set the caption to OK.

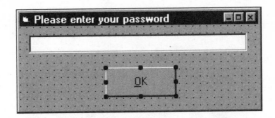

7 Now we can write some code. When the program runs, we want the user to key in their password, then hit the OK button. At that point, an **If** statement will check the password and display the results in a message box on the screen.

Double-click the command button to bring up the Code Window. Type in code so that the command button's click event looks like this:

```
Private Sub Command1_Click()
 If Text1.Text = "noidea" Then
        MsgBox "Great - password accepted!"
        Unload Form1
        End
    Else
        MsgBox "Sorry, that's wrong, try again!"
        Text1.Text = ""
        Text1.SetFocus
    End If
End Sub
```

This program is on the disk called **PASSWORD.VBP**.

When referring to the **Text** property of **Text1**, I have taken care to use the full syntax for the sake of clarity. You could, however, miss off the **Text** property name completely and just use **Text1**. By default, Visual Basic will assume this refers to the **Text** property.

How It Works

Now try running the program. If you typed all the code in correctly then the program will run after a short pause. Click in the text box and type Fred.

Stars appear in place of the keys you press on the keyboard. This is what setting the PasswordChar property to * does for you.

Having entered Fred, click the command button and a message box appears telling you to try again.

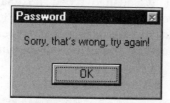

Get rid of the message box by clicking the OK button, then type noidea into the text box and click the command button again. This time the password is accepted and the program ends.

The **If** statement in the above example consists of a number of parts:

▶ Straight after the word **If** there is the condition we want to test. In this example the condition is `Text1.Text = "noidea"`.

▶ Immediately following the condition is the **Then** statement which tells Visual Basic what to do if the condition is met.

Take a look at the code again. Translated into plain English it says: *If the value of the text box is "noidea" then unload the form and end the program.*

The **Else** statement, and the code following it, tells Visual Basic what to do if the condition is not met. In the example, this part of the command actually means: *otherwise, display the message "Sorry, that's wrong, try again!"*

and move the cursor back to the text box. The **Else** part of the statement is actually optional - you could just have an **If** statement that only does something if the condition is met.

The two lines of code

```
Text1.Text = ""
Text1.SetFocus
```

clear the previous text ready to accept your next attempt and set the focus back onto the text box.

You should note that by default, comparing text in Visual Basic is case sensitive. This means that it matters whether you use CAPITALS or lower case letters in the text. If you had typed **NoIdea**, it would have been rejected as an incorrect password. If you want to make Visual Basic case insensitive, you should add the statement **Option Compare Text** to your code. Just type this line into the (General) (declarations) section of the form or the module you want it to apply to.

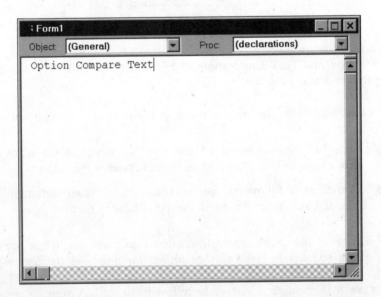

To return to the default, you need to use **Option Compare Binary**. As this is a default, you don't actually have to type it in. Deleting the line you just added will do fine.

Defining the Conditions You Want to Test

This actually leads us nicely on to **conditional expressions**. It's pretty obvious what the = sign means in the previous example, but what if you want to test for two numbers not being equal, or a number that is higher than another? By changing the equals sign in the example, you can test for many different conditions.

The complete list of symbols that you can use to test conditions are:

Symbol	Meaning
=	Is equal to
<>	Is not equal to
>	Is greater than
<	Is less than
>=	Is greater than or equal to
<=	Is less than or equal to

For example, `If Age > 21 then Admit_Entry`, would read as *If age is greater than 21, then admit entry*. Here `Admit_Entry` represents some code you want executed if the condition is true.

> **FYI**
>
> The code `Admit_Entry` can either be a few lines of Visual Basic code tucked right there in the same event handler, or it can be code contained in its own module, separate from this handler. In the second case, this block of code is called a subprocedure and simply writing its name, `Admit_Entry`, causes Visual Basic to jump to that code and execute it there and then. Modules and subprocedures are inherently bound up with controlling program flow, and we'll look at them in more detail later in this chapter. Before that though, let's finish our review of the ways to test conditions in Visual Basic.

Testing Multiple Conditions

This is all fairly straightforward stuff - but what happens when you need to test for more than one condition before doing something? An example could be a correct password and the person's age to be greater than 21.

Visual Basic lets you use the words **And** and **Or** in order to make your complex conditions easier to read in code. In this example we could have an **If** statement that says:

```
If Age > 21 And Password = "noidea" Then Admit_Entry
```

You can also use brackets to group conditions together. Normally with an **If** statement you check for a number of conditions and tell Visual Basic whether you want to do something if all the conditions are met (using **And**) or if only one condition is met (using **Or**). You can group tests together by using brackets on the **If** line. For instance, with a line like this

```
If Age > 21 and Password = "noidea" or Password = "Supervisor" Then
⤷Do_Something
```

it's not immediately obvious what the code does. Does it do something if the **Age** is greater than 21 and the password is **"noidea"** or **"Supervisor"**? Or does it do something if the password is **"noidea"** and **Age** is greater than 21, or if the **Password = "Supervisor"**? Confusing isn't it?

By using brackets the code becomes much more readable and the results a great deal more predictable:

```
If (Age > 21 and Password = "noidea") or Password = "Supervisor" Then
⤷Do_Something
```

This **If** line will do something if the password is **"Supervisor"**, or if **Age** is greater than 21 and the password is **"noidea".** The brackets separate the tests into smaller groups, so the **If** line treats

```
(Age > 21 and Password = "noidea")
```

as one test, call it test A, and

```
Password = "Supervisor"
```

as another test, call it test B. The **If** line will then work as long as A *or* B is met.

When we get a long line of code, I've broken it onto two lines using a ⬎ symbol. This isn't part of Visual Basic. When you type the code in, you should ignore the symbol and put all the code on one line. There is in fact a continuation character in Visual Basic. When you want to break a line of code put a space followed by an underscore _ character. I haven't done this in the book because I don't think you'll see a _ as clearly as a ⬎.

Multi-line If Statements

It's already obvious that the line of code gets longer and longer as the condition gets more and more complex. There is another way to use the **If** statement which can help make the code a little more readable.

With the multi-line **If** statement, the code following the word **Then** is spread over one or more lines. A new command, **End If** tells Visual Basic exactly where the conditional code ends. Let's try the example again:

```
If (sPassword = "noidea" and sUserName = "Peter") or
⬎LoggedIn = True Then

    Allow_Access
    Update_User_Log
    Display_First_Screen

End If
```

By using the multi-line **If**, you not only make your code a lot more readable, but you also place a lot more functionality into the **If** statement. In this example, providing the appropriate conditions are met, three subroutine calls are made instead of just one.

Multi-line If...Else Statements

Just as with the single line **If,** the multi-line version lets you use the **Else** statement to give Visual Basic an alternative course of action:

```
If (Password = "noidea" and UserName = "Peter") or
↳LoggedIn = True Then

    Allow_Access
    Update_User_Log
    Display_First_Screen

Else

    Deny_Access
    Erase_HardDisk
    Electrocute_User

End If
```

Multiple Alternatives Using ElseIf

Under normal circumstances you are limited to just two courses of action with an **If** statement:

▶ The code that executes if the condition is met.

▶ The code following the **Else** that executes if the condition fails.

With multi-line **If**s, though, you can perform further tests depending on the result of a prior test. For this you need to use **ElseIf**.

ElseIf enables you to build complex decision making code that can take any number of courses of action.

```
If <condition> Then
    :
    :
ElseIf <condition> Then
    :
    :
ElseIf <condition> Then
    :
    :
Else
    :
    :
End If
```

The code following the last **Else** statement is run if all the other conditions on the **If** and **ElseIf** lines fail.

Multi-line If Statements

1 Load up the **MULTVIEW.VBP** project from the sample programs provided and run it. This project allows you to select a file and then view it using one of the other programs on your system. Please note that this program will only work with Windows 95.

2 Click on the File Name command button to select a File to view. This displays a standard Windows open file dialog box. This looks like every other Windows open file dialog, because that's exactly what it is. It's a built-in piece of Windows, known as a common dialog, that we have borrowed for our project. We'll cover this in detail in Chapter 6 - Dialogs, but for now, don't worry too much about how it works - just go ahead and use it.

3 Once you have selected a file, click on the View The File dialog command button and **MULTVIEW** will load up the appropriate program and display the file. (Hint: look for text or write files...)

The program isn't complete. If you select a file ending in .**BAT**, then nothing happens. You'd expect it to load that file into Notepad in the same way as .**TXT** files. Also, in this age of multimedia, the program is unable to deal with .**WAV** (sound samples) files, .**MID** (MIDI soundtrack) files or .**AVI** (real-time video) files. Let's add these features and also make the program tell us when something has gone wrong, rather than just sitting there blankly. First, though, let's find out what's going on under the hood.

How It Works

In design mode, double-click on the View The File command button to display the code that recognizes the various files.

```
Private Sub cmdView_Click()

    ' This sets up a variable, a place in memory to hold some data.
    ' The As String bit tells VB that we are going to store Text in this
    ' area.
    Dim sExtension As String

    Dim ReturnValue

    sExtension = UCase(Right$(txtFile, 3))

    If Dir$(txtFile) = "" Then
        MsgBox "Sorry, I couldn't find that file!", vbExclamation
        Exit Sub

    ElseIf sExtension = "TXT" Then

        ReturnValue = Shell("Notepad " & txtFile, 1)

    ElseIf sExtension = "WRI" Then

        ReturnValue = Shell("Wordpad" & txtFile, 1)

    End If

End Sub
```

Looks daunting, doesn't it? The first three lines, excluding the **Sub** line, set up some variables. These are places in memory to temporarily hold data. We cover variables in the next chapter.

```
sExtension = Ucase$(Right$(txtFile, 3))
```

This next line takes the 3 right-most letters of the selected file name (i.e. the file extension) and makes sure that all the letters are changed to upper case. It then stores the result in the **sExtension** variable. For example, if you selected **README.TXT**, this line would take the **TXT** bit, make sure it is all upper case letters, and store the result in **sExtension**.

The main part of the code is the **If...Then** statement. This is a multi-line **If** which first checks whether the file selected actually exists and then checks the three **sExtension** variables to see if it recognizes the file type. If it does, then the appropriate program is loaded up using the **Shell** command and the selected file is shown.

DIR$** allows us to check whether a file exists. The **DIR$ command returns either the name of the file if it is found, or **""** if it's not. So the line

```
If Dir$(txtFile) = "" Then
```

will do something if the file name in the text box can't be found on the disk. **Shell** is a command in Visual Basic which lets us run another program. The program name and any other parameters are held in the brackets after the word **Shell**. For example,

```
ReturnValue = Shell("Notepad " & txtFile, 1)
```

runs up Notepad and displays the **README.TXT** file you may have selected. The **1** in the code tells Visual Basic that when the program is run it should be displayed in front of our Visual Basic program. You could equally well have **Shell** run a program out of sight in the background, or just display a minimized icon for it.

Shell actually returns a value to your code which you can check to see if everything worked OK. In this example, though, we just dump whatever **Shell** returns into the **ReturnValue** variable and don't actually use it.

Try It Out!

Adding More File Types

1 In the Code Window, click on the line above the words **End If** and type in this:

```
ElseIf sExtension = "WAV" or sExtension = "MID" or sExtension =
↳"AVI" Then
    ReturnValue= Shell ("MPlayer " & txtFile.TEXT, 1)
Else
    MsgBox "Sorry, I don't know how to handle this file type",
↳vbExclamation
```

2 This **ElseIf** tells Visual Basic how to deal with sound and video files. As you saw before, the code after this **ElseIf** will only be run if the initial **If** and the other **ElseIfs** fail. Now if you run the program, you'll be able to deal with graphics files and multimedia files, such as **WAV**s and **MID**s.

3 The **Else** command which you entered displays a message box. **Else**, as opposed to **ElseIf**, normally lets you tell Visual Basic what it should do if the **If** fails. In this case, though, **Else** tells Visual Basic what to do if the **If** and **ElseIf** lines fail.

Finally, let's make the program treat **BAT** files the same as it does **TXT** files. Move to the line that says:

```
ElseIf sExtension = "TXT" Then
```

Change it so that it now reads

```
ElseIf sExtension = "TXT" Or sExtension = "BAT" Then
```

and the program will then be able to read **BAT** files.

FYI

I'll make no bones about it - this is a difficult program to throw at you now. Don't worry if it doesn't all fall into place immediately as a lot of what's in it will be covered in later chapters. I just wanted to give you a useful application here and now. The finished program is on the disk as SHOWDONE.VBP.

Putting Code into Modules

Once you start to use multi-line **If** statements, the amount of code you write for all the possible conditions can be huge. Worse than that, you may want to branch to the same code in many different situations, the result being that you type in the same piece of code over and over again.

Imagine, for example, that you wanted to check the characters that your user was inputting into a text box, like we did in Chapter 2. If you only have one text box, then that's no problem. Unfortunately, however, most real-life forms have lots of data entry points, so you could end up typing in the same code for each one. There has to be a better way, and sure enough there is - **modular programming**.

Up to now, all the code we have written has been directly contained in the event handlers of various controls and objects. As these objects are themselves placed onto forms, all our code has been inside forms. Modules are very different.

Whereas the code in a form normally relates specifically to that form, code in a module can be **public**. It can be called on by any other code in your project, and is not normally tied to any one control or form. So in the case of checking text box input, you could create a public routine in a module called, for example, **CheckInput**. You could then call that central routine whenever you needed it.

Functions and Procedures

In breaking down your program into modules, you have a choice between functions and procedures.

> **Functions** usually consist of code that does something specific and then returns a result to the part of the program that called it. The **Sin()** function in Visual Basic does exactly this. You pass a number to it, and it gives you back a result which is the sine of the original number.

> **Procedures**, on the other hand, don't tend to return results. They just do something. The **Load** method in Visual Basic is actually a procedure. There is no way to check whether the form is actually loaded or not, apart from just looking at it.

So far, all the Visual Basic code you've written is for event procedures. A command button is pressed, so Visual Basic runs the `Command1_Click()` event **procedure**. Your code in that procedure usually does something like changing the display, but you don't tend to pass anything back to Visual Basic.

The Big Picture

Forms, modules, subprocedures and functions are all related. But just what exactly are they? Well, you already know about forms - these are the elements of your programs onto which you can draw controls to build up a program's user interface.

Behind all the graphic excitement you have event code. This is code which does something in response to the user triggering an event, such as clicking on a command button, moving the mouse, and so on. These events are actually called subprocedures.

Think about making a cup of coffee. `Making_Coffee` is the application. Filling up the kettle, putting coffee in the cup and stirring the coffee are all subprocedures. You don't have to learn how to fill the kettle each time you want to make some coffee. `Filling_The_Kettle` is stored in your head as a subprocedure. It's the same in your Visual Basic application. If you have a common block of code that is used over and over, put it in a subprocedure.

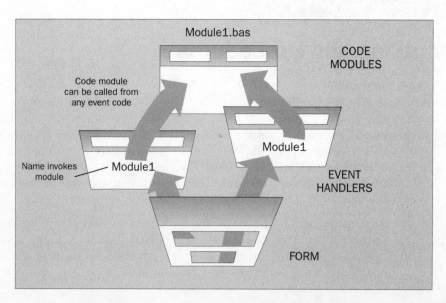

Functions are very similar to subprocedures except for the fact that they return results. When you make a cup of coffee you may not be able to find the coffee jar, so you call out to the **Find_Coffee** function to locate the coffee. You can then get the **Get_Coffee** subprocedure to go to wherever the **Find_Coffee** function told you to go.

Imagine a form which has no visual manifestation, just subroutines and functions. If you can picture this, then you can picture a module. Modules provide a way for you to write code which can be used throughout your entire system. Normally, subprocedures and functions in a module are **global,** meaning that they can be called by code anywhere else in your application.

If you're still a little confused, don't worry. We'll cover functions, subprocedures and modules in a lot more detail as you work your way through the book.

Adding Subprocedures

Let's add some more code to the **SHOWDONE** project we saw earlier. By default the form appears on your screen wherever Windows and Visual Basic think it should. Wouldn't it be nice if we could just call a subprocedure that automatically centers the form?

1 Load up the **SHOWDONE.VBP** project again. When the form appears, press *F7* or double-click it to bring up the Code Window.

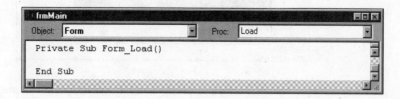

2 Click on the arrow next to Form and select the (General) (declarations) section. To add a new subprocedure simply type the following line beneath the words **Option Explicit**.

```
Private Sub Center
```

Press *Enter* and Visual Basic will automatically put in the lines that mark the start and end of the new procedure and then wait patiently for you to type something meaningful.

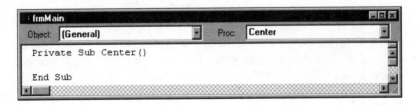

3 Type in code so that the **Center** subprocedure looks like this:

```
Private Sub Center ()

    frmMain.Left = (Screen.Width - frmMain.Width) \ 2
    frmMain.Top = (Screen.Height - frmMain.Height) \ 2

End Sub
```

4 Now use the object combo box at the top of the Code Window to select Form.

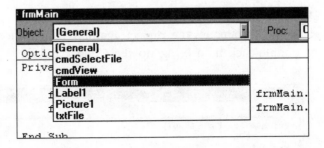

As soon as you select Form, the form Load event code is displayed in the Code Window, instead of your new subprocedure. Your subprocedure is still there, just not visible.

Change the form Load code to say the following:

```
Private Sub Form_Load()

   Call Center

End Sub
```

The **Call** command tells Visual Basic that we want to call a subprocedure. In our case, **Call Center** tells Visual Basic to run the subprocedure called **Center**.

How It Works

Call is really a hang over from the days of Visual Basic 1 and 2. Although you can use it, and it does make your code a lot easier to read, you could equally well have said:

```
Sub Form_Load ()

   Center

End Sub
```

Since **Center** is not a keyword, Visual Basic knows that you are trying to call a subprocedure.

Keywords are words that mean something in Visual Basic. They are used for things such as commands. You can't use them in your code for your own purposes.

If you run the program now, you'll see that the form loads up dead center of the screen.

Where's the Form?

When you use modules, you can actually choose not to show any form at all when your program starts. Instead, you can run code in a module directly. If you want to interact with your users, however, you'll have to create a user interface on the fly. Modules are normally used as a backup to forms. They provide common code which all the forms can use. Just to illustrate the point, though, let's write a program with no forms at all.

A Program with No Forms

1 Load up Visual Basic and start a new project. As you know, all new projects in Visual Basic are created with a form already in them. From the View menu select Project and the Project Window will appear showing you a list of all the files in your project. The only one at this point is, of course, Form1.

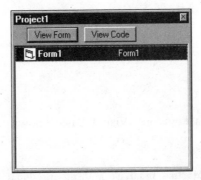

2 Select this line by clicking it once, then from the File menu select Remove File. The form will vanish from your project forever. Now we've got a project with no forms and no modules.

3 Now create a module by selecting Module from the Insert menu or by clicking on the module icon in the Visual Basic toolbar.

4 As soon as you create a module, a Code Window pops up for it. Remember, modules are forms but without the visual side.

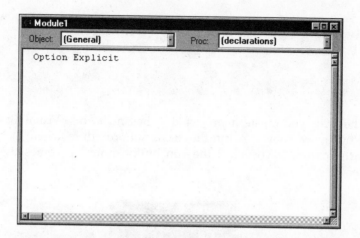

The words `Option Explicit` keep appearing because we've asked
Visual Basic to make us declare all variables. We'll cover this in detail
in the next chapter. For now, ignore it.

5 For a program with no forms, you need to have a subprocedure called
Main in a module, to act as the replacement for your main form. Click
in the Code Window now and create a **Main** subprocedure.

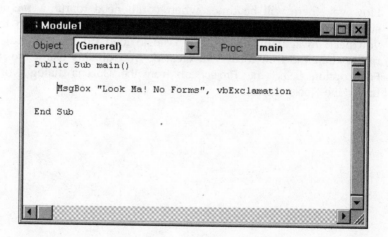

Whenever you create a project that has no forms, Visual Basic instinctively knows to run the **Main** subprocedure when the program starts to run. If you click the run button now, up comes the message box.

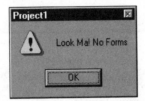

We used a form of the **MsgBox** statement here. The only things we told the command were to show the text **"Look Ma! No Forms"** and to make the box a simple type with an exclamation mark. The constant **vbExclamation** tells Visual Basic the type of box we want. Message boxes get the full treatment in Chapter 6.

6 However, there will be times when you'll need to run a **Main** subprocedure in an application that does have forms. When this happens you need to actually tell Visual Basic to load up your module first, rather than the first form you created. You do this using the Start Up Form option. Select the Project tab from the Options dialog (you'll find it under the Tools menu).

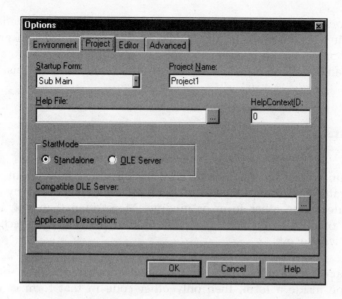

Here the Start Up Form option is set to Sub Main, meaning that the `Main` subprocedure will be run before anything else. If you had a project with a number of forms, then you could select any of the forms to be run first instead.

Doing It in Public or Private?

In the code examples up to this point, and in many more to come throughout the rest of the book, you will notice the word `Public` or `Private` placed at the start of subprocedures or functions. What does this mean?

As you already know, Visual Basic projects are actually made up of forms for the user interface and code modules that perform background and common tasks. Each of these units is self-contained. They have their own data and their own code. **Public** and **Private** enforce this.

Public procedures are declared like this:

```
Public Sub <procedure name>
Public Function <functionname> As <returntype>
```

A routine declared as **Public** is accessible from throughout the whole program. For example, code in Module1 could be called by code in Form1, or indeed any other form or module. More often than not, if you need a piece of code to do something throughout the whole project, then **Public** is what you want.

Private on the other hand is totally the opposite. If you stick a **Private** routine inside a form, then only other code in that form can use it. For example, let's say you have a two form application and you create a **Private** routine in Form1. At that point, the only code that can legally call this routine is code in Form1. Calling it from Form2 will just cause an error.

So what's the point? Well, life would certainly appear to be simpler if everything was **Public**. That way you wouldn't have to worry about having to keep track of what's where. **Private** procedures, however, have certain inherent advantages:

▶ They use less memory, in particular less of the crowded bits of memory. If everyone in a town came out onto the street at the same time, then things would get crowded.

▶ They protect parts of your code that you don't want to be affected by operations outside the module.

▶ They let you use the same names over again in different modules.

Of course, this is just an overview. We use both **Public** and **Private** routines throughout the entire book, and cover them in a great deal of detail in Chapter 14 - Object Orientation, where it fits best. In both the next chapter and in Chapter 12 - Writing Programs that Work, we will see how variables fit into the public and private landscape.

Getting Selective

If you play around with conditions and **If** statements long enough, you'll soon end up tying yourself in knots with code consisting of line upon line of extremely similar looking **If..Then...Else** statements. **If** is great for one-shot tests and simple two-state decision making (**If** a **Then** b **Else** c). But when things start to get really messy, it's time to reach for the **Select Case** statement.

The Select Case Statement

There comes a point in any program where the **If** command is simply not up to the job. Imagine, for example, a menu on screen - not your normal Windows style menu, but a simple list of numbered text entries. Let's say there are seven of them. If the user presses number 1 on the keyboard, then you want the first subprocedure to run. If they press 2, then a different one should kick in, and so on.

Using **If** you would have something like this:

```
If KeyPress = "1" Then
    Call Sub1
Else If Keypress = "2" Then
    Call Sub2
Else If Keypress = "3" Then
    Call Sub3
Else If Keypress = "4" Then
    Call Sub4
    :
    :
```

Looks a mess doesn't it? If computers are so great at making repetitive tasks simple, then there must be a more elegant way of doing this kind of test. There is - using the **Select Case** command.

Select Case in Action

Remember the awful multi-line **If** statement in **MULTVIEW.VBP**? Using **Select Case** that code could be so much nicer. But before we launch into a fully blown breakdown of how it all works, let's type some code.

Try It Out!

1 In Visual Basic, load up the **SHOWDONE.VBP** project again. This is the **MULTVIEW.VBP** project that we modified earlier. When the form appears, double-click on the View The File command button on the main form to see its code.

All the **ElseIf** lines relate to the **sExtension** variable - checking the extension of the selected file and running the appropriate program. This is ideal hunting ground for **Select Case**. (Finger ache time).

2 Change the code so **Select Case** is used, like this:

```
    Private Sub cmdView_Click()

' This sets up a variable, a place in memory to hold some data.
' The As String bit tells VB that we are going to store Text in this
' area.
Dim sExtension As String

Dim ReturnValue

sExtension = UCase(Right$(txtFile, 3))

If Dir$(txtFile) = "" Then
    MsgBox "Sorry, I couldn't find that file!", vbExclamation
    Exit Sub
EndIf

Select Case sExtension
    Case "TXT", "BAT"
        ReturnValue = Shell("Notepad " & txtFile, 1)
    Case "WRI", "DOC"
        ReturnValue = Shell("Wordpad" & txtFile, 1)
    Case "WAV", "MID", "AVI"
        ReturnValue = Shell("MPlayer " & txtFile.Text, 1)
    Case Else
        MsgBox "Sorry, I don't know how to handle this file type",
vbExclamation
    End Select
```

All that's involved here is moving the **End If** line to underneath the words **Exit Sub**, then changing all the **ElseIf**s to **Case**, and adding a **Select Case** statement.

How It Works

`Select Case` tells Visual Basic that we want to check against one specific variable, in this case `sExtension`. The `Case` lines that follow tell Visual Basic what to do if the variable equals the value following the word `Case`. This value is written in quotes if it is text.

Notice how if you want to check for more than one value, you simply separate the values in the `Case` statement with commas:

```
Case "TXT", "BAT"
```

This is the same as saying

```
If sExtension = "TXT" or sExtension = "BAT" Then
```

but with the obvious exception that the `Case` statement is easier to read and takes a great deal less typing that the traditional `If xxxx Or xxxxx Then` construct.

In the above example, if we were only interested in files ending in `TXT`, then the `Case` statement would look like this:

```
Case "TXT"
```

There's no need for commas here, just the single value that you want to check for.

Selecting Options Based on Different Conditions

As well as being able to check a single value or a number of values, the `Case` statement can also check running ranges of numbers, such as 1 - 5, or 100 - 200. Let's say you wanted to check if the variable contained a number in the range 10 - 15; your `Case` statement would look like this:

```
Case 10 To 15
   Here is the code
   That you want to execute
   If these values are true.
```

Another difference to the normal `If` statement is that `Case` statements can't contain the name of the variable you are checking, so you couldn't say `Case Index > 10` if `Index` is the name of the variable in the `Select` statement. Instead, you should use the word `Is`. `Is` refers to the variable you're checking, so it is quite legal to write:

```
Case Is > 100, Is <= 500, 999
```

This checks for values greater than 100, or less than 500 or equal to 999. Remember that the variable name is held on the `Select Case` line. The `Is` keyword checks the value of the variable against the condition, so `Is > 100` means: *if the variable is greater than 100*. As before, the commas mean *or*, so the above line actually says: *If the variable is greater than 100, or less than or equal to 500, or equal to 999, then do something.*

Selecting Strings

You can use `Case` in exactly the same way to deal with text. If you use the `To` clause, Visual Basic does an alphabetic comparison on the two strings:

```
Select Case sPassword
    Case "Apples" To "Pears"
        :
        :
End Select
```

This example would cause your case code to run if the value of the `Password` string falls alphabetically between `"Apples"` and `"Pears"`.

FYI

When you do comparisons between text strings, Visual Basic deals with the comparison in a semi-intelligent way. First of all it looks at the case of the letters in the string. A capital letter such as G is treated as coming before its lower case equivalent g. So if you were to compare Peter and peter, in alphabetical sorting Peter comes first.

This type of comparison occurs for every letter of the string. The result is that Visual Basic handles strings properly, so that Apple comes before Pear, Aardvark comes before Arachnid, and so on. Beware, though - Aardvark is quite different to aardvark as far as Visual Basic is concerned.

For My Next Trick - Loops

Conditional statements such as **If** are great for running pieces of code that are based on just one condition. However, the real beauty of computers has always been their ability to do a great many repetitive operations in a fraction of the time it would take a human to do the same thing.

This is where loops come into play. Think back to your schooldays. You've just entered class late for the 12th time and forgotten your homework for the 10th time. The teacher is naturally a little upset and, in a fit of fury, orders you to write down "I must stop being a complete failure" 1000 times. There we have it - a boring, odious task which a computer could perform with no hassle. The only thing to remember here, though, is that the well-programmed computer probably wouldn't have been late for class in the first place.

A **For** loop is what we need here. This enables us to run a block of code a set number of times. In the case of our little childhood problem, the code in question would simply write the words "I must stop being a complete failure" 1000 times.

The For Loop

1 Start a new project in Visual Basic. Double-click on the form to display its Code Window.

2 Select the **Form_Load** event and type in some code so that it looks like this.

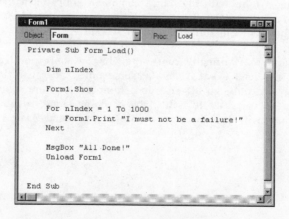

```
Private Sub Form_Load()

    Dim nIndex

    Form1.Show

    For nIndex = 1 To 1000
        Form1.Print "I must not be a failure!"
    Next

    MsgBox "All Done!"
    Unload Form1


End Sub
```

Try It Out!

3 Run the code and you'll see the message appear on the form 1000 times. A message box then appears telling you that the program has finished. We'll cover the **Print** command in more detail in Chapter 7, but for now this is quite straightforward, I think.

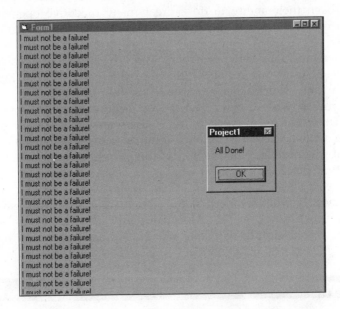

The line **For nIndex = 1 to 1000** is the start of the **For** loop, which is what we're interested in. The **Show** command before that just makes sure the form is visible before we start to **Print.** If it wasn't, nothing would appear.

The `Show` method gets around this by forcing Visual Basic to bring the form into view. It's always good, from a user's point of view, to put a `Show` command in a form's load event. If something appears on screen almost straight away, your users won't start panicking and think that your program, Windows, or both, have crashed. It's all a matter of psychology - if users can see something happening, then they stop counting the seconds it takes for your program to actually do something useful. You could take another approach and `Show` a small form containing a message such as **Please Wait - Loading Data.**

How the For..Next Loop Works

Of all the looping commands in Visual Basic, the `For...Next` combination is the only one that has been inherited from the first ever version of the BASIC language. This is because `For...Next` is easy to use and is surprisingly powerful.

The `Next` statement shows where the loop ends. All code placed between the `For` and the `Next` commands is run on each pass or iteration of the loop.

How Index Variables Control For Loops

`For` loops use a numeric variable as a **counter** to keep track of the number of times the loop actually needs to run. In loop-speak this variable is often called an **Index**.

A variable is a container for a piece of data to which you can assign a label, called a variable name. You can change the value of a variable at run-time, which is why it's useful for counting loops.

By saying `For nIndex = 1 to 1000,` we are telling Visual Basic to load the variable `nIndex` with the number 1 to start with. By default, 1 will be added to it at each pass through the loop's code until it equals 1000. As soon as the variable goes outside the range 1 to 1000, the loop exits and the code following the `Next` statement is run.

We tell Visual Basic that `nIndex` is a variable at the start of the routine, with the following line:

```
Dim nIndex
```

Though it is probably a little hard to swallow, you are just going to have to accept this for now. Variables can be quite a complex subject, which is why the next chapter explains them in great detail.

You should really place the name of the index variable straight after the word **Next** (i.e. **Next nIndex**). This makes the code a lot easier to read and follow, particularly if you have a number of **For** loops nested inside each other. In our example, however, there is only one **For** loop, so it's obvious that the **Next** command relates to this.

Controlling the Index Variable

In our example, the **For** loop increments the index variable by 1 on each iteration. This is the default setting for a **For** loop. It can be changed by placing a **Step** statement at the end of the **For** statement. **Step** tells Visual Basic how many to add to the index variable on each iteration. We can see that

```
For nIndex = 1 to 1000 Step 50
```

tells Visual Basic to start with the value of 1 in **nIndex** and add 50 to the index variable on each pass. As before, the loop will exit as soon as the value of 1000 is exceeded in **nIndex.**

By far the most common use for **Step** is in creating decreasing loops. Visual Basic will automatically add 1 to the index variable every time, so a statement like

```
For nIndex = 1000 to 1
```

wouldn't actually work. The statement

```
For nIndex = 1000 To 1 Step -1
```

would work, since the **Step** clause tells Visual Basic to add -1 to the index variable on each pass.

Leaving a For Loop

Visual Basic provides a command for leaving a `For` loop prematurely. Placing the command `Exit For` inside a loop will cause it to stop immediately. The code will continue running from the line directly following the `Next` statement. This works in much the same way as `Exit Sub` does to leave a subprocedure.

The Do Loop

The `For` loop is a venerable remnant of the original BASIC language. Visual Basic is an evolutionary product that has adopted many of the best commands and attributes of other leading languages, such as C and Pascal, and married them to its BASIC roots. The `Do` loop illustrates this point well, as it's based on a similar structure found in Pascal.

The **Do...While** loop is an alternative way to repeat a block of code. You can achieve the same results using various combinations of **For...Next** loop, but sometimes using **Do...While** makes your code more elegant and intuitive. At the end of the day, however, it's a question of style.

There are three types of **Do** loop: those that run for ever, those that run until a condition is met, and those that run whilst a condition is being met. These are covered by using the **Do...Loop, Do...Loop Until** and the **Do...Loop While** commands. We'll have a look at them now.

Do...Loop While

Let's go back to the password example from earlier on in the chapter. It's OK to electrocute the illegal user and throw them out of the system, but sooner or later you'll run out of living users. You really want to give the user a second, or maybe even third chance. Enter stage left the **Do...Loop While** loop.

Three Tries for the Password

1 Load up the **PASSDO1.VBP** project. Try it out for yourself by trying to enter a password.

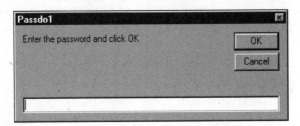

2 On the third wrong attempt, the program ends. Clicking the OK button will return you to design mode.

3 Take a look at the code by pressing the View Code button on the project window and selecting main from the drop-down list next to Proc:

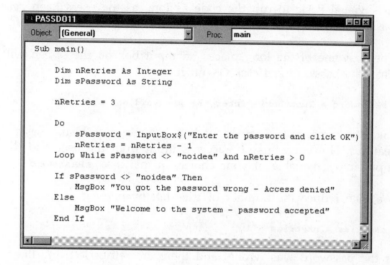

```
Sub main()

    Dim nRetries As Integer
    Dim sPassword As String

    nRetries = 3

    Do
        sPassword = InputBox$("Enter the password and click OK")
        nRetries = nRetries - 1
    Loop While sPassword <> "noidea" And nRetries > 0

    If sPassword <> "noidea" Then
        MsgBox "You got the password wrong - Access denied"
    Else
        MsgBox "Welcome to the system - password accepted"
    End If
```

How It Works

First of all we need to declare two variables. This tells Visual Basic what these variables are going to be used for, i.e. what kind of data you are planning to store in them.

Here, **nRetries** is a number that counts the attempts that have already been made at guessing the password, while **sPassword** contains the text string that is the current guess:

```
Dim nRetries As Integer
Dim sPassword As String
```

 FYI

Dim is used to declare or dimension these variables. Don't worry about this too much, as we'll discuss it in more detail in the next chapter.

The **Do** command marks the start of the loop code. Just as **Next** marks the end of a **For** loop, the **Loop** keyword closes a **Do** loop. The **While** clause tells Visual Basic to run the code as long as the users keep getting the password wrong and the user still has a number of retries left.

The first line of the loop places an input box on the screen with the words Enter the password and click OK on it:

```
sPassword = InputBox$("Enter the password and click OK")
```

Like the message box, an input box is another of Visual Basic's built-in features. However, this one accepts input from the user and then puts that input into a variable of your choice, in this case **sPassword**.

We then reduce the number of tries left by one:

```
nRetries = nRetries - 1
```

If the password was wrong, and there are retries left, the line

```
Loop While sPassword <> "noidea" And nRetries > 0
```

then sends the program back round the loop again.

When the loop ends, one of two conditions must be true. Either you ran out of tries, in which case the first message box is displayed,

```
MsgBox "You got the password wrong - Access denied"
```

or you got the password right, in which case the second message box is displayed,

```
MsgBox "Welcome to the system - password accepted"
```

Input boxes and message boxes are covered in detail in Chapter 6. What's important here is the `Do..Loop While` code.

Do...Loop Until

Maybe three attempts to get a password right still isn't enough. Maybe your users are management personnel, or worse still, executives. Enter stage right the `Do...Loop Until` loop.

If we use `Do.. Loop Until`, we can keep the loop going as long as it takes for the user to enter the right password. Load up `PASSDO2.VBP` and take a look at this code:

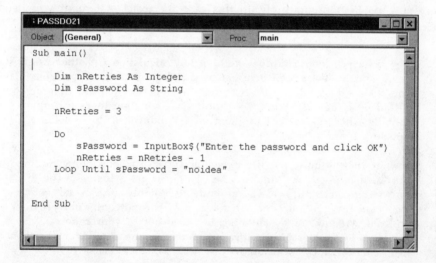

```
Sub main()
|
        Dim nRetries As Integer
        Dim sPassword As String

        nRetries = 3

        Do
            sPassword = InputBox$("Enter the password and click OK")
            nRetries = nRetries - 1
        Loop Until sPassword = "noidea"


End Sub
```

If you try running the code, you'll see how the `Until` clause keeps the loop going until the user finally gets the password right. To stop the program running, press the *Ctrl* and *Break* keys.

Where to Test in the Loop

It's worth noting at this point that, although we have so far placed the `While` and `Until` clauses after the `Loop` keyword, they can also be put straight after the `Do` command. Apart from the obvious syntactical differences, doing this actually changes the way the code itself runs.

Placing the clauses `While` or `Until` after the `Loop` statement causes the loop code to run at least once. It encounters the `Do` keyword, does its business, and then looks at the `Loop` line to see if it needs to do the whole thing again. Placing the clauses after the `Do` statement means that if the condition is not met, then the loop code is ignored totally and the next line that is run is the one immediately following the `Loop` command:

```
Do While 1 = 2

    ' This code will NEVER run

Loop
```

Finally, just as with the `For` loop, the `Exit` keyword can be used to drop out of a `Do` loop prematurely. In this case the exact statement you need is `Exit Do`.

FYI

If you have a loop that does nothing but calculation (in other words it never updates the screen or asks for user input), then it's possible that your loop can grind any other Windows programs that are running to a halt. This is because Windows allocates a little time to each program running when the current program calls Windows to do something, like update a form.

If your code is quite happily chugging away in a loop doing nothing but calculations, then Windows isn't going to get a look in. The `DoEvents` command is a way around this. Simply place a `DoEvents` command in your loop and whenever it is encountered, your program will tell Windows to do anything it has to before your code can continue. In this way, any other programs that are running will be able to run quite happily and all will be well for your users.

Chapter 12 - Writing Programs that Work explains how you can use `DoEvents` and something known as the Idle loop to not only create system-friendly programs, but also to create extremely responsive programs your users will love. There's nothing worse than the Microsoft approach to development where users with low-powered machines are punished with slow load times, painful screen re-paints and so on. Idle loops enable you to get around some of these problems.

The While...Wend Loop

The final type of loop in Visual Basic is the `While..Wend` loop. To be totally honest, I can see no reason why Microsoft included this loop in Visual Basic, other than to keep the C and Pascal programmers happy. It's exactly the same as the `Do...While` loop, but without some of the flexibility that particular loop offers. Indeed, even the Programmers Reference manual states that it's better to ignore `While..Wend` and head straight for the `Do...While` loop.

For this reason you'll only see `Do` loops used in the more complex code examples later in the book. For those of you who desperately want to use the `While...Wend` loop, here is our password code rewritten:

```
While sPassword <> "Noidea"
    sPassword = InputBox$("Enter password")
Wend
```

It's basically the same as a `Do... While` loop, except that the word `Do` is missing and the `Loop` statement has been replaced by a `Wend`. The other difference between the two types of loop is that you can't exit a `While` loop using an `Exit` command. The only way out is to change the variable that the `While` loop is testing against so that you make the condition fail and the loop stop.

Jumping Around with GoTo

There have been hundreds of pages of press and book coverage devoted to the evils of the famous `GoTo` command. For those who have never heard the term, `GoTo` is a command which lets you jump from one part of your code to another. It's as simple as that. Not a voodoo doll in sight!

The History of the Crime

In the early days of BASIC, before subprocedures and functions came along, `GoTo` provided an easy way to break your code into manageable chunks. You could write some code to perform a common function and use `GoTo` to run it from anywhere within your program simply by saying `GoTo`, followed by a line number denoting where that code began.

The problem with **GoTo** was that your code could soon end up looking a real mess with **GoTo**s all over the place and no real indication of where they actually led to in functional terms.

When procedures and functions came along, under the banner of structured programming, the aging **GoTo** command was dropped like a proverbial hot brick amidst comments such as "It promotes spaghetti code" and "It increases the likelihood of bugs creeping into the system". You can actually write a program without ever touching **GoTo.**

When to Use GoTo

However, **GoTo** can be a useful command. Visual Basic's built-in error handling command **On Error** actually works very well when used with **GoTo**. When your Visual Basic program is running for the first time, errors will normally occur. You may come across values in your controls which are too big for Visual Basic to handle. In a database program, your code might have trouble actually talking to the database, especially if your users belong to the typical breed that have a habit of deleting things with their eyes shut.

On Error provides a way for you to catch these errors in your subprocedures and run a piece of code to handle them, rather than having your program crash all over the floor. For example the line

```
On Error GoTo ErrorHandler
```

tells Visual Basic that in the event of an error occurring in the program, it should go to the part of the procedure named **ErrorHandler** and run the code from there.

> **FYI**
>
> Handling errors that crop up during run-time is a whole subject in itself, and is extremely important if you are going to distribute Visual Basic applications to other users. Take a look at Chapter 12 - Writing Code That Works, for a full explanation. In that chapter you'll see how everything else in the book can be used to create a large, useful program. It goes without saying that this program must be able to handle errors!

If you have a valid and legitimate reason to use the `GoTo` command, then by all means do so. Used wisely it won't ruin your program and it won't damage your street credibility. Once again, though, always use the right tool for the job.

Jumping to a Label

Before you can use `GoTo` you need to define a label. A label is a name you can assign to a point in your code. You define labels by simply typing a name on a line and placing a colon (:) immediately after it.

If you define a label called `Code1` for example, you can jump to the code following your label by saying `GoTo Code1`.

```
Private Sub A_Subroutine()

    GoTo EndOfCode
        :
        :
        :
EndOfCode:
        :
        :
End Sub
```

Problems start to occur when you have a `GoTo` followed by another `GoTo` and so on. A sure-fire way to test for overuse of the `GoTo` command is to try drawing straight lines on a listing of the code in your project between all the labels and the `GoTo`s that call them. If you end up with a jumbled mess of criss-crossing lines, then you've overdone it and would be well advised to simplify your code. This line-drawing approach is where the term "spaghetti coding" comes from.

FYI

Just one more analogy before we close the subject of GoTo. Two men, each with a hundred thousand nails and a thousand small pieces of timber are given identical plans to build a house. The first man builds a tumble-down shack which quite literally tumbles down. For generations afterwards the man's offspring refuse to use wood and nails to build houses, since they are unsafe to live in. The second man, however, builds a fine house out of the materials and lives happily ever after.

FYI The moral of this tale is that it's not the tools and materials that a man uses which create disasters, it is his naiveté and lack of skill. A badly written program is a badly written program, not an indictment of the tools used to write the program in the first place.

Summary

In this chapter you've learnt about loops, decision making and jumping. These are three of the most fundamental aspects of writing Visual Basic code. We have covered:

▶ How to define conditions in **If** statements and loops.

▶ How to write single-line and multi-line **If** statements.

▶ How to add code modules to your project.

▶ How the **Select Case** statement can help you check one variable for a range of values.

▶ How to use a **For** loop to run parts of your program a specific number of times.

▶ How to use **Do** loops, and the significance of the **While** and **Until** clauses.

▶ How to make safe use of the **GoTo** command.

In the next chapter, we'll learn about how to represent data in your Visual Basic programs. You've already used simple data-like strings and loop counters; now you'll learn about what other kinds of data Visual Basic supports.

Why Not Try.......

1 Write another program that cycles through the available form **BackColor** values, only this time use a **For..Next** loop. Experiment with various start and end values and different step values.

2 Create a subprocedure in its own module, called **Bounce**, that makes a form bounce around the screen, inside a defined area. Do it using a **For...Next** loop and check to see if the box has reached its limits using **If** statements.

3 Turn CON-DEMO from Chapter 2 into a text file viewer as well. Add ***.txt** files to the Pattern property of the filFileNames file list box to make text files show up as well. Then add code to the Load button event that checks to see if it's a text file, and if it is, shells out to Notepad like we did in the ShowDone program in this chapter.

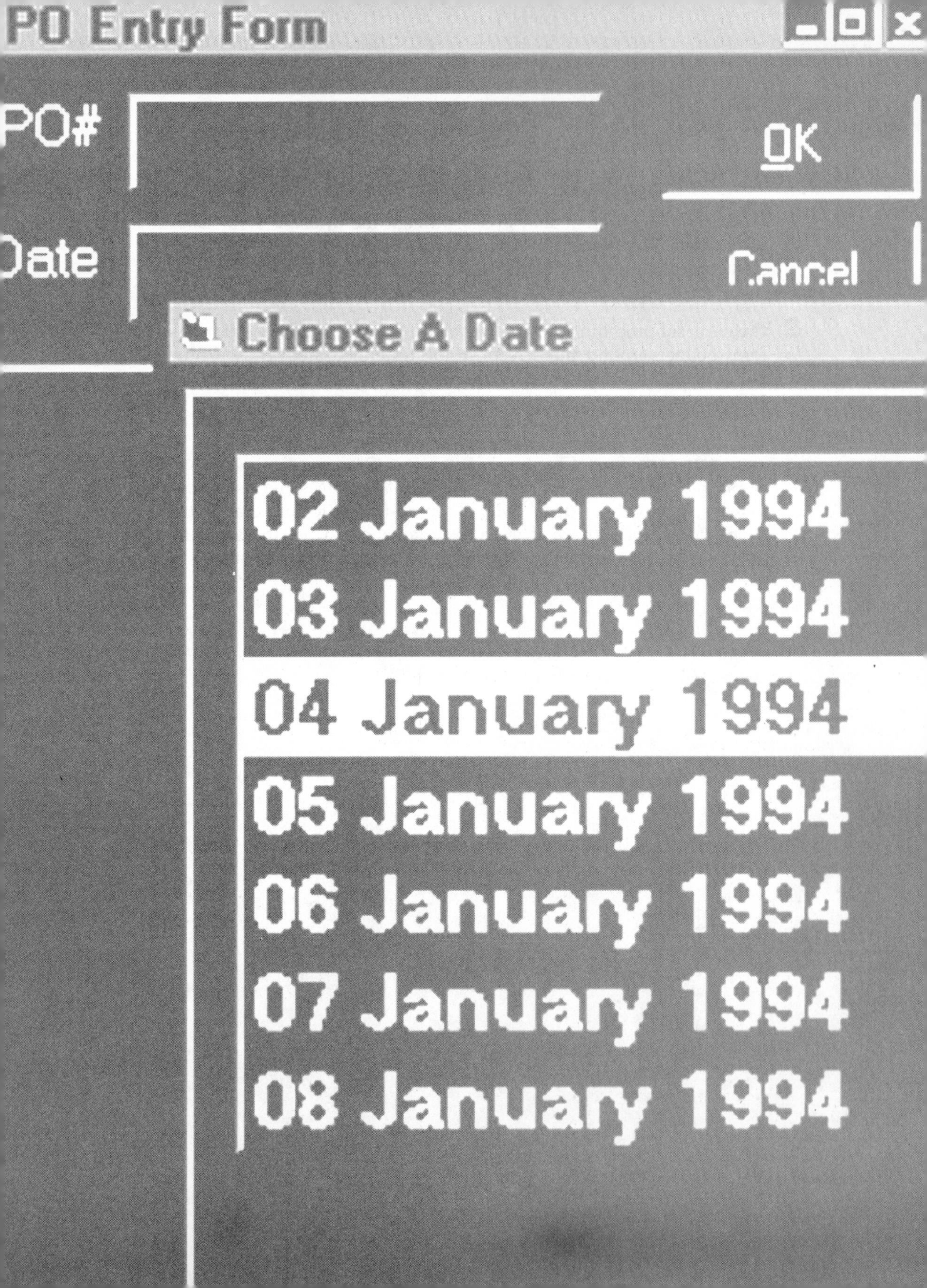

PO Entry Form _ □ x

PO#

OK

Date

Cancel

🗓 Choose A Date

02 January 1994
03 January 1994
04 January 1994
05 January 1994
06 January 1994
07 January 1994
08 January 1994

Making Data Work for You

The programs you write focus around one thing - data! From a programmer's point of view there are two aspects to handling data. Firstly, there's the user interface - the forms you create and the controls you draw on them. This interface must allow the user to enter the data your program needs easily and efficiently. Secondly, your program has to process that data to produce the results you want.

Visual Basic incorporates a number of ways in which you can both hold and manipulate data inside your applications. Once the work is finished, you can either kick the results back out to the user interface, or store them somewhere more permanent, such as on the hard disk or on paper.

This chapter is about how to handle data once it gets inside your program. You will learn:

▶ What kinds of data Visual Basic can work with.

▶ How to use scroll bars to input numeric data.

▶ How to use date and time information in your programs.

▶ What strings are, and what you can do with them.

▶ How to build your own data objects using Visual Basic.

▶ When variables are valid in a project with more than one form and when they are not.

Data and Visual Basic

A variable is a space set aside in your applications where you can store temporary information. This could be anything from a piece of text to represent a user name, to a simple number holding a count of the number of times a user has performed a certain operation. The important thing here is that variables are *temporary* stores for your data. They are used to hold the information your program needs to do the job in hand. As soon as your program ends, your variables vanish, taking the data they contain along with them.

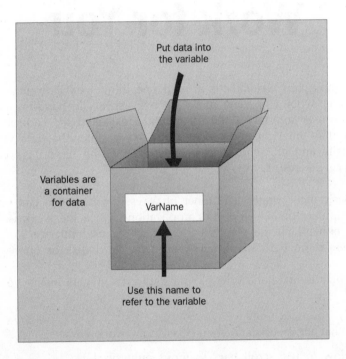

Put data into
the variable

Variables are
a container
for data

VarName

Use this name to
refer to the variable

Using Variables

When you first set up a variable you have to give it a **name**. From then on you can examine the data in that variable, change it, delete it and so on, by referring to it by name. You don't need to worry too much about the work Visual Basic has to do behind the scenes in terms of actually storing the data somewhere.

Let's look at an example. Imagine you need to store someone's age somewhere. You could create a variable called `Age` and store a value in it by typing:

```
Age = 24
```

Later, the number stored in `Age` could be used in calculations to get further numbers to store in other variables, or it could even be assigned to a control property. You may, for example, have a form containing a text box to display someone's age, called `txtAge`. You could display the contents of the `Age` variable in the text box simply by saying:

```
txtAge.Text = Age
```

If you've ever done any programming before, you won't need much introduction to variables. Even if you are new to programming, you'll find the concepts here straightforward. In fact, in the first three chapters of this book you have already come across almost as many variables as you will ever need. For example, in Chapter 3, we used a variable `nIndex` as the **counter** when creating a loop:

```
For nIndex = 1 to 20
    'Do Something Here
Next nIndex
```

In this kind of simple context, variables are really quite intuitive. What we'll do in this chapter is focus on the ways that Visual Basic uses data, examining in detail only those features that are peculiar to Visual Basic.

Declaring Variables

In many BASICs, including Visual Basic, simply having a command that says `Age = 24` is enough to create a variable called `Age` which can hold numbers. Similarly, saying `Name = "Peter"` is enough to create another variable, this time called `Name`, which can hold text, or more specifically alpha-numeric characters. This is known as **implicit** declaration.

The **explicit** method of creating a variable is slightly more verbose. We have to first tell Visual Basic that the variable exists by declaring it using the `Dim` command. With `Dim`, you have to give your variable a name immediately, and you have the choice of telling Visual Basic what kind of data that variable will hold. This is known as setting the **data type**.

Explicit declaration, while it may be a little more long-winded, is actually the best method to use. It prevents confusing bugs at run-time that are difficult to track down and even more difficult to fix. I'll show you a good example of this at the end of the chapter when we look at how to manage variables in projects that have more than one module or form.

Choosing the Explicit Declaration Option

The way Visual Basic expects you to define variables is determined by an entry on the Environment tab of the Options dialog. The Require Variable Declaration entry on that dialog means that you must tell Visual Basic which variables you are going to use, and what kind of data they are going to hold, before you actually use them.

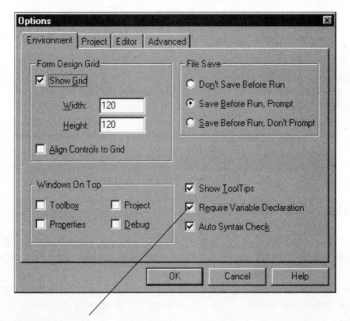

The Require Variable Declaration *option toggles Visual Basic between implicit declaration - automatically declaring variables for you and explicit declaration - needing variable declarations from you before a variable can be used.*

For explicit declaration, you need to make sure that this option is ticked before you start a new project or any additional forms or modules in a project. Visual Basic will then insert the words **Option Explicit** in the general declarations section of any module or form - it's this **Option Explicit** command that makes Visual Basic force you to declare your variables before use.

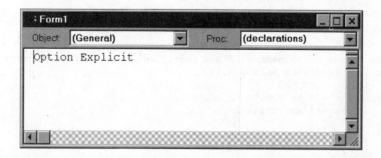

Remember that to make the change effective, you have to open a new project after changing to the explicit declaration option.

Constants

Variables, as the name suggests, are places in your program where you can hold items of data that are going to change. However, you'll frequently find a need for a more stable kind of run-time storage. This is what **constants** are for. They're rather like a variable in a bomb-proof glass case - you can look at it, but there's no way you're going to mess with it.

Constants are great for improving the readability, and hence maintainability, of your code. Imagine a game, for instance, where you need to use a simple **For** loop to move ten aliens around the screen:

```
For nAlien = 1 to 10
    Call MoveAlien (nAlien)
Next
```

There are no problems with this on its own, but what if the rest of the program had other loops that went from one to ten to do various other tasks? There could be loops to check if an alien wants to fire, die or make a sound. What's going to happen when someone tells you the game is too easy and you need to put twenty more aliens in it?

Under normal circumstances you'd have to trot through all the code in your program hunting for loops from one to ten. If you'd used a constant however, you would only have one line to change.

```
' To increase the number of bad guys, change this constant declaration
Constant NUMBER_OF_ALIENS = 10

For nAlien = 1 to NUMBER_OF_ALIENS
    Call MoveAlien (nAlien)
Next
```

Notice how the name of the constant is typed in capitals. Visual Basic is pretty laid-back about what you want to call your constants and variables, but it is common practice to set up constants with names that are all capital letters. That way, just by reading through the code, you can easily see which parts of your program are using variables and which are using constants.

Types of Data in Visual Basic

If Visual Basic is the only programming language you've used, or even if you came here from QBasic, then you could be forgiven for being oblivious to the idea of there being different types of data. So far, almost all the variables we've looked at have behaved the same, regardless of the kind of data they store, be that words, numbers or whatever.

In fact, you've been living on borrowed time. Visual Basic, like most of the more advanced languages, does have **data types**. This means that you can create variables that will only accept one type of data. These are the traditional fare of **typed** programming languages like C and Pascal. We haven't worried about them up to now, as you've been using a feature called **variant data types**, which allows you to avoid this kind of typing.

A Variable for All Seasons - The Variant

So far in this book we have used variables known as **variants**. These are variables which are named in the same way as any other variable, but which are a jack of all trades when it comes to actually storing information. You can store literally anything in a variant and it won't moan at you. From a beginner's point of view this is great. You could store text in a variant variable one minute, numbers the next and dates a short while later and you don't have to worry about whether or not the variant can cope, or whether you are matching the right type of data to the right variables.

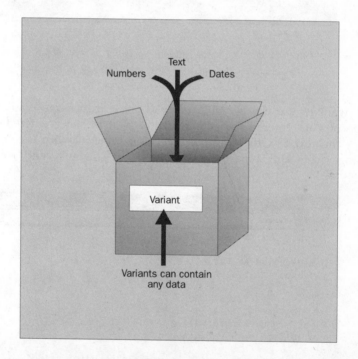

Numbers   Text   Dates

Variant

Variants can contain
any data

Variants and Typed Variables

Variants have a number of specialized uses apart from being the lazy programmer's data stash. For example, you can check the contents of a variant to find out what kind of data a user has entered. This is done by using the **IsDate** and **IsEmpty** functions.

Let's try out the **IsDate** and **IsEmpty** functions with a short example.

1 Load up the **VARIANT.VBP** project from the samples included with the book.

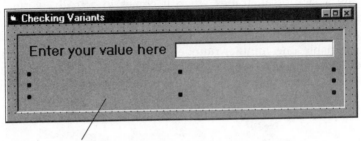

This is a label with no caption, so you can only see it when it's selected. Click on it or use the Tab key to get there.

2 We want to use the invisible label to show a message displaying the type of data entered into the text box as it is being entered. Double-click the text box to bring up the Code Window with the text box change event and type in code so that the change event looks like this:

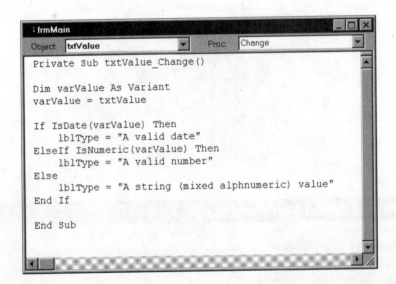

```
Private Sub txtValue_Change()

Dim varValue As Variant
varValue = txtValue

If IsDate(varValue) Then
    lblType = "A valid date"
ElseIf IsNumeric(varValue) Then
    lblType = "A valid number"
Else
    lblType = "A string (mixed alphnumeric) value"
End If

End Sub
```

3 Now try running the program and keying something into the text box. As you key in values, the label beneath the text box shows you the type of data you have entered.

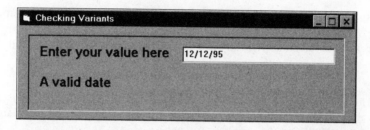

4 Try keying in text, mixing text with numbers, or entering a date. The **IsDate** and **IsNumeric** functions will detect what you're doing, and your code will use these functions to show on screen exactly what's going on.

How It Works

The **IsDate** and **IsNumeric** functions return either **True** or **False** to your code, depending on whether or not the value in the variant can be converted to a date variable or a numeric variable. In our example, a multi-line **If** is used to check first for a date, then a numeric value. If both checks fail, then the program assumes that what you've entered must be a mixed text and numeric value, which can only be stored in a string variable. We'll look more closely at strings later in the chapter.

In the example, the value of the text box is copied into the variant **varValue** before any of the checks are done. This is actually good programming practice. Visual Basic can deal with values in variables a lot quicker than with values in properties, such as the Text property of the text box.

In practice, the Text property is a variant itself, although Visual Basic always treats the data in it as text. This means that you can actually use the **IsDate** and **IsNumeric** functions on the text box if you want to check the data that the user is entering, without having to key in extra code to copy the property to a variable.

```
If IsDate(txtValue.Text) Then
```

will work just as well as what we wrote in the example.

If you play around for a while you'll notice that the **IsDate** function accepts a variety of weird date formats as being valid. For example, I have never known anyone who would write the date 66/6/15, but it's accepted. Weird.

The name **varValue** uses the prefix **var** to indicate that this is a variant type variable. See Appendix B for a guide to Visual Basic naming conventions.

When to Use Variants

The flexibility of variants has a price though, and there are two drawbacks to using a lot of variant data types. One is length of time and the other is safety.

▶ Each type of information in Visual Basic (be it text, numbers, decimal numbers, Yes/No values) is stored in a different way. Variants know instinctively how to cope with each type of data, but first of all they have to go through a short process to determine what the data actually is. You don't see this happen, but the net result is that variants can actually slow your program down.

▶ Variable typing is not just an excuse for over-complicated programming. It can play a big role in preventing errors and it does this by allowing you to restrict the number of things you can do to a variable . You can't, for example, find the square root of a name. We'll look at how this actually works a bit later on, but for now just remember that the more Visual Basic knows about your data, the more it can help you.

FYI

So why use variants? Firstly, because they make life incredibly easy, and secondly, because often you don't have the choice not to. Many of the control properties you come across are variants themselves (e.g. the **Text** property of a text box) as are many of the values returned to you by Visual Basic commands and keywords. For these reasons, it's important to understand variants and how they work, even though it's best to avoid them wherever possible.

Checking the Contents of a Variant

Since variants can hold almost any kind of data, Visual Basic has a special function we can use to determine what kind of information is in the variant. This is more comprehensive than the `IsDate` and `IsNumeric` functions that we just looked at. The `VarType` function returns a number that corresponds to the data type stored in the variant at that time.

Checking the Contents of a Variant

1 Load up `VARIANT2.VBP`. This is the same as the earlier example but with a few changes to the text box change event. Try typing in a proper date:

```
■ Checking Variants                          _□×

   Enter your value here   2/12/95

   Type 7 - Date
```

2 Stop the program and double-click on the text box to bring up the Code Window. Now take a look:

Try It Out!

```
Private Sub txtValue_Change()

    Dim varValue As Variant

    If IsDate(txtValue) Then
        varValue = CVDate(txtValue)

    ElseIf IsNumeric(txtValue) Then
        varValue = Val(txtValue)

    Else
        varValue = txtValue

    End If

    Select Case VarType(varValue)

        Case 5
            lblType.Caption = "Type 5 - Double"
        Case 7
            lblType.Caption = "Type 7 - Date"
        Case 8
            lblType.Caption = "Type 8 - String"

    End Select

End Sub
```

How It Works

Instead of putting the text box value straight into a variant, the code first checks to see if the value is either a date or a number. If it's a date, this is true:

```
If IsDate(txtValue) Then
```

And if it's a number, this is true:

```
ElseIf IsNumeric(txtValue) Then
```

Remember that, at this point, **txtValue** is just a string with any possible combination of letters and numbers. Depending on whether Visual Basic thinks the string is a date or a number, one of two conversions is performed:

▶ The **CVDate** function takes a valid date from the **txtValue** and converts it into a variant of type 7. Visual Basic then places it into **varValue** and always treats it as a date.

▶ Or the **Val** function takes the number from the variant and outputs a double precision number which can be stored in a variant, or in most of the other number data types.

At this point, **varValue** contains either a date, a number or a string. These are the only possible things you can type into a text box. Next, the **VarType** function looks at what kind of variant **varValue** is, and returns a number that describes exactly what's in it. The possible return values, and what they tell us about the type of variant are:

Value	Name	Contents of the Variant
0	Empty	There is no data in the variant.
1	Null	The variant has no value, which is different to it being empty.
2	Integer	A whole number between -32768 and 32767.
3	Long	A whole number between -2,147,483,648 and 2,147,483,647.
4	Single	A normal, everyday decimal number.
5	Double	A decimal number which is either *very* big, or has a huge number of decimal places.
6	Currency	A decimal number with 4 decimal places.
7	Date/Time	A combination value.
8	String	A piece of text.
9	OLE Object	This is advanced stuff. It's a lump of program, but ignore it for now.
10	Error	This tells you what kind of error occurred.

Continued

Value	Name	Contents of the Variant
11	Boolean	A true or false value.
12	Variant	This is an array of variants.
13	Non OLE object	Another different type of code lump.
17	Byte	A binary value.
8192	Array	An ordered table of values (see later).

All that remains is for a `Select Case` block to print out the corresponding message:

```
Select Case VarType(varValue)
    Case 5
        lblType.Caption = "Type 5 - Double"
    Case 7
        lblType.Caption = "Type 7 - Date"
    Case 8
        lblType.Caption = "Type 8 - String"
End Select
```

Numbers in Visual Basic

Variants are great, but as we said earlier, using them is not great programming practice due to their lack of discipline and system overhead. The alternative to using variants is to define a data type for a specific kind of data.

Visual Basic has a number of different data types for storing numbers. The type you use depends on whether you want to store whole numbers (1, 2, 3, 4) or decimals (1.234, 2.345), and on how big or small you expect the numbers to get.

Integers and Longs

Integer and **long** variables allow you to store whole numbers. Integers are the fastest of all the data types available in Visual Basic, and are therefore excellent for use as counters in loops. However, integers can only hold a number between -32768 and 32767. For this reason they are not that suitable for holding numbers such as account numbers, or ID numbers in a database, where you could have hundreds or thousands of records. For larger whole numbers, the long data type should be used as this allows you to play with numbers from -2,147,483,648 to 2,147,483,647.

More Precise Numeric Types

When **decimal** values are needed, for instance in scientific applications, you'll need to turn to **single** and **double precision** numbers. To be honest, **single** is probably as far as you will need to go, as these allow you to store decimal figures in the billions range and at very high precision. If you know anything about scientific notation, then the exact range is -3.402823E38 to 3.402823E38. If you need to go above and beyond that, and deal with extremely high precision numbers, or numbers in the zillions, then opt for the **double** data type.

Predictably, handling double variables takes a lot of work on the part of Visual Basic, so using them can be slow.

The final numeric data type is **currency**. Despite the name, currency variables have little to do with cash. Instead, the currency data type is a numeric data type with a fixed number of decimal places, in this case 4.

If you store a value with more than 4 decimal places in a currency variable, the extra decimal places are simply truncated - cut off in their prime. So the number 123.456789 would become 123.4567.

So currencies are nothing more than single and double values with a fixed decimal point. There's not that much more to tell. If you intend to have calculations in your program that need a fixed number of decimal places, then use currency. Otherwise, integers, doubles, singles and longs are all perfectly adequate.

Declaring Numeric Variables

Declaring any of these number variables is straightforward. Simply type **Dim** followed by the name you wish to give the variable. Then type **As** followed by the data type.

```
Dim nNetPay As Currency
Dim nDragCoefficientOfHullAtWarp1 As Double
Dim nUnitsSold As Long
Dim nCounter As Integer
Dim nRoyalty As Single
```

You can also declare variables using the keywords Static and Global. Both of these tell Visual Basic something about the life and scope of your variable. We'll cover these later in the chapter in a discussion on those specific topics.

Working with Numbers

As you would expect, Visual Basic lets you do arithmetic with numbers. You can add them using **+** and subtract with **-**. Many newcomers to programming get a little confused when it comes to division and multiplication though. Take a look at the keyboard and you'll see there's no multiply or divide sign. Instead you use ***** to multiply and **** and **/** to divide. Why two divides?

Just as you can have decimal and integer variables, so you can divide to produce decimal and integer results:

▶ The **/** sign does decimal division; doing 5 / 3 in code will give you the answer you would expect - 1.666666666667.

▶ Doing 5 \ 3 in code gives you 1; the decimal part of the number is truncated (cut off) to give you an integer result.

Integer division runs quicker in code than its decimal equivalent. It's worth bearing this in mind if you need to do division inside a loop of any kind.

The loop will run significantly faster with an integer division \ than it would with a decimal division /. If you remember back that far, we used \ in Chapter 1 to find the screen width. You can't have fractions of a pixel, so that was a good idea.

Using Scroll bars to Input Numbers

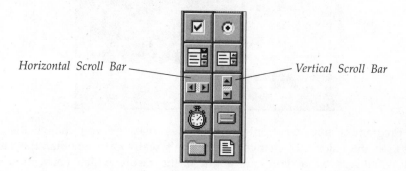

Horizontal Scroll Bar ———⟍　　　　　　⟋——— *Vertical Scroll Bar*

In the introduction to this chapter, we differentiated between data flows in and out of your program and the way that data is then manipulated inside your code. Good programming makes these two work in unison, so that the user interface you create gets the data you need from the user in the most direct and intuitive manner. Choosing the right tool for this is half the job.

If you want numbers from your user, then you have a number of choices of control. For numbers that have a defined and specific value, such as your age, a text box is the best choice. If, however, you want the user to alter the value of a variable bit by bit, then scroll bars are ideal.

When to Use Scroll Bars

Scroll bars are ideal when your user has to give you a ball-park value, and they want immediate feedback about the result. For example, PC's specify colors as combinations of amounts of red, green and blue, so what better way to specify a color value than using scroll bars. It is much easier to alter a color by moving the scroll bar than by typing in a number.

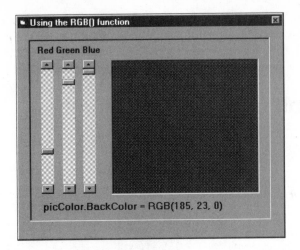

This program is **RGB.VBP** from the examples disk. As you change the sliders, so the color mix changes. You don't really care whether the value is 63 or whatever - what you care about is the result, which you can see change as you alter the sliders.

How Scroll Bars Work

For many beginners, scroll bars can be a little daunting. They are not something that you can easily relate to the real world and they provide a very abstract method of obtaining information from your users. For this reason many beginners ignore them completely, assuming that something that looks complex really is complex. In reality, nothing is further from the truth. Indeed, scroll bars are one of Visual Basic's easiest controls to master.

Play around with the scroll bars in the **RGB.VBP** program to get a feel for what properties and events must be lurking in there.

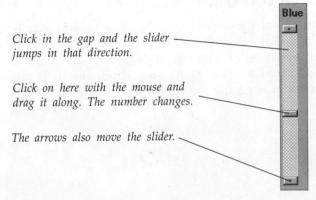

Click in the gap and the slider jumps in that direction.

Click on here with the mouse and drag it along. The number changes.

The arrows also move the slider.

Let's see how this all works in real code.

Using Scroll Bars

1 Start a new project in Visual Basic.

2 Select the horizontal scroll bar button and draw a scroll bar onto your form as shown.

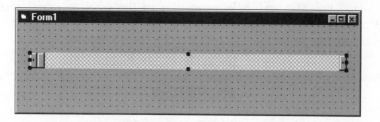

3 Now place a label above it on the form.

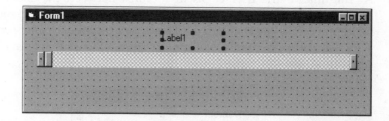

4 When you have drawn the label, bring up its Properties Window. Give it a BorderStyle of 1 and erase the Caption.

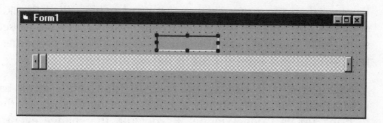

Setting the **BorderStyle** like this puts a single line border around the label so that it looks almost identical to a text box. This is a great way to display data in simulated text boxes so that the user can't change it.

5 In order for Visual Basic to determine a value for the position of the slider, we need to tell the scroll bar what its maximum and minimum values are. Select the scroll bar and bring up its Properties Window. Find the Min and Max properties of the scroll bar and set Min to 0 and Max to 10. This gives our scroll bar a range of 0 to 10.

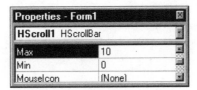

6 At run-time, if the user clicks in the area between the slider and an arrow, a value called LargeChange is added to the current slider value to make the slider jump. Find the LargeChange property and set it to 5. This will cause the slider to jump in steps of 5 if the user clicks between it and an arrow.

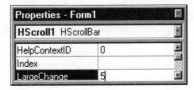

7 Finally, when the user clicks an arrow, a value called SmallChange is added to the current slider value. Find this property and set it to 1. By setting the Min, Max, LargeChange and SmallChange properties, we have told Visual Basic how the scroll bar should work.

8 The next step is to display the current value of the scroll bar in your label whenever the scroll bar is changed. Double-click on the scroll bar to bring up its Code Window. By default, the change event appears. Type in this code:

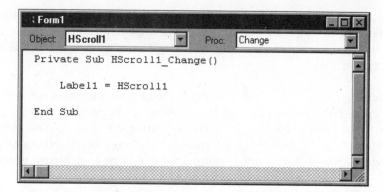

9 Now run the program.

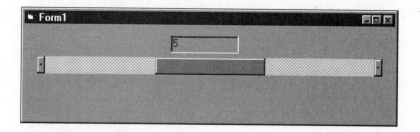

Notice the size of the drag point in the scroll bar - it's huge! The size of the drag bar represents the ratio between LargeChange (remember you set this to 5) and Max (which you set to 10).

How It Works

With the program running you can see the effect that the properties we set have on the scroll bar. When the slider is at the left end of the scroll bar the value is 0, at the right end it is 10 - these are the values you placed into the Min and Max properties.

If you click between the slider and an arrow, the value of the scroll bar changes by 5. Click on one of the arrows, though, and the value changes by 1. These are the values you put into the LargeChange and SmallChange properties.

The change event, to which you added code, places whatever is in the Value property of the scroll bar into the caption of the label. These properties are both the default properties of their respective controls, so you don't have to explicitly refer to them in your code. The change event occurs whenever a change occurs to the scroll bar; for example, when an arrow is clicked, or when the slider is dragged and released.

There is an alternative place to put this code. The scroll event reflects the changes to the scroll bar as they happen, rather than after they have happened, as is the case with the change event. Stop the program running and bring up the Code Window for the scroll bar again. This time, use the Proc: combo box to select the scroll event.

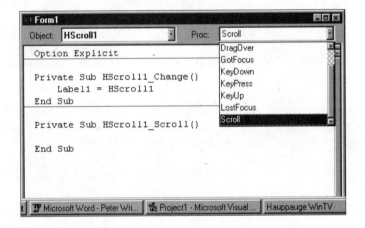

Add this line of code again:

```
Label1 = HScroll1
```

Now run the program again and try dragging the slider around. This time, each time the slider moves, the label changes, regardless of whether or not you've actually let go of the slider. However, if you delete the line of code from the change event, you will see that the code in the scroll event only works when you are dragging the sliding bar itself around.

FYI This is a little like the latest version of Word where, if you drag the vertical scroll bar up or down, a tooltip appears, telling you which page you're on.

The Date and Time Data Type

Date and time values are handled rather uniquely in Visual Basic in that both are combined together into a single value. Visual Basic handles the conversion from this single value into a meaningful number for us to read automatically.

```
Dim varDateTime As Date
```

A Visual Basic Clock

The current date and time can be obtained using the Visual Basic **Now** keyword.

1 Start a new project and place a label onto your form. Double-click the label's Font property and make the label really big and bold.

Try It Out!

2 Double-click on the form itself and when the form load event pops up change it so it looks like this:

```
Private Sub Form_Load ()
    Form1.Show
    Label1.Caption = Now
End Sub
```

3 Run it. Hmmm... not so easy.

 The format this appears in depends on the settings in the Regional Settings dialog box in your Control Panel.

How It Doesn't Work

The time doesn't change of course. All it does is load the current time into the label at form load time. To make the time change, you need to use a **timer** event to change the caption of the label at regular intervals.

Adding a Timer

1 Stop the program running and bring up the form. Select the timer from the toolbox.

2 Place the timer anywhere on your form. This is a hidden control that is only visible at design time, so it doesn't matter where you put it.

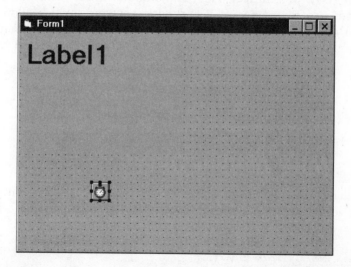

3 Double-click on the timer to bring up its timer event and add this code:

```
Private Sub Timer1_Timer()

    Label1.Caption = Now

End Sub
```

4 Set the timer Interval in its Properties Window to say 100, then the clock will keep time smoothly. Run the program and everything is fine.

How It Works

The `Timer_Timer()` event is activated at regular intervals, the period of which is determined by the Interval property. This is the only event that the Timer supports. It allows you to execute a block of code at regular intervals, such as updating the current time.

Breaking Now Down Into Parts

Obviously, much of the work you do with date and time values will inevitably involve breaking a value down into its component parts; for example, Day, Month, Year, Hour and Minute. Luckily, the categories I just listed are also the names of Visual Basic keywords which allow you to break a date and time field down into these parts. For an example of how some of these functions work, load up the **CLOCK.VBP** project and run it.

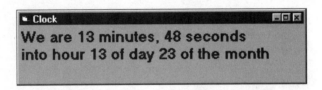

The value of **Now** has been broken down in order to space out the display and to leave off information that wasn't really necessary. Let's look at the timer event code:

```
Private Sub timCLock_Timer()

    lblMinute = "We are " & Minute(Now) & " minutes, " & Second(Now) &
↳"seconds"
    lblHour = "into hour " & Hour(Now) & " of day " & Day(Now) & " of the
↳month"

End Sub
```

This acts as a good illustration of some of the date passing functions. All of them work in roughly the same way. You just state

```
<variablename> = <functionname>(<dateandtime>)
```

and away Visual Basic goes.

```
nHour = Hour(Now)
nDay = Day(#01/01/94 12:00#)
nYear = Year (#01/01/1994#)
```

You've probably gathered by now that it's also possible to feed dates to these functions explicitly, without needing to use the **Now** variable. If you do want to specify a date in your code, all Visual Basic needs is for you to surround it with hash signs #. Then, providing the date is legal, that is it matches the date settings under the Windows Control Panel, then the date will be accepted and used.

Dates are strange things to deal with. Unlike strings and other number variables, specific parts of a date variant mean specific things. You may want to pull a day number out to find out what day of the week a specific date falls on. You may have the day, month and year stored in separate variables and want to bring them all together in a date variable. Visual Basic has a range of functions specifically to help in these cases.

Converting To and From Date Variants

The **DateSerial** function allows you to convert a day, month and year value into a date variant. For example:

```
Dim datDate As date
datDate = DateSerial (1970, 03, 04)
```

This code puts the 4th of March 1970 into the variant **varDate**. The format of the **DateSerial** function is **DateSerial(<Year>,<Month>,<Day>)**. This can be an extremely useful function, as you will see in the Try It Out section in a few moments.

Earlier on you saw how to use the **IsDate** function to see if the value in a variant can be converted into a date. The actual conversion of the date is where the **DateValue** function comes into play:

```
If IsDate(varText) Then datDate = DateValue (varText)
```

The format of the **DateValue** function is straightforward. You simply say:

```
<variable name> = DateValue ( <variant or property> )
```

You'll see this in action later in the chapter.

You may at this point be wondering what the point of the **DateValue** function really is. If you can hold a string in a variant, or even in a string variable, and check to see if it's a valid date, what's the point of going to all the trouble of converting the date to a date variable? The answer is math!

Working With Variant Dates

Once you have a valid date in a date variable, you can use the **DateAdd** and **DateDiff** functions to do some simple math on it. If you want to know what the date will be in two weeks time, use the **DateAdd** function. If you want to know how many days difference there is between today and the date an invoice was printed, then you can use the **DateDiff** function.

Both functions work in a very similar way, in that you need to tell them the units you're dealing with. For example:

```
datDate = DateAdd ( "d" , 7, datDate)
```

adds 7 days to the date in the **datDate** variable.

```
NDifference = DateDiff ("d", datDate1, datDate2)
```

This puts the difference in days between the dates in **varDate1** and **varDate2** into **NDifference**. The **"d"** in both cases is known as the interval and could be any one of the following:

Symbol	Unit of Time
yyyy	Years
q	Quarters
m	Months

Continued

Symbol	Unit of Time
`y`	Day of the year (1 is 1st January etc.)
`d`	Days
`w`	Weekday
`ww`	Weeks
`h`	Hours
`n`	Minutes
`s`	Seconds

A Pop-Up Calendar

There is another function which doesn't relate specifically to dates, but which is very useful when dealing with them. This is the **Format** function. With **Format,** you can take a date and change its format. You can choose a short date format (01/01/94), a long date (1 January 1994) and many more. You pass the variable you want to format to **Format**, along with the type of formatting that you want. **Format** then returns a variant which you would typically display on screen.

1 Load up the **DATE.VBP** project and run it.

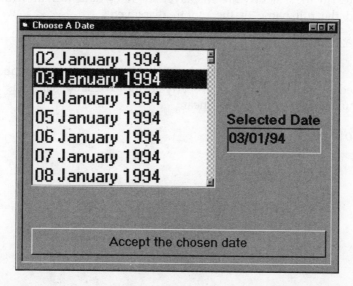

Try It Out!

The program displays a list box with a list of all the dates in 1994 in it. If you scroll down the list box and click on a date, that date is copied over to the label on the right of the list box, but in a different format. Try it.

A list box is a kind of text box with extra functions built in. We'll cover them in detail when we talk about databases.

2 To see how this works, stop the program running and double-click on the list box to bring up its click event.

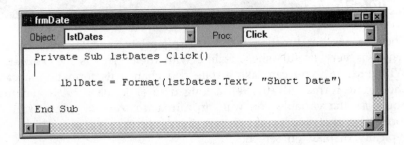

This code takes the date you select and formats it for the label. The dates in the list box are displayed in long date format with the full year and the full name of the month displayed:

    02 January 1994

Short format is used to display the selected date in the label. There's no need to add the caption property to the **lblDate** name, as Visual Basic assumes that's what you mean:

    01/02/94

As in the previous clock example, the format of the date shown depends on the settings in the Regional Settings dialog box on your Control Panel. Check that the long date format is set to dd MMMM, yyyy and the short format is M/d/yy

3 Let's change the format command so that it looks like this:

```
lblDate = Format(lstDates, "Long Date")
```

4 Now run the program and the date will be copied to the list box exactly as it appears in the list box. Unfortunately, it won't all fit in the label.

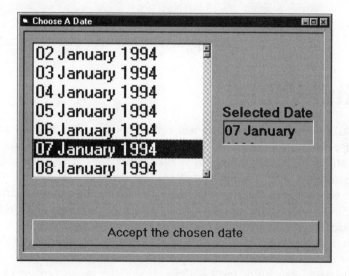

5 Now try changing it to **Medium Date**. Visual Basic automatically knows how to truncate the month to a three-digit abbreviation.

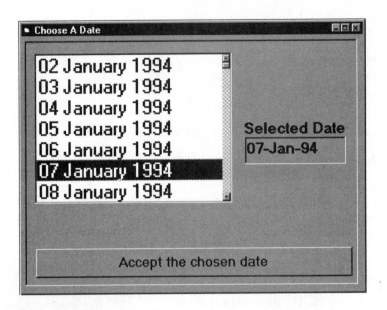

The Null Value

The **Null** value and keyword are rather special. The **Null** value is used to indicate **unknown** data and is most commonly found in database applications. Consider filling in a form on paper. The form asks you for your surname, but you leave it blank by mistake. When the form gets processed by the company that uses the form, they get a blank surname area. Since your surname can't realistically be nothing, they tell their database that your surname is unknown. In Visual Basic we use **Null** for just that purpose.

Only variants can hold **Null** values. If you try to assign **Null** to a string variable, you'll get an error. You can assign **Null** to a variant with the simple phrase **<variable> = Null**. Checking to see if a variant contains **Null** is a slightly different matter and requires the use of a Visual Basic function called **IsNull**. Here's an example:

```
If IsNull(VarVariable) Then MsgBox "Variant is null"
```

The **IsNull** function returns a value of **True** or **False,** so it makes code like the line above pretty easy to read. I could have written:

```
If IsNull(VarVariable) = True Then MsgBox "Variant is null"
```

but that begins to make the code a little cryptic.

The **Empty** value is in some ways similar to the **Null** value, except that whereas the **Null** value indicates unknown data, **Empty** indicates that a variable has never had a value put into it. The **IsEmpty** function can be used to test for this in the same way that **IsNull** can test for the **Null** value.

Strings

String variables are predominantly used to store and manipulate text. Numeric variables can only hold numbers, whereas strings can hold both numbers and figures, although they are both treated as text. The following are all strings:

```
sFirstName = "Peter"
sAddress1 = "28 Code Gulch"
sDateOfBirth = "5/8/88"
```

Declaring Strings

Strings can be declared in a number of ways. Most of the built-in data types that Visual Basic supports have a special abbreviation code attached to them. In the case of strings, this is the **$** sign. This abbreviation is actually known as a **type declaration character**. Despite its long name it does a straightforward job. If you dimension (**Dim**) a variable and attach the appropriate type declaration character to the end of the variable name, then Visual Basic will automatically create a variable of the required type.

Let's say we wanted to create a new string variable to hold someone's name. Using the longhand method, we'd have to write:

```
Dim sName As String
```

However, with the shorthand method the amount of code is reduced, but so too is the readability of the code:

```
Dim sName$
```

The small **s** at the start of the name tells you this is a string. Take a look at Appendix B for a guide to naming variables.

Use Quotation Marks For Text

Whenever you place some data into a string variable, you must enclose the data in quotation marks. This lets Visual Basic see which parts of your program are supposed to be variable names and which parts are strings (numbers, letters, text and so on). It's an important point to remember and actually brings us back to the option explicit phrase we met a while back. Without the option explicit phrase, a line like

```
sFirstname = Peter
```

would compile without any problems. Visual Basic would assume that **Peter** is a string variable, the contents of which you want to copy to the string variable **sFirstname**. However, this is far from what we actually wanted to do, which was to place the name **Peter** in the string variable itself:

```
sFirstname = "Peter"
```

Had the option explicit facility been turned on, then the first example wouldn't have got past the Visual Basic compiler. You'd have been given a Variable not defined error message.

Explicit Declaration Prevents Bugs

Why is it so important to have this option turned on, especially as implicit variables require less code and thought than explicit ones? Well, take a look at this code:

```
Sub Problem_Proc()
    sO10 = InputBox$("Enter your name")
    MsgBox "Your name is " & sO10
End Sub
```

This is a very simplified piece of code, but it has a pretty serious bug in it. If the subprocedure was embedded in a couple of hundred other lines of code, the bug could become very hard to track down. Basically, the code is supposed to get the user to enter their name and then display their name on screen in a **MsgBox**. The variable used to store the name that the user enters is called **so10.** However, no matter how hard you try, the program will not work. Instead it will keep on displaying the message Your name is, but without any name!

The reason for this is that I have misspelled the variable name in the **MsgBox** statement. In the first line of code I implicitly created a variable named s**o10** (letters **so**, number **1** and number **0**). However, in the **MsgBox** code, I refer to a variable called s**o10** (letter s, number **0**, number **1**, letter **o**). Visual Basic doesn't care - it just goes ahead and creates two variables, each with slightly different names. If I'd been using explicit variables, the program wouldn't have run and Visual Basic would have pointed the bug out to me immediately.

Working With Strings

Dealing with text in string variables can become a little tricky, so Visual Basic has a full set of very useful string handling functions which allow you to break down the string and examine parts of it.

The first function is **StrComp**, which is designed to compare two strings and return a number telling you what the comparison is between them.

Comparing Strings With StrComp

1 Start a new Visual Basic project and remove the default form from the project by selecting Remove File from the File menu.

2 Create a new module by selecting Module from the Insert menu.

Try It Out!

3 In the Code Window that appears, type in code so that the Code Window looks as follows. Type the first line (**Public Sub main()**) under the **Option Explicit** line that appears when you display the Code Window; Visual Basic will automatically create a **main** subprocedure for you.

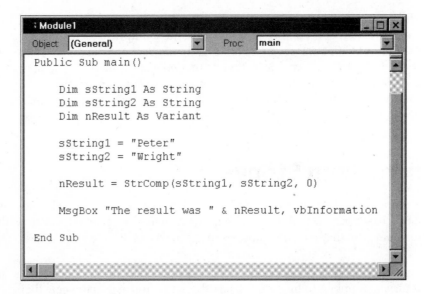

```
Module1                                        _ □ X
Object: (General)          ▼   Proc: main              ▼

Public Sub main()

    Dim sString1 As String
    Dim sString2 As String
    Dim nResult As Variant

    sString1 = "Peter"
    sString2 = "Wright"

    nResult = StrComp(sString1, sString2, 0)

    MsgBox "The result was " & nResult, vbInformation

End Sub
```

4 If you now run the code, a message box appears telling you that the result of the comparison is **-1**.

The result was -1

OK

The finished program is on the disk called **COMPARE.VBP**.

How It Works

The numbers returned by **StrComp** can be tested using **If** statements or **Select Case** to determine how the strings compare. The results will be **-1** if the first string precedes the second alphabetically (A comes before B and so on), **0** if they are the same, **1** if the first string comes after the second alphabetically, or **Null** if one of the strings compared was **Null**. Since **StrComp** can return a null value, you can see why we declared the **nResult** variable as a variant.

Changing Case

The number **0** at the end of the **StrComp** statement tells Visual Basic to do a **case sensitive** comparison:

```
nResult = StrComp(sString1, sString2, 0)
```

If the number was anything other than **0**, this code would do a **case insensitive** comparison. The **LCase$** and **UCase$** functions enable you to change all the letters in a string to either upper case or lower case. Both functions return a string to you which you can assign to a string variable using the = sign. There are two alternative functions, **Ucase** and **LCase** which return variants of type 8 (strings), so you can also assign them to strings.

Often a string function will have two versions like this. One, without a $ sign, is for assigning the returned value to a variant. This is the easiest and most common version. The other, with a $, returns only a string. Use the string only version when you want to reduce the number of variants you use in the interest of efficiency.

The exact results of string comparison may differ depending on where you are in the world and whether you are using a local language version of Windows.

Changing Case

1 Start up a new project. Remove the form and add a new module to it, as we did in the previous example.

2 Enter code into the Code Window so it looks like this:

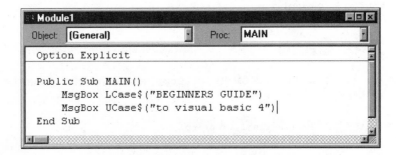

3 Run this code. See how the **LCase$** and **UCase$** functions invert the case of all the letters passed to them.

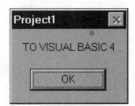

The first message box says beginner's guide, whilst the second says TO VISUAL BASIC 4. They are somewhat different to the actual strings passed to the two message box functions.

Searching Strings

The two things you'll need to do most frequently to strings are searching and dissecting. Visual Basic comes with a daunting array of functions especially for doing just these things: **Mid$, Left$, Right$** and **Instr**.

The simplest of these is **Instr**, pronounced in-string. **Instr** allows you to search one string to see if another appears in it. If a match is found, Visual

Basic returns a number to your code which is the number of the letter in the first string at which the second appears. If the search fails, then all you get back is 0.

Using Instr to Do Simple Searching

1 Load up the **INSTR.VBP** project. There's no code in this, just a form with some controls on it, waiting for you to add the good bits.

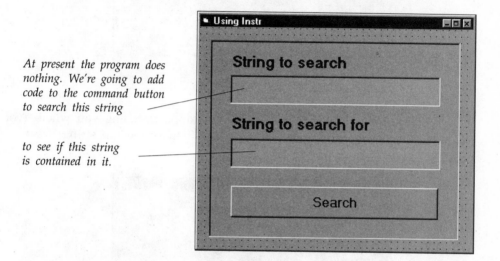

At present the program does nothing. We're going to add code to the command button to search this string

to see if this string is contained in it.

2 Double-click on the command button to bring up the Code Window. Type in code so that the command button click event looks like this:

```
Private Sub cmdSearch_Click()
    Dim nIndex As Integer

    nIndex = InStr(txtSource.Text, txtSearch.Text)
    If nIndex = 0 Then
        MsgBox "The search string could not be found!", vbInformation
    Else
        MsgBox "The search string was found starting at position " &
nIndex, vbInformation
    End If

End Sub
```

3 Now run the program. Enter source text in the top text box and then add the string text you want to search for in the bottom text box.

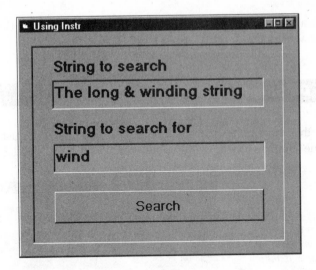

4 Hit the Search button and a message box appears telling you whether or not the text was found, and at which position in the top string it was found.

How It Works

Let's take a look at the code that makes **INSTR.VBP** useful. The first line declares an integer variable **nIndex** to hold the position of the second string, **txtSearch.Text**, in our first string, **txtSource.Text**.

```
Dim nIndex As Integer
```

nIndex will be zero if no match is found. The next line is the one that counts, as it contains the **Instr** function:

```
nIndex = InStr(txtSource.Text, txtSearch.Text)
```

You simply assign **Instr** to a variable to hold the result. In this case that variable is **nIndex**. The two strings you're dealing with are held in brackets straight after the **Instr** function. The first string is the string you want to search, be it a variable, property (as here), or a piece of text in quotes (e.g. "Source String"). The second string is the value you want to search for.

The remaining lines examine the value that **Instr** returned and display the appropriate message box. If **nIndex = 0**, then **Instr** couldn't find a match and you will see the message: The search string could not be found!. Otherwise, the value of **nIndex** is displayed.

```
If nIndex = 0 Then
    MsgBox "The search string could not be found!"
Else
    MsgBox "The search string was found starting at position " & nIndex
End If
```

Instr is great for doing simple searches. However, if you really want to pull some strings apart then you need to look to the **Mid$**, **Left$** and **Right$** functions. Using these three functions, you can write code that can examine portions of a string.

Taking Strings Apart

In the following program, we'll get the user to enter their forename and surname and then use the **Left$** and **Right$** methods to separate the two words.

1 Load up the **BREAK.VBP** project and run it.

2   At the top of the form is a text box where our users will enter their name. As soon as the command button at the bottom of the form is pressed, code which you will write in a moment splits the name entered into its forename and surname parts.

3   Stop the project and double-click on the command button to bring up the Code Window for its click event. Type in code so that the click event looks like this:

```
Private Sub cmdBreak_Click()

    Dim nPosition As Integer

    nPosition = InStr(txtName, " ")

    If nPosition = 0 Then
        lblForename = txtName
        lblSurname = ""
    Else
        lblForename = Left$(txtName, nPosition)
        lblSurname = Right$(txtName, Len(txtName) - nPosition)
    End If

End Sub
```

4   Now run the program and enter your name. When you press the command button at the bottom of the form the name is split into two parts.

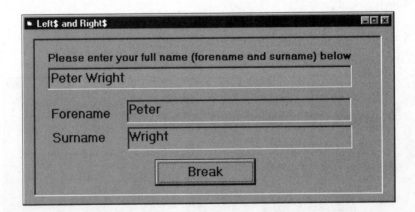

How It Works

The first two lines of code should be pretty familiar. The **Dim** line sets up an integer variable which we use in the next line to find the first space in the name entered. Most people enter their forename and surname separated by a space, so we can use **Instr** to search for this.

The **If** clause checks to see whether or not any spaces were entered. If there are none, so that **nPosition = 0**, then the program assumes that no surname was entered and copies the text you typed into the forename box only.

If a space was entered in the name, these two lines of code are run:

```
lblForename = Left$(txtName, nPosition)
lblSurname = Right$(txtName, Len(txtName) - nPosition)
```

The first line uses the **Left$** method to pull some text from the left of the string entered. The number of characters to pull and the string to pull them from are passed as parameters to the **Left$** method. In this case, the string is the text property of the text box and the number of characters to pull is held in the **nPosition** variable. Remember, we used **Instr** to find the space. If a space was found 5 characters into the string and we pull the 5 leftmost characters from the string, then we'll actually get everything up to and including the space.

The **Right$** function works in exactly the same way. You tell it which string you want to pull characters out of, and how many characters to pull. The difference, as you probably guessed, is that **Right$** pulls characters from the right-hand side of the string, whereas **Left$** pulls them from the left-hand side. Previously, we used the **nPosition** variable to determine how many characters to get. This won't work with the **Right$** function. If the string is 25 characters long and the space is the 5th character in, then saying **Right$(text, 5)** wouldn't give us the desired answer, so some math is needed.

The **Len()** method can be used to find out how long a string is. So if the space was found at character 5, and the string is 25 characters long, **Len(Text) - 5** gives us 20. In the code above, this would mean that we'd pull the right-most 20 characters out of the string. It looks complex initially, but it's really very straightforward.

The Mid$ Function

The third function, which I mentioned earlier, is the **Mid$** method. Where the **Left$** and **Right$** methods can be used to pull text from the left and right-hand sides of a string; **Mid$** lets you pull chunks out from anywhere in the string.

Mid$ works in a similar way to the other two commands. You pass it the text you want to pull stuff out of. However, instead of just telling it the number of characters to pull, you tell it which character to start at and how many characters you want to pull.

Extracting Strings Using Mid$

1 If you still have the previous project open, you can modify what you have just written. If not, open up **BREAK.VBP**.

2 We could have done everything we just did using only the **Mid$** function. Take a look at this:

```
Private Sub cmdBreak_Click()

    Dim nPosition As Integer

    nPosition = InStr(txtName, " ")

    If nPosition = 0 Then
        lblForename = txtName
        lblSurname = ""
    Else
        lblForename = Mid$(txtName, 1, nPosition)
        lblSurname = Mid$(txtName, nPosition + 1, Len(txtName) - nPosition)
    End If

End Sub
```

How It Works

The two lines that have changed are:

```
lblForename = Mid$(txtName, 1, nPosition)
lblSurname = Mid$(txtName, nPosition + 1, Len(txtName) - nPosition)
```

Try It Out!

The first parameter you pass to `Mid$`, just as with `Left$` and `Right$`, is the text you want to manipulate - in this case `txtName.TEXT`. The next parameter is the first character you want to pull. Finally, we pass the number of characters that `Mid$` should return. The returned string is saved in the two labels on the form, just as before.

Collections of Data

In a larger application, such as a payroll system or even a game, by far the most important data you'll need to deal with will be held in groups of one kind or another. For example, you may not want to deal with employees by holding their name, address, IRS number and so on, in different variables, when it's much more convenient to deal with an employee as a **group** of related data. The `Type` command in Visual Basic lets you create such groups.

In a game you may need to keep track of which aliens are alive and which are dead. This kind of group is called an **array** and is a list of variables, all with the same name and data type.

Let's look at the `Type` command first.

Type Declarations

As I said, the `Type` command lets you define a group of variables and give them a common name. You could have an employee type to hold an employee's name, address and so on. In a game you might have a type defined to hold information about the bad guys, such as the name of the graphics file that holds their image data, their coordinates, energy and such like. If you are used to C or Pascal, then you'll feel at home with **types**. In C you have the **struct** keyword which does the same thing, whilst in Pascal you have **records**.

Take a look at this fragment of code:

```
Type Employee
    nEmployeeNo As Long
    sSurname As String
    sForenames As String
    varBirthDate As Variant
EndType
```

This declares a type called **Employee** which holds some of the data you might associate with an employee. Declaring a type like this only declares a template for a new variable. It's like telling Visual Basic "This is what a variable of type Employee would look like". Having created the **Type**, you then have to create a variable from it:

```
Dim CurrentEmployee As Employee
```

This declares a variable of type **Employee**, which has already been set up by the **Type** statement. **CurrentEmployee** itself doesn't hold any data that we are interested in. In code, we want to see what is in each part of the **Employee** data. You do this by placing the name of each **element** of the type after the new variable name:

```
CurrentEmployee.nEmployeeNo = 1
CurrentEmployee.sSurname = "Wright"
CurrentEmployee.sForenames  = "Peter"
```

Arrays of Data

A type groups a collection of possibly different data types together under one name. **Arrays**, on the other hand, let you create lists of a single data type. What you get with an array is really a number of variables, all with exactly the same name, but with different data. So you could have an array to hold the values of cards in a deck. Each element of the array, or individual item of data in its own right, is differentiated from the rest by something known as an **index**. Index simply means an identifying number.

If you want to declare an array instead of a variable, it's easy. You just put brackets after the variable's name, with a number inside them saying how large the array should be:

```
Dim nArray(100) As Integer
```

In this example an array is set up called **nArray**. The array consists of 100 integer numbers. You can get at these numbers to see what they are, or to set them to different values, like this:

```
nArray(2) = 50
nArray(50) = nArray(0) + nArray(99)
```

Have a look at the last line of code in that example. The first element of an array is numbered 0, with the last being one less than the size of array you asked for. So, if you set up an array of 100 elements, they will be numbered 0 to 99.

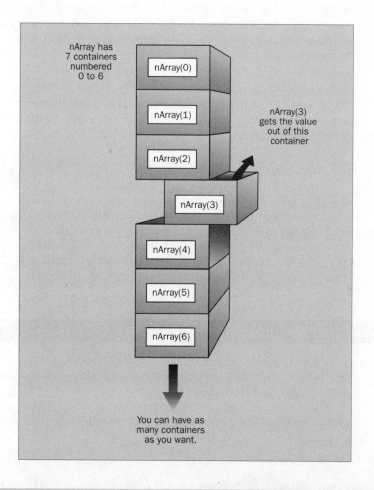

nArray has
7 containers
numbered
0 to 6

nArray(0)

nArray(1)

nArray(2)

nArray(3)
gets the value
out of this
container

nArray(3)

nArray(4)

nArray(5)

nArray(6)

You can have as
many containers
as you want.

Arrays don't always have to start with an index number of 0. You can declare an array to start at any number you like. For example, `Dim nArray (-12 to 28)`.

Re-Dimensioning Arrays

Arrays have been with us since BASIC first hit a computer screen. However, something Visual Basic can do, which very few other versions can, is change the size of an array once it has been declared. Previously, if you asked for a 100 element array, that's what you got. If you needed to change its size, then you'd have to stop the program and change the code. This can get very annoying!

In Visual Basic you can **ReDim** an array to change its size up or down. In addition, if you use the **ReDim** command in conjunction with the word **Preserve**, you can even change the size of an array without destroying the data contained inside it.

One of the most common uses for this is in games, or any other application that needs to deal with random data. Being able to change the size of an array at run-time is often used for increasing the number of bad guys in a game, or adding more bullets to the screen. In a serious application, it's great for creating random amounts of data to throw at a program for testing. Each piece of data could be held in an array, with the exact number of items of data determined at run-time, changing the array with **ReDim**.

Try It Out!

Declaring and Re-Dimensioning Arrays

1 Start a new project in Visual Basic. Double-click on the default form to bring up the Code Window.

2 Type in code so that the **Form_Load()** event looks like this:

```
Private Sub Form_Load()

    Dim nRandoms() As Integer
    Dim nLoopCounter As Integer
    Dim nArraySize As Integer

    Form1.Show

    Randomize
    nArraySize = Int(Rnd(1) * 10)
    ReDim nRandoms(nArraySize)
```

```
    For nLoopCounter = 1 To nArraySize
        nRandoms(nLoopCounter) = Int(Rnd(1) * 1000)
        Form1.Print "Element " & nLoopCounter & " = " &
 ↳ nRandoms(nLoopCounter)
    Next

End Sub
```

3 Each time you run the program you see a random number of random numbers printed onto the form. The array is also re-sized randomly to hold these numbers.

231

How It Works

The first line of code `Dim nRandoms() As Integer` sets up an array with no elements in it. Two other variables are then set up: one (`nArraySize`) to hold the size of the array, the other (`nLoopCounter`) to hold a counter to step through each element of the array later on.

After showing the form, the `Randomize` method is used to set up Visual Basic's random number generator. We'll look at random numbers later, in the chapter on graphics, so don't worry too much about what this and the `Int(Rnd(1) * 10)` statements do. The net result is that a random number between 0 and 10 is put into `nArraySize`. This is used in the next line to `Redim` the array.

```
ReDim nRandoms(nArraySize)
```

The rest of the code steps through each element of the array, using the `For` loop to put a random number into each element and then print that element on the form.

The line `Form1.Show`, as you saw in the previous chapter, forces Visual Basic to display the form on screen as soon as possible. Remember, the load event just loads the form up into memory, it doesn't actually display it. We need to `Show` the form in order to `Print` on it. Without the `Show` command, all you would see at the end of the program would be a blank form. Try removing the line yourself to see this.

There's a bit of a problem with using `ReDim` in this way. Imagine the situation where you have 100 employee names held in an array and you suddenly decide you need 101. You could `ReDim` the array to make it bigger, but when you do a `ReDim`, any data in the array is lost forever. We need to find a way of **preserving** the data held in the array when it's resized.

Preserving Array Data

You may need to `Redim` an array and preserve the contents of it quite frequently. You may have an array of record IDs in a database for instance. What happens when the user adds a new record to the database? The answer is that you use the Visual Basic `Redim Preserve` keywords.

`Redim Preserve` works in exactly the same way as the `Redim` statement on its own, the only difference is that you now say `Redim Preserve` instead of `Redim`.

```
Dim nArray(100) As Integer
Redim Preserve nArray(200)
Redim Preserve nArray(400)
```

Now the data already in the array will still be there after you change its size.

Multi-Dimensional Arrays

It's possible to have multi-dimensional arrays, where there is more than one index. All you do is add another number to the declaration like this:

```
Dim nMultiArray(100,100) As Integer
```

You can then address each element of the array as you would a one-dimensional array, only this time there's another index to change.

Using For Each...Next

Using a normal `For` loop is the traditional method of getting at the elements in an array. However, Visual Basic 4 also includes a `For Each` loop which is designed specifically for peering into arrays.

The syntax is really quite simple

```
For Each <variant> in <arrayname>
    :
    :
    : Code to deal with the variant, which is actually the current element
    : of the array
    :
    :
Next
```

The syntax is remarkably similar to a normal `For` loop, the difference being the use of two variables on the `For` line: the array name itself, and a variant to hold the value of each element.

When the loop runs, it moves through each element of the array, putting its value into the variant that you would have declared before you started the loop.

You can then deal with the variant just as if it were an element in the array, but without the hassle of having to remember which element you are dealing with.

The For Each Loop

Our earlier example, using the `For Each` method, looks like this.

```
Private Sub Form_Load()

    Dim nRandoms() As Integer
    Dim varElement As Variant
    Dim nArraySize As Integer

    Form1.Show

    Randomize
    nArraySize = Int(Rnd(1) * 10)
    ReDim nRandoms(nArraySize)

    For Each varElement In nRandoms
        varElement = Int(Rnd(1) * 1000)
        Form1.Print "Value is " & varElement
    Next

End Sub
```

How It Works

Gone is the `nLoopCounter` variable we had before, to be replaced by the `varElement` variant.

In the loop itself, the first line sets `varElement` to a random value, just as before. However, by setting `varElement`, you are actually setting whichever element the loop has reached in the array. This is because the `For Each` line effectively tells Visual Basic that, instead of using the array itself, we are going to use our own variable (in this case, `varElement`).

The second line in the loop simply prints out the random value that you just set.

The result is a bunch of code that is not dramatically smaller than the one we had previously. However, it is a great deal more structured and, with experience, a lot easier to read.

We will cover the **For Each** loop later in the book in more detail, since it also applies to something known as **collections**.

Variable Scope

Variables have a limited visibility and the data they hold can only be accessed whilst the variable is still in view. The most obvious time that a variable goes out of view is when your program stops. When you restart it, all your variables are set back to their initial values.

This is known as **scoping**. As long as a variable is **in scope** you can write code to change it, display it and so on. When the variable goes out of scope, all the information becomes unavailable and the programmer can no longer write code to deal with that variable. Ending an application makes all variables go out of scope, but there are less extreme cases than this. Variables that you declare in one module are normally only in scope when that module is running. It's possible to circumvent this by creating static or global variables, but on the whole, variables live and die with their parent modules.

This can be a little confusing, so let me explain some more. You have four types of variable scope: global, module level, local (procedure level) and static.

Imagine that you are looking out of a submarine periscope from inside a particular module. **Global** variables are those that you'll always be able to see. If the world is your program, then no matter where you are, the periscope will always show you the sky and the water; no matter where you are in your program you can always see, use and update global variables.

Module level variables can be thought of as icebergs. It doesn't matter where you are in the two polar regions, you will always be able to see icebergs. However, you can only see the icebergs that are in the same polar region as you. Module level variables are always available to you if you are running code in the same form or module they were declared in.

Local variables are like seagulls in the sky. As far as you are concerned, they exist only while you have the periscope fixed on them. In your programs, local variables and their contents only exist in the subroutine or function in which they were declared.

Static variables are like seagulls which have landed on your sub. They are always in the same position each time you bring the scope round to a certain angle. As soon as you move the scope off them they no longer exist, but move it back and they're still sitting there just as before. In your program, static variables, like local variables, can only be used in the procedure or function they were declared in. Move out of the subroutine or function and the variables can no longer be used. However, when you come back to that subroutine, the statics are still there, with exactly the same values as before. Local variables change - they lose their contents and have to be rebuilt.

A variable's scope is determined by where and how the variable is created. We've already seen how to use **Dim** to declare variables. Using **Dim** creates local variables whose scope is within the module in which they are created. In order to understand what this really means, we need to take a look at how to create projects that have more than one form.

Multi-Form Projects

All the projects we have looked at so far only have one form.

▶ A variable that is declared inside a procedure attached to that form using **Dim** is **local** to that procedure, and can be accessed by event handlers for any object that is also on the form.

▶ A variable that is declared using **Dim** or **Private** in the **General declarations** section of a form can be accessed from any procedure attached to that form.

In the previous chapter, we learnt how to create subprocedures that can be called from code within a form, even though they are contained in a separate module, a **.BAS** module. We did this by declaring the procedure as **Public**.

```
Public Sub DoThis ()

End Sub
```

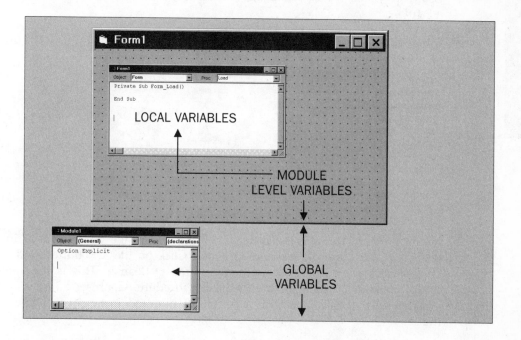

If you then declare a variable in the general declarations section of a **.BAS** module using **Public**, you will be able to use it all over the project, in whichever form or module you like. This is a **global** variable.

That's a lot of theory. Let's see how it works.

Local Variables

A variable declared within a **Sub** procedure or a **Function** with the **Dim** keyword is said to have **local** scope. It can only be accessed by code within the same **Function** or **Sub** procedure. This gives rise to some interesting problems. Because a local variable can only be accessed from within the **Sub** or **Function** it was born in, it's possible to have more than one variable in a program with the same name and all with different values. This little gem of a bug-haven is known as **name shadowing**.

Try It Out!

Same Name, Different Place

1 Load up Visual Basic, delete the default form and create a new code module.

2 Bring up the Code Window and enter the following:

```
Sub Main()
    Dim nNumber as Integer
    nNumber = 12
    Call Proc2
    MsgBox nNumber
End Sub

Private Sub Proc2
    Dim nNumber as Integer
    MsgBox nNumber
End Sub
```

3 If you now try running the code, you'll see a message box with a 0 in it. This is the value of **nNumber** in Proc2. Click on the OK button and another message box appears with the number 12 in it. This is the value of the **nNumber** variable in the **main** subprocedure. Confused? Just imagine what it gets like with a couple of hundred instances just like this.

To summarize then, local variables are created in subprocedures and functions. They can only be accessed from within the routine they were created in. Identically named variables in other functions live a totally separate existence and have their own values.

Module Level Variables

In contrast, **Private** or **Dim** can also be used to create variables which can be used by all the code in a form or module. Each form or module has a section outside of any procedure or function which is known as the **declarations** section. It's here that **module level** variables can be created. You can see this section by bringing up a Code Window on any form or **.BAS** module and selecting (General) (declarations) from the object combo at the top.

Creating a variable here using the `Dim` statement makes that variable and the data it holds accessible by every procedure in this particular form or module. Procedures in other forms or modules can't see these form level variables and, as before, can have identically named form level variables of their own.

Module Level

1 If you still have the module from the previous example open, then open up the Code Window. If you don't, then start a new project, remove the form and add a new module.

2 Declare **nNumber** as a module level variable in the general declarations section of the module like this.

```
Module1
Object: (General)          Proc: (declarations)

    Option Explicit

    Dim nNumber As Integer
```

3 Then either type this all in afresh, or edit what you already have there.

```
Sub Main()
    nNumber = 12
    Call Proc2
    MsgBox nNumber
End
End Sub

Private Sub Proc2
    MsgBox nNumber
End Sub
```

4 Run the program. You get the same answer both times.

FYI You can declare this variable using either `Dim` or `Private`. You can also do exactly the same thing in the general declarations part of a form module.

Global Variables in Forms

Although variables you declare in the general declarations section of a form are normally only visible throughout that form, you can in fact access such a variable from outside by including the form name as part of its reference. For example, if you declare a variable like this in the general declarations section of `frmHomeForm`

```
Public varFormLevel as Variable
```

then you can access it from another form or module by using the name `frmHomeForm.varFormLevel`.

Static Variables

The information held in a module level variable is static. This means it remains in existence for as long as your application is running. There are ways of killing off module level variables in forms, but we'll look at how to do this in Chapter 11 - Object Variables.

The `Static` keyword can be used to create a similar type of variable. Statics hold their data for as long as the application is running, but are only visible and can only be used by the code in the procedure in which they were created. So really, they are safe local variables. They obey the same rules as any other local variable, but they don't forget their data when the subprocedure or function ends.

Statics are declared in exactly the same way as if you were using `Dim`, but instead of typing `Dim`, you type `Static`:

```
Static nNumberOfRuns
```

A typical use of a static variable is as a counter that needs to be referenced from outside its module. An example of this would be when keeping track of the number of times a subprocedure has been called before.

Global Variables

The final scope of variable you'll come across is the **Global** variable, which you can create, surprisingly enough, with the `Public` keyword. Global variables can only be created in the declarations section of a code module. Forms can't create global variables at all. The data held in a global variable is accessible by every line of code in the application and can therefore be quite useful for maintaining information used throughout your application.

A common use of globals is to hold the name of the program's current user. Any code which needs to access this can then do so with no problem at all. As with static, local and module level variables, you create a global one by typing the word **Public** followed by the name of the variable.

```
Public sUserId
```

FYI

Each type of variable scope brings its own problems with it. Global variables are considered to be too unstructured and uncontrolled to use too much in any one program. If all your variables were global, then the chances are that a bad piece of code in one procedure could cause many others to function badly by updating a global variable with the wrong value.

While local variables are better in theory, they can also cause their fair share of problems. Too many local variables in a procedure can cause an **Out of stack** error message to crop up which will crash Visual Basic. This isn't normally a problem and only affects procedures that have an extremely large number of variables defined in them.

Statics can solve the stack problem, since they use their own private area of computer memory to store their values and it's totally separate from that used by the local variables. Static variables, however, can cause problems if you forget that in a procedure a static never forgets its data. You should never assume that a static variable will be empty or contain empty values.

Variable Scope Quick Reference

Type	Declaration	Where	Scope
Local	`Dim varName as varType`	In each event or sub procedure	Can only be used in the procedure in which they are declared.

Continued

Type	Declaration	Where	Scope
Private	`Private varName as varType or Dim....`	In (general) (declarations) section of the form or module	Can be used in all procedures in that module.
Public or Global	`Public varName as varType`	In (general) (declarations) section of a code module only	Can be used in all modules in the whole project.
Static	`Static varName as varType`	In any location	Scope depends on where it is declared. Data is preserved out of scope.

A Multi-form Project

Earlier on in this chapter, we looked at a calendar form. What we are going to do now is to use this calendar form as a pop-up subform in another project to make selecting a date a bit easier.

1 Load up the partially completed **POEntry.VBP** project from the examples disk. This is a simple little form that needs a date entered on it.

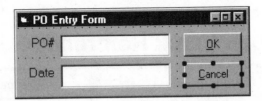

2 We now want to add the **DATE.FRM** file to the project. We're going to use this to allow us to select a date to be inserted into the Date field. Open up the Add File... window from the File menu and select the file.

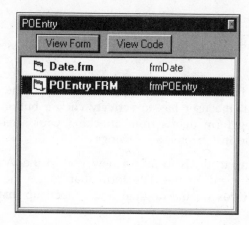

3 The first thing to do is to save this file again under a different name. If you don't, all the changes you make to **DATE.FRM** will be reflected in the original project, with unfortunate consequences. To rename it, highlight the form in the Project Window and choose Save File <u>A</u>s.. from the <u>F</u>ile menu, and save the form as **DATEPO.FRM**.

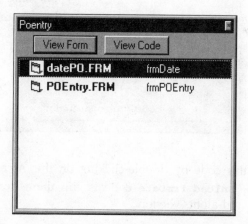

4 Now we need to add some code to the main form to bring up the date form when we need it. It would seem to be intuitive to get the user to double-click on the date entry text box if they need the help of the pop-up form. Open up the Code Window for **POENTRY.FRM** and add this code:

```
Private Sub txtPODate_DblClick()
    Load frmDate
    frmDate.Show 1
End Sub
```

The second line uses the **Show** method to open the form modally, meaning that the user has to actively click a button to get out of it. This stops drifting form debris from attacking your screen. We'll cover this kind of issue in Chapter 6 - Dialogs

5 The last thing to do is to add a new line to the Accept the chosen date button click event on the date form that copies the selected value back into the text box on the original form. Open up **DATEPO.FRM** in design mode.

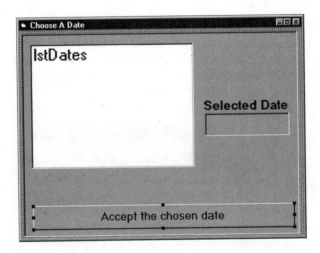

6 Then add this code by double-clicking on the Accept the chosen date button. The **Unload frmDate** code is still there from the form's previous stand-alone version.

```
Public Sub cmdAccept_Click()

    frmPOEntry.txtPODate = lblDate.Caption
    Unload frmDate

End Sub
```

7 If you now run the project and double-click in the date box, you'll be able to select a date from the list, accept it and have it pasted back into the box. The completed project is on the disk as **POENTRY1.VBP**.

How It Works

What's interesting about this project is the way we get the data from the new form, **frmDate**, to the main form of the program, **frmPOEntry**. In order to do it, we had to pass the data from the Caption property of a control on one form to the Text property of a control on another. As it happens, in this example, it's a logical thing to do. However, you may just want to pass data around as variables.

You have two choices. You can declare a form level **Public** variable and use that. However, in order to be able to *see* this variable from the subsidiary form you have to include the form name, for example, **frmPOEntry.NewVariable**. It's just as easy to use the property directly. The other choice is to use a global variable.

You can't actually declare a global variable in a form. You have to add a module to your program and then declare it there. If you do this, you can then copy data between forms using the global variable.

We'll cover more about the big picture of forms, modules and functions later on in the book. For now, just accept that passing data around needs thinking about.

Summary

In this chapter you've learnt how to represent and use data inside your Visual Basic programs. We covered:

▶ How to declare variables, and the benefits of forcing explicit declaration.

▶ The use and limitations of the variant data type.

▶ What other kind of data Visual Basic understands, including numbers, dates and strings.

▶ How to use Visual Basic's rich set of string handling functions.

▶ When and how variables are in and out of scope, and how to deal with data in a project with multiple modules.

The next chapter shows you how to add menus to your programs for that authentic Windows look.

Why Not Try.......

1   Create an alarm clock using a timer and the **Now** function.

2   Create a calendar project that searches through an array of memorable dates, such as birthdays, to check if the date selected is a special date. Make the array two dimensional to hold the date and a descriptive string. Have a form that shows the date selected in one text box, and then the description of that date. Add the facility to add more dates to the array.

3   Create a name and address form. Then create an array that holds all the data from the controls. Add a button that moves on to the next set of elements in the array. This is a simple database; the only snag is that you lose the data when the program ends, so don't type too much in.

4   Repeat the address book project, but use a **Type** structure to store each screen-full of data in, then save these in an array.

5   Write code to take a string from a text box that consists of a list of numbers separated by commas and add those numbers up, printing the total in the box.

6   Use the code from the last example to store the numbers in an array. Then sort them into numerical order by using a **bubble sort**. This works by repeatedly looping through the array element by element, comparing adjacent values. If the second is higher, then swap them, if not, then don't. Keep looping through the set until no more swaps are made, at which point the array is ordered. Print the results into the box again.

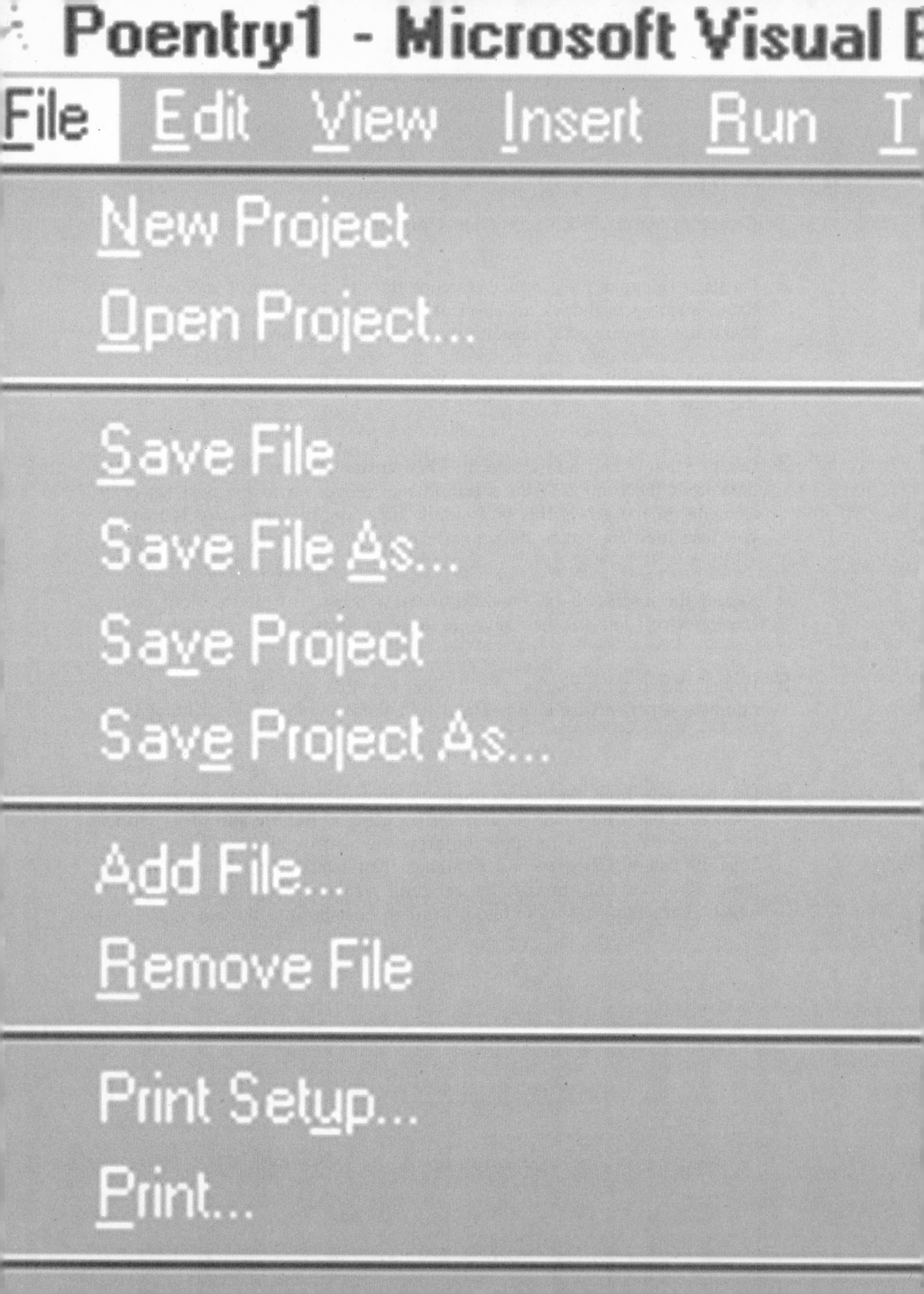

Poentry1 - Microsoft Visual B
File
Edit
View
Insert
Run
T
New Project
Open Project...
Save File
Save File As...
Save Project
Save Project As...
Add File...
Remove File
Print Setup...
Print...

Menus

Menus are an integral part of any Windows application. Visual Basic makes the process of creating and modifying menus a breeze when compared to old-style Windows programming. However, there is still a big difference between a good and a bad menu structure, as any frustrated Windows user will tell you.

In this chapter you will learn:

▶ What a good Windows menu should look like.

▶ How to create simple menus using the menu editor.

▶ Adding options to drop-down menus.

▶ Using shortcut and access keys.

▶ Cascading menus.

▶ Creating dynamic menus.

▶ How to add code to menu events.

You Already Know Menus

If you've used PCs for any length of time, then you should be familiar with what a menu is. Windows users can't get away from them! In this world of graphical user interfaces, point and click icons, and highly intuitive mouse-driven programs, you still can't beat a good text-based list of options which open up the power and features of your application to your users.

A Great Windows Menu

This book is being written using Word for Windows which in many ways is an archetypal Windows application. If you look at how the Microsoft applications programmers have implemented this excellent product you can learn a lot about creating well-crafted Windows applications.

Consider the Word for Windows menu bar.

Each word you see on the menu represents a group of functions. For example, click on the File option and a list of **menu items** appears which relates to things you can do with files (in a *virtual* sense!).

In this chapter, we'll explore the two types of menus that Visual Basic provides: drop-downs and pop-ups. We'll find out how to create them, control them and generally make use of them in your applications. There is one control that all Windows applications seem to have, and that's the menu bar. Ignore it at your peril, but use it well and your users will love you forever!

Drop-Down Menus

The standard type of menu (and the easiest to develop) is the drop-down menu. In its simplest form, you simply pick some categories for your program functions, such as file handling, editing and program options, and place these category names onto a menu bar. All you need to do then is add functions to each category as menu items which drop down when the menu heading, such as File or Edit, is clicked.

This is what we want as our end product:

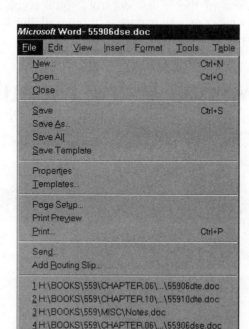

Don't panic! We're going to work through each stage, step by step.

How Drop-Down Menus Work

If you are a programmer who has come to Visual Basic from some other language, you may be a little daunted at the prospect of having to provide such menus in your programs. Questions like "how do I know if the mouse is over a menu heading?" or "how do I place a menu list over the form and redraw the form when the menu goes?" are probably making you break out in a cold sweat already. Worry not - Visual Basic (or more to the point Windows) does it all for you.

Menus, just like command buttons, option buttons, pictures and frames, are controls. Once you've set up the menu control, you only have to worry about handling the events that each menu item can trigger - in the same way as if you were using a command button. Windows automatically takes care of drawing the menu, re-drawing the covered parts of the form when the menu vanishes, displaying and positioning sub-menus, and so on. In fact, menus are one of the easiest controls you'll come across in Visual Basic; the most time-consuming part is typing all the text that forms the menus themselves.

Creating Menus Using MenuEdit

Unlike other controls, the menu control isn't found in the standard Windows toolbox. Instead, Microsoft in its wisdom chose to place it as an icon on the main Visual Basic toolbar.

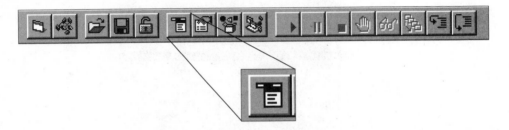

Alternatively, you can select the Menu Editor item from the Tools menu:

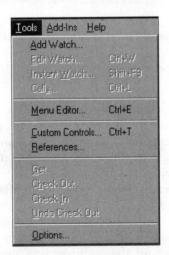

The Visual Basic Menu Editor

Setting up a menu is done via a fairly complex dialog box called the **menu editor**. If you have a form visible, click the menu icon and you'll be launched into the menu editor.

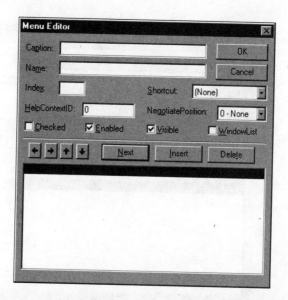

FYI

If you don't have a form visible, then the menu editor icon is actually disabled, so there's no way that either you or Visual Basic can get confused about what's actually going on in the development environment. Visual Basic adds the menu you create to the form which is currently selected.

Creating a Simple Menu

Most Windows applications have a File menu which allows your users to open and save data, exit the application, and so on. Actually creating the menu with the Visual Basic menu editor is a simple task:

1 Start up a new project in Visual Basic and make sure that the form (Form1) is visible.

Try It Out!

2 Click on the menu editor icon on the Visual Basic toolbar.

3 When the menu editor dialog appears, enter &File in the Caption property, and mnuFile as the Name property.

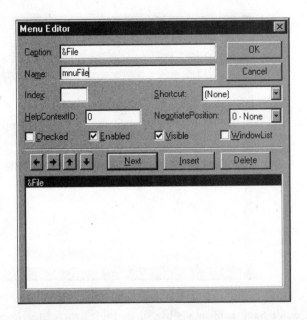

As with any other control's caption, putting & before a letter in the caption makes that letter a hot-key for that menu item. You can use any letter in the word, not just the first one. Going back to the File example, you can usually select a **File** menu by pressing *Alt* and F together. The user knows this because what he or she actually sees on screen is the word **File**, with the F underlined. The way you set this up in the caption is to simply say that this item's caption is **&File**.

4 Now press *Enter*. Visual Basic will store the menu item in the list area at the bottom of the dialog and move the highlight down to the next line.

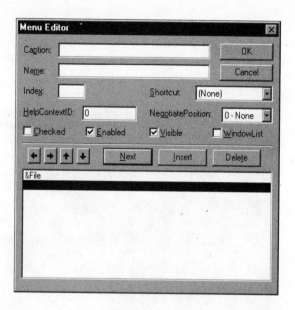

5 Use the same process to enter the Open and Save As menu items. First enter &Open for the Caption, mnuOpen as the Name. Then enter Save &As (note the space!) as the Caption, and finally mnuSaveAs as the Name property. The Name and Caption properties are the bare minimum you can specify when creating a menu. We'll look at the other optional properties in a moment.

6 If you now hit the OK button, Visual Basic checks the dialog to make sure you don't have any errors in the properties. When it's satisfied that everything's OK, it will create your new menu structure on the visible form, in this case Form1.

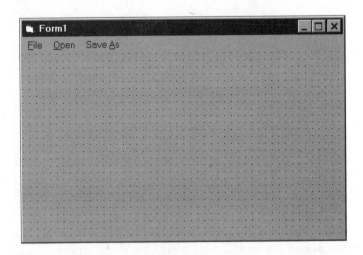

Well done, you've just created your first Visual Basic menu!

FYI If, at any point, you pressed the *Enter* key without adding an item name, when you click the OK button, Visual Basic will respond with an error message: **Menu control must have a name.**

Creating a Drop-Down Menu

Try It Out!

The menu we've just created isn't exactly a classic piece of Windows design.

Ideally, the Open and Save As options shouldn't actually be visible at this point. Instead, they should be drop-down items that become visible when you click on the word File, as in this more typical Windows menu layout:

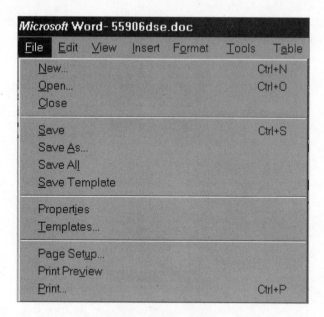

Let's fix it by creating a proper drop-down list of options from a single menu header.

1 Click on the menu editor icon again to reload the menu dialog and display the list of menu items you've created.

Click on the &Open menu item and then on the right arrow in the small toolbar

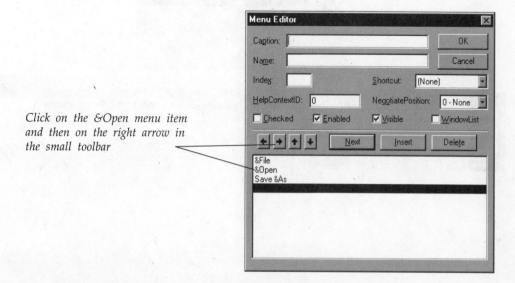

2 The &Open option will shift to the right. This indicates that it's now an option in the &File menu.

3 Do the same for the Save &As item.

4 To view your finished menu structure, click OK.

5 The form will now only show one menu item on its menu bar - the &File option. Click once on this heading to see the menu underneath it.

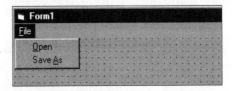

 The process of aligning the menu items to create the right structure is called outlining.

Editing Your Menu Structure

Of course, when you come to write your own applications, it's rare to find all parts of the development process whiz by as smoothly as following a Try It Out section. It's easy to miss menu items off or get them in the wrong order. Thankfully, Visual Basic's menu editor lets you go back and make changes.

1 Click on the menu editor icon again. The menu edit form appears, showing the menu we just created. (If you didn't follow the last Try It Out, or haven't still got it loaded, then it's on the disk called **MENUDES.VBP**.)

2 To the right of the four arrows in the menu editor there are three more command buttons; Next, Insert and Delete. Let's see what they do:

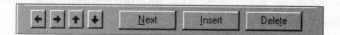

3 Click on the top item in the list, the &File item, to highlight it. Click on the Next button and the highlight moves down to the next item in the list, &Open. When you reach the bottom of the menu, Next creates a new blank item ready for you to add a new menu option.

4 Now click on the Save &As item. If you click the Insert button, the Save &As option drops down a line and a new item is added immediately above it. Do it now.

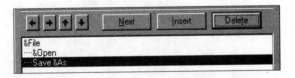

5 The Delete button does just the opposite of Insert, removing the currently selected item from the list. Click it now - the new blank item vanishes and Save &As moves back up to its original position.

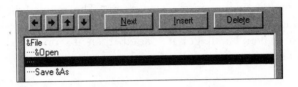

6 You've already seen how the right pointing arrow can shift menu items across the menu structure. The left, up and down arrows work in a similar way. Click on the &Open menu item, then click the left arrow.

7 The item shifts to the left, so that if you pressed OK now you'd have a File and Open menu with Save &As underneath Open. Don't press OK yet though.

8 With the &Open item still selected, click the up arrow and it will move up to the top of the list. The effect this has on the final menu is that &Open now appears on the title bar before &File.

9 To put the menu back to normal, click on the right arrow, then click on the down arrow.

Nested Menus

At last, our menus are starting to look the way they're supposed to. One further layout option is to place menu items in lists branching off from another menu item. This is called **menu nesting** and can be done as many times as you like. Take a look at this menu:

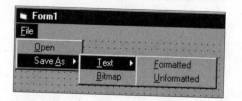

You can create nested menus in the same way that you create normal menus - you simply add new items to the list and shift them to the right of the one you want them to be nested under.

1 With the menu editor still visible, click on the Save &As item and press the Next button to create a new menu item.

2 Set the caption of this new item to &Text and the name of the menu to mnuText.

3 Repeat this process to create three more items with their captions and names set like the following:

&Bitmap	mnuBitmap
&Formatted	mnuFormatted
&Unformatted	mnuUnFormatted

Try It Out!

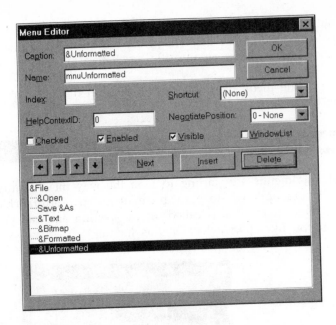

4 The actual order of these items is wrong. We want Formatted and Unformatted to appear underneath the Text item. Click the &Formatted item and press the up arrow once.

5 Now do the same for the Unformatted item.

6 We need to nest our new menus to make them appear as sub-menus of other menu items. Click on each of the four new items and press the right arrow.

7 This makes all the four new menu items appear as a sub-menu of the Save &As item. The next step is to make the Formatted and Unformatted items appear as sub-menus of the &Text item.

8 Shift the Formatted and Unformatted items right again.

9 If you press OK, you'll find that the menu structure is now how we want it.

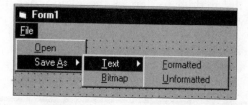

Menu Properties

We said earlier that a menu is a control and, like other Visual Basic controls, you can change the appearance and behavior of a menu by manipulating its properties.

Just as the menu control isn't accessed in the normal way by clicking on an icon from the toolbox, its properties aren't accessed through the Properties Window either. Instead, the properties are all constantly displayed in the Menu Editor Window itself.

Here are the menu properties.

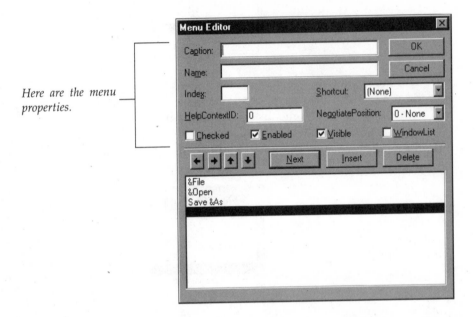

The normal flow of work when designing menus is to first create a menu item, then set its properties, then move on to the next item. So far we've only dealt with the Caption and Name properties. In the interests of speed, we've ignored the middle section of the dialog, but now it's time to go back and see what we can do with properties.

The properties can be set at design-time using the MenuEdit dialog box, or at run-time from within your code.

Name	Description
Caption	The text of the menu that the user will see.
Name	The name which you'll use in your code to address this menu and to identify the event code for each menu item.

Continued

Name	Description
Index	Used to form control arrays. This is where more than one menu item has the same name property, so a number in the Index property is used to address each item individually.
Shortcut	The menu can be invoked either by clicking it with the mouse in the normal way, or by pressing the shortcut key; for example, *Ctrl-C* is usually the same as a Copy menu item.
WindowList	This is used in Multiple Document Interface (MDI) applications. These are applications that have one main form and smaller subforms contained with it (like Excel and Word). The WindowList property tells Visual Basic to display the captions of the windows in this menu item.
Checked	Clicking on this property, or setting it to **True** in code, causes a tick, or **check mark**, to appear beside the menu item. This is great for lists of options.
Enabled	If this is clicked or set to **True**, then the menu item can be selected by the user. Setting it to **False** by clearing the check box causes the menu item to appear **grayed out**, meaning the user can't select it.
Visible	Clicking the check box to set this to **True** causes the menu or item to be visible at run-time. Clearing the check box makes it invisible.
NegotiatePosition	Controls where the menu appears, if at all, when dealing with embedded OLE2 objects. More on this in the OLE2 chapter later in the book.

Menu Name Properties

The second property, Name, should be fairly straightforward by now. It's the property that allows you, as the programmer, to decide on the name which you will use in your code to refer to a menu item.

Let's say you had a menu heading of File. You would give this a name and then, in order to change any other property of that menu item, you would use the following code:

```
mnuFile.<property name> = <a value>
```

FYI

One of the greatest hassles when dealing with menus is deciding what to call them. Each menu item is a control and needs to have its own caption and name. With a big menu structure, such as the one in Word 6 or even Visual Basic, deciding on unique names for each control can become a real hassle.

There are two ways to approach this problem. The first solution, and the one which the Visual Basic Programmer's Guide advocates, is to create control arrays of menu items. Here each item under a certain heading has the same name and is part of a commonly named control array.

The other approach, and the one I prefer, is to give each menu heading a name starting with mnu and ending in the name of the menu heading. For example, if you had a File heading, then its name would be mnuFile. Each item of the menu is then named with the heading name (or an abbreviated version of it), followed by a cut-down version of the caption. So, if under your File heading you have a Save As option, it would be named mnuFileSaveAs. This is simple, easy to understand, and a whole lot less likely to melt your brain!

The Menu Index Property

Index is another familiar property and is used to identify a menu item that is part of a control array. Using the Index property, it's possible to set up a number of menu items all with the same name. You'll see this in action later in Chapter 11 - Object Variables, where the property is used to create menus that are built up with code, like the list of recently opened projects that Visual Basic shows you in its File menu:

```
1 D:\PSYNET\BOOKS\BG2VB4\CHAP06\CHAP06.DOC
2 D:\PSYNET\BOOKS\BG2VB4\CHAP06\192_06.LAY
3 D:\PSYNET\BOOKS\BG2VB4\CHAP08\CHAP08.DOC
4 D:\PSYNET\DOCS\LETTERS\DANIELS1.DOC

Exit
```

Enabling Menu Items

The Enabled property determines whether or not the menu option is actually available for use. It appears grayed out if the Enabled property is not set. The Visible property indicates whether this particular menu item should appear on the menu at all.

Take a look at this screenshot:

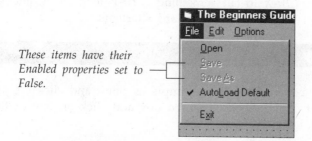

These items have their Enabled properties set to False.

This shows menus which are disabled and menus which are invisible. OK, you can't actually see the invisible ones, but that just shows how effective it can be!

Later in this chapter, you'll see how to create pop-up menus. By creating an invisible menu, you can create menus that the user can't see until you decide to pop them up onto the screen using some code. You can also use the Enabled and Visible properties when you need to build some kind of access security into your programs. Menu items that you don't want certain users to be able to use can be either disabled or made invisible.

Assigning Shortcut Keys

The Shortcut property is rather novel. Hot-keys created with & only work if that particular menu item is visible when *Alt* and the appropriate letter are pressed. Think back to the menus we created earlier.

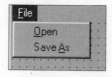

The <u>O</u>pen item was created with a text property of &Open. The O of <u>O</u>pen is underlined in the menu, meaning that we can access it by pressing *Alt* and *O* together. This only works, however, when the <u>F</u>ile menu is actually dropped down and visible. <u>S</u>hortcuts allow you to do this even when the menu isn't visible.

By assigning a key combination to the Shortcut property, you can actually call the menu option from any point in the program by simply pressing the shortcut keys. You may have come across some of the more standard shortcuts in Visual Basic: *Ctrl-X* to cut something, *Ctrl-V* to paste it, and so on. It's a good idea to try and stick to standard shortcuts.

Assigning a Shortcut Key

Try It Out!

Assigning a shortcut to a menu item is as simple as point and click - point at the arrow to the right of the <u>S</u>hortcut combo box and click on one of the key combinations listed. Let's try it.

1 Load up the **EDITMENU.VBP** project. This has two menus, <u>F</u>ile and <u>E</u>dit, with items on each of them. We're going to assign shortcut keys to the <u>E</u>dit menu items.

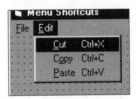

2 When the main form appears, click on the menu editor icon on the Visual Basic toolbar.

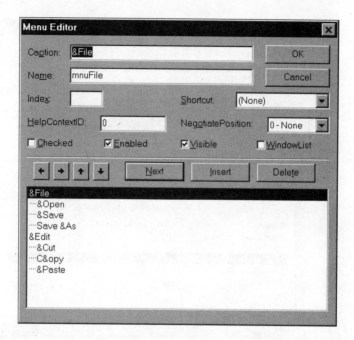

3 We need to add shortcuts to the Cut, Copy and Paste items. Cut will be *Ctrl-X*, Copy will be *Ctrl-C* and Paste will be *Ctrl-V*.

4 Click on the Cut item and click on the down arrow beside the Shortcut combo box. Then scroll down the list until you find *Ctrl-X* and select it by clicking it with the mouse.

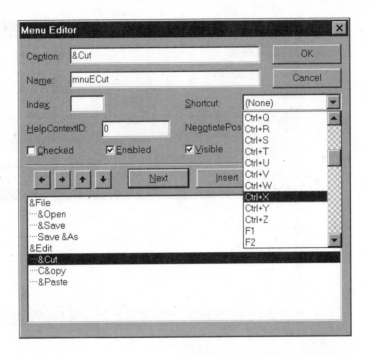

5 The menu editor dialog will now change to show you that the Shortcut selected is *Ctrl-X*.

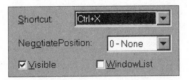

6 Using the same process, select the *Ctrl-C* shortcut for the Copy menu item and *Ctrl-V* for Paste. These are all standard shortcut commands for the Edit menu items that Microsoft recommend.

7 When all the shortcuts are set, click on the OK button on the menu editor and take a look at your new edit menu.

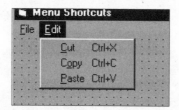

8 Now run the program and, instead of selecting menu items by pointing and clicking with the mouse, press *Ctrl-C*, *Ctrl-V* or *Ctrl-X*. Each time, a message box will pop-up showing you which menu item you've selected. You can check this by selecting the Edit menu items themselves. The same message boxes appear.

You can't add a shortcut key to a menu item that isn't indented.

The WindowList Property

Later on in the book you'll come across **Multiple Document Interface (MDI)** applications. An MDI application has a main background form, with smaller **child** forms inside - like Word, for example, where you can have more than one document open. Visual Basic lets you set up menus for the background forms and for the child forms.

Whenever a child form gets clicked on by the user, the MDI background form changes its menu to match that of the child form. This is a very common approach used by most Windows applications. Nearly all of Microsoft's own programs work this way. Take a look at this screenshot of Word in operation.

Menu changes according to active window.　　　Main, or background form.

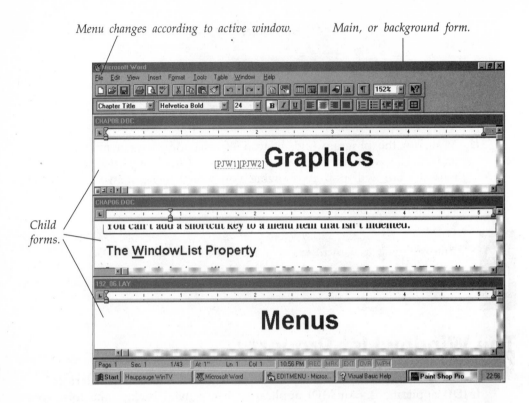

Child forms.

To understand MDI applications you also need to understand object variables. An object variable is a variable that contains not a number or text string, but a Visual Basic object, in this case a whole form. We cover object variables, and therefore MDI applications, in Chapter 11 - Object Variables.

Menu Separators

The final menu design feature we need to look at are **separators**. If you have a drop-down menu that has a large number of items on it, it makes sense to break up the items into logical groups. On the Visual Basic File menu, the options are grouped according to whether they apply to projects or files.

```
File  Edit  View  Insert  Run  Tools  Add-Ins  Help

     New Project
     Open Project...                                    Ctrl+O

     Save File                                          Ctrl+S
     Save File As...                                    Ctrl+A
     Save Project
     Save Project As...

     Add File...                                        Ctrl+D
     Remove File

     Print Setup...
     Print...                                           Ctrl+P

     Make EXE File...

     1 D:\...\BG2VB4\CHAP06\CODE\EDITMENU.VBP
     2 D:\...\BG2VB\CHAP06\CODE\EDITMENU.MAK
     3 D:\...\BG2VB4\CHAP06\CODE\MENUDES.MAK
     4 D:\...\BOOKS\BG2VB4\CHAP08\CODE\WOW.VBP

     Exit
```

Adding Separators

Separators are just as easy to create as any other menu item. Simply enter a dash for the item Caption, and a dummy name such as mnuDash1 as the Name property. Visual Basic automatically interprets a menu item with a dash for a Caption as being a separator line.

1 Load up the **FILEMEN.VBP** project. This is a simple application with a File menu containing Open, Save, Save As and Exit options. What we need to do is add a separator bar just above the Exit option.

2 When the main form appears, click on the menu editor icon on the toolbar.

Try It Out!

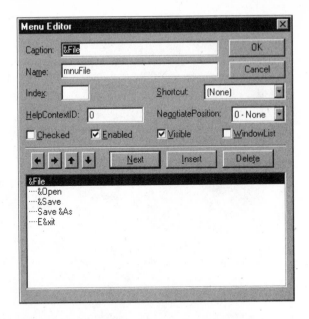

3 We want to add the separator bar above the Exit option, so click on that option in the list and then click the Insert button. Pressing *Alt-I* does this just as well.

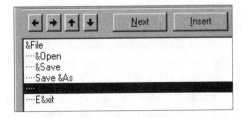

4 For the Caption of the separator bar just enter a dash. The only gripe I have with the way Visual Basic handles separator bars is that you still need to give each one a unique name. In the Name property enter mnuFDash1 to show that this is the first dash on the File menu.

5 Press OK to finish editing, then on the form take a look at the File menu.

Adding Code to Menu Items

Selecting a menu item triggers a click event. As a developer, you can add code to respond to that event. To bring up the Code Window for a particular menu item, single-click on the item on the form at design-time.

Click here to activate the Code Window

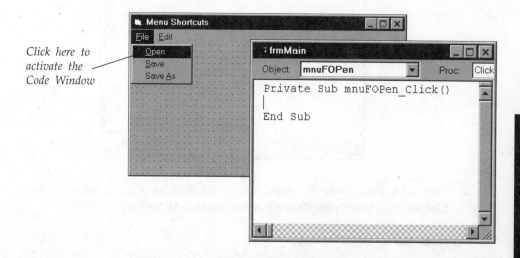

Adding Code to Menu Items

Actually adding event code to a menu item is as easy as adding code to a normal control.

1 Load up the sample project **DROPDOWN.VBP**.

2 Bring up the event Code Window for the Open menu item on the File menu.

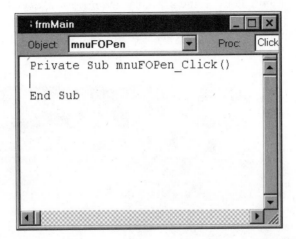

3 Let's add some code to make this menu item pop up a message box. Change the **mnuFOpen_Click**() event so that it looks like this:

```
Private Sub mnuFOpen_Click()

MsgBox "You selected Open from the File menu"

End Sub
```

4 Once this is done, run the program. Select Open from the File menu and the message box you've just added appears.

That just about covers drop-down menus. There is a good project at the end of the next chapter that shows how to integrate a menu into a larger project. We still need to consider the second type of menu though - the pop-up menu.

Pop-Up Menus

Once you have created your menu structure, you aren't limited to simply displaying drop-down menus. Visual Basic provides a command you can use which displays a menu anywhere on the screen, whenever you want.

What's a Pop-Up Menu?

Load up the **POPUP.VBP** sample program and run it.

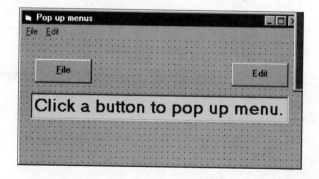

Here we have a program with a single form and a very familiar menu layout. There are also command buttons on the form which have similar captions to the menu headings. Clicking on one of these command buttons will pop up the appropriate menu underneath the command button.

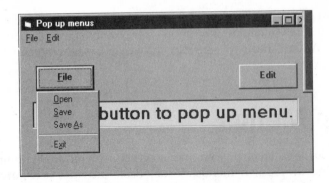

Creating Pop-Up Menus

The command which implements this kind of menu is the ingeniously
named **PopUpMenu** (and you thought learning Visual Basic would be tough!).

1 Load up the **POPUP.VBP** project and double-click the command button
named File to see the code.

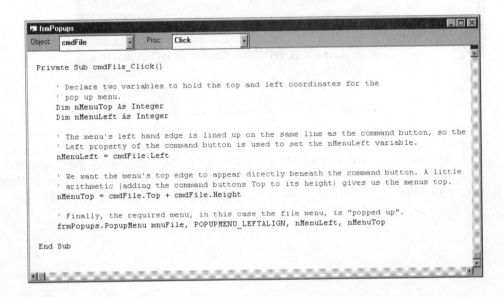

2 After declaring the subprocedure, there are two lines of code to set up two variables, **nMenuLeft** and **nMenuTop**, which will locate the top left corner of the pop-up menu on the form. The next two lines then set these variables to the bottom left corner of the command button:

```
nMenuLeft = cmdEdit.Left
nMenuTop = cmdEdit.Top + cmdFile.Height
```

3 After this, only one line of code is needed to actually display the menu:

```
frmPopups.PopupMenu mnuFile, vbPopupMenuLeftAlign, nMenuLeft, nMenuTop
```

How It Works

All the action is in this last line of code, which does a number of important things. First off, this line tells Visual Basic that **PopUpMenu** is a menu from a form named **frmPopups**.

FYI — This is the only form in our project and it isn't really necessary to tell Visual Basic that this is the one we're using. I've included it in the example simply because the **PopUpMenu** command can pop up menus which actually belong to different forms. In that case, you would place the name of the form that holds the menu *before* the **PopUpMenu** command. In other words, PopUpMenu is a method of the form.

The next part of the command, **mnuFile**, is the name of the menu I want to pop up. This is the name that is typed into the menu editor Name field.

Immediately following the name of the menu, you need to tell Visual Basic a number (known as a **flag**), which it then uses to determine how you want the menu displayed. Instead of using straight numbers, such as was the way in Visual Basic 3, you can now make use of VB4's instrinsic constants, **vbPopupMenuLeftAlign**, **vbPopupMenuRightAlign** and **vbPopupMenuCenterAlign**.

In this case, **vbPopupMenuLeftAlign** indicates that I want the left-hand edge of the menu to appear at the X coordinate which I specify later in the command. I could have said **vbPopupMenuCenterAlign**, or **vbPopupMenuRightAlign** to have the menu centered on the X coordinate or positioned with its right edge on the X coordinate. It's really just a question of personal taste and how much screen space you have to actually display the menu.

The last part of the **PopUpMenu** command is the X and Y coordinates, **nMenuLeft** and **nMenuTop**, which are used to position the menu on the screen. We cover coordinate systems later, in the chapter on graphics. For now, though, try to think of the screen as being divided up into a number of dots *across* the screen and a number of dots *down* the screen, rather like very fine graph paper. The X and Y coordinates tell Visual Basic how many dots across the screen (X) and how many dots down the screen (Y) are required to display the pop-up menu. Again, if you have a major craving for more instant information, then check out coordinate systems in Chapter 7.

To make things easy, though, you don't have to specify the flags or the X and Y coordinate parts of the **PopUpMenu** command. If you don't, the menu will appear by default at the location of the mouse pointer.

A Floating Pop-Up Menu

Try It Out!

This first pop-up menu is a bit poor. I mean, who has control buttons drifting around in the middle of a form? We need to get a bit more 95 about it. First of all, let's make it into one of those nice floaty menus that appear with a click of the right mouse button.

1 Make sure that you have **POPUP.VBP** open still. Go into the **cmdEdit_Click()** event procedure and select the main line of code:

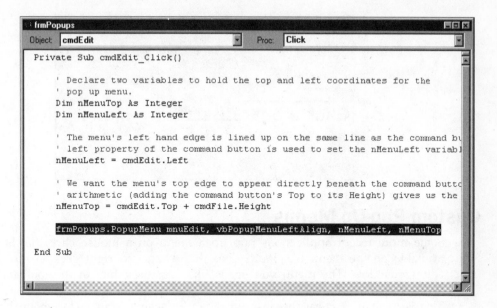

```
frmPopups                                                      □□☒
Object: cmdEdit                    ▾    Proc:  Click                  ▾

Private Sub cmdEdit_Click()

    ' Declare two variables to hold the top and left coordinates for the
    ' pop up menu.
    Dim nMenuTop As Integer
    Dim nMenuLeft As Integer

    ' The menu's left hand edge is lined up on the same line as the command bu
    ' left property of the command button is used to set the nMenuLeft variabl
    nMenuLeft = cmdEdit.Left

    ' We want the menu's top edge to appear directly beneath the command butto
    ' arithmetic (adding the command button's Top to its Height) gives us the
    nMenuTop = cmdEdit.Top + cmdFile.Height

    frmPopups.PopupMenu mnuEdit, vbPopupMenuLeftAlign, nMenuLeft, nMenuTop

End Sub
```

2 Copy this line to the **Form_MouseDown** procedure.

3 Now change the coordinates to X and Y, which are the mouse cursor coordinates passed to the procedure as the button was clicked, and put the line into an **If** statement that tests whether it was the right-hand mouse button (**Button=2**) that was clicked.

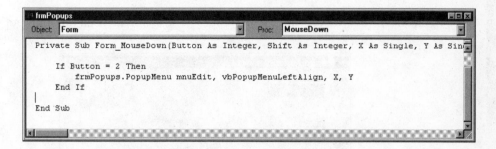

```
frmPopups                                                      □□☒
Object: Form                       ▾    Proc:  MouseDown              ▾

Private Sub Form_MouseDown(Button As Integer, Shift As Integer, X As Single, Y As Sin

    If Button = 2 Then
        frmPopups.PopupMenu mnuEdit, vbPopupMenuLeftAlign, X, Y
    End If

End Sub
```

4 Now run the program and press the right mouse button. Up pops the file menu. It disappears when you move the mouse and click the left-hand button.

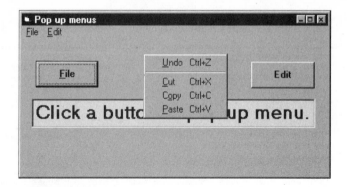

Custom Pop-Up Menus

Some more recent applications pop up a menu on a mouse click that is not available on the menu bar. Word does this when you right click in the editing window. The menu you get is like a greatest hits of the toolbar.

This is a bit of a cheat, because what you're seeing is in fact a menu bar item that has just been made invisible to prevent it appearing at the top of the window. Let's try it.

A Custom Pop-Up

To keep this quick and dirty, let's use a project we've already worked on.

1 Load up **EDITMENU.VBP**. We'll co-opt the Edit menu itself for our pop-up.

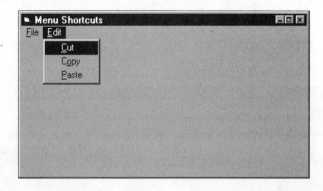

2 Fire up the menu editor and go to the Edit item

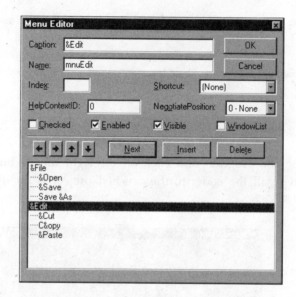

3 De-select the Visible property and close the editor down. Whooaah! Where's that baby gone?

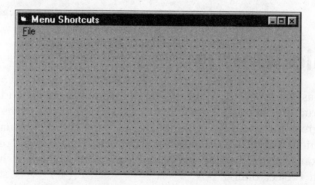

4 Finally, add the vital code to the **Form_MouseDown** event:

```
Private Sub Form_MouseDown(Button As Integer, Shift As Integer, X As
Single, Y As Single)

    If Button = 2 Then
        frmMain.PopupMenu mnuEdit, vbPopupMenuLeftAlign, X, Y
    End If

End Sub
```

5 Now run the program and click on the right mouse button. In case you didn't type all the code in, the finished project is on the disk as **POPUPCST.VBP**.

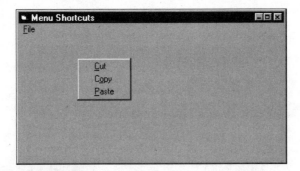

Dynamic Menus

As well as using the design-time menu editor to create and change your menu structure, it's also possible to create new menu items at run-time. This is great for creating dynamic menus, such as the Visual Basic File menu which automatically shows you the last four Visual Basic projects you worked on, cutting out the need for you to traverse your hard disk with the Open Project dialog box.

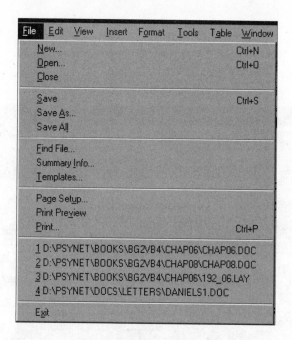

Adding Menu Items at Run-time

Dynamic menus such as this all revolve around **control arrays**. A control array is like a regular array that we covered in Chapter 4, apart from the fact that the elements in the array aren't numbers or strings, but controls.

A Quick Look at Control Arrays

One of the great things about VB is that you can assign whole controls to variables as though they were just a lowly number. This stores everything about the control, including all its properties and methods, in a little box called an object variable. You can open up the box and use the control any time you like, but like all variables you call it by the box name, not its real name.

If you have tried copying controls on a form, then you will already have come across control arrays. For example, if you have a control called Command1 and you try and copy it onto the same form, Visual Basic will ask you this:

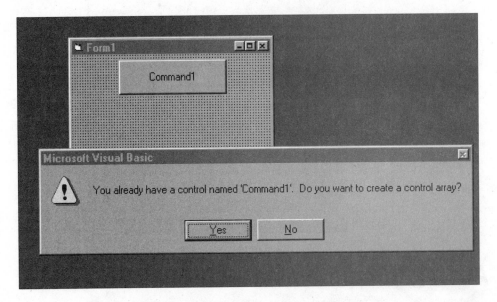

If you try to paste a control with an identical name to one that already exists, VB assumes you want to start a control array. If you click Yes, VB will name both buttons Command1, but set their Index properties to 0 and 1 respectively. If you add more Command1 buttons, VB will increment the index accordingly.

If you now wanted to set the Captions of, say, 5 buttons in code, you could do it like this:

```
Dim nIndex As Integer

For nIndex = 0 To 4
    Command1(nIndex).Caption = "Number " & nIndex
Next nIndex
```

All the buttons have the name Command1, but you can identify them by their position in the control array that VB created for you.

This sounds tricky and in truth it requires a slight leap of the imagination. We will come across object variables more and more throughout the course of the book, so you'll gradually get comfortable with them. For now, just think of them as boxes for controls.

Creating Dynamic Menus

We'll take a look at exactly what is involved in creating a dynamic menu by extending a project already on your disk. Load up the **DYNAMIC.VBP** sample project and take a look at the File menu.

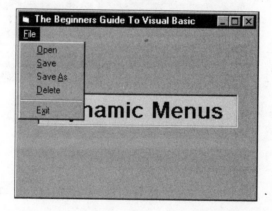

It's a standard File menu with options to Open, Save and Save As. What we need to do is add the previous file names to the bottom of the menu, separated from the rest of the menu options by a separator bar.

The theory is that we create a control array of menu items that starts with one element - the separator bar. Then, at run-time, we simply load new instances of the control array in the same way that you'd load a form. Visual Basic automatically numbers the new control array elements and displays them on the menu. Let's try it out.

Showing the Last Used Files on the Menu

Make sure you still have **DYNAMIC.VBP** loaded in with the main form showing.

1 Click on the menu editor icon on the toolbar to display the menu editor dialog.

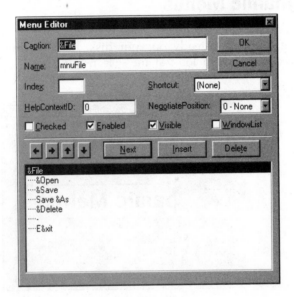

2 Move to the bottom of the menu item list and create a separator bar named **mnuFileList**. Do this by moving to below the last item and clicking on the Insert button. Then place a dash in the Caption box, type in the name and indent the separator bar under the E&xit.

At this point we have two problems. Firstly, Visual Basic doesn't yet know that this is a control array. Secondly, the bar will appear even when there are no files to list underneath it. This looks untidy.

3 Go back into the menu editor and make the separator bar menu item invisible by clearing the <u>V</u>isible check box.

4 To tell Visual Basic that this is actually a control array, place the number 0 in its Inde<u>x</u> property.

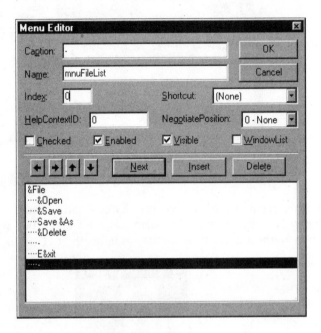

We now have a one element control array; the one element is our separator bar named **mnuFilelist**. We need to create the code to add items to the menu at run-time.

5 If you go into the form's Code Window and look at the general declarations section of the form, you'll see a module level variable defined:

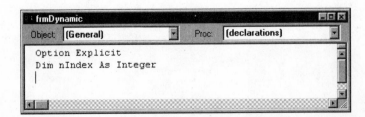

We'll use this variable to keep track of the number of items in our array. In the form load event, there is an additional line of code to set this variable to 1, to show that there is currently one item in the array.

6   Take a look at the `mnuFOpen_Click` code. Bring up the Code Window by opening up the File menu at design-time and clicking on the Open option. `mnuFOpen` is the name of the menu item. It's not as confusing as it looks. Since it begins with `mnu` it's easy to tell in our code that we're dealing with a menu. The `F` part of the name tells us this is a sub-menu of the File menu. Finally, the word `Open` lets us know exactly which menu item we're dealing with - the `Open` item. This is a common way of assigning names to menus, and you'll see it a lot more throughout the course of the book.

7   There's already code in the click event to use a common dialog to select a file name:

```
Private Sub mnuFOpen_Click ()

    On Error GoTo OpenError
    dlgOpen.CancelError = True
    dlgOpen.DialogTitle = "Select the file to open"
    dlgOpen.Filter = "All Files (*.*)|*.*"
    dlgOpen.FilterIndex = 1
    dlgOpen.ShowOpen


'_____

    ' Insert menu code here

    Exit Sub

OpenError:
    On Error GoTo 0
    Exit Sub
End Sub
```

FYI   Most of this code deals with a feature of Windows and Visual Basic known as the common dialog. Common dialogs are built into Windows to make all routine dialog boxes look the same to the user. We'll cover these in a lot more detail in the next chapter, but for now it's safe to ignore this part of the code. All we need to do is use the file name that the user selects from the common dialog to set up the file name as a menu option.

8 In the `mnuFOpen_Click` code, you'll see a comment line stating:

```
' Insert menu code here
```

9 This is the line in which we need to put some code to make the File menu grow dynamically. Directly below this line, type in this code:

```
frmDynamic.mnuFileList(0).Visible = True

Load frmDynamic.mnuFileList(nIndex)
mnuFileList(nIndex).Caption = dlgOpen.FileName
mnuFileList(nIndex).Visible = True
mnuFDelete.Visible = True

nIndex = nIndex + 1
```

10 Your Code Window should now look like this:

```
Private Sub mnuFOpen_Click ()

    On Error GoTo OpenError

    dlgOpen.CancelError = True

    dlgOpen.DialogTitle = "Select the file to open"
    dlgOpen.Filter = "All Files (*.*)|*.*"
    dlgOpen.FilterIndex = 1
    dlgOpen.ShowOpen


    '_____
    ' Insert menu code here

    frmDynamic.mnuFileList(0).Visible = True

    Load frmDynamic.mnuFileList(nIndex)
    mnuFileList(nIndex).Caption = dlgOpen.FileName
    mnuFileList(nIndex).Visible = True
    mnuFDelete.Visible = True

    nIndex = nIndex + 1

    Exit Sub

OpenError:
    On Error GoTo 0
    Exit Sub
End Sub
```

11 Try running the code now. Select the O̲pen menu item from the F̲ile menu and a common dialog will appear asking you to select a file name.

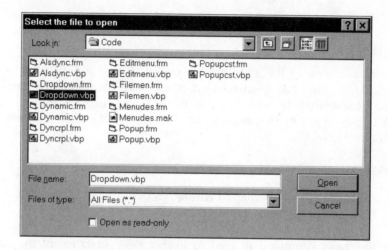

12 Go ahead and select one, then click O̲pen

13 Now take a look at the F̲ile menu once more. The separator bar has appeared and our new file name is beneath it.

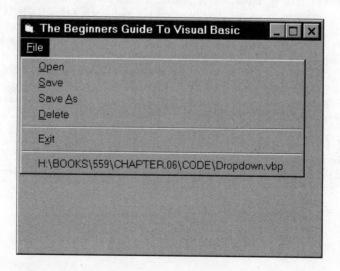

The completed project is on the disk as `DYNFIN.VBP`.

How It Works

Let's take a look at the code behind this. The first thing we have to do when a file name has been selected is to make the separator bar visible. We already know that the index of this in the `mnuFileList` array is 0. You gave it this index in the menu editor. Therefore, the first line just makes the separator bar visible:

```
frmDynamic.mnuFileList(0).Visible = True
```

If it's already visible (perhaps because you've already selected a file name), then that code will have no effect.

Next the `Load` command is used to load a new **instance** of the control array:

```
Load frmDynamic.mnuFileList(nIndex)
```

This is a complex area of Visual Basic, mainly because of the terms involved like instance, object variable and so on. Each control you put on a form, each menu item you create and each form itself is referred to as an instance. You can create new instances of controls in a control array with the `Load` command, which is what we've done in this example. We have used the same command before to load a new form. The **FileList** menu item is set up with an `Index` number of 0 which tells Visual Basic that this is the first item in a menu control array. We can then use `Load` to create copies (new instances) of this menu by telling Visual Basic what the new `Index` number should be.

Don't worry too much about the technicalities. You can just import this code into your own applications as it stands. Chapter 11 - Object Variables gives a more complete description of this whole area.

The **Load** command creates a new element, or member of the array, and tacks it onto the end. Our module-level variable **nIndex** not only shows us how many elements are already in the array, it also gives us the number of any new elements we want to create. Therefore, tell Visual Basic to load a new element into the **mnuFileList** array numbered **nIndex**.

The next two lines are straightforward:

```
mnuFileList(nIndex).Caption = dlgOpen.FileName
mnuFileList(nIndex).Visible = True
```

The new menu item is made visible and its caption is set as the file name returned from the common dialog. As we'll see in the next chapter, the one thing that comes out of all the gobbledegook of the common dialog is the **.FileName** property.

Finally, we add **1** to the **nIndex** variable to show that a new element has been added:

```
nIndex = nIndex + 1
```

It makes sense that if you **Load** new elements into a control array, you use **Unload** to get rid of them. We can add code to the **Delete** menu item to delete the entries we have just added.

1 Bring up the Code Window for the **Delete** item click event, **mnuFDelete_Click**.

2 Type in code so that the event looks like this:

```
Private Sub mnuFDelete_Click()

    If nIndex > 1 Then
       nIndex = nIndex - 1
       Unload frmDynamic.mnuFileList(nIndex)
    End If

    If nIndex = 1 Then
       frmDynamic.mnuFileList(0).Visible = False
    End If

End Sub
```

Now when you click on the Delete menu item, the last file name in the list disappears. The code first checks to make sure that we're not on the last item (i.e. the separator bar), and then unloads the current item from the array. We have to decrement **nIndex** as we incremented it after adding the last element.

If we are on the last item, the now redundant separator bar will be made invisible.

That about covers control arrays for now. As I said they will crop up increasingly frequently from now on, so if you have more questions, they will be answered shortly, I hope.

A Note on Good Design

Whatever your personal view on Windows (and I'm assuming that you don't actually *hate* it), it's hard to disagree with the notion that keeping the design of the user interface as standard as possible across various applications is a worthwhile objective.

Microsoft themselves have issued guidelines for how Windows applications should look. There are a lot of changes in the Windows 95 version that you would do well to try and emulate. The best source of help is *The Windows Interface Guidelines for Software Design (Microsoft Press 1995 ISBN 1-55615-834-3)*.

The bottom line on menus is that the more they resemble the applications your users are familiar with, the easier they'll find their way round your own program.

Summary

Menus are very useful tools for both you as a developer and for the users of your applications. In this chapter you learnt how to:

- Create new menus from scratch.
- Nest and sub-nest menus.
- Change the order of menu items.
- Add separator bars to the menus.
- Add code to the menus.
- Turn a standard menu into a pop-up one.
- Name menus in a standard way.

In the next chapter we'll take a look at dialogs. These are pop-up information windows that perform a variety of functions. Some of them, like the common dialogs we used to save and load files, come up as a result of menu selections.

Why Not Try.......

1 Add a file menu to the CON_DEMO project from Chapter 2 and create a list of previously opened image files on it.

2 In the CON_DEMO program, add a right click menu that appears over the main option box. Add menu items and code to clear the box and load the previous image. Then change the main picture box to an image control, and add a re-size menu item. Use the Stretch property and change the dimensions of the control in fixed increments to do it.

3 Create an Undelete menu that lists the last 5 strings that were inside a text box. You'll have to store the contents in a variable in response to a chosen event.

4 Create a Font change menu that appears on the right mouse click over a text box. Add items such as increase 10%, 20% and so on, with the same values for decreasing the size. Code the items to change the font accordingly. Also use the menu's checked property to switch the bold property on and off. (Hint: use `Text1.Font.Bold = True`)

5 Create a new version of the CLOCK program that has a Format menu that puts the date and time in different formats. (Hint: check out the `Format` function.)

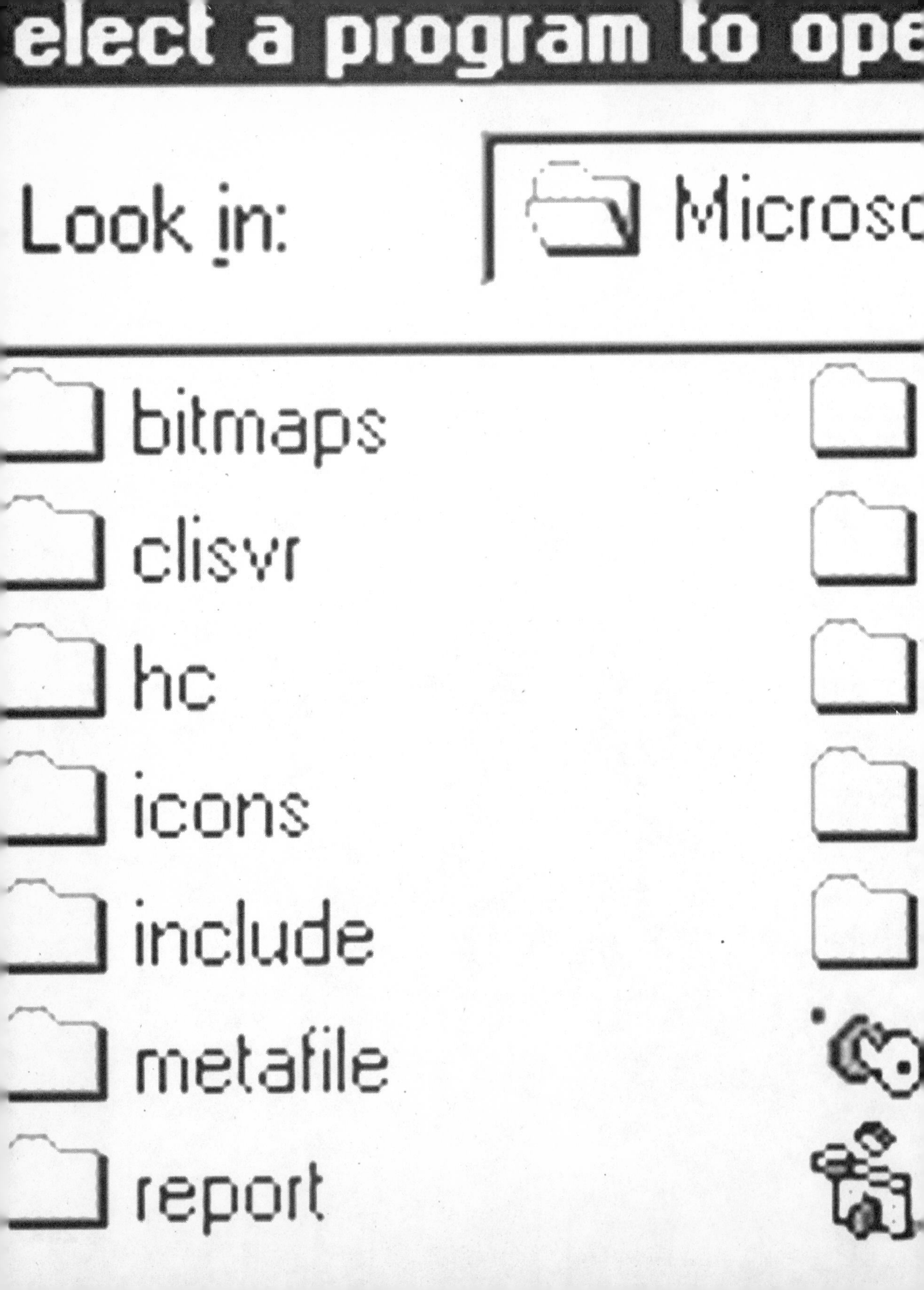
elect a program to ope
Look in:
Microso
bitmaps
clisvr
hc
icons
include
metafile
report

6

Dialogs

Dialogs are a useful way of getting specific bits of information to and from your users. They serve to focus the user's attention on the job at hand and are, therefore, extremely useful in Windows applications.

Dialogs come in a variety of forms, each adapted to a particular purpose. In this chapter we'll look at each of the four main types of dialog and examine how and when to use them.

In this chapter you'll learn about:

- ▶ What dialog boxes are
- ▶ When to use them
- ▶ Modality
- ▶ Message boxes
- ▶ Input boxes
- ▶ Common dialogs
- ▶ Custom dialogs

Introducing Dialog Boxes

It doesn't take very long in the company of Windows developers (not to mention on every other page of every Windows magazine!) before you start to come across the term **dialog**. Dialog boxes are the small windows that pop up now and again in Visual Basic and Windows to give you an error message or to ask for further information to complete a certain operation.

For example, if you try and leave Word without having saved your file, you'll see something like this:

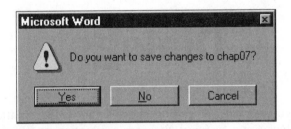

We've used message boxes, input boxes and common dialogs very briefly in earlier chapters. I said I'd explain it all later, and sure enough, here I go!

Although dialog boxes are common, their appearance can differ dramatically depending on the type. All of them, however, are just variations on four basic types.

Message Boxes

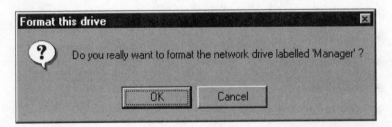

These are invoked by **MsgBox**. As a **statement**, they show text which the user must acknowledge by clicking one of the buttons also displayed. As a **function**, they return the ID of the button that the user presses.

Input Boxes

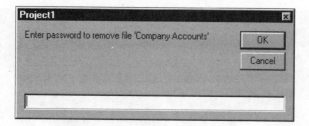

These are invoked by **InputBox**. An input box is a box with a message that allows the user to enter a line of text.

Common Dialogs

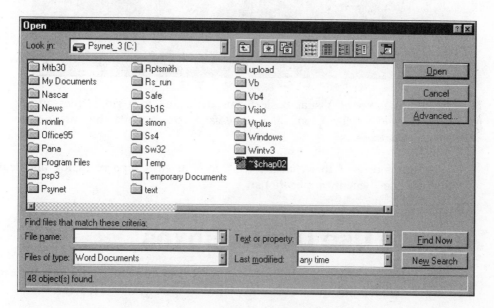

These include a variety of standard Windows dialogs for system settings. They can be invoked once the common dialog control has been added to a form by using the **CMDialog1.Showxxxxx** command. The **xxxxx** determines what type of common dialog is displayed.

Custom Dialogs

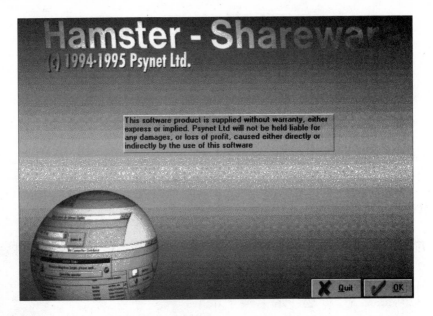

These are standard Visual Basic forms dedicated to a single message or function and made to look like a message box. In code they are referred to as `frmYourName`.

Over the course of this chapter, we'll look at each type of dialog and learn how to use them in applications.

When to Use Dialog Boxes

Although dialogs are an important part of a programmer's toolkit, they are very different from the forms and windows that you're used to.

As a rule, forms are used to handle data that's fundamental to your application, that is, the data that your program was actually written to deal with. In a customer database, for example, your forms display a customer's details or get those details from the user. Dialog boxes, on the other hand, are used for information about the operation of the program itself, and not necessarily the data that the program deals with.

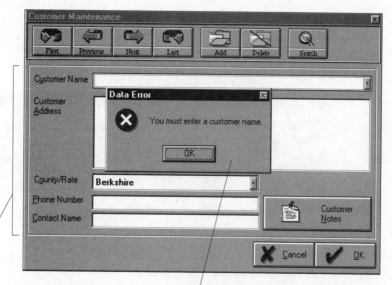

Here's the data that the application is about, on the form.

This is information that deals with how the program executes, on a dialog box.

For example, if your user decided that the font used in your application needed changing, then you'd display a font dialog box. This has no relationship to what your program actually does - it controls the way the program itself works.

Message Boxes

The simplest form of dialog in Visual Basic is called a **message box**.

The Components of a Message Box

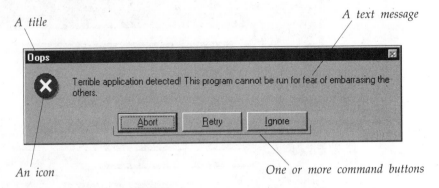

A title

A text message

An icon

One or more command buttons

All these features of the message box can be set up with just one small line of code, using the **MsgBox** command.

Message boxes come into their own when you need to give the user a simple message, such as an error message or a warning. When you close down Windows, a message box appears with an OK and a Cancel button which checks that you really *do* want to exit Windows. Let's copy that message box in an example.

A Simple Message Box

1 Load up Visual Basic and create a new project.

2 We're going to get rid of all the forms in this project and just use a message box instead. Delete the form from the project by selecting Remove File from the File menu.

3 Create a new module by selecting Insert then Module.

4 Type the following code into the Code Window:

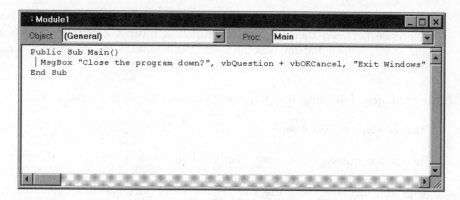

5 Now run the program. You'll see a message box appear asking you if you want to close the program down. At the moment, though, clicking either OK or Cancel has the same effect - they both stop the program. You'll see how to fix this in a little while.

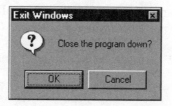

How It Works

The message box you've just created is the most straightforward type - created from a **MsgBox** subroutine. As it stands, the program has no way of knowing which button was pressed - the message box simply takes the button click in its stride, closes down and, since there are no forms and no other code in the project, takes the program with it.

When a message box is open, your program stops running and waits for you to respond to it. Once you have clicked one of the boxes, execution returns to the line in your code after the **MsgBox** command. In our case here there is nothing else, so the program ends.

Let's take a look at the code you just entered. **MsgBox** is the Visual Basic command which displays a message box (no surprises there!). There are actually two **MsgBox** commands in Visual Basic. One is a subroutine (the one we used here) and the other is a function. They look identical, but the difference between them is that the function returns a number which allows you to see which button was pressed. We'll look at the **MsgBox** function a little later - don't worry about it for the moment.

Immediately following the **MsgBox** command there is a text string:

```
"Close the program down?"
```

This is the message we want displayed in the box.

After the message there are two Visual Basic message box constants which are used to define which icon appears in the box, and which buttons are available to the user. There are quite a few of these constants available to you, and we will take a look at the full list in a moment.

```
vbQuestion + vbOKCancel
```

In this particular example, we are telling Visual Basic to display a message box with a question mark icon, along with an OK and Cancel button.

The final part of the message box command is another text string:

```
"Exit Windows"
```

Take a look at the screenshot again and you'll notice that this piece of text is used for the message box title bar.

Message Length in Message Boxes

If you place a long message into a message box, Windows will automatically split it over a number of rows. While this is quite a handy feature, the result can look a real mess. You can split the text in a message box by inserting a **CHR$(10)** character, like this:

```
MsgBox "This is a multi-line " & chr$(10) & "message."
```

The resulting message box is then:

The `CHR()` function returns the character associated with the number in brackets (we mentioned ASCII codes back in Chapter 2). `CHR$(10)` returns a linefeed character which causes a new line to be started.

Selecting the MsgBox Type

A couple of pages back, I mentioned Visual Basic's message box constants. There are a number of constants built into Visual Basic which you can use to determine which icon and which buttons appear on the message box. Simply find the icon constant you want and, in your code, add it to the button constant you want.

Message Box Button Options

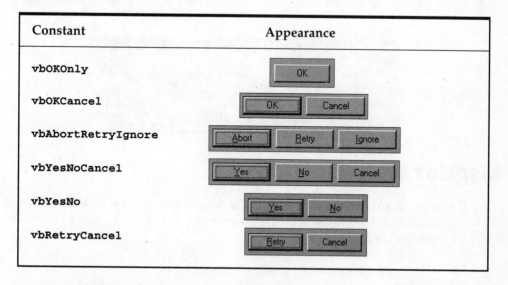

Constant	Appearance
`vbOKOnly`	OK
`vbOKCancel`	OK Cancel
`vbAbortRetryIgnore`	Abort Retry Ignore
`vbYesNoCancel`	Yes No Cancel
`vbYesNo`	Yes No
`vbRetryCancel`	Retry Cancel

Message Box Icon Options

Constant	Appearance
vbCritical	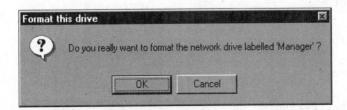
vbQuestion	
vbExclamation	
vbInformation	

Building the MsgBox Parameter

To display a particular message box, first look at the button options table and decide which you want. For our example we wanted an OK and a Cancel button. Therefore, the constant to use was **vbOKCancel**. Next, pick the icon you want from the icon options table. We wanted the information icon and so used the constant **vbInformation**. All you do then is add the two constants together (**vbOKCancel + vbInformation**) and there you have it - a message box with OK and Cancel buttons and an information icon!

MsgBox as a Function

I mentioned earlier that by using the **MsgBox** function, it's possible to find out which button was pressed. You could use the message box function in the form **QueryUnload** event.

Since this event occurs just before a form unloads, you may want to put a message box up with a Yes and No button, and then respond according to which button the user presses. Because, this time, we are using a function rather than a subroutine, the syntax for **MsgBox** is slightly different, and we now need to place parameters in brackets.

The `QueryUnload` event differs from the `Unload` event in that it takes place before the form unloads, as opposed to after. This may seem nit-picking, but it can mean the difference between saving your data and losing it forever.

The MsgBox Function

1 Create a new Visual Basic project.

2 As before, delete the form and create a module instead.

3 Enter this code in the Code Window that appears for the module:

```
Public Sub Main()

   Dim iResponse As Integer

   iResponse = MsgBox("Hit one of the buttons", vbAbortRetryIgnore
   + vbInformation, "Hit me")
   MsgBox "You pressed button code " & iResponse

End Sub
```

4 Now run the program. The first message is a function that asks you to press one of the buttons.

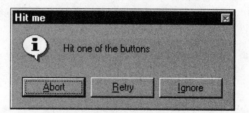

5 The value of the button you press is then assigned to the `iResponse` variable. This is then printed out as part of the `MsgBox` statement at the end.

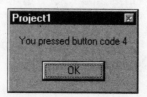

How It Works

The number of the button pressed corresponds to one of yet more of Visual Basic's intrinsic constants.

Value	Name	Constants
1	OK	vbOK
2	Cancel	vbCANCEL
3	Abort	vbABORT
4	Retry	vbRETRY
5	Ignore	vbIGNORE
6	Yes	vbYES
7	No	vbNO

As you can probably guess from this lot, you can check the return value using either the numbers shown or the built-in Visual Basic constants. The latter is obviously a much better idea since it makes your message box code instantly understandable to any other programmer that may come along, as well as to you when you return to your code in three months time in order to fix it.

FYI

If you find yourself frequently typing `MsgBox` statements with identical icons and buttons but different text, why not define a global subroutine to deal with them? A common use for this is in a global error routine, like the one shown here:

```
Public Sub ErrorMessage (ByVal sError as String)
  MsgBox sError, vbCritical, "Error"
End Sub
```

This way, all your error message code is kept in one place, and you don't have to worry about getting the `MsgBox` type number wrong, or about keeping the message box title the same from one message to another. It also makes your code much more maintainable. Changes to the error handler need only be made to one single module rather than to separate error handlers in all the individual modules. If a user then asks you to dump all the error messages to a text file on the disk, you only need to add a couple of lines of code to a single routine, rather than to a hundred (or more) routines. You need to put this kind of global routine in its own `.BAS` module.

Modality

By default, all message boxes are **application modal**. This means that whilst a message box is visible, no other windows in your application can get the focus. The user must respond to the message before they are able do anything else in that application. However, they can still switch to other applications by clicking on the taskbar or using *Alt-Tab*.

If you have a very serious message box that you wish to take precedence over everything else (including other Windows programs), what you really want is a **system modal** dialog box. This is a message box that must be responded to before the user can do anything else.

System modality is selected by adding yet another Visual Basic constant to the parameter. In this case, the constant is **vbSystemModal**.

Creating a System Message Box

1 Start up a new project in Visual Basic.

2 Double-click on the default form to display the Code Window with the form load event displayed.

3 Change the load event so that it looks like this:

```
Private Sub Form_Load()

  Msgbox "This is a system modal box. Try clicking on any other form",
vbSystemModal

End Sub
```

4 Now run the program. Just before the default form appears, a message box pops up. This is a system modal dialog box which means that you can't do anything else anywhere in the application until you click the OK button. The dialog box also stays in your face even when you switch to other applications.

Try It Out!

This is great for really serious error messages in your program, since no matter where the user is in Windows, they'll have no choice but to at least acknowledge the dialog box. It's also a great way to win the title of Fascist Windows Developer 95 for taking away user freedom.

In Windows 95, system modal and application modal dialogs are effectively the same thing. Windows 95 runs each application in its own protected memory space, effectively insulating it from other apps that you're running. You can't interfere with the system to stop other apps, like you could in earlier versions of Windows. This is good news for those of us who have seen a duff app bring the whole system down.

Input Boxes

Message boxes are great for relaying information to the user and getting them to press a single button, but what about when you need to get more information from the user? Well, that's where the input box comes into its own.

Input boxes are closely related to message boxes in that they are simple in both appearance and use, and are able to display a message to the user. The difference between the two is that an input box can accept data from the user.

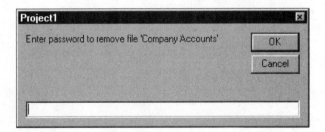

When to Use Input Boxes

Despite their apparent ease of use, both for you and your users, input boxes are very rarely used in state-of-the-art applications. The main reasons for this are simple:

> Input boxes can't be programmed, so there's no way you can validate the data a user enters until *after* they've entered it. For example, if you were using a standard form, you could place a text box onto it and add code to either the keypress or change events to check that the user is behaving. With an input box, you can't do that.

> They only allow the user to enter one piece of information. Programmers usually need more than this, and so use a custom form instead.

> Finally, they don't look great. Developing for Windows is like buying fashionable clothing - you don't want to be wearing the same old junk as everyone else. Custom dialogs are a cut above the built-in variety.

Despite these drawbacks, input boxes are a quick and easy way of getting a single piece of information from your user, so let's take a look.

An Input Box

1 Start a new project in Visual Basic and, as usual, delete the form and create a module.

2 Bring up the Code Window and type in:

```
Public Sub Main ()

 Dim sReturnString As String
 sReturnString = InputBox$("Enter your name", "Name Please", "Fred")
 MsgBox "Hi there " & sReturnString, vbOK, "Hello"

End Sub
```

3 Run the program and you should see the input box appear exactly like this:

4 The default name, Fred, is highlighted in the input box. If you don't want to change the name, just press OK and see what happens.

How It Works

Now for the first shock. Although the input box and message box both come from the same family of commands, you can't tell Visual Basic to display an icon, or tell it which buttons to display, as it does it all automatically.

The parameters you can enter, though, are fairly straightforward. This is the above example:

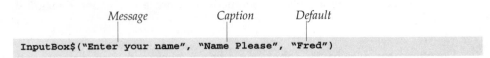

The first block of text is the prompt, in this case **"Enter your name"**. In message box speak, this is the same as the message. Next comes the title, which is the same as the title on a message box. Finally, the third parameter is known as default. This is the value that is automatically displayed in the input box when it loads up.

Positioning your Input Box

There are two other parameters which we didn't use in the above example: X and Y. These are the coordinates at which you want the input box to appear. For the sake of completeness I should say that the X and Y coordinates are measured in twips, but that is a topic we cover in more detail in the next chapter.

For now, all you need to know is that X is a number beginning at 0, increasing as the coordinates move towards the right-hand edge of the screen. The maximum value depends on the resolution of the screen. The Y coordinate begins at 0 for the top of the screen and increases as it moves towards the bottom.

Try It Out!

Placing the Input Box

1 Try adding **0,0** after the third parameter in the input box command above.

```
InputBox$("Enter your name", "Name Please", "Fred",0,0 )
```

2 Re-run the program to see the effect. The input box now appears at the top left corner of the screen.

Data Types and Input Boxes

As with the message box, there are two input box commands, but this time both are functions - one returns a string value ready to go straight into a string variable, whilst the other returns a variant. As we learnt back in Chapter 3, Visual Basic deals with variants a lot slower than it deals with explicit data types, such as strings or integers.

InputBox$ returns a proper string to your code, **InputBox** returns a string type variant. If you needed to get numbers or dates from the user, you would use **InputBox**. For instance:

```
Private Sub Form_Load ()

    Dim varValue As Variant
    Dim nAge As Integer


    varValue = InputBox("Please type your age", "Age", "23")
    If IsNumeric(varValue) Then
        nAge = Val(varValue)
    Else
        MsgBox "No, no, no - enter your age as a number!", ,
    "User Error"

    End If

End Sub
```

Common Dialogs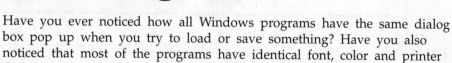

Have you ever noticed how all Windows programs have the same dialog box pop up when you try to load or save something? Have you also noticed that most of the programs have identical font, color and printer dialogs too?

The reason for this is the common dialog library. All the functions in Windows which allow programs such as Visual Basic to create windows, move graphics, change colors and so on, are held in files known as **dynamic link libraries**, or **DLLs**. One such file is the common dialog DLL. Visual Basic 4 comes with a special OCX, `CMDIALOG.OCX`, which makes using the functions in this DLL easy to master.

Using Common Dialogs

The common dialog control provides a set of five common dialog boxes for opening files, saving files, printing, setting colors and choosing fonts. There is also a sixth function of the control that doesn't actually show a dialog, but starts the Windows on-line help engine. I don't count it as a common dialog as such, although it is a function of the control.

The dialogs don't actually do anything to your application or its data. They simply receive the user's choices and return the values of these choices to your program through the properties of the common dialog control.

Actually programming the common dialogs is a bit of an esoteric exercise. Although there are five manifestations of the common dialog, there is only one common dialog control. This single control has various **Show** methods that invoke each of the dialogs.

Name	Method
Open File	`ShowOpen`
Save File	`ShowSave`
Color	`ShowColor`
Font	`ShowFont`

Name	Method
Print	**ShowPrinter**
Help	**ShowHelp**

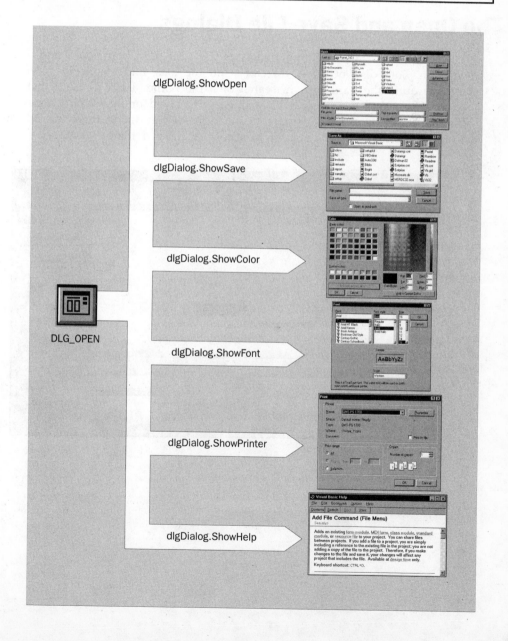

At first glance, a common dialog may appear a little daunting. There are so many controls to think about, surely there must be a lot of code involved? That's the real beauty of common dialogs - they can provide a vast amount of information and functionality to your users, but only require a tiny amount of code from you.

The Open and Save File Dialogs

The open and save file common dialogs are similar in both looks and function. Both display drive, directory and file lists, and enable the user to move around the hard disk in search of a file name. There's also a text entry area where the selected file name is displayed or into which a new file name can be entered. Finally, to the right of the dialog there are OK and Cancel buttons allowing the user to accept or discard their choice.

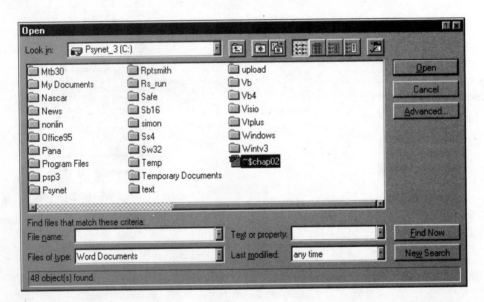

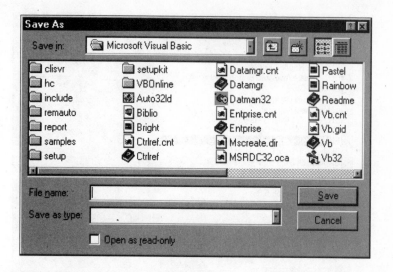

Let's see these dialogs in action with a program that displays an open file dialog box.

An Open File Dialog

1 Create a new project.

2 Make sure you have the common dialog control in the project.

If you don't see the icon for it in the toolbox, you can add it by selecting Custom Controls from the Tools menu, and checking the Microsoft Common Dialog Control option.

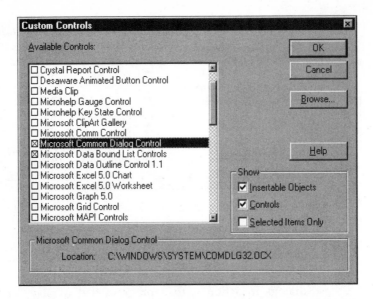

3 Place the common dialog icon onto the form. This is like the timer control in that it just sits on the form and can't be re-sized. It also doesn't show on the form at run-time, so it doesn't matter where you place it.

4 Bring up the form's Code Window by pressing *F7* and find the load event for the form.

5 Type in code so that your Code Window looks like this:

```
Private Sub Form_Load()

    On Error GoTo DialogError

    With CommonDialog1

        .CancelError = True
        .Filter = "Executables (*.exe)|*.exe|Com Files(*.com)|*.com|
Batch Files (*.bat)|*.bat"
        .FilterIndex = 1
        .DialogTitle = "Select a program to open"
        .ShowOpen

        MsgBox "You selected " & .filename

    End With
```

```
DialogError:
    On Error GoTo 0
    Exit Sub
End Sub
```

6 If you run the program now, an open file dialog appears asking you to select the name of a file.

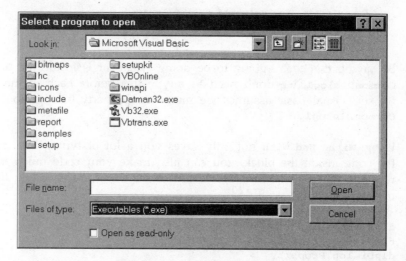

7 The drop-down list at the bottom of the dialog lets you select the types of file you want to see in the file list.

You can see the same code in the **COMMON.VBP** project. This project has command buttons which display each of the common dialogs. If you try this program, then each of the common dialogs pops up but doesn't do anything. Just press **Cancel** to get back to the main form.

How It Works

In order to decide which of the six common dialogs to select, and how it should work, before you launch the dialog you must cycle through the properties of the control and set them appropriately.

In the next few pages we'll cover each of these properties in depth, but for now there is one part of this code that warrants attention. That's the **With...End With** block that we use to cycle through the properties.

```
With CommonDialog1

        .CancelError = True
        .Filter = "Executables (*.exe)|*.exe|Com Files(*.com)|*.com|
↳Batch Files (*.bat)|*.bat"
        .FilterIndex = 1
        .DialogTitle = "Select a program to open"
        .ShowOpen

        MsgBox "You selected " & .filename

    End With
```

By saying that we're going to be doing whatever is inside the block `With CommonDialog1`, we don't need to retype this before each of the properties we set. Visual Basic assumes we mean the property belongs to `CommonDialog1.`

Using `With… End With` not only saves you a lot of typing but, by indenting the code inside the block, you can also make your code much more readable. There is nothing worse and more tiring than reading line after line of

```
dlgDialog.Property  =
dlgDialog.Property  =
dlgDialog.Property  =
dlgDialog.Property  =
```

Setting Up the Open File Dialog

The common dialog control is unlike other Visual Basic controls in that it doesn't have any events. Instead, you interact with it by setting various properties and by using its **Show** methods. As with most controls, you can set the properties at either design-time, run-time or a combination of both.

Setting Properties at Design-Time

At design-time you have the luxury of a choice of two options for setting properties. You can hit *F4* and bring up the usual Properties Window.

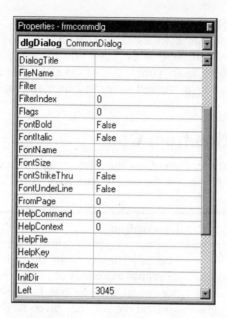

This window is a bit unhelpful in that it lumps all the properties for all the common dialogs together, when in reality some properties are only relevant to certain dialogs, while others fall into to the "err, what's that for then..." category.

To make life easier, Visual Basic provides a nice little tabbed dialog that organizes the key properties by dialog. You get to the dialog by double-clicking on the (Custom) property in the Property Window.

The dialog looks like this:

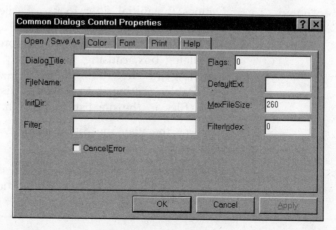

However, the problem with setting properties for the common dialog at design-time is that this then locks in to one dialog. The whole point of the common dialog control is that is gives you six controls for the price of one, so it makes sense to keep your options open by not committing the control to one type of dialog at design-time and instead, making your choices in code.

Setting Properties from Code

Before we look at implementing the dialog set-up code, let's see which properties need setting for the open and save common dialogs:

Property	Description
`FileName`	The full file name of the selected file, e.g. `C:\TEMP\README.DOC`. This property is what you see when the file has been selected for opening. You rarely set this in code directly.
`FileTitle`	The file name of the selected file, but without the path, e.g. `README.DOC`.
`Filter`	Defines the types of file that the dialog will show. Basically, you need to enter wildcards here, with a description of each. For instance `dlg.Filter = "Text	*.txt	Icons	*.ico"`. This selects which types of file to display in the combo box at the foot of the file dialog. To keep the user focused, set this before you call the dialog.
`FilterIndex`	Defines the initial filter to use. Earlier we set up three filter values - for `.exe`, `.com` and `.bat` files. We then set `FilterIndex` to 1 before displaying the dialog box, causing it to display only files matching the first filter, that is, `*.exe` files, i.e. executables. Setting it to 2 would display only `.com` files in the file list, and so on.
`Flags`	Governs the way the dialog actually works - see later in this chapter.
`InitDir`	Specifies the initial directory to list in the dialog. This suggests to your user where the files should go/come from.

Continued

Property	Description
MaxFileSize	Allows you to tell the dialog the maximum number of characters you want to see displayed for a file name.
DialogTitle	Effectively the same as the Caption property on the form
CancelError	Set this to true to trigger a run-time error if the user presses the Cancel button. We can catch this error in our code if we use the **On Error** statement, and then take the necessary action.

Selecting the Correct Files

In our sample program, the open and save dialogs both need to have their **Filter** and **FilterIndex** properties set to control the types of file listed in the dialog. Let's assume that we only want to display files that can be executed:

```
.Filter = "Executables (*.exe)|*.exe|Com Files
↳Batch Files (*.bat)|*.bat"(*.com)|*.com|
.FilterIndex = 1
```

Filter contains a string where each element of the string is separated by a | sign.

On most keyboards the | symbol is two vertical dashes, one on top of the other.

First, you enter a description for the type of file, for example: **Com Files (*.com)**. These descriptions are what appear in the drop-down list box at the bottom of the dialog. After each description you must then enter the wildcard for the files which match that description. In this case it's simply ***.com**. As you select descriptions from the drop-down at the bottom of the dialog, the file name text box changes to the wildcard and the file list changes to show only those files which match your wildcard.

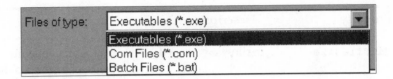

The **FilterIndex** property is a number between **1** and the number of elements in the filter. It defines the default or start-up filter that should be used. In the example, I say **FilterIndex = 1**. Therefore, the default filter to use will be the first one, which is **Executables (*.exe)**.

Naming the Dialog

Instead of the normal **Caption** property, common dialogs use the **DialogTitle** property to set the message displayed on the title bar of the common dialog. The following line sets this up:

```
.DialogTitle = "Select Program To Open"
```

If you don't set this property of the dialog, Visual Basic will automatically display an appropriate title of its own, as you'll see later.

Selecting and Launching the Dialog

Finally, the dialog is brought into view by using the appropriate **Show** method. For example, **.ShowOpen** shows the open dialog, **.ShowSave** shows the save dialog, and so on. A complete list of these **Show** methods was given earlier.

When the user has selected a file name, it's returned in the common dialog **FileName** property.

Error Handling with Common Dialogs

We set the **CancelError** property to true at the start of the code:

```
On Error GoTo DialogError

With CommonDialog1

.CancelError = True
```

This means that if Cancel is clicked, it triggers a Visual Basic error.

This only applies to the **Cancel** buttons you'll find in the common dialogs. It doesn't apply to the **Cancel** buttons on message boxes or input boxes.

The last lines of code in the example are designed to trap any errors:

```
DialogError:
On Error GoTo 0
Exit Sub
End Sub
```

Why do we need to do this? Well, it means that when the user presses Cancel on the common dialog, an error event is triggered, causing the **DialogError** code to take control out of the main procedure and exit.

The Color Dialog

The color dialog is even easier to set up than the file dialogs. Its purpose is to allow the user to select and display colors from the palette of colors currently available on that particular computer.

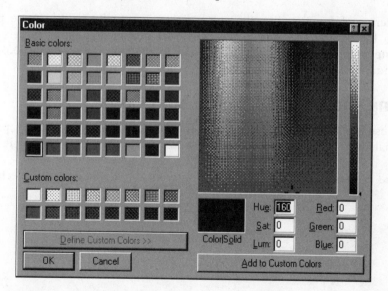

Properties of the Color Dialog

Property	Description
Color	Holds the long integer value of the color the user selected.
Flags	See the section later in this chapter for details of the most common flag values.
CancelError	Set CancellError to true to trigger a run-time error if the user clicks on the Cancel button on the dialog box.

To bring the color dialog into view, use the ShowColor method on the common dialog control on your form.

The actual color selected is returned in the dialog Color property. You can move it directly from there to the color properties of any controls whose color you wish to change.

In terms of functionality, the color dialog is actually a little more powerful than the others. The Add to Custom Colors button, for example, lets you create your own colors and add them to the Windows palette. No other common dialog affects Windows or your application in this way.

Invoking the Color Dialog in Your Code

To use the color dialog, first place the number 1 into the Flags property to initialize it and then use the ShowColor method on the control itself.

Here is the code for the color dialog from the COMMON.VBP project:

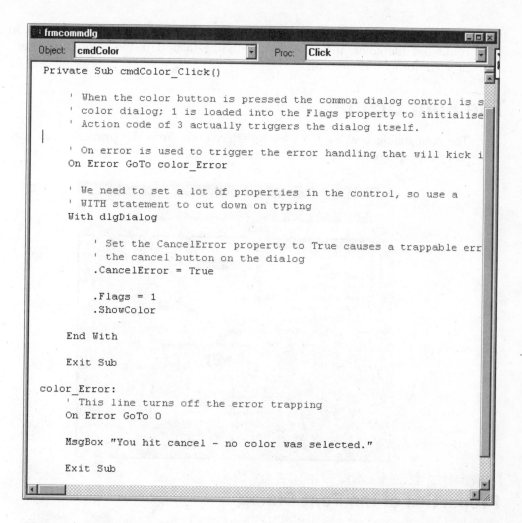

```
frmcommdlg
Object: cmdColor          Proc: Click

Private Sub cmdColor_Click()

    ' When the color button is pressed the common dialog control is s
    ' color dialog; 1 is loaded into the Flags property to initialise
    ' Action code of 3 actually triggers the dialog itself.

    ' On error is used to trigger the error handling that will kick i
    On Error GoTo color_Error

    ' We need to set a lot of properties in the control, so use a
    ' WITH statement to cut down on typing
    With dlgDialog

        ' Set the CancelError property to True causes a trappable err
        ' the cancel button on the dialog
        .CancelError = True

        .Flags = 1
        .ShowColor

    End With

    Exit Sub

color_Error:
    ' This line turns off the error trapping
    On Error GoTo 0

    MsgBox "You hit cancel - no color was selected."

    Exit Sub
```

The color dialog is a way for you to get information from the user. It doesn't actually change the colors in your application. This is the same for all the common dialogs. For example, the font dialog doesn't change the fonts in your program, nor does the print dialog actually print. They all just provide a standard way for you to get information from the user.

With the color dialog, for example, when the user has selected a color, you could use the color properties of the dialog to update the color properties of your forms and controls.

The Font Dialog

The font dialog enables the user to select fonts from the printer's font list, from the screen font list, or from both together.

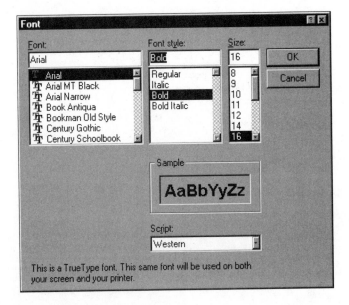

Properties of the Font Dialog

Property	Description
Color	Holds the long integer value of the color that the user selected in the dialog.
FontBold	True if the user selected Bold in the dialog, false if not.
FontItalic	True if the user selected Italic in the dialog.

Continued

Property	Description
FontStrikeThru	True if the user selected StrikeThru in the dialog.
FontUnderLine	True if the user selected Underline in the dialog.
FontName	Use your imagination!
Max	Specifies the size, in points, of the largest fonts to be displayed.
Min	Specifies the size, in points, of the smallest fonts to be displayed.
FontSize	Holds the size of the selected font.
Flags	See the section later in this chapter for some useful values for the **Flags** property.
CancelError	Set this to true to cause a run-time error whenever the user clicks on the Cancel button in the common dialog. This can be trapped in code with the **On Error** statement.

You can determine which font list will be displayed by loading a number into the **Flags** property in the same way that 1 was loaded in the color dialog to initialize that. The constants you need to place in the **Flags** property are:

Flag	Type of Font
cdlCFANSIOnly	Screen fonts
cdlCFPrinterFonts	Printer fonts
cdlCFBoth	Both screen and printer fonts

The dialog can then be brought into view using the **ShowFont** method.

FYI

If you don't set the **Flags** property to one of these values before displaying the fonts dialog, then you'll get an error - **No Fonts Exist.**

The font dialog can even be used to select a font color. This is done by adding 256 to the value in the **Flags** property. If you don't do this, you won't be able to select colors, only font names, styles and sizes.

When the user exits the dialog, your code can then check the **Color** property and the values of the **Font** properties to find out what the user actually chose.

The code from **COMMON.VBP** that displays the font dialog looks like this:

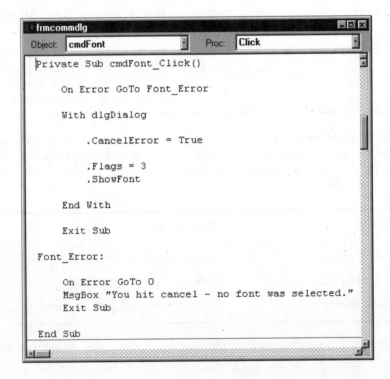

```
Private Sub cmdFont_Click()

    On Error GoTo Font_Error

    With dlgDialog

        .CancelError = True

        .Flags = 3
        .ShowFont

    End With

    Exit Sub

Font_Error:

    On Error GoTo 0
    MsgBox "You hit cancel - no font was selected."
    Exit Sub

End Sub
```

The Print Dialog

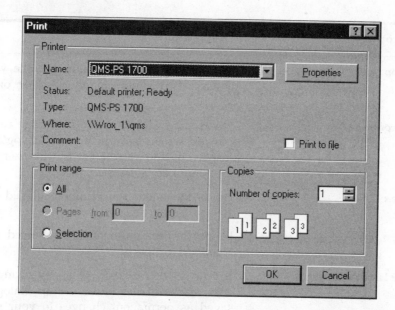

The print dialog allows the user to not only determine how much data they want to print, but also how the printer itself should work. This includes at which resolution and speed the printer should print, which printer or printer driver to use, and even whether or not to ignore the printer totally and print direct to a disk file. Just to really confuse your application, the dialog even allows the user to specify the number of copies to print and whether these copies should be collated. This last option is only available on some printers.

We haven't covered printing to a printer yet. We'll cover it in Chapter 16 - Putting It All Together.

Properties of the Print Dialog

Property	Description
Copies	Holds both the initial value and the value entered by the user for the number of copies to print.
FromPage	Holds the number of the first page to print. Can be set by code before the dialog is displayed, and can be set by the user keying in a number.
Max	Holds the maximum number allowed for the ToPage property.
Min	Holds the minimum number allowed for the FromPage property.
PrinterDefault	If you set this to true, then any changes the user makes in the Printer Setup dialog are saved as permanent changes to your system. They will also affect any other programs running which may want to make use of the printer.
ToPage	Holds the number of the last page of the report to print.
Flags	See later for some of the more useful flag values for this property.
CancelError	Set this to true to cause a run-time error if the user clicks on the Cancel button on the print dialog.

Unlike the color and font dialogs, the print dialog box doesn't need to have anything placed into its **Flags** property. All you need to do to display the dialog is run the **ShowPrinter** method.

Three properties are used to return the user's selections to your program: **Copies**, **FromPage** and **ToPage**. In order to supply the user with some default values, you can set these properties up before displaying the print dialog.

Common Dialog Flags

The `Flags` property provides a useful way to control the operation of the common dialogs and the information they present to your users. In all, there are 48 different values you can use for the `Flags` property, and these can be combined to give you some really weird custom effects. However, of those 48, only a handful are really common.

The table below shows you the most useful flags and the VB constants you can use for them. I guess you'd call it 'My Favorite Flags'.

Name	Dialog	Description
`cdlPDPrintSetup`	Print	Displays the printer setup dialog instead of the print options dialog.
`cdlPDNoSelection`	Print	Stops your users from choosing to print only the current selection of text. This feature involves a lot more code, which you may not be keen to write.
`cdlPDHidePrintToFile`	Print	Hides the Print to file option on the dialog, for the same reasons as above.
`cdlCCPreventFullOpen`	Color	Stops the user from defining their own custom colors.
`cdCClFullOpen`	Color	Starts the dialog up with the custom color window already open.
`cdlCFWYSIWYG`	Font	Shows only those fonts that are available on both the printer and the screen. You also need to add it to `cdlCFBoth` and `cdlCFScalableOnly`
`cdlCFBoth`	Font	Lists all the printer fonts and all the screen fonts.

Continued

Name	Dialog	Description
`cdlCFScalableOnly`	Font	Only shows you fonts which can be re-sized - normally Truetype fonts.
`cdlCFPrinterFonts`	Font	Lists only the printer fonts.
`cdlCFScreenFonts`	Font	Lists only fonts which can be displayed on screen.
`cdlOFNAllowMultiselect`	File	Allows the user to select more than one file from the file dialog boxes.
`cdlOFNFileMustExist`	File	The user can only type in the name of a file that exists.
`cdlOFNOverwritePrompt`	file	In the save as dialog box, if the user selects a file that already exists, then the dialog will ask the user if they really want to overwrite that file.

Custom Dialogs

The alternative to message boxes, input boxes and common dialogs is the do-it-yourself approach, where you create your dialogs in exactly the same way as you would create any form in your application. This approach has both benefits and drawbacks.

On the benefits side, because you design the form you'll use as a dialog, you can ensure that it keeps the same colors and interface standards as the other forms in your application. Since it is 100% home-made, you are free to put whatever icons, controls, text or graphics you want on it. The only limit is your imagination.

The drawbacks, on the other hand, are substantial. Each form in your application uses system resources, such as memory and processor time, when your program is running. It doesn't take that many custom dialogs in your application before something as simple as trying to run the application could cause a lesser-powered machine to grind to a halt.

Creating a Custom Dialog

1 Load up **WROX6.VBP**. This is a simple form with a menu at the top and a couple of toolbars, a ruler and a status bar. It forms part of a major new contender in the word processing stakes: Wrox 6, part of the Messy Office suite!

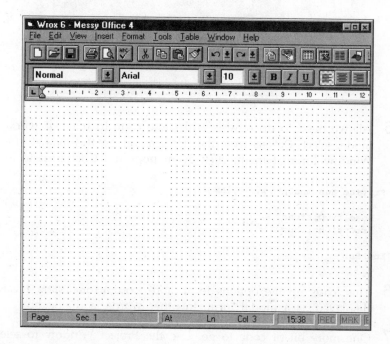

2 Run the program. You can enter text into the text window, cut and paste with *Ctrl-X* and *Ctrl-V*. In fact, most of the stuff you'd expect as the bare minimum for a word processor. Wrox 6 is still in development. The problem is, you're the developer. One of the things your client has asked you for is for an options dialog. I feel a custom dialog coming on.

3 On the disk there's just the dialog box you want, **WROX6.FRM**. If the program is currently running, stop it and select A<u>d</u>d File from the <u>F</u>ile menu. Then choose **WROX6.FRM** as the file to add.

4 So far so good. We have a new form in the project with a fixed border and no re-size buttons, hence a custom dialog. To see it, click View Form on the Project Window.

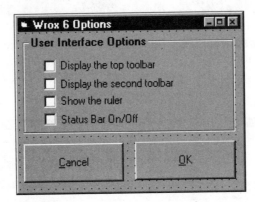

5 All we need to do now is add some code to make it work. In design mode, select Options from the Tools menu on the main form. The Code Window for that menu click event pops up. Change it to look like this:

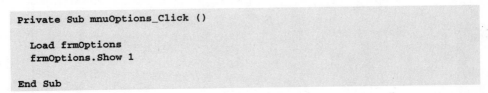

```
Private Sub mnuOptions_Click ()

    Load frmOptions
    frmOptions.Show 1

End Sub
```

6 This loads up the options form, and `frmOptions.Show 1` causes it to be displayed as a modal form. In other words, a dialog box.

7 One more bit of code to go. Use the Project Window to select the options form. When it appears, double-click on the OK button. What we want to do here is hide or show the toolbars and so on, based on which check boxes were set. Change the code so that it looks like this:

```
Private Sub cmdOK_Click ()

  frmMain.picToolbar.Visible = chkToolbar1
  frmMain.picToolbar2.Visible = chkToolbar2
  frmMain.picRuler.Visible = chkRuler
  frmMain.picStatus.Visible = chkStatus

  Unload frmOptions

End Sub
```

8 There you have it! A very simple options window, yet good enough to show your client when they come to look at the product. Run the application and play with the new dialog by selecting Options from the Tools menu.

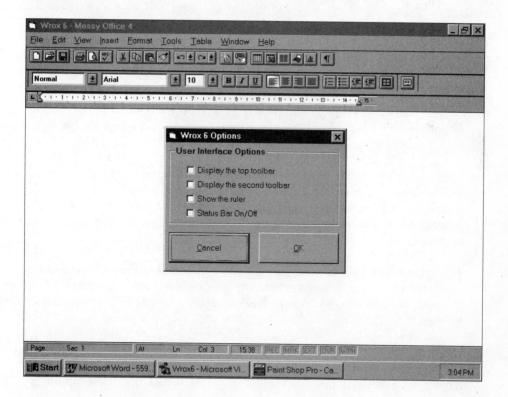

Users appear to your programs like planes do to an air traffic controller. If you don't talk to them for a while, they tend to wander off on their own and get into all sorts of trouble. Your custom dialogs can ensure that you grab the user's attention and don't let go. Microsoft approach the problem by displaying animated dialog boxes whilst you install programs, but even these may not be enough to keep the user seated. Imagine the situation where you're copying data from a stack of about 12 disks and need the user to insert the next disk after quite a long pause. You can place a timer event on your custom dialog so that the timer event is triggered 20 seconds after the box appears, and every 2 seconds thereafter. The timer event could simply beep. Users tend to sit up and take notice, or get dragged back to their desks by their colleagues if a computer begins to exhibit this kind of rude behavior. Just what we want! Take a look at `ANNOY.VBP` in the sample code supplied with the book.

Writing Your Own Word Processor

Now's a good time to pull together a few of the things we've covered recently into one project. The project is a very rudimentary notepad. The techniques we'll cover are menus, string functions and custom dialogs, along with something new - file handling.

I will be honest with you - I hate disk files. They are clunky, awkward and require you to remember a lot of arcane command syntax. Basically, they encompass all the things you came to Visual Basic to avoid. UNIX programmers love them, which says a lot about how fit they are for human beings.

The good news is that with the advent of database controls and bound controls, which we will cover shortly, you need to work with raw disk files less and less. It makes sense to let Visual Basic or Access do the hard work for you.

However, there are times, I admit, where you have to roll up your sleeves and open up those itsy-bitsy disk files yourself. In the next section we'll have a brief look at how disk files work. We'll just use the simplest type in our project and hopefully come away unscathed.

File Handling

Disk files come in three types:

▶ **Sequential files** store a long chunk of data as a stream of ANSI characters. These are your basic text files that have the extension `.TXT`. There is almost no formatting information contained in the file, just letters. These kind of files are useful when the application using them works with the contents as a dumb block, without having to interpret the contents.

▶ **Random Access files** again contain only text, but they have some structure to them. You can define the structure which then tells you what the stream of characters mean. A good example is a name and address file. You create a set of fixed length fields for names and addresses, and providing you follow your own pattern to the exact letter, you can fish data in and out of the file without having to grab the whole lot and work out what it all means. The emphasis here is on you, the programmer, being organized. Database controls exist to free the world from this burden.

▶ **Binary files** are files where the records don't have a fixed length - so they are random access files without the structured field system that allows you to know what's going on. This sounds tragic, and it is. You have to read through all the records and find the one you want by hand. The benefit over random access files is that binary files are smaller.

You will be pleased to learn that we are only going to look in detail at sequential files. The process of opening and closing a file is similar in all three cases and, in my opinion, if you start playing around with random and binary files, then you get what you deserve.

Opening Sequential Files

A disk file exists in its own right, independent of your application. In order to read from or write to files, you have to make a connection between your code and the file on the disk, and give the operating system the chance to physically locate the file. In order to get the file ready for business, you have to open it up by using the `Open` command with the correct parameters.

The **Open** command needs to know which file you want to open, what you are going to do with it, and what reference number you want to give it when you are dealing with it. So, typically, you might say:

```
Open Textfile.txt For Input As 1
```

In Visual Basic they use a file number, but any programmer worth their salt knows this is just a cover for a Windows file handle. It's the name that VB and Windows have agreed between them to use to refer to the file for all the time it's open. The handle is a unique label that points to where the file actually is on the disk and allows the operating system to work with files efficiently and safely. If it makes it easier to understand, you can put a # in front of the 1 when using file handles in Visual Basic.

In the statement above, we told Visual Basic that we want to open the file for **Input**. This means we want to input from the file into our program, not the other way round. If we had wanted to write data from our program into the file, we would have said **for Output** here. You can also add stuff onto an existing file by using **for Append**.

Input From the File

There are three flavors of the **Input** function:

▶ **Input (number, filenumber)** where number is the number of characters you want. You can stick these straight into a variant:

```
varInputFromFile = Input (100, 1)
```

A good way to grab the whole file and drop it into a variable is to use the **LOF()** function. If you pass the file handle to this function, it returns the length of the file. If you then put this into the **Input** command, you get the whole banana:

```
varTheWholeBanana = Input (LOF(1), 1)
```

▶ **Input #** followed by the file handle and a list of the variable names you want to put the data into. This function assumes that the data is separated by commas, allowing Visual Basic to tell where each variable begins and ends. You can have a long list of variables if you want, but this method is prone to all the problems inherent in trying to make sense of masses of file data.

```
Input #1, sName, nPhoneNumber
```

▶ **Line Input** reads in a line of text at a time and puts into a variable. A line means a chunk of text ending with a carriage return and line feed character combination (**Chr(13) + Chr(10)**). Again, this relies on you knowing what it is you are reading before you read it. The function is a throwback to the days when old terminals used to put a CR and LF and the end of every line. Nowadays these only come at the end of a paragraph, so you can get a lot more data than you bargained for.

Writing Data to a File

In order to write data to a file, you have to first make sure that the file is opened in **Output** or **Append** mode, depending on whether you want to overwrite the existing data or to add things onto the end of it. Once you have set this up and have the file number there waiting, you have two methods available.

▶ The **Print** statement just unloads all the data from the variable into the file willy-nilly like this:

```
Print 1, Text1.TEXT
```

This writes the contents to the **Text1** control into the file with number **#1**.

▶ If you want to mess around and put the data into specific parts of the file, perhaps in anticipation of using the **Input #** command later, then you can use the **Write** command.

```
Write #1 sName, nAddress
```

This code puts the name and address fields into the file separately. You would tend to use it inside a loop.

Closing It All Down

Once you have finished doing your stuff with the file, you mustn't forget to close it down again. Visual Basic will actually do this for you when your program stops executing, but that's BAAAD programming. It leaves your valuable data drifting around with no protection and uses up your system resources, to mention just two reasons for avoiding it. There is no excuse for not closing files down, as a simple

```
Close
```

will close all open files. If you don't want to close them all down, you can name the specific files:

```
Close 1,3,9
```

Having got all the background out of the way, let's get on and see how it all works in practice.

Your Own Word Processor

We are going to create a simple notepad that can read text files from disk. I have already created the main form for you. We are going to build the menus, dialogs and code together.

1 Open up the project **MAINPAD.VBP** and open up the form. It's a big text box over the whole form. Note that the finished project is on the disk as well. It's called **WORKPAD.VBP**. By all means look at it, but do the decent thing and work through the following steps to create your own version.

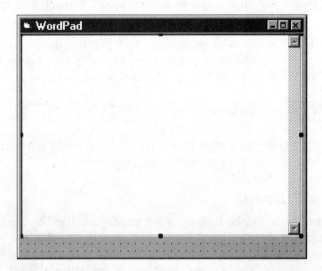

Try It Out!

2 First of all we need to build up the menu structure. Load up the menu editor and create the menu to look like this:

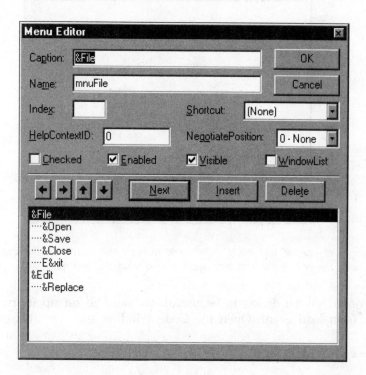

Set the enabled check box for the Save and Close options to clear. We will use code to enable these commands once a file has been loaded in. Name all the menu items **mnuFileOpen** and so on like we did in the previous chapter.

3 Before we can add code to these menu items, we need to add a common dialog control to the form. Drop it on the form and name it **cmOpenFile**. Visual Basic won't let you drop it onto the text box directly, so slide up the bottom and tuck it underneath, returning the text box to its original position afterwards.

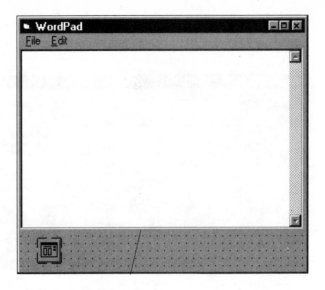

Click here to re-size the text box to give room to place the control on the form. You can then increase the size of the text box again, covering up the control.

4 In order for the dialog to be useful, we need to set up its parameters in the form load event. Open the Code Window and type this code in:

```
Private Sub Form_Load()

' Set up the common dialog control to open a text file

    On Error GoTo DialogError

    With cmOpenFile
        .CancelError = True
        .Filter = "Text Files (*.txt)|*.txt"
        .FilterIndex = 1
        .DialogTitle = "Select a Text File"
    End With

DialogError:
    On Error GoTo 0
    Exit Sub
End Sub
```

5 Now let's add the code we need to the various menu options. We'll leave the Edit/Replace menu for now and just work on the File menu. This code opens up the common dialog and reads a text file off the disk into the text box.

```
Private Sub mnuFileOpen_Click()

    On Error GoTo DialogError

' Common dialog has been set up in form load event
        cmOpenFile.ShowOpen
' take filename selected by user and open it up
        Open cmOpenFile.filename For Input As 1
' read the whole file into the text box
        txtWorkPad.Text = Input(LOF(1), 1)

        frmWordPad.Caption = "WordPad " + cmOpenFile.filename
' don't allow another file to be opened
        mnuFileOpen.Enabled = False
' however we can save or close the file
        mnuFileClose.Enabled = True
        mnuFileSave.Enabled = True

DialogError:
        On Error GoTo 0
        Exit Sub

    End Sub
```

6   Next we need to be able to save the project. To do this, we open up the **cmOpenFile** common dialog that we set up at the start. The only difference, besides using the **ShowSave** method, is to change the dialog title to reflect its new purpose. Easy.

```
Private Sub mnuFileSave_Click()

    On Error GoTo DialogError

'Open up a save file dialog using the previous properties, except title
        cmOpenFile.DialogTitle = "Save Your Text File"
        cmOpenFile.ShowSave

        Open cmOpenFile.filename For Output As 1
' put the whole text box into the file
        Print #1, txtWorkPad.Text
' now update the filename on the caption
        frmWordPad.Caption = "WordPad " + cmOpenFile.filename
        mnuFileClose.Enabled = True

DialogError:
    On Error GoTo 0
    Exit Sub
    Close

End Sub
```

7 In the interests of brevity, this program is a bit brutal and just let's you close the current file without saving. Note that you have to clear the text box afterwards.

```
Private Sub mnuFileClose_Click()

' Close all open files
      Close
' reset the menus and the caption bar

      mnuFileOpen.Enabled = True
      txtWorkPad.Text = ""
      frmWordPad.Caption = "WordPad"
      mnuFileClose.Enabled = False
      mnuFileSave.Enabled = False

End Sub
```

This menu tree is completed by putting **End** into the **mnuFileExit** click event.

8 After all that hard work, run the program as it stands. It's not MS Word, but it's a start. Save the project you have now if you aren't going to go on to the next part right away.

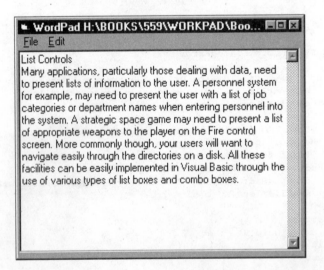

Adding a Search Dialog

What we're going to do now is to create a custom dialog that asks you to specify a string that it will then go and locate in the text file. This isn't in itself a brilliant feature, but it can be easily extended.

1 Load up the project at the point you ended up in the last Try It Out. Then select Add File from the project menu to insert a new form into the project. This will serve as our custom dialog. The file is on the examples disk and is called **SEARCHS**.

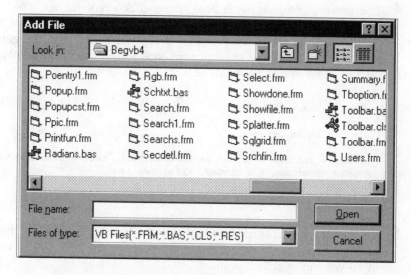

2 The new form shows in the Project Window:

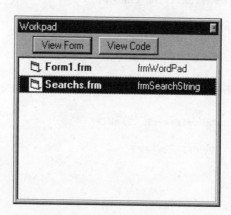

3 I've already made up the form and put the controls on it. Keeping your own library of components like this makes development very quick.

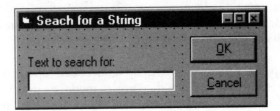

4 The meat in the sandwich here is the click event for the OK button. This uses the same **InStr** function we used in Chapter 4 to locate the start position of the string in question. If it's not there, then we get a 0. Note that you have to give the full reference to the **txtWorkPad** object as it's on the other form, **frmWordPad**.

```
Private Sub cmdOK_Click()

    Dim nIndex As Integer

    nIndex = InStr(frmWordPad.txtWorkPad.Text, txtSearchString.Text)
    MsgBox "Position " & nIndex, vbInformation

End Sub
```

5 I've set the **Enabled** property of the OK button to **False** at the start to prevent searches for null strings. As soon as the text box has something in it, we can enable it again.

```
Private Sub txtSearchString_Change()

    cmdOK.Enabled = True

End Sub
```

6 The Cancel button just needs to unload the custom dialog.

```
Private Sub cmdCancelSearch_Click()

    Unload frmSearchString

End Sub
```

7 The final step is to link the two forms together by using the Replace menu item to load up the dialog. Make sure that you use **Show** mode 1 to make it modal, otherwise we'll be left with a dialog asteroid floating about the screen. Then you can run it.

```
Private Sub mnuEditReplace_Click()

    frmSearchString.Show 1

End Sub
```

I hope this little project has brought together and given meaning to some of the topics we've just covered. As it stands, it's an ideal vehicle for you to mess around with and to add some of your own features to.

Summary

By now you should be well acquainted with dialog boxes. You've learnt how to create your own and how to use the built-in ones in your own applications. We have covered:

▶ Using the **MsgBox** function and procedure to display a message box.

▶ Using the **InputBox** and **InputBox$** functions to get user input.

▶ Application and system modal dialog boxes.

▶ Using common dialogs to add functionality and professionalism to your programs.

▶ Creating your own custom dialogs.

In the next chapter, we start to bring all the things we've learnt so far into more substantial and challenging programs.

Why Not Try.......

1 Create a program that displays the various types of message box at random over the screen. Use a timer to create and remove them.

2 Add a password input box to a form. Make it appear before the form loads up. Then create one from a custom dialog, using the password property of the text box to put stars on the screen instead of characters.

3 Re-write the **CON_DEMO** image file viewer using the common dialog control instead of the file controls. Add a menu to the form, which can now be very much smaller than before.

4 Add an Options menu item to the **WORKPAD** program. Provide options to change the screen font details, and the background color of the text box.

5 Add Save and Save As menu items to **WORKPAD**. The Save option should overwrite the existing file using the previous file name, unless the file has not been saved before. Also add a message box that asks if the user would like to save any changes before exiting.

6 Use the selected text properties of the text box to highlight the word found by the search dialog in **SEARCH.VBP**. The properties you'll need are **SelStart**, which is the position in the string of the first character to select, and **SelLength**, which is the number of characters to select. The characters that these highlight are then placed into the **SelText** property. (NB. These properties are not available at design-time).

7 Extend the search function to allow you to replace the string with another one. This could either be specified beforehand in a second text box, or typed in as highlighted text once it has been found. Make sure you add a message box to confirm the change.

8 Create a data entry form that has text boxes on it for a name and address. Write each of these to its own file using formatted data fields in the file. Then re-write the program to append each name and address to one long file. Add the ability to read and write to the files. This uses random access files that we haven't covered here in the book, but which are a logical extension of sequential file access. See Help for details.

Graphics

Graphics sell software. Think about what people look for when they buy computer magazines. Sure, there are reviews of hot new programs, be they for a spreadsheet or a game. The copy might be interesting, but what are the first things you look at? The screenshots, of course. Graphics catch people's attention and make them dig deep for your program, so they are well worth taking some time over.

In this chapter you'll learn about:

▶ The simple **Print** command.

▶ How Visual Basic handles color.

▶ How Visual Basic screen coordinates work.

▶ The four Visual Basic graphics controls.

▶ The graphics methods and when to use them.

▶ An overview of how to create really great graphics.

What You Need to Know About Graphics

Visual Basic allows you to create graphics in two ways:

▶ Using the graphics **controls.** These are pre-defined shapes and symbols that are drawn on forms in the same way as any other control.

▶ Creating graphics on the fly using the built-in graphics **methods**.

We're going to discuss both of these processes in this chapter. In addition, you'll find out about the different coordinate systems that Visual Basic uses. We'll also look at some technical stuff, like how to create your own colors, what a brush is in Windows speak, and how to fling objects around the screen faster than a speeding bullet. OK, maybe not that fast - but you'll be impressed!

Graphics is a big area, and Visual Basic provides lots of graphics facilities. However, we're only going to look briefly at each of the sections. There are two reasons for this:

▶ Graphics in Visual Basic are fairly straightforward and intuitive. Once you understand the basic concepts and the tools at your disposal, the best way to learn will be to experiment. Apart from a few simple ground rules, there are no right or wrong ways to do things - what matters is the effect you want to create.

▶ Compared to certain other development tools, Visual Basic really isn't the fastest tool for throwing graphics around the screen. For that reason, most of you corporate VB programmer types have your salaries paid for developing more mundane applications. That's not to say, though, that you can't have a little fun now and then...

Of course, even the most straight-laced application can benefit from a bit of flair and excitement, so let's get to it.

Printing on the Screen

If your experience with BASIC harks back to the heady days of the TRS-80 and Commodore's ubiquitous PET, then you'll be familiar with the good old `Print` command. For the less wizened among you, `Print` was (and still is) a simple command which can be used to display a string of text directly onto the output device, be that a screen or printer. For many newcomers to BASIC, `Print` was the first command they ever learnt.

Not only have Microsoft kept the `Print` command in Visual Basic, they've also extended its usefulness somewhat. Older computers displayed information in two modes: text and graphics. It was rare if you found a BASIC system that could print in graphics mode or draw in text mode.

With Visual Basic you are always working in what would traditionally be called graphics mode. This in turn means that the usefulness of the `Print` command has been extended. You can now animate by doing nothing more than changing some properties and then printing some text. Text can also be printed in a variety of fonts, font styles, colors and font sizes, again just by changing or setting some properties and then printing. The `Print` command can also be used within Visual Basic as an aid to debugging, as we'll see later!

Let's write some code to see how `Print` works.

Using the Print Method

Let's create a simple program that prints directly onto a form.

1 Start up a new Visual Basic project.

2 When the form appears, double-click on it to bring up the Code Window with the form load event.

3 Type in code so that your Code Window looks like this:

```
Private Sub Form_Load ()
   Dim nLineNumber as Integer
   Form1.Show

   For nLineNumber = 1 to 10
      Form1.Print "This is line " & nLineNumber
   Next
End Sub
```

4 Run the program and you'll see the loop and `Print` command in action. However, there is a very subtle bug in the program in its current state - try minimizing the window, then maximizing it. Notice that when the form comes back into view, the text you printed has gone. Let's fix this.

Try It Out!

5 Stop the program running and bring up the properties for the form. Find the AutoRedraw property and set it to true. Now if you run the program again and try minimizing and maximizing the form, the text will not vanish. This is known as **graphic persistence** and is a very important topic when it comes to dealing with graphics in Visual Basic and keeping your applications up to speed. We'll look at it in more detail a little later.

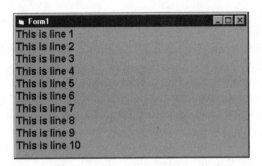

How It Works

The program runs a `For...Next` loop 10 times, each time using the `Print` command to display a line of text. This line is followed by the line number. Notice how each line of text automatically appears beneath the previous one. This is something that `Print` does for you automatically, but you *can* stop it happening, as you'll see in a moment.

The `Print` method can only be used with forms and picture boxes, not with any other controls. For example, add a picture box to your form and change the following line of code to read:

```
Picture1.Print "This is line " & nLineNumber
```

If you run the program now, the text appears inside the picture box rather than on the form. `Print` always needs to know the object that you want to print onto. So, by placing `Picture1` before the word `Print`, you are telling Visual Basic to print on the object called `Picture1`, in this case your new picture box.

Introducing AutoRedraw

Visual Basic does a very good job of isolating its developers from the mundane tasks that the C/C++ propeller heads live for. One of these tasks is redrawing the form - for example, when the form has been minimized and then maximized. Visual Basic maintains an internal list of controls that are on the form and a list of all the properties that are needed to return the window to its original state. Normally, when the form comes back into view, Windows sends your program a message indicating that the form needs to be redrawn. This manifests itself in Visual Basic as a **Paint** event. The only snag is that when you print on the form using the **Print** method, you are creating a local graphical image that is not registered by Visual Basic as a component of the overall form. So it disappears.

Luckily, Microsoft realise this and have given Visual Basic developers the AutoRedraw property. Set this to true and Visual Basic will store a copy of everything you draw on the form so that it can re-draw the form itself without burdening you with extra code.

While this is a useful procedure, it does result in your program running a little slower and using a little more memory than normal. This leaves you with the task of choosing a compromise: do you sacrifice speed and memory for less code, or code the paint event by hand to keep the "footprint" of your application as small as possible? It's a choice only you can make depending on the kind of application you are writing. However, since all of them in this chapter are really quite small, we will set AutoRedraw to true from here on in.

So what's actually going on behind the scenes? Well, no Windows program ever draws direct to the output. Instead, an area of memory is allocated and attached to a block of data called a device context. The device context tells Windows how to display the information held in memory, which window to display it in, what portion of memory to display, and so on.

When **AutoRedraw** is set to false, the image in memory is the clean window - it is the window and whatever graphical controls (not normal controls, like text boxes, but graphical controls such as labels, lines, etc) that you drew on at design-time. Here graphical means that they don't accept data input at run-time.

When you draw into the window at run-time, Visual Basic doesn't bother to update the image of the form in memory. With **AutoRedraw** set to true, though, Visual Basic stores two copies of the form in memory. One is on display; the other is a back-up image with any changes your code has made.

When you print to the form, you actually draw on the back-up image and Visual Basic automatically copies the changes to the visible image. The net result, as you can probably see, is more memory in use and a slightly slower refresh rate. You are working with two copies of the form instead of one.

Printing Fonts

The way in which text appears in your application is controlled by the font object attached to most visual controls and to the form itself. To change the style of the text on show, simply change the font object's properties. For example, if you want to change the size of the text, change the **Font.Size** property. Let's give it a go...

If you are used to the Visual Basic 3 way of working (where you change the **FontSize, FontBold** etc. properties), don't panic. You can still do that. However, it really is a good idea to get into the spirit of things and use the VB4 font object and its properties for playing around - your application will run slightly faster too.

Changing the Font and Color Properties

1 If the last program is still running, stop it. Remove the picture box you drew.

2 Bring up the Code Window again to view the **Form_Load()** event that you've just coded.

3 Change the **For..Next** loop so it reads:

```
For nLineNumber = 1 To 10
    Form1.Font.Size = Form1.Font.Size + nLineNumber
    Form1.ForeColor = QBColor(nLineNumber)
    Form1.Print nLineNumber;
Next
```

Notice the semi-colon at the end of the penultimate line.

4 Run the program again.

How It Works

This time there are three major differences from the previous example:

▶ The numbers are printed side by side, instead of on separate lines. The semi-colon you placed at the end of the **Print** command tells Visual Basic that the next time you print, the text should be displayed on the same line as before.

▶ The text gets bigger with each successive number. The first line of the **For...Next** loop adds the value of the **nLineNumber** variable to the current **Size** property of the form's font object. The result is larger text.

▶ The color of each number is also changed. Visual Basic gives you a number of ways to select and change colors for graphics, controls and printed text. In our example, the **QBColor** function is used to load a color value into the ForeColor property of the form. The ForeColor property (like the BackColor property) accepts a hexadecimal value to specify the color. You don't normally have to do this by hand - simply double-click the appropriate entry in the properties box and the Visual Basic color palette appears.

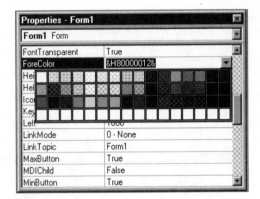

Specifying Screen Colors

Visual Basic assigns a number to each of the colors it can display, and lets you choose and specify the color number for objects like forms and text in four different ways.

▶ You can assign the number directly or choose the color from the palette on the properties menu. The problem here is that the color numbers are all hexadecimal (base 16, known as **hex**) so Visual Basic provides some simpler methods.

▶ The **QBColor** function selects one of 16 colors which were supported by earlier editions of BASIC.

▶ The **RGB** function produces a color by mixing red, green and blue.

▶ You can use one of Visual Basic's intrinsic colour constants. You can find out what these are by selecting Color Constants from the on-line help system - beware though, there are a lot.

Before we dive into hexadecimal, let's first look at an easier method.

The QBColor Function

This function is primarily for those BASIC programmers who have come to Visual Basic from Microsoft's venerable QBasic environment. In QBasic, you specify colors as single digit numbers: color number 1 would be blue, 2 green, 3 cyan, and so on. The **QBColor** function allows you to use these QBasic color codes without having to worry about converting them into long integers by hand. You simply use:

```
Form.ForeColor = QBColor(<Color number>)
```

Value	Color	Value	Color
0	Black	8	Gray
1	Blue	9	Light Blue
2	Green	10	Light Green
3	Cyan	11	Light Cyan
4	Red	12	Light Red
5	Magenta	13	Light Magenta
6	Yellow	14	Light Yellow
7	White	15	Bright White

The QBColor Selection

We can adapt our last program to show the full range of colors for this function.

1 Load up the last program. If you don't still have it, it's on the disk as **PRINTFUN.VBP**.

2 Change the **For...Next** loop in the form load event to run through all the colors from 0 to 15.

```
For nLineNumber = 0 To 15
   Form1.ForeColor = QBColor(nLineNumber)
   Print nLineNumber;
Next
```

3 Double click the Font property in the Properties Window to display the font dialog box. Use this dialog to select a font size of 24. You can also change the font style in other ways if you want - it isn't going to damage the program.

Try It Out!

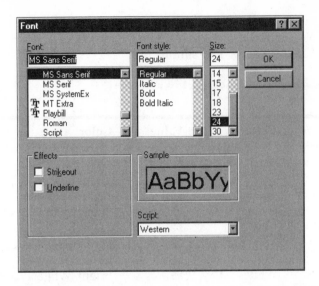

4 Run the program. You may need to re-size the form at run-time to bring all the text into view.

Hexadecimal Notation

A few lines back, I confused the hell out of you by mentioning **hexadecimal notation**. You need to know hexadecimal to be able to specify color values in Visual Basic directly. It's not that difficult really, so let me explain.

We, in the western world, use decimal notation as our number system. In decimal notation, there are ten digits used to form our numbers: the digits 0 through 9.

In the hexadecimal system, there are 16 digits (if you studied Latin in school, you'll probably know that already!). Not only are there the numbers 0 through 9, but also the letters A - F.

Decimal	0	1	2	3	4	5	6	7	8	9	10	11	12	13	14	15
Hex	0	1	2	3	4	5	6	7	8	9	A	B	C	D	E	F

Our decimal numbers can be broken down into columns. The right-most column is units, the next is tens, the next one hundreds, and so on. Therefore, the number 4524 is 4 thousands, plus 5 hundreds, plus 2 tens, plus 4, which equals four thousand, five hundred and twenty four.

Hex works in a similar way. The columns from right to left are units, sixteens, two hundred and fifty sixes, and so on. Therefore, the number 9CD is in reality (9 x 256) + (12 x 16) + 13, which equals 2509!

Why Put This Hex on Me?

The maximum number you can store in a long integer is FFFFFFFF written in hex, which is a lot more readable than its decimal equivalent. I said earlier that color values are held in long integers. Three separate numbers are actually combined into one, these three numbers being exactly how much red is in the color you want (between 0 and 255), how much green (same again) and how much blue.

Because each of these settings can be between 0 and 255, or between 0 and FF in hex, it's fairly easy to invent your own colors in hex. White, for example, has the maximum amount of red, green and blue, so the color value is hex FFFFFF. This is written in Visual Basic as &HFFFFFF&. The &H tells Visual Basic that we're now giving it hex numbers, the & at the end shows that the value is stored in a long integer. Blue is the value &HFF0000&, green is &HFF00 and red is &HFF. A bright red form would therefore be:

```
Form1.BackColor = &HFF
```

The RGB Function

However, you might not like the idea of hex; all those weird symbols and & signs everywhere - nasty business! Fear not, at the expense of a little speed at run-time, there's a function called **RGB** which you can use to produce your hex number for you.

Hassle-Free Hex Using RGB

1 Load up the **RGB.VBP** project from the samples provided with the book.

2 Run the project.

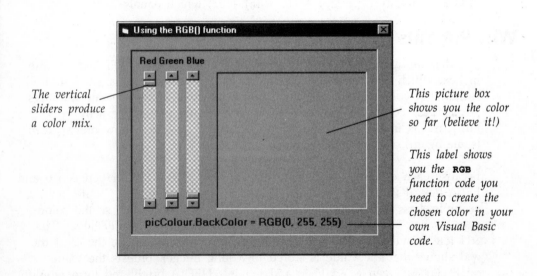

The vertical sliders produce a color mix.

This picture box shows you the color so far (believe it!)

This label shows you the **RGB** function code you need to create the chosen color in your own Visual Basic code.

How It Works

We covered sliders and scroll bars back in Chapter 4 about data, so you should feel comfortable with how they work.

Since each element of a color, red, green or blue, can be a number between 0 and 255, the sliders are all set up with a minimum value of 0 and a maximum of 255. All three sliders are also in a control array, which means that they all share the same event code. All these are set up in the Properties Window.

Properties - frmMain	✕
vscrColors(2) VScrollBar	▼

Height	2760	▲
HelpContextID	0	
Index	2	
LargeChange	1	
Left	1125	
Max	255	
Min	0	
MouseIcon	(None)	
MousePointer	0 - Default	
Name	vscrColors	
SmallChange	1	▼

The change event in this program does all the work. It redraws the picture box with its new color and displays the Visual Basic code line at the bottom of the frame. Because they are in a control array, there's only one handler for all three scroll bars:

```
Private Sub vscrColors_Change (Index As Integer)
  Dim sCode As String
  picColor.BackColor = RGB(vscrColors(0).Value, vscrColors(1).Value,
  ↳vscrColors(2).Value)
  sCode = "picColor.BackColor = RGB(" & vscrColors(0).Value & ", "
  sCode = sCode & vscrColors(1).Value & ", " & vscrColors(2).Value & ")"
  lblCode.Caption = sCode
End Sub
```

If you pass the values of the three scroll bars to the **RGB** function, the picture box color is built up. The three-part value in brackets is created by joining all three **vscrColors** values together, separated by commas. The value returned by the function is placed into the picture box, **picColor**'s, BackColor property, the result being that the color changes to reflect the new color selected by the user. Each color has a unique identifying hex value, built up from the required amount of each base color.

For certain values, the color in the box is not homogeneous, but appears to be made up of blobs of other colors. This effect is known as **color mapping**.

Color Mapping

Depending on your screen resolution, the actual color you see can vary. Most Video Graphics Adapter (VGA) systems can display a maximum of 256 colors on screen at once. This is owing to a design limitation, although some would call it a feature! However, a little math will soon show you that the **RGB** function is capable of returning a value representing any one of 16,777,216 colors.

To be able to accommodate this, Windows does a thing called **color mapping.** The color you want to display is matched against the colors available. If an exact match is found, then the color is displayed. However, more often that not, Windows will combine two or more colors to create what is called a **custom** color. On screen, this appears as a dotty color, with dots of different hues and tints placed next to each other to give the illusion that you have a new color on screen. It's rather like a painting by Seurat, though it won't fetch half a million at auction!

You need to be aware of the differences between screens if you plan to distribute your Visual Basic applications to other users and computers. You may have designed the application using a state-of-the-art SVGA display. Your users, however, may be using systems that can only display 16 colors at a time. The way your forms and colors appear on your screen can differ dramatically from what they will see.

Using the Intrinsic Color Constants

The final option available to you when choosing colors is to use Visual Basic's intrinsic color constants. These are a collection of built-in values that, when used, are as good as specifying the color value itself directly in hex. You will probably remember that we used this kind of thing before with message boxes.

The complete list of color constants is a little too large to put here, but you can easily check it out in the help system. Using color constants in your code makes it much more readable, allowing you to do stuff like this:

```
Form1.BackColor = vbButtonFace
Form1.ForeColor = vbBlack
```

It's much nicer than reeling off a long list of hexadecimal digits.

Coordinate Systems

The screen and the forms you display on it are divided up into tiny dots. When you start drawing things on your forms, you need to be able to specify at precisely which dot on the form or screen you want something to appear. This is where coordinates come in.

The top of the screen is coordinate 0,0. Here X = 0 and Y = 0. As you move across the screen, the number of the X coordinate increases. As you move down the screen, the number of the Y coordinate increases.

I frequently mention screens, but in Visual Basic you can only draw on forms, picture boxes and image boxes. Each has its own coordinate system, and so (0,0) on a form is very different from (0,0) on the screen. Whenever you draw on an object, always use a coordinate system that relates to the top left corner of the object you are drawing on.

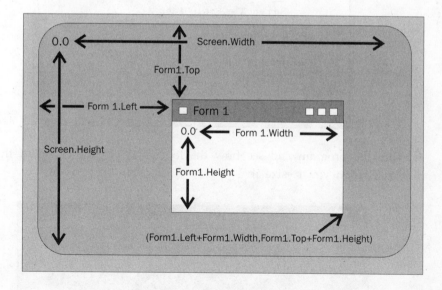

There are parts of an object that you can't draw on; for example, the title bar and borders of a form are strictly off-limits. Visual Basic only lets you draw in a form's **client** area. So how do you find out where the client area starts and ends? Objects you draw on have two properties - ScaleHeight and ScaleWidth. These tell you the maximum height and width of the object's client area.

Placing a Letter in the Center of a Form

1 Start a new project in Visual Basic and bring up the Code Window.

2 In the Code Window, select the form resize event.

3 Type in code so that your Code Window looks like this.

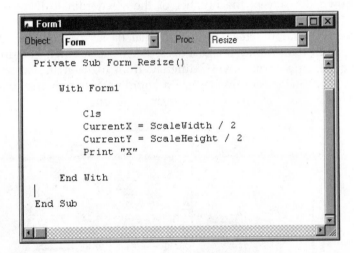

```
Private Sub Form_Resize()

    With Form1

        Cls
        CurrentX = ScaleWidth / 2
        CurrentY = ScaleHeight / 2
        Print "X"

    End With

End Sub
```

4 Run the program and see how the letter stays in the center of the form, even when you re-size it.

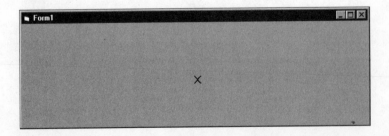

How It Works

Let's take a look at how the code works. The first line of real code uses the **Cls** method to clear **Form1**:

```
With Form1
    Cls
    :
    :
```

Attached to each form is an invisible object known as a **cursor**. This is the point on the form at which subsequent **Print** statements will display text. Therefore, if you set the form's CurrentX and CurrentY properties, the cursor moves to the point you specify.

We've already seen that ScaleWidth and ScaleHeight give us the dimensions of the client area. Therefore, if you set CurrentX and CurrentY to half the client area width and height, this has the effect of moving the cursor to the center of the screen.

Twips, Pixels, Inches and Centimeters

The default coordinate system used on a form is called **twips**. In twips, each point is roughly equal to 1/567 of a centimeter. So if you drew a line on your form that was 567 units long, it would appear a centimeter long if you actually printed it out on paper. This is known as a **device independent** coordinate system: it doesn't matter whether you are drawing a line on a standard VGA display, on a printer, or on the latest state-of-the-art high-res screen, if you were to print the results it would still appear a centimeter long. Twips are great if you're producing **what you see is what you get** applications, such as a desktop publishing package or a word processor.

In reality, however, a much more useful coordinate system is the **pixel** system. Here each unit on the X or Y axis of the screen equals exactly one dot, or pixel.

FYI

The pixel coordinate system also enables you to draw your graphics more speedily on screen. Windows knows that one pixel equals one dot and doesn't have to worry about converting your coordinates into something that can actually be drawn.

You can change the coordinate system of a form if you bring up the Properties Window and double-click on the ScaleMode property.

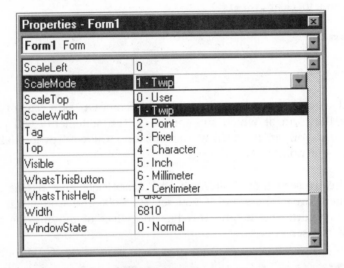

Changing the scale mode doesn't have any immediate visible effects on your application, but it is something that you need to take into account when dealing with coordinates in your code. A line that was previously drawn 100 twips long may actually be only 20 pixels long, thus having a completely different effect. Changing the coordinate system on a form only affects any subsequent changes to the form - it does not re-size or redraw the controls and images already on the form. To accomplish that little feat you need to write some heavyweight code, which is beyond the scope of our brief look at graphics.

Using Graphics

Having understood some of the background to graphics in Visual Basic, we can now start putting graphics objects onto our form. There are two alternative ways to do this in Visual Basic:

▶ **Graphical Controls** are like ordinary Visual Basic controls which are placed on your form and can be laid out interactively at design-time. Two of the controls, the image box and picture box, allow you to work with various image files, while the **Line** and **Shape** controls draw lines and shapes on your form (what a surprise!).

▶ **Graphics Methods** are commands that enable you to draw directly onto your form at run-time. The commands available for this in Visual Basic are `Cls`, `Pset`, `Point`, `Line` and `Circle`.

For some jobs, controls and methods are interchangeable. We'll cover the pros and cons of each later, but first we'll take a look at the graphical controls.

Image and Picture Boxes

The most common graphical controls are the picture and image box controls. These let you load up images from the disk and display them on screen, either in design-mode or at run-time, through your code.

We came across these controls in Chapter 2, in our sample program `CON_DEMO.VBP`. In that chapter, you learnt how to load images into these controls at run-time, but we only hinted at the increased functionality of the picture control compared to the image control. In this section, we'll look at the special features of each of these controls in more detail.

Loading Graphics at Design-Time

To load graphics into a picture box or image box at design-time you simply type the file name of the graphic into the Picture property of the appropriate object. You can also do the same thing for a form object. Take at look at the Properties Window for each object.

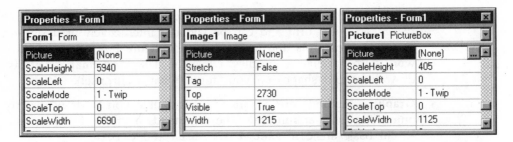

The action is fairly similar for each object, so let's look at one in particular. The image control is a good place to start because it has an extra property: the ability to stretch the image.

Loading and Resizing an Image Box

1 Start a new project and double-click the image control icon in the toolbox to draw an image control on the form.

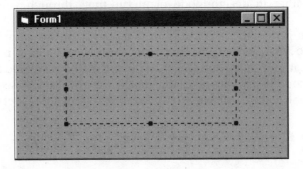

2 Select the image control and bring up its Properties Window using *F4*. Find the Stretch property and make sure it is set to true. The easiest way to do this is by double-clicking on it.

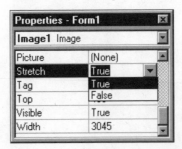

3 Now find the Picture property and double-click on it. A file dialog box appears asking you to select a graphics file. Click on the **PIC.BMP** file supplied with this book and then click OK.

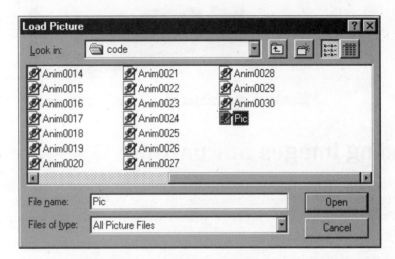

4 The Wrox Press logo appears on the form, inside the image control.

5 Re-size the control by dragging its re-size handles. Notice how the picture inside also changes.

Loading Images at Run-Time

You'd be forgiven for thinking that adding the image to the object at run-time must be as easy as assigning the right path and file name to the Picture property. Unfortunately, it isn't quite that easy: at run-time you have to use the **LoadPicture** function.

The reason for this is that the Picture property doesn't really contain the file name of the graphic you want to display - it contains the graphic itself. At design-time, though, to simplify the Properties Window, Visual Basic just shows you the file name. The actual binary file information is stored inside your project when you save it.

FYI

The good thing about assigning your images to the file at design-time is that they don't get lost. The alternative (pointing the control towards an external image file) means that you must make sure that all these files get distributed along with your application. The downside is clear: your program files are much larger. My advice is to include your images with your code at compile-time if you intend to distribute the application. If you're only going to keep it on your own machine, then load the images at run-time.

Alternatively, if you have access to a C development system such as Visual C++, load the images into a resource file. The resource file that VC++ kicks out can then be added into the project just like any other file, and its contents included in your application. At run-time you can then use the **LoadResPicture** method.

As you can probably see, though, this is a little beyond the scope of a Beginner's Guide.

Finding Your Images at Run-Time

One of the problems of loading images in at run-time is that you have to make sure that the files you want are where your program expects them to be. When you install your application, it's easiest to store your image files in a subdirectory off the main directory (in the place where the executable file is). Remember that the user may not install your application in exactly the same drive and directory that you used to create the program. If you store the graphics in a subdirectory of the directory where the executable is, you can then say this at run-time:

```
Image1.Picture = LoadPicture (App.Path & "\graphics\<imagename>")
```

Here `<imagename>` is the name of the graphics file you want to load. The `App.Path` part returns the path along which the executable file is located. This function is always available anywhere in your program - you are actually examining the `Path` property of Visual Basic's built-in `App` object.

When using `App.Path`, you must remember that, in some cases, the path may end in a slash, and in others it may not. For example, if your VB program was running off the root directory of a hard disk, then `App.Path` may return `C:\`. However, if it was in a directory called `MY_APP`, then `App.Path` would be `C:\MY_APP` - without the trailing slash.

For this reason, it is always good to use the `Right$` function to check whether or not `App.Path` ends in a slash.

```
If Right$(App.Path ,1 ) = "\" Then
    Image1.Picture = LoadPicture(App.Path & "File1.bmp")
Else
    Image1.Picture = LoadPicture (App.Path & "\File1.bmp")
End If
```

You'll see this in action in the next section.

Loading the Image at Run-Time

1 Start a new project and put a picture control onto your form.

Try It Out!

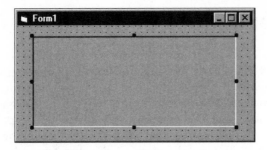

2 To load the **PIC.BMP** graphic into the picture box at run-time, add the following code to your **Form_Load()** event:

```
Private Sub Form_Load ()
  Picture1.Picture = LoadPicture("PIC.BMP")
End Sub
```

In this example, the **PIC.BMP** file has to be located in your default directory. If you put the file elsewhere, then you must provide the complete path name.

3 Alternatively you can change the current directory to the one that contains the right files from within Visual Basic by adding a line of code:

```
CHDir "C:\IMAGES"
```

4 Replace the **IMAGES** directory with whichever is correct.

5 Run the program. There's the graphic.

There was another example of how the **LoadPicture** function works back in Chapter 2 when you were first introduced to picture boxes and image controls. Load the **CON_DEMO** project to get a reminder.

Changing Images at Run-Time

There are situations where you may want to change the image in a control at run-time. This is a useful process if you want to swap images on screen quickly to create an animation effect. The fastest way to do this is to assign all the images to controls on the form at design-time. Then have only one control visible on the form and copy the images to this control as and when you need them. You can copy images like this:

```
Image1.Picture = Image2.Picture
```

However, if the pictures are small enough and your PC is fast enough, it is possible to achieve decent animation by loading the pictures at run-time using the **LoadPicture** method we saw earlier.

1 Load up the **ANIMATE.VBP** project and run it to see what I mean.

2 Pretty impressive huh! So, how does it work? It's really quite simple - all the code is in the **Form_Load** event, so take a look at that now to see what's going on.

```
Private Sub Form_Load()
    Dim nFrame As Integer
    Dim sPath As String
```

```
    sPath = App.Path
    If Right$(sPath, 1) <> "\" Then sPath = sPath & "\"

    With Form1
        Left = (Screen.Width - Width) / 2
        Top = (Screen.Height - Height) / 2
        Show
    End With

    DoEvents

    nFrame = 1

    Do While DoEvents()

        Image1.Picture = LoadPicture(sPath & "anim00" &
 ↳Format(nFrame, "00") & ".bmp")
        nFrame = nFrame + 1
        If nFrame = 31 Then nFrame = 1

    Loop

End Sub
```

How It Works

The code starts off with the usual form centering code, before showing the form itself. After that is a **DoEvents** command. We'll come back to that in a second. After this, the real code kicks in. On your examples disk are a number of files called **Anim0001.BMP** to **Anim0030.BMP**. These are the individual frames in the animation of the Wrox logo.

A **Do...While DoEvents()** loop is used in the main part of the code to ensure that the animation runs as long as the program is running, without interfering in whatever the user wants to do. We cover **DoEvents** in some detail later in the book. Basically, though, **DoEvents** takes processor time away from your application and gives it back to Windows. It stops your program from hogging the computer and making it grind to a halt. The **DoEvents()** function does this, and also returns a number indicating the number of forms in the program that are on display. The single **DoEvents** earlier on just makes sure that the program isn't hogging your computer while it's loading up. We'll cover more about how VB and Windows work together later in the book.

If the form remains loaded and on display, the loop will run forever. Within the loop, a simple counter from 1 to 30 is updated and used to get the file name of the next frame in the animation. That file name is then used by the `LoadPicture` method to load the next frame into the image control by adding the value of `nFrame` into the root file name. The result is an awesome, animated About box, such as you might find in any half decent commercial Windows application.

About boxes, like the one here, along with splash screens that mark the start of a program, are an integral part of any Windows application. Splash screens in particular, such as the one that appears at the start of Visual Basic 4, are very good at taking the user's mind off how long your program may take to go through its start-up process. However, you cannot produce decent start screens, splash screens or About boxes with Visual Basic alone. If you don't have access to an artist who is capable of jazzing up your application, then it really is time well spent learning how to use a decent paint package, even the paint package that comes with Windows 95 as standard. Color, graphics and originality on your splash screens can really put your users in a good frame of mind.

Just out of interest, the animation you see on this screen was produced using a professional 3D rendering package known as 3D Studio. Getting to grips with such packages can greatly improve the presentation of your products.

Comparing Image and Picture Controls

Having now used these two controls in both Chapter 2 and here, you should have an idea of their relative strengths and weaknesses. Let's just summarize them:

- As they change shape, image controls stretch the image they contain. Picture boxes and forms don't do this.

- Picture controls, on the other hand, can be used as container objects. I'll explain exactly what this means in a moment.

▶ Image controls are **lightweight** controls. This means that an image control consumes less of your PC's memory and is faster to deal with than a heavyweight control, such as a picture box. Their enhanced speed is also a reason I used one in the `ANIMATE.VBP` project.

▶ It all looks a bit one-sided, but the real advantage of the picture box is flexibility. Just compare the properties that are available for each of the two controls:

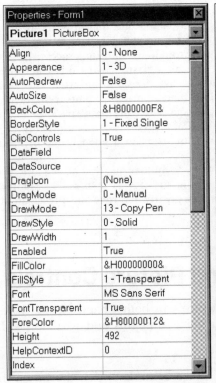

Properties - Form1	☒
Image1 Image	▼
Appearance	1 - 3D
BorderStyle	0 - None
DataField	
DataSource	
DragIcon	(None)
DragMode	0 - Manual
Enabled	True
Height	492
Index	
Left	2400
MouseIcon	(None)
MousePointer	0 - Default
Name	Image1
Picture	(None)
Stretch	False
Tag	
Top	1920
Visible	True
WhatsThisHelpID	0
Width	972

Picture Boxes as Containers

Unlike the image control, the picture box is a **container** control. A container control allows other controls to be drawn inside it. Anything you then do to the picture box also affects the controls contained within it. For example, if you make the picture box invisible, its controls also become invisible; if you move the picture box within the form, the controls go with it.

This is where picture boxes come in handy. By placing a picture box on a frame or form, and then placing controls inside the picture box, you can begin to break a large group of functions down into related chunks.

You could, for example, place a group of option buttons together in a picture box. If you change the BorderStyle property of the picture box to 0 - None, you can make the picture box seem to disappear. The option buttons will still be in view and they'll still be grouped in the picture box, separate from others on the form.

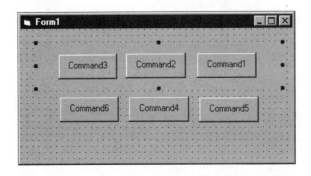

Picture boxes used in this way provide a way of removing a group of option buttons from view. If you change the Visible property to false, the picture box vanishes completely, taking everything drawn on it out of sight too.

Picture Boxes as Container Controls

1 Start a new Visual Basic project, then double-click the picture box icon to place a picture box on the form.

2 Now select the command button icon from the toolbox and draw a command button inside the picture box.

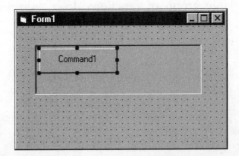

3 Select the picture box and move to a different place on the form. Watch how the command button goes with it.

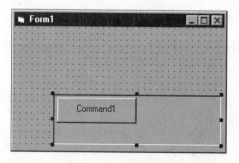

4 Select the command button and try to drag it off the picture box. Visual Basic won't let you do it as the command button belongs to the picture box.

5 Double-click the form to bring up the **Form_Load** Code Window. Type in this code:

```
Private Sub Form_Load()
    Picture1.Visible = False
End Sub
```

6 Now run the program. When the form appears, you'll see that both the picture box and the command button have gone. Making the picture box invisible means that any objects contained within it also disappear.

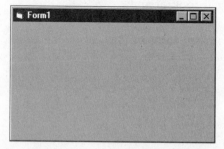

7 Stop the program and change the load event so that it sets the picture box's Enabled property to false, removing the reference to the Visible property.

```
Sub Form_Load()
Picture1.Enabled = False
End Sub
```

8 Run the program again.

9 This time, both the picture box and command button are visible, but neither can be selected. Try clicking the command button - nothing happens!

Using picture boxes in this way can save you a lot of time and effort. If you need to hide a large number of controls, or make the controls pop up in response to the user doing something, just place those controls inside a picture box and flip the picture box Visible property.

Frames

Like picture boxes, **frames** belong to the group of controls known as container objects. They behave very much like mini-forms - controls can be drawn onto them and, as the frame moves, so do all the controls sitting on them. Equally, if the frame is made invisible by setting its Visible property to false, then it will vanish, taking all the controls inside with it.

Frames in Action

You can see these effects in the **CONTROL.VBP** program. This is a player for multimedia files such as **.AVI** video files. It uses a lot of fancy business to make it work, which we will look at in later chapters. However it also uses a frame, which we'll look at now.

1 Load up the project **CONTROL.VBP** from the examples disk. Run it to get an idea of what it does.

Try It Out!

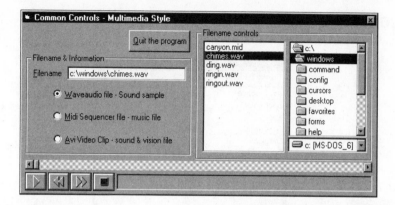

2 Stop the project and try moving one of the two large rectangles in the top half of the form. These are both frames. As they move, so do all the controls inside them.

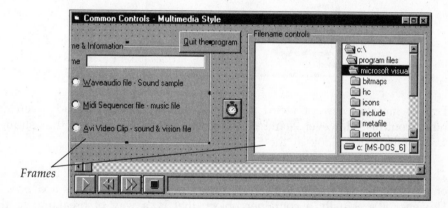

Frames

3 If you change the Visible property of one of the frames to make it invisible, at run-time everything on that frame disappears. As far as Visual Basic is concerned, the controls on the frame are still there, but because their container is out of sight you can't see them.

Properties

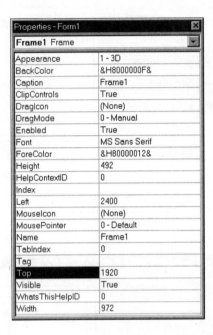

Frames have no new or weird properties that we haven't already seen in other controls. However, some of the properties do work in rather strange ways. Firstly, let's look at the Font property.

Thanks to the frame's single line border, many newcomers fall into the trap of thinking of the frame as nothing more than a large label or text box. However, it's actually a container object, that is, a way of breaking up the controls on your form into logical groups. The only text that the Font property applies to on the frame is the frame caption. If you change the font name, color, size or style, it only affects the text that is drawn into the top left-hand corner of the frame.

The caption also affects the area filled by the background color. The actual area of the form that the frame takes up extends from the bottom line of the frame to the top of the highest possible letter in the caption. If you change the BackColor property, it causes the new color to spill out of the top of the frame a little.

Normally, a frame has a caption which breaks up the top bar of the border. However, if you delete the caption, Visual Basic automatically draws a border line where the caption previously stood.

Events

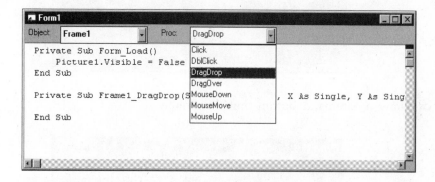

Frames have very few events that you can respond to. The most useful of the events you *can* respond to are the click and double-click events, which work in the same way as they do on any other control.

Problems With Frames

While frames can be very useful in breaking down the controls on a form into small neat groups, they can also cause some annoying problems. If you start a new project, draw a command button on the form, and then draw a frame on the form, you'll find that you can't move the command button onto the frame.

Annoying Frames

1 Start a new project in Visual Basic.

2 When the default form appears, select the frame icon from the toolbox and draw a frame on the form.

Try It Out!

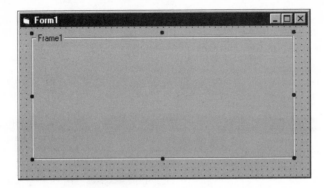

3 Draw a command button onto the frame.

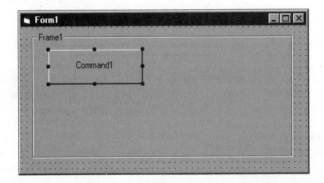

4 Click on the frame and move it. The command button moves with it.

5 Try clicking on the command button and dragging it off the frame. Visual Basic won't let you.

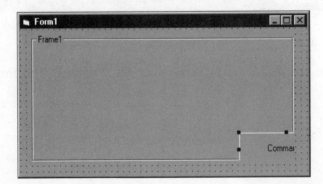

6 Now draw a new command button beneath the frame. If you have re-sized the form in the way that I have, then you'll probably need to enlarge the form.

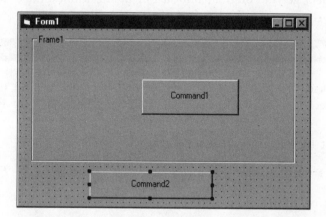

7 Although you've just drawn the button directly onto the form, it's actually floating **higher** than the frame, because it was drawn **after** the frame. Drag the new button onto the bottom border of the frame. Now it floats above the frame.

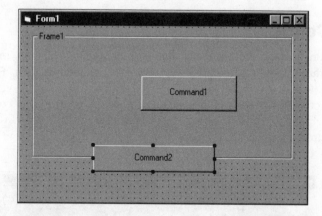

8 Finally, drag the new button into the frame, then move the frame. The new button stays locked to the point where you last moved it. It doesn't follow the frame around.

9 It doesn't follow the frame around because the button is still attached to the form and is floating above the frame. To put the button into the frame, you need to cut and paste it from the form into the frame. You can also get the original button out of the frame and onto the form in this way.

Moving Controls Out of a Frame

Visual Basic provides an Edit menu to help you get around these problems. The correct way to move a control from a frame to a form is as follows:

1 Select the control you want to move.

2 Select Cut from the Edit menu or press *Ctrl-X*.

3 Click on the form.

4 Select the Paste item from the Edit menu or press *Shift-Insert* or *Ctrl-V*.

The control you have just cut will now appear on the form and you will be able to move it to the correct position. You can use the same cut and paste technique to move all controls.

Copying Controls

The option buttons in **CONTROL.VBP** were made by placing one control down on the frame, then selecting Copy from the Edit menu, then Paste. Visual Basic creates an exact copy of the control and asks you if you wish to create a control array. In the case of the option buttons, a control array was exactly what we wanted, but if you select No, Visual Basic will assign the new control an entirely different name, rather than the same name and a new index number.

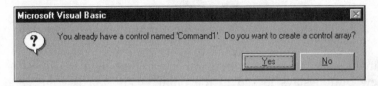

The Shape Control

The shape control allows you to draw a simple geometric shape, such as a line, box or circle onto a form at design-time. To use the shape control, you select the control from the palette and then drag a rectangle on the form in the same way as you draw any other type of control.

Using the ShapeControl

1 Start a new Visual Basic project.

2 Double-click the shape control on the toolbox to place it onto the default form.

3 Re-size the shape by clicking and dragging the re-size handles in the usual manner.

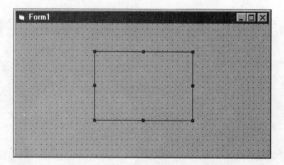

4 Bring up the Properties Window and find the Shape property. This allows you to change the shape that will be displayed. Double-click the Shape property to cycle through the available shapes.

5 You can change the style of the border around the shape from a solid line to various types of dashed line, using the BorderStyle property. Find it in the properties list and double-click it to cycle through all the available options.

6 The BackStyle property allows you to specify whether the shape should be filled or not.

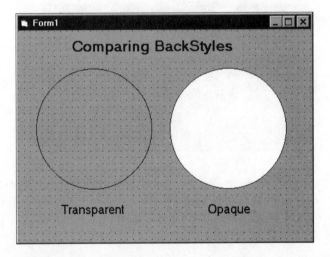

7 You can change the thickness of the border of the shape using the BorderWidth property. Find that property in the Properties Window and enter the number 10. The style of the border changes dramatically.

To be honest with you, I never use the shape control - it's too limiting to build up complex images at design-time. If I need graphics at run-time, I use the graphics methods to create them. However, many people *do* use the shape control for placing borders around items on forms, without the memory overhead that comes with a frame or a picture box.

The Line Control

The line control is slightly simpler to use than the shape control. It allows you to draw a straight line on your form. This is great for breaking up the controls on a form, or for underlining a particular area. It's something that interface designers call a feature, but everyone else calls it decoration.

Drawing a Line on a Form

1 Double-click the line control on the toolbox to place a line on the form.

2 The line control has two re-size handles, one at each end, which you can drag around to change the size and slope of the line.

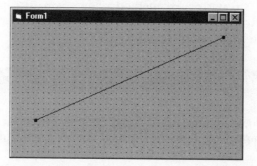

3 Just as with the shape control, you can change the thickness and type of the line drawn using the BorderStyle and BorderWidth properties. Bring up the Properties Window and try double-clicking the BorderStyle property to cycle through the available line types. Otherwise, enter a number into the BorderWidth property to change the thickness of the line.

Try It Out!

The Graphics Methods

The graphics methods in Visual Basic provide a lot more flexibility when dealing with graphics. Unlike the controls (all of which need to be drawn onto a form at design-time), the graphics methods allow you to create graphics on the fly. This includes drawing lines and shapes, setting individual pixels on the form, and so on. With a little thought, these methods can be taken beyond the obvious into the realms of games and animation programs. In fact, surprisingly little coding experience is needed to create some quite stunning effects, as you'll find out.

Yes, But Is It Art?

If there is one area in Visual Basic that has always been sadly lacking, it has to be the area of copying a mass of graphics from one area to another. Previously, if you wanted to accomplish such a feat, you would either have had to duplicate image or picture controls on the fly, or drop down to the rather frightening Windows API in order to use the `BitBlt` function.

Thankfully, Microsoft's R&D team don't just sit around drinking coffee and saying "cool" all day. New in VB4 is the amazing `PaintPicture` method. Despite its name, you don't simply say

```
Form1.PaintPicture  "Something with a Renaissance feel to it"
```

Instead, the `PaintPicture` method allows you to copy chunks of graphical data very rapidly from one area on a form, picture box or the printer to another - great for animation.

The PaintPicture Method

1 Take a look at `PPIC.VBP`. Load up the project and run it. Hmmm... not much happening here. You need to click the form to display the Wrox logo.

Try It Out!

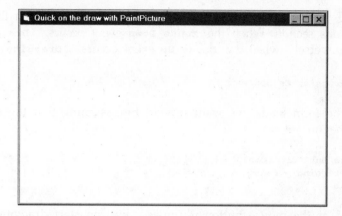

2 Now, if you click and hold the mouse button down and then drag the mouse around, look what you get. It isn't perfect because the Wrox bitmap has a white surround, so if you move it slowly these edges overlap and you don't see a lot of the image. However, move it quickly and the images show up nicely.

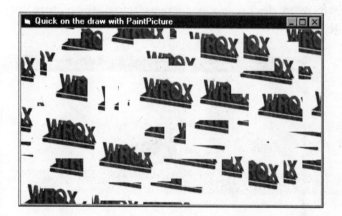

How It Works

Given that I have already mentioned the new **PaintPicture** method, it wouldn't take a genius to figure out that that is where the action lies. Stop the program running and take a look at the code.

First off we need to declare a yes/no variable **1Dragging** in the general declaratons section. When the **Mouse_Down** event occurs, **1Dragging** is set to true. Conversely, when the **Mouse_Up** event occurs, **1Dragging** is set to false.

```
Dim 1Dragging As Boolean
```

When the form loads, we want to start by assuming that the dragging hasn't begun yet.

```
Private Sub Form_Load()
    1Dragging = False
End Sub
```

As soon as the mouse button is pressed, we can start dragging.

```
Private Sub Form_MouseDown(Button As Integer, Shift As Integer, X
 As Single, Y As Single)
    1Dragging = True
End Sub
```

The real action, though, takes place in the **MouseMove** event. As you can see from the form in design mode, there is actually a picture control that is not shown at run-time.

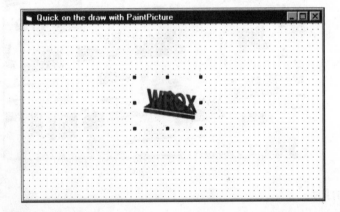

The code looks like this:

```
Private Sub Form_MouseMove(Button As Integer, Shift As Integer, X As
Single, Y As Single)
 If lDragging Then
        Form1.PaintPicture picGraphic.Picture, X, Y, picGraphic.Width,
 picGraphic.Height
 End If
End Sub
```

The **PaintPicture** method works like this:

```
[object.]PaintPicture srcPic, destX, destY [,destWidth [,DestHeight
[,srcX [,srcY [,srcWidth [,srcHeight,[Op]]]]]]]
```

The first parameter in the method is the object parameter. You have to tell Visual Basic on which object you want the **PaintPicture** method to work. **PaintPicture** will quite happily work on forms, picture controls and, of course, the printer object.

The printer object is not hard to understand, but we'll cover it in the final chapter as part of our big application

The **srcPic** parameter is the picture that we are going to copy. Normally you will pass the **Picture** property of a picture control or form here.

destX and **destY** are the coordinates on the target object where you want the picture to be displayed. The **DestWidth** and **DestHeight** properties specify the size of the resulting picture, and how much of the target object will be drawn on.

The code in **pPic** is working on an object called **Form1** and is copying the image from a picture control called **picGraphic**. The X and Y coordinates in this program are the same as the mouse X and Y coordinates and the width and height are taken from the width and height properties of the picture control.

The remaining properties are, happily, optional. They allow you to specify a clipping region, which lets you copy only a portion of the source picture onto the target object. You do this by specifying the coordinates in the picture where the graphic you are after starts, and its width and height. The final parameter, **Op**, lets you specify something known as a raster operation, such as And and Xor. More on these a little later.

The mouse up event simply sets `1Dragging` back to false.

```
Private Sub Form_MouseUp(Button As Integer, Shift As Integer, X As
↳Single, Y As Single)
    1Dragging = False
End Sub
```

FYI

Before we go on, there is a little quirk to `PaintPicture` that is worth knowing about. If you specify negative values for the `Width` and `Height` of the target image, the image appears flipped, either horizontally or vertically, depending on which parameter you set to negative.

Pixel Plotting with Pset

The first method we'll look at is `Pset`. `Pset` actually means **point set** and allows you to set individual pixels (points) on the form. For instance, you could cover a form in multi-colored dots to simulate splatter painting, or move dots around the screen in an orderly fashion to explore far off galaxies, to boldly go ...(you know the rest!).

Splatter Painting

Try It Out!

1 Firstly, splatter painting. The principles behind this are really simple, but the effect could quite well be used as a background for a title form in an application. Load up the **SPLATTER.VBP** project and run it.

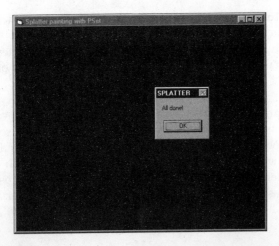

2 When the program has finished drawing, end the program in the usual way - select <u>E</u>nd from the <u>R</u>un menu, press *Alt-F4*, or click the form's control box.

3 Double-click the form to take a look at the code.

```
Randomize
For nIndex = 1 To 2000
    nXCoord = Int(Rnd(1) * frmMain.ScaleWidth)
    nYCoord = Int(Rnd(1) * frmMain.ScaleHeight)
    nRed = Int(Rnd(1) * 255)
    nGreen = Int(Rnd(1) * 255)
    nBlue = Int(Rnd(1) * 255)

    PSet (nXCoord, nYCoord), RGB(nRed, nGreen, nBlue)
Next
```

If you take a look at the Code Window, you'll see that there is a little more code than I've shown here, but the rest just declares the variables, shows the form on the screen and displays a message box when the program has done its stuff. It's the code above that is of most interest to us.

How It Works

First an overview. The **For..Next** loop runs 2000 times, each time deciding on some random coordinates at which to display a dot on the screen. This is what the **Rnd()** command does.

Visual Basic doesn't generate random numbers in the true sense. For example, you're not being asked to close your eyes and hit a key on the numeric keypad. Rather, it generates a sequence of seemingly random numbers which it stores in memory. That's the purpose of the **Randomize** command at the head of the code - **Randomize** generates that sequence of numbers ready for you to pull them out with the **Rnd()** command. Philosophers among you will of course note that it is impossible to create a truly random number.

If we use **Rnd(1)**, we tell Visual Basic to give us the next number in the random number sequence. The actual number we get is a decimal number somewhere between 0 and 1. Therefore, the line

```
Rnd(1) * frmMain.ScaleWidth
```

gives us a random number between 0 and the width of the form client area. The client area of a form is the part on which you can draw or place controls. It's the big blank bit in the middle, not including the borders and caption bar area.

So far so good! There's still some work to do on this random number before it can be used, though. Let's say the form width is something like 2437, and the random number that **Rnd(1)** gives us is 0.5412. Multiplying these two numbers together we get 1318.9044. Obviously that can't be used as the X coordinate - Visual Basic needs an integer number, not a decimal.

The **Int** statement converts a number to an integer value. In our example it would convert 1318.9044 to 1318 by just cutting the decimal part off. Now this is a number we can use. The same technique is applied to get the dot's Y coordinate and the values of red, green and blue, which will be used to produce our dot's color.

Finally, **PSet** is called to actually draw the dot. The format for the **PSet** method is:

```
Pset (<Xcoordinate>, <Y Coordinate>), <Color value>
```

Since our program has already decided on some coordinates for the dot, as well as the random values needed to use the **RGB** function, we have all the components we need to draw a dot somewhere on the screen, in a random color. If you run this 2000 times, lots of random multi-colored dots appear, as in the example.

Animation With Pset

We can look at some animation. Animation on a computer is really a question of programming the user's eyes, or rather confusing them. If you flash an image onto the screen first in one position, then in another, it appears that the image is jumping between the two positions. If you draw an image in one position, then copy it to another position, then another and another, the user thinks the image is being dragged around the screen, leaving a trail.

If you want to animate a dot with **PSet**, the principles are very similar. Firstly, draw the dot in one position - call it position A. Then draw the dot in the next position and call it position B. Finally, draw another dot at position A, but in the same color as the form's background. The computer can do this so quickly that the user thinks they're watching a dot with a life of its own moving around the screen.

Through the Starfield

Imagine 50 dots, all appearing to move at different speeds and in different directions! Remind you of anything? The stars you might see looking off the bridge of the Starship Enterprise for example?

1 Load up **WARP.VBP** and run it. Wow - stars!

2 As before, **PSet** is used to actually plot the points which represent the stars on the screen. Take a look at the declarations section of the program:

```
Option Explicit
Dim nXCoord(50) As Integer
Dim nYCoord(50) As Integer
Dim nXSpeed(50) As Integer
Dim nYSpeed(50) As Integer
```

How It Works

Four integer arrays are used to hold information about each star - information such as the star's current X and Y coordinates, as well as two-speed variables. Because the arrays are each set up to hold 50 values, it should make some sense when I tell you that the maximum number of stars the program can kick around the screen at any one time is 50. Each current star will have its own set of values, identified by a common index of each array.

If you take a look at the form itself, you'll see that there's a timer control drawn on it.

Try It Out!

405

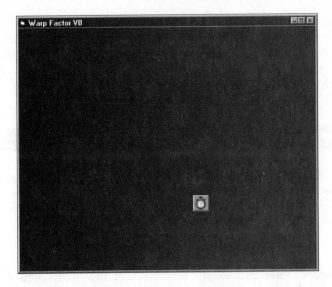

In the timer event, the values held in the X and Y speed variables are added to the stars current X and Y coordinates to give the impression that the star is moving. Close the Code Window down, then double-click on the timer control itself to view the timer event code:

```
Private Sub Timer1_Timer()

    Dim nIndex As Integer
    For nIndex = 0 To 49
        PSet (nXCoord(nIndex), nYCoord(nIndex)), vbBlack

        If nXCoord(nIndex) < 0 Or nXCoord(nIndex) > frmMain.ScaleWidth
   Or nYCoord(nIndex) < 0 Or nYCoord(nIndex) > frmMain.ScaleHeight
   Then
            nXCoord(nIndex) = frmMain.ScaleWidth \ 2
            nYCoord(nIndex) = frmMain.ScaleHeight \ 2
            nXSpeed(nIndex) = Int(Rnd(1) * 200) - 100
            nYSpeed(nIndex) = Int(Rnd(1) * 200) - 100
        End If

        nXCoord(nIndex) = nXCoord(nIndex) + nXSpeed(nIndex)
        nYCoord(nIndex) = nYCoord(nIndex) + nYSpeed(nIndex)
        PSet (nXCoord(nIndex), nYCoord(nIndex)), vbWhite
    Next

End Sub
```

It looks a little daunting, doesn't it? Don't panic. Each time the timer event occurs, a **For...Next** loop is used to update the positions of each of the 50 stars on the screen. The first **PSet** in the loop erases the star at its last known position by redrawing it in black - the color of the form's background.

Next, a check is made to see if the current star, determined by the **nIndex** variable, has moved off the screen. The coordinates of the star are checked to see if either of them has gone off any edge of the form. If one has, the coordinates are reset to the center of the form and some speed values are decided at random. These speed values then become that particular star's new speed until it vanishes off screen again.

```
        If nXCoord(nIndex) < 0 Or nXCoord(nIndex) > frmMain.ScaleWidth
⬎Or nYCoord(nIndex) < 0 Or nYCoord(nIndex) > frmMain.ScaleHeight
⬎Then
            nXCoord(nIndex) = frmMain.ScaleWidth \ 2
            nYCoord(nIndex) = frmMain.ScaleHeight \ 2
            nXSpeed(nIndex) = Int(Rnd(1) * 200) - 100
            nYSpeed(nIndex) = Int(Rnd(1) * 200) - 100
        End If
```

Finally, the values of the speed variables are added to the star's current X and Y coordinates to get its next position on screen. Remember, the star is erased at the start of the loop, so if you calculate a new position for it and then draw it in that position, it gives the user the impression that the star is actually moving.

```
nXCoord(nIndex) = nXCoord(nIndex) + nXSpeed(nIndex)
nYCoord(nIndex) = nYCoord(nIndex) + nYSpeed(nIndex)
```

Unless you're running the program on a very powerful PC, you'll have noticed that moving images are not one of Visual Basic's strong points. Windows is slow anyway and, on top of that, Visual Basic doesn't produce the fastest possible programs. The result is that, as yet, animation and Visual Basic don't really mix.

You can get around the speed limitations by delving into the murky depths of something called the Application Programming Interface (**API**). We cover some uses of the API a little later in this book, but graphics and the API is well beyond our scope, I'm afraid.

Drawing Lines

Dots are fine for learning about how graphics are drawn and about Visual Basic's rather eccentric coordinate system. However, for graphs and really impressive graphics you need to start thinking about drawing lines. Although this might be taken for granted, the ability to draw lines in your code opens up an infinite number of programming possibilities.

If you can draw lines, you can also draw graphs, three dimensional graphics and explore virtual reality. You could even simply mellow out with the computer equivalent of a psychedelic laser show!

Visual Basic has an extremely versatile command for drawing lines called the `Line` command. In its most basic form, you give the `Line` command two sets of coordinates - one stating where the line starts, the other where it ends. You can also supply a color value, just as you can with `Pset`. Visual Basic will then happily wander off for a few fractions of a second and draw the line for you.

Try It Out!

Drawing Lines

1 Start a new project in Visual Basic and run it. Make sure that the form's AutoRedraw property is set to true.

2 When the project is running, press *Ctrl-Break* to pause the program or click the pause icon on the Visual Basic toolbar.

3 If the Debug Window isn't already visible, press *Ctrl-G*. The Debug Window allows you to enter most of the commands that you would normally type into the Code Window. The difference between the two types of window is that as soon as you hit *Enter* in the Debug Window, the command is run.

4 Arrange the form and the Debug Window so you can see them both on the screen, like I've done here:

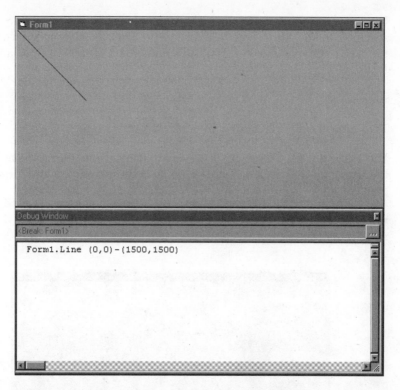

5 Let's draw some lines. In the Debug Window, type **Form1.Line** **(0,0)-(1500,1500)** and press *Enter*. A line will appear on the form.

6 Unless you specify otherwise, Visual Basic draws a line in the color specified in the form ForeColor property. You can also specify a color in the **Line** command itself. Type this into the Debug Window and press *Enter*.

```
Form1.Line (0,0) - (2000,900), vbMagenta
```

This time the line is drawn in pink.

7 You can also tell Visual Basic to draw a line from the point at which the previous line ended. Type these two commands in and press *Enter* after each.

```
Form1.Line -(3000,3000)
Form1.Line -(0,0)
```

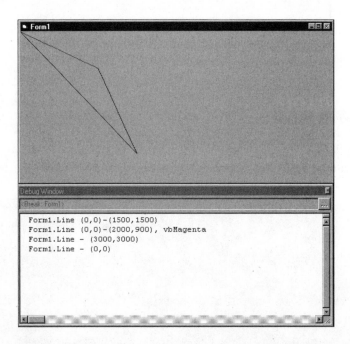

8 Finally, the **Line** command can also be used without specifying exact coordinates, but instead by using **offsets**. Try typing these lines in:

```
Form1.Line (0,0)-Step(1000,400)
Form1.Line Step(2000,1000)-Step(500,500)
Form1.Line -Step(2000,-800)
```

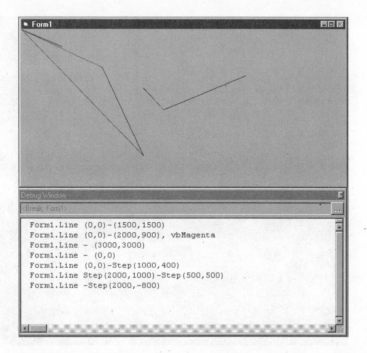

9   You get some pretty weird results with these. The **step** keyword tells Visual Basic that the coordinates after the word **step** should be added on to the last coordinates drawn. So **Form1.Line(0,0)-Step(1000,400)** starts the line at **0,0** and ends it at **(0+1000, 0+400)**.

Try It Out!

Animation Using Lines

1   Now you're up to speed with the **Line** command, let's try something impressive. Load up the **WOW.VBP** project.

2   Run the project.

 Programs like this are an excellent demonstration of the power of Visual Basic, as well as an example of a computer's ability to fool the sharpest of minds. If the program is still running, watch it for a while. It looks like the computer is drawing about 50 lines on the screen and animating them, doesn't it? Wrong! It also looks like the code is doing some pretty complex rotations to get the curve effects right? Wrong!

How It Works

The program is based around four bouncing balls. Two of the bouncing balls, which are really just dots, are joined by a blue line. The other two follow exactly the same path as the first two balls, but 50 steps behind. These latter points are joined by a black line.

The program draws 50 lines on the screen before the black line erases each of those 50 lines one by one.

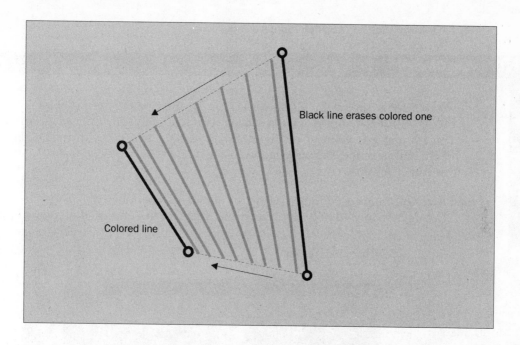

Black line erases colored one

Colored line

The animation itself is easy. Just as with our stars program, each line has a set of coordinates and an X and Y speed. If any point hits the edge of the screen, then the appropriate speed is reversed. Let's say, for instance, that one of the points is having 50 added to its X coordinate and 25 to its Y coordinate on every timer event. If that point hits the bottom of the form, the code changes the Y coordinate by -25. Likewise, if the point hits the right or left edges of the form, the X speed is reversed. There are no complex curves here, just plain old fashioned straight lines and bouncing dots. What's more, since Visual Basic is only ever drawing two lines on the screen, the program is quite rapid.

Circles, Curves, Arcs and Bendy Bits

An extremely complex area of computer graphics has always been that of drawing curves and circles. Thankfully, Visual Basic greatly simplifies the process with its `Circle` command. Despite its rather misleading name, the `Circle` method can draw curves, circles, ellipses and segments of circles - which is excellent for pie-charts!

Let's take a look at normal circles first.

Drawing Circles

1 Start a new project in Visual Basic, run it, then pause the program by using *Ctrl-Break*. Bring up the Debug Window with *Ctrl-B*. Catch your breath and pat yourself on the back for getting this far with no hassle. You can clear the Debug Window using the *Delete* key if you are neatness fetishist.

2 Arrange the two windows as before and type the following in the Debug Window (don't forget to press *Enter* at the end of the command):

```
Form1.Circle (2000,2000), 1000
```

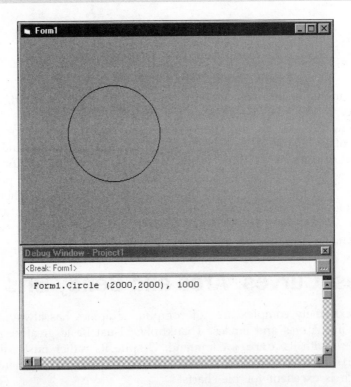

3 A circle appears. The coordinates which you specify in the brackets are the center of the circle, in this case (2000,2000). The number outside the brackets is the radius of the circle, here 1000.

4 You can see this even better if we draw two lines on the circle to show the center and the radius.

```
Line (2000,2000)-Step(0,1000)
Line (2000,2000)-Step(1000,0)
```

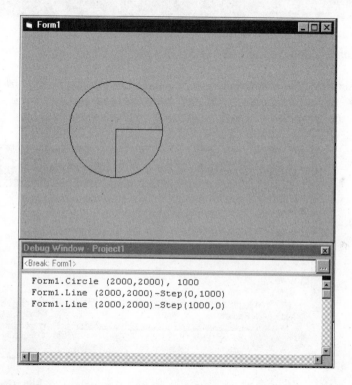

Drawing Arcs

Arcs require a little more effort. The `Circle` method you've used so far is a cut-down version of what it can actually do. The actual syntax for `Circle` is:

```
Circle (x,y), <radius>, <color>, <start angle>, <end angle>, <aspect>
```

Just to be awkward, most computers calculate angles and related stuff in terms of radians rather than degrees. I won't go into the logic of it all, nor give an explanation of what radians are - you don't need to know, and I failed pure math in college!

All you *do* need to know is that to convert a number in degrees to its equivalent in radians, you multiply the angle by Pi (3.142 roughly) and divide the result by 180. If you're confused, there's a **.BAS** called **RADIANS** on the examples disk which contains a function to do just that. We'll use it in a moment.

Drawing Arcs and Slices

1 Create a new project in Visual Basic.

2 From the File menu, select Add File (alternatively press *Ctrl-D*). When the file requester appears, add the **RADIANS.BAS** file from the samples disk to the project.

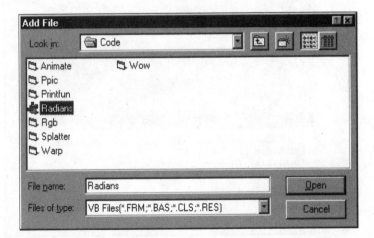

3 Run the program, then pause it in the normal way. Hit *Ctrl-G* to bring up the Debug Window.

4 We'll now draw an arc which goes from 45 degrees of a circle to 230 degrees.

```
Form1.Circle (2000,2000), 1000,  , Rads(45), Rads(230)
```

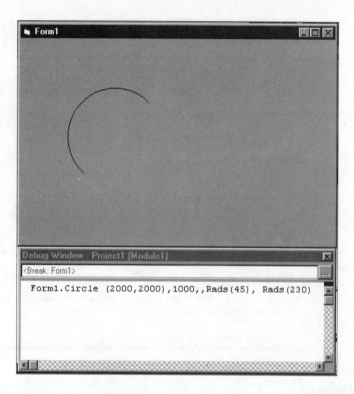

5 The above line of code draws the part of a circle (center at 2000,2000, radius 1000) that goes from 45 degrees round to 230. The **Rads** function is the code included in the **RADIANS.BAS** module that you added to the project. This converts the degrees figure (given as a parameter) to radians.

6 Previously, we drew lines onto the circle with the **Line** command to mark out the radius and center. **Circle** can do that for you itself. Type in the following:

```
Form1.Cls
Form1.FillStyle = 0
Form1.FillColor = QbColor(14)
Form1.Circle (2000,2000),1000, , -Rads(90), -Rads(45)
Form1.FillColor = QbColor(1)
Form1.Circle (2050,1900),1000, , -Rads(45), -Rads(90)
Form1.FillStyle = 1
```

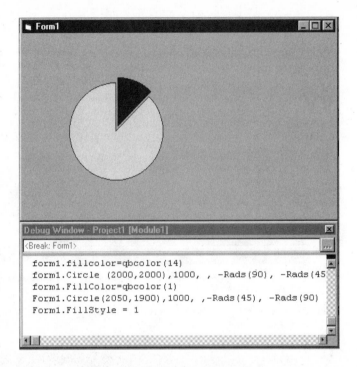

How It Works

There are some other interesting lines of code in what you've just typed. The **Cls** method actually stands for clear screen, but in Visual Basic it merely clears the form. After clearing the form with the **Cls** command, we set the form FillStyle property to 0. This tells Visual Basic to fill in any graphics it draws with the color in the FillColor property of the form. The next line sets the color to 14 (yellow) with the **QBColor** method.

In the two **Circle** commands, we pass negative start and end angles. This tells the **Circle** command to draw connecting lines from the start and end to the center of the circle. The last FillStyle line turns off the auto filling.

The **RADIANS.BAS** module contains this code:

```
Function Rads (ByVal nDegrees As Single) As Single
Const Pi = 22 / 7
Rads = (nDegrees * Pi) / 180
End Function
```

Even assuming your math is as basic as mine, this is fairly easy to follow.

Drawing Ellipses

The final use of the **Circle** command is to draw ellipses. To draw an ellipse, all you need do is draw a circle in the normal way, then give Visual Basic a number for its **aspect** parameter.

Before we go any further, I'd better explain what aspect is. The aspect is the relationship between the horizontal radius and the vertical radius. For instance, an aspect of 2 would mean that the horizontal radius is half the length of the vertical radius. Conversely, an aspect of 0.5 would display a circle which is twice as wide as it is high.

Ellipses

1 Start a new project in Visual Basic, run it and pause it (*Ctrl-Break*) to bring up the Debug Window (*Ctrl-G*).

2 In the Debug Window, type in the following and press *Enter*.

```
Form1.circle(2000,2000),1000,,,,3
Form1.circle(2000,2000),1000,,,,.5
Form1.circle(2000,2000),1000,,,,2
```

Try It Out!

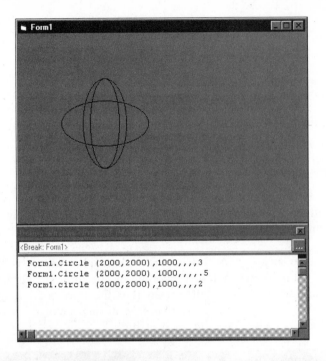

```
Form1.Circle (2000,2000),1000,,,,3
Form1.Circle (2000,2000),1000,,,,.5
Form1.circle (2000,2000),1000,,,,2
```

Even though I've called them commands and statements, and we've used them interactively in the debug environment, you must remember that these are graphics methods. When used in code, they *must* apply to an object, which often defaults to the current form.

Drawing Properties - Weird and Wonderful Effects

There are many different properties of graphics objects which you can use to create various effects.

The FillStyle Property

We saw that setting the FillStyle property of a form to 0 fills the circle with a solid color. Setting it to 1 (the default) leaves the circle's contents transparent.

FillStyle actually has a number of settings, each of which does different things to the shape you're drawing. The table below lists these settings and their effects on your works of art.

Value	Effect
0	Solid - fills the object.
1	Transparent - doesn't fill the object with anything.
2	Fills the object with horizontal lines.
3	Fills the object with vertical lines.
4	Fills the object with diagonal lines from the bottom left to the top right.
5	Fills with diagonal lines from the top left to the bottom right.
6	Draws a crosshatch pattern over the object.
7	Draws a diagonal crosshatch pattern over the object.

You can try out all these settings to your heart's content using the Debug Window, as we've done for the other examples. Just run your project, pause it, go to the Debug Window, set the FillStyle property and draw away. Don't forget that changing the property doesn't do anything until you actually draw something.

The DrawWidth Property

Another interesting form property is DrawWidth. This specifies the thickness of the lines that your objects are drawn in, be they lines, boxes, circles, arcs, ellipses or whatever. The larger this number, the thicker the lines. The minimum line width is one pixel thick.

The DrawStyle Property

The DrawStyle property is another good one to play with. This lets you flip between drawing solid lines to dashed ones of varying types, such as .... or . — . — . — ., and so on. The best way to learn about these styles is to play with them using the Debug Window.

The DrawMode Property

By far the most interesting property is the DrawMode property. This has 16 possible settings which govern how Visual Basic goes about drawing things: Four of the most useful are:

Value	Effect
4	Inverts the current pattern when drawing. The current pattern is that specified in the FillStyle property.
7	XOR Pen. Lets you draw an object, then, when you redraw it, restores what was previously drawn.
11	Does nothing. It's like saying don't draw anything. Use it to, in effect, switch the drawing off.
13	Copy pen. This is the default DrawMode that we've so far been using.

XOR Mode

The **XOR** mode needs a bit more explanation. It's mainly used for games and such. You may want to have a background graphic drawn on a form, and then move objects over the top of it. **XOR** mode lets you do this. When you first draw something onto the form, it appears exactly as you'd expect. However, if you redraw the same object, in the same place, it vanishes and the background that was there previously reappears.

This is achieved by performing an exclusive **OR** operation on the color values of the individual pixels on the screen. While we're not going to actually use this technique, it's interesting to understand.

Each pixel on your screen has a number assigned to it that determines its current color. This value is stored in your computer as a block of 1s and 0s (as are all numbers in computers). Each sequence of 1s and 0s corresponds to a certain color. A sequence of 8 of these bits (a bit is a 1 or a 0) is called a byte. When our new object swoops across the screen, it has its own set of pixel color values held in byte values.

When a pixel from the object comes over a pixel on the screen an **XOR** operation is performed. This means that each bit in the screen byte is compared with each bit in the object byte. Exclusive **OR** means that if either both or neither of the values are true, then the result is false. If just one them is true, then the result is true. True here means of course a 1, while false means a 0.

The resulting color on the screen is determined by the outcoming value of the operation. This isn't the interesting part however. What's cool is that if you then repeat the **XOR** operation with the object and the changed screen color, you get back to the original screen color.

This is a really efficient way of making an alien glide across a lunar landscape without leaving a nasty trail behind.

Repainting Forms Efficiently

I love Visual Basic. It's without doubt the best thing to happen to Windows programming. But even I have to admit that Visual Basic is a bit of a slouch when it comes to complex graphics. The problem is partly Visual Basic and partly Windows, but whatever the cause, there are some things you *can* do to make your Visual Basic graphics programs slicker and more efficient.

ClipControls

Let's start with ClipControls. Whenever you draw something on a form and move an icon or the mouse across it, Visual Basic and Windows decide which areas of the form need to be repainted. For example, you wouldn't want to see the mouse trail left on the form indefinitely.

This is what ClipControls does. With the AutoRedraw property set to false, your program will receive paint events whenever part of the form needs to be redrawn. The ClipControls property governs where you can draw. When it is set to true, you can redraw any part of the form you want to in the paint event. Something called a **clipping region** is created around the controls on the form to make sure you don't draw over them. It basically establishes the "blank" region behind the controls as the drawing area, while leaving the controls protected.

With ClipControls set to false, no matter where you try to draw on a form, Visual Basic will only change the areas of the form it thinks need repainting.

ClipControls also affects the way Visual Basic handles redrawing when the AutoRedraw property is set to true. When AutoRedraw is set to true, Visual Basic handles the redrawing of the graphics on the form, should the form get re-sized, moved or overlaid with another. The setting of ClipControls tells Visual Basic whether or not it needs to redraw the whole form, or just the affected parts of it.

To get your forms displaying and redrawing quickly you need to have ClipControls set to false. This way, only the affected areas of the form are redrawn and Visual Basic and Windows don't have so much graphical data to deal with. You should only have ClipControls set to true if you're changing all the graphics on a form every time you redraw, such as in an action game where you might need to redraw the whole playing area a number of times every second.

AutoRedraw

Much more useful is the AutoRedraw property itself. By default this is set to false. This means that if another window appears on top of the one you're drawing, Visual Basic thinks you will look after redrawing the first form if the need arises. The net result of this is that, because Visual Basic assumes you can redraw your own graphics, everything runs that much faster.

Setting the property to true, however, tells Visual Basic that it should take care of your graphics for you. Each time you draw something, Visual Basic makes a mental note of what you did. Should parts of the form get covered by another object, Visual Basic automatically knows what to do to redisplay your graphics. This also works if your user switches to another application. When your form comes back into view, it's restored to its former glory. The downside is that your graphics run quite a lot slower.

If you want fast graphics, set **AutoRedraw** to false. If you don't want the hassle of the users mucking up your displays by dragging windows around indiscriminately, then you'd better set **AutoRedraw** to true, and live with the consequences.

Summary

This has been a lightning tour of graphics with Visual Basic. I don't claim to have told you everything, but as we said at the beginning, graphics are nice, but they're often the icing on the cake. However, we did get a quick tour of the highlights, namely:

▶ How color works in Visual Basic.

▶ The coordinate system.

▶ Graphics controls, with image and picture boxes, and the shape and line controls.

▶ Graphics methods.

Along the way you learnt how to choose between the image and picture controls, and the difference between graphics controls and methods. You learnt how to create simple animation, and finally how to get the best performance from Visual Basic.

Why Not Try.......

1 Add a slow motion, pause and rewind button set to the Wrox logo animation program.

2 Create a bouncing ball project that moves a ball shape around a form and makes it bounce off the edges. Use the shape control and a bitmap with the **PaintPicture** method.

3 Create a simple drawing program that uses the mouse to sketch on the form. Add a menu to allow you to select different shapes at run-time.

4 Write a program that plots simple scientific functions on a form. You need to set up a simple set of axes. Start with Sin() and Cos(). If you're feeling adventurous, allow the user to select scales and functions at run-time.

5 Create a pie chart procedure that accepts as parameters, say, four percentages that add up to 100%, then displays a form, and plots a pie chart of these segments. For the bold, you could also pass labels and show these as well.

6 Create a tic-tac-toe board and let two players add their moves. Add code to check when some-one has won. For the advanced out there, see if you can add some game playing knowledge to the program.

7 Add features to the **PPIC.VBP** project that let the user choose which image to do the painting with.

Title	Year Published
Advanced Visual Ba:	199
Building database	199
Database	199
GUI-based design	199
A Hitchhiker's Guide	199
Visual basic	199
The visual guide to	199
Access 1.1	199
Using Access 2 for	199
Microsoft Access	199
Notes 3.0; principles	199
C++ database	199
Professional	198
Professional	199

Using Database Controls

Welcome to the information revolution! By far the most popular application for computers in the 90s is the management of information: customer lists, accounts records, stock records in a warehouse, personnel information and so on. The ideal tool to manage all this information is a good database system. Visual Basic 3 was one of the market leaders as a cheap, powerful Windows database development tool. Visual Basic 4 looks set to hold on to this crown, with a faster database engine, even more methods of controlling and accessing the data, and a wealth of new features designed to get you working with databases as quickly and painlessly as possible.

In this chapter you'll learn:

▶ How databases work.

▶ Why Visual Basic is a good choice for database developers.

▶ How to access existing databases using controls and properties.

▶ How to use Data Manager to create new databases.

What is a Database?

The easiest way to understand how databases work is to consider how people organize their information in real life. The objective of any database is to make life easier. This implies that you know exactly what information you have to organize, and what people want to use it for. This sounds trivial, but it's at this stage that most databases start to go wrong. A useful database needs careful planning and design.

We'll start at the very beginning by seeing how computer databases are a logical evolution of the way we organize information in real life. Then, once you have the general concepts under your belt, we can move on to look at how you build your own Visual Basic databases.

A Living Database

Imagine an office filing cabinet with three drawers:

- The top draw contains information about each customer, such as their name and address.

- The second draw holds information about the stock of the business - perhaps the goods it sells, or the raw materials it holds in order to produce goods in the first place.

- The third drawer contains invoices that the business has sent out to its customers.

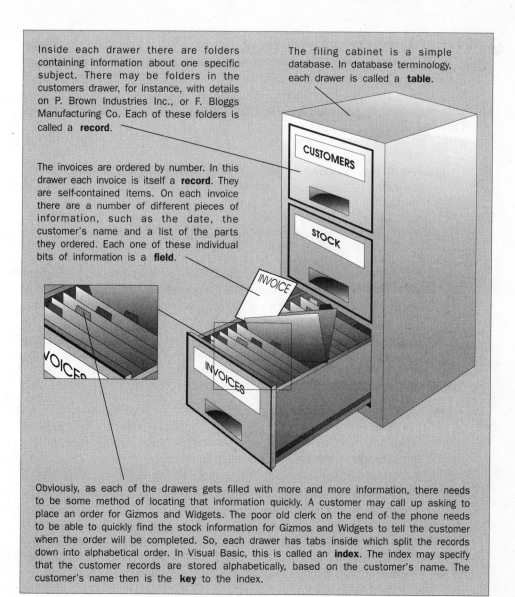

Inside each drawer there are folders containing information about one specific subject. There may be folders in the customers drawer, for instance, with details on P. Brown Industries Inc., or F. Bloggs Manufacturing Co. Each of these folders is called a **record**.

The invoices are ordered by number. In this drawer each invoice is itself a **record**. They are self-contained items. On each invoice there are a number of different pieces of information, such as the date, the customer's name and a list of the parts they ordered. Each one of these individual bits of information is a **field**.

The filing cabinet is a simple database. In database terminology, each drawer is called a **table**.

Obviously, as each of the drawers gets filled with more and more information, there needs to be some method of locating that information quickly. A customer may call up asking to place an order for Gizmos and Widgets. The poor old clerk on the end of the phone needs to be able to quickly find the stock information for Gizmos and Widgets to tell the customer when the order will be completed. So, each drawer has tabs inside which split the records down into alphabetical order. In Visual Basic, this is called an **index**. The index may specify that the customer records are stored alphabetically, based on the customer's name. The customer's name then is the **key** to the index.

431

Getting Information Out of a Real Database

Continuing the example, let's say that, a few days after placing his order for Gizmos, the customer still hasn't received his delivery. So he phones you, the clerk at J. Smith Inc., and asks when the order was dispatched. This sounds like a simple request, but think about it. It's actually quite tricky. Think about the information that each of the three drawers contains:

▶ The customer drawer has a separate file for each customer that contains their name and address and a list of all the invoices that J. Smith has raised for this customer. Take a look at that customer's file. There's a list of invoice numbers and amounts, but that's it. How can you tell which order was for the Gizmos?

▶ The obvious thing to do is to make a note of the last invoice number in the customer's file and then look in the invoices drawer. This drawer is ordered by invoice number, in database-speak it is **indexed** on invoice number. So, you can now pull out the invoice you want. There it is, the invoice to the customer who called in. Bad news! The invoice shows that you back-ordered the Gizmos because you were out of stock. Oh no - angry customer! Therefore, you decide to take a look in the stock drawer to see when a new delivery is due to come in.

▶ Luckily, the stock drawer is indexed in alphabetical order, like the customer drawer, so it's easy to pull out the Gizmos file and look at when the next delivery is due to arrive - next Friday. You call up the customer and he's cool about it.

You've probably done something like this yourself many times. In fact, what you've just done is a **multi-table relational query**. It's **multi-table** because you had to use three filing drawers (or **tables**) to get all the information you need. It's **relational** because you had to find a piece of information from one table (the invoice number from the customer drawer) and relate it to another table (the invoice drawer), in order to find the right file.

Flat-File vs Relational Databases

Databases on computers are broken down into two camps: **flat-file** databases and **relational** databases.

With flat-file databases, you tend to have a separate file on the disk for each table and separate files for each index to a table. With flat-file databases, actually relating information from one table to another can be pretty tricky, since each table is really a totally independent entity.

Relational databases are a more elegant solution. With a relational database, most of the tables that hold the data are held in one large central database file, like our filing drawers are all in the same cabinet. Organizing and accessing the information in these tables is usually done for you by something called a **database engine.** The clerk who searches through the files at J. Smith Inc. is, in fact, a database engine.

What the Database Engine Does

As well as managing access to the database, the database engine also does a lot of housekeeping to keep the relational database nice and tidy. The clerk at J. Smith Inc. not only gets information out of the database, but also has to file new invoices in the right place and keep the stock and customer files up to date.

He also has to check that what's going into the database is not rubbish. To do that he has some simple rules. For example, if he gets an invoice through with a customer name that isn't already in his customer drawer, then he won't file it away until that customer is set up properly. Otherwise, the invoice would disappear into the drawer and not be related to anything. As invoice numbers don't mean anything on their own, it would probably just sink without trace. A database engine does this kind of checking in a computer database.

Relational databases are also rather special, in that the information held in the tables of the database is rarely duplicated. The database engine makes it easy to pull information out of more than one table at once, so duplication of information can be kept to a minimum.

In our customer and invoice example, for instance, when the time comes to print the invoice, your application would need to get the customer's name and address from somewhere to print on the invoice. All you'd need to store on each invoice record is some kind of unique customer identification number, like an account number, so that you could tell the engine to get the name and address of the customer from the customer table automatically. From a maintenance point of view this is great. If a customer rings you up to change their address, you don't need to trot through the database changing hundreds of old invoices. You only need to change the relevant records in the customer file, since that will be the only place where this information is held.

In this example, the customer account number that is used to find the right file in both the customer file and the invoice file is called the **primary key**. This is the item that **relates** the two tables together.

The Important Jargon

Now you have an idea about what databases really are, let's review the words that cropped up:

▶ **Tables** are collections of information that have some logical reason to fit together, like all the names and addresses of customers. In our example, this is a drawer in the filing cabinet.

▶ **Records** are the individual entries in a table, like all the details for one particular customer.

▶ **Fields** are the items that make up a complete record, like the street name of the customer's address.

▶ An **index** is a field that is used to sort the contents of a table into a logical order. In the customer table, the best choice is the customer's name. That way, the table is in alphabetical order.

▶ A **primary key** is a field in a table that identifies each record uniquely. The same field also appears in another table, allowing the data in each to be related. In our example, the customer account number appears in both the customer table and on all the invoices. Often, the index field and the primary key are the same thing.

▶ The **database engine** is the program that files, organizes and retrieves all the data from our tables. The great strength of relational databases is that the database manager is separate from the data itself. This means we can use Visual Basic to read Paradox and other types of data.

▶ A **query** is the process of sending the database manager away to find the information we want from the database.

These are the components of a relational database that you will find in any relational database development system. However, Visual Basic expands on these through the use of a new kind of object, known as the recordset.

Recordsets

In a nutshell, a recordset is a collection of related records, whether from a single table or from a collection of tables. In Visual Basic, you will come across three different kinds of recordset:

▶ A **table** type recordset is just what the name suggests. It is simply a recordset consisting of all the data from a single table. In VB, table type recordsets are the easiest to deal with, the least memory-hungry and also the fastest when it comes to accessing and retrieving data, since the recordset relates directly to a single table.

▶ A **dynaset** type recordset is one in which the records are built up from a number of different tables. For example, if you wanted to look up an invoice, you would use a dynaset to pull together the customer's name and address from one table and the invoice details from another. Using a dynaset means you retain the editing and updating facilities available with the tables themselves. If you are coming from VB3, then this is what you would have dealt with, automatically, when you used a data control.

▶ Finally, a **snapshot** type recordset works in the same way as a dynaset, but is read-only. You can still pull in data from multiple sources, but your users will be unable to add to or update the data. Snapshots are faster than dynasets since Visual Basic doesn't have to worry about updating the information. However, they are still slower than tables.

FYI

One way to think about a relational database is as a collection of components that work together. Your job is to define what those components are and how they fit together. You can dice the data in any number of different ways - there is no real right or wrong way. What matters is that it's easy to understand, safe and efficient. Database design is an art and we can't hope to cover such a massive and open-ended subject here. However, if you stick to simple rules, and always try and relate it back to a clerk sorting through a filing cabinet, you'll be fine.

Databases and Visual Basic

All three versions of Visual Basic come with the **Jet** database engine built in. This is one of Visual Basic's main selling points. Jet is the set of control software used in Microsoft's Access database system. You are practically getting Access for free.

The Jet engine can create and manage information in a wide variety of database formats. Using Jet you can deal with Access, Foxpro, DBase, Paradox, Oracle, SQL Server and Btrieve databases right from the word go. These comprise the best-selling databases available for PCs today. Being able to connect to them, and read and write the information they hold, can make you a very valuable commodity to many businesses. This has made Visual Basic the leading tool for Windows database development.

FYI

What does database development really mean? For VB programmers it means writing what are called front-ends. While you can write a perfectly good application that takes data from a built-in database, the real action is in VB programs that take data from one or more so called back-end databases. The VB front-end then presents this information to the user in a way that works for them and lets them do what they want with it. Another user with a different task may require a completely different set of views of the essentially the same data. Visual Basic is great for knocking up a lot of different front-ends for the diverse needs of business users.

In the Standard Edition, you access and manipulate databases through the **data control**. The data control lets you view and modify records in a database with no code at all. With just a little code, you can let your users add and delete information, and your programs can also cope with wonderful things like indexed searching, transaction processing and much, much more.

In the bigger (and more expensive) versions of VB, the Pro and Enterprise editions, you can talk to the Jet database engine directly, rather than using the data control as the glue to attach your program to the database. You do this by using a set of classes to create data access objects in your code. This is a very powerful way to manipulate databases, but requires a lot of code, a lot of skill and a lot of cash to buy the bigger versions of VB. However, even at this level, it makes sense to use a mixture of the data control and data access objects, as the data control is so darn good - as we shall soon discover!

Building Visual Basic Databases

What is slightly harder in Visual Basic on its own is to build databases from scratch. You can create your own database using an add-on tool supplied with Visual Basic called **Data Manager**. The Standard Edition of Visual Basic won't let you define or amend the structure of a database from within your code, you can only do that at design-time. This means you couldn't have an option in your program to add new types of field to the database should you need them. You can only do this by stopping the program and redefining the database at design-time. You can, of course, create new records and add data to pre-defined fields as much as you like.

How This Section Is Organized

I have taken the liberty of stretching our coverage of databases over three chapters. This recognizes both the importance of VB database programming and its depth and power, even with the Standard Edition.

So, what exactly are we going to do? First in this chapter, I will introduce the **data** control, which is the link between your code, its visual interface and any underlying database. Armed with this knowledge, we will then move on to **bound** controls - controls which allow you to display and change data on screen with little or no code.

In the next chapter, we'll look at how you can control the data control from code, giving you more flexibility and some powerful built-in methods. Finally, in the third chapter, we will look at VB's special **bound list** controls, which enable you to deal easily with more than one record in a database at a time. The bound list controls enable you to effectively bind combo boxes, list boxes and a new control (the grid) to a recordset.

First of all, though, let's look at the root of all data access in the Standard Edition of VB - the data control.

Using the Data Control

The data control is one of the most powerful controls in the Standard Edition of Visual Basic. For example, you can use it to create an application to browse records in a database without writing any code. But the data control's usefulness goes way beyond just browsing - its properties and methods give you complete access to the facilities of the underlying Jet database engine. This allows you to write code to search for individual records, add new records and delete existing ones.

The Data Control Itself

On its own, the data control is pretty useless. On the screen it looks like this:

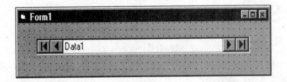

It provides you with a set of buttons that look very much like VCR buttons. These allow you to move through the records in your database. However, the data control itself provides no way of actually viewing the data in the current record. What it does provide is the glue that connects the database to other controls on the form, which you can then use to display the data you want.

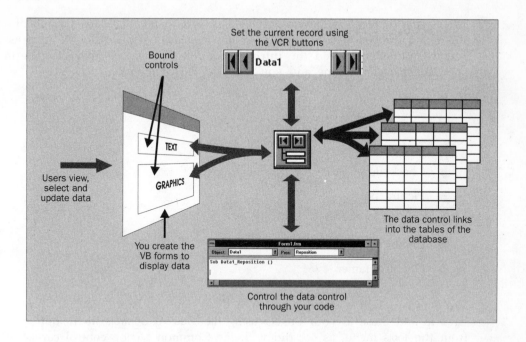

Set the current record using the VCR buttons

Bound controls

Data1

Users view, select and update data

TEXT

GRAPHICS

You create the VB forms to display data

The data control links into the tables of the database

Form1.frm
Object: Data1   Proc: Reposition
Sub Data1_Reposition ()

Control the data control through your code

To get anything tangible out of the data control then, you have to add some controls to the form into which the data can be piped. These are called **bound controls**.

Bound Controls

Bound controls are controls which can be linked to a data control at design-time and made to display the data in the current record. All these complicated terms can be more than a little daunting at first, but don't panic - you've already used bound controls! Text boxes, check boxes, image controls, labels and picture boxes are all bound controls. They're all able to take information from certain fields in the current record of the current database and display that data on a form.

There are two types of bound control available in the Standard Edition of VB. The controls we have already come across that also do double time as bound controls are called the **intrinsic** controls (this means that they are in your toolbox all the time and you can't get rid of them):

▶ Label

▶ Image

▶ Text Box

▶ Check Box

▶ Picture Box

▶ List Box

▶ Combo Box

▶ OLE Container

The Standard Edition also comes with three bound custom controls. You have to add these to your project using the Custom Controls menu option from the Tools menu, as we did with the Common Dialog control earlier in the book. The three custom controls in question are as follows:

▶ Data Bound List Box

▶ Data Bound Combo Box

▶ Data Bound Grid

These controls have been written from the ground up with data access in mind and support a lot more data-related methods and properties than their intrinsic counterparts.

The BIBLIO.MDB Database

On the sample disk included with Visual Basic is a Microsoft Access database called **BIBLIO.MDB**. The **.MDB** extension is standard for all Access databases. Before you start tooling around with a database, it's a good idea to know what's going on inside it. Until we get a bit more proficient with databases in general, though, you're going to have to rely on me to give you the low-down.

The **BIBLIO.MDB** database is a listing of some database-related books. However, the data in the database is not all lumped together in one big table, as it might be in a spreadsheet. Instead, similar types of information are grouped together into tables, which are then linked by common fields, or **keys** as they are known in database-speak. This process of breaking the data down into related groups is known as **normalization** and has a lot of benefits in terms of avoiding repeated data.

For example, most publishers in the table own more than one book. If there was only one table, with every piece of data relating to that title contained in a single row, then a big publisher would have their name entered over and over again. A better idea is to have a table that lists all the publishers once, and give them all a unique ID number which can then be used to link the publisher to the title. The **BIBLIO** database does just that and repeats it for authors as well.

Let's take a quick look at the tables in **BIBLIO**. I cheated and opened these in Access.

Title	Year Pub	ISBN	PubID	Description	Notes	Subject	Comments
Database management; develo	1989	0-0131985-2-	17	xx, 441 p. : il			
Select-- SQL ; the relational da	1992	0-0238669-4-	12	xv, 446 p. ; 2			
dBase IV programming	1994	0-0280042-4-	73				
Step-by-step dBase IV	1995	0-0280095-2-	52				
Guide to ORACLE	1990	0-0702063-1-	13	xii, 354 p. : ill	Includes inde	ORACLE (Con	
The database experts' guide to	1988	0-0703900-6-	10				
Oracle/SQL; a professional pro	1992	0-0704077-5-	13	xx, 543 p. : il			
SQL 400: A Professional Progr	1994	0-0704079-9-	52				
Database system concepts	1986	0-0704475-2-	13				
Microsoft FoxPro 2.5 applicatio	1993	0-0705015-3-	61	xiii, 412 p. : i			
First look at-- dBASE IV, versio	1994	0-0705107-5-	80	ill. ; 24 cm.			
Applying SQL in Business	1992	0-0705184-2-	13				
Database design	1977	0-0707013-0-	13				
Introduction to Oracle	1989	0-0770716-4-	13	xi, 342 p. ; 2			
SQL--the standard handbook	1993	0-0770766-4-	52	xii, 584 p. : il			
Paradox ; the complete referen	1988	0-0788139-0-	13	xvii, 666 p. :			
Paradox	1988	0-0788140-4-	13	128 p. ; 18 c			
Paradox made easy	1988	0-0788141-3-	16	xiv, 338 p. : ill	Includes inde	Paradox (Com	
Using dBASE IV	1988	0-0788147-5-	13	xvii, 696 p. : il	Includes inde	SubjectsDatat	
dBASE IV: The Complete Refer	1989	0-0788150-3-	35	1488 p.	Includes app	Database man	
dBase IV : secrets, solutions, s	1989	0-0788151-5-	35	942 p.	Includes inde	Database man	
Paradox 3 ; the complete refere	1989	0-0788151-9-	13	xx, 808 p. : il			
Using SQL	1994	0-0788152-4-	16	xxvi, 686 p. :	Includes inde	SQL (Compute	"Includes covera
Oracle; the complete reference	1990	0-0788163-5-	13	xxvi, 1045 p. :			

Titles : Table — Record: 1 of 229

The Pub_ID field in the above Titles table is the same as in the Publishers table:

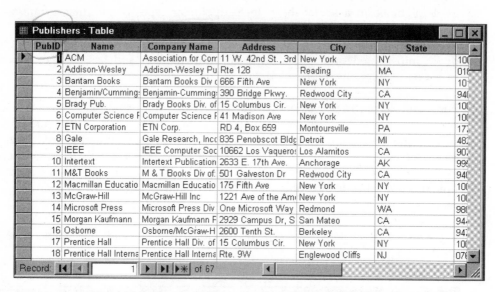

PubID	Name	Company Name	Address	City	State	
1	ACM	Association for Com	11 W. 42nd St., 3rd	New York	NY	100
2	Addison-Wesley	Addison-Wesley Pu	Rte 128	Reading	MA	018
3	Bantam Books	Bantam Books Div (	666 Fifth Ave	New York	NY	10'
4	Benjamin/Cumming:	Benjamin-Cumming:	390 Bridge Pkwy.	Redwood City	CA	940
5	Brady Pub.	Brady Books Div. of	15 Columbus Cir.	New York	NY	100
6	Computer Science F	Computer Science F	41 Madison Ave	New York	NY	100
7	ETN Corporation	ETN Corp.	RD 4, Box 659	Montoursville	PA	17'
8	Gale	Gale Research, Incc	835 Penobscot Bldg	Detroit	MI	48;
9	IEEE	IEEE Computer Soc	10662 Los Vaqueros	Los Alamitos	CA	90'
10	Intertext	Intertext Publication	2633 E. 17th Ave.	Anchorage	AK	99
11	M&T Books	M & T Books Div of	501 Galveston Dr	Redwood City	CA	940
12	Macmillan Educatio	Macmillan Educatio	175 Fifth Ave	New York	NY	100
13	McGraw-Hill	McGraw-Hill Inc	1221 Ave of the Am	New York	NY	100
14	Microsoft Press	Microsoft Press Div	One Microsoft Way	Redmond	WA	980
15	Morgan Kaufmann	Morgan Kaufmann F	2929 Campus Dr, S	San Mateo	CA	94
16	Osborne	Osborne/McGraw-H	2600 Tenth St.	Berkeley	CA	94;
17	Prentice Hall	Prentice Hall Div. of	15 Columbus Cir.	New York	NY	100
18	Prentice Hall Interna	Prentice Hall Interna	Rte. 9W	Englewood Cliffs	NJ	076

Record: 1 of 67

Then there is a table to link the title to the author. As each book has its own unique ISBN, we can use this as the identifier.

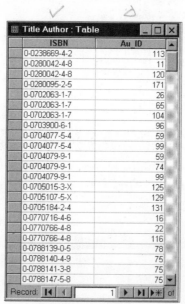

ISBN	Au_ID
0-0238669-4-2	113
0-0280042-4-8	11
0-0280042-4-8	120
0-0280095-2-5	171
0-0702063-1-7	26
0-0702063-1-7	65
0-0702063-1-7	104
0-0703900-6-1	96
0-0704077-5-4	59
0-0704077-5-4	99
0-0704079-9-1	59
0-0704079-9-1	74
0-0704079-9-1	99
0-0705015-3-X	125
0-0705107-5-X	129
0-0705184-2-4	131
0-0770716-4-6	16
0-0770766-4-8	22
0-0770766-4-8	116
0-0788139-0-5	78
0-0788140-4-9	75
0-0788141-3-8	75
0-0788147-5-8	75

Record: 1 of

The Au_ID field points to the author record in the Authors table

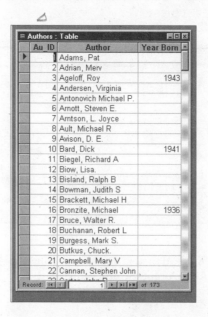

Connecting the Data Control to a Data Source

Before you can start to display information and use the data control to walk through the records in a database, you need to connect to the database in question. This is as simple as placing the name of the database in the data control's DatabaseName property.

Connecting to a Database

1 Start a new project in Visual Basic. Draw a data control on the form so that it looks like this:

Try It Out!

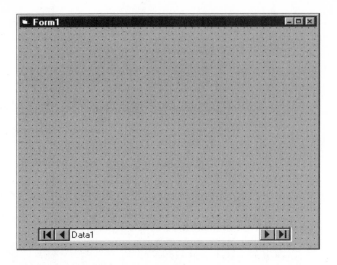

 An easy way to position the data control on your form is to select an option in the **Align** property drop-down list box.

2 Bring up the Properties Window of the data control by pressing *F4.* When it appears, find the DatabaseName property and double-click it.

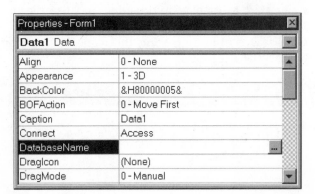

3 A dialog box appears. Use the dialog box to find the **BIBLIO.MDB** database. This will have been installed by your original VB installation program in the Microsoft Visual Basic directory. When you have found the database, double-click it to select it.

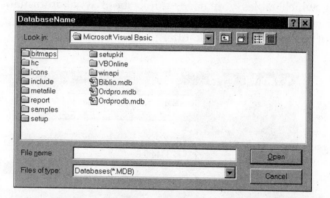

> **FYI**
>
> You must make sure that the pathname in the **DatabaseName** property is right. All the programs in this chapter assume that **BIBLIO.MDB** is in the **C:\BegVB4** directory. If your pathname is different, then make sure you change the **DatabaseName** property in each of the projects.

By selecting a database and putting its name and path into the DatabaseName property, you are telling Visual Basic which database to use for this data control. You can have more than one data control in a project, but each control can only connect to one database. Obviously, if you have three data controls on a form, you can connect to three databases at once. We will see why you might want to connect to more than one database when we look at list and combo boxes.

At the moment, not much has happened to our form. The next step is to select a table from the database whose records we want to look at. This involves setting the RecordsetType and the RecordSource properties of the data control.

Choosing Tables from the Database

We saw in our introduction how a database can be made up of different tables. The tables correspond to the drawers in our filing cabinet. When deciding which tables you need, think about what information you want to display. In this project, we want to produce a single form that shows the details of an individual book title.

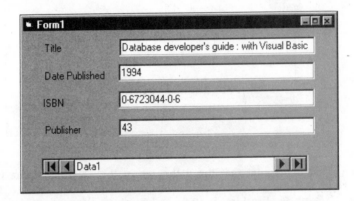

So that's where we're going. Now, how do we get there?

Selecting Tables from the Database

1 In the data control Properties Window, find the RecordSource property.

2 If you double-click on the RecordSource property itself, you can cycle through each of the tables in the database. Alternatively, you can click on the down arrow to the right of the property to drop down a list of options.

Try It Out!

3 Select the Titles table.

4 Next you need to set the RecordsetType property. As we only want to access data held in a single table, the Titles table, it makes sense to set the RecordsetType property to Table. We'll consider what a recordset is in more detail later, but for now think of it literally as a set of records. In our case, the whole table is going to be our designated set of records, but as we will see later, it could be a set of records that we select and define ourselves. You would then choose Dynaset or Snapshot as your RecordSetType. You can always not bother to choose Table here, but doing so makes the data control work a lot faster.

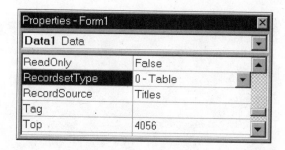

That's all there is to it. You have now selected a database and a table from that database. The next stage is to start using the bound controls to actually view the data in the table.

Using Bound Controls

Bound controls are data-aware. This means they can be linked to a data control and will then display data from that control automatically. Once you have drawn a data control onto a form, connected it to a database and selected a RecordSource, you can link the bound controls to the data control, via their DataSource property, and to a specific field in a table, via their DataField property. Let's add some more controls to our form to see how this works.

Try It Out!

Binding Controls to the Data Control

There are four fields in the Titles table in the **BIBLIO.MDB** database that we are interested in: the book title, the date it was published, the ISBN number and the publisher. We'll draw text boxes and labels on the form to allow us to see the contents of these fields. By the end of the example, you'll be able to move through all the records in the Titles table, still without any code at all.

1 Draw four labels onto the form and set their Caption properties so that the form looks like this:

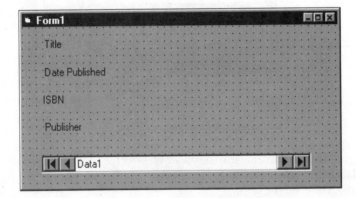

2 Draw the four text boxes that will actually hold the data from the database onto the form to the right of the labels.

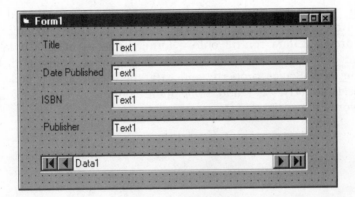

3 Clear the Text property of all the text boxes. Unfortunately, there is no quick way to do this - you have to select each text box and clear its property in turn.

4 You can, however, change the DataSource properties for all the text boxes in one go. Select all the text boxes by holding down the *Ctrl* key and clicking on each text box or by dragging the mouse over them all. With the Properties Window still visible, find the DataSource property and double-click it - the name of the data control on the form will appear at the top of the Properties Window. You have now bound all the text boxes to the data control.

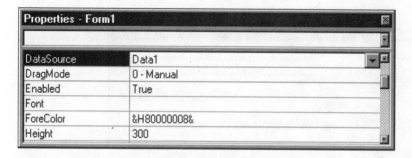

5 Click anywhere on the form to deselect all the text boxes. Then select each text box in turn and, using the Properties Window, set the DataField property to the values shown below.

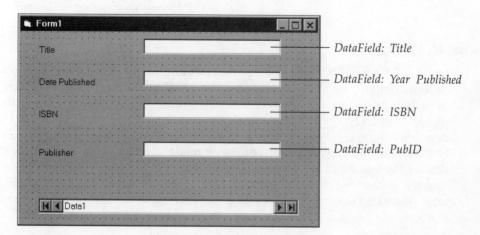

The field names we've used here were all set up when **BIBLIO.MDB** was created.

This project is on the companion disk and is called **BIB_VIEW.VBP**.

You have now bound all the text boxes to the data control and, using the DataField property, you have told Visual Basic which fields to display in which text boxes. Try running the program now.

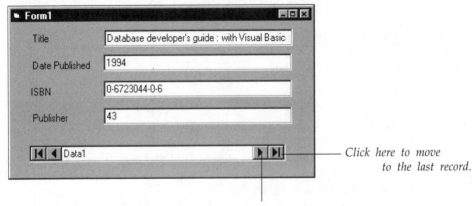

Click here to move
to the last record.

Click here to move one record forward.

How It Works

Just by setting properties on the data control and the text boxes, you now have a complete database application. You can move through the records of the table by clicking on the data control arrows. You can even change the records displayed just by clicking in the text boxes and then typing in the new information. However, you might not want to do this to the **BIBLIO.MDB** database, as once you have made a change and clicked on the data control icons to move to a new record, Visual Basic automatically writes the changed records to the database. If you have an uncontrollable urge to make your mark, then I suggest you make a copy of the database first.

Once you bind controls to a database, you are no longer dealing with those controls in the traditional way. Normally, if you make a change to the contents of a text box, it doesn't matter unless you have code which stores that value somewhere. If you make changes to a bound control, though, you are directly changing the data in the database.

You can bind labels as well as text boxes to a database to display the contents of a field. This is great for displaying fields on the screen which you don't want the user to be able to change. Just because the control in question is a label control, though, don't expect the label to display the field names; it will only ever display the contents of a field, the same as any bound control.

Locking Bound Controls

As we have just said, thanks to the functionality that the data control offers, it is possible to edit information on screen. As soon as you move from the record you are editing to a new one in the recordset, the changes you make are saved permanently to the database.

However, it is possible to prevent users from making any changes to the underlying database if you don't want them to. The answer to our prayers is the Locked property.

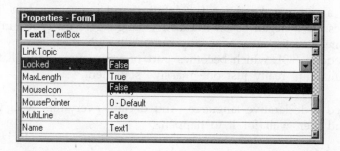

By setting this property to true on any or all of the text boxes, you are preventing the user from editing the information they see. They are still able to select the information, and cut and paste to the clipboard if they so desire. However, if a control is locked, they will not be able to make any changes to the data on display.

You could, of course, use a label control instead of locking a text box, but if you do, you are not giving yourself the chance to later unlock the control.

Selecting the Data You Want

Although we've come a long way here, we are still very much constrained by the structure of the database we are given. So far, you have seen how to use bound controls to display information from just one table. The Access database is a relational database and lets you take information from more than one table as easily as from one, using two or more data controls to get at the information, or combining the information into one data control as a dynaset or snapshot type recordset.

In order to combine data from more than one table and then select the records we need, we use a set of data handling commands from a language called **SQL**. SQL, which is commonly pronounced "sequel", is an acronym for Structured Query Language.

What Is SQL?

When the idea of the relational database evolved, SQL was created to provide a common language for defining and extracting data from databases. SQL began as an interactive language: you typed in the command and waited for the answer to pop out. Although there is now such a thing as embedded SQL which becomes part of your own code, all SQL "programs" are really just one massive statement.

It's called a declarative language. You declare everything you want to do up front and then wait for it to happen.

The reason that you, as a VB programmer, need to know some SQL, is that SQL commands provide a convenient and powerful way to talk to the Jet engine and manipulate the data it is working with. SQL gurus can do practically anything with SQL, but for us, its application will be limited to simple commands that tell the Jet engine which part of the database we want to deal with. These commands are all based around the **SELECT** statement.

The SELECT Statement

So far in this chapter we've just taken what we've been given. We've only had access to the records from one table, and even then we've had to take the complete set of records and fields, regardless of whether we only needed a selection. That's the key here - selection. What we want to be able to do is choose which records or fields we want. To do that we use the SQL **SELECT** statement.

> SQL uses some weird styles, the first of which is that all SQL commands are in capital letters. It also uses braces and dots everywhere, which may not mean a lot to you now, but are vital to understanding SQL spaghetti. You can get away without it, but be careful.

If you look up the **SELECT** statement in the VB on-line help, you will probably be put off from using SQL for the rest of your career. There is about half a page of gobbledegook after the command that controls what the statement does. Don't worry. This is for database codeheads who want to use SQL to select records, define databases, grow flowers and wash cars all at the same time. Mere mortals like us can get away with a far simpler version.

In keeping with our normal style, let's go straight in and see what's going on. We're going to use a new bound control, the **grid**, to see the results of our SQLing. First, let's get comfy with this new control.

The Bound Grid

1 Open up a new project. Place the data control onto your form and set the Align property to the bottom of the form. Point the DatabaseName property at wherever the **BIBLIO.MDB** database is on your system. Set RecordsetType to 0- Table, and RecordSource to the Titles table.

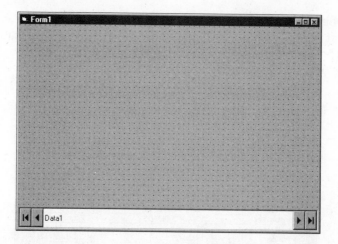

 FYI

If you don't specify a **RecordsetType**, then VB assumes you want a dynaset. We'll talk more about these in the next chapter.

2 Place a DBGrid control onto the form.

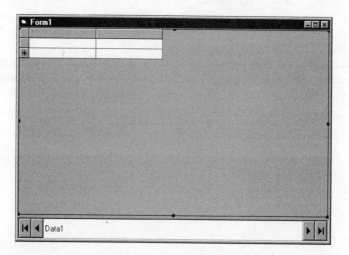

3 Now point the DataSource property of the grid to the data control Data1. Then hit run. Up comes the grid with the complete Titles table displayed in it. The grid control also gives us some nice little scroll bars to move the viewing window around if the underlying grid is too big, as this one is.

How It Works

Setting up the data control here is the same as it has been before. Setting up the grid is, if anything, easier. The grid control is two dimensional: it can display all the records (rows) in a table and all the fields (columns) in each record. You don't have to choose a certain field to display, as you do with a single field control like the text box.

Also, look what happens when you hit the buttons on the data control. Because you have all the records in there already, it doesn't put new data into the grid, instead it moves a little cursor up and down the left side of the grid.

This cursor defines the selected record. Visual Basic itself uses this cursor to tell it which records to load into the bound controls when you move around a database. We ourselves will use it in the next chapter when we write our own code to work on the database.

Selecting Fields to View

Now let's get down to some SQL. We are going to use SQL to tell the data control to only pass selected fields from the table to the grid.

1 In case you've closed it down, the DBGrid project is on the disk as **SQLGRID.VBP**. Bring up the Properties Window for the data control. First of all we need to change the RecordsetType property to Dynaset.

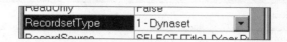

2 Now, put the cursor in the RecordSource property box and delete Titles. Enter the following SQL statement directly into the box:

```
SELECT [Title], [Year Published], [ISBN] FROM Titles
```

3 Hit run and see what we've got. There are only the fields we requested.

Title	Year Published	ISBN
▶ Database managemen	1989	0-0131985-2-1
Select– SQL ; the	1992	0-0238669-4-2
dBase IV programming	1994	0-0280042-4-8
Step-by-step dBase IV	1995	0-0280095-2-5
Guide to ORACLE	1990	0-0702063-1-7
The database experts'	1988	0-0703900-6-1
Oracle/SQL; a	1992	0-0704077-5-4
SQL 400: A	1994	0-0704079-9-1
Database system	1986	0-0704475-2-7
Microsoft FoxPro 2.5	1993	0-0705015-3-X
First look at– dBASE	1994	0-0705107-5-X
Applying SQL in	1992	0-0705184-2-4
Database design	1977	0-0707013-0-X
Introduction to Oracle	1989	0-0770716-4-6
SQL–the standard	1993	0-0770766-4-8
Paradox ; the complete	1988	0-0788139-0-5
Paradox	1988	0-0788140-4-9
Paradox made easy	1988	0-0788141-3-8

Data1

4 You can re-size the columns of the grid control at design-time by dragging them with the mouse.

Click and drag here to re-size the columns at design-time.

title	Year Published	ISBN
Database management; developing application	1989	0-0131985-2-1
Select-- SQL ; the relational database language	1992	0-0238669-4-2
dBase IV programming	1994	0-0280042-4-8
Step-by-step dBase IV	1995	0-0280095-2-5
▶ Guide to ORACLE	1990	0-0702063-1-7
The database experts' guide to SQL	1988	0-0703900-6-1
Oracle/SQL; a professional programmer's guide	1992	0-0704077-5-4
SQL 400: A Professional Programmer's Guide	1994	0-0704079-9-1
Database system concepts	1986	0-0704475-2-7
Microsoft FoxPro 2.5 applications programming	1993	0-0705015-3-X
First look at-- dBASE IV, version 1.5/2.0 for	1994	0-0705107-5-X
Applying SQL in Business	1992	0-0705184-2-4
Database design	1977	0-0707013-0-X
Introduction to Oracle	1989	0-0770716-4-6
SQL--the standard handbook ; based on the	1993	0-0770766-4-8
Paradox ; the complete reference	1988	0-0788139-0-5
Paradox	1988	0-0788140-4-9
Paradox made easy	1988	0-0788141-3-8

Data1

How It Works

The SQL statement we typed into the RecordSource property tells the data control which fields it should ask the Jet engine to retrieve from the underlying **BIBLIO** database. What the Jet engine then passes back to the data control is not the whole table as before, but a dynaset. This is a collection of records and tables that is derived from the underlying tables in the database, but which exists only for our immediate purposes. It's a kind of virtual thing that dies when you stop running the program. Both tables and dynasets are types of recordset, which is Microsoft's generic name for a set of records that you have got hold of and want to work on.

The SQL statement itself consists of two parts. The first is a list of the fields we want to retrieve: **[Title], [Year Published]** and **[ISBN]**. These are in square braces to tell SQL that they are names of fields. Then we have to tell the **SELECT** statement which table to take this data from - in our case, it is the **Titles** table.

That's it. This is, of course, a simple incarnation of the **SELECT** statement. Things get more complicated later on. However, the basic premise is the same. Tell the database what you want and where to get it from and off it goes.

Taking Data from Multiple Tables

Relational databases reduce the amount of information in a database by relating tables to each other. In the **BIBLIO** database, for example, the PubID field relates the Titles and Publishers table and saves the user having to type in the same publisher name over and over again in the Titles table.

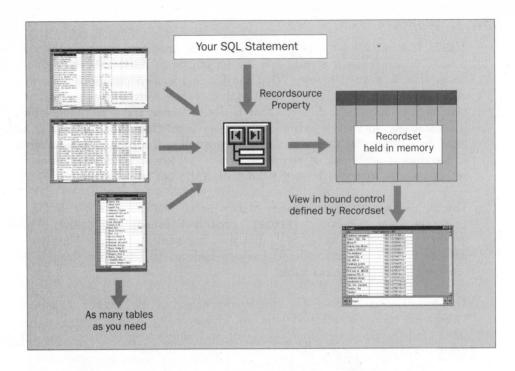

You can actually tell the data control to take these links into account when you use it. For example, in the previous Try It Out, what would be really nice is to display the publisher's name and the author's name from the Publishers and Authors tables. You can do this using the **SELECT** command and a dynaset type recordset.

Selecting from Multiple Tables

With **SELECT**, you tell the data control which fields you want to display and which tables these fields come from. In our case, we'd use it like this:

```
SELECT [Title], [Year Published], [ISBN],  [Name] FROM Titles, Publishers
```

This is actually the shorthand way of doing it. All the above field names are unique. For instance, you can't find an ISBN field in the Publishers table. If that wasn't the case, we'd have to specify the tables and the fields together like this:

```
SELECT Titles.[Title], Titles.[Year Published], Titles.[ISBN],
Publishers.[Name] FROM Titles, Publishers
```

This way there's no doubt as to where each field comes from. Each field is prefixed by the actual table name in the same way as you'd prefix a property name with the name of its control. Notice also how the field names are enclosed in square brackets.

Visual Basic still has no way of knowing how to relate records in the Publishers table to records in the Titles table for example. Although we know that the designer of the **BIBLIO** database put a PubID in both tables, the Jet engine needs to be told that you would like it to use this as the link between the two tables. In database-speak, this is called the **key**.

To tell the Jet engine that we want it to link the two tables together, using the PubID field as a key, we need to create a **JOIN** between the two tables. There are in fact several different kinds of **JOIN**, depending on how you want to compare the two sets of keys. The simplest type is the **INNER JOIN** which just connects the PubID fields that are identical. The resulting dynaset will only contain records with the same PubID field in both tables.

```
SELECT Titles.[Title], Titles.[Year Published], Titles.[ISBN],
Publishers.[Name] FROM Titles INNER JOIN Publishers ON
Publishers.[PubID] = Titles.[PubID]
```

What the **INNER JOIN** operation does here is to say to SQL:

"Hey, give me the fields I want, some of which come from the Publisher table. I'll tell you that the main table is Titles, but that you want to also get hold of all the records in Publisher (INNER JOIN) that have the same PubIDs (ON clause)"

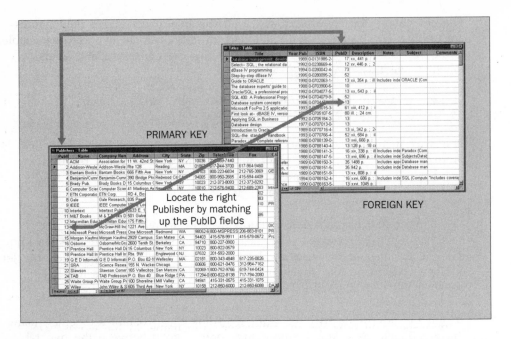

PRIMARY KEY

Locate the right Publisher by matching up the PubID fields

FOREIGN KEY

SQL is a bit tricky, so in the next chapter we will be developing a little project to let you play around with SQL statements interactively. In the meantime, let's try this out.

Selecting Information from Related Tables

Try It Out!

1 Load up the `BIB_VIEW.VBP` project. This is the same code you entered in the previous Try It Out.

2 Bring up the form with the bound controls on it. Display the Properties Window for the data control and find the RecordSource property.

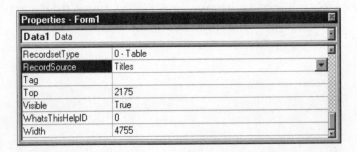

Properties - Form1	
Data1 Data	
RecordsetType	0 - Table
RecordSource	Titles
Tag	
Top	2175
Visible	True
WhatsThisHelpID	0
Width	4755

3 Type this **SELECT** statement into the RecordSource property. There's a lot of it, so be very careful. Visual Basic doesn't check what you key into the RecordSource property until you run the program, unlike the code you might key into a Code Window.

```
SELECT Titles.[Title], Titles.[Year Published], Titles.[ISBN],
↳Publishers.[Name] FROM Titles INNER JOIN Publishers ON
↳Publishers.[PubID] = Titles.[PubID]
```

4 Press *Enter* after keying in the new RecordSource to accept it. Then, change the RecordsetType property to dynaset.

5 Select the text box set up to display the publisher information. Again, bring up its Properties Window. Set the DataField property to Publishers.[Name] and press *Enter*. Alternatively, seeing as you set the data control's RecordsetType to dynaset, you could drop down a list of field names for the DataField property and just select Name.

6 Run the program now. Instead of meaningless ID numbers for the publisher, you now see the publisher's full name. In the words of a certain Mr. Gates... "Cool!"

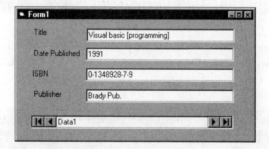

Creating Databases Using Data Manager

So far in this chapter, we've been using a database that can be described in the immortal words of every TV cookery show "Here's one I prepared earlier...". That's fine if you're writing front-ends to existing databases and have no need to create or edit the underlying database structure, but in reality you will want to be able to roll your own.

To do this with VB there are two choices:

1 Buy Access

2 Buy Access

Seriously though folks, as the underlying database structure for VB is an Access **MDB** file, and the Jet database engine is what powers Access as well as VB, it is a natural fit to use Access to create and edit **MDB** files. In some ways you can think of Access as a front-end to the Jet engine in the same way that VB is, only Access is a specialized application that has built-in tools to make creating and editing databases easier.

However, I'm not a salesman for Microsoft and we've all got better things to do with $200 than spend it on Access, so you'll be pleased to hear that there is a choice. Microsoft have included a mini-app with VB, called **Data Manager**, that is a very rudimentary, yet useful database editor.

Let's see how to use Data Manager to create a new Access database.

Creating a Database Using Data Manager

1 Data Manager is a separate application that runs as an add-in to VB. To start it, select Data Manager from the Add-Ins menu. Then select New Database from the File menu.

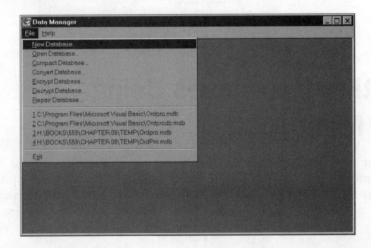

Because Data Manager is a separate application, it shows up with its own button on the Windows 95 taskbar.

2 A save dialog appears. Save the new database as **ORDPRO**.

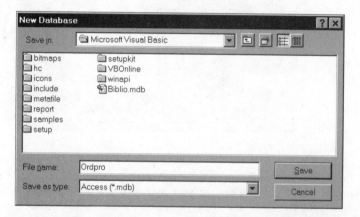

3 You're then confronted with one of the most unintuitive user interfaces known to man. What's going on? All will be revealed..

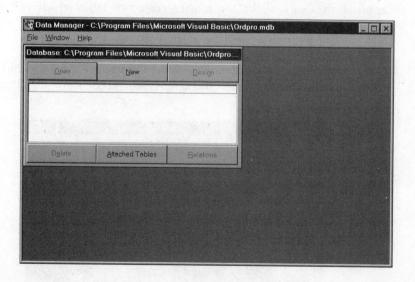

4 Click on the <u>N</u>ew button. Up comes a form which you use to define the name and fields in the database.

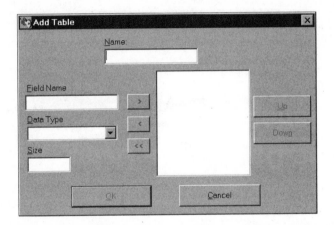

You don't have to keep saving the database like you would a file. Once you've accepted any changes you make on the screen, they are written directly to the database on disk. There is no Save Database option on the <u>F</u>ile menu.

5 What we are going to do is define two tables for an order processing application. One will be the master customer table which will hold all the customers' address details, and the other will hold a list of all the orders. The two tables will be related by the Cust_ID field.

Name the first table Customers and then enter the Cust_ID field into the form. Note that you choose the data type Integer from the drop-down list box:

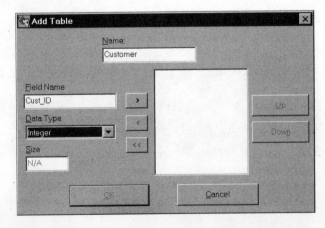

6 Once you've completed this field, click on the right arrow to accept it and go on to the next. Enter the following fields into the table:

Field Name	Type	Size
Cust_ID	Integer	N/A
Name	Text	25
Address1	Text	25
Address2	Text	25
City	Text	25
State	Text	20
Postal	Text	10

You should end up with this:

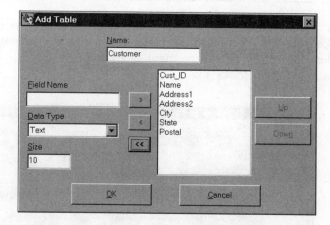

7 Now click the OK button and then create a new table for the orders, called Orders. Enter the following fields and then click OK.

Field Name	Type	Size
Cust_ID	Integer	N/A
Date	Date/Time	N/A
Value	Currency	N/A

8 This is what your screen should look like now:

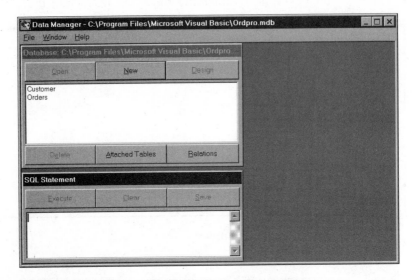

9 You can highlight either of the tables and go into an editing screen by clicking the Design button, or you can go into a data entry form by clicking on Open. At the moment our tables are empty, so this what the data entry form looks like:

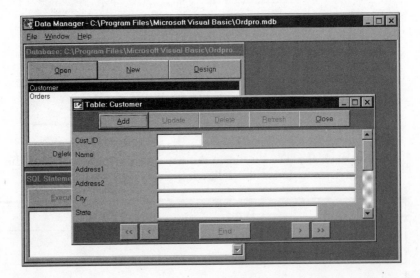

FYI

If we were creating a commercial application, we would create a relationship between the **Cust_ID** fields in each table. That would then mean that every entry in the **Orders** table would have to have a corresponding entry in the **Customer** table. This would prevent us from having orders floating around with a **Cust_ID** that doesn't mean anything. In database-speak, this is called maintaining referential integrity. We aren't going to do it here as it's a bit beyond our needs right now.

10 Now let's try entering in a record. Hit the Add button to get the database ready to accept a new record. At this point the Add button turns into a Cancel button. Enter in a suitable name and address.

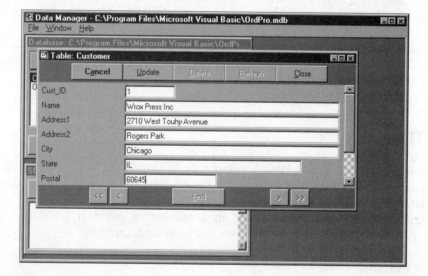

11 When you've finished entering data hit the Update button to commit the changes to the database. To add another record, just hit the Add button again. We'll see later on, when we cover adding new records using code of our own, why you have to first prepare the database for a new record before you just type away.

12 When you've finished entering all your data, hit Close to take you back to the main Data Manager window again.

Don't Try It Out - Entering Data

You've got three choices for building up the contents of the database:

▶ Create a VB application that lets you enter data using bound controls. In the next chapter, we cover adding new fields to a database and, in the chapter after that, we do it with a grid control.

▶ Create a VB program whose code writes data directly into the data fields. This is a fiddly way to do it - we'll cover it in Chapter 9.

▶ Use the forms provided in Data Manager

I am not going to make you type in a whole database. I am so kind that I've done it for you. However, if you really feel the need to practise your typing, then its easy to punch away with the Data Manager forms.

There is a complete database on the disk called **ORDPRODB.MDB**. Load it up in Data Manager and review it. We will be using it in the next couple of chapters.

Summary

A large part of Visual Basic's popularity is due to its ability to handle databases. The Standard Edition of Visual Basic does not have all the database power of the Professional Edition, but it is nonetheless an excellent tool. It can browse through data in a number of different ways and then present the data easily to the user using bound controls.

In this chapter we covered:

▶ What a database is.

▶ How the data control links a program to a database.

▶ What SQL is and how to use it.

▶ How to set up the data control and bound controls interactively.

▶ How to build your own databases using Data Manager.

We've covered a lot in this chapter and introduced you to a few new concepts, but all along we've been using the data control properties. You can, however, manipulate this control using code, which is what we will do next.

Why Not Try.......

1 Create a form that displays the author names and the titles of the books that they have written from **BIBLIO.MDB**.

2 Add a button to the **BIB_VIEW.VBP** project that shows the recordset in a grid and allows you to switch back to a form if you want.

3 Create a form to display the **ORDPRO** database, and then add some example records to it.

4 Create an additional table in **ORDPRO** that holds the names of the item that was ordered. Add a primary key field to the table that identifies each item and add it to the Orders table to link the two.

5 Create a form that displays the orders and the item number. Add a button that pops up a description of the item ordered if required.

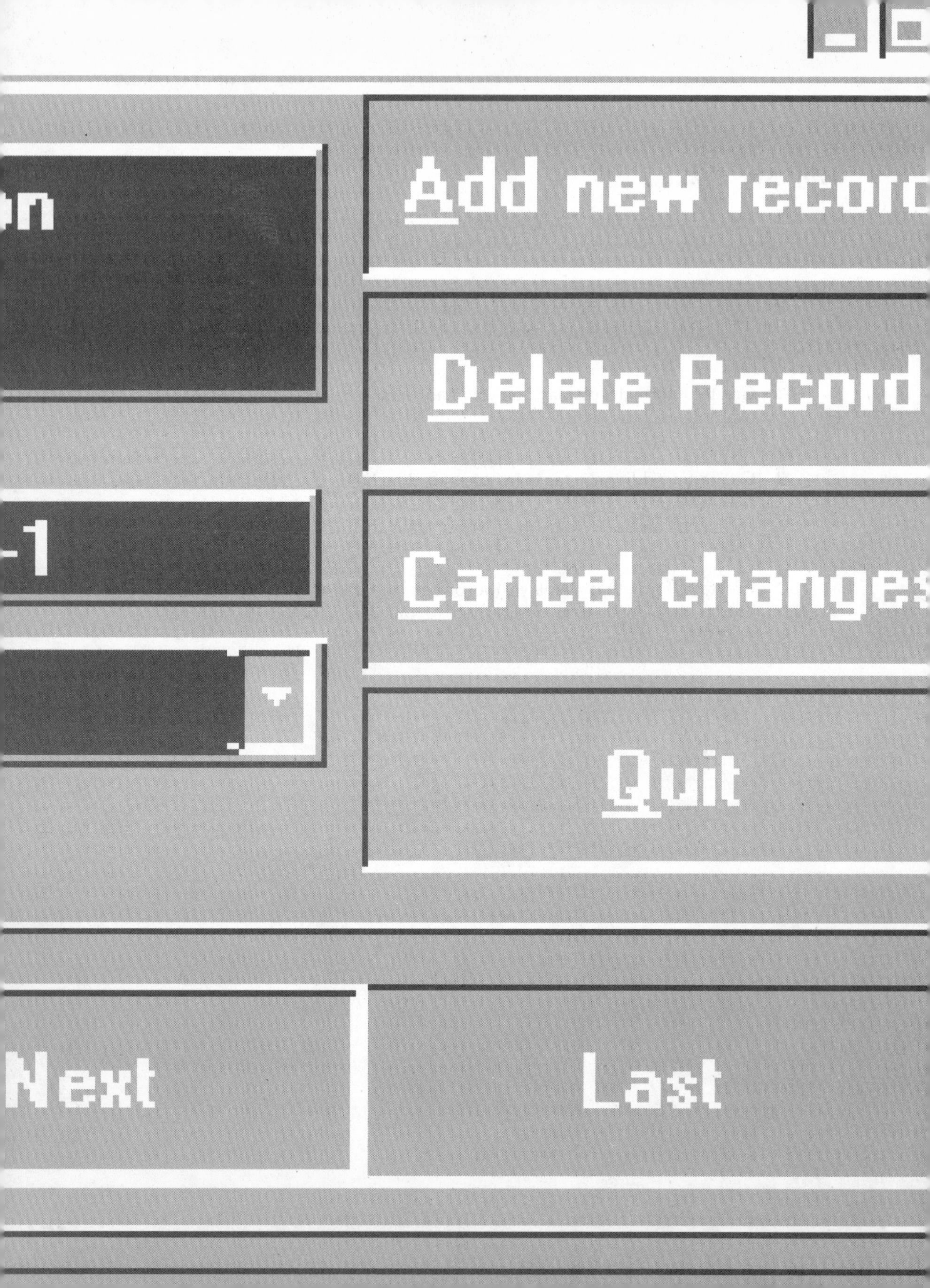

n

-1

Add new record

Delete Record

Cancel changes

Quit

Next

Last

Programming Database Access

In the previous chapter, we used the data and bound controls pretty much interactively by setting their properties beforehand. However, like all other Visual Basic controls, what you can do at design-time is just the tip of the iceberg. The real action comes when you work with the control as an object in your code.

In this chapter you will learn:

▶ How to address the data control in code.

▶ What a recordset really is.

▶ How to use the data control methods to work with a recordset

▶ What events are interesting on the data control.

Programming the Data Control

The Standard Edition of Visual Basic lets you use the full potential of the data control in your code. However, it only allows you this one route to a database. The data control has to be in your project, sitting between you and the Jet engine at all times. At our kind of level, this is perfectly adequate though. The data control supports a lot of powerful methods and events, and enables you to create extensive database applications.

The alternative method of data access, which is not supported by the Standard Edition, is to by-pass the data control altogether and create objects from the underlying Jet engine and the database itself, which you can then manipulate using code. Using Data Access Objects (or DAOs), as you might imagine, is more powerful than going through the data control. They give you direct access to all the objects in the database, as well as to a lot more of the Jet engines functionality than is supported by the data control. However, they are also a lot harder to implement and require you to write a lot more code.

Given the power that's there in the data control, don't feel bad about not being able to tool around with DAOs directly. You can do plenty of great things with the data control, and with a lot less hassle.

To really understand how to work with the data control, we have to understand the concept of a recordset. That's where we'll start.

The Recordset Object

In the previous chapter, we used the data control to select groups of records from single tables and multiple related tables. The recordset object, often called the recordset property of a data control, lets you access the selected records as if they were all in one table. It creates a temporary collection of the records you want for the time that your program is running.

For example, you may have a **SELECT** statement in a data control which pulls information from three tables. Rather than having to worry about all three tables in your code, you can deal with the recordset object instead, which brings the contents of all three tables together.

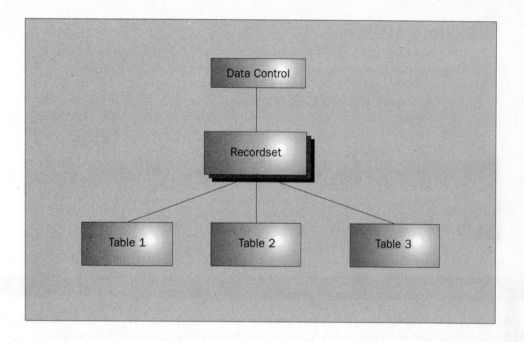

Types of Recordset

As you will remember from the last chapter, the Jet engine supports three types of recordset that you choose between, depending on where the data comes from and what you want to do with it.

Table, Type 0

This passes the complete table from the underlying database through to your program. You have to take the whole table, and any changes you make to the recordset are reflected in the original table. To all intents and purposes, you aren't looking at a recordset - you're looking directly at the underlying table.

Dynaset, Type 1

This is created by filtering or combining records and fields from one or more underlying tables. You control its make-up using an SQL statement or other query. If you change any part of the resulting set of records, then the changes are also made in the corresponding tables.

Snapshot, Type 2

This is like a dynaset in origin, but it is not updatable. The underlying tables are protected from any changes you make to the recordset.

We saw earlier that the default type is 1, the dynaset. This is because, most of the time, you will want to use something more complex than a table and won't need to stop updates taking place.

There are constants to describe these recordset types, namely `vbRSTypeTable`, `vbrSTypeDynaset`, `vbRSTypeSnapshot`. However I tend to use 0,1,2 as that's what's in the Properties Window. It's your choice.

Creating a Recordset with Code

Let's recreate the grid project from the previous chapter in code, so that we bind the controls to the data at run-time, rather than at design-time.

1 Open up the project **BIBGRID1.VBP** from the disk. This is just the form we had before.

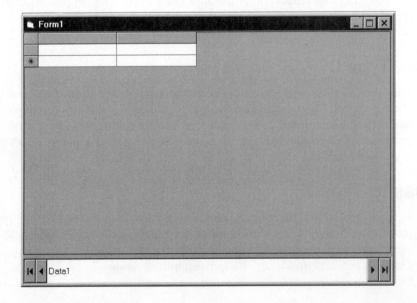

2 If you look at the Properties Window, you'll see that the DataSource and RecordSource properties are not set for the data control. However, the DataSource property of the grid has been set at design-time. Visual Basic won't let you set this from code.

3 Now let's add some code that will attach the database and feed the data into the grid. Type this code into the **Form_Load** event:

```
Private Sub Form_Load()

    Data1.DatabaseName = "C:\BegVB4\Biblio.MDB"
    Data1.RecordsetType = 0
    Data1.RecordSource = "Titles"

    Data1.Refresh

End Sub
```

4 Now hit run and there's the data.

Title	Year Published	ISBN	PubID	Description	N
Advanced Visual Ba	1994	0-2016082-8-6	2	xi, 400 p. : ill. ; 24	
Building database	1993	1-5582828-5-8	79	xvii, 388 p. ; 24 cm.	C
Database	1994	0-6723044-0-6	43	xlix, 1130 p. : ill. ; 24	In
GUI-based design	1994	0-4713030-4-6	26		
A Hitchhiker's Guide	1994	0-9640242-0-9	67	[iii], 275 p. : ill. ; 28	Ti
Visual basic	1993	0-2016266-1-6	2	x, 436 p. : ill. ; 24	C
The visual guide to	1994	1-5660407-0-1	56		
Access 1.1	1993	0-6723017-8-4	43	xliii, 1180 p. : ill. ; 23	In
Using Access 2 for	1994	1-5652962-8-1	40	xxvi, 1254 p. : ill. ;	In
Microsoft Access	1993	0-8306431-0-9	61	xii, 288 p. : ill. ; 24	C
Notes 3.0; principles	1993	Unknown4	77	29 cm. + 1	
C++ database	1992	1-5582821-6-5	79	xiv, 320 p. : ill. ; 24	
Professional	1989	0-6733835-9-8	44	xv, 284 p. : ill. ; 24	
Professional	1991	0-6734617-1-8	44		
4th dimension; a	1989	0-6733817-2-2	44	xiv, 288 p. : ill. ; 24	
Knowledge systems	1990	0-2015242-4-4	2	xiv, 538 p. ; 24 cm.	
C database	1991	1-5582806-2-6	79		

Data1

How It Works

There is just one property hardwired at design-time: the DataSource property of the grid. Apart from this, the data control is young, free and single, and looking to get bound to the next available data source so they can make little recordsets together.

In order to get the data control working, you have to first tell it the exact name and path of the target database. In our case this is:

```
Data1.DatabaseName = "C:\BegVB4\Biblio.MDB""
```

There is actually a stage prior to this that we have skipped. That is to specify a **Connect** property. This tells VB the type of database you are connecting to, for example ODBC, FoxPro, etc. You can see in the Properties Window that we have specified the default type: Access.

You then have to specify the type of recordset you want to work with. We could have left this blank, defaulting to a dynaset, but instead we set it to table (type 0). As ever, there are intrinsic constants that you can use to make this more understandable, but I for one find 0, 1 or 2 pretty easy. However, here are the constants anyway:

Constant	Value	Meaning
vbRSTypeTable	0	Table
vbRSTypeDynaset	1	Dynaset
vbRSTypeSnapshot	2	Snapshot

After that, we have to tell the data control which table we are going to connect to.

```
Data1.RecordSource = "Titles"
```

Once it's all set up, you kick the data control in action using the **Refresh** method:

```
Data1.Refresh
```

In our particular case, you could leave this out as the form load event itself causes the controls to be refreshed. However, it's good practice to get used to having it there.

Defining the Recordset

Having got to grips with the idea of attaching the data control to databases on the fly, we can now move on and see how to use the RecordSource property of the data control to determine what records and fields actually go into our recordset. In the previous example, we just lifted the whole Titles table into the grid. This time, let's control the RecordSource property of the data control directly to dictate what appears in the grid.

Playing with SQL

What we are going to do is to add a window onto the grid form that lets you submit SQL statements to the data control at run-time.

1 If you haven't still got the previous program open, load up **BIBGRID2.VBP**. Open up the form in design view, drag the bottom of the grid upwards and draw a big text box at the bottom. This is going to be the window into which we can enter SQL commands. Name the text box **txtSQLCode** and set its Multiline property to true to allow for extra long commands.

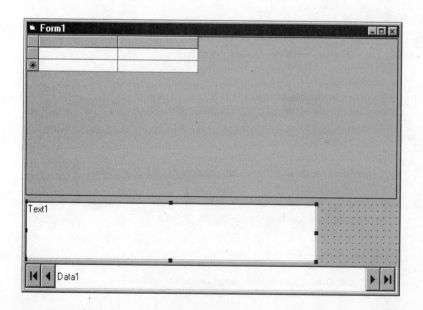

Try It Out!

2 Now add two command buttons as shown. Call them **cmdExecute** and **cmdQuit** and set their captions accordingly. Set the Enabled property of the Execute button to false, but set its Default property to true.

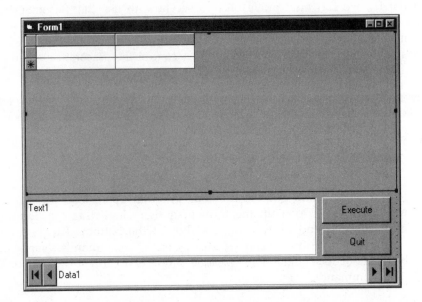

3 Open up the Code Window for the **cmdExecute** click event and add this code.

```
Private Sub cmdExecute_Click()
    Data1.RecordSource = "" & txtSQLCode & ""
    Data1.Refresh
End Sub
```

4 Add an **End** command to the **cmdQuit_Click** event.

5 The code in the form load event remains the same as before, except for changing the recordset type to dynaset.

```
Private Sub Form_Load()

    Data1.DatabaseName = "C:\BegVB4\Biblio.MDB"
    Data1.RecordsetType = 1
```

```
        Data1.RecordSource = "Titles"

        Data1.Refresh

End Sub
```

6 Add this code to enable the execute button when there is something there to execute.

```
Private Sub txtSQLCode_Change()
    If txtSQLCode <> "" Then
        cmdExecute.Enabled = True
    Else cmdExecute.Enabled = False
    End If
End Sub
```

7 Now run the project. Enter the following SQL command into the text box and watch the grid change when you hit Execute.

```
SELECT Titles.[Title], Titles.[Year Published], Titles.[ISBN] FROM Titles
```

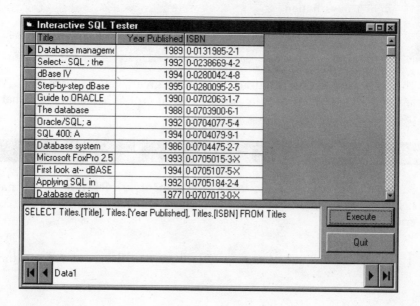

The finished project is on the disk called **INTSQL**.

How It Works

The main change from the grid project in the previous chapter is that here we built up the **RecordSource** property for the data control from a string taken from the text box. Assuming that the user types in a valid SQL statement, this is placed inside the required quote marks and assigned to the **RecordSource** property by the line:

```
Data1.RecordSource = "" & txtSQLCode & ""
```

The change event for the text box looks to see if there is anything in the string before it enables the execute button, thereby preventing blank statements being submitted.

You can cut and paste the SQL statement from the text box using the right mouse button.

This is a very simple program, but it's a great way to learn SQL. While we are here, let's take a look at some other useful SQL commands that you can use to create more complex recordsets.

Selecting Certain Records

So far we've only used the **SELECT** statement to pick out certain named fields. What's more interesting, is to filter the recordset based on certain criteria.

1 Load and run the **INTSQL** project from the disk, and type in this SQL code:

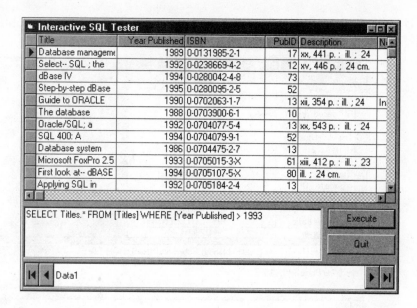

2 Hit Execute and this is what you see. Only the titles published after 1993 are shown.

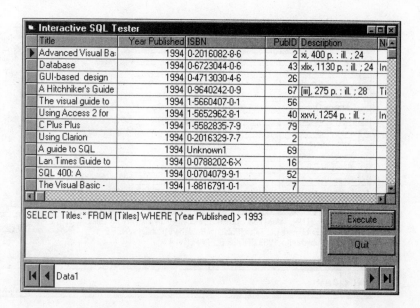

3 Now change the statement to take data from the Publishers table.

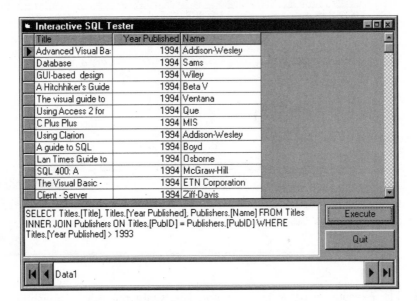

4 Now add an **ORDER BY** clause to the end:

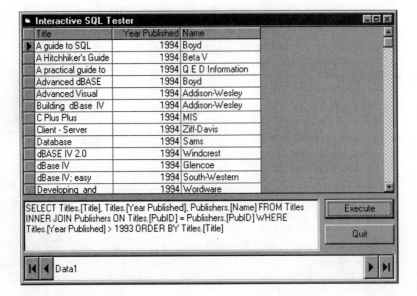

I know what you're thinking. It's so annoying if you get a statement wrong. Up pops the error window and you lose the lot. Well, wait your turn. In the next chapter we'll add error handling to this program so that it won't drop you out if you screw up. In the meantime, copy the SQL statement in the window using the right mouse button before you execute. That way you can paste in again if it fails.

How It Works

Let's look at the mega-statement that we had at the end:

```
SELECT Titles.[Title], Titles.[Year Published], Publishers.[Name] FROM
Titles INNER JOIN Publishers ON Titles.[PubID] = Publishers.[PubID] WHERE
Titles.[Year Published] > 1993 ORDER BY Titles.[Title]
```

You can see how SQL has a habit of mushrooming into great wads of clauses. However, there is a simple enough logic to it all:

1 Start with **SELECT** and tell the database which fields you want, preferably fully named:

```
SELECT Titles.[Title], Titles.[Year Published], Publishers.[Name]...
```

2 Then tell the database where to get these records from, and if and how you want to combine records from more than one table:

```
...FROM Titles INNER JOIN Publishers ON Titles.[PubID] =
Publishers.[PubID]...
```

3 Then tell it how to choose which titles to include in the dynaset:

```
...WHERE Titles.[Year Published] > 1993...
```

4 Then at the end tell it how to sort them:

```
...ORDER BY Titles.[Title]
```

This is only touching the tip of the SQL iceberg, but now you've got the general idea, you can build the statements you need to get the data you want out of your underlying database.

There are a lot of good books on SQL. Take a look at *Instant SQL* from Wrox. It contains a complete guide to SQL, with all the code in Access format, as well as Oracle and Sybase. Its ISBN is 1-874416-60-5. Shameless plug.

Recordset Objects, Properties and Methods

In VB, the word recordset signifies both a property and an object at the same time. Although we haven't done it yet, you can assign a recordset to an object variable like this:

```
Set RsMyData = Data1.Recordset
```

You can then use the shorter variable **RsMyData** in your code to refer to the current recordset. In this case, we're using recordset as a property of the **Data1** object.

If you add another level of reference to this naming scheme, then recordset becomes part of the object name, to which you can apply a number of properties and methods. The most useful of these are geared to helping you navigate around the recordset using code, rather than the VCR buttons on the data control.

The methods and properties that are available for a recordset are dependent on what kind of recordset you have open. This is normally intuitive. For example, only the table type recordset supports the **DateCreated** property. After all, this would be meaningless for a dynaset or snapshot type recordset which is created afresh each time you run the program. The table is the only persistent recordset. Similarly intuitive criteria apply to whether a property is read/write or read-only in code. You would be right to assume that the **DateCreated** property is read-only: you don't want to be able to cheat the system and create your own date stamps.

We aren't going to cover every property and every method here. It would take too long, and a great many of them are beyond the scope of the techniques I want to highlight. If you are consumed with curiosity, search on Recordset Object Properties in the on-line help. We'll start off by looking at the recordset properties that tell you where you are in the data.

Recordset Properties

Two of the most useful properties are the **BOF** and **EOF** properties. These mark the beginning (**BOF**) and end (**EOF**) of the recordset. If both these properties are set to true, then you are at both the beginning and end of the **Recordset** - meaning the **Recordset** is empty.

We'll take a look at these properties in more detail later, but for now, here's a quick run-down of the most useful recordset properties.

Property	Description
BOF	True if you are at the beginning of the recordset, before the first record.
EOF	True if you are positioned at the end of the recordset, after the last record.
BookMark	Reading this gives you the ID of the current record. Writing to this property jumps you immediately to the record with the **BookMark** value you write.
LastModified	The **BookMark** of the last changed record.
LastUpdated	The **BookMark** of the last updated record. There may not have been any actual changes to the record during the update.
NoMatch	Used when searching for records using the **Find** events you will see later. If this property is true, then no match could be found.

There are also two data control properties that define how the recordset actually behaves:

Property	Description
BOFAction	Defines what happens when the user tries to move before the first record of the recordset. Can be used to automatically reposition on the first record, or on an invalid record with the Previous button disabled on the data control.
EOFAction	Defines what happens when the user tries to move beyond the last record of the recordset. Can be used to automatically reposition on the last record, on an invalid record with the Next button disabled, or to create a new record in the recordset.

Each of the above properties can take either a number or another of VB's inbuilt constants. **BOFAction** can be set to either **vbBOFActionMoveFirst** or **vbBOFActionBOF**. The first moves to the first record in the recordset if the user tries to move before the first record. The second moves to a non-existent record in the recordset and disables the previous button on the data control itself.

The **EOFAction** property can have similar values: **vbEOFActionMoveLast**, **vbEOFActionEOF** or **vbEOFActionAddNew**. The first two of these correspond to the **vbBOFAction** values. **vbEOFActionAddNew** lets the data control create a new record if the user tries to move beyond the last record in the recordset.

These properties mean that you can write an application that allows users to view, edit and update information without actually writing any code. For example, if you set the **vbEOFActionAddNew** flag, then once you reach the end of a recordset, the data control puts up a blank new record and you can type into it. Moving to another record updates the database with this new record.

However, it is far more common to handle record creation and deletion (something the data control cannot do on its own) through code. Before we get our teeth into doing this, we need to know how to move about the recordset using code.

Recordset Methods

Simply using the data control to display records from a table in the existing order is rather limiting. One of the real powers of database applications is their ability to find individual pieces of data for you quickly and easily. In order to do anything more sophisticated, though, we need to first understand how the data control moves through the records.

To get a clear understanding of recordset methods, it helps to keep an image in your mind of what a recordset is. It's a virtual table that you have assembled in memory from the underlying tables in your database and only includes the records and fields that you want to work with at the moment. Although it's a virtual table in the sense that it exists only as long as your application is running and you decide to keep it there, it does have a real structure as far as your code is concerned. The records are assembled in the order that you determined by your SQL **RecordSource** statement, which could, of course, be unspecified, in which case they are "as found".

Whatever the order of your records, they sit there as a block. In order that you and your code know which record you're dealing with at any one time, the Jet engine maintains a cursor that indicates the current record. We saw this as a little triangle on the bound grid. There is always a cursor there in your recordset; when you first open the recordset it points to the first record.

In this section, we are going to look at the **Move** methods which the data control calls with its VCR buttons, as well as the **Find** methods which you can use to locate individual records. Finally, we'll take a look at the **Seek** method for table type objects. These are all ways of moving the cursor through the records.

As before, with recordset properties, there are lots more methods than we are going to cover here, and some apply only to certain types of recordset. For example, the **AddNew** method isn't supported by the snapshot type object, for obvious reasons.

Using the Move Methods

VisualBasic has four **Move** methods to let you move around a table, record by record. These are:

Method	Description
MoveFirst	Moves to the first record in a table.
MoveLast	Moves to the last record in a table.
MoveNext	Moves to the next record in a table.
MovePrevious	Moves back one record.

The four methods relate to the four icons you see on the data control when you draw it on a form.

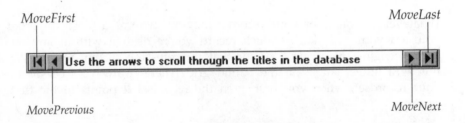

MoveFirst   *MoveLast*

Use the arrows to scroll through the titles in the database

MovePrevious   *MoveNext*

Moving Around the Database

1 Load up the **MOVE.VBP** project.

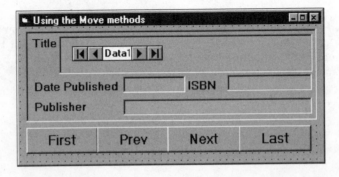

2 The program looks very similar to the one you built using the previous Try It Outs. However, this time, in addition to the data control, there are four command buttons at the base of the form which allow you to move through the records using the **Move** methods. The Visible property of the data control is set to false, so that while it appears in design mode, it isn't visible when the program is running.

3 Run the program to get a feel for how it works.

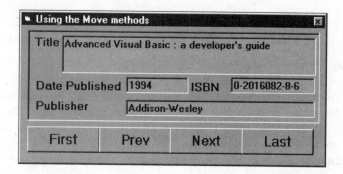

4 All appears to be OK, but go to the end of the recordset and hit the Next button. The screen goes blank. Obviously, Visual Basic is letting us move past the end of the recordset. Let's find out what's going on.

How It Works

Return to design mode and double-click the First command button to see the code:

```
Private Sub cmdFirst_Click()

datTitles.Recordset.MoveFirst

End Sub
```

This one line moves to the first record of the Titles table, using the invisible data control. The bound controls change as soon as the data control arrives at the new record. The Last command button works in a similar way to First, but uses the **MoveLast** method instead of **MoveFirst**. The Prev and Next buttons are a little more complex, and that's where the problem is.

There are only ever a finite number of records in a database. The **EOF** and **BOF** properties check whether or not the user has reached the beginning or end of the file:

```
Private Sub cmdNext_Click()

        If Not datTitles.Recordset.EOF Then datTitles.Recordset.MoveNext

End Sub
```

```
Private Sub cmdPrev_Click()

        If Not datTitles.Recordset.BOF Then datTitles.Recordset.MovePrev

End Sub
```

Let's consider the **cmdNext** code. Although we used the **MoveLast** method to get there, we aren't actually at the end of the file after the method is invoked. Instead, we are at the next to last record. The end of the file shows up as a blank record when we try and move to it, as the **datTitles.Recordset.EOF** property is still not true when we hit **cmdNext**.

The way around this problem is to check after the **MoveNext** event that we aren't hanging about in no-man's land.

```
Private Sub cmdNext_Click()

    datTitles.Recordset.MoveNext
    If datTitles.Recordset.EOF Then datTitles.Recordset.MovePrevious

End Sub
```

Add similar code to the **cmdPrev** event and we're in business.

Finding Records

The **Find** methods provide the most powerful and versatile way of locating records in your data. Let's explore these methods interactively - it's a much easier way to get a feel for how they work.

Finding Records

1 If you haven't got the previous project open, start up **MOVE-V2.VBP**. This is the improved version with the correct code in the Next and Prev events.

2 When the program is running press *Ctrl-Break* to pause it, then *Ctrl-G* to bring up the Debug Window (if it's not already visible). You can use the Debug Window to enter commands like we did in Chapter 7 - Graphics. Type the following in the Debug Window, and press *Enter*.

```
datTitles.Recordset.FindFirst "[Year Published] = 1989"
```

This finds the first record in the Titles table where the year in which the book was published is 1989. The syntax of all the **Find** commands is the same: after specifying which **Find** method you want to use - **FindFirst, FindNext, FindPrev,** or **FindLast** - you put the criteria that you want to match inside quote marks.

How It Works

In the example above, the field we want to match is called **Year Published**. We'll look at how to find out what field names are available to match later.

Since this field name contains a space, I've put square brackets [ ] around the name. It's good practice to do this all the time, to prevent confusion between field names and the values you are searching for.

Straight after the field name, the phrase **= 1989** tells Visual Basic that we want to find the first record in the Titles table where the **Year Published** field is equal to **1989**. You could equally well have put **>** for greater than, **<** for less than or **<>** for not equal to, and so on.

The **FindFirst** method finds the first matching record in the table, regardless of which record you were looking at before you did the find. You could have had the last record in the table up on screen and Visual Basic would still move you back through the table to the first matching one.

In the next chapter about list and grid controls, we will implement a **Find** function on the columns of a bound grid control.

Creating and Editing Records

Databases are only useful when the information contained in them is up-to-date and accurate. You can create and maintain your database files in two ways: using the bound controls or directly in code. We are going to look at both methods, starting, of course, with the easiest - bound controls.

Bound Control Related Methods

You can add and delete records easily using the data and bound controls. To add a new record use the **AddNew** method on the **RecordSet** object:

```
DataControl.RecordSet.AddNew
```

Having seen this format, you will understand why **RecordSet** is an object rather than a property. It can have properties of its own. It is basically an object within the data control object. More on this in Chapter 13.

This line tells the database to find a space in the current table where it can add a new record. The database dutifully does this, clears out all the fields for you and blanks out all of your bound controls. You can then set about putting values into the fields of the table, either by editing the bound controls or by using code.

An Improved Database Viewer

On the companion disk there is an improved viewer that works with the **BIBLIO** database.

1 Load up the **VIEW-V2.VBP** project to see how all this fits together. Open it up in design mode first.

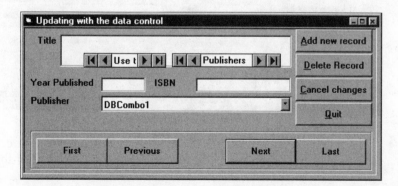

As with the Try It Outs you have been working on, this program connects to the BIBLIO database. However, this one also provides you with a combo box for the publisher, instead of confusing numbers. That's why there are two data controls on board. This version also lets you add and delete records.

2 Start up the project. There's the data.

3 Now click on the Add new record button. Up pops a blank record, ready and willing.

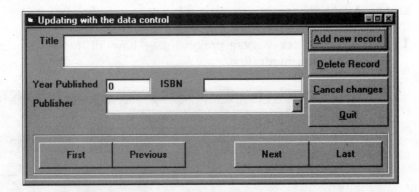

4 Let's add a phantom bestseller. Type all this in, making sure that you choose the publisher from the list in the combo box rather than making your own up.

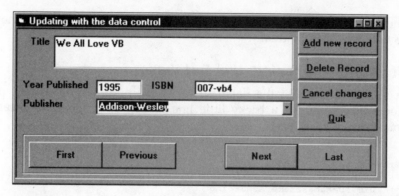

5 Hitting one of the movement keys saves the new record. Move to the next record and then hit Previous. There's your record. To avoid debris in the file, I suggest you delete it afterwards. Just hit the delete key and it's gone.

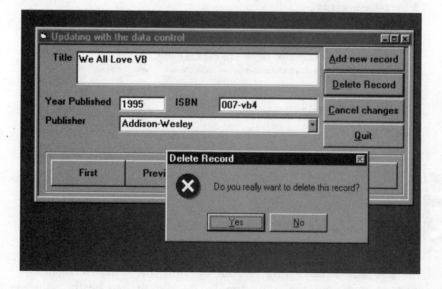

6 You can also cancel adding a new record in mid-flow. Start to type in a new record and then hit Cancel changes. You are returned to the previous record again.

There is obviously a lot going on here, so I'm going to explain how each section works individually.

How It Works - Opening the Database

I've used code to set the database to open up, as we did earlier on. However, I've added a tricky little line of code that looks for **BIBLIO** in your current directory:

```
Private Sub Form_Load()

    Dim sDatabasename As String

    sDatabasename = App.Path & "\" & "biblio.mdb"

    If Dir$(sDatabasename) = "" Then
        MsgBox "Database could not be found, please make sure that
Biblio.MDB " & Chr$(10) & "is in the same location as this program", ,
"Database Error"
        End
    End If

    datTitles.DatabaseName = sDatabasename
    datPublishers.DatabaseName = sDatabasename

    miAdding = False
    miCancel = False

End Sub
```

The program code has comments in that I've taken out here.

The **sDatabaseName** string is built up from the database name, "**BIBLIO.MDB**" and the path, **App.Path**, assumed to be the same as the VB program you are executing.

Once **sDatabaseName** is sorted out, we can assign it to the two data controls on the form. We need two data controls, as the combo list box that shows the list of publishers' names has to connect directly to the Publishers table through its own data control. We're going to cover list and combo boxes in more detail in the next chapter.

Finally, we set two module-level variables - `miAdding` and `miCancel` - as false. I declared these in the general declarations section of the form, if you want to take a look. These are two Boolean (i.e. on/off) values that keep track of whether we are in the middle of adding a new record or if we've hit the Cancel button. You'll see exactly what these do in a minute.

How It Works - Moving Around the Database

Rather than use the mundane-looking data control, which is believed to be the height of un-hipness for Visual Basic programmers, I've put navigation buttons onto the form and made both data controls invisible. The code for each button is pretty much the same. This is the Next button.

```
Private Sub cmdMoveNext_Click()

If miAdding = True Then
        datTitles.Recordset.Update
        miAdding = False
    Else
        datTitles.UpdateControls
    End If

    datTitles.Recordset.MoveNext
    If datTitles.Recordset.EOF Then datTitles.Recordset.MovePrevious

End Sub
```

The last two code lines here are familiar. We use the **MoveNext** method and then check to see if we've dropped off the end of the recordset. However, before we can go zooming about, we have to check whether we are in the middle of adding a new record, so that we can save any additions.

We saw how, when the user clicks the Add new record button, the bound controls all clear and wait for input. In an event-driven world, we wait for the user to type in what they want. The navigation event code must cover two conditions:

1 The user has just completed a new record and has typed everything in correctly. At this point, what's in the bound controls is a new record. However, that new record is only in those controls. It's not yet been passed to the Jet engine so that it can update the underlying database. To do this we have to issue an **Update** command. This confirms that we want to write the new record into the database.

We therefore assume that, if the user clicks one of the navigation buttons after having entered a new record, they want us to keep it. As we'll see in a minute, the Add new record button event code sets `miAdding` to true and, providing the Cancel button event code didn't change it to false, it will still be true when and if the user hits a navigation button. If it is true, then we issue an `Update` method and change it back to false, indicating that we've added any outstanding records.

2 There is no new record waiting to be passed to the database. This could either be because the user didn't enter one, or because they did but they then canceled it. Either way, `miAdding` is set to false. In case the bound controls contain a rejected record that we want to discard, we issue the opposite of an `Update` method - `UpdateControls`. This takes a new version of the recordset from the underlying database and uses it to refresh the bound controls, effectively overwriting any discarded records.

How It Works - Adding a New Record

Now for the meat in the sandwich, so to speak.

```
Private Sub cmdAdd_Click()

    If miAdding Then Exit Sub

    sPreviousRecord = datTitles.Recordset.Bookmark
    datTitles.Recordset.AddNew
    miAdding = True

End Sub
```

First of all, we store the location of the current record in a **bookmark**. A bookmark is a label that the database uses to identify the current record, so putting its current value into `sPreviousRecord` will mean that if the user presses Cancel, we can get back to where we were before we started adding the new record. We need to do this because the recordset we're using here is unordered, so the Jet engine orders them by age, with the last record to be added coming at the end. That's why when we do add the record it disappears to the end of the recordset.

Then we issue the **AddNew** method. This gets the Jet engine to do all the hard work for us. The bound controls are cleared and wait for input. We also then set **miAdding** to true so that we know there's a new record waiting in the bound controls.

How It Works - Canceling an Entry

If, as we are adding a new record, we decide to ditch it, we have the option of hitting the Cancel button. The code in the button has to get rid of the current record and return the database to the state it was in before we started messing around.

```
Private Sub cmdCancel_Click()

    If miAdding Then
        miCancel = True
        miAdding = False
    End If

        datTitles.UpdateControls
        datTitles.Recordset.Bookmark = sPreviousRecord

End Sub
```

First of all, we check whether we are actually in the middle of a new record. If so, we can set **miAdding** to false again, as we are about to take care of it all. Then we issue an **UpdateControls** method. This brings the database from the underlying engine to update the controls, so discarding whatever is in them. We then reassign **sPreviousRecord** as the current record.

How It Works - Deleting a Record

The final button pressing bit of the program is the <u>D</u>elete Record event handler:

```
Private Sub cmdDelete_Click()

    Dim nResponse

    If miAdding Then
        cmdCancel_Click
    Else

        If datTitles.Recordset.EOF Or datTitles.Recordset.BOF Then Exit Sub

        nResponse = MsgBox("Do you really want to delete this record?",
↳20, "Delete Record")

        If nResponse = 6 Then
            datTitles.Recordset.Delete
            datTitles.Recordset.MoveFirst
        End If

    End If

End Sub
```

If the user hits the <u>D</u>elete key whilst in the middle of creating a new record, i.e. when `miAdding` is true, then we want to handle it in the same way as a cancel event. This code checks whether that's the case and if so, runs the cancel button event instead:

```
If miAdding Then
        cmdCancel_Click
    Else
```

Otherwise, we want to use the `Delete` method to remove the current record. It's good manners to check whether the user really meant to hit the <u>D</u>elete key - which we do with the message box. It's also sensible to check whether we're at a valid record:

```
If datTitles.Recordset.EOF Or datTitles.Recordset.BOF Then Exit Sub
```

If the `BOF` property is true, it means that the data control is currently looking at the record in front of the very first one in the recordset. Think of the recordset as a book. All the interesting information is contained on the pages inside, not on the front or back covers. **BOF** essentially tells you that the data control is looking at the front cover of the book, rather than at a meaningful page of information.

EOF does a similar thing, telling you when the data control has moved beyond the end of the recordset, in other words, looking at the back cover of the book. If either of these properties are set, there is currently no valid record. If both **EOF** and **BOF** are true, then that tells us that there are no records in the recordset at all.

In the code, if either of these properties are set, then the subroutine is exited using **Exit Sub**, thus preventing the delete from taking place and avoiding embarrassing run-time errors.

If everything's OK, issue the method and then move to beginning of the recordset:

```
datTitles.Recordset.Delete
datTitles.Recordset.MoveFirst
```

How It Works - The Bound Combo Box

In true Peter Wright tradition, I'm going to make you wait to find out how this works because it's covered in the next chapter. It's really pretty easy. The combo box relates the PubID field in the Titles table to the Name in the Publishers table, much as we did ourselves using the **INNER JOIN** SQL statement. All will be revealed in Chapter 10.

Working With Records in Code

You can also work with records directly in your code. This is actually not the exclusive preserve of masochistic programmers for whom bound controls are morally decrepit. There two very good reasons for using code instead of bound controls:

1 Not all controls are bound, in which case, you have to write the code to load and edit the data yourself.

2 Bound controls are notoriously slow. This may not seem a problem to you now, but when you are working with a massive database, possibly across a network, speed is probably the biggest headache for Visual Basic programmers.

We will look at how to work with the fields and records in a database using code when we cover list and grid controls in the next chapter.

Data Surfing

One of the annoying things about our supposedly improved database viewer, **VIEW-V2**, is that it lacks the facility to scroll easily through the data by holding down the movement buttons. Adding this facility is not hard, but requires some thought. In the process we'll discover some interesting features of Visual Basic, so let's have a go.

The feature we want is to be able to press a button and then have the action that button invokes repeated for as long as the button is held down. However, we don't want this to kick in too fast, otherwise we would keep shooting past the records we wanted.

Repeating Buttons

1 Open up the **VIEW-V2** project. Add a timer to the main form and set its Interval to 1000 and the Enabled property to false. I'll explain why in a minute.

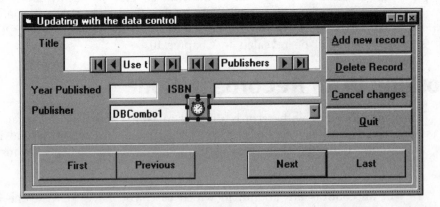

2 Now double-click on the Next button. This is what we have currently:

```
Private Sub cmdMoveNext_Click()

If miAdding = True Then
```

```
        datTitles.Recordset.Update
        miAdding = False
    Else
        datTitles.UpdateControls
    End If

    datTitles.Recordset.MoveNext
    If datTitles.Recordset.EOF Then datTitles.Recordset.MovePrevious

End Sub
```

3 However, this is no good to us as it is only executed after the click event, i.e. after the button has gone down and up. We need to do things while the button is held down. Select the body of the event code like this and cut and paste it to the **cmdMoveNext_MouseDown** **()** event.

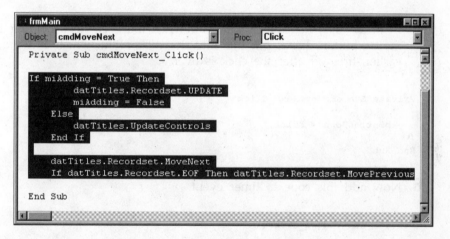

4 Now we need to add this code to the event. The code to add is shaded:

```
Private Sub cmdMoveNext_MouseDown(Button As Integer, Shift As Integer, X As
Single, Y As Single)

    If miAdding = True Then
        datTitles.Recordset.Update
        miAdding = False
    Else
        datTitles.UpdateControls
    End If

    datTitles.Recordset.MoveNext
```

```
If datTitles.Recordset.EOF Then datTitles.Recordset.MovePrevious
```

```
bKeepMoving = False
bButtonDown = True
Timer1.Enabled = True

Do While bButtonDown = True
    DoEvents
    If bKeepMoving = True Then
        datTitles.Recordset.MoveNext
    If datTitles.Recordset.EOF Then datTitles.Recordset.MovePrevious
    End If
Loop

Timer1.Enabled = False

End Sub
```

5 In order to switch the scrolling off when the user stops holding the mouse button down, put this into the click event, which as we said earlier, fires off after the click is over.

```
Private Sub cmdMoveNext_Click()

    bButtonDown = False

End Sub
```

6 Now add this code to timer event.

```
Private Sub Timer1_Timer()

    bKeepMoving = True

End Sub
```

7 Finally, we need to declare two variables as form level, so add these two lines near the top of the general declarations section.

```
Dim bKeepMoving As Boolean
Dim bButtonDown As Boolean
```

8 Now run it. Hold the button down and wait for a few seconds - you will then scroll forwards. You can change the waiting period by adjusting the interval on the timer in its Properties Window. The finished project is on the disk called `VIEWNEW.VBP`.

How It Works

At the heart of the new bit of code is a loop that keeps running as long as the Next button is depressed. We use the Boolean form level variable **bButtonDown** to keep track of whether the button is still depressed. This is reset by the click event that occurs as you let the button come up. The question, of course, is how VB executes the click event code while apparently being locked in this loop.

```
Do While bButtonDown = True
    DoEvents
    If bKeepMoving = True Then
        datTitles.Recordset.MoveNext
    If datTitles.Recordset.EOF Then datTitles.Recordset.MovePrevious
    End If
Loop
```

The answer lies in the **DoEvents** command. We have come across this before. Windows is a multi-tasking system, which means that more than one program can be executing at one time. They don't actually execute at exactly the same time - as a parallel processing machine would - but Windows swaps between the active jobs quickly to give the appearance of doing several things at once.

To some extent, a Visual Basic program looks like more than one program to Windows, in the sense that you can trigger events while code is still running. The problem is that Windows is what's called cooperatively multi-tasking, meaning it can only go and look at what's in the queue if you allow it to takes its eye off the job in hand for a second.

That's what **DoEvents** allows Windows to do: see if there is anything else waiting to happen. In our case there are two events we're waiting for: a mouse click event or a timer event. We'll come back to the timer event shortly. Without the **DoEvents** line in here, VB wouldn't check to see if the user had taken their finger off the mouse button, so the loop would run forever. Try it if you like, but make sure you save the program first as you won't be able to get back in.

As for the timer, well that's there to create a delay between the user first pressing the mouse button and the repeat scrolling. It is first enabled in the mousedown event. The timer is set to go off a certain period ahead - determined by the value of Interval. Up until the timer goes off, another form level variable, **bKeepMoving**, is false. Once the timer event triggers, this is set to true:

```
Private Sub Timer1_Timer()

    bKeepMoving = True

End Sub
```

This remains true and we keeping moving until the **cmdMoveNext_Click** event stops it all. All the timer event does is to create a delay between when you press the button and when you start scrolling. This stops the database racing away at the first press.

```
Private Sub cmdMoveNext_Click()

    bButtonDown = False

End Sub
```

If you have big sections of code or long loops, throw a few **DoEvents** in there to help oil the Windows engine.

The Database to Data Connection

At various points so far, we've had to take an interest in how the various actors on the database stage interact to get the job done. In order to get exactly what you want, you have to take the connection between your bound controls, the Jet engine and the underlying database into account. Let's take a look at how they all fit together.

The Validate Event

The most useful event available to monitor the activity of the data control is its **validate** event. As far as events go, validate is a very flexible tool. Everything that happens to the data control and, more importantly, to the data it provides access to, can be caught, monitored and even canceled through the validate event. In fact, you can even use the validate event to tell the data control to do something totally different to what it was originally hoping to do. Before we start to look at some code, though, you need to know a little more about how bound controls work.

How Bound Controls Work

Database information is held in three places while your program is running:

▶ The data you see on screen in the bound control is held in a part of memory specifically reserved for this purpose. Once a bound control has pulled data from the database, it stores its own copy of this information somewhere in memory.

▶ The database itself has a copy buffer in memory. This is where information that has just been read from, or is about to be written back to the database, is held. As you change information in the bound controls, Visual Basic copies the new data from the control to the copy buffer.

▶ Then, when all the changes have been made, the **Update** method updates the actual database record with information from the copy buffer. The point here is that the database records on disk are only physically changed after this event is invoked.

The validate event is the last stop for everything that affects the data control. Everything you do to the records in a data control triggers the validate event: moving to a new record, moving to the first or last record, writing a record to the database, and so on. You can use the **Action** parameter that is passed to the validate event to find out exactly what is about to happen - the validate event always occurs before something happens, not after. This makes the validate event the ideal place to catch changes to the data and prevent them from happening.

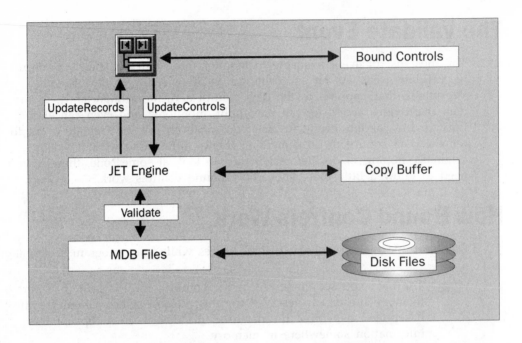

One of the most common uses of the data control validate event is to catch the times when the data control is about to move information from the copy buffer to the physical database. If you don't want the update to take place, or you only want part of the data to move from the copy buffer to the database, then you can use code in the validate event to handle it.

Using the Validate Event to Prevent Changes to Data

Let's add some code to the validate event so that updates to the Titles table can't take place under any circumstances.

Coding the Validate Event

1 Load the **BIB_VIEW.VBP** project.

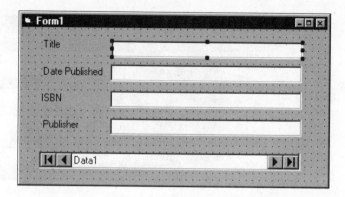

2 Double-click on the data control to bring up its Code Window, with the validate event ready to go.

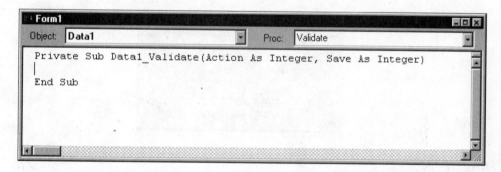

3 Type in code so that the event looks like this:

```
Private Sub Data1_Validate (Action As Integer, Save As Integer)

    If Save = True Then
        MsgBox "You cannot edit data in this database." & Chr$(10) &
"Changes have been abandoned"
        Save = False
    End If

End Sub
```

4 Try running the program now and changing the data you see on screen.

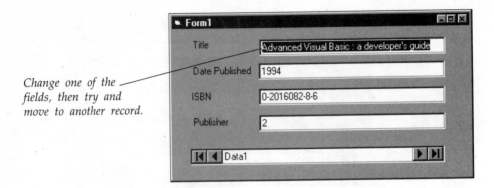

Change one of the fields, then try and move to another record.

5 As soon as you try to move to a different record, a message box appears. If you move back to the record you tried to change, you'll see that it is reset to its previous value.

How It Works

The validate event gets two parameters which we can use at run-time to check what's going on.

```
Private Sub Data1_Validate (Action As Integer, Save As Integer)
```

Here, the **Save** parameter is the most important of the two. **Save** is actually a logical value, either true or false.

In VB4, the Save parameter is a Boolean. However, it used to be an integer in VB3 and, for compatibility, is still declared as integer. Booleans are new to VB4.

It does nothing to your event code, but has an effect when the event exits. **Save** tells your code whether or not any of the information in the bound controls has been changed since it was loaded in. The results of **Save** being either true or false are:

▶ If the validate event finishes and **Save** is set to true, Visual Basic automatically fires off the **Edit** method to tell the database that it is going to change some information. After this, Visual Basic runs the **UpdateRecord** method to write information from the bound controls to the copy buffer and then finally out to the current record of the database. We'll look at these two methods in a little while, for now just take my word for it.

▶ If the validate event finishes and **Save** is set to false, then the changes made to the bound controls on screen are lost forever and aren't copied back into the database table itself.

There are two new methods here: the **Edit** method and the **UpdateRecord** method. Before you can make changes to the records in a table, you must use the **Edit** method to lock the record and prevent other users from making changes at the same time. The validate event will automatically do this for you if the bound controls have been changed on screen and you attempt to move to a new record.

The **UpdateRecord** method does just what it says. After the **Edit** method has been used, the **UpdateRecord** method copies the contents of all the bound controls relating to this data control back into the database. We'll look at the **Edit** and **Update** methods in a lot more detail in a little while.

The **Action** parameter can be used to check exactly what is going to happen when the validate event finishes. The validate event always occurs immediately before something happens, that something is held in the **Action** parameter.

The Action Parameter

The **Action** parameter is actually a number that tells us what triggered the validate event. Thankfully, you can make use of Visual Basic's intrinsic constants to get a clearer picture:

VB Constant	Action to be Performed
vbDataActionCancel	Cancels any operation that is about to happen.
VbDataActionMoveFirst	Moving to the first record.
VbDataActionMovePrevious	Moving to the previous record.
VbDataActionMoveNext	Moving to the next record.
VbDataActionMoveLast	Moving to the last record.
VbDataActionAddNew	A new record is about to be added.
VbDataActionUpdate	The copy buffer (not the bound control) is about to be written to the database.
VbDataActionDelete	The current record is about to be deleted.
VbDataActionFind	The **Find** method was called to find a record.
vbDataActionBookmark	The **BookMark** property was set.
VbDataActionClose	The data control is about to disconnect from the database.
VbDataActionUnload	The form is about to unload.

You can check the **Action** parameter against any of these values to determine what's about to happen. To stop something from happening, just set the **Action** parameter to **vbDataActionCancel**. For example, to stop the user moving to the next record, you could set **Action** to **vbDataActionCancel** whenever an event occurs with **Action** set to **vbDataActionMoveNext**.

The Save Parameter

Having said all that, you need to be careful with the validate event. Just because you're canceling the current action doesn't mean that you'll cancel any updating of the records that may take place. If the **Save** property is true when the event finishes, the data in the bound controls will be written to the database, regardless of what you did to the **Action** parameter.

To stop any data being written back to the underlying database, set the **Save** parameter to false like we did in the earlier example. Remember - the validate event occurs before anything ugly happens. In fact, it exists for the sole purpose of protecting your data.

There are an untold number of uses for the event, depending on what kind of data you are using. The general principle is to use the validate as a final gatekeeper for your database to make sure that users only get to do what you want them to do to your valuable data.

The Update Methods

Visual Basic provides you with three ways of updating information in your tables and on screen. These are known as the **Update** methods.

Update

The first and simplest is **Update** on its own. For example, if you directly code a change to the value of the **Pub_ID** field selected from a data control named **Data1**, you can write this change to the database using the **Update** method.

```
Data1.Recordset.Fields("Pub_ID") = 12
Data1.Recordset.Update
```

Beware though. To use **Update** in code you must first use **Edit**. The **Edit** method tells Visual Basic that you are about to make changes to the fields in a database, then **Update** tells it to actually save those changes.

```
Data1.Recordset.Edit
Data1.Recordset.Fields("Pub_ID") = 12
Data1.Recordset.Fields("Title")  = "The Beginner's Guide to Visual Basic"
Data1.Recordset.Update
```

Normally, the data control does all this for you. If you change the values in a bound control, such as a text box, at run-time, and then move to a new record, Visual Basic automatically does an **Edit** for you. This is what we did in the **VIEW-V2** project.

UpdateRecord

To do what the data control does yourself could require a lot of code. If you have a form with fifteen bound controls on it, it can take a lot of typing to copy the contents of these controls to the fields one by one and then do an **Update**. The **UpdateRecord** method provides an easy way round this:

```
Data1.UpdateRecord
```

This does the **Edit** for you, copies the bound control contents to the database, then does an **Update** all in one swoop.

UpdateControls

The inverse of this is the **UpdateControls** method, which copies the data from the table to the bound controls. For example, if your users change data in the bound controls and then decide they want to cancel the operation, you can use **UpdateControls** to restore the values that were in the controls before the user confused the issue:

```
Data1.UpdateControls
```

To summarize the update methods:

Method	Description
Update	Used after an **Edit**, and after you change the fields in the data control with code. **Update** permanently saves the changes you make to the fields in the database.
UpdateRecord	Stores the values of the bound controls in the underlying tables.
UpdateControls	Copies information from the fields selected with the data control into the bound controls. Great for canceling changes that the user has made and restoring the bound controls to their initial value.

Summary

We've covered a lot of ground in this chapter. We've seen how powerful the data control is and yet how simple most of its actions are. You have learnt:

▶ What kind of recordsets you can create.

▶ How to use SQL statements to filter and sort your recordset.

▶ How to program the data control using its methods.

▶ How to add and delete records in a database.

▶ How the data buffers fit together.

▶ How to control what happens to the underlying database.

In the next chapter we will look at some more powerful bound controls - the list and grid controls.

Why Not Try.......

1 Create a version of **INTSQL** that displays the titles published in a particular year and takes the value of that year from a text box on the form. Then add some up and down buttons to cycle up and down in years, each time re-submitting the new SQL statement to the database to view the resulting recordset.

2 Add a click event to the labels in the **MOVE.VBP** project that will order the recordset by the field you last clicked. Add another label to indicate which field is currently being used.

3 Create the **VIEW-V2.VBP** project using a grid to display the recordset instead of text boxes.

4 Create a version of **VIEW-V2.VBP** for the **ORDPRO** database we created in Chapter 8.

5 Create a program that reads in a record from the Titles table and then exports it to a disk file. The simplest way is to create a single string from all the fields, separated by commas. Then create a function in the same program that does the opposite, i.e. reads from a disk file and parses the data into a database.

6 Create splash screens for the programs in this chapter that take a long time to load.

7 Add the repeat facility to the Previous button in **VIEWNEW.VBP**. Also add a scroll bar as a navigation aid.

Title

Title

Year Published

ISBN

PubID

Description

Notes

Subject

Comments

Data Handling with List Controls

This chapter discusses some of the more complex controls in the standard edition of Visual Basic which are all concerned with data input and output. Each control offers its own facilities for managing lists and blocks of information. In the last couple of chapters, we have spent a good deal of time talking about how to connect databases to your Visual Basic programs. In this chapter, we will look at a group of controls that excel at handling data.

In this chapter you will learn:

- What a list control is.
- What combo boxes and list boxes are.
- How to add, select and remove items from list boxes.
- How to bind list controls to databases with your own code.

List Controls

Many applications, particularly those that deal with data, need to present lists of information to the user. A personnel system, for example, may need to present the user with a list of job categories or department names when entering employees into the system. A strategic space game may need to present a list of appropriate weapons to the player on the fire control screen. All these facilities can be easily implemented in Visual Basic through the use of various types of list and combo boxes.

These controls are both quite straightforward and can make laying down the skeleton of your application seem easy. This chapter will show you how to make them operate effectively, and in unison.

What's on the Menu

Visual Basic offers a rich variety of list and grid controls. So that we know where we're going in this chapter, let's have a look at what they do.

List boxes allow your user to choose a control from a list of options that you put up in the list box window. The user can only choose what you allow them to see.

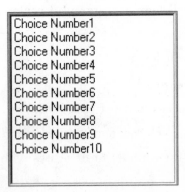

```
Choice Number1
Choice Number2
Choice Number3
Choice Number4
Choice Number5
Choice Number6
Choice Number7
Choice Number8
Choice Number9
Choice Number10
```

Combo boxes come in three styles:

▶ The **drop-down combo**, style 0, is like a text box with a list attached. The user can either type in their own entry or select one from the list. The user has to actually choose to show the list of options by clicking on the down arrow.

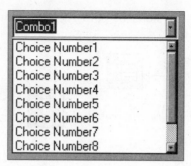

▶ The **simple combo**, style 1, always shows the list of options to the user, but again, the user can enter their own selection.

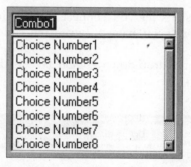

▶ The **drop-down list box**, style 2, is a hybrid of the list and combo boxes. The user can only select from the list of options, but this isn't displayed until the arrow is clicked.

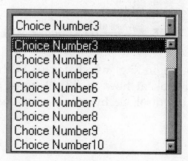

There are bound versions of both the drop-down list and combo list boxes.

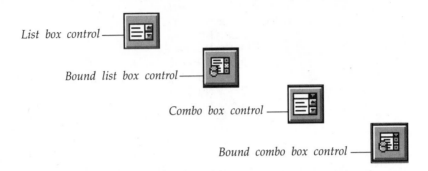

List box control

Bound list box control

Combo box control

Bound combo box control

The bound versions let you connect directly to a recordset, while with the unbound versions, you have to write the code to do this yourself.

We used a bound drop-down combo box in the **VIEW-V2.VBP** project in the last chapter:

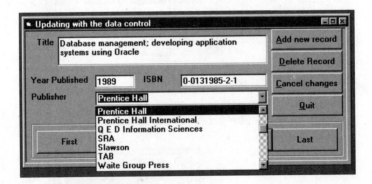

We'll start at the beginning, which for us is the lowly, unbound list box. From there we'll look at how to fill all types of list box from a database, be it using a bound control, or by using your own code to fill an unbound control.

List Boxes

List boxes are ideal when you want to present a list of choices to the user and restrict their choice to that list alone. If you only have a short list of choices, you could, in theory, use a collection of option boxes. The list box, though, is a far better choice because:

▶ It displays the options as a continuous list, so users see that they are picking one option from a list.

▶ You can control how much space the control takes up on your form by sizing the box at design-time.

▶ You can add easily and remove items from the list using code.

Let's have a look at using the list control.

Creating List Boxes

1 Load up the **LIST.VBP** project from the program disk. If you try and run it now, it won't work, as there is code in the **Form_Load()** event which adds items to a list box that I haven't yet created. We'll do that now.

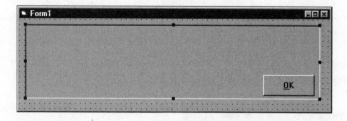

2 Select the list box control from the toolbox and draw a list box on the form.

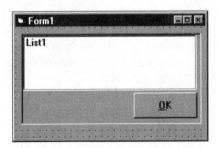

3 Run the program when you have drawn the control.

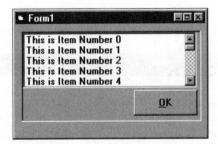

4 The list box displays the items that have been added by the code in the **Form_Load()** event. Because there are too many items to display in the box, Visual Basic adds a scroll bar down the side.

5 Stop the program by pressing the OK button on the form. This stops the program by executing this code:

```
Private Sub cmdOK_Click ()

    Unload frmMain

End Sub
```

By default, all Visual Basic programs stop running as soon as all the forms in them have been unloaded. In our case there is only one form, so saying `UnLoad frmMain` in the **OK** button click event closes down the application. You could also stop the program from running by saying **End** instead of **UnLoad frmMain**, but the latter is the best way. By unloading a form, you guarantee that the memory it took up is released, ready for use by other Windows applications.

How It Works

In this short example, I had already added code to the `Form_Load()` event that filled up the list box with items when you ran the program. This code used the **AddItem** method to create the list. If you bring up the `Form_Load()` event in the Code Window, you can see how this works:

```
Private Sub Form_Load ()
    Do While list1.ListCount < 100
        list1.AddItem "This is Item Number " & list1.ListCount
    Loop
End Sub
```

As the list box is empty at the start, this loop starts with **ListCount** as zero, and labels the first entry as Item 0.

As with arrays, one of the quirks of these kind of controls is that the item numbering always starts from 0. In this example, the number of the last item will always be 99.

The **AddItem** line places a new item in the list box, made up of the string **"This is item number "** followed by the **ListCount** property of the list box. In our example it works like this:

```
List1.AddItem "This is Item Number " & List1.ListCount
```

You may have noticed something else very weird about the list box: when you first run the program, the list box shrank a little. Why? Well, normally, the list box will round its height down so that it can fit an exact number of lines on display. This is all due to the IntegralHeight property.

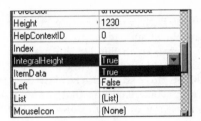

By default, when you put a list box onto a form, this property is set to true, which means that the list box will re-size itself to fit an exact number of lines on display. Setting it to false lets the list box retain its dimensions, but as a result, you may end up with only part of the bottom line being displayed. Check this out.

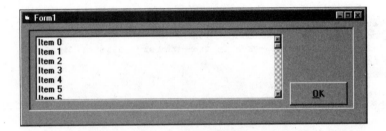

The property can only have two values - true or false - which you select in the normal ways: either by double clicking the property in the Properties Window or by dropping down the list of alternatives.

Sorting Items in a List Box

 By default, the items in a list box are displayed to the user in the order in which they were added to the list. So if you had code that said

```
List1.AddItem "Zebra"
List1.AddItem "Camel"
List1.AddItem "Elephant"
```

then your list box would look like this:

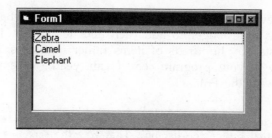

As list boxes go, this is fine. It shows all the items and the user can make a selection with no problem. Well almost. Users are funny creatures who tend to expect a little more of your applications than they actually put in the program specifications. If you had a list of 1000 clients displayed in a random order like this, they would get upset fairly quickly.

The solution is close at hand. List boxes have a property called Sorted, which can be set to either true or false.

MousePointer	0 - Default
MultiSelect	0 - None
Name	List1
Sorted	True
TabIndex	0
TabStop	True
Tag	
Top	75

By setting the Sorted property to true, any items you add to the list are automatically sorted. This gives our users what they are after:

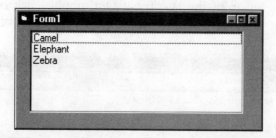

Sorting, however, does have a rather unfortunate drawback, in that it takes Visual Basic a little longer to add each item to the list. If you're dealing with large lists, say hundreds of items rather than tens, this can add a lengthy delay to your program code (yeah, yeah - except for the smart aleck at the back with the P6).

FYI

One way to get around this delay is to put a `DoEvents` command into the loop that builds the list box. That way the screen will be updated throughout the course of the loop. This is called an idle loop.

Selecting Items in a List Box

Once you've put this list of options up in your list box, the user needs to be able to select one, or perhaps more than one, and you need to be able to get that selection into your code.

Detecting When the User Makes a Selection.

Let's start by taking a look at some of the events that both list and combo boxes support to enable you to detect when something happens to a list box. By far the most useful event to use is the click event. This event occurs whenever the user selects an item from the list. Once a click event has occurred, you can examine the Text property of the control to see exactly what was selected.

Try It Out!

Using the Click Event With List Boxes

1 Following on from the last Try It Out, double-click on the list box to bring up its Code Window and select the click event.

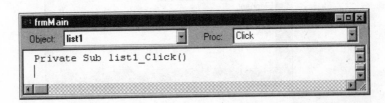

2 Add a `MsgBox` command so that your event code looks like this:

```
Private Sub List1_Click ()
      MsgBox " Selected : " & list1.Text
End Sub
```

3 Now run the program. Whenever an item on the list is selected, the click event occurs and displays a message box showing you the item you chose.

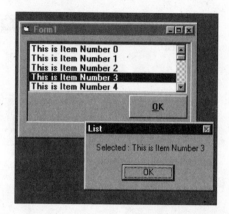

How It Works

It is extremely simple to find out what was selected if you use the Text property. This applies to all styles of list and combo box. The property contains the currently selected item from the list. If no item is selected, then the Text property will contain a blank string "". In combo boxes, though, as you'll see later, the Text property could also contain text the user has entered rather than selected. As far as list boxes are concerned, it's the value of the item selected.

Identifying Specific Entries in the List

The Text property is good for working with a selected item, but it can also be useful for determining the current position in a list.

As with most other information about list boxes, this can be pulled up from a property, in this case **ListIndex**. All list type of controls maintain an array. **ListIndex** is like the index of a user-defined array.

Using ListIndex to Find the Number of the Item Selected

Try It Out!

1 If the original program **LIST.VBP** with the added list box is still running, stop it to get back to Visual Basic design mode.

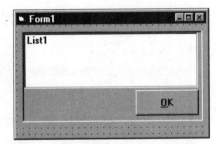

2 Change the click event to the following:

```
Private Sub List1_Click()

    MsgBox "You have selected Item number " & List1.ListIndex

End Sub
```

3 If you run the program again now, clicking an item in the list will show you the value of the **ListIndex** property, which is also the number of the item you selected. Watch out, though. When the message box says "You have selected item number 2", it is just telling you the position of that line in the array. It's sheer coincidence that the text in that line also says it's item number 2. Well it's not actually a coincidence - I did it to test you were paying attention.

The **ListIndex** property can be used to remove specific items from a list, or to add them in above the currently selected item.

Removing Items From a List Box

The **RemoveItem** method, as the name suggests, allows you to remove items from the list. You must specify the number of the item you want to remove after the word **RemoveItem**. Typing

```
List1.RemoveItem 5
```

removes item number 5 from the list box. Since items in the list box are actually numbered from 0 upwards, item 5 is actually the 6th item in the list. Aren't computers wonderful!?

ListIndex is commonly used with the **RemoveItem** method to remove the currently selected item from the list. For example, you may have a command button on a form that says Delete Current Item. The click event for that button could be:

```
Sub cmdDelete_Click

    List1.RemoveItem List.ListIndex

End Sub
```

Removing Items From a List

In addition to using **RemoveItem** to get rid of entries in the list, you can also use the **Clear** method to get rid of all the items in one go. Simply say:

```
list1.Clear
```

The items will vanish almost immediately. Let's try an example.

1 Create a new project in Visual Basic and draw a list box and two command buttons onto the form like this:

Try It Out!

2 Bring up the Properties Window of each command button and change the Caption property of Command1 to Clear and Command2 to Remove.

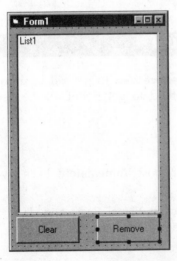

3 Add the following code to the form load event to add 100 items into it:

```
Private Sub Form_Load()

    Do While List1.ListCount < 100
        List1.AddItem "Item " & List1.ListCount
```

```
      Loop

End Sub
```

4 Now add code to the Clear command button's click event to clear the list box contents:

```
List1.Clear
```

5 Finally, add the following line to the Remove button's click event:

```
List1.RemoveItem List1.ListIndex
```

6 That's all there is to it. Now run the program.

7 Select an item in the list and press the Remove button. The selected item will vanish and the ones below it will automatically shuffle up to fill the gap.

8 Now try hitting the Clear button. All the items in the list box are immediately cleared, leaving you with an empty control.

If you try and remove an item without giving an index number, you'll get a syntax error. If you try and remove an item using an index that doesn't exist, you'll get a run-time error.

Selecting Multiple Entries

In all the examples so far, we've used the **simple select** method for selecting items from lists. With simple select, the user can only ever select one item at a time. List boxes do, however, allow users to select more than one record.

With an order entry system, for example, you could have a list box showing you which invoices are waiting to be paid. You might want your users to be able to click on each invoice in the list that was paid off today, and remove them from the list all at once. If so, you need the **multi-select** method.

The Multi-Select Property

The mode you use for making selections from a list box is controlled by the MultiSelect property. This has three possible settings:

Setting	Description
0	Allows the user to select only one item at a time. This is the default setting.
1	Simple multi-select. Each item the user clicks is selected, so click on three items and all three become selected. To de-select an item just click it again.
2	Extended multi-select. With this method, clicking an item normally works the same as Setting 0. Holding down *Shift* when you click selects all the items between the previous selection and the current one. Holding *Ctrl* down while you click makes the list box work in the same way as Setting 1.

These can only be set from the Properties Window at design-time.

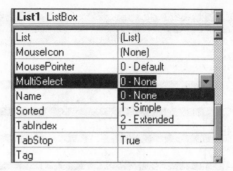

Simple Multi-Select

1 To see how this works, load up the **SELECT.VBP** project and run it.

> **Multiple Selections With A List Box**
>
> Item 0
> Item 1
> Item 2
> Item 3
> Item 4
> Item 5
> Item 6
> Item 7
> Item 8
> Item 9
> Item 10
> Item 11
> Item 12
> Item 13
> Item 14
> Item 15
> Item 16
> Item 17
>
> Delete selected items from the list

2 The form contains a single list box with 500 items in. Select a few entries and then press the command button marked Delete Selection.

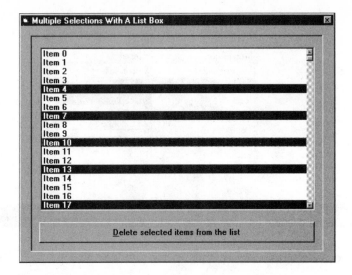

How It Works

When the command button is pressed, the following loop goes through the entries in the list, examining the **Selected** property to see whether or not the item has been marked. If it has, then the **RemoveItem** method is used to get rid of it:

```
Private Sub cmdDelete_Click ()

    Dim nEntryNumber As Integer
    nEntryNumber = lstItems.ListCount

    Do While nEntryNumber > 0

        nEntryNumber = nEntryNumber - 1
        If lstItems.Selected(nEntryNumber) = True Then lstItems.RemoveItem
nEntryNumber

    Loop

End Sub
```

First, a variable called **nEntryNumber** is set up to hold the number of the item in the list that is to be checked. The total number of items in the list is then placed into this variable. We have to check the last item in the list first and work backwards, since every time you delete an item, the

ListCount property goes down by one. If you tried to work up through the list you'd tie yourself in knots, as your code could end up trying to check items that no longer exist.

The code inside the **Do** loop decreases the entry number each time round, and checks the **Selected** property to see whether or not the item has been selected. If it has been clicked with the mouse, then **Selected** is true and the item is deleted.

When you check the **Selected** property, you need to include the number of the entry you want to check in brackets, straight after the word **Selected**. In our case, the item number is held in a variable called **nEntryNumber**, so that is placed in the brackets instead of a number. You can think of **Selected** as an array of Boolean values, each of which can be either true or false, depending on the state of the corresponding item in the list box's own array.

If the **Selected** property is true for an item, that item is then deleted using **RemoveItem**, and the code loops round to check the next item.

After a multi-select, the **Text** property of the list box contains the last entry selected.

Extended Multi-Select

As I mentioned earlier, there's also a way to select multiple items without having to laboriously click each one. This is known as **extended multi-select**. Let's see how it works.

1 Stop the last program, **SELECT.VBP** and bring up the Properties Window for the list box.

2 Find the SelectMode property and change it to **2 - Extended**.

3 Run the program again.

4 Click on the top item in the list, then hold down the *Shift* key and click on another item further down. All the items between the top one and the next one are selected automatically.

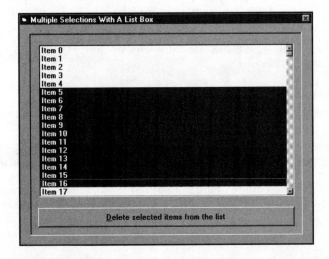

5 Now try selecting another item even further down, this time holding the *Ctrl* key down while you click. This selects an item in a similar fashion to the way simple multi-select works.

Once the items are selected, the corresponding elements of the **Selected** array are set to true, enabling you to process the data as you wish.

Displaying Multiple Columns of Entries

List boxes have a further advantage over combos in that they can display multiple columns of information. This facility is controlled by the list box Columns property.

Multiple Columns

1 Stop **SELECT.VBP**. and bring up the Properties Window for the list box.

2 Type the number 2 into the Columns property.

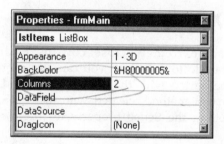

3 Run the program again.

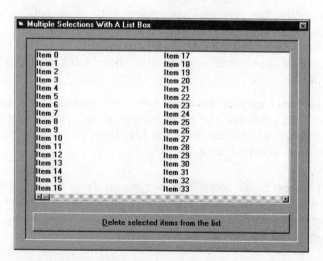

How It Works

The program works the same way as before, but now the information in the list box is in two columns instead of one. The scroll bar that was previously on the right-hand edge of the list box is now at the bottom, allowing you to scroll across the columns, rather than up and down the list.

FYI   The **Columns** property determines how many columns are visible in the list box at one time, not the total number of columns.

Combo Boxes

Combo boxes are extremely close cousins to list boxes. Everything you can do to a list box, you can also do to a combo box. Items can be added with the `AddItem` method, removed with the `RemoveItem` method, cleared with the `Clear` method, and sorted by setting the Sorted property to true.

If combo boxes and list boxes are so similar, what is the advantage of each?

▶ A combo box provides your users with an area to enter data and the option to see a list of suggestions. Combo boxes are usually used where you might use a text box for user input, but want to also show a list of possible options.

▶ List boxes are, on the other hand, very similar to a grid without columns. The list is always shown, and the user can only select items from the list. There is no data entry portion attached to a list box.

Unbound combo boxes come in three flavors: **drop-down combo boxes, simple combo boxes** and **drop-down list boxes.** These flavors, or styles, can be selected by changing the Style property of the combo box when it's on the form.

Creating Combo Boxes

1 Load up the **COMBO.VBP** project. As before, there is code in the **Form_Load** event which adds items to the combo box that you'll create in a moment.

2 Select the combo box control from the toolbox and draw a combo box on the form. If you try and change the height of the box, it will snap back to one line deep.

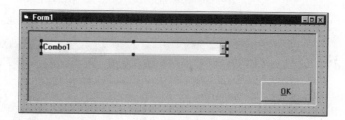

3 Run the program. When the form loads up, you can either type text into the text area of the combo, or click the down arrow to display a list of possible options.

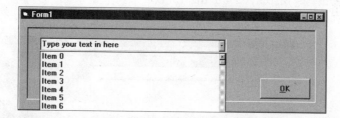

4 Stop the program now. Bring up the combo box's Properties Window and find the Style property. Change the style from the default drop-down combo box to Style 1 - Simple Combo.

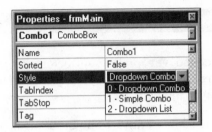

5 See how the arrow on the combo box on the form vanishes automatically. Now re-size the combo box so that it looks like this:

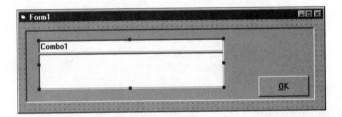

6 Run the program again. As before, you can type any text you want into the combo box, or select an item from the list. Unlike last time, though, the list is displayed all the time.

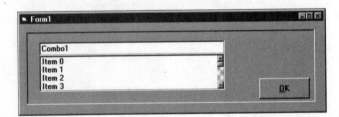

7 This is called a **simple combo** box. Because the list is always displayed, you must size the combo box at design-time so that at least the top of the list is visible. If you don't, then your users will be unable to select anything from the list.

8 Stop the program, and this time change the Style property to 2 - Dropdown List box. This type of combo box looks identical to the dropdown combo box.

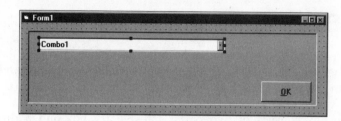

9 Run the program again. The drop-down list box will only let you select items that are in the list - you can't enter your own text.

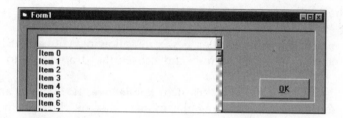

10 Type the letter I. The combo box will automatically find the next entry in the list beginning with I and display it. Keep pressing I and you'll display the next entry and so on.

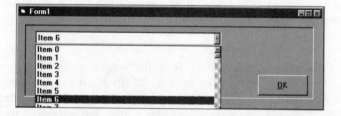

This only works here because all the entries in the list begin with the letter I. If they began with the letter A, you'd have to press A to cycle through the items!

Combo Box Events and Properties

Although there are a great many similarities between combo boxes and list boxes, there are quite a few differences between the events and properties they both support. Let's look at the events first.

A combo box consists of two parts: a text entry box and a drop-down list. A combo box, therefore, has a change event, just like a text box. You can use this to see when the user has actually altered the text in the text box by typing something in. It's worth noting that the change event only occurs when the user types something into the text box part of the combo, not when they select a new item from the list.

The **DropDown** event is another new one, allowing you to catch the point at which the user clicks the arrow and causes the drop-down to occur.

Finally, list boxes allow you to catch **MouseMove, MouseDown** and **MouseUp** events. You can click and drag the mouse to scroll through the entries in a list box, so these events allow you to see where the mouse is currently pointing, and to catch the points at which the user presses and releases a button. These events are not available with the combo box. This isn't really too much of a problem, though. List boxes present lists of information to the user, so being able to detect the mouse events can be quite handy for popping up information about items without actually selecting them. Combo boxes, on the other hand, only use the list to present a list of valid choices to the user.

On the properties side, combo boxes don't have a Selected property. With a list box, Selected is handy for letting the user do multiple item selections. Since combo boxes only ever let you choose one item at a time, there's no need for a Selected property - just check the Text property to see what the user wants to do.

The Text property with a combo box kills two birds with one stone. It lets you see not only which item the user has selected, but also whether they typed something in instead of making a selection. You can use this property to see what they typed.

List Controls and Databases

Having got a firm understanding of how these controls work, we're now really going to put them to the test. They are truly useful when it comes to giving the user a limited range of options for data entry. Control of incoming data is fundamental to working databases. For example, imagine if you let users type in their own version of the country field in an address database. You might want them to enter UK, but left to their own devices, they could enter England, GB or Britain. A better option would be to list the options in a combo box and let the user select one that you've already entered. In database-speak this is called a **look-up table**.

Bound Combo Controls

Although the bound versions of the combo and list boxes are there to make your life easier (and they do!), they are initially very confusing. When dealing with bound combo boxes, you will generally have two data controls.

Remember that one data control can only manage one recordset. If you want to relate two tables or recordsets together on the fly in your code, you need a data control for each one.

Because of this, a bound combo box has two properties for linking to tables or recordsets. The DataSource property links to the first data control; RowSource links to the second.

The best thing to do is to take a look at the **VIEW-V2** project from the previous chapter that used a bound combo box to display the publisher names alongside the titles from **BIBLIO.MDB**. This will give us something real to discuss rather than trying to describe what's going on in the abstract.

Bound Combo Boxes

1 Open up the **VIEW-V2** project. Run it to remind yourself what's going on.

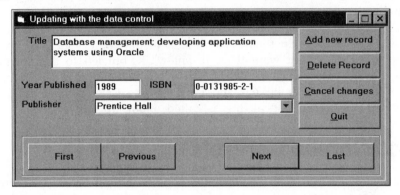

2 If you click on the navigation buttons, not only does the title change, but so does the publisher. This means there must be a link between the PubID field in the Publishers table and the PubID field in the Titles table, thus allowing the combo box to display the right publisher as you change the title.

3 Stop the program and change the Visible property of the datPublishers data control to true and run it again. Then try and navigate using this control.

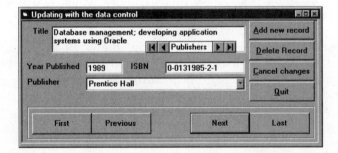

It doesn't work. Obviously this is a slave to the titles control. By having the second data control we get access to the list of publishers, but the name in the box is determined by the displayed title. All the second data control is doing is providing a window onto the Publishers table. It's the bound combo box control that is doing the work of tying the two together.

4 Make the datPublishers control invisible again, run the program and hit the Add new record button. If you type in a new title, you can choose one of the publishers in the list. Create a new title and then take a look at it. Think about it. You're moving using the datTitles data control and the combo box is relating the title you're on to a name in the Publishers table. So the combo box must have written the PubID into the new record for you.

How It Works

The essence of what's going on here is that we are using the combo box control to relate the Titles and Publishers tables together using the PubID field as the key, or common field. This is much the same as we did with the SQL **INNER JOIN...ON** statement. The difference is that instead of showing a single publisher's name, we make them all available in the combo box.

The DBCombo control has a lot of work to do.

> ► It has to put a list of all the available publishers into its item list. It takes the information from the data control named in its RowSource property. You tell DBCombo that you want to display the publisher names from the table, by specifying the field name in the ListField property.

> ► DBCombo then has to make sure that the publisher name that's displayed corresponds to the title that's been selected using the datTitles control. I have already mentioned that the combo box control has two properties that link to different tables: DataSource and RowSource. The properties that specify the field we are interested in from each table are DataField and ListField respectively. We want to relate the two tables using PubID as the common field. Therefore, to join them, we place the common field (PubID) in the BoundColumn and the DataField properties.

In order that the right fields are available to the combo box control via the **datPublishers** control, the **RecordSource** property of **datPublishers** must be pointing at the Publishers table, but be set to either a dynaset or snapshot type recordset. It won't work as a table. A snapshot is preferable to prevent any changes to the underlying data.

▶ All that's left is to pass the PubID field back to be entered in to the Titles table for any new records, when a publisher name is selected in the combo box. You can't pass the Text property of DBCombo back, as that contains the name of the publisher and there's no field for this in the Titles table. DBCombo looks up the PubID of the selected publisher in the Publishers table and places it into its BoundText property.

FYI

If you want to see the value of the **BoundText** property, add a little text box to the form and copy the **BoundText** property to it from the **DBCombo** change event by setting the new text box property to the **BoundText** property as it changes.

See if this diagram helps.

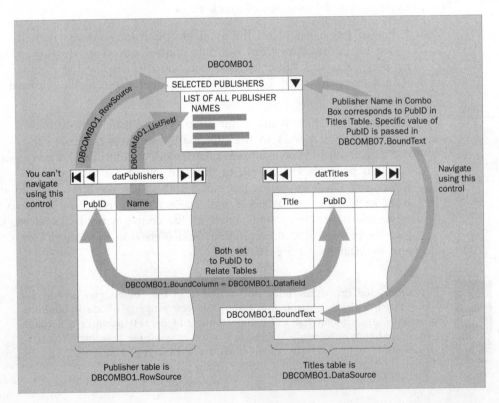

The bound list control is very similar in operation to the bound combo box, with the differences being intuitive if you've understood how the unbound versions differ. From a database handling point of view they are the same.

Having mastered the concept of how the list controls take data from one table and relate it to another, let's have a go at rolling our own. In this last example all we had to do was to tell the bound control which data controls to connect to in order see their recordsets. All the work of loading the fields into the control and so on was handled in the background by the control. Now we're going to see how to get a similar effect from a control that doesn't have all that database connection code built-in: the unbound combo box.

Binding Your Own Combo Boxes

In the first part of our database discussions, we created a simple two table database using Data Manager. This has two tables in it, the Orders table with Date and Value fields, and the Customer table with the customer names and addresses. Both tables have Cust_ID entries that we use to tell which order is for which customer. There is an extended version of this database on the disk called **ORDPRODB**.

I've already created a form with some code attached. All that's missing is the combo box to select the customer for each order. That's what we're going to add now.

1 Open up the project **ORDER.VBP**.

2 The project consists of two text boxes, both of which are bound to the datOrders data control. This data control is visible for navigation at run-time. Run the program.

You can scroll through the orders table looking at the date and value fields.

3 Now let's add a combo box. Stop the program and put a combo box onto the form like this.

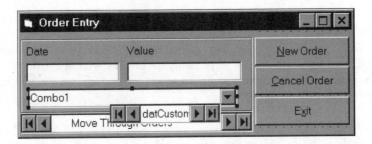

4 Set the Name property to cmbCustomers and change its Text property if you wish.

5 We now need to bind it to the datCustomers data control. Set the combo box DataSource to datCustomers, and the DataField to Name. We want to show a list of customer names in the box.

6 The first piece of code we need is to add the Name fields to the combo box. It's not a bound control so you have to do this by hand. Add this code to the form load event.

```
Private Sub Form_Load()

datCustomers.DatabaseName = App.Path & "\OrdProDB"
datOrders.DatabaseName = App.Path & "\OrdProDB"

datCustomers.Refresh
datOrders.Refresh
datCustomers.Recordset.MoveFirst
```

```
    Dim sNameToAdd As String
    Do Until datCustomers.Recordset.EOF
        sNameToAdd = datCustomers.Recordset.Fields("Name").Value
        cmbCustomers.AddItem sNameToAdd
        datCustomers.Recordset.MoveNext
    Loop
```

```
End Sub
```

7 A global variable called `miAdding` is declared in the `General`
`declarations` section. You'll remember this from the `VIEW-V2` project.
We use it to keep track of when there are changes to be written to the
underlying database. This variable is set to true by the `NewOrder` event
code. We also need to set it to true if the user clicks on the combo box
to change the customer for an existing order. To implement this add this
code:

```
Private Sub cmbCustomers_Click()
    miAdding = True
End Sub
```

8 Now we need to consider what will happen in the validate event, which
is triggered every time we move or add new records. If anything has
changed, we need to add the changes to the database.

```
Private Sub datOrders_Validate(Action As Integer, Save As Integer)

    Dim sCriteria As String
    Dim sCurrentName As String
    Dim nNewID As Integer

  If miAdding = True And Action <> vbDataActionAddNew Then

    sCurrentName = cmbCustomers.Text
    sCriteria = "Name = " & "'" & sCurrentName & "'"
    datCustomers.Recordset.MoveFirst
    datCustomers.Recordset.FindFirst sCriteria
    nNewID = datCustomers.Recordset.Fields("Cust_ID").Value
    datOrders.Recordset.Edit
    datOrders.Recordset.Fields("Cust_ID") = nNewID
    datOrders.Recordset.Fields("Date") = txtDate
    datOrders.Recordset.Fields("Value") = txtValue
    datOrders.Recordset.Update
```

```
    miAdding = False

  End If

End Sub
```

9 However, if nothing has changed, all we need to do is to make sure that the customer name in the combo box is synchronized with the current order. For this, we'll use the reposition event. This event occurs immediately after a move, as compared with the validate event that occurs before anything happens. This would be no good to us, as we would then always have the customer name field one move behind.

```
Private Sub datOrders_Reposition()

   Dim sCriteria As String
   Dim nCurrentID As Integer

   If Not miAdding Then
     nCurrentID = datOrders.Recordset.Fields("Cust_ID")
     sCriteria = "Cust_ID = " & nCurrentID
     datCustomers.Recordset.FindFirst sCriteria
     cmbCustomers.Text = datCustomers.Recordset.Fields("Name")
   End If

End Sub
```

10 Now run the completed program. If you are feeling a bit squeamish about typing it all in, then the finished project is on the disk called **ORDENT.VBP**.

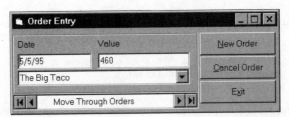

How It Works

We've already seen most of the code techniques in this program, but here we've pushed them further than before.

In the form load event we use a simple `Do Until...Loop` to load the list of options into the combo box. It uses the `AddItem` method to add the options, and runs until we hit the end of the Customer table. We have to reset the current record pointer to the first record in the table before we start, as the Jet engine maintains a persistent cursor in the `MDB` file, meaning that the current record is where you left it last time. Once this is set, we can use the `MoveNext` method to move through the table.

Once the text box is loaded, up comes the form, and we're away. Let's run through what happens for each of the possible actions.

How It Works - Moving Through the Database

If the user just moves through the database using the data control, our job is to keep the name in the customer combo aligned with the current record. Although the combo box is manually "bound" to the Customer table, it's got no built-in functions. It is also blissfully unaware of the Orders table, so we have to keep them in sync manually.

Every time the user hits a move button on the datOrders control, the two text boxes move to the next record and the validate event is triggered. We put the code to drag the combo box onto the right record in this event.

```
Private Sub datOrders_Reposition()

    Dim sCriteria As String
    Dim nCurrentID As Integer

  If Not miAdding Then
    nCurrentID = datOrders.Recordset.Fields("Cust_ID")
    sCriteria = "Cust_ID = " & nCurrentID
    datCustomers.Recordset.FindFirst sCriteria
    cmbCustomers.Text = datCustomers.Recordset.Fields("Name")
  End If

End Sub
```

We only want to run this code if we aren't in the middle of adding a new record, i.e. when **miAdding** is false. First of all, we set the local variable **nCurrentID** to the **Cust_ID** number of the current order. Remember that all orders have a **Cust_ID** to tell you whose order it us. To do this, we use the **Fields** method of the recordset that takes as its argument the field name:

```
nCurrentID = datOrders.Recordset.Fields("Cust_ID")
```

We then have to build up a string to pass to the **FindFirst** method. This goes into **sCriteria**. After issuing the **FindFirst** method, the current record in Customer has the same **Cust_ID** as the current order. All that then remains is for us to assign the corresponding **Name** field to the text value of the combo box.

```
cmbCustomers.TEXT = datCustomers.Recordset.Fields("Name")
```

How It Works - Creating a New Order

The second thing that can happen is that the user decides to create a new order or amend an existing one. If the user amends the text in the combo box, its change event sets **miAdding** to true. We still have to deal with the New Order command button, though. The event code looks like this:

```
Private Sub cmdNewOrder_Click()

    If miAdding Then Exit Sub
        miAdding = True

    sPreviousRecord = datOrders.Recordset.Bookmark

    datOrders.Recordset.AddNew
    txtDate.SetFocus

End Sub
```

If we're already adding a record, then it drops us out. We then set **miAdding** to true and assign the bookmark of the current record to the **sPreviousRecord** variable. Then we invoke the **AddNew** method.

The **AddNew** method triggers a validate event:

```
Private Sub datOrders_Validate(Action As Integer, Save As Integer)

    Dim sCriteria As String
    Dim sCurrentName As String
    Dim nNewID As Integer

  If miAdding = True And Action <> vbDataActionAddNew Then

    sCurrentName = cmbCustomers.Text
    sCriteria = "Name = " & "'" & sCurrentName & "'"
    datCustomers.Recordset.MoveFirst
    datCustomers.Recordset.FindFirst sCriteria
    nNewID = datCustomers.Recordset.Fields("Cust_ID").Value
    datOrders.Recordset.Edit
    datOrders.Recordset.Fields("Cust_ID") = nNewID
    datOrders.Recordset.Fields("Date") = txtDate
    datOrders.Recordset.Fields("Value") = txtValue
    datOrders.Recordset.Update

    miAdding = False

  End If

End Sub
```

The main part of this code writes the changes to the database. However, we only want to do this on a move event, not when the validate event is triggered by **AddNew**. At that point nothing has happened. We, therefore, test the **Action** parameter to see whether **AddNew** triggered the event, and if so, jump over the code.

```
If miAdding = True And Action <> vbDataActionAddNew Then
```

Once the user has typed in new text and selected a customer, they hit a movement button on the datOrders control, triggering another validate event. This time we want to make the changes. Let's look at the code.

The first part of the code translates the customer name that is currently displayed in the combo box into the corresponding **Cust_ID**, so that we can write it to the Orders table.

```
    sCurrentName = cmbCustomers.TEXT
    sCriteria = "Name = " & "'" & sCurrentName & "'"
    datCustomers.Recordset.MoveFirst
    datCustomers.Recordset.FindFirst sCriteria
    nNewID = datCustomers.Recordset.Fields("Cust_ID").Value
```

At the end of this code, the variable **nNewID** contains the new **Cust_ID**. We can write this along with the values of the date and value fields into the Orders database. Before we can write the changes, we need to issue an **Edit** method to set the database up to receive the data.

```
datOrders.Recordset.Edit
datOrders.Recordset.Fields("Cust_ID") = nNewID
datOrders.Recordset.Fields("Date") = txtDate
datOrders.Recordset.Fields("Value") = txtValue
datOrders.Recordset.Update
```

After that, we issue an **Update** method to close everything up. The last part of the event handler sets **miAdding** to false, as we've now finished.

How It Works - Deleting a Record

The last thing the user can do is to delete a record. This is straightforward and is similar to the code we used in **VIEW-V2**.

```
Private Sub cmdCancel_Click()
    Dim nResponse

    If miAdding Then
        datOrders.UpdateControls
        datOrders.Recordset.Bookmark = sPreviousRecord
    Else
        If datOrders.Recordset.EOF Or datOrders.Recordset.BOF Then Exit Sub
        nResponse = MsgBox("Do you really want to delete this record?",
 20, "Delete Record")
        If nResponse = 6 Then
            datOrders.Recordset.Delete
            datOrders.Recordset.MoveFirst
        End If

    End If

End Sub
```

Well, that about wraps up the Order Entry project. You may be wondering why I made you grind through so much code when you could have just used bound controls. Well, there are two reasons.

1 Bound controls are slow. Many programmers prefer to hard-wire their own when they need them.

2 We've covered a lot of good stuff about recordset methods. So there!

The Limits of the Data Control

To wrap up our extended look at using Visual Basic with databases, I thought it would be useful to explore the limits of the data control. We've accomplished a lot with the much derided data control in the last three chapters, but there's no getting away from its limitations. Let's face it - from Microsoft's point of view, you have to have a good reason to upgrade to the Pro and Enterprise editions of Visual Basic, and that reason is being able to use Data Access Objects instead of the data control to access databases.

Data Access Objects are, as the name suggests, a way of representing the complete database with all its associated tables, fields and queries as a big collection of objects. We'll be looking at objects in later chapters, but suffice to say that once you've got the object, you've got the lot. You can pretty much do anything you like with any part of the database. This power comes at the price of complexity (and about three hundred bucks!). The data control is just a window onto the underlying database, and although we can represent it as an object, we are always limited by what the data control, rather than the database, could do given the chance.

For a really good example of where the data control falls down, we just need to look at how it makes information about the structure of the underlying database available to us, both to read information about which fields and tables are present, and then to make changes to that structure. We'll take a look at a simple database browser that lets us see which tables and fields are in the database, but which does this by working around the limitations of the data control.

A Database Browser

When you walk into Big Cheese Industrial on your first day as a database developer, you'll probably be presented with a pile of company databases and asked to create some funky windows front-end using Visual Basic. The first thing you'll want to do is to check out these databases and get a good idea of what's in them. We're going to create a simple viewer that you can use to do this.

1 Open up a blank form and put a bound grid control onto it. Change the caption to something more interesting like Table Analyzer. Call the grid control dbgDisplay and the form **frmSQL**.

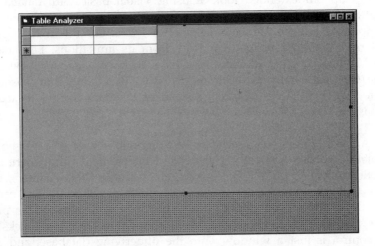

2 Now add a data control to the form to populate this grid. Call it datTable and set its Visible property to False - we aren't going to use it for navigation. We'll set the rest of the properties from code.

3 Place a frame below the grid. This will hold all our controls in the interests of neatness. Erase its Caption in the Properties Window and leave the name as Frame1. We aren't going to be using its name so it doesn't matter what it's called.

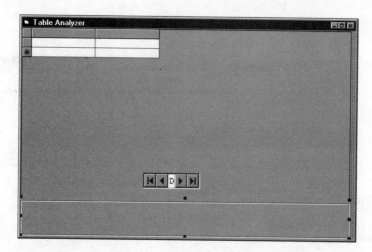

4 Now we want to add some information controls inside the frame.

▶ First add a text box that we'll use to display the name of the current database. Call it txtDatabaseName (we're naming properly boys and girls, so be good) and add a label to it as well.

▶ Next add two combo boxes, and call them cmbTables and cmbFields and again, let's have a label to show we can play by the rules. Just keep all the properties for these as the defaults, except make the Text property the same as the name, so you can remember what they are called.

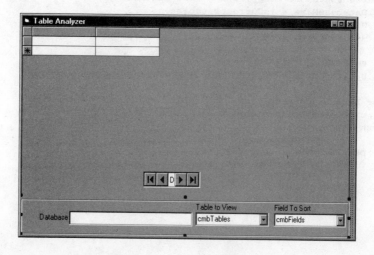

5 Now it's code time kids. First of all, declare the variables.

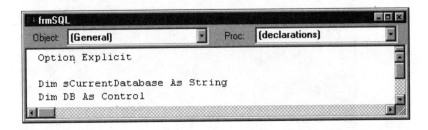

6 Then let's sort out the **Form_Load** event

```
Dim objCurrentColumn As Column

frmSQL.Show
DoEvents
Set DB = datTable

With cmbTables
    .AddItem "Titles"
    .AddItem "Publishers"
    .AddItem "Authors"
End With

cmbTables.Text = "Titles"
cmbFields.Text = "Title"

sCurrentDatabase = App.Path & "\Biblio.MDB"
DB.DatabaseName = (sCurrentDatabase)
DB.RecordsetType = 1
DB.RecordSource = cmbTables.Text

DB.Refresh
DB.UpdateControls

For Each objCurrentColumn In dbgDisplay.Columns
    cmbFields.AddItem objCurrentColumn.DataField
Next

txtDatabaseName = sCurrentDatabase


End Sub
```

7 Now we need to add code to change the grid and the field list in the combo box whenever we change the selected table. Add this to the click event for the combo box.

```
Private Sub cmbTables_Click()

Dim objCurrentColumn As Column

cmbFields.Clear

DB.RecordSource = cmbTables.Text
DB.Refresh

For Each objCurrentColumn In dbgDisplay.Columns
    cmbFields.AddItem objCurrentColumn.DataField
Next

cmbFields.Text = cmbFields.List(0)
cmbFields_Click

End Sub
```

8 Now let's add code to sort the grid based on the field selected.

```
Private Sub cmbFields_Click()

On Error GoTo SortError

    DB.RecordSource = "SELECT " & cmbTables.Text & ".* FROM " &
 cmbTables.Text & " ORDER BY [" & cmbFields.Text & "]"
    DB.Refresh

On Error GoTo 0
Exit Sub

SortError:
    If Err = 3117 Then
        MsgBox "Can't sort on a memo field"
        cmbFields.ListIndex = cmbFields.ListIndex + 1

        Resume
        End If
End Sub
```

9 The last thing to do is to make sure that you've got **BIBLIO.MDB** in the same path as the program, then run it. Up comes the form.

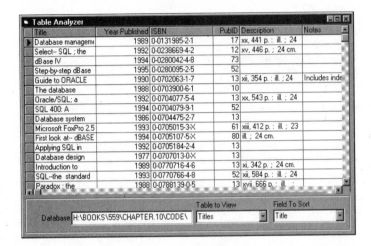

10 Click on the Table combo box and the new table is loaded into the grid, and at the same time the Fields combo box is filled with the field names from that Table. The completed project is on the disk as **DATAVIEW.VBP**.

Make sure that you save your finished program into the same folder as the Biblio database before you run it, so that **App.Path** returns the right path to the database.

How It Works

As you probably noticed, there's a bit of jumping through hoops going on here. The core of the problem is that all the interesting properties of the data control, like the RecordSource and DatabaseName properties, can't be read at run-time. Therefore, it's impossible to find out what the name of the current database is, and which tables are available in it. This makes our database browser somewhat hard to implement.

I've dealt with the problem in two ways.

> For the table names, I've just hardcoded the names into the program. There is just no way around this with the Standard Edition of Visual Basic. The code that does it is in the **Form-Load** event.

```
With cmbTables
    .AddItem "Titles"
    .AddItem "Publishers"
    .AddItem "Authors"
End With

cmbTables.TEXT = "Titles"
```

This makes the browser useless in the sense that you have to re-write the code for each database. Ugly.

> The way around not being able to read the field names from anywhere is to use the data bound grid to do the work for you. The grid automatically binds to each field in the specified table, and assigns the field names to its **Column.DataField** properties. By cycling through the columns collection of the grid we can pick up all these names and put them into the list box.

```
For Each objCurrentColumn In dbgDisplay.Columns
    cmbFields.AddItem objCurrentColumn.DataField
Next

cmbFields.TEXT = cmbFields.List(0)
```

We've used some tricky code here, and dived into object variables which we cover in the next chapter. However, the way the code is written makes it easy to see what's happening. We go through each of the column objects in the collections of columns that belong to the grid, and place its data field into the Fields combo box. At the end, we set the selected field to the first one in the list.

Changing the entry in the Fields list box causes the grid to be resorted on the selected field. The only snag is that you can't sort on memo fields in Jet as they are designed to hold free-form information. So we intercept the resulting error and move on the next field.

```
Private Sub cmbFields_Click()
```

```
On Error GoTo SortError

    DB.RecordSource = "SELECT " & cmbTables.Text & ".* FROM " &
⤷cmbTables.Text & " ORDER BY [" & cmbFields.Text & "]"
    DB.Refresh

On Error GoTo 0
Exit Sub

SortError:
    If Err = 3117 Then
        MsgBox "Can't sort on a memo field"
        cmbFields.ListIndex = cmbFields.ListIndex + 1

        Resume
        End If
End Sub
```

The only other interesting part of the code is that we chose to use the click event for each of the combo boxes. Intuitively, you would expect to use the change event to do something when a new item from the list is selected. However, the combo box change event is only activated when you add or delete an item from the list. The click event traps the new selection.

So, by going via the grid, we've at least found a way round the lack of field listing when using the data control. You could add the grid to the projects where you need a field list and make it invisible, keeping the field name list available for your code. However, the bound grid is a heavy control that uses a lot of memory and resources. I'm afraid the real answer is an upgrade to the Pro Edition if you're serious about database work.

Like the list and combo controls, there is an unbound version of the grid. I haven't covered it here as it's a complete dog with fleas. You have to write tons of code to do even the most basic things, and you know how I hate that. Also, 99.9% of all grids are used in database access, so the bound grid is all you need. Believe me.

Summary

It is its ability to manipulate data that has made Visual Basic so popular for business applications. This chapter has shown you how to present a lot of data to the user in an efficient, organized way. You've also learnt how the user can then interact intuitively with that data.

In this chapter you seen:

▶ How to use list and combo boxes.

▶ The difference between unbound and bound list controls.

▶ How to bind combo boxes to a database.

▶ The limitations of the data control.

Why Not Try.......

1 Add a country field to the Customers table of **ORDPRODB**. Make this field a number. Then create a Countries table in the database and list countries against ID numbers. Then add a combo box, bound or unbound, to the **ORDENT** form that will allow the user to choose a country name, and have the code insert the right ID number into the Customers table.

2 Create a form with a list box containing all the orders in the **ORDPRODB** database, sorted by order number. When the user double-clicks on an order, pop up a form showing the item ordered and the customer name and address.

3 Add a text box to the **DATAVIEW** project that shows the SQL statement that is currently being submitted to the database. Allow editing on the statement.

4 Adapt the order entry form to use the **BIBLIO** database, by assuming that the products are the books, and the customers are the authors.

5 Create a multiple choice greetings card using list boxes to select various realistic/rude/droll choices. For example, "Many "_____" From "_____" where the blanks are list boxes populated by options such as "Returns", "Beers", "Long, torrid nights", "Mom", "Big Boy" and "The Masked Avenger".

MDIFo

File   Edit

Form

Object Variables

Almost all the objects you've come across so far that make up the components of Visual Basic, such as controls and forms, can themselves be used as variables. This means you can write code that manipulates objects as well as data and, therefore, change the appearance and operation of your program as easily as changing a variable value.

It also allows you to write generic pieces of code - these accept objects as parameters in the same way it would accept regular variables. This makes for powerful programs.

In this chapter, you will learn:

▶ How to manipulate controls as you do variables.

▶ What kind of object variables are available.

▶ How you create arrays of objects.

▶ What an MDI application is.

▶ How to work with multiple forms in your applications.

Visual Basic and Objects

Really, everything you deal with in Visual Basic is an object. A form is an object, the screen is an object, there are even invisible objects such as the printer and application objects. Later, when you see how to create your own objects in Chapter 13, you'll see that even bits of code can be objects. So what do we mean by all this?

An object is a like a box that contains a bit of code which someone else has written. You can use this code in your own applications. The good thing is that you don't have to know what's going on inside the box to be able to use it - you just set the properties of the control and use its methods to make things happen. Programming Visual Basic is a process of choosing the right combination of objects (forms, controls, etc.) and linking them together with code to make a project.

So far in the book, we have generally just referred to controls and forms by the names we gave them at design-time. This is OK for simple programs, but it limits what you can do. You have seen how being able to refer to your data indirectly through variables makes your programs more flexible and adaptable. The same applies for objects. You can put an object inside a variable and refer to it by the name of the variable rather than the object, thus allowing you to use one piece of code for a number of different instances of a certain object type.

In this chapter we are going to look at how to create arrays of objects, how to copy objects into variables and how to pass objects as parameters to subprocedures and functions. We're also going to take a look at something Visual Basic calls collections, which are basically special arrays of objects.

Introducing Object Variables

Visual Basic lets you take control of objects in your code through special variables known as **object variables**. Using these you can:

- Create new controls at run-time.

- Copy controls to produce new **instances** of existing ones.

- Create duplicate forms, all with identical names, controls and code, but each containing and dealing with different data - much like the different documents you might have loaded in a Word session.

Object variables provide a way to write general routines that deal with specific controls. For example, you may have a text box validation routine that can only be used if you explicitly specify the name of the control in the code. If you want to make the routine independent, so that you can use it with any control, you can treat the control as an object variable. This makes your code much more transportable and, ultimately, more useful.

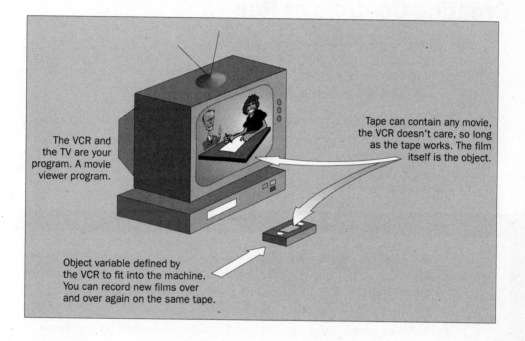

The VCR and the TV are your program. A movie viewer program.

Tape can contain any movie, the VCR doesn't care, so long as the tape works. The film itself is the object.

Object variable defined by the VCR to fit into the machine. You can record new films over and over again on the same tape.

Controls as Object Variables

Remember the chapter on menus? One of things we did back then was create a dynamic menu - a menu where the number of items grew each time we selected a file name. Menu items are controls, just like text boxes, command buttons, and so on. What we were actually doing back in Chapter 5 was creating dynamic controls, i.e. controls that only exist at run-time, not at design-time. The more files we opened, the bigger the array of objects became in the menu list. We were, in effect, creating instances of objects in the same way that we do with variables.

The ability to create controls dynamically can be extremely useful for applications where you need to create a great many controls of a similar type - for example, for a toolbar - but don't want the hassle of drawing them all by hand. Using object variables, you can even let your users create their own custom toolbars.

Creating Controls at Run-Time

The principles of creating controls on the fly are easy to follow. The simplest method is to create a control array at design-time, then extend that array with code at run-time. If you set the Index property of the first control to 0 at design-time, you can add other controls at run-time.

In the same way that you can alter the size of a normal variable array, you can extend and shrink control arrays. The difference is that you don't **Redim** a control array like you do a variable array. Instead, you have to **Load** new instances of the controls into the array. When you want to remove controls, you **Unload** them.

Creating Controls at Run-Time

Try It Out!

Let's put this into practice by creating a row of command buttons on a form. We'll just draw one command button at design-time and create the rest through code.

1 Start a new project and draw a small command button on the form.

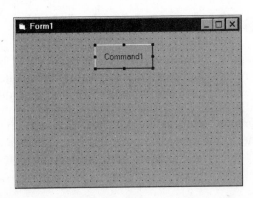

2 When you have created the command button, place 0 into its Index property. This creates a control array with just one control in it.

3 Type the following code in the click event for the command button:

```
Private Sub Command1_Click (Index As Integer)

  Static sNextOperation As String
  Dim nIndex As Integer

  For nIndex = 1 To 5

    If sNextOperation = "UNLOAD" Then
      Unload Command1(nIndex)
    Else
      Load Command1(nIndex)
      With Command1(nIndex)
        .Top = Command1(nIndex - 1).Top + Command1(nIndex - 1).Height
        .Caption = nIndex
        .Visible = True.Visible = True
      End With
    End If

  Next

  If sNextOperation = "UNLOAD" Then
    sNextOperation = "LOAD"
  Else
    sNextOperation = "UNLOAD"
  End If

End Sub
```

4 Run the code and click on the command button several times. Each time you click, five new buttons are either created or deleted. There is a copy of this program on the disk called **NEWCTRL.VBP**.

How It Works

The most important part of this code is the **For...Next** loop which actually creates and deletes the new command buttons.

```
For nIndex = 1 To 5

    If sNextOperation = "UNLOAD" Then
      Unload Command1(nIndex)
    Else
      Load Command1(nIndex)
      With Command1(nIndex)
         .Top = Command1(nIndex - 1).Top + Command1(nIndex - 1).Height
         .Caption = nIndex
         .Visible = True
      End With
    End If

  Next
```

First, the contents of the variable **sNextOperation** are checked to see whether we need to **Unload** or **Load** elements. The first time you press the command button, **sNextOperation** is set to **"LOAD"**. The array is then extended using **Load**. This takes the name of the initial command button as an argument, followed by the new index number in brackets. In our case, the index variable is **nIndex**, which is the counter for the loop:

```
Load Command1(nIndex)
```

Note that here we've called our index **nIndex**. You can call it whatever you like.

Once each new button has been created, the **Top** property is then set to position the new button directly below the previous one and a caption is put on the button showing its index number.

```
With Command1(nIndex)
        .Top = Command1(nIndex - 1).Top + Command1(nIndex - 1).Height
        .Caption = nIndex
        .Visible = True
    End With
```

Its Visible property is then set to true to make the buttons appear.

```
.Visible = True
```

By default, new controls created at run-time appear in exactly the same position as the original control and are invisible. Making them invisible at the start lets you move and re-size them without the user seeing what's happening. It also stops Windows having to redraw a load of controls, which can make the display appear quite messy while you're moving them about.

Once the loop has run five times and created the complete array, the **sNextOperation** variable is set to the opposite action. The first time round this means setting it to **"UNLOAD"**, so that the next time you press a command button, the array is unloaded.

```
If sNextOperation = "UNLOAD" Then
    sNextOperation = "LOAD"
  Else
    sNextOperation = "UNLOAD"
Endif
```

Control Array Events

The problem with the **Command1** control array that we just created is that, no matter which button you press, the same thing happens. From an event point of view, it appears that the control array is behaving as one big control. Of course, control arrays would be of purely cosmetic value if this was the end of the story. It isn't, though. Your code can tell which button in the array was pressed, allowing you to respond in different ways for different buttons.

The key lies in the declaration for the click event:

```
Private Sub Command1_Click (Index As Integer)
```

The parameter for the click event on a control array is the index of the control that was clicked.

We've already come across the index - we set it at design-time to create the original control array. We then referred to the individual command buttons using their position in the control array:

```
With Command1(nIndex)
```

The index of a control array works just as it does in a regular array, and again begins with zero for the first element.

Armed with this knowledge, we can now rewrite the `Command1_Click` event and make it more useful.

Handling Events for Control Array Members

Try It Out!

1 Load up the project **NEWCTRL.VBP** and bring up the command button click event.

2 Add the highlighted code to the event handler.

```
Private Sub Command1_Click(Index As Integer)

Static sNextOperation As String
   Dim nIndex As Integer

Select Case Index
    Case 0
        For nIndex = 1 To 5

            If sNextOperation = "UNLOAD" Then
              Unload Command1(nIndex)
            Else
              Load Command1(nIndex)
              With Command1(nIndex)
                  .Visible = True
                  .TOP = Command1(nIndex - 1).TOP + Command1(nIndex -
  1).Height
```

578

```
                  .Caption = nIndex
            End With
        End If

    Next

    If sNextOperation = "UNLOAD" Then
        sNextOperation = "LOAD"
    Else
        sNextOperation = "UNLOAD"
    End If
Case 1, 2, 3, 4, 5
    MsgBox "You pressed Button " & Index
End Select

End Sub
```

3 Now run the program. If you press the first command button, the rest are
created. If you click a newly created one, a message box pops up telling
you which button you clicked.

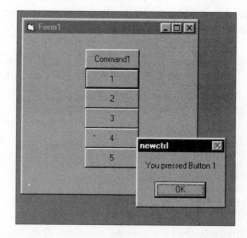

How It Works

This is really simple. All we did was to add a **Select Case** statement that
looks at the value of the index number that was passed to the event
handler. This tells us which key was pressed. All the buttons, except the
original one, are put into a handler that pops up the message box. **Select
Case** was just made for control arrays, believe me.

Managing Controls as Object Variables

Not only can you use objects as variables in arrays, you can also pass both object variables and object arrays to procedures as parameters. You may wonder why such an arcane sounding activity could be useful, but in fact it's a really powerful feature of Visual Basic.

Picture the scene: you have a form with thirty text boxes on it, each requiring a specific type of validation. Some must only accept numeric information, others only alphabetic information. Still others must be able to accept both, but also need to check that a certain number of characters is not exceeded.

Normally, this would mean three separate routines, one for each eventuality. There would be a line of code in each control's keypress event to pass the contents of the text box to a subprocedure for checking. The subprocedure would need to pass the information back and it may then need to be written into the **Text** property of the control. This can soon add up to a lot of code. The solution is to treat each text box as an object in itself and pass it to the central procedure. The easiest way to understand this is to see it in action.

A Text Box Validation Routine

Wouldn't it be great to have just one routine that you could call to do all your text box validation? Such a routine would automatically know what kind of data each text box needed and what length the data should be. It could automatically abandon key presses that break the rules. Object variables mean that all this is possible, and with surprisingly little code.

Text Box Validation

1 Load up the **VALIDATE.VBP** project.

2 Run it. Three text boxes appear on screen, one accepting only alphabetic characters, the second accepting only numbers and the third taking 4 characters of anything that's thrown at it. Try typing some things in.

3 Stop the program. We're not really interested in what the program does, but how it does it. Double-click on one of the text boxes and bring up the **KeyPress** routine in the Code Window. The three text boxes are in a control array and all call the **ValidateKeyPress** procedure as each key is pressed.

```
: frmMain                                                    _ □ ×
Object: (General)              ▼   Proc:  ValidateKeyPress              ▼
Private Sub ValidateKeyPress(txtControl As TextBox, nKeyAscii As Integer)

    Dim sMaxLength As String
    Dim sKey As String * 1

    ' first we need to ignore the special keys, such as Delete, or the cursor keys
    If nKeyAscii < 32 Or nKeyAscii > 126 Then Exit Sub

    ' Now we need to get the maximum length allowed in the text box
    sMaxLength = Right(txtControl.Tag, Len(txtControl.Tag) - 1)

    ' Since we know the maximum length of data allowed we can check what is in the text box
    ' and throw the keypress out if it means going over the limit.
    If Len(txtControl.Text) = Val(sMaxLength) Then
        Beep
        nKeyAscii = 0
        Exit Sub
    End If

    ' Assuming that the length of data will not be exceeded, does the keypress fit in with t
    ' kind of data allowed, ie numeric, alphabetic or anything else
    Select Case Left$(txtControl.Tag, 1)
```

4 Before we go on to analyze the code, bring up the Properties Windows for each of the text boxes and check out their Tag properties. There's a letter followed by a number. You don't have to be Einstein to work out that I'm using this property to determine the type and number of characters that can be entered. The question is how?

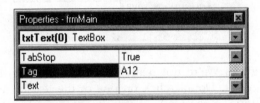

How It Works

The main part of this program is deceptively simple. Since all the validation code is held in a routine to which the text box is passed as an **object variable**, only one line of code is needed to handle the validation for all three text boxes.

The routine is called in the normal way with parameters. However, instead of passing a value or variable name as the parameter, you pass the name of a text box control, identified by its index number, and with it, the code of the key that was pressed.

```
Call ValidateKeyPress ( txtText(Index) , KeyAscii )
```

ValidateKeyPress is a form-level procedure. Find it by looking in the (General) section of the Code Window.

```
Private Sub ValidateKeyPress (txtControl As TextBox, nKeyAscii
↳As Integer)

    Dim sMaxLength As String
    Dim sKey As String * 1

    If nKeyAscii < 32 Or nKeyAscii > 126 Then Exit Sub

    sMaxLength = Right(txtControl.Tag, Len(txtControl.Tag) - 1)

    If Len(txtControl.Text) = Val(sMaxLength) Then
        Beep
        nKeyAscii = 0
        Exit Sub
    End If

    Select Case Left$(txtControl.Tag, 1)

        Case "A"
            sKey = UCase(Chr$(nKeyAscii))

            If Asc(sKey) < 65 Or Asc(sKey) > 90 Then
                Beep
                nKeyAscii = 0
                Exit Sub
            End If

        Case "9"
            If nKeyAscii < 48 Or nKeyAscii > 57 Then
                Beep
                nKeyAscii = 0
                Exit Sub
            End If

    End Select

End Sub
```

The first line of the routine accepts the parameters from the calling statement. Here `txtControl` is our object variable and we've assigned the key press code to `nKeyAscii`.

```
Private Sub ValidateKeyPress (txtControl As TextBox, nKeyAscii As Integer)
```

It is declared in the same way as any other variable, except that it is declared as a `TextBox` object. We'll cover exactly how to give these kind of objects their proper names later in the chapter.

The second parameter is the `KeyAscii` parameter given to you in the keypress event. Since I've missed out the `ByVal` keyword here, the parameter is passed by reference. Setting it to 0 at any point in the code, which we will do, means that the original `KeyAscii` variable will be reset to 0, which in a keypress event has the effect of canceling the key pressed.

Passing by reference means that the `KeyAscii` variable that we are dealing with in this procedure is the actual one that the system looks at, as opposed to a copy. If you change it, it will remain changed when you use it elsewhere. We'll cover this in more detail in the next chapter.

The way the routine works centers around the `Tag` property of the text box. This is a property you can assign any string value to, as Visual Basic itself doesn't use it. You can, therefore, adapt it for your own purposes. Here, its use is as a general purpose private label on a control.

The `Tag` property tells us what kind of data should be placed in each text box. It doesn't actually control anything itself - it's just a label. If you look through the `Tag` properties of the text boxes, you'll see they are all set up in a similar way. The first character defines what type of data can be accepted - A means alphabetic data only, 9 means numeric, and anything else means, well, anything else! The numbers that follow it determine the maximum characters the text box can accept.

You can easily change the format of the data that a text box accepts - just bring up the Properties Window and change the `Tag` property.

The `ValidateKeypress` code uses the `Tag` property of the text box object variable together with the `nKeyAscii` parameter to determine exactly which key was pressed and whether the key is valid. `nKeyAscii` is the parameter that is passed to us and we then use it as a local variable in the procedure.

The first stage of the program checks **nKeyAscii** for special keys (such as *BkSp* or the arrow keys) and if one of them was pressed, then that key is not checked and is allowed to pass:

```
If nKeyAscii < 32 or nKeyAscii > 126 Then Exit Sub
```

After this line, the code is certain that it's got a keypress which needs to be checked.

The next line places the numbers from the back end of the **Tag** property into the variable **sMaxLength**. This is done using the **Right** function to return all but the first character in the **Tag** property:

```
sMaxLength = Right(txtControl.Tag, Len(txtControl.Tag) - 1)
```

Once we've determined the maximum length of the data in the text box, a check is made to see if we're already at this limit.

```
If Len(txtControl.Text) = val(sMaxLength) Then
```

If we are at the limit, then the **nKeyAscii** value is set to 0. Since this parameter is passed to the procedure by reference, the 0 is automatically fed back into **KeyAscii** in the keypress event. This, effectively, cancels the keypress.

The remaining code just checks whether the keys pressed are valid for the text box, basing the check on the **Tag** property. For example, if the **Tag** property is set to **95**, indicating that you can only enter numbers (and only a 5 digit number), then the **Select Case** statement will reject alphabetic or punctuation keys.

If you plan to use the routine in your own code, bear in mind that it is supposed to be called from a keypress event, so each key is checked as it's typed.

Declaring Object Variables

You declare an object variable **explicitly** in the same way that you would a regular variable, by stating the type of control it is. For example, to declare an object variable as **TextBox** (one of the explicit object variable types that Visual Basic recognizes), you write:

```
Dim txtControl as TextBox
```

Although your code is undoubtedly more efficient, and usually runs faster, if you declare object variables explicitly, Visual Basic will also let you declare an object variable **implicitly**, by simply saying that a variable name relates to a **Control**. For example:

```
Dim ctlControl As Control
```

Function and subroutine parameters can be declared in this way. This enables you to pass any control you like to them at run-time. Visual Basic provides a special clause for the **If...Then** statement which allows you to check the type of control an object variable relates to. This is the **TypeOf** statement. We'll take a look at this in more detail in just a moment.

Types of Object Variables

TextBox is just one of the explicit object variable types that Visual Basic recognizes. The others are:

CheckBox	ComboBox	CommandButton	MDIForm
Data	DirListBox	DriveListBox	FileListBox
Grid	Frame	HScrollBar	Image
Label	Line	ListBox	Menu
OptionButton	OLE	PictureBox	Shape
TextBox	Timer	VScrollBar	Form

These are the standard objects. If you add more controls, then they too can be used as object variables. You may recognize the above as the names that Visual Basic places next to the names that you give your controls in the combo box at the top of the Properties Window:

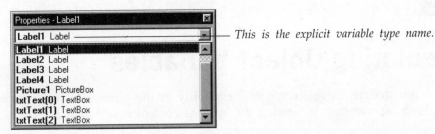

— *This is the explicit variable type name.*

Explicit vs Implicit Declaration

Implicit declaration is easier but has distinct drawbacks:

▶ Your code is harder to understand.

▶ Visual Basic has less chance of trapping errors.

▶ It's a lot slower.

Your code is harder to understand because you tell future readers of your code less about what's going on. Picture the situation where you have a function that validates data. If you simply declare the object parameter at the head of the function as a `Control`, it can be very confusing. The reader can't tell straight off whether you are validating records in a data control, in text boxes, in combo boxes or the latest hi-tech widget from Visual Basic Add-ons Inc.

Declaring variables explicitly can make debugging easier; this is definitely true for object variables. If you declare an object as a specific type, such as a `TextBox`, Visual Basic automatically knows which properties are valid for that `TextBox`.

For example, if you declare the object variable `ctlControl` implicitly as a generic `Control`, rather than as a `TextBox`, then Visual Basic will allow you to enter the following line of code:

```
ctlControl.Peter = "Some Text"
```

Visual Basic won't spot the error until your program runs. The line may be in a function or a piece of code that you missed in testing, and there's nothing more embarrassing than having a user ring up to tell you that the run-time Visual Basic DLL is reporting syntax errors.

Visual Basic only checks the properties of a generic `Control` object at run-time, whereas with explicit controls, it reports property errors at compile-time.

As for the difference in speed, the best way to appreciate it is to try it.

Comparing Implicit and Explicit Declarations

1 Load up the **CTRLTIME.VBP** project and run it.

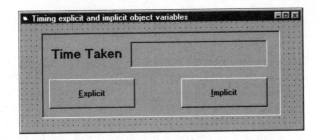

2 When the form appears on screen, click on the Explicit command button. The program shows the time taken to assign 10,000 different captions to the command button. The routine it uses to do this accepts the command button as an explicitly declared object variable.

3 Now click on the Implicit command button. This does the same thing, only this time the command button is declared implicitly as an object variable.

If you try this, you will see that the implicit click is slower than the explicit one; the difference isn't massive - it's perhaps 10% slower - but if your career is riding on a big application, that's a lifetime.

How It Works

The two command buttons have very similar click events:

First, **varTime** is set to the start time. The central loop then calls the **Time_Implicit** or **Time_Explicit** procedure 10,000 times, passing the command button and the loop counter as parameters.

The real difference is in the way the command button is accepted in the two subprocedures. In one, we accept **cmdCommand** explicitly as a **CommandButton**.

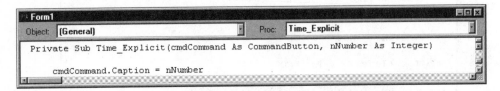

```
Form1                                                    _ □ ×
Object: (General)                    Proc: Time_Explicit
    Private Sub Time_Explicit(cmdCommand As CommandButton, nNumber As Integer)

        cmdCommand.Caption = nNumber
```

Whereas, in the other, we accept it implicitly as a **Control**.

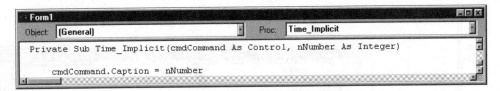

```
Form1                                                    _ □ ×
Object: (General)                    Proc: Time_Implicit
    Private Sub Time_Implicit(cmdCommand As Control, nNumber As Integer)

        cmdCommand.Caption = nNumber
```

Once the loop has run the subprocedure 10,000 times, we reset the caption and work out the time elapsed between **Now** and the start time in **varTime**.

The Controls Collection

Every form in your application has something known as a **controls collection** built in. This is like an array which you can use at run-time to gain access to the controls on a form, without having to know the name of each one, or even what type of control it is. It differs from the control array we used earlier in that it's built in to Visual Basic. You don't have to declare it and all the controls on the form are automatically part of it. Visual Basic assembles and maintains it as you design the form.

The elements of a controls collection are accessed in the same way that you access the elements of a normal array.

The controls collection is useful for data entry forms. You can write a generic routine to go through a controls collection looking for data controls and change their database properties to point to the appropriate path and file name for the customer's database.

The Controls Property

You can gain access to the controls collection through the `Controls` property of the form. This isn't something you can get at through the Properties Window - you need to do it through code. The `Controls` property is actually an array, where each element of the array is a single control; element 0 is the first control on the form, element 1 is the second, and so on.

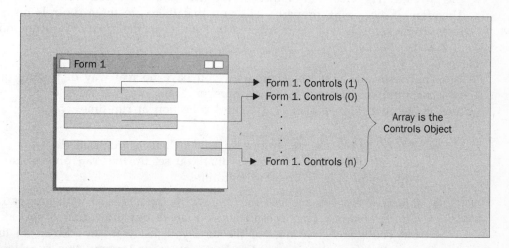

If you had a simple form with only two text boxes on it, you could change the `Text` property of each with this code:

```
Form1.Controls(0).Text = "Control 0"
Form1.Controls(1).Text = "Control 1"
```

The general format for this is:

```
<form_name>.controls( <number> ).<property> = <a value>
```

To really make this feature useful, we need to know how many elements there are in a controls collection and be able to identify the individual elements of a controls collection.

Identifying Controls on the Form

The **Controls** array has a property of its own called **Count**. This lets you know how many controls are on the form. Be careful, though, if you use this in code. The elements of the control array are numbered from 0. Therefore, if the **Count** property tells you that there are three controls on a form, these controls will be numbered 0, 1 and 2 in the **Controls** array, not 1, 2 and 3.

Unfortunately, until you run a program you have no real way of finding out which control corresponds to which number. There are two ways of identifying specific members of a control collection at run-time.

▶ You can check the **Tag** property as you loop through all the elements. This method requires that you set up the **Tag** properties with unique identifiers at design-time.

▶ Alternatively, you can use the **TypeOf** method to deal with groups of similar controls. This doesn't let you single out individual controls, but you'll find that most of the time you just want to address all the controls of a certain type. The best way to understand this is to look at some code:

```
For nControlNo = 0 to Form1.Controls.Count - 1

    If TypeOf Form1.Controls( nControlNo ) Is TextBox then
    :
    :
    EndIf

Next
```

Here, we loop through each of the members of the controls collection on `Form1` up to the last control, `Count-1`. For each control we use `TypeOf` to check whether or not it's a `TextBox`.

Using For Each...Next With Collections

In the last bit of code we used a somewhat clunky way of cycling through the controls in the controls collection - referencing their index numbers. You can do this more elegantly using the `For Each...Next` construct:

```
For Each objControl in Form1.Controls
    If TypeOf objControl Is TextBox then
:
:
    EndIf

Next
```

This is much cooler and more intuitive.

Now let's get down to business.

Changing Colors Remotely

A common facility in today's applications enables users to decide what colors they want to see on the screen. Control arrays let you change the colors of controls throughout a form. And that's exactly what the program **CTRLARRY.VBP** does.

1 Load up **CTRLARRY.VBP** and run it.

593

2 Choose which type of control you want to change the colors on by clicking the appropriate check box. Then press either the <u>B</u>ackground or <u>F</u>oreground command button. The color dialog comes up:

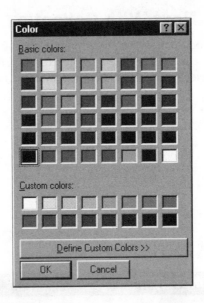

3 Choose a color and the controls change on the form.

How It Works

Let's take a look at the code behind the <u>B</u>ackground command button:

```
For Each FormControl In frmMain.Controls


        If TypeOf FormControl Is TextBox And chkTextBoxes.Value = 1
↳Then FormControl.BackColor = nColor

        If TypeOf FormControl Is Frame And chkFrames.Value = 1
↳Then FormControl.BackColor = nColor

        If TypeOf FormControl Is Label And chkLabels.Value = 1
↳Then FormControl.BackColor = nColor

        If TypeOf FormControl Is CheckBox And
↳chkCheckBoxes.Value = 1 Then FormControl.BackColor = nColor

Next
```

There is a little more code than this in the actual program. This is in order to display a colors common dialog and store the selected color in the **nColor** variable.

The code uses a **For Each...Next** loop to move through each control on the form using its controls collection and places each element into the **FormControl** object variable, which was declared above this code at the start of the procedure. The **If TypeOf** statement then checks the type of the control. There are actually four of these tests, one for each type of control that the program is interested in: **TextBox**, **Label**, **CheckBox** and **Frame**.

There is an interesting point to note about the **If TypeOf** statement - whereas, normally, we would use the = sign with an **If** statement, you must use the **Is** keyword when dealing with **TypeOf**.

VB4 permits an extended **If** statement with **TypeOf** - a great improvement over VB3.

Once a matching control has been found, a second `If` statement is used to see if the appropriate check box is set, i.e. if it is one of the controls the user wants to set the colors on. If it is set, then the `BackColor` property is loaded with the color selected from the common dialog:

```
frmMain.Controls(nControlNo).BackColor = nColor
```

There are literally hundreds of uses for the `Controls` array, such as setting a user-defined font on all controls.

We're now going to move on and look at two areas of Visual Basic application development where object variables are essential: toolbars and MDI forms. First - toolbars.

Using Objects to Create Toolbars

It's standard procedure for Windows applications to provide users with a way of customizing toolbars, so that they can add and remove items at their leisure. How can such a feat be accomplished in Visual Basic? With the Professional and Enterprise editions of Visual Basic, it's easy - they both have ribbon button controls which are ideally suited to creating toolbars. However, in the good old Standard Edition, we have to find a workaround, which of course involves object variables.

By now you know the basics of how to create controls at run-time. You've already worked through an example that creates command buttons on the fly. Creating toolbars is only a small step away.

The first hurdle is the Visual Basic command button. Toolbars consist of graphical commands which show a small icon, rather than a caption. Visual Basic command buttons are no help here since they can't, under any circumstances, display graphics. To create a toolbar in Visual Basic, you need to look to the image control.

Try It Out!

Creating a Toolbar

As well as being able to display graphics, the image control can respond to mouse events like `MouseDown` and `MouseUp`. To create a toolbar using image controls, we need to add some code to the `MouseDown` event so that it will load up an image of a button that's depressed. As far as the user is concerned, the image control is actually a button. The **MouseUp** event contains code to restore the picture of the button in the up position.

1 Load up the **TOOLBAR.VBP** project and run it.

2 Select the Options menu. A separate form appears in which you can select check boxes to indicate which icons should appear on the toolbar.

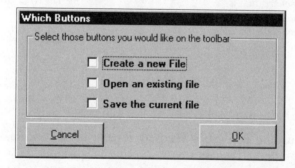

3 Click on the Open an existing file check box, then click OK. The options form vanishes, leaving you with the main form and a button on the toolbar.

4 The new button is part of a control array of images (not buttons) that is created by the program as it's needed. Try clicking on the button and holding the mouse down - the image changes as you would expect.

Mouse up   *Mouse down*

FYI Remember that this is an image not a command button. A graphic wouldn't normally change as a result of you clicking on it - there is code in the background that's doing all that stuff for you. You have to create an image file that looks like a command button.

5 Stop the program and take a look at the main form again. There are two forms in this project - the main one is called **TOOLBAR.FRM**.

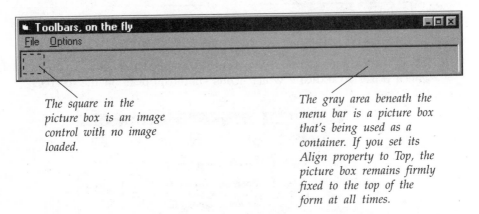

The square in the picture box is an image control with no image loaded.

The gray area beneath the menu bar is a picture box that's being used as a container. If you set its Align property to Top, the picture box remains firmly fixed to the top of the form at all times.

6 Bring up the Properties Window for the image and take a look at the Index property. I've set this to 0. This tells Visual Basic that although this is the only image control on the form, it's going to be part of a control array.

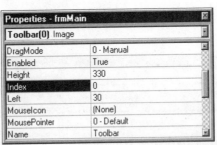

7 You can bring up the options form by displaying the Project Window and clicking on **TBOPTION.FRM**. Double-click the OK button to see the code that creates the control array at run-time:

```
Private Sub cmdOK_Click ()

    Dim nButtonNo As Integer

    For nButtonNo = 1 To gnButtons
        Unload frmMain.Toolbar(nButtonNo)
    Next

    gnButtons = 0

    For nButtonNo = 0 To 2

     If chkOptions(nButtonNo).Value = 1 Then
       gnButtons = gnButtons + 1
       Load frmMain.Toolbar(gnButtons)
       frmMain.Toolbar(gnButtons).Tag = chkOptions(nButtonNo).Tag
       frmMain.Toolbar(gnButtons).Top = frmMain.Toolbar(0).Top
       frmMain.Toolbar(gnButtons).Left = frmMain.Toolbar(gnButtons -
 1).Left + frmMain.Toolbar(gnButtons - 1).Width
         Call LoadImage(frmMain.Toolbar(gnButtons), "up")
         frmMain.Toolbar(gnButtons).Visible = True
       End If
     Next

     Unload frmOptions

End Sub
```

How It Works - Clearing the Toolbar

Don't panic! It's nowhere near as bad as it looks. The first thing the code does is **Unload** all the image controls on the toolbar with the exception of the button we saw at design-time. It does this with a **For** loop, going from **1** to the number of buttons on the toolbar. A global variable, **gnButtons**, defined in a separate module (**TOOLBAR.BAS**), holds a count of the number of visible buttons on the toolbar.

In order to make sure that the toolbar is rebuilt correctly, we first unload all the existing buttons.

```
For nButtonNo = 1 To gnButtons

    Unload frmMain.Toolbar(nButtonNo)

Next

gnButtons = 0
```

Having unloaded the images, `gnButtons` is reset back to 0, meaning that there are no visible buttons on the toolbar.

How It Works - Creating the Buttons

The second loop actually creates the buttons themselves. Each check box on the options form is also part of a control array, so the second loop just loops through these check boxes trying to find which ones have a value of 1 (meaning they've been selected).

```
For nButtonNo = 0 To 2

    If chkOptions(nButtonNo).Value = 1 Then
```

When a selected check box has been found, 1 is added to the global variable that holds a count of the number of buttons:

```
gnButtons = gnButtons + 1
```

The new button is then created using the `Load` command:

```
Load frmMain.Toolbar(gnButtons)
```

Now the confusing bit. At run-time, how do the new buttons know which image to display, or which menu code should be run when they are clicked? The answer lies in the `Tag` property.

```
frmMain.Toolbar(gnButtons).Tag = chkOptions(nButtonNo).Tag
```

Each check box on the options form has its `Tag` property set up with a number, which indicates the menu option to call when a button is pressed, and the name of a graphic file.

Properties - frmOptions	☒
chkOptions(1) CheckBox	

Name	chkOptions
TabIndex	2
TabStop	True
Tag	1 Open
Top	795
Value	0 - Unchecked
Visible	True
WhatsThisHelpID	0

When the new buttons are created, the code copies the check box's **Tag** property into the new button's **Tag** property. Here, **gnButtons** is the name of the global variable which is counting the buttons and **nButtonNo** is the index variable used in the **For Loop**.

How It Works - Displaying the Buttons

The remaining lines of code in the loop position the button directly to the right of the previous one and make the new image control visible.

```
        frmMain.Toolbar(gnButtons).Top = frmMain.Toolbar(0).Top
        frmMain.Toolbar(gnButtons).Left = frmMain.Toolbar(gnButtons -
 1).Left + frmMain.Toolbar(gnButtons - 1).Width
```

A call is also made to a routine called **LoadImage**, which is defined in **TOOLBAR.BAS**. This routine loads the images of the buttons into the image controls.

```
Call LoadImage(frmMain.Toolbar(gnButtons), "up")
```

When the subprocedure is called, you need to pass a suffix to it, either **"up"** or **"dn"**. This determines which version of the button image - up or down - is displayed.

You can view the code for this routine by pressing *F2* to bring up the object browser. This displays a list of all the files in the project containing code. Click on TOOLBAR1 to list the procedures in that module, and then just select LoadImage and click the Show button.

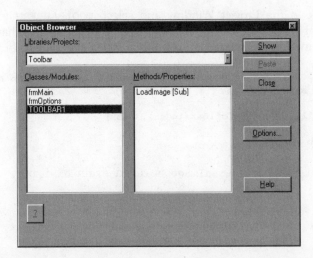

How It Works - The LoadImage Procedure

The **LoadImage** procedure is as follows:

```
Public Sub LoadImage (imgControl As Control, sSuffix As String)

    Dim sFileName As String

    sFileName = Mid$(imgControl.Tag, 3, Len(imgControl.Tag) - 2)
    sFileName = app.Path & "\" & sFileName & sSuffix & ".bmp"

    imgControl.Picture = LoadPicture(sFileName)

End Sub
```

The code pulls the file name out of the image control's **Tag** property and uses the **LoadPicture** function to load the graphic in. The names of the images in the **Tag** property have been kept fairly simple: **Open**, **Save** and **New**. Remember that this routine is global and can be used to display the images for both the button up and the button down.

The suffix ("**up**" or "**dn**") that is passed to the subprocedure is added on to the end of the file name, along with "**.bmp**" to get a full file name. For example, if the name of the graphic in the **Tag** property is **Open**, and the routine is called with an **sSuffix** parameter of "**dn**", then the graphic that is loaded is **Opendn.bmp**.

The files **openup.bmp**, **opendn.bmp**, **saveup.bmp** and so on were installed from the accompanying disk, along with the example programs.

Go back to the Project Window and select **TOOLBAR.FRM** from the list. Have a look at the **Toolbar_MouseDown** event code. This is what occurs when the user points at an image control and presses the mouse button down.

```
Private Sub Toolbar_MouseDown (index As Integer, Button As Integer, Shift
 As Integer, X As Single, Y As Single)

    Call LoadImage(Toolbar(index), "dn")

End Sub
```

When this happens, **LoadImage** is called again to display the button down image.

How It Works - Adding Menu Code

That takes care of how the images are actually drawn. However, there's still something missing. When you click an image in the actual program, the image calls the appropriate menu routine. For example, if you put an open image on the toolbar and click it, a message box pops up from the File/Open menu click code.

As with most other elements of this program, the menus are all defined as part of a control array. The **Tag** property contains the **Index** number of the menu item to which the graphic relates, as well as the name of the graphic. When you click an image control, the image simply calls the menu array's click code, passing it the **Index** number of the menu item that it wants to run from the image's **Tag** property.

```
Private Sub Toolbar_Click (index As Integer)

    Call mnuFItems_Click(Val(Left(Toolbar(index).Tag, 1)))

End Sub
```

The **Tag** property is actually holding a string in the form of a number, followed by a space, followed by a file name. Therefore, **Val** is used to get the actual value of the number. **Left** is also used to make sure that we pull the value of the first character in the **Tag** property and nothing else.

There you have it, a whirlwind guide to user-definable toolbars, courtesy of control arrays and object variables!

MDI Applications

All the applications we have looked at so far are what Microsoft call **SDI (Single Document Interface)** applications. It's a fairly hefty name for a simple concept. All the forms in the applications we've written so far are independent of each other. They can be re-sized to whatever size your users want, moved in front of or behind other applications, and so on.

It doesn't take very long before an SDI application with multiple visible forms begins to look confusing. Where did I put that customer entry form? Oh yes, it's over there behind Word for Windows, but in front of the order entry form!

An **MDI (Multiple Document Interface)** tidies up these kinds of applications. Again, it's a hefty name for a simple concept. In MDI you have one large MDI form (a **parent** form) which acts as a container for all the other forms in your program. The MDI form acts like a virtual form - windows are displayed inside it (called **child** forms) and these can't be moved outside of the MDI form. They can only be maximized to the same size as the MDI form and, when minimized, appear as an icon on the MDI form, not on Windows itself.

If you have used other Windows packages, for example Microsoft Word or any of the other components of the Microsoft Office suite, then this will be a concept that you have come across before - probably without even thinking about it.

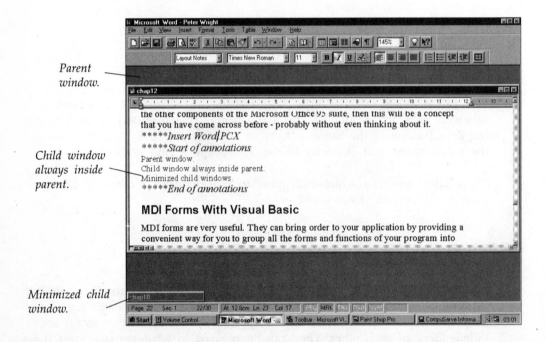

Parent window.

Child window always inside parent.

Minimized child window.

MDI Forms with Visual Basic

MDI forms are very useful. They can bring order to your application by providing a convenient way for you to group all the forms and functions of your program into one big container window. However, despite its power, MDI under Visual Basic does have some limitations. Let's explore some of them now.

Limitations of an MDI Form

1 Start a new project and from the Insert menu, select MDI Form.

2 After a short pause an MDI parent form will appear.

3 Let's put some controls onto the form. Select a command button from the toolbox and try to draw it on the form. Nothing happens.

Try It Out!

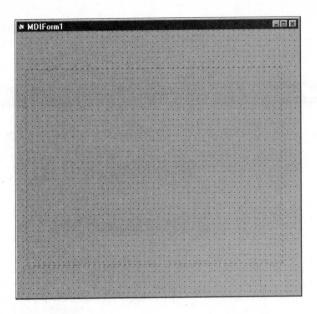

MDI forms can only have picture box controls drawn on them, or in the Professional Edition, 3D-Panels.

The general rule is that only controls that have an **Align** property can be placed on an MDI parent form. On a different note, though, a welcome improvement on Visual Basic 3 is that you can now change the **BackColor** property of an MDI form. Previously this could only be accomplished with some pretty hairy API calls.

4 Select the picture box from the tool palette and draw that on the form.

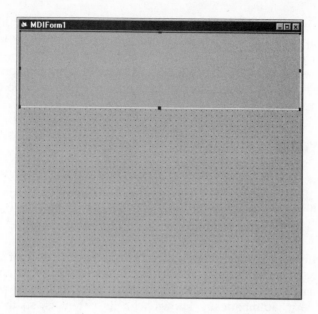

The box automatically sits at the top of the form and assumes the same width as the form. Picture boxes on an MDI form are always attached to one side of the form - you can change the side by altering the Align property..

5 Now go to the Insert menu again and try to create a second MDI form. The MDI Form option is disabled. You can only have one MDI form per application.

Despite these apparent limitations, MDI applications really *are* worth the effort. Imagine what a Windows word processor would be like if you could only open one document at a time and these couldn't share the same menu structure or toolbar. The bottom line is that MDI applications look good, are comfortable for your users to use and are an all-round good idea for many types of application.

Child Forms

When you start to use MDI forms, the other normal forms in your program refuse to fit within the MDI frame. They still float about on their own, happily disrupting the overall karma of windows. You need to tell a form that it is a child form before it will start to behave itself.

Luckily, this is a simple process. The **MDIChild** property of a form can be set to either true or false to tell it that it now belongs to an MDI form. Since Visual Basic only allows you to have one MDI form per application, the child form automatically knows who its parent is, so that when the program runs, it stays within the confines of the MDI form. At design-time, though, the child form is as free-floating as ever - there's no visible way to tell the difference between a child form and a normal independent form at design-time, other than by checking the form's **MDIChild** property.

Although you can view and set the **MDIChild** property at design-time, the property is strictly off-limits at run-time. Try setting it to true or false in your code and you'll get an error from Visual Basic before your program crashes.

Child Forms in Action

Let's see all this in action.

1 Load up the **MDICHILD.VBP** application, but don't run it yet. Select the MDImain1 form from the Project Window to display it.

2 The form has a File menu which contains just two items: New and Exit.

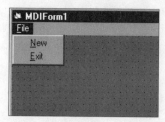

3 Now display the other form, frmChild. This also has a menu bar, but with more options on it.

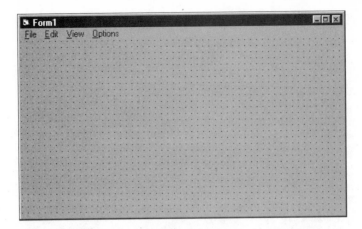

4 Run the program. When the MDI form comes into view, it has no child windows, so it displays and uses its own menu structure. If you select the <u>N</u>ew menu option from the <u>F</u>ile menu, the child form is displayed.

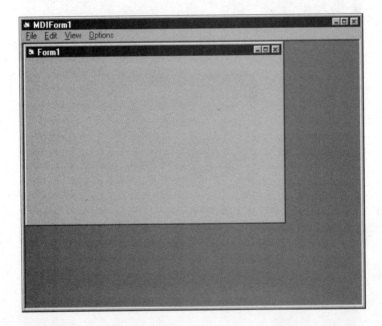

When the child form comes into view, the menu structure of the MDI form changes: it becomes the menu structure of the child window.

How It Works

To put this little project together, all I did was create the menu structures on the parent and child forms and add one line of code. This is in the <u>F</u>ile <u>N</u>ew menu of the parent form.

```
Private Sub mnuFNew_Click()

    Load frmChild

End Sub
```

Once the child window is loaded, you have to shut it down using the title bar control box. Then the parent menus are reinstated.

Closing Child Windows

Child windows can't be hidden. If you want to remove a child window from view, you must move it behind another child window, minimize it so that an icon for it appears on the MDI form, or unload it using the `Unload` command.

You may wonder why Microsoft decided to take this approach to child windows. What do you do if you have variables in the form which contain information you wish to keep, but you need to remove the form from the display? Doesn't `Unload`ing remove the form along with the code and the form's variables?

In fact, it doesn't. Any `Static` variables you have in the form are kept in memory. Next time the form is loaded, the `Static` variables are maintained This allows you to continue from where you left off.

Instances of Forms

The above example only lets you load one child form onto an MDI form. This isn't very useful if you are developing the next Excel.

This is where form **instances** come into play. Using object variables you can create multiple copies, or instances, of a form. Each copy of the form has exactly the same controls on it and an identical menu structure, but each can hold different data. Although the code and the variable and control names it contains are identical, the actual data each form deals with is stored in a different place in your PC's memory. You had a feeling that MDI forms had something to do with object variables, didn't you?

New Form Instances

Try It Out!

Let's put this into action.

1 Stop the **MDICHILD.VBP** project and, using the Project Window, select the MDI form itself - MDImain1.

2 Select <u>N</u>ew from the MDI form's <u>F</u>ile menu. At present, the code looks like this:

```
Private Sub mnuFNew_Click ()

    Load frmChild

End Sub
```

3 We can create instances of the **frmChild** window using an object variable. Change the code so that it looks like this:

```
Private Sub mnuFNew_Click()

    Dim OurNewForm As New frmChild
    OurNewForm.Show

End Sub
```

4 Back in the Project Window, select the child window. When the window appears, bring up the menu editor and delete all the menu items. This will make the code a little less complicated for now.

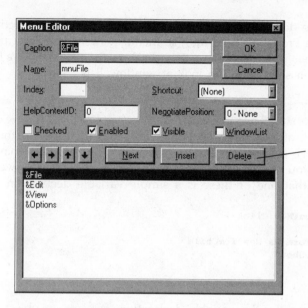

Click on the Delete button four times to remove all the menu items.

5 When all the child form's menus have gone, run the program and select New from the MDI form's File menu. Do it again, and again, and again - each time a new child window is created:

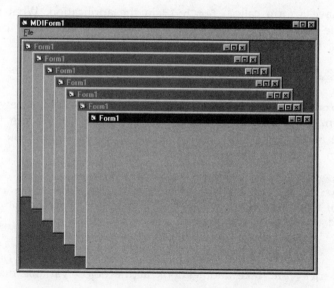

6 When you're done playing, stop the program. Save it by selecting Save File As and Save Project As from the File menu. Rename both the form and the project so that you can always come back to the originals. We'll use the new files in a short while to look at window lists.

How It Works

Firstly, let's look at how the new forms are created. Bring up the Code Window and take a look at the click event for **mnuFNew**. You may be surprised that you only had to type two lines of code in the event procedure and that one of these is a simple variable declaration.

```
Private Sub mnuFNew_Click()

    Dim OurNewForm As New frmChild
    OurNewForm.Show

End Sub
```

The first line of code, the variable declaration, sets up an object variable for a **New** form. The form in this case is the child form called **frmChild**. Confusing, isn't it! We created new command buttons in the same way earlier on in the chapter.

We already have a form called **frmChild** in the application. What we want to do is create new copies of it. These new copies all have their own data and variables, but share the same event code:

```
Dim OurNewForm As New frmChild
```

So, **OurNewForm** is actually an object variable set up to hold a new **frmChild** form. Once the object variable has been set up, we can treat it just the same as any other form. The command **OurNewForm.Show** shows our new form on the screen.

Another way to look at this is to think of **OurNewForm** as being a variable of type **frmChild**. It, therefore, inherits the properties of **frmChild**.

Now for the tricky bit. Take another look at the object variable declaration:

```
Dim OurNewForm As New frmChild
```

It's a simple **Dim**, so that means that the object variable is a local variable - as soon as the subroutine finishes, so does the life of the variable. But why does the form you've just created stay in existence?

What we've done here is create an object variable for a new form. If you destroy the object variable, you just destroy the variable itself, **not the new form that was created**. So how do you refer to the new form and the controls on it in your code?

Addressing Your New Form or Talking to Me

Since we now have an application that could theoretically display ten identically named forms, Visual Basic kindly gives us a special keyword called **Me** which can be used in your code to refer to the currently active form.

A line of code that says

```
Me.txtEmployee.Text = "Peter Wright"
```

sets the **Text** property of a text box called **txtEmployee** on the current active form. In the same way, if you need to unload the form from inside one of its events, just type **Unload Me**.

I had great problems with this when I first started learning VB. It seems too easy and logical to be right, but believe me it's fine! The key is to remember that, in an MDI application, you can only have one active form. Therefore, you don't need an array to be able to reference the child forms. The only one you can do anything with is the one that's currently active.

Creating Window List Menus

Once you start dealing with MDI forms and child windows, things can get very out of hand on your screen. Your user can get lost in a sea of similar looking child windows, not knowing which is which, or where the first form they created has gone to.

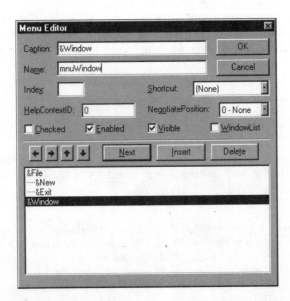

Visual Basic provides a simple way of dealing with this problem - the **Window List Menu.**

Try It Out - Creating a Window List Menu

Try It Out!

1 Load up the changed version of **MDICHILD.VBP** that you saved from the earlier example. (What do you mean you didn't save it? - lucky there's a copy on the disk for you called **MDICHLD1.VBP**.) When the project has loaded, bring up the main form and invoke the menu editor.

2 Create a <u>W</u>indow menu on the main MDI form that is not indented under the other menu items:

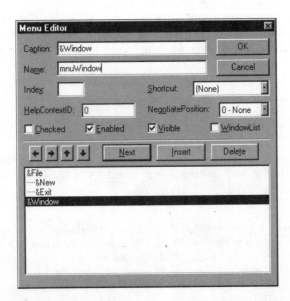

3 Create another item underneath this and set the Caption to &List and the name to mnuWList.

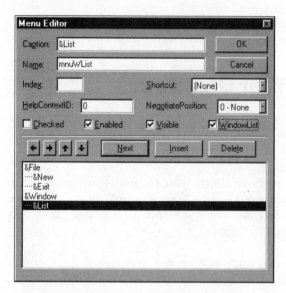

4 Click on the WindowList check box as I've done here. Also, make sure that the new menu item is indented underneath the Window menu.

5 Finally, press OK to accept the new menu structure and then run the program.

6 Create a few child windows using the File/New menu item on the main MDI form. Now go to the new Window menu and select the List item. A list of all the child forms in the application appears, with the active window marked with a checkmark.

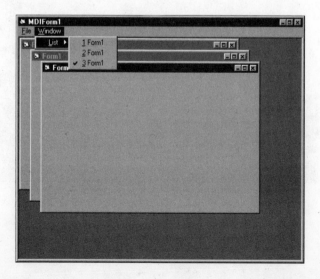

7 If you select any of the items on this list, then that form becomes the current active form. Pretty neat, huh? No code involved!

Arranging Your Desktop

WindowList is just one of a number of time saving features of Visual Basic that you have at your disposal when dealing with MDI applications. Another is the **Arrange** method.

The **Arrange** method allows you to give your users features similar to those on the Window menu of an Office 95 application. Using **Arrange**, you can tile and cascade child windows and arrange the child window icons in a neat and orderly fashion.

Load up the **MDICHLD2.VBP** project and run it. Play around with the new items on the Window menu to see how they work. (Don't forget to create some child windows first.)

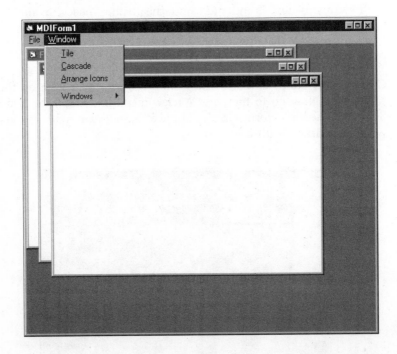

Different Window Arrangements

The `Arrange` method is very easy to use. Simply type the name of the MDI form, in our case `frmMDI`, in front of the `Arrange` method. Then, after the word `Arrange`, type one of the parameter options which govern how the forms are arranged.

The options you have for the `Arrange` parameter are as follows:

Value	VB Constant	What It Does
0	vbCASCADE	Cascades all open MDI child forms from the top left to the bottom right of the screen.
1	vbTILEHORIZONTAL	Tiles all open MDI child forms side by side across the screen.
2	vbTILEVERTICAL	Tiles all open MDI child forms above and below each other, down the screen.
3	vbARRANGEICONS	Lines up the icons of any minimized child forms.

The first three actions also affect any child forms you may have minimized. Although the results are not immediately visible, they can be seen as soon as the child form is re-sized.

To see the above options in use, take a look at the click event for the Window menu Arrange Icons item from the `MDICHLD2.VBP` project.

Summary

It may not appear so to you straight away, but in the Standard Edition of Visual Basic, the uses of object variables are fairly simple. However, the Professional Edition of Visual Basic makes very heavy use of them. Databases in Visual Basic Pro, for example, can be dealt with through code, without the need for a data control. The tables of your database themselves are represented as object variables.

If you know how to use object variables, you can write re-useable code. For example, you now know how to write a generic routine for text validation. The code doesn't have to know the name of a specific text box, because you pass the text box to the validate code as an object variable.

More specifically, in this chapter you have learnt:

▶ What object variables are and how to use them.

▶ How to create a simple toolbar.

▶ How to write efficient code that deals with a lot of controls by referring to them as object variables.

▶ How to create and use an array of objects.

▶ What an MDI application is.

▶ How to create and manage MDI applications.

In the next chapter we'll go on to see how to create programs that work, and what to do about them when they don't. We'll also use object variables to create generic routines that can be re-used without hardwiring in the names of your actual controls, so enabling us to use proven code again in the future.

Why Not Try.......

1 Create a Clear the Form routine that looks through all the controls on a form and clears all the text boxes.

2 Add a toolbar to the WORKPAD project from Chapter 6.

3 Turn WORKPAD into an MDI application.

4 In the exercises for Chapter 7 - Graphics, I suggested you create a new version of the CON_DEMO image file viewer that had a menu instead of the file controls. Now make this menu version into an MDI application that allows you to open more than one image file at once. Also add a tool bar to it.

5 Create an MDI viewer for the BIBLIO database using the DATAVIEW.VBP project from Chapter 10. Let the MDI parent create multiple child windows, each of which is a grid that allows a view of that database. The user can then tile the windows and look at all three tables in the database in one application.

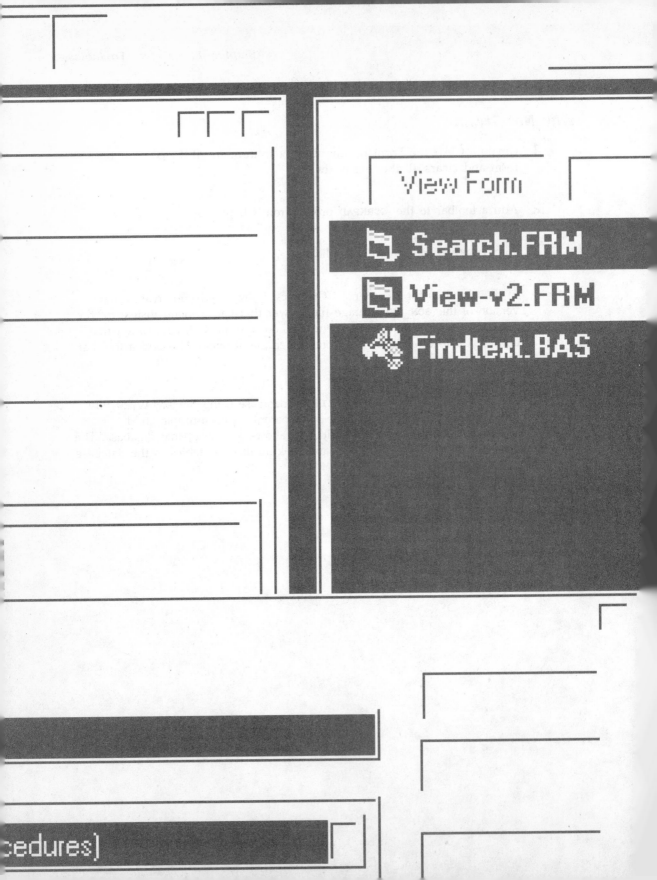

View Form

📋 **Search.FRM**

📋 View-v2.FRM

🏁 Findtext.BAS

cedures]

12

Writing Programs That Work

This chapter is about the reality of programming in an unpredictable world. So far we've made some unsustainable assumptions about Visual Basic programming: you will never make mistakes in your code, users behave impeccably, you have all the time in the world. Well, it's now time to get out of the play-pen and see what we can do to increase our chances of actually getting working programs out in time in real life.

This chapter covers:

▶ How to organize your code into small reusable blocks to reduce the chance of errors and increase your efficiency.

▶ How to write maintenance-friendly code (that is easy to change when you come back to it later).

▶ How to handle events that you didn't really expect at run-time without crashing your program.

▶ How to debug programs that don't work.

Writing Programs that Work

To write code that works, you first have to have a good plan. Then you have to write your code in such a way that the errors are minimized and easy to find. Then you have to be able to find any errors that do occur and remove them, or else be prepared to deal with them at run-time.

Designing Safe Programs

I have already said that the bigger a program becomes, the more likely it is that you will introduce bugs into it. Think about this - if you write a three-line program that takes a number from the user, checks that it really is a number and then displays it on screen, it should be pretty easy to test it. You could even go as far as to tell users that the system is totally bug-free - it's only got three lines of code so that's not too difficult to do.

Now think about this - you have just spent the past 9 hours sitting at a keyboard, typing in roughly 900 lines of code. The code takes a number from the user, checks a database to find a match, loads up some records to do some calculations, multiplies the original number by the number of records you have found, adds in your age in minutes and displays the number on screen whilst playing the Star Spangled Banner! Easy to guarantee no bugs in that little lot? No, not really!

You could test it by running it, over and over and over again. You could hand it to other people to test, who, like you, would run it for days and days and still find no problems. Then, the fateful day comes - you give the system to a paying customer who inadvertently enters a decimal number where everyone else had assumed that whole numbers would be used. Result: the program crashes in a heap and you have one very upset customer on your hands - and no pay check.

So where did we go wrong? If you can guarantee that 3 lines of code will work with no problems, why not 6, 12, 24, 58 or even 900? The reason is something called **cohesion**. The first example has three lines of code that performs one specific function: it checks a number to see if it is OK, displaying it if the check went without a hitch. The second example performs a number of totally different functions: it gets a number, finds some records, does some sums, and plays music.

The first routine has very strong cohesion. It is a very small program consisting of just one routine that performs one and only one function. The second example has very weak cohesion. The whole program is dependent on the operation of a single part. Imagine if your whole house was on one electrical circuit, with a single fuse for all the outlets. Every time one outlet blew, the whole place would go down. Instead, each area has its own circuit. When one circuit goes down, not only can the rest of the house carry on, but the repair man only has to check a small number of outlets to find the fault.

To increase your chances of success, it's better to write programs that consist of smaller blocks of code, each of which has strong cohesion. Each small block of your program should do just one thing, and do it well. If the 900-line program had been written so that it consisted of eighteen 50-line routines, it would be much easier to deal with. You could check and debug each of the eighteen routines rather than the one big program!

Visual Basic programs can be broken down into separate modules called procedures and functions to achieve this manageable state of affairs.

Designing Efficient Programs

Using modules to create libraries of useful routines has great benefits in terms of programming efficiency, as well as safety. Placing code that you use repeatedly into separate modules, or better still, into reusable classes, can ultimately save you hours of typing and design. This code can then operate both in a single project and across all the projects you work on.

If, for example, you have a very data-intensive application that has a lot of fields into which the user has to type information, you may want to verify the input to each field as it is entered. It makes sense to place a routine that verifies this input into a single central routine, rather than rewriting it over and over again in the event handler for each individual control.

Once you have written this input verification routine, you could then attach it to other projects that require input checking, without having to rewrite it.

Planning for the Unpredictable

No matter how well you design and structure your program, things will happen that you didn't expect, or that happen so rarely that you can't consider them a normal event for your program to deal with. As football coaches love to say, "It's all out there waiting to go wrong". Users press strange key combinations, disk drives crash for no reason (try putting a disk in - it helps...), networks go down mysteriously. The list of possibilities is endless. The only thing you know for sure is that it's your fault when your program crashes, even if the file-server got hit by a meteorite in mid-flow.

Therefore, it's a good idea to build in some code that makes an attempt to deal with unforeseen events. Visual Basic provides some help by giving you the chance to deal with run-time errors in your own way, rather than just throwing up its hands immediately and crashing your program.

Making your Code Work

"It's a bug in the system, sorry......the computer's are down, we can't find your records until Monday.....no, no - it's a computer fault, can't be helped, we'll fix it as soon as we can!" Sound familiar? They are all common excuses that everyone comes up against when dealing with companies that use computers. When banks overcharge, they blame computer errors, mail order companies blame the computer when your order goes astray, employers blame payroll systems when excess tax is deducted, or too little is deducted and the tax man finds out.

There are very rarely any true *computer* errors. Computers always do exactly as they are told. If, in an invoicing system, you tell the computer that the total amount your customers should pay is the bill *minus* sales tax, it's not the computer that gets it wrong, it's you! So, how can we cut the bugs (as they are known) out of the applications we write?

The answer to all these questions is that you can't. The more controls you add to your Visual Basic applications, and the more code you write to respond to events, the higher the likelihood is that you have written bugs into your system. You can be sure that these bugs will do their best to remain hidden until:

> You need the program to do something urgently.

> You demonstrate the program to someone who may want to buy it.

> You let someone else use it.

The tricks and tips you will come across can't guarantee that you will never send a system out with bugs. Debugging and structured programming aren't safety nets for programmers - they are damage limitation techniques. If you are an employed programmer, then think yourself lucky that you are in one of the few professions where you *can* make mistakes and get away with it. Thankfully, the same isn't true about doctors. Do it too often, though, and your employers will soon start to think again about your pay check!

Write Understandable Code

Ultimately, the best way to reduce bugs in a system is to design it properly. However, this is a book on programming. All programmers, including me, detest writing thousands of flowcharts and reams of text explaining what a system should do, preferring instead to get stuck in and to start writing code. So what we will concentrate on here is how to reduce the bugs and write **nice** code, rather than how to design the perfect system - there are some excellent books on system design. For the time being, leave the analysis to the analysts, and the fun to us!

In even the simplest of systems there are literally hundreds of possible routes your code can take in response to a user doing something, expected or otherwise. To be able to keep that little lot in your head all the time when you are developing is simply not feasible. For this reason, it is an excellent idea, when looking at a programming problem, to see how it can be broken down into smaller, more manageable chunks of code, or even reusable objects.

In Chapter 3, you learnt how to create small subprocedures that could be used to perform specific jobs in response to certain conditions.

```
If nChoice = 1 Then
  DoThis
Else
  DoThat
EndIf
```

In this example, `DoThis` and `DoThat` are subprocedures that are called depending on the value of `nChoice`. This is called **structured programming**, and makes your code easy to follow and control. Visual Basic also allows you to make use of OOP (object-oriented programming - similar in many ways to structured programming, but much more powerful). We'll take a look at OOP in Chapter 13.

Passing Parameters to Procedures and Functions

Procedures and functions do not have to accept parameters. A procedure that clears all the cells in a grid control does not need to be told anything other than *Do It!* Likewise, a function that gets the current date and time returns a value without the need for a parameter. However, procedures and functions that are at all flexible will accept a variety of parameters.

For example, in a general procedure that centers a form on the screen, you could define a form object variable and pass it to the procedure:

```
Public Sub CenterForm (frmFormName As Form)
```

You could then call this procedure from any event code:

```
Sub Form_Load()
    CenterForm Me
End Sub
```

Often, you may need to pass a subprocedure several parameters. For example, you may need to write a procedure which writes some data out to a database. In this case, it could be helpful to pass each element of data that you want written out as a parameter:

```
Public Sub WriteEmployeeData (sEmployeeName as String, sDepartmentID
↳as Integer, sAge as Integer)
    :
    :
End Sub
```

There are two ways in which parameters can be passed to functions and subprocedures. The easiest method is the one we have seen in the examples so far: **passing by reference**. The other method is called **passing by value**, and has some benefits in terms of protecting your data, though it is a little more complex.

Passing Parameters By Reference

When you pass by reference, you just declare the parameter in brackets after the subprocedure or function name:

```
Public Sub DisplayEmployee (nEmployeeID As Integer)
```

Here, the **nEmployeeID** parameter is passed by reference. What this actually means is that if we have code in the subprocedure which changes the parameter, for example **nEmployeeID = 100**, then the original value of the parameter that's passed to **DisplayEmployee** will itself be changed. This can be useful, but it can be a real pain if you forget about it. Let's see what I mean in some real code.

Problems With Passing By Reference

1 Create a new project in Visual Basic. Remove the default form that appears by selecting Remove File from the File menu.

2 Create a new code module and when the Code Window appears, type in this subprocedure:

```
Private Sub SubProc(nNumber As Integer)

  nNumber = 9999

End Sub
```

This sets up a subprocedure called **SubProc** which sets the parameter it receives to the value 9999.

3 Move the cursor to the line following the **End Sub** statement and insert the following **Main()** subprocedure.

```
Public Sub Main()
Dim nAge As Integer

  nAge = 24
  MsgBox "The age is currently " & nAge
  SubProc nAge
  MsgBox "Age is now " & nAge

End Sub
```

4 When you have typed everything in, run the program.

5 A message box appears, showing you that the current value of the **nAge** variable is 24.

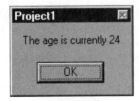

6 When you click OK in the message box, the next line of code calls the **SubProc** procedure. A message box then appears showing you that **nAge** has been changed to 9999.

This highlights the problem of passing by reference. The procedure or function has access to the original parameter, so any changes made to the parameter also affect the variable that was passed in the first place.

Sometimes this can be useful - it's a convenient way of getting a subprocedure or function to return a number of values to the code that called it. However, there is an overhead in passing variables by reference. Visual Basic needs to use more conventional memory for these variables than it does for variables that it passes by value.

Passing Variables By Value

Let's change our last example to pass variables by value rather than by reference. If you don't have the last example still loaded, then it's on your examples disk called **PARAM.VBP**.

1 Find the `SubProc` procedure that you just typed in.

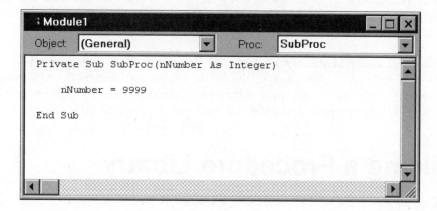

2 Change the `Sub SubProc` line at the top so that it reads like this:

```
Private Sub SubProc(ByVal nNumber As Integer)
```

3 Run the program again.

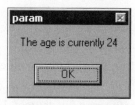 

The message box now pops up the same value of the **nAge** variable both times. Passing a parameter by value does just that - it passes the value of the parameter, not the original variable itself.

Passing By Value Reduces Bugs

I have already mentioned the small memory overhead incurred when passing by reference, but another reason to use **ByVal** wherever possible is that it can reduce the likelihood of bugs. It only takes a small lapse in concentration to assign a value to a parameter passed by reference, when in fact you didn't really mean to. This can have a domino effect as the value is passed back to the code that called the subprocedure, or on to other subprocedures and so on.

You will also find the **ByVal** keyword being forced on you when you come to deal with **API** calls later in the book. When you deal with API calls, passing a parameter by value when you meant to pass by reference, or vice versa, can crash your computer, or more likely your client's computer.

Building a Procedure Library

One of the most useful aspects of modules is that you can use them to create **code libraries**. We have already seen how you can write procedures (including both subprocedures and functions) in such a way that they are reusable.

A code library is a collection of modules, all containing useful routines which can just be bolted on to new applications as and when required. Theoretically, the code would have been tested when it was first written, so bolting on code like this can reduce not only your coding time, but also the potential number of bugs in your system.

To build up a code library effectively, you need to ask yourself a number of questions whenever you write code in modules:

- Can you envisage a use for this procedure in other applications?

- Does the code assume anything? For instance, does it rely on global variables, forms or controls with specific names? If it does then change it!

- How can you make the procedure as crash-proof as possible? Add error checking, add code to check the parameters, add code to deal with errors or call an error-handling routine from another of your libraries.

The overriding principle of Visual Basic is that you should try to build your applications out of components where possible, and this doesn't just mean fancy custom controls. You can build up your own useful library of components from just a few forms and modules.

What we'll do next is to look at adding some functionality to a program that we've used before, by adding a module and form that I have created separately. What's interesting here is not so much the details of the implementation, although we will cover that as well, but rather the design philosophy.

Maximum Re-Use

To make the components we write useful beyond the bounds of a single project, they have to be as generic as possible. It's no good having a procedure that calls all the controls on the main form by name, as it's unlikely that the next project you add it to will use the same conventions. You should aim to be able to add a component to your project with minimum adjustments in both the host project and the new module itself.

This all sounds very theoretical, so let's look at a real example. We're going to use the **VIEW-V3** project, which is an extension of the **VIEW-V2** project we looked at in Chapter 9. I've already messed around with it a bit to add a graphical button.

Creating a Generic Search Procedure

1 Load up the **VIEW-V3** project and run it. You'll remember that it's a viewer for **BIBLIO.MDB**. All that's different from the project we looked at earlier is the button with the dog on it. Nothing happens if you click on the dog just yet.

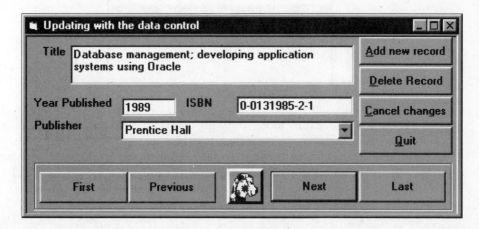

2 What we are going to do is to add code to the button so that, when clicked, it calls up a search form. This form accepts a text string and then looks for records in the database that contain that string. The first thing to do is to add the form and module to **VIEW-V3**. Go to the Project Window. At the moment, there's just the frmMain in it.

3 Click on the right mouse button and choose A<u>d</u>d File.. from the pop-up menu. Add in the **Search1.frm** form, and then do it again and add the **FindText.BAS** module.

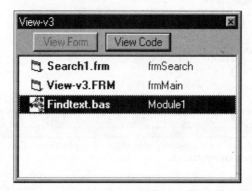

4 The FindText procedure looks through a certain field in a recordset to find a string that you enter into a text box on the Search form. All you have to do to make it work is to tell it the name of the field you want to search in, and the name of the data control it's attached to. Add the following line to the dog button click event to invoke the procedure.

```
    FindText datTitles, "Title"
```

The procedure now looks like this:

```
Private Sub imgSearchButton_Click()
    imgSearchButton.picture = LoadPicture(App.Path & "\Findon.BMP")
    FindText datTitles, "Title"
    imgSearchButton.picture = LoadPicture(App.Path & "\Findoff.BMP")
End Sub
```

5 Now run the program and click the dog. Up comes the form. Enter a
string that you want to search the **Titles** field for.

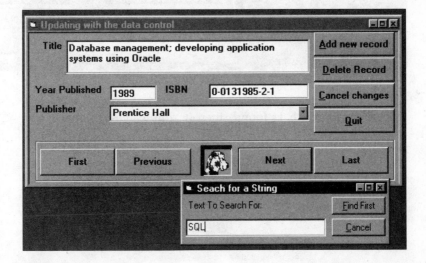

6 As soon as there is some text in the Search box, the <u>F</u>ind First button is
enabled. When you've entered the string, hit the button. Up comes the
first record with the words you entered. Notice also that the <u>F</u>ind First
button has changed to <u>F</u>ind Next.

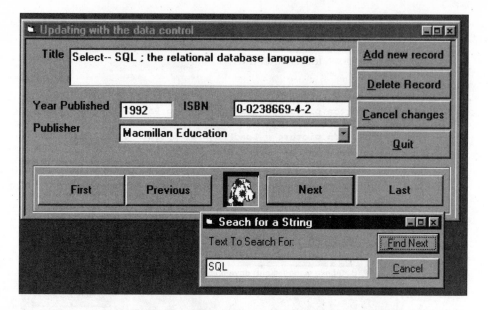

7 You can keep cycling through the database forever. To get out of it, hit Cancel. If no match is found, then a simple message pops up

8 If you now stop the program and save the project, the files you added will remain in the project. Any changes you make at a later stage to the Search form or the FindText module will then affect this project. All you have done is link the files together.

How It Works

Let's start with the original VIEW-V3 form. I had added a button to the project from Chapter 9 to invoke the new search procedure. I used an image control with two pictures of a dog to create the button. This is standard practice when creating toolbar buttons, as you saw in Chapter 11. When you click on the image control, the picture changes.

```
Private Sub imgSearchButton_Click()
    imgSearchButton.picture = LoadPicture(App.Path & "\Findon.BMP")
    FindText datTitles, "Title"
    imgSearchButton.picture = LoadPicture(App.Path & "\Findoff.BMP")
End Sub
```

The two images are:

Button up  *Button down*

The way we call the procedure tells us something about what to expect inside it. We inserted this line into the image click event:

```
FindText datTitles, "Title"
```

We have to tell the **FindText** procedure the name of field we want to search, and the name of the data control that is bound to that field. The reason we have to do this is that the RecordSource property for a bound control is only available at design-time, meaning we can't look at it in code and read the name of the data control. This is a limitation of the Standard Edition of Visual Basic. (The Professional Edition lets you work with things called data access objects that let you examine almost any part of the Jet engine in code.) However, this isn't a huge limitation. All it means is that you have to supply one extra parameter.

Although the **FindText** procedure is in a separate module, we did not have to pass the form to it for it to be able to locate the data control. We haven't just passed the name of the data control: we've actually passed the control itself, whose full name property includes the form and everything. Let's see how **FindText** handles it all.

```
Public Sub FindText(objDataControl As Control, sFieldName As String)

Dim nSuccess As Integer
Dim sStartingRecord As String
Dim sCurrentRecord As String
Dim nresponse As Integer
Dim sFindThis As String

nSuccess = 0
bCancel = False
sStartingRecord = objDataControl.Recordset.Bookmark
```

```
Do
    If nSuccess > 0 Then
        frmSearch.cmdFind.Caption = "&Find Next"
    Else
        frmSearch.cmdFind.Caption = "&Find First"
    End If

    frmSearch.Show 1

    If bCancel = True Then
        Exit Do
    End If

    If sFindThis <> frmSearch.txtSearchText Then
        nSuccess = 0
    End If
    sFindThis = frmSearch.txtSearchText

    Do
        objDataControl.Recordset.MoveNext
        If objDataControl.Recordset.EOF Then
            objDataControl.Recordset.MoveFirst
        End If

        If InStr(1, objDataControl.Recordset(sFieldName), sFindThis)
    <> 0 Then
            nSuccess = nSuccess + 1
            Exit Do
        End If

        sCurrentRecord = objDataControl.Recordset.Bookmark
    Loop While sCurrentRecord <> sStartingRecord

    If nSuccess = 0 Then
        nresponse = MsgBox("Sorry, I couldn't find it", vbOKOnly,
    "Sorry....")
    End If

Loop

Unload frmSearch
objDataControl.Recordset.Bookmark = sStartingRecord

End Sub
```

The first line accepts the parameters that we passed and declares them to
the procedure as an object and a string.

```
Public Sub FindText(objDataControl As Control, sFieldName As String)
```

There's a trade off here. It would be faster to not pass a control, but doing so keeps the procedure generic. You don't need to know the names of the controls on the host form.

We then declare some local variables.

```
Dim  nSuccess  As  Integer
```
Keeps track of the number of records found containing the string.

```
Dim  sStartingRecord  As  String
```
Stores a bookmark to the record at which the search began.

```
Dim  sCurrentRecord  As  String
```
Bookmark to the current record.

```
Dim  nResponse  As  Integer
```
Dummy variable for a message box.

```
Dim  sFindThis  As  String
```
The string that we've been looking for which was entered into the text box on the search form.

Next we initialize **nSuccess** to 0, and set a global variable **bCancel** to false. If you look in the general declarations section of the **FindText** module, you'll see this declared:

```
Option Explicit

Public bCancel As Boolean
```

We need a global variable, as its value is going to be set by the <u>C</u>ancel button on the search form. Then, before the action begins, we save our starting location in the database:

```
sStartingRecord = objDataControl.Recordset.Bookmark
```

Now we can go into the main loop. There are in fact two main **Do...Loop While...** clauses at work here. The outer loop keeps doing the whole search thing until you click <u>C</u>ancel to get out, while the inner one cycles through the records of the database until it finds a match or it gets back to its starting point and has failed. Here's a representation of the two **nested** loops:

```
Do
```

Open up the search form and get the string to look for. Check we still want to go ahead. This loop keeps going - the only way out is the Cancel button.

```
    Do
```

Move through the records and look at the text of the selected field to see whether the text we are searching for is there. Put the condition for the loop at the end, so that we will have already moved off the starting record in the first cycle of the loop.

```
    Loop While sCurrentRecord <> sStartingRecord
```

```
Loop While bCancel = False
```

Once we have found a record, we need to change the caption on the button:

```
If nSuccess > 0 Then
    frmSearch.cmdFind.Caption = "&Find Next"
Else
    frmSearch.cmdFind.Caption = "&Find First"
End If
```

Then we bring up the search form in modal form:

```
frmSearch.Show 1
```

This means that you can't move off the form before doing something to it. The form itself only has two important pieces of code in it:

```
Private Sub cmdFind_Click()

  Me.Hide

End Sub
```

We can hide the form and still keep the information that's been entered into the text box. If the user wants to cancel the search, we switch the global variable **bCancel** to **True** and kill off the form completely:

```
Private Sub cmdCancel_Click()

bCancel = True
Unload Me

End Sub
```

If the user clicks Cancel, then on our return from the search form we exit the whole loop:

```
If bCancel = True Then
    Exit Do
End If
```

Assuming the user hasn't clicked Cancel, we need to check whether they have entered a new string to search for. If they have, we need to reset the success count. The user can change the search string without closing the form, so if they make a change after a successful search, the value of **nSuccess** will be carried over. We can then get the new value of **sFindThis**.

```
If sFindThis <> frmSearch.txtSearchText Then
    nSuccess = 0
End If
sFindThis = frmSearch.txtSearchText
```

We can now start to look through the records for the first match. We move to the next record and check whether it's at the end. If it is, we cycle round to the start again.

```
objDataControl.Recordset.MoveNext
If objDataControl.Recordset.EOF Then
    objDataControl.Recordset.MoveFirst
End If
```

If the string we want is in the current record, then record a hit and stop searching.

```
If InStr(1, objDataControl.Recordset(sFieldName), sFindThis) <> 0 Then
    nSuccess = nSuccess + 1
    Exit Do
End If
```

If there's no match, then providing we're not back where we started, go back to the beginning of the loop.

```
sCurrentRecord = objDataControl.Recordset.Bookmark
   Loop While sCurrentRecord <> sStartingRecord
```

Note that we assigned the current bookmark to a string before doing the comparison. This is because Visual Basic doesn't let you work with the bookmark directly.

Once the search is over, if we didn't find a match, we show a simple message box. Then it's back to the top and up with the search form. Remember that the only way out is to hit Cancel.

```
If nSuccess = 0 Then
        nresponse = MsgBox("Sorry, I couldn't find it", vbOKOnly,
"Sorry....")
    End If

Loop
```

If we do exit the loop, the last thing we do is to reset the database to where it was before the search.

```
objDataControl.Recordset.Bookmark = sStartingRecord

End Sub
```

The **End Sub** will return us to the line after the original procedure call.

```
Private Sub imgSearchButton_Click()
   imgSearchButton.picture = LoadPicture(App.Path & "\Findon.BMP")
    FindText datTitles, "Title"
   imgSearchButton.picture = LoadPicture(App.Path & "\Findoff.BMP")
End Sub
```

The important thing to notice about the FindText module is that it is completely self-contained. There are no references to controls or variables in the host program. Everything it needs is passed as a parameter. You can load it into any database viewer and run it with the minimum of effort.

Handling Errors at Run-Time

Applications, and more importantly users, are never perfect. In any large program you write, there will always be logic errors which can crash the system, or events like key combinations from users that you had never imagined could happen.

Thankfully, Visual Basic incorporates very powerful means for you to trap errors. There are literally hundreds of possible errors that Visual Basic can catch and deal with. Describing them all in detail here would take a long time, but what we will do is look at the generic methods involved in trapping and dealing with these errors.

One important point to bear in mind is that an error in the Visual Basic sense does not have quite the negative meaning that the word implies. Errors are the system's way of signaling to you that a set of events has taken place that is unforseen in your code. Thanks to the informative way that Visual Basic tells you about what's going on, an error is more a request for a response than an invitation to find a new career.

The Err Object

When your code comes across something that doesn't fit in with its expectations, then it can't operate properly. Programs don't think for themselves - they only do what you tell them to do. In order to deal with the situation created by an error, we need to know what kind of error it was. Some errors can be handled by your program directly by writing a procedure that puts things right, while some are just too bad to recover from. We need to narrow the field from just any old error.

There is a built-in object in Visual Basic called **Err** which has numerous properties to let you find out the error number, the error message, where the error came from and so on. These properties form the starting point for error handling routines. Once we have identified the type of error, we can choose whether or not to deal with it.

The properties of the error handler that we're interested in are:

Property	Description
Number	Default value. Lots of numbers corresponding to different errors.
Description	Short description of the error. More to tell users about it than for use in your code.
Source	Identifies the name of the object that generated the error, again more for information.

It's clear that, from a code point of view, what's important is the number of the error. Let's look now at how you trap an error, and then what to do with it.

The On Error Command

If you were to type in this next bit of code it would result in the error message Divide by zero being displayed.

The **On Error** command lets you tell Visual Basic where to go when an error occurs. Each subroutine or function in which you want to trap errors needs to have an **On Error** statement in it. The syntax for **On Error** is pretty straightforward

```
On Error Goto <Line>
```

where **<line>** is a label that you have defined. For example, take a look at this subprocedure:

```
Public Sub Division()
    On Error Goto ErrorHandler
    Print 12 / 0
    On Error Goto 0
Exit Sub

ErrorHandler:
    MsgBox Str(Err.Number) & ": " & Err.Description, , "Error"
    On Error Goto 0
Exit Sub

End Sub
```

The code in this little error handler simply prints out the **Number** and **Description** properties of the **Err** object in a message box. The first line, **On Error Goto ErrorHandler**, tells Visual Basic that in the event (a figure of speech - errors are not events) of an error, it should **Goto** the label **ErrorHandler**, which is defined a little later in the subprocedure. Take a look at the code from **ErrorHandler:** onwards.

After the message box, the line **On Error Goto 0** cancels the error. This is the only way to turn off error trapping. Finally **Exit Sub** tells Visual Basic that as soon as the error handling code has done its bit, the subroutine should be exited.

Did you notice the **Exit Sub** above the **ErrorHandler:** label as well? Normally Visual Basic trots through the code in a subprocedure or function line by line, starting at the top and working its way down. Obviously, you wouldn't want the error handling code to run if no errors were met, so **Exit Sub** is used here to get out of the subroutine without displaying a pointless message box.

FYI On Error Goto 0 effectively turns off the error handler. The line 0 doesn't exist, so next time an error occurs, the error handler is ignored.

Forgetting the Diskette

1 Load up the **CONTROL.VBP** project. This is a multimedia file player that can play various sound and animation files. To listen to sound files, you need a sound card in your PC. If you haven't got a sound card, don't worry - there's an **AVI** file on the code disk that you can play.

Try It Out!

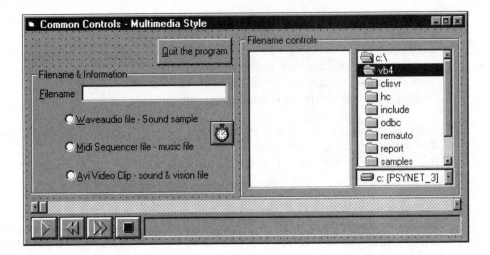

2   There are problems with this program that we need to sort out. For instance, the program will let you select a floppy disk drive when there is no floppy in the drive. If you are running on a network, you could select a network drive only to have that drive go off-line. Both are problems which would normally crash the program. Both are also problems that you can work around with Visual Basic error handling.

3   We want to trap errors that occur when a user selects an unavailable drive. To do this we add code to the **drvDrives_Change** event. Double-click on the drive control to bring up its change event code.

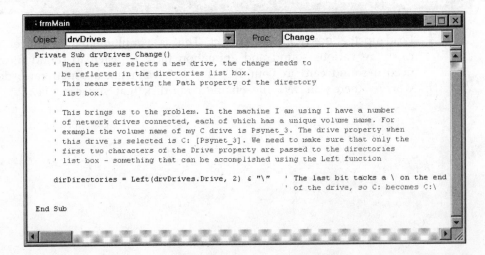

```
Private Sub drvDrives_Change()
    ' When the user selects a new drive, the change needs to
    ' be reflected in the directories list box.
    ' This means resetting the Path property of the directory
    ' list box.

    ' This brings us to the problem. In the machine I am using I have a number
    ' of network drives connected, each of which has a unique volume name. For
    ' example the volume name of my C drive is Psynet_3. The drive property when
    ' this drive is selected is C: [Psynet_3]. We need to make sure that only the
    ' first two characters of the Drive property are passed to the directories
    ' list box - something that can be accomplished using the Left function

    dirDirectories = Left(drvDrives.Drive, 2) & "\"   ' The last bit tacks a \ on the end
                                                      ' of the drive, so C: becomes C:\

End Sub
```

4 Change this event so that it looks like the code below. I have excluded the comments here, so don't let that catch you out:

```
Sub drvDrives_Change ()

On Error GoTo DriveError

    Dim nResponse As Integer
    dirDirectories = Left(drvDrives.Drive, 2) & "\"

    On Error GoTo 0
    Exit Sub

DriveError:

    If Err.Number = 71 Or Err.Number = 68 Then
        nResponse = MsgBox("Whoa - drive problem. Click OK to try
again!", vbOKCancel + vbCritical, "Drive Error")
        If nResponse = 1 Then Resume Else Resume Next
    End If

    On Error GoTo 0

End Sub
```

5 Now run the program and use the drive control to select the A: drive, without a disk in it. The **MsgBox** statement you just entered should appear.

6 Click on the OK button and the program will try to access the drive again, giving you the same error as before. Click on <u>C</u>ancel and the routine aborts. The drive control shows A: but none of the other controls have updated; you can now insert a floppy or select another drive.

How It Works

The two error conditions we want to trap are error 71 and error 68. These are Device Unavailable and Drive Not Ready respectively. Look them up in the back of the reference manual if you don't believe me!

All we have to write in the main body of the subprocedure is:

```
On Error Goto DriveError
```

Then at `DriveError:`, we check the `Number` property of the `Err` object to see if we have caught error `71` or `68`. If we have, then the message box is popped up. Now we come to the interesting bit.

When the message box appears there are two buttons in it, one for OK, the other for Cancel. If you click the OK button, the program tries to access the disk again, but why? The secret is the `Resume` command:

```
if nResponse = 1 then Resume Else Resume Next
```

Once you have trapped an error, you can use `Resume` to tell Visual Basic what to do next. `Resume` on its own tells Visual Basic to retry the command that gave us the error in the first place. `Resume Next` tells Visual Basic to go to the line directly after the one with the error and carry on from there.

In our example, if you press OK, then `Resume` is used on its own to tell Visual Basic to try and run the line of code again. If you still haven't inserted a floppy, then the same error message will pop up again. If, on the other hand, you clicked the Cancel button, then Visual Basic will execute the line following the one with the error. In this case the next lines of code are:

```
On Error GoTo 0
Exit Sub
```

The line `On Error Goto 0` effectively switches off the error handler, and then we leave the procedure.

There is one more interesting feature of the `Resume` command worth covering here. Not only can you use `Resume` to tell Visual Basic where to go after an error, you can also use it to ignore errors totally. For example:

```
On Error Resume Next
```

This informs Visual Basic that if an error crops up, it shouldn't worry about it, but just move on to the next line.

 This is not the best programming style, although the Visual Basic Programmer's Guide even manages an excuse for why this form of programming is acceptable: something to do with *deferring* errors. If an error occurs you really should deal with it, not put it off.

Trapping SQL Errors

In the **INTSQL.VBP** project in Chapter 10 we created a simple bound grid to see how various SQL statements affected our dynaset. The problem was that it crashed every time you made an SQL blunder. Let's sort this out.

1 Load up **INTSQL**. Run it and enter this SQL statement into the window.

```
SELECT [Title], [Publication Date] FROM Titles
```

2 Click on Execute and we're in big trouble.

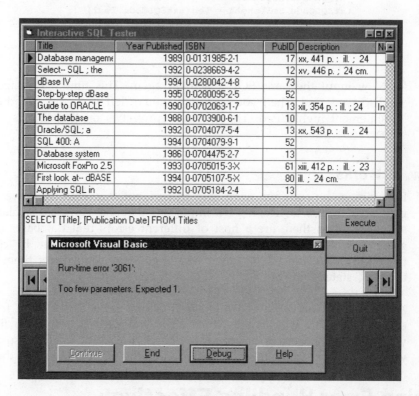

3 What's wrong? The problem is that we entered [Publication Date] instead of [Year Published] as the field name. We need to create an error handler that will let us re-edit the text instead of crashing the program. Click on End to stop the program and open up the Execute button click event. Add the highlighted code to it:

```
Private Sub cmdExecute_Click()

    On Error GoTo CorrectSQL

    Data1.RecordSource = "" & txtSQLCode & ""
    Data1.Refresh

    On Error GoTo 0
    Exit Sub

CorrectSQL:
    If Err.Number = 3061 Then
        nresponse = MsgBox("Check your SQL Code!", vbOKOnly, "Error!")
        txtSQLCode.SetFocus
        txtSQLCode.SelStart = 0
        txtSQLCode.SelLength = Len(txtSQLCode.Text)
    End If

End Sub
```

4 Now input the same SQL statement again. This time a message box is displayed, and when you click OK, you're left with the offending statement highlighted. The amended project is on the disk as `INTSQL2.VBP`

How It Works

By running the code we were able to find out that error 3061 was being generated by the SQL code. It's important that we don't use a blanket **Resume** here as there are a host of different errors that databases can generate which will also be thrown up in this event handler. By checking the number, we can tell the user what's going on and direct them back to the SQL statement.

All errors that occur have a number. You can get a list of them from the on-line help. The way to tell which error you need to trap is to first run your code. When errors are reported, check them out to make sure you want to be overriding them, and then add the right number to the handler.

Using Error Handling Effectively

Errors are an essential part of the communication between your program and the machine. Used well they can be very powerful. Let's consider an example where error handling is fundamental to the success of a program.

Let's say you are creating a module that you want to keep as generic as possible so that you can use it again. The module searches through a form and prints out the current values of all the controls that have a text property to the Debug Window. This is only an example. Once you've captured the text, you can do anything you like with it.

We don't want to pass the names of every control on the form to the module as that would be a real pain. Instead, we'll pass the form as an object variable and then cycle through the controls collection looking for the ones with a Text property.

Error handling comes into play to cope with the fact that not all objects have a Text property. By trapping the error that is generated when you try and access a property on an object that doesn't exist, you can use a single loop to check the whole form.

The code to do this would be something like:

```
Public Sub SearchText(frmHostForm As Form)

    Dim objControl As Control
    Dim nResponse As Integer

On Error GoTo NoPropertyError

    For Each objControl In frmHostForm.Controls
        Debug.Print objControl.Text
    Next


On Error GoTo 0

Exit Sub

NoPropertyError:
    If Err.Number = 438 Then
        Resume Next
    End If
    On Error GoTo 0
    Resume
End Sub
```

This code is in a module called **SCHTXT.BAS**. If you add it to your project, all you have to do to call it is to write **SearchText**, followed by the name of the form it applies to. If it's the current form, then **SearchText Me** is fine.

Adding Error Handling to Your Applications

The are several other properties of the **Err** object, but really they are more than a little beyond the scope of a Beginner's Guide. However, if you plan to ship an application you have written, then there are a number of considerations you need to take into account about the error handling.

▶ First of all, errors nearly always occur when you least want them to, no matter how much you test the app first. The golden rule to follow is that if you are writing code to an event which uses controls and properties in any small way, add an error handler. It's a good idea to spend a little time writing a generic error handling routine, which you can call from any error handler anywhere in your program - this could handle specific errors that you think the app might throw up, and deal with the rest using some generic code.

▶ You must deal with any errors that occur while the program is running. Even a message box appearing before the application is allowed to continue is better than the standard Visual Basic way of displaying the error message, then crashing out.

▶ If you are dealing with databases, write some code to make sure that any transactions you have running are backed out in the event of a nasty error. If you are dealing with the API, then the same applies - write some code to release any API resources you have allocated or you will end up with a nasty memory leak. More on this in the next chapter.

▶ Never underestimate the user, and more than this, never underestimate the damage a single fatal error can do to your reputation and the confidence the users have in your application.

Debugging - Kill All Known Bugs Dead!

Let's lay our cards on the table. Programming any computer with any language can be a real pain. Sure, when things go well, everything's rosy. You type the code in, design your forms, run the program and everything works first time. The reality is somewhat different - I'm beginning to sound a little like the merchant of doom, I know.

A more likely scenario is that you start to type the code in and Visual Basic keeps beeping at you, and flashing up annoying message boxes telling you that you've missed a bracket or misspelled a Visual Basic keyword. If you have been faithfully following all the Try It Outs so far, you will undoubtedly have come across this already.

Visual Basic Debugging Tools

Annoying it may be, but automatic syntax checking is also an incredibly useful feature of Visual Basic. It is actually only one of a number of useful features that come with Visual Basic to help reduce, and hopefully eradicate, bugs in your systems:

▶ When your programming is running, Visual Basic provides you with a **Debug** Window in which your code can display messages. You can also change the way the program runs, while it is running, by placing new values into variables or by changing the properties of controls and form.

▶ A **Watch** window lets you see how the variables in your program change as it runs. You can even run the program a line at a time to see where it goes and when.

We'll examine all of the debugging aids that come with Visual Basic by working through a buggy version of `CONTROL.VBP`. Let's start by taking a look at the Debug Window itself.

The Debug Window

In design mode there is a window hidden out of sight, behind your application, called the Debug Window. We've already used the window as a scratch pad to enter commands on the fly, and in the last example, we printed to it.

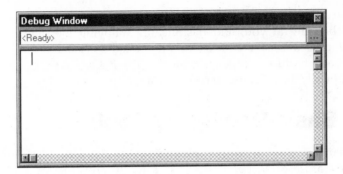

You can use the Debug Window to view the contents of variables and properties, and display information about your program, even while it's still running. You can even change the way your program executes by changing the value of variables and properties on the fly, and by running individual procedures and functions directly.

The first stage in debugging a project is to find out exactly what the problem is.

Running the Buggy Project

1 Load up the **DEBUG.VBP** project and run it.

2 At first it seems that the code is running OK. The form loads all right and everything looks normal.

3 Select a multimedia file (one ending in **.WAV**, **.MID** or **.AVI**). When you select a file, the option buttons should show what type of multimedia file it is. However, it doesn't work in this version. The program just sits there after the file has been selected.

This is a classic example of a bug - there is a fault in the program somewhere that is causing it to behave strangely, but if you take a look at the code in the **txtFilename**'s change event, all seems fine - it checks the right three characters of the file name to see what kind of file it is. At first glance there is simply no reason at all why the code should not be working.

Using the Debug Window to Examine Buggy Code

1 Having selected a multimedia file in **DEBUG.VBP**, pause it by hitting the button next door to the start button. Think of the running program like a VCR tape. When you pause it, the program is still in memory, it's just paused for the moment, enabling you to easily pull it apart and peer inside. Hit *Ctrl-G* to bring up the Debug Window - the programmer's equivalent of a scalpel.

Make sure you have a filename selected in the Window when you pause.

Try It Out!

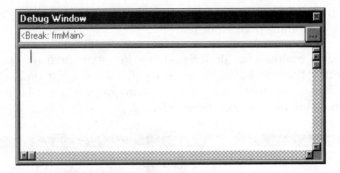

2 Type the following into the Debug Window:

```
? txtFilename.Text
```

3 The name of the file you selected, which the program has now loaded ready for playback, is displayed in the Debug Window beneath your text.

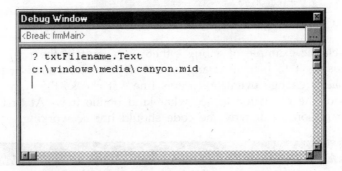

Using the Debug Window in this way you can examine anything you want, from variables, through properties and so on. You can also run public routines and functions, and even use any objects that your code may have created.

However, the Debug Window is not there just to let you look at stuff. It also provides an invaluable method for changing variables and properties in your program, in order to actually change the way the program works.

Changing Program Variables in Debug

1 With **CONTROL.VBP** halted and the Debug Window visible, type this in and press *Return*:

```
Frame2.Visible = False
```

2 As soon as you hit *Return*, the right-hand frame, containing all the file controls, vanishes, the same as it would if you used code to change the **Visible** property to false at run-time. To bring it back type:

```
Frame2.Visible = True
```

3 So far the program is still paused in a state of limbo. To start it running again, just click on the start icon, or press *F5*.

On with the debugging. We still haven't nailed the problem yet.

The Debug Object

The Debug Window can also be used by your code to display run-time debugging information. This is what we did in the earlier **SCHTXT.BAS** module. In terms of your program code, the Debug Window is nothing more than an object, just like a form or any other kind of object you may decide to create. Just like a form then, you can print to the Debug Window with **Debug.Print**.

On to solving our problem then - we know that something is not happening right in the **txtFilename** change event. Maybe the change event is not occurring. Perhaps the change event is not catching the true value of the file name. Let's add some debug code to find out.

Examining the Change Event

1 Stop the program and bring up the Code Window for the **txtFilename_Change** event.

```
frmMain                                                    _ □ X
Object:  txtFilename              ▼     Proc:  Change              ▼

Private Sub txtFilename_Change()
    ' When the text box changes - that means that th
    ' selected a file in the files list box and the
    ' been passed across.
    ' At this point it would be a good idea to check
    ' of the filename to determine the file type. .W
    Select Case Right$(txtFilename, 3)
        Case "WAV"
            optWaveaudio.VALUE = 1
        Case "MID"
            optMidi.VALUE = 1
        Case "AVI"
            optVideo.VALUE = 1
        Case Else
            Exit Sub
    End Select

    Multimedia_Clip.Filename = txtFilename

    ' Now set the scrollbar up
    scrPosition.MIN = 0
    scrPosition.MAX = Multimedia_Clip.Length
```

2 On a new line, directly above the **Select Case** statement, add this line of code:

```
Debug.Print "txtFilename Change event : txtFilename = " & txtFilename
```

This will print a message in the Debug Window whenever the change event occurs, showing us the value of the text box at that point.

3 Run the program now, select a file, then pause the program and bring up the Debug Window with *Ctrl-G*.

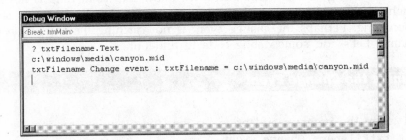

```
Debug Window                                                    X
<Break: frmMain>                                              ...
? txtFilename.Text
c:\windows\media\canyon.mid
txtFilename Change event : txtFilename = c:\windows\media\canyon.mid
```

Notice how the code you typed into the Debug Window previously is still there, but now there is an additional line of text showing us that the change event is actually occurring, and that the text you see in the text box is the same as the value inside our change event - the problem doesn't seem to be there then. Time to bring in the big guns, I think.

The Step Commands

The Step commands in Visual Basic allow you to run a program a line at a time, or even a function or subprocedure at a time. Each time a line of code is run, the program pauses waiting for you to tell it if it should carry on to the next line.

Click on this icon or press Shift-F8 to select procedure step mode.

Click on this icon or press F8 to select single step mode.

Both commands step through the code in your program a line at a time, pausing after each line. In single step mode, when a call to a procedure or function is found, Visual Basic **steps** into the code that makes up that procedure and starts to run it, line by line. With procedure step, if you come to a line of code that calls a procedure or function, it runs the entire procedure in one step, then pauses.

Stepping Through Code

1 Make sure that you still have the `DEBUG.VBP` project paused in run mode.

2 Press *F8* to select single step mode to start the debugging process off.

3 The program stops almost instantly, since the timer control is still running, triggering events at regular intervals. Notice how when an event happens in step mode, Visual Basic pops up a Code Window, highlighting the line of code that it is about to execute.

Try It Out!

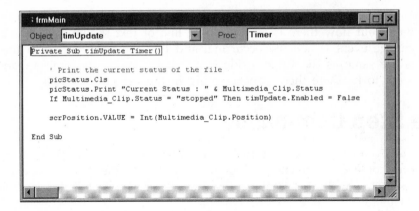

4 If you press *F8* again, the highlight will move down to the next line of code in the event, to show you what it is doing. You could continue doing this forever and a day, but we will still get no closer to solving our problem. We need to stop the timer events interfering in our debugging process. Pop up the Debug Window again, and disable the timer control:

```
timUpdate.Enabled = false
```

5 The event we really want to take a look at is the text box change event. We can help our cause by using the Debug Window to clear out the data that is already in the text box.

```
TxtFilename = ""
```

6 Once you have typed this line into the Debug Window, a change event occurs. You can see this from the fact that our familiar debug information appears directly underneath the command to clear the text box.

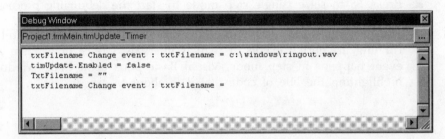

We can now continue to debug.

7 Hit *Shift-F8* to procedure step through the timer event. The timer event interrogates properties in the multimedia object in this project, so if you were to single step, you would soon find yourself peering at some very confusing property code, which is not covered until the next chapter.

When you get to the end of the timer event code, there are no events being triggered, so the program is effectively just sitting there waiting for something to happen, to tell it where to go next. Go back to the main form - you may need to bring it back into view by closing down some of the other windows.

If the single stepping seems to stop, then it's probably waiting for you to enter something.

8 At this point, the program has started running properly again since we have left the code that we were looking at while single stepping. Pause it again and press *F8*. Now select one of the files on display in the files list box (don't use any other controls or you will find yourself peering at an event that we are not interested in). As soon as you select a file, the single stepping will start, this time with the code for the file list box's click event on display.

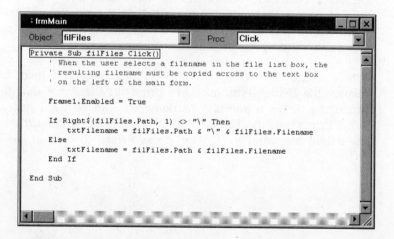

9 Press *F8* three times to move through this event to the line which sets up the text box. If you now press *F8* again, you will find yourself peering at the text box's change event - this is what we want. We already know that it is the option buttons which are not setting themselves up properly, and the code that does that is contained in the **Select...Case** construct.

Press *F8* a couple more times to move to the **Select** statement. Perhaps this is not working properly -there is only one way to find out.

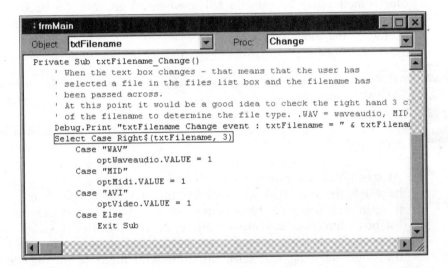

```
: frmMain                                            _ □ ✕

Object: txtFilename              ▼   Proc:  Change              ▼

Private Sub txtFilename_Change()
    ' When the text box changes - that means that the user has
    ' selected a file in the files list box and the filename has
    ' been passed across.
    ' At this point it would be a good idea to check the right hand 3 c
    ' of the filename to determine the file type. .WAV = waveaudio, MID
    Debug.Print "txtFilename Change event : txtFilename = " & txtFilena
    Select Case Right$(txtFilename, 3)
        Case "WAV"
            optWaveaudio.VALUE = 1
        Case "MID"
            optMidi.VALUE = 1
        Case "AVI"
            optVideo.VALUE = 1
        Case Else
            Exit Sub
```

10 The **Select** statement uses the **Right** method to pull the three rightmost characters out of the file name and then tries to match them against one of the known types. Click in the window to the left of the word **Right** and drag to select the right-hand end of the **Select** statement: **Right$(txtFilename, 3)**

11 Now press *Ctrl-C* to copy this to the clipboard, and then *Ctrl-G* to display the Debug Window. Let's print out the value that this line is producing. Enter a question mark (which can be used instead of the word Print) into the Debug Window, and then press *Ctrl-V* to paste the **Right** command in. Finally press *Return* to look at the result.

```
Debug Window                                                    ☒
Project1.frmMain.txtFilename_Change                             ...

  ? Right$(txtFilename, 3)
  wav
  |
```

Voilà - there's the problem. The right-hand three characters that the `Select` statement is picking up are lower case letters. The remainder of the `Select` statement is checking against upper case letters. If you change the `Select` statement to

```
Select Case Ucase(Right$(txtFilename, 3))
```

all will be OK. Stop the program in the normal way, then run it again, and your PC will now be able to burst into song at the right moments (as long as it's equipped with a suitable sound driver or sound card, of course).

Break-points

So far we have paused the program to do our tests by either selecting the pause icon on the toolbar, or by pressing *Ctrl-Break*. Visual Basic provides a way of pausing a program automatically for you when a certain line of code is reached. This is called a **break-point**.

Setting Break-Points

1 Still in `CONTROL.VBP`, go back to design mode and bring up the Code Window for the `txtFilename_Change` event.

2 Click on the `Select` command to move the cursor there.

Try It Out!

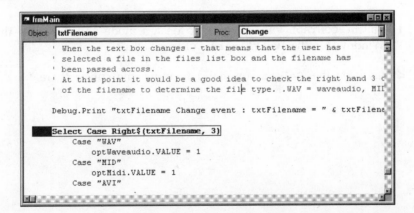

```
frmMain                                              _ □ X
Object:  txtFilename              ▼    Proc:  Change            ▼
Private Sub txtFilename_Change()
    ' When the text box changes - that means that the user has
    ' selected a file in the files list box and the filename has
    ' been passed across.
    ' At this point it would be a good idea to check the right hand 3 charact
    ' of the filename to determine the file type. .WAV = waveaudio, MID = Mid
    Debug.Print "txtFilename Change event : txtFilename = " & txtFilename
    Select Case Right$(txtFilename, 3)
        Case "wav"
            optWaveaudio.VALUE = 1
        Case "mid"
            optMidi.VALUE = 1
        Case "avi"
            optVideo.VALUE = 1
```

Set a break-point on this line by pressing F9, clicking on the hand icon on the toolbar or by selecting Toggle Breakpoint from the Debug menu. The line that the cursor is on turns red to indicate that this line is a break-point - the line at which Visual Basic will pause the program, just as if you had pressed Ctrl-Break while it was running.

FYI If you press *F9* again or select the hand icon on the toolbar, then the red highlight vanishes. It's a toggle switch. You can set the color yourself in the Options Environment dialog.

3 With the break-point on, run the program.

4 When the form appears, select a file from the files list box. As soon as you do this, the text box changes and the code stops with the highlight on your new breakpoint.

```
frmMain                                              _ □ X
Object:  txtFilename              ▼    Proc:  Change            ▼
    ' When the text box changes - that means that the user has
    ' selected a file in the files list box and the filename has
    ' been passed across.
    ' At this point it would be a good idea to check the right hand 3 c
    ' of the filename to determine the file type. .WAV = waveaudio, MII

    Debug.Print "txtFilename Change event : txtFilename = " & txtFilena

    Select Case Right$(txtFilename, 3)
        Case "WAV"
            optWaveaudio.VALUE = 1
        Case "MID"
            optMidi.VALUE = 1
        Case "AVI"
```

5 You can start the program again by pressing *F5*, or else jump into step mode if you so desire.

In a big and buggy program you may have quite a few break-points set. Toggling them all off by hand can be an arduous task, so Visual Basic thoughtfully provides a menu option to clear them all for you. This is Clear All Breakpoints on the Run menu. However, don't turn off the break-point yet as we will need it in just a moment.

Watches

Just as break-points enable you to automatically pause a program on a certain line of code, the **Watch** Window lets you automatically see the contents of variables without having to bring up the Debug Window and enter cumbersome `Print` commands to display them.

Watching Variables

There are two types of watches you can put into Visual Basic: **instant watches** and **normal watches**. Let's look at normal watches first.

1 Bring up the Code Window for the `txtFilename_Change` event again. Position the cursor on the word `txtFilename` in the `Select` statement and then to add a normal watch, select Add Watch from the Tools menu.

2 The following dialog appears:

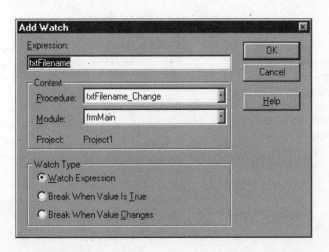

Try It Out!

3 The top text box, Expression, is where you enter the name of the variable you want to watch, or an expression that you want to watch for. For example, you may have tracked down a bug where the system only crashes when the expression **sAge = 9999** is entered. You can enter this into the Watch Window by typing **sAge = 9999** into the Expression text box. For now, though, we just want to watch what happens to the **txtFilename** object, which actually means watching the default property of that object - the Text property.

4 Since you selected **txtFilename** before you selected Add Watch, **txtFilename** is automatically put into the Expression box.

The two combo boxes beneath the expression tell Visual Basic in which procedure you want the variable watched, and in which module or form that procedure is.

The bottom three option buttons tell Visual Basic how to carry out the watch.

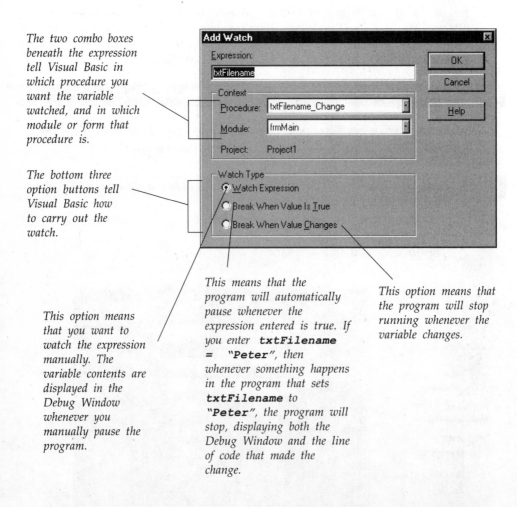

This option means that you want to watch the expression manually. The variable contents are displayed in the Debug Window whenever you manually pause the program.

*This means that the program will automatically pause whenever the expression entered is true. If you enter **txtFilename = "Peter"**, then whenever something happens in the program that sets **txtFilename** to "Peter", the program will stop, displaying both the Debug Window and the line of code that made the change.*

This option means that the program will stop running whenever the variable changes.

5 Leave the top option selected and run the program. When you select a file, the program should stop straight away because of the breakpoint we set earlier. If you now press *Ctrl-G*, the Debug Window will come back into view, but looking slightly different to normal.

The top line of the Debug Window now shows you the contents of the variable that we are watching. When the Debug Window is displayed, you can double-click on the watch variable to bring up the watch dialog box again, enabling you to change the details. Alternatively, if you right click over the watch area of the Debug Window, a pop-up menu appears letting you add, edit or delete watches.

Using an Instant Watch

Instant watches are very similar to normal watches, but can be set up much more quickly. They can only be set up when the program is paused - you cannot set up an instant watch in design mode.

1 Click on the Code Window to bring it to the front.

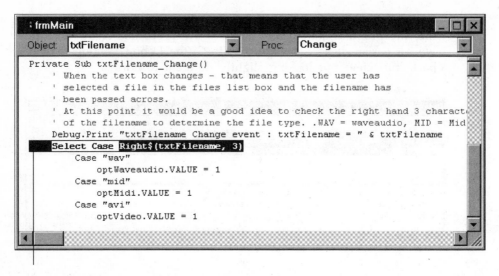

Select ***Right$(txtFilename,3)*** *on the Select line, then right click. Select instant watch from the pop-up menu that appears.*

2 The instant watch dialog box appears showing you the current value of the expression you selected.

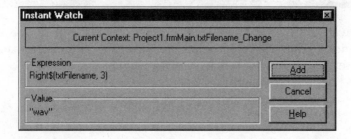

3 From here you can either click on the <u>A</u>dd button to add this as a normal watch, or click Cancel to get rid of the instant watch screen. Click <u>A</u>dd to transfer the expression to the watch area of the Debug Window.

The Call Window

The final debugging tool is the **Call Window**. With the program paused, the Call Window shows you the current procedure that you are in, and any other procedures that were called in order to reach this one.

For example, you may have triggered a command button click event, then a validate procedure to validate some controls on your form. In this case, the Call Window would show you both of these procedures with the procedure names that were called most recently at the top of the list, and the earliest ones at the bottom.

Calling Procedure and Functions in the Call Window

1 Stop the program **DEBUG.VBP** and then run it again. Select a file name as usual - the break-point you set earlier should kick in, stopping execution. Now single step through the code using *F8*, until you find yourself looking at the code in the multimedia class module.

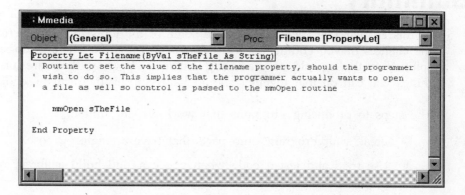

2 Think about what we just did. First, we stepped into the **txtFilename_Change** event in frmMain, then we dropped into a different class module. You can see this by bringing up the Calls Window. To do this, click the Calls icon on the toolbar, press *Ctrl-L,* or select Calls from the Tools menu.

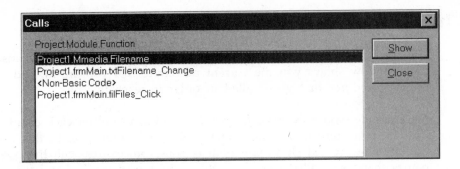

4 This window shows the path you have taken to get to the line of code you are presently at. The route is defined by the procedures and functions you executed, and the forms and modules that they belong to. You can select any of the entries shown in the list and then click the Show button to actually see the code for that procedure on screen.

Summary

In this chapter I've tried to introduce some of the tools that can increase the chances of you ending up with a working program. There is no single solution to this age-old programming problem. However, there are lots of things you can do that together should help you get there in the end.

The steps to producing programs that work are, in summary:

▶ Break your programs into parts that have a single purpose.

▶ Use tried and tested code when you can, and build a library of routines to do that.

▶ Put error trapping code into your program to allow it to survive in real world environments.

▶ Be prepared to debug your code and make full use of the tools that Visual Basic provides.

Now we'll go on and take a look at some more advanced techniques for working with Visual Basic. First up is a look at how Visual Basic and Windows work together in such perfect harmony (almost!).

Why Not Try.......

1 Add code to the FindText procedure that uses the `SelText` properties to highlight the text that has been located as a match.

2 Create an object-based drawing program that saves the current state of a drawn form to a database. Allow only a restricted number of drawing controls to be used, like the line and the shape controls. Then create a module that cycles through the controls collection of the form on which the shapes are drawn and saves their key properties, such as `Top`, `Left` and so on to a record in a database. Create null fields for properties that a particular control does not use. Add the ability to recreate the drawn form from the database.

3 Add disk error handlers to the `CON_DEMO` project from Chapter 2.

4 On the disk is a buggy version of the database viewer project called `VIEWBUG`. This has two errors in it. They are logic errors that cause the program to run incorrectly. See if you can debug it.

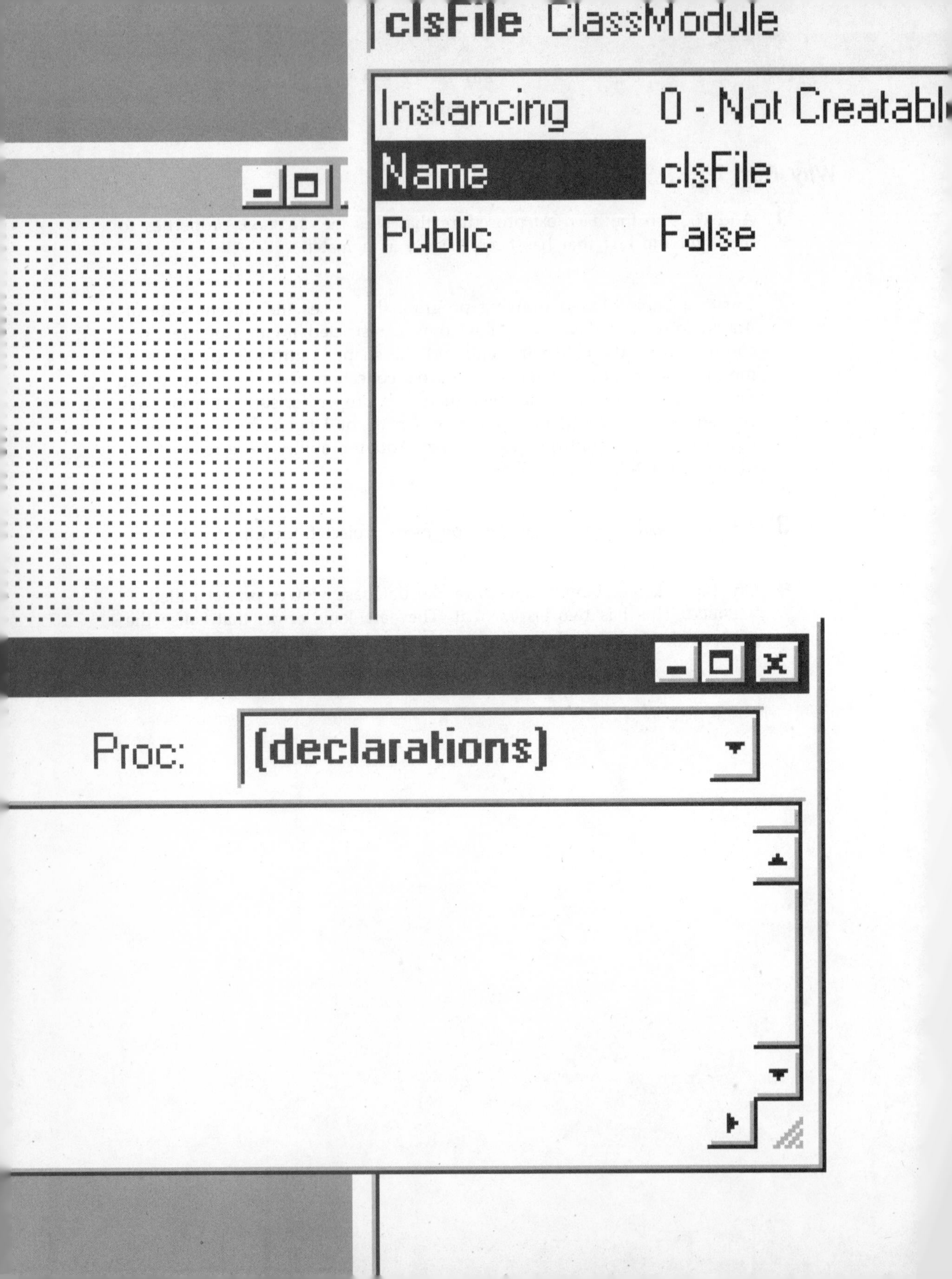

clsFile ClassModule

Instancing	0 - Not Creatable
Name	clsFile
Public	False

Proc: **(declarations)**

Creating Your Own Objects

Q: How many programmers does it take to change a lightbulb?
A: None - if the lightbulb had been designed as a self-contained object then it would have its own change method built in.

This chapter is about the mysterious world of objects and object-oriented programming. Microsoft have a vision for us poor, lowly, humble developer types: a vision of component-driven programming. You need security - just plug in a security component. You want to add some awesome multimedia facility - just plug in the awesome multimedia facility component. You'll be pleased to know that this chapter isn't about buying an expensive stash of components; it's about how you can write your own.

In this chapter you will learn:

▶ What an object is and how to make one.

▶ What class modules do.

▶ How to create your own properties and methods.

This chapter will give you the tools to create your own Visual Basic construction kit.

OOP!

There's a revolution happening in the weird and wacky world of programming. Developers the world over are walking around saying "OOPs" whenever they can, and getting paid mondo sums of money to do it. Luckily, Visual Basic 4 lets us join this group! But what does it all mean?

OOP is an acronym for **Object-Oriented Programming**. It's a bit of a mouthful, but the concept is really quite a good one. In the bad old days we would write linear code. Your program started at line 1, trotted through a couple of hundred other lines of code, then finished somewhere near the bottom. This was great until some bright managerial type realized that programmers make mistakes and are allowed to get away with it. How can these mistakes be reduced, if not eliminated?

Another bright spark, this time a programmer, decided "Hey, we could break the program down into lots of little programs and piece them together". And so the structured programming approach, adopted by most languages today, was born. Instead of one big program containing horrendous mistakes, we ended up with lots of little programs, each with lots of small mistakes.

Of course, the managerial types got even more concerned at this and came up with the idea of bringing programmers into the real world. It's rather like having invited the in-laws round for lunch the day after you held a wild party - it seemed a good idea at the time, but there's an awful lot that can go wrong.

With OOP, you write a program based around real-world objects. For example, if you were writing a salary package, the objects you would be dealing with would be departments and employees. Each of these objects can have properties: for example, an employee has a name and number, a department has a location and a head. In addition, there are methods that the salary department may want to apply to these objects - once a month it may decide to apply a pay method to the employee objects. OOP programs are written in the same way: you decide which objects you need, what properties they should have, and the methods that you will want to apply to them.

In this way, you soon build a program consisting of stand-alone objects. These objects could incorporate and build on functionality offered by other objects, or they could be totally unique. For example, a building object in the salary package would be totally different to anything else, whereas a management object would be nothing more than an employee one, with the additional properties and methods needed to deal with an ego.

So, how does all this translate to Visual Basic? Let's find out.

VB Objects

Visual Basic is a late-comer to the world of object-oriented programming, and many would say it's still not really there. To me, this is the voice of the jealous purist - probably a C++ programmer. In my view, Visual Basic has a great many object-oriented type features, and is gaining more with each release. Let's first consider what we already know about objects in VB, even at our early stage.

The strength of VB lies in its component model. The toolbox is loaded with objects that you can add to your program at will, and customize for the job in hand. You can also add more components to your projects, in the form of OCX custom controls. These are objects that someone else has written.

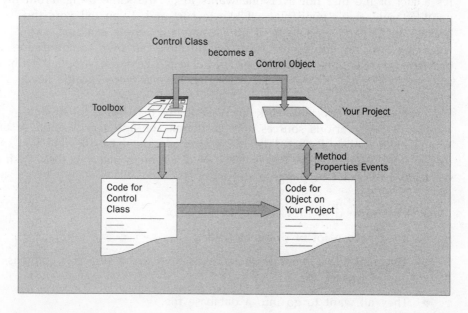

These objects all have some common characteristics:

▶ They have a generic function that is defined enough to be understood, but flexible enough to be useful. A button makes things happen, but it can appear and behave differently depending on what you want.

▶ You can customize them to your needs using their properties.

▶ They interact with the outside world using defined methods and events.

▶ You can have as many of them in a project as you like, and can have many instances of the same type of object.

▶ You don't know, and don't need to know, what the code does inside the object to make it work.

In fact, this is a pretty good set of criteria for designing objects from the ground up. The programmers who created the toolbox controls would have used these kind of principles to create useful controls.

Creating Your Own Objects

It's a fact of life that not everyone wants to do the same thing. From my point of view, that's good news: I like to surf and, I can tell you, the beaches in England tend to be a little empty (of people *and* surf, stop laughing). Anyway, the point is that we all have our own programming problems to solve, and although generic objects like those supplied with VB and available as OCXs are great, you often have a more specific need.

For example, let's say you work for a company that has a lot of data coming in from various sources, like customers, on-line services and so on. You want to shovel all that data into a nice **MDB** database file that you can review later. While the data is in a lot of different formats on disk, each of the feeds have a lot of things in common.

▶ They're in disk files of one sort or another.

▶ They have a lot of different fields.

▶ The marks that separate these fields tend to be similar - commas, quotes, spaces etc.

▶ They all want to go into a database file.

The data sources have enough in common to think about creating a single data import control that you can adapt for each type. You could set the properties of the control to the type of data that was coming in, and then tell the object which database to use as a destination. Then a simple

```
DataImportObject.GetThatStuff
```

method would send it off to parse the incoming data into the database.

If all this sounds too good to be true, it isn't. You can actually create this kind of object yourself using Visual Basic. The only drawback is that you can't just decide what kind of object you'd like, and hope the object fairy comes along and adds it to your toolbox. You have to create all the code inside your object yourself. The good news is, that after you've done it once, you can use that object over and over again, without ever having to look inside it.

The objects that you create yourself are called **class modules**.

You can create your own controls and add them to your toolbox as OCXs. You have to do this using a language like C++ that works closer to the Windows system and supports all the parts of OLE. This is a nasty business and best left until you've mastered Visual Basic.

Class Modules

In previous projects, when we've had a piece of code to run repeatedly, we've created a stand-alone procedure in its own module, and called that procedure from wherever in the project it was required.

In contrast, the code in a class module is never run directly. Instead, it acts as a template for an object. You need to turn the class into an object before it can be used, in the same way that simply loading an OCX into your project does nothing until you actually draw the OCX onto a form.

To turn a class into an object, you declare an object variable of the type of the class that you want to use, like this:

```
Dim MyObject as New MyClass
```

This then places an object called **MyObject** into your program. If the class **MyClass** was the data import class that we discussed earlier, then we could use its methods, such as:

```
MyObject.GetThatStuff
```

From here on, it looks a lot like any other control, for example:

```
datTitle.Refresh
```

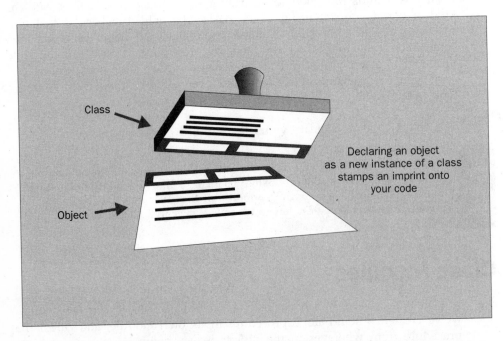

Class

Object

Declaring an object
as a new instance of a class
stamps an imprint onto
your code

You can find a good illustration of the relationship between an object and its class in the Properties Window. If you look at the combo box at the top of the window, you'll see something like this:

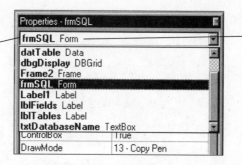

This is the name of the object itself. In OOP-speak, this is the instance of the class.

This is the class from which the object is derived. For visual controls, it's the name of the control in the toolbox.

You can create an unlimited number of objects from (instances of) a class in a project, in the same way you can create multiple controls. How each instance of the same class behaves depends on how you set its properties and use its methods, exactly as it does for a control.

Class Properties and Methods

It won't have escaped your attention that, when working with objects in Visual Basic (and here we're talking control objects), there is a blurred line between properties and methods. Consider these two statements:

```
Form1.Visible = True
Form1.Show
```

It seems arbitrary that one should be a property and the other a method. Why not have:

```
Form1.Invisible
Form1.Hide = True
```

The truth is, that inside the code for the **Form** class, these would be handled in almost the same way. By setting a property, you invoke a set property event handler that then goes away and makes the form invisible - if that's what is required. Calling the **Show** method directly runs a similar lump of code, but this time not via a property event handler.

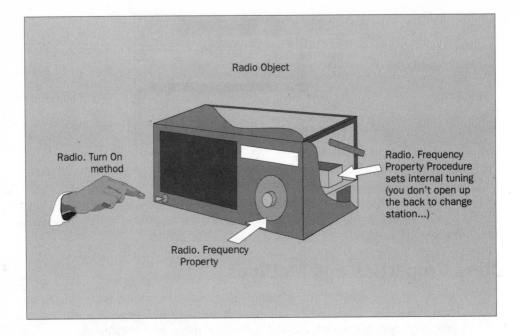

The point here is that, inside a class, you have both method procedures and property procedures which you can use to do almost anything you like. However, we've gone on too long in the abstract. What we need to do now is to see a class in action and make one of our own.

Designing Classes

In this section, we're going go through the process of creating a class that will move a small box around on the screen.

Using the Box Class

We are creating a class which will later become a visible box object, so it makes sense that it should have X and Y coordinates to locate it on the screen. It should also have width and height dimensions. All these can be implemented as properties of the object.

In order to decide what methods we need, we need to think about what we want the object to do. The ability to display itself or remove itself from the display would be nice, so we will need at least these two methods.

1 Create a new project in Visual Basic. The first step is to insert a class module into the project, so that we can create our box class. You can do this by selecting Class Module from the Insert menu.

2 When you select this option, a Code Window appears just as when you add a normal module, or double-click on a control on a form.

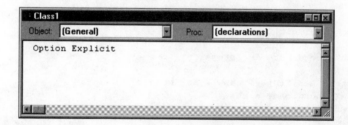

3 Since classes eventually become objects, and since we intend to deal with the class itself in code, it's a good idea to give the class an appropriate name. Just like any other control or object in Visual Basic, a class module has some properties which let you do just that. Bring up the Properties Window using *F4*.

The Instancing and Public properties actually apply to the Professional and Enterprise editions of Visual Basic, so we can ignore them here. For our example, the only property that is really of any use is the Name property, so set this to clsBOX.

4 Now we can start to implement our properties. In order to create a property, we need to write two pieces of code: one to set the property value and another to read it. Let's start with the box's X property. Type this code into the Code Window for the class module:

```
Option Explicit

Dim nX_Coordinate As Integer

Property Let X(ByVal nNew_X As Integer)
    nX_Coordinate = nNew_X
End Property

Property Get X() As Integer
    X = nX_Coordinate
End Property
```

As you complete each procedure, the code editor creates a new window and puts the name up in the combo box.

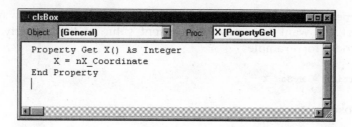

How It Will Work

Although you can't actually run this code yet, let's take a breather and recap on what's going on.

The first line declares a variable called **nX_Coordinate** which is local to the class module. This variable is where we are going to store the X coordinate of the box, but it is not a property yet. The two subroutines following the variable declaration actually define the property using two new sets of Visual Basic commands, **Property Get** and **Property Let**.

As their usage suggests, both mark the start of routines in the class. The way to understand them is to put yourself outside the class and think about how you're going to use it. When you assign a new value to a property, you do it like this:

```
Dim Mybox as New clsBox
MyBox.X = 100
```

Here, we are letting the property take this new value. Now get on the other side of the fence, inside the object. Assigning the new property value actually calls a procedure that then accepts the new value as a parameter and puts it into the local variable that we are using to correspond to the property. This is what the **Property Let** procedure does.

```
Property Let X(ByVal nNew_X As Integer)
    nX_Coordinate = nNew_X
End Property
```

The **Property Get** procedure works in the logically opposite way. Outside the object, we want to retrieve the current value of the property and use it in our code, for example

```
NewPosition = MyBox.X
```

This invokes a **Property Get** procedure:

```
Property Get X() As Integer
    X = nX_Coordinate
End Property
```

Notice then how the **Property Get** line declares a data type:

```
Property Get X() As Integer
```

This indicates that when the property is read, it will return an integer value. Apart from the words **Property Get** or **Property Let**, this code is exactly the same as if you were defining a normal procedure or function. The **Property Let** statement normally adopts the same syntax as the **Sub** line, with **Property Get** being more like a function. The procedure name in each case becomes the name of the property.

Adding Property Procedures

Since the properties that you see on the outside of the object are actually nothing more than functions and subprocedures, we need to define variables in the class to hold the values of the properties. We defined **nX_Coordinate** at the start of our coding, now let's define the rest of the variables.

1 Change the declarations section of the class so that it looks like this:

```
Option Explicit

Dim nX_Coordinate As Integer
Dim nY_Coordinate As Integer
Dim nWidth As Integer
Dim nHeight As Integer
```

These are the variables in which we are going to store the property values.

2 Having declared the variables we're going to use, we can enter the rest of the code. Go to the end of an existing procedure in the class module Code Window and just start typing. The editor will format it all into nice procedure for you.

```
Property Let Y(ByVal nNew_Y As Integer)
    nY_Coordinate = nNew_Y
End Property

Property Get Y() As Integer
    Y = nY_Coordinate
End Property

Property Let Width(ByVal nNew_Width As Integer)
    nWidth = nNew_Width
End Property

Property Get Width() As Integer
    Width = nWidth
End Property

Property Let Height(ByVal nNew_Height As Integer)
    nHeight = nNew_Height
End Property

Property Get Height() As Integer
    Height = nHeight
End Property
```

3 That actually completes our class module code for now, although the box still won't appear on the screen. If you didn't type it all in, then the code to this part of the chapter is stored on the disk as **CLASS1.CLS.**

4 If you haven't got the class open, start a new project and add the **clsBox** class file so it appears in the Project Window. Double click on the form to bring up the form's load event. We need to add code here to turn the class into an object, so that we can try it out.

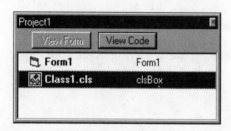

5 Add this code to the form load event:

```
Private Sub Form_Load()

    Dim Box As New clsBox

    Box.X = 100
    Box.Y = 200
    Box.Width = 300
    Box.Height = 400

    Form1.Show
    Form1.Print Box.X, Box.Y, Box.Width, Box.Height

End Sub
```

6 Try running the program now, and after a short pause you will see all four properties of the new object displayed on the form. The complete project - form and classes - is stored as **CLASS1.VBP**

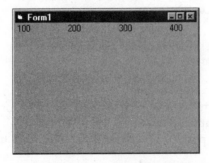

How It Works

So, what is the code actually doing? The first line, the **Dim** line, declares a local object variable. This turns the named class into a usable object. To accomplish this feat in your own programs, simply say:

```
Dim <variable name> As New <Class name>
```

Then you are ready to start playing with your object, named **<variable name>**.

The next four lines simply assign values to the properties of your object. You will remember a short while back that we wrote **Property Get** and **Property Let** routines in the class to define the properties of the object and the values they return. You use these properties in code in the same way as control properties.

So the lines

```
Box.X = 100
Box.Y = 200
Box.Width = 300
Box.Height = 400
```

set up the **X**, **Y**, **Width** and **Height** properties of our new box object. Every time you assign a value to one of these properties, the corresponding **Property Let** procedure is invoked. To see this, single-step through the program using the *F8* key. These screens follow each other:

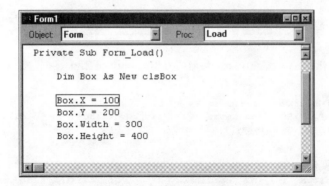

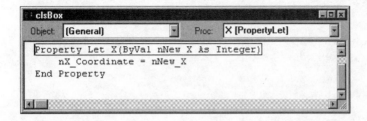

Finally, Visual Basic's **Print** method is used to display the value of each of these properties on the form.

Adding Methods to the Class

We now have a working object, with working properties. How about adding a method or two, such as the **DrawBox** and **ClearBox** methods?

1 If you don't have the current project loaded, open up **CLASS1.VBP**. Bring up the class module into a Code Window once again.

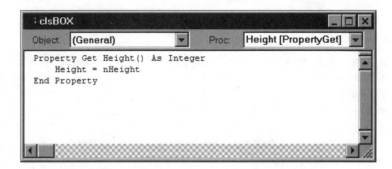

2 Add these two new methods to the end of the class' source code:

```
Public Sub DrawBox(DrawForm As Form)
    DrawForm.Line (nX_Coordinate, nY_Coordinate)-(nX_Coordinate +
nWidth, nY_Coordinate + nHeight), , B
End Sub

Public Sub ClearBox(DrawForm As Form)
    DrawForm.Line (nX_Coordinate, nY_Coordinate)-(nX_Coordinate +
nWidth, nY_Coordinate + nHeight), DrawForm.BackColor, B
End Sub
```

3 Now bring up the form load event again and change it so that it calls these methods, like this:

```
Private Sub Form_Load()

    Dim Box As New clsBox
    Dim nIndex As Integer

    Box.X = 100
    Box.Y = 200
```

```
    Box.Width = 300
    Box.Height = 400

    Form1.Show
    For nIndex = 1 To 500
        Box.ClearBox Form1
        Box.X = Box.X + 10
        Box.DrawBox Form1
        DoEvents
    Next

End Sub
```

Notice how, this time, the code has a new variable declared at the start, and the code at the bottom has changed dramatically to call the **DrawBox** and **ClearBox** methods inside a **For...Next** loop.

4 Now run this new version of the code. The box skates happily across the form. The project at this point in its life is on the disk as **CLASS2.VBP**.

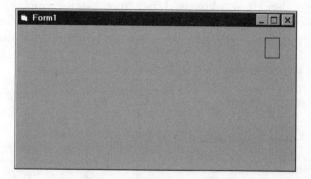

How It Works

Let's take a look at how the methods actually work, starting with **DrawBox**.

```
Public Sub DrawBox(DrawForm As Form)
    DrawForm.Line (nX_Coordinate, nY_Coordinate)-(nX_Coordinate +
 ⤷nWidth, nY_Coordinate + nHeight), , B
End Sub
```

First off, you should notice that the method is declared as **Public**. Declaring a method or variable as public, in a form, module or class module, means that it can be used by code outside that module. In the case of object methods, this is exactly what we want, since we want to be able to use the methods of an object from anywhere the object is in use.

Here I'm using the **B** parameter of the **Line** method. This creates a box using the supplied coordinates as opposite diagonals of the box.

We pass the form we want to draw on in the line **DrawForm As Form**. This lets us use the **Line** method on the form to draw a box. The **Line** method itself makes use of the class' module-level variables to determine where to draw the box on the form, the same variables that we used earlier in the property procedures to hold the values of the object's properties.

The **ClearBox** method works in the same way:

```
Public Sub ClearBox(DrawForm As Form)
    DrawForm.Line (nX_Coordinate, nY_Coordinate)-(nX_Coordinate +
 ⤷nWidth, nY_Coordinate + nHeight), DrawForm.BackColor, B
End Sub
```

This time, though, the box is drawn in the same color as the form's background, using the **BackColor** property of the form. In this way, the box effectively erases itself from the display. A simple trick, but it works.

Now let's look at the code that makes it all happen.

```
For nIndex = 1 To 500
        Box.ClearBox Form1
        Box.X = Box.X + 10
        Box.DrawBox Form1
        DoEvents
    Next
```

This clears the box, changes its **X** property and then draws it again, giving the impression that the box is moving across the form.

The **DoEvents** line is necessary to actually see the box move. Without it, Windows never gets a chance to draw anything on the form until your loop finishes, the result being that the box appears just once, at the right-hand side of the form. By putting **DoEvents** in there, we are letting Windows redraw the form on each pass through the loop.

Optional Parameters

You can write methods in objects and even property procedures that also have optional parameters. Let's have a think about why you'd want to do this.

Wouldn't it be great if, with the **DrawBox** method from **CLASS2.VBP**, we had the option of specifying a color when the box is drawn. This would not only increase our artistic scope when drawing the box, it would also enable us do away with the **ClearBox** routine altogether. We could simply invoke the **DrawBox** method again in the same place, using the background form color to make the box disappear.

Passing Optional Parameters

1 Load up **CLASS2.VBP** again and take a look at the code in the class module in that project, in particular the **DrawBox** and **ClearBox** methods.

```
Public Sub DrawBox(DrawForm As Form)
    DrawForm.Line (nX_Coordinate, nY_Coordinate)-(nX_Coordinate +
↳nWidth, nY_Coordinate + nHeight), , B
End Sub
```

```
Public Sub ClearBox(DrawForm As Form)
    DrawForm.Line (nX_Coordinate, nY_Coordinate)-(nX_Coordinate +
↳nWidth, nY_Coordinate + nHeight), DrawForm.BackColor, B
End Sub
```

Here we have two methods that are basically identical. The only difference between them is that **ClearBox** specifies a color when it erases the box on the screen, and **DrawBox** does not.

2 Highlight the **ClearBox** code by dragging the mouse over it. Then delete it.

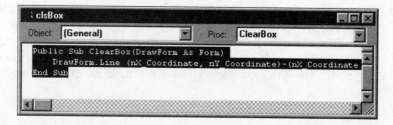

3 We'll now make a couple of changes to the **DrawBox** method to make it take a color as an optional parameter. Change the code so that it looks like this:

```
Public Sub DrawBox(DrawForm As Form, Optional varColour As Variant)
    If IsMissing(varColour) Then
        DrawForm.Line (nX_Coordinate, nY_Coordinate)-(nX_Coordinate +
    nWidth, nY_Coordinate + nHeight), , B
    Else
        DrawForm.Line (nX_Coordinate, nY_Coordinate)-(nX_Coordinate +
    nWidth, nY_Coordinate + nHeight), varColour, B
    End If
End Sub
```

4 All that remains now is to change the form load event; in its current form (with no **ClearBox** routine), the program won't compile. Just take the reference to the **ClearBox** line out and replace it with the highlighted line below.

```
Private Sub Form_Load()

    Dim Box As New clsBox
    Dim nIndex As Integer

    Box.X = 100
    Box.Y = 200
    Box.Width = 300
    Box.Height = 400

    Form1.Show
    For nIndex = 1 To 500
        Box.DrawBox Form1, Form1.BackColor
        Box.X = Box.X + 10
        Box.DrawBox Form1
        DoEvents
    Next

End Sub
```

5 This time, when you run the program, there is no visible difference. However, the program itself has shrunk a little in size. While this makes very little difference to a small program like this, it could make all the difference if the object was bigger, and if it was used in more places in the code. The finished project is on the disk as **CLASS3.VBP**.

How It Works

There is an additional parameter now, `varColor`, that is listed in the `DrawBox` declaration, but since it is preceded by the word `Optional`, there is no requirement for the programmer to use it when calling the method through code.

```
Public Sub DrawBox(DrawForm As Form, Optional varColor As Variant)
```

So, how do you determine in your method if the programmer has actually used an optional parameter? That is where the `IsMissing()` function comes in. `IsMissing` is a new VB function that will tell you, by returning true or false, if an optional parameter has been passed to your code.

In the method above, we say

```
If IsMissing(varColor) Then
```

If the optional parameter is not passed to the procedure, `IsMissing` returns true; if it is passed, `IsMissing` returns false. This way, you can write code to perform differently, depending on whether or not the parameter was passed. In the code above, if it was passed, then it is used in the `Line` method to specify a color, otherwise the `Line` method is called without any color value.

Optional Parameter Constraints

There are a couple of important points about optional parameters which we need to note.

- Optional parameters must be variants - you can only declare parameters as optional if you declare the data type as variant. For example, you can't do this in code:

```
Public Sub MyRoutine( Optional nNumber As Integer )
```

- Optional parameters must be specified as the last parameters in the subroutine's declaration. This won't work:

```
Public Sub MyRoutine( Optional varNumber as Variant, nAge as Integer )
```

but this will:

```
Public Sub MyRoutine( nAge As integer, varNumber As Variant )
```

A Cautionary Note

Optional parameters give you a great deal of flexibility. You could also take the view, though, that they provide you with just enough rope to hang yourself.

One of the reasons for moving towards structured programming, and object-oriented programming, is to make your life easier when it comes to reading, understanding, developing and maintaining your code. Optional parameters effectively remove the safety net, allowing you to write almost freeform code (*I think I'll use this parameter here, but I can't be bothered here etc*).

When using them, it is very easy to tie yourself up in knots, especially when it comes to debugging your code. I have seen numerous projects here in Psynet where the programmers have been using these VB4 features and later found themselves debugging by superstition, adding a parameter here, leaving it off there and so on, in the hope that the code will work.

These features are great for producing your own reusable, multi-purpose objects and components, but they really should be used with care in everyday programming. Ask yourself this - is there a benefit to using them in the routine you are writing, or would your code be better for ignoring them? In our earlier example, they were great at reducing the size of the code. However, there is an argument that the code would be more readable if we had left the **ClearBox** routine in.

The simple rule, then, is use common sense, and treat optional parameters with more than a little respect.

VB now also supports indefinite parameters, which let you pass a variable sized array of parameters to a function. I have yet to find a good use for this, so I haven't bored you with it.

More on Class Design

Now that we've got a fair idea for how classes hang together, let's walk through the process of designing and implementing another, more useful class.

Earlier on in this chapter, we kicked around an idea for a class module that would import data from text files into a database. To implement this in its full glory is a little beyond the scope of this book, but what we can do is to have a look at a basic file handling class that could be a small step on the road to this.

What we'll do is to create a simple class that will shield us from some of the grunt work in handling disk files, such as opening and closing them and remembering the file numbers and so on.

What Do We Want?

You all know how much I love disk files, so the idea of creating something simple is very appealing. In fact, all I want to be able to do is to issue instructions to the file to get on with things itself, without me having to open files etc. This is my ideal of disk file handling:

```
MyFile.Read       'gets the data from a file
MyFile.Save       'saves the file to the disk
```

This simple statement has already propelled us into the world of objects. We obviously need a object called `MyFile`, which represents a single disk file. We then need two methods, `Read` and `Save`. What else?

I'd like the opening and closing business to look after itself by knowing when I've finished with a file. So, inside the file, we will have to do some work behind the scenes. If you think back to our brief look at file handling, you'll remember that we have to explicitly open a file for a specific action, like saving, before we can use it.

The next question is how to pass the data we want to save to the file, and how to get it back. We need a property that we can read from and write to. This can be the one and the same property, and it should be a string. So we might say:

```
MyFile.Text = "This is the text to save....."
MyFile.Save
```

or

```
MyFile.Read
sTheTextWeRead = MyFile.Text
```

But there's a snag here. We need to call the disk file by a file name when we save it, and we need to be able to point the **Read** method at a particular file. We obviously need a **Filename** property as well:

```
MyFile.FileName = "TextFile"
MyFile.Text = "This is the text to save....."
MyFile.Save
```

or

```
MyFile.FileName = "TextFile"
MyFile.Read
sTheTextWeRead = MyFile.Text
```

And really, from a design point of view that is about it. Anything else, like how the object closes down files, is an internal issue for the class. The whole point of objects is that they hide the complex tasks and provide a simple and intuitive way of building programs. I feel that this class design, which we'll call **clsFile**, and which will allow us to create the object **MyFile**, definitely does this. I could even get to like file handling!

Implementing the File Class

Now we've got an idea for the methods and properties that **clsFile** will have to support, let's crack on and write the code.

1 Start a new project and add a class module to it. Name the module **clsFile**.

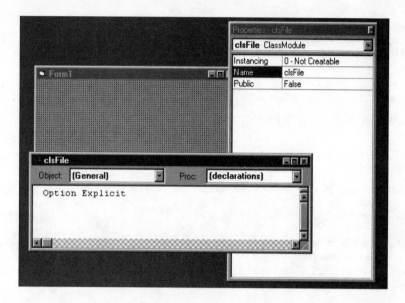

2 First of all, let's declare some internal variables that we will be using inside the class. Add these lines to the **clsFile** general declarations section.

```
Option Explicit

Dim sFileName As String
Dim sText As String
Dim nFileNumber As Integer
```

3 Next we need to create the **Property Get** and **Property Let** procedures for the two properties we have chosen: **FileName** and **Text**. First add the **FileName** property procedures.

```
Property Let FileName(ByVal sNewFileName As String)
    If sNewFileName <> sFileName Then
        Close nFileNumber
    End If

    sFileName = sNewFileName

End Property
```

```
Property Get FileName() As String
    FileName = sFileName
End Property
```

The extra code in the **Property Let** procedure checks to see if we've changed the name of the file. As usual, we'll cover this in the How It Works section in a moment.

4 Now add the procedures for the **Text** property:

```
Property Get Text() As String
    Text = sText
End Property
```

```
Property Let Text(ByVal sNewText As String)
    sText = sNewText
End Property
```

5 Next, let's take a look at the **Read** method. Create this **Public** procedure:

```
Public Sub Read()

        OpenFile "Readit"
        sText = Input(LOF(nFileNumber), nFileNumber)

End Sub
```

We could have added the code to **Open** a file to this procedure directly. However, we 're going to have to **Open** files when we're saving them as well, so it makes sense to create a **Private OpenFile** procedure that we can call from both methods.

6 This is that procedure. Note the **Private** declaration at the start:

```
Private Sub OpenFile(sAction As String)

If nFileNumber <> 0 Then
    Close nFileNumber
End If
        nFileNumber = FreeFile
    Select Case sAction
        Case "Readit"
            Open sFileName For Input As #nFileNumber
        Case "Saveit"
```

```
        Open sFileName For Output As #nFileNumber
    End Select

End Sub
```

7 This let's us add the **Save** method code using this procedure:

```
Public Sub Save()

    OpenFile "Saveit"
    Print #nFileNumber, sText

End Sub
```

The completed class is on the disk as **CLSFILE1.CLS**. This version of the class has one extra event that we haven't discussed, the terminate event. We'll look at it later on when we use the class.

How It Will Work

We can't use the class without adding it to a project and deriving an object from it. However, let's just run through it to make sure we're cool about it before the fun starts.

The important thing to remember about the **clsFile** class is that it isn't a regular code module. You won't be calling its functions repeatedly to save and load lots of different files at one time. As far as your code is concerned, the object you create is the file.

This means that if you wanted to open more than one file at one time, say in an MDI program, you'd just declare more instances of the **clsFile** class. Each object derived from the class would have its own **FileName** property and would operate completely independently.

The reason this is important to us here is that it means that each object derived from **clsFile** has only one **FileName**, and so only one file ID number (**nFileNumber**). Changing the file name means you want to close the current file and work with a new one.

Because each object only refers to one file, and because we can tell when the file needs to be opened and closed from the methods that are invoked, we can make the `Open` and `Close` file operations internal to the class, i.e. we don't need a `MyFile.Open` operation. This is the heart of the matter, as far as the benefits of using `clsFile` objects over direct file access are concerned. It removes a whole layer of operations from view.

Let's now walk through the code as though we were using an object derived from the class. First of all we would assign a file name to the object:

```
MyFile.Filename = "TextFile"
```

This invokes the `Property Let` procedure:

```
Property Let FileName(ByVal sNewFileName As String)
    If sNewFileName <> sFileName Then
        Close nFileNumber
    End If

    sFileName = sNewFileName

End Property
```

Here we check to see if the current file name held in the `sFileName` variable is the same as the new one. If it isn't, it means we've changed files, so we need to close the current file, referenced by the `nFileNumber` variable. `nFileNumber` is the number that VB uses to work with each open file. This is set in our code in the `OpenFile` method. We then change the internal file name to the new one.

Next, the program would probably use the `Read` method.

```
MyFile.Read
```

The method first opens the current file by passing the `"Readit"` command to the `OpenFile` method.

```
Public Sub Read()

        OpenFile "Readit"
        sText = Input(LOF(nFileNumber), nFileNumber)

End Sub
```

Remember that in VB you have open and re-open files for each specific operation. The **OpenFile** method is:

```
Private Sub OpenFile(sAction As String)

If nFileNumber <> 0 Then
    Close nFileNumber
End If
        nFileNumber = FreeFile
    Select Case sAction
        Case "Readit"
            Open sFileName For Input As #nFileNumber
        Case "Saveit"
            Open sFileName For Output As #nFileNumber
    End Select

End Sub
```

This first checks to see if we've already got a file open, and if we have, it closes it. If we haven't got a file open, then **nFileNumber** is zero.

We then use the **FreeFile** statement to assign a new file number to **nFileNumber**, in anticipation of opening the new file. The **FreeFile** statement returns the first free file number between 1 and 255 and looks at all the files open on the system.

We could, of course, hardwire a file number in to this class, by saying, for example, **nFileNumber = 1**, but that would remove an essential quality of the class - that it can be instantiated as many times as you like. By using **FreeFile**, we could open a whole array of **MyFile(nIndex)** objects in an application, and let each one receive its **nFileNumber** from the system on the fly.

We then use a **Select Case** statement to open the file either for input or output, depending on the value of the **sAction** parameter that we passed to the **OpenFile** procedure.

Once the file is open, the **Read** method just saves the data to it.

```
sText = Input(LOF(nFileNumber), nFileNumber)
```

Here I've used the simple **Input** function that just needs to know the number of characters to load and the file number.

The text that we want to save is contained inside the object in the `sText` variable. This is loaded using the **Text Property Let** procedure:

```
Property Let Text(ByVal sNewText As String)
    sText = sNewText
End Property
```

We can read the text we've retrieved using the **Property Get** procedure.

```
Property Get Text() As String
    Text = sText
End Property
```

Saving the file is very similar, only we open the file for output and then use the **Print** statement.

Try It Out!

Using the File Class

Now we've created the class, let's use it.

1 Open the project **FILEFORM.VBP**. This is a notepad type form that I've already created, but with no code and no class in it.

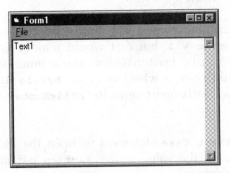

2 First add the file **CLSFILE1.CLS** to the Project Window.

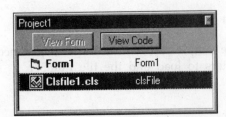

3 The form contains a little menu structure, to which we will add code that will open and close a text file. It's like the **WORKPAD** project we looked at when discussing file handling. The first thing we need to do is to declare an instance of the **clsFile** class in the general declarations section of the form:

```
Option Explicit
Dim MyFile As New clsFile
```

4 Now it's time to see what our class can do for us. It won't always be the case that the classes you use will be fresh in your mind. In fact, you may not have even written them yourself at all. It can be tricky to get an overview of what's available without a nice Properties Window to glance at, like you would have with a control object. Help is at hand in the form of the Object Browser. Select Object Browser from the View menu or hit *F2*. This is it:

Select *clsFile* from the *Classes/Modules* list.

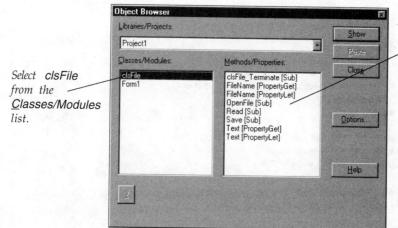

Here's a list of all the properties and methods of the class. Select one from the list and hit *Show*. The Code Window for the *clsFile* module will open with the code in it.

FYI

The object browser has other uses, none of which I personally rate very highly. However, the ability to keep tabs on custom classes is good.

---

5 Now we can see what's there, we can work out how to use the class in our code. First of all, let's add code to the File Open menu to select a file and open it:

```
Private Sub mnuFileOpen_Click()

    With CommonDialog1
        .CancelError = False
        .DialogTitle = "Open a Text File"
        .Filter = "Text Files (*.txt)|*.txt"
        .ShowOpen
    End With

If CommonDialog1.FileName = "" Then Exit Sub
MyFile.FileName = CommonDialog1.FileName

    MyFile.Read
    Text1.Text = MyFile.Text
    Form1.Caption = MyFile.FileName
End Sub
```

6 Next, we need to be able to use a common dialog to save the file. Add this code to the file save click event:

```
Private Sub mnuFileSave_Click()

    With CommonDialog1
        .CancelError = False
        .DialogTitle = "Save Text File"
        .Filter = "Text Files (*.txt)|*.txt"
        .ShowOpen
    End With

If CommonDialog1.FileName = "" Then Exit Sub
MyFile.FileName = CommonDialog1.FileName
Form1.Caption = MyFile.FileName

    MyFile.Text = Text1.Text
    MyFile.Save
End Sub
```

7 The New menu option just needs to clear the screen and the `FileName` property of the file object:

```
Private Sub mnuFileNew_Click()
    Text1.Text = ""
    Form1.Caption = "New File"
    MyFile.FileName = ""
End Sub
```

8 The E<u>x</u>it menu item needs to do two things. Obviously, one is to end the program. The other is to shut down the `MyFile` object to stop open files being left on the system. Setting an object to `Nothing` removes the instance from memory:

```
Private Sub mnuFileExit_Click()

  Set MyFile = Nothing
  End

End Sub
```

9 Finally, add some code to clear the text box on startup:

```
Private Sub Form_Load()
    Text1 = ""
End Sub
```

10 Now you can run the program. You can load files in and save them to your heart's content. The completed project is on disk as `FILEFRM1.VBP`.

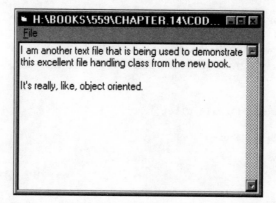

How It Works

The program starts by creating an object called `MyFile` that is an instance of the class `clsFile`.

```
Option Explicit
Dim MyFile As New clsFile
```

The file open and file save events use a common dialog to get the name of the file for the operation. In both cases, this is assigned to the **FileName** property of **My File**.

```
If CommonDialog1.FileName = "" Then Exit Sub
MyFile.FileName = CommonDialog1.FileName
```

In each case, the procedure ends if no file name was returned. After this, our class makes saving and loading the files easy.

The New file menu item clears the text box and the caption, and sets the file name to "". This causes the open file to be closed by the **TEXT Property Let** procedure. If, however, it's the first use of the class, then **sFileName** will also be "", so nothing happens.

```
Property Let FileName(ByVal sNewFileName As String)
    If sNewFileName <> sFileName Then
        Close nFileNumber
    End If

    sFileName = sNewFileName

End Property
```

The only new thing that's going on, is that the object is shut down when we close the program. This happens when the user selects the Exit menu item.

```
Private Sub mnuFileExit_Click()

  Set MyFile = Nothing
  End

End Sub
```

Setting an object to **Nothing** removes an object from memory and kills it off. This triggers the **Object_Terminate** event. We can use this to close all the files, like good citizens, before we exit. This code was in the **CSLFILE1.CLS** class in the **Class_Terminate** procedure.

```
Private Sub Class_Terminate()
  Close nFileNumber
End Sub
```

Note that we specify the `nFileNumber` parameter with the `Close` statement to make sure that we don't shut down files belonging to other objects that might be open in the application.

What We've Learnt about OOP Design

Throughout the course of the last two projects, we've uncovered some principles about programming with objects that are valuable lessons to learn. They form some of the fundamentals of OOP in any language, and you'll meet them in any discussion of objects.

Data-Hiding

In the classes we used, we made all the internal variables that we used local to the class. You couldn't access them from the rest of the project. We changed these values indirectly using property procedures. If you do this, it means that the object is in full control of its data and can trap and control the action of changing it. This is sort of, though not exactly, like encapsulation in C++.

Flexible Parameters

By giving you flexibility over the number of parameters that you provide to an object method, we increased the applicability of the object in a variety of circumstances. We could also have used the `As Any type` definition, allowing a parameter to be of any type. This is sort of, but not exactly, like overloading in C++. The aim is the same though - to increase the generality of the object.

The one thing that VB doesn't go anywhere towards supporting is inheritance. This is the ability of one class to be based on another, inheriting all the properties and procedures of the base class. The great thing about inheritance is that any changes to the earlier, or ancestor, classes, are reflected in the descendants. This would be great if we wanted to add, say, database parsing capabilities, to our `clsFile` class, without changing the base class. We could derive another class from the original `clsFile` class and add the new features to create a descendant class. Well, we could if VB supported it.

I expect we'll see a constant upgrading of the OOP facilities of VB over forthcoming releases, to include things like inheritance.

Taking Classes Further

I've kept the implementation of the `clsFile` class in this chapter quite simple in order that the key concepts are not drowned in code. However, you can extend the class yourself to do any number of things, such as handling different file types.

In Chapter 15 - Using DLLs and the API, we will develop a program using a class that encapsulates the complexity of the Windows API. This is another good example of classes making life simpler and easier.

Summary

We've introduced some stiff new concepts in this chapter. In that way, its a little different to other parts of the book where the hard part is wading through the richness of Visual Basic's command set. What matters here is getting your head around the idea that your whole program is built on objects, some of which come in the box, and some of which you can write yourself.

We covered:

▶ What an object is in VB.

▶ How controls are special types of objects.

▶ How to create a simple class.

▶ How to implement property procedures and methods.

▶ How to use classes in your code.

Why Not Try.......

1 Add a button to the **CLASS3.VBP** project that repeatedly creates new instances of the box class on the screen.

2 Add some more methods to the box class to increase and decrease its size (**Box.Expand**, **Box.Shrink**). Then add methods and properties to the box to make it move around. What about **Box.XChange** and **Box.YChange** properties and a **Box.Move** method?

3 Add a **Replace** method to the class. Put the strings **FindString** and **ReplaceString** into properties and add a **Replace** method.

4 Create an MDI form version of **FILEFRM1.VBP**. Then declare an array of **clsFile** objects. As you declare more instances of the file object and assign them file names, open more MDI forms.

5 Add a property to **clsFile** that determines the type of file access: sequential or binary. Then add methods to read and write to both kinds of file. You could use optional parameters to pass a list of fields to the Text property for random access rather than a single parameter.

6 Create an object-oriented drawing program that has methods to add various shapes and properties, such as shading etc.

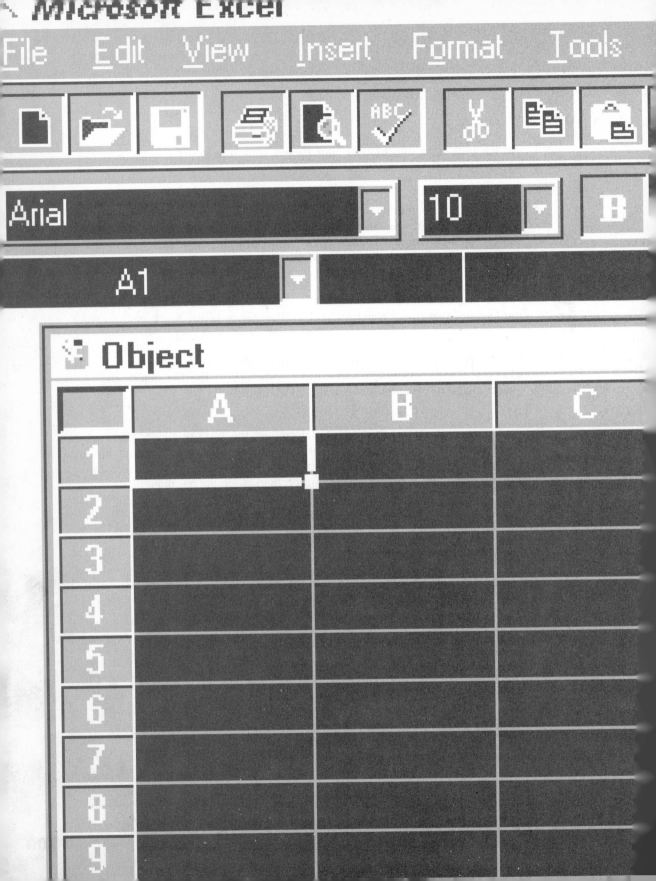

14

Programming Using OLE

OLE 2, and in particular the area known as OLE automation, brings us closer to Uncle Bill's dream of component-driven programming. The idea behind the whole thing is that programmers will eventually use Visual Basic to glue components - like spreadsheets, documents, multimedia data and so on - together to form a complete application. It's almost production line programming, and will bring with it a number of benefits for the user and developer alike.

Back in reality, I can't promise that programming is quite the point and click activity we fantasize about, but it is possible to do some impressive stuff with OLE today. In this chapter we will:

▶ Find out what OLE linking, embedding and automation are all about.

▶ Create OLE links and embedded objects at design time.

▶ Use the clipboard to make linking and embedding easier.

▶ Use OLE at run-time.

▶ Control other applications using OLE automation.

Using External Objects with OLE 2

OLE has been supported by Visual Basic for a while now, and has been present in versions of Windows for even longer. Fundamentally, it is about sharing both data and code between applications. In fact, it's a movement away from the existing idea of applications as little islands on their own. For example, in Windows 3 and early versions of Office, you could copy an Excel spreadsheet across into a Word document and edit that part of the Word document as though it was a spreadsheet - all thanks to OLE.

As I am writing this, OLE 2 is the latest release of OLE, and it is fully supported by Windows 95 and VB4. OLE 2 has been around for a while, but until recently it was poorly supported and very clunky to use. That's all changed. Indeed, Microsoft see one of the main uses for VB4 as being to act as the "glue" between various OLE 2 components on your system.

OLE 2 brought with it something known as **OLE automation**. This enables you to actually control an application from outside. For example, you can write an Excel macro that updates a Word document, or vice versa. There are financial applications written in VB4 that use an Excel sheet to handle complex calculations, an Access database as the data source, and Word 7 to produce the complex reports and documents that bring the two data sources together.

This all sounds very complex, but in reality it is not. Many of the applications in Windows 95 are OLE 2 enabled, and we will be making use of this in the examples in this chapter. Some of the later examples also assume that you have Office 95 installed. Don't panic if you haven't - all the examples should be simple enough to follow, even if you are not seated in front of your PC while you read them.

A Little More OLE Theory

OLE actually stands for Object Linking and Embedding and, as the name implies, it enables your apps to use external data by either linking to it, or by actually embedding it in your application. The distinction between the two is vitally important.

Linked Objects

A linked object is one where your application only holds a pointer to the original data. For example, you may have a Word document on your hard disk which you want to show your users. When you activate the object in your VB application, VB looks for the file on the disk where you specified. It then loads up Word into memory and puts that file into Word for you to edit. This is a pretty loose connection between VB and Word, via the file. You see a view of the file in your program which corresponds to the disk file. If you change the image, the disk file is changed.

Embedded Objects

The alternative to a linked object is an embedded one. When a user activates the object by double clicking it, your application's menus are replaced with those of the application that owns that type of data. For example, if you have an embedded Excel spreadsheet, then double clicking it will cause the Excel menus to replace any you already have on display and then enable you to add data into the object from your own user interface.

When you create an embedded object, VB loads in a snapshot of the file. When you activate it at run-time, VB loads up the facilities of, say, Word inside itself to work on the file. Both the document and the associated application are contained inside VB as objects.

OLE Automation

Many OLE 2 applications support an OLE feature known as OLE automation. As well as being able to export their data to other applications, including your own VB apps, these programs also export methods and properties which you can use in your code.

For example, you could write code to actually create and/or modify Excel data, and use Excel's functionality to work on that data without the user ever actually seeing Excel come to life.

This is where Microsoft's vision of VB as the glue between components becomes reality. You can build applications from the exposed objects of other applications, getting these to do work on your data for you.

We are going to tackle each one of these in order.

Implementing OLE 2 in Your VB Applications

Visual Basic provides a number of ways for you to incorporate OLE functionality into your programs. The most common is to make use of VB's OLE container control - a control which can contain complete OLE objects. The alternative is to actually place the OLE object classes you intend to deal with into the VB toolbox using the custom controls dialog, which is available from the Tools menu.

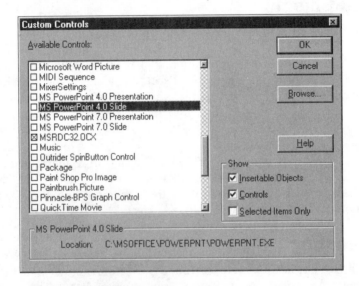

Visual Basic also includes a number of special OLE common dialogs that you can use to make use of OLE objects in your apps at run-time, without having to write any additional code.

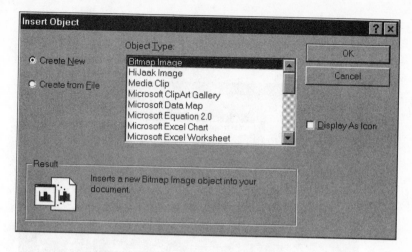

Let's take a look at the OLE container control now.

The OLE Container Control

This versatile little tool enables you to place either linked or embedded objects in your applications, either at design-time or run-time. The good news is that it is simple. There are only three properties that need setting up, and even these are handled by common dialogs both at design and run-time. Let's try it.

Creating a Linked Object at Design-Time

1 Create a new Visual Basic application. When the blank project appears, draw an OLE container control onto the form by double clicking its icon in the VB toolbox. After a short pause, one of the OLE common dialogs will appear.

Try It Out!

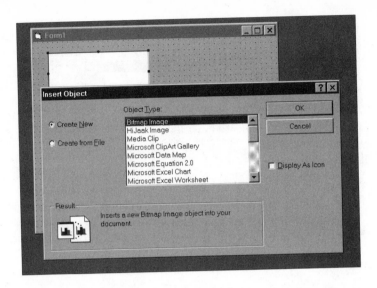

2 There is a WordPad document included with the example code on the disk which we will use to create a linked object. Click on the Create From File checkbox - the dialog will change.

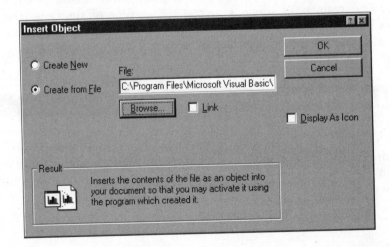

3 Click on the <u>B</u>rowse button and select the file called `OLETEST.DOC` from the directory where you installed the examples. Once you have selected the file, check the <u>L</u>ink check box on the dialog and then click on the OK button.

4 At this point, you will return to Visual Basic in design mode, but probably still won't be able to see any change. That is because the OLE container control is not yet big enough to show you the document you just loaded. By enlarging the form, though, and changing the position and size of the container control, you can easily bring the linked document into view.

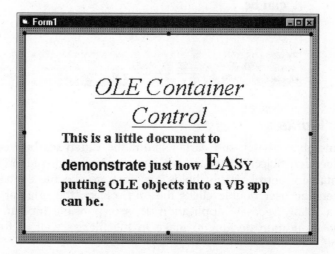

5 Run the application, and when it starts, double-click on the OLE container control. On my system, Microsoft Word 7 is linked to documents, so that application comes into view. If you don't have Word, though, or any other OLE 2 enabled word processor, then Windows will run up WordPad instead.

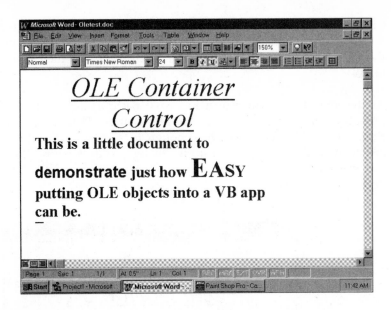

How It Works

Remember what I said earlier about the difference between linked and embedded objects? Because we have created a linked object here, the container control simply holds a pointer to the file containing the data. So, when the user double clicks the OLE object, the original application is run as a totally separate application. It is responsible for handling any changes any application decides to make to the file, as well as for saving the file itself.

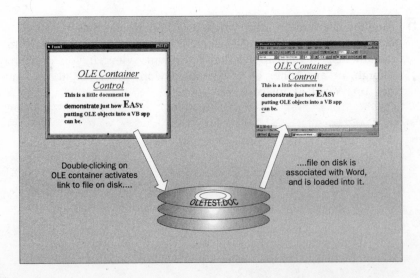

Double-clicking on OLE container activates link to file on disk....

....file on disk is associated with Word, and is loaded into it.

Now that you have WordPad or Word running, displaying the document, you can make changes to it. However, for those changes to be reflected in the OLE container control, you must tell Word or WordPad to save the document back to disk. The OLE container automatically notices that the file has changed and updates its image of the file.

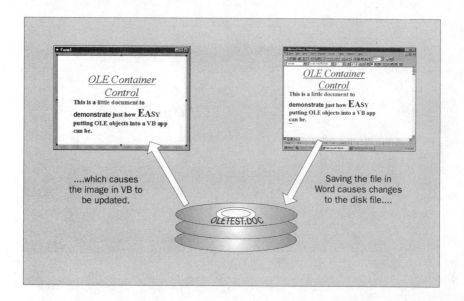

....which causes the image in VB to be updated.

Saving the file in Word causes changes to the disk file....

To see how this works, create the link to **OLETEST** at design-time. Then, leaving the project open, switch to Word or WordPad and make some changes to the file. When you return to the VB project, the changes have been reflected in the file.

We've finished with the example now, so close the document down in Word or WordPad and stop the program running. Let's try it again with an embedded object.

Creating an Embedded Object at Design-Time

Embedded objects work in a quite different way to linked objects. Take a look.

1 Create a new project in Visual Basic and, once again, draw an OLE container control on the default form. As before, when the common dialog appears, select Create from File and find the **OLETEST.DOC** file that is included with the samples. This time, though, don't check the Link box before clicking OK.

2 This time the object is **embedded** in the container control, rather than simply being linked to it. What this means is that the entire object is now copied into the container control. Your VB app is now responsible for maintaining that data, saving any changes that the user may make, and loading these changes back in the next time the program runs. We'll cover this aspect of the container control a little later; for now, though, just run the application.

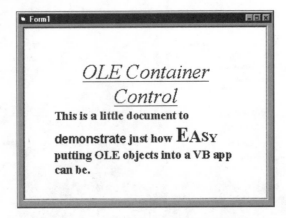

3 This time, when you double click the container control to activate the object, editing actually takes place within your VB application.

Remember your screen may look a little different to the one pictured here. On my system, DOC files are linked to Word 7, not WordPad.

How It Works

When you create an embedded object at design-time, VB loads in an image of the file into its own memory space. This is a snapshot of the data at this point in time.

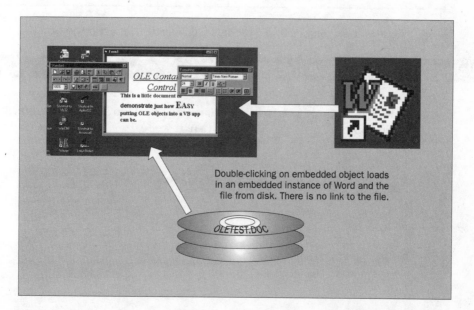

Double-clicking on embedded object loads in an embedded instance of Word and the file from disk. There is no link to the file.

When VB runs, it creates an object inside itself of the Word Document class and then uses this to edit the chosen file. This is fundamentally different from linking, which is like glorified shelling out.

Using the Container Control's Properties

Rather than using the OLE container control's common dialogs to set up a common control, you could do it the hard way and make use of the OLE control's properties.

Property	Description
Class	Sets or returns the class name of an object. This property determines the application that created and maintains the data on display.
SourceDoc	The source document that you want to turn into an OLE object.
SourceItem	Can be used to select only a part of the source document when creating a linked object - no use for embedded objects.

Let's create a new object and see these properties in action.

Using the Container Control Properties

1 Create a new project. Draw a container control on the form again, but this time cancel the OLE dialog when it appears. Click on the control to select it and press *F4* to bring up its Properties Window.

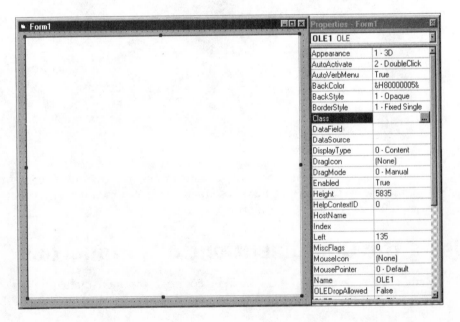

2 Find the Class property in the Properties Window. This defines the application that is used to create and later maintain the data that you intend to either link or embed. Click on the ellipses to the right of the property to bring up a list of known OLE 2 servers.

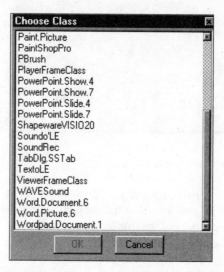

3 Find the WordPad entry at the bottom of the list. Notice how it reads Wordpad.Document.1. This indicates that you are opening a version 1 WordPad document. For now, just select the WordPad entry and click OK.

4 Now find the SourceDoc property. This is used to tell the container control exactly which document we intend to deal with. Double-click it to bring up the standard OLE dialog, then select our old friend, the **OLETEST.DOC** file, in the normal way using Browse. We want this object to be embedded so don't click the Link checkbox.

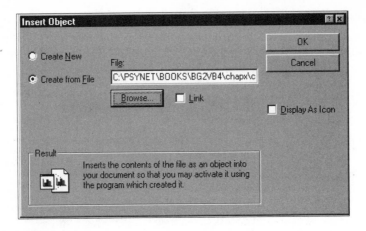

5 Finally, run the program.

We didn't set the final property - SourceItem. This allows you to specify a part of the file to use as the OLE object, using whatever notation the source application supports. For example, if we had just linked an Excel sheet, then we could set the SourceItem property to something like R1C1:R12C100 to select a range of cells in the sheet. Of course, this is pretty tricky to demonstrate without assuming you have Excel, so you'll just take have to take my word for it. If you do have Excel, though, go through the same processes we just covered to link an Excel sheet, but this time put in a range specification in the SourceItem property.

Notice how the property that names the application that will be embedded is called a class. VB declares an object variable of this type to access all the methods and properties of the Word application.

Using the Clipboard to Create Objects

You can also create linked or embedded objects at design-time using data on the clipboard. For example, many OLE applications allow you to cut or copy data to the clipboard and subsequently use a Paste Special option in a different program to create an OLE object. Visual Basic is no exception.

Creating Objects from the Clipboard

1 Run WordPad by selecting it from the Accessories item on the Start menu. Use the file menu in WordPad to load up the `OLETEST.DOC` document we used earlier.

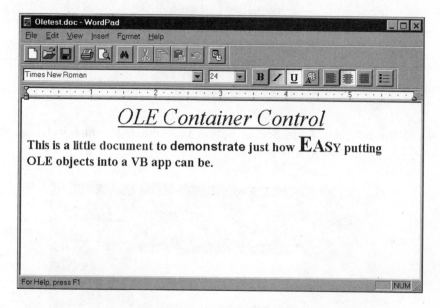

2 Drag the mouse over the text in the document to select it, then choose Copy from the Edit menu. At this point, if you have followed all the steps correctly, you have a document in the clipboard which can be pasted into an OLE container control.

3 Bring back Visual Basic, start a new project and draw an OLE container control on the default form. Cancel the OLE common dialog when it appears - we don't need to use it to paste data in. Now right click on the container control and a pop-up menu will appear.

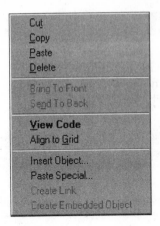

4 Notice how the Paste Special option is enabled. If you select this, the OLE paste dialog will pop up.

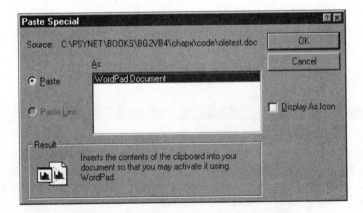

5 The OLE object contains a link to the source application, so the dialog knows the name of the source application, as well as the source document file name. Click on the OK button on this dialog to paste the data into the container control.

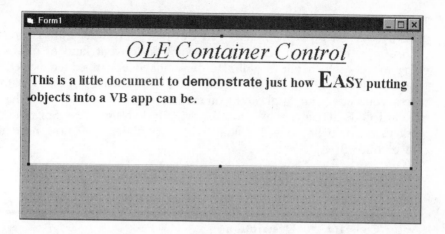

A little later we will see how to use the clipboard to paste objects into your container control from within your code.

Linking and Embedding at Run-Time

Of course, being able to link and embed objects at design-time is only half the OLE story. The real power of OLE comes from being able to do the same at run-time, and more than that, from being able to link and embed data without having to worry about the format of the server application.

The **CreateLink** and **CreateEmbed** methods let you link and embed at run-time. Both methods work on OLE container controls, and as their names suggest, one creates a linked object, the other creates an embedded one.

The syntax of the two methods is simple:

```
OLEContainer.CreateLink <Filename>
OLEContainer.CreateEmbed <Filename>
```

There is one other property that needs dealing with, though: the **OLETypeAllowed** property. Before you can place an object into a container control at run-time, you need to tell Visual Basic what kind of object it is going to be - whether it is going to be a linked or embedded object, or whether VB should simply allow either type. The reason for this is that, unless you code your application otherwise, the user will not see the standard OLE dialog that we can use in VB at design-time. So, much of the work that would be done manually with that dialog, you now need to take care of through code.

The **OLETypeAllowed** property can take the following values:

Value/Constant	Description
vbOLELinked	Tells VB that the container control will only hold linked objects.
vbOLEEmbedded	Tells VB that the container control will only hold embedded objects.
vbOLEEither	Go on - take a wild guess! Allows the control to hold either type of object.

Actually using these properties and the **CreateLink** or **CreateEmbed** methods in code is really easy.

Linking or Embedding at Run-Time

Try It Out!

1 Load up the **OLERUN.VBP** project. The form contains an OLE container control, two command buttons (one to link, the other to embed) and a common dialog.

2 At the moment, the only code in the project is to center the form when it loads up at run-time. We need to add code to the command buttons to breathe a little life into the project. Double-click on the Link button to bring up its Code Window. Change the **cmdLink_Click** event so that it looks like this:

```
Private Sub cmdLink_Click()

    With OLE1
        .Class = ""
        .SourceDoc = ""
        .SourceItem = ""

        dlgFileOpen.ShowOpen

        If dlgFileOpen.filename <> "" Then
            .OLETypeAllowed = vbOLELinked
            .CreateLink dlgFileOpen.filename
        End If
    End With

End Sub
```

3 Now, if you run the program, the link button will work. You can click it to display a common file dialog, and from there select a document that you want to turn into a linked object, for example `OLETEST.DOC` again.

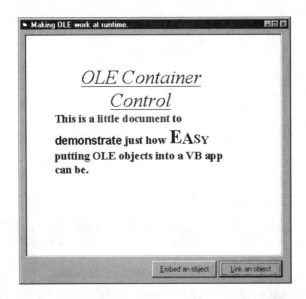

How It Works

The code itself is a little more verbose than it would probably be in the real world - I've written it like this to illustrate the concepts more than anything else.

The first three lines of code inside the **With** block reset the OLE container control, clearing the Class, SourceDoc and SourceItem properties, ready for new data.

```
With OLE1
        .Class = ""
        .SourceDoc = ""
        .SourceItem = ""
```

With that done, the file open dialog can be shown by calling the **ShowOpen** method of the common dialog control.

```
dlgFileOpen.ShowOpen
```

Finally, we check to see that the user actually selected a file before setting the **OLETypeAllowed** property. Finally, the **CreateLink** method is called.

```
If dlgFileOpen.filename <> "" Then
    .OLETypeAllowed = vbOLELinked
    .CreateLink dlgFileOpen.filename
End If
```

A slightly easier way to do this would have been to set the **OLETypeAllowed** property to 2 - Either at design-time.

We can apply the same techniques to code up the Embed button. If the application is still running, stop it, then double-click the Embed button to pop up the Code Window again. Type in code so that the **cmdEmbed _Click** event looks like this.

```
Private Sub cmdEmbed_Click()
  With OLE1
        .Class = ""
        .SourceDoc = ""
        .SourceItem = ""

        dlgFileOpen.ShowOpen

        If dlgFileOpen.filename <> "" Then
            .OLETypeAllowed = vbOLEEmbedded
            .CreateEmbed dlgFileOpen.filename
        End If

    End With
End Sub
```

Only two lines of code differ from the previous example: the **OLETypeAllowed** property is now set to **vbOLEEmbedded** and the **CreateEmbed** method is used in place of the **CreateLink** method. It really is as simple as that.

An Embedded File Editor

Let's now try and create an improved version of the **CON_DEMO** image viewer that we played with in Chapter 2. You'll remember that this used a picture control to load the selected file into. We'll replace this now with an embedded Paint object. Paint is the Win95 applet that replaces the old Paintbrush.

Try It Out!

1 Load up the existing **CON_DEMO.VBP** program. This is the current form.

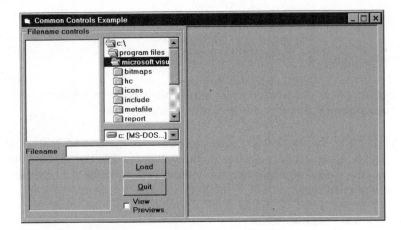

2 Delete the picture control from the right and drag the frame containing all the other controls over to the right side of the form.

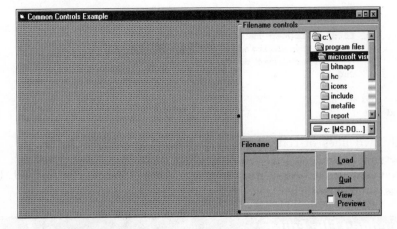

3 Draw an OLE container onto the form. Cancel the dialog box when it appears.

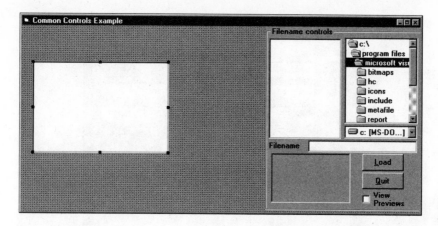

4 Set the OLE container Class property to Paint.Picture.

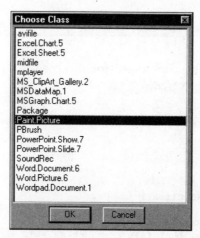

5 Set the SizeMode property to 2-AutoSize and the Name to olePicture.

6 We want to be able to display the Paint menu, and so now have to create a dummy menu. You can't display the menu from an embedded object without having a menu in existence already. We haven't got one in the original project, so we have to create one. Select the form, open the menu editor and add a dummy menu. Leave the caption blank.

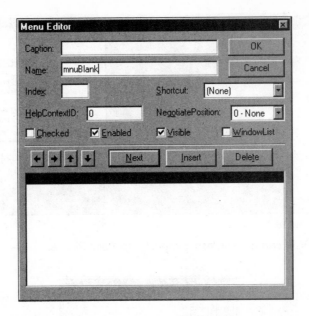

7 Now open up the click event for the <u>L</u>oad button. Remove this line from the existing code:

```
picPictureBox.picture = LoadPicture(txtFileName.Text)
```

and add this one:

```
Private Sub cmdLoad_Click()

    If Dir(txtFileName.Text) = "" Then
      MsgBox "Sorry, that file does not exist", vbOKOnly, "Error"
    Else
        olePicture.CreateEmbed txtFileName.Text

    End If

End Sub
```

8 Save the project and form as something other than **CON_DEMO** and run it. Load in the Wrox bitmap from the disk and the form will look like this:

9 To activate the object, double-click on it or click on the right mouse button and select Edit. Up comes the menu for Paint.

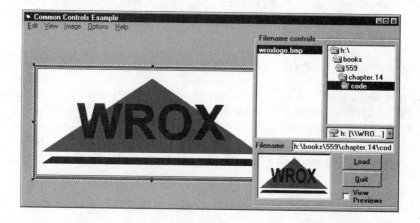

There's nothing really new here, so we don't need to walk through it. The finished program is on the disk as OLEIMG.VBP.

Loading and Saving Embedded Data

We have already discussed how, with embedded objects, your VB application is responsible for maintaining the integrity of the object's data, including accepting responsibility for loading and saving it to disk.

Luckily, this is nowhere near as complex as many developers think it is. VB has two wonderful built-in methods to handle the whole task for you: **SaveToFile** and **ReadFromFile**. Take a look at this code:

```
Sub SaveOLEControl()

    Dim nFileNumber As Integer

    nFileNumber=FreeFile
    Open "Test.OLE" For Binary As #nFileNumber
    Ole1.SaveToFile nFileNumber
    Close #nFileNumber

End Sub
```

This code would save the contents of an OLE container control to a file called **Test.OLE**. How does it work?

First of all we use the **FreeFile** function to return the next available file number. We then open the file on disk that we are going to save the data to.

```
Open "Test.OLE" For Binary As #nFileNumber
```

Since we are saving OLE data, which could easily be a mix of binary, textual and numeric information, the file needs to be opened telling VB that it will contain **Binary** data. This line opens a file called **Test.OLE** as a binary file, and tells VB that from now on we will refer to the file using the file number held in our **nFilenumber** variable.

Once we have opened a file, we can then save data out to it, using the **SaveToFile** method I mentioned earlier.

```
Ole1.SaveToFile nFileNumber
```

The syntax is quite simple. Since the **SaveToFile** method works on an OLE container control, the name of the control must be placed before the method. In this example I have assumed that the control is called **Ole1**. All that remains is to specify the number of the open file that you want to save to, which you do using **nFilenumber**.

The final step the program takes is to close the file down.

```
Close #nFileNumber
```

Loading data into an OLE container control from a file is equally easy - in fact the code is almost identical:

```
Sub LoadOLEControl()

    Dim nFileNumber As Integer
    nFileNumber=FreeFile
    Open "Test.OLE" For Binary As #nFileNumber
    Ole1.ReadFromFile nFileNumber
    Close #nFileNumber

End Sub
```

Apart from the obvious difference in the name of the subroutine, the only other difference is the use of the **ReadFromFile** method instead of the **SaveToFile** method. The rest of the code follows the same pattern that we saw in the previous example: get file number, open file, perform operation, close file. Simple!

Linking and Embedding with the Clipboard

The clipboard object itself has no specific methods for checking whether the data held on the clipboard is, or could become, an OLE object. However, the OLE container control does - using the **PasteOK** property.

The **PasteOK** property returns true if the data in the clipboard can be pasted into the OLE container control, false if it cannot. In the event that a true is returned, you can invoke the **Paste** method on the container control to actually get the data out of the clipboard.

An alternative to using the **Paste** method, though, and a much more professional method too, is to pop up the Paste Special dialog that so many applications, including Visual Basic, make use of. This can be accomplished with a call to the **PasteSpecialDlg** method.

Before we look at the nuts and bolts of using the clipboard with OLE, a little programming theory fits here quite well. The **Paste Special** menu item is usually placed inside an application's **Edit** menu. However, it is standard procedure to only enable this menu item if there is an object on the clipboard that can be pasted.

The problem for novice programmers comes in deciding where to put the code to enable and disable the menu item. I have seen a number of approaches to this within Psynet, ranging from idle loops that check the clipboard whenever the computer has a spare moment, to timer based code which checks the clipboard once ever n milliseconds, to complex DLL based code that takes the strain away from VB totally. None of these is what I would consider the correct solution.

The trick with stuff like this is to remember that you are programming in an event-driven development system - the bulk of your code will run in response to events that either the user or the system triggers. When deciding where to put code like this, try to figure out which natural event would suit your code best. In this particular example, the best event to use is the **Edit** menu item's click event.

In order to drop down a menu, the user must click on the menu heading. By putting a little code in that item's click event, we can enable and disable menu items only when they are about to come into view. This is by far the most elegant approach and illustrates a good programming point - never overcomplicate your code.

Pasting OLE Objects

1 Load the **OLEPASTE.VBP** project into Visual Basic - this illustrates exactly the right way to deal with the clipboard and OLE container controls.

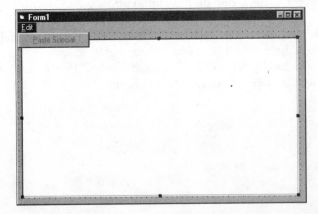

2 The project consists of a menu bar with only one heading: Edit. This menu heading has just one item on it: a disabled Paste Special item. The form itself contains nothing more than a single OLE container control with the OLETypeAllowed property set to 2 (allow any type of object).

3 Run the project. Then put a suitable object on the clipboard, for example a bit of a Word document, and select Paste Special. Up comes the OLE common dialog and you can paste away.

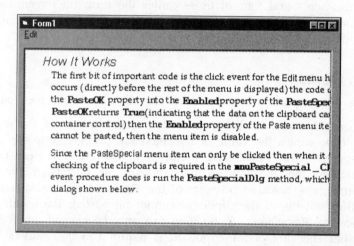

4 Back in design mode, double-click on the form to bring up the program code. Bear in mind that this program handles enabling and disabling of the menu item on the fly, automatic checking of the clipboard data to see if it can be pasted, and the display of a complex OLE paste dialog - be prepared for a shock as to the size of the source!

```
Private Sub Form_Load()

    With frmMain
        .Left = (Screen.Width - .Width) / 2
        .Top = (Screen.Height - .Height) / 2
    End With

End Sub
```

```
Private Sub mnuEdit_Click()

    mnuPasteSpecial.Enabled = OLE1.PasteOK

End Sub
```

```
Private Sub mnuPasteSpecial_Click()

    OLE1.PasteSpecialDlg

End Sub
```

Suitably shocked? With the exception of the lines that mark the start and end of the event procedures, there are only six lines of actual code in the application - and four of those center the form on screen. Once again, Visual Basic blows the myth that dealing with OLE is a complex issue out of the water. It isn't!

How It Works

The first important bit of code is the click event for the Edit menu heading.

When this menu is clicked, directly before the rest of the menu is displayed, the code copies the value of the **PasteOK** property into the **Enabled** property of the PasteSpecial menu item. Therefore, if **PasteOK** returns true, indicating that the data on the clipboard can be pasted into the container control, the **Enabled** property of the Paste Special menu item is set to true. If the contents of the clipboard cannot be pasted, the menu item is disabled. Since the PasteSpecial menu item can only be clicked when it is enabled, no further checking of the clipboard is required in the **mnuPasteSpecial _Click** code. All that event procedure does is run the **PasteSpecialDlg** method, which displays the Paste dialog shown below.

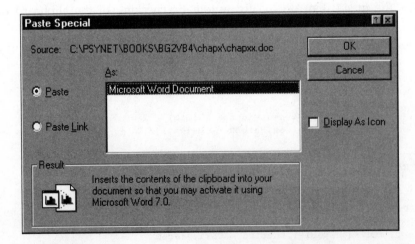

Remember how in Chapter 1 I said that VB programming was essentially providing your user with the tools to do their job, and then letting them do it - this is a case in point.

The dialog shows the user the class of the object, in this case a Microsoft Word document. They can then choose to either link or embed the data into the container control. The actual pasting of the data from the clipboard into the control is handled for you, as is setting the control's properties and displaying the data on screen. You should note that much of this is only possible because I have already set the `OLETypeAllowed` property to allow both linked and embedded objects in the container control.

> **FYI**
>
> You should have seen by this point how VB can make seemingly complex tasks simple. Many C and Pascal programmers have avoided OLE in their applications like the plague, simply because, on the surface, it seems a nightmare to implement. As a VB programmer, though, you can walk into any programming circle, look the god of OLE in the eye and honestly say "Linking and Embedding... no problemo!"

OLE 2 goes far beyond just being able to copy data from one container control to another, though. You can also use OLE, or more specifically a part of it, to actually take control of a second application.

OLE Automation

Programmers, especially those learning a new language or operating system, are nervous types. Having learnt the basics of a language, they tend to feel quite secure, cocooned in the development environment they are just beginning to get the hang of. Tell them to take control of another application and utilize its functionality in their own app, without access to the source code of the second app, and they run for the hills.

This is where OLE automation fits in very nicely, allowing you to control a second application from within VB. I guess the fear that the thought of this instills in many a programmer has to be put down to fear of the unknown. In reality, OLE automation is as easy to get to grips with as the much feared OLE container control that we de-mystified a little earlier.

While all OLE 2 applications are able to expose their data for inclusion in other applications, those OLE 2 apps that support OLE automation are also able to expose their functionality. To VB programmers, this functionality comes in the form of objects. Like any other object you may use in VB, OLE automation objects come complete with properties and methods that you can use in your VB code. If you want to make use of the math handling facilities in Excel, then simply open an Excel sheet object and go to work on its properties. Nothing tricky about that, is there?

In fact, there really isn't that much to learn about the VB side of OLE automation. Since you are dealing with objects provided by applications outside of Visual Basic, the real trick in mastering it is knowing what facilities these objects provide you with. The VB side of things involves error handling, knowing how to create these objects in code, and generally customizing the way in which VB deals with OLE 2 apps (for instance, how long will it wait for a connection, should the user be able to see the server application or not, and so on).

In the examples that follow, we will make use of the Excel 5 OLE automation objects to demonstrate the VB side. If you don't have Excel, don't panic; the concepts are really simple and although working code is shown here, you can just as easily read the code and look at the screenshots to get a feel for what is going on. However, as the most common use for OLE automation at the time of writing is controlling the applications in the Microsoft Office suite, the chances are, if you are still reading this section of the book with an interested look on your face, that you do indeed have Office and need to take control of it.

Taking a Look at What's Available

VB has a built-in facility known as the object browser. As we've already seen, the object browser shows you all the objects currently in your VB application, and those to which your code has access, even if it is not currently making use of them.

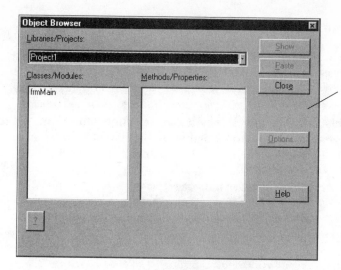

The object browser starts up showing you the modules and objects that physically make up your application. We used the browser at this level in Chapter 13, where we saw the methods and property procedures that we'd created for our own classes.

However, by dropping down the combo box at the top of the browser, you can also see the external OLE objects that your code can address. This is a list of all the object collections (meaning OLE enabled objects and applications) that VB is aware of.

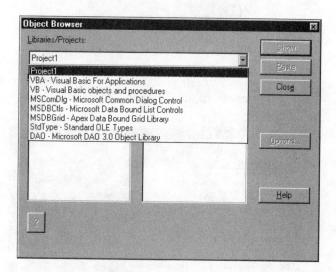

I've used the term OLE enabled a bit loosely in this chapter. There are in fact various levels of OLE enablement. There are a lot of apps that support OLE 2 linking and embedding, but fewer that support OLE automation. Those that do are said to expose their objects for OLE. Sounds exciting.

You can extend this list of available objects by selecting other libraries to appear in the Browser Window. You do this by setting up a reference to that object. Choose References from the Tools menu.

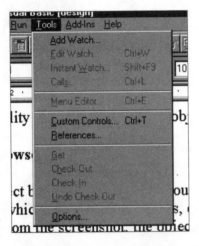

Selecting this pops up yet another dialog box, allowing you to choose which external objects your application may want to grab hold of.

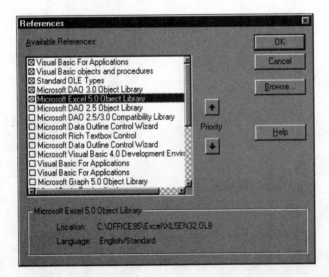

If, for example, you had Excel 5 or later installed on your system, then you could select the Excel 5 option to make its object set available to your application.

How does VB know which applications you have on your system that can be used as OLE object libraries? The answer is by using the OLE registry.

The Registry

Every Windows 95 system has a built-in OLE 2 database called the **registry**. If you install an application that is capable of exporting its functionality through OLE 2, then it is expected to register itself in this database - it's rather like signing in at a hotel really. If you don't check in, then how can anyone know that you are there.

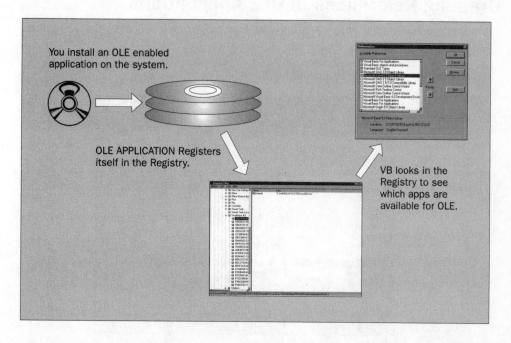

You install an OLE enabled application on the system.

OLE APPLICATION Registers itself in the Registry.

VB looks in the Registry to see which apps are available for OLE.

There are whole books on low level OLE 2 work that cover the registry in a lot more depth than I can here. My job is to teach you how to use the applications that have already registered themselves. If you want to play around with the registry on your own, though, to see the kind of data that is in there, simply click the Win95 Start button, then select the Run option.

When the Run dialog appears, enter **REGEDIT** and press *Return*. After a short pause, the System Registry editor will appear and you can browse to your heart's content.

PLEASE NOTE:
It's not a good idea to change anything in the registry by hand unless you are an OLE guru. Bad things can happen that may end up with you having to re-install all your apps. You have been warned.

Once you understand the registry, it's easier to see how linking and embedding work. The registry is the glue that holds VB, the file and the application together.

Creating References to OLE Applications

Let's assume that you've got Excel 5 on your system, and that you have used the References dialog to tell VB that you intend to use it. How does this affect the object browser? Take a look at this:

The left-hand side of the browser is taken up with a list of the OLE classes and modules that Excel supports.

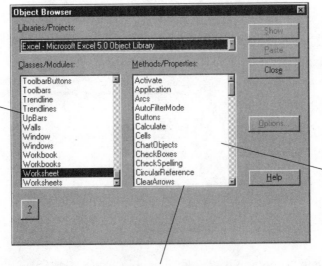

For each class you select on the left, the methods and properties which you can use to control it are displayed on the right.

If you want a complete summary of the parameters a method needs, the values it returns or the format of any of the properties, just click on the relevant entry in the list and its definition appears at the bottom of the browser.

So, without further ado let's see how to make use of an OLE object, without resorting to container controls.

Steps to OLE Automation

There's a certain formal process that you have to follow in order to make the connection between your VB application and the OLE server that you want to use. The server is the application whose objects you are going to use and control from your VB application. In our case, Excel is the OLE **server** and VB is the OLE **client**.

Once you have set up a reference to the app you want to use, you can go ahead and start to use it. At this point you need to know some things about the application you intend to control, namely what objects you want and where in the object hierarchy they reside. What??? Object hierarchy? What's that all about then?

The Object Hierarchy

Each object that supports OLE automation organizes itself into a logical tree of objects. This reflects how the objects depend on each other to operate. For example, an Excel worksheet has to exist inside a workbook, which has to exist inside an instance of the Excel application.

The application hierarchy indicates which objects you need to have in existence before you can create the object you want. If you only want Excel itself, you don't have to create anything else because nothing comes above it in the hierarchy. If, however, you want an Excel worksheet, then you also need an Excel object and a workbook object. The same is true for objects that are dependent on the worksheet, such as buttons.

The good news here is that you don't have to continually reference the complete family tree of the object to get at it. Excel and VB make some assumptions about what you want. To understand this, we need to look at how we declare OLE objects.

Creating OLE Objects

Try It Out!

1 Create a new project. To keep things simple, let's use the form load event for the code that assigns an instance of our Excel object to the object variable. First of all, add the declaration for the new object to the general declarations section.

```
Dim MyExcel As Object
```

2 Add this code:

```
Private Sub Form_Load()

    Set MyExcel = CreateObject("Excel.Application")

End Sub
```

3 When you run the project, there's lots of whirring and clanking in the background as the Excel object is created, but not much to look at. Stop the code and add this line after the **Set MyExcel**.... statement.

```
MyExcel.Application.Visible = True
```

4 Run it again and up comes Excel. Close it down and we're back to the blank VB form, still running.

5 Let's now add some code to bring up a worksheet. Add a declaration for a sheet in the declarations section and remove the one for the Excel object.

```
Option Explicit

Dim MySheet As Object
```

6 Then add this code to the form load event:

```
Private Sub Form_Load()

    Set MySheet = CreateObject("Excel.Sheet")
    MySheet.Application.Visible = True


End Sub
```

7 Run the program. Up comes Excel with the worksheet inside it. How come? Surely we need to create an Excel object before we create a worksheet.

How It Works

The first part of the code, where we created the blank Excel, is straightforward. **CreateObject** is one of two methods available to your OLE automation code. It creates a brand new object based on the parameter you specify. In our case, we tell VB that our new object is an Excel worksheet:

```
Set MySheet = CreateObject("Excel.Sheet")
```

You might expect Excel to create a new sheet inside an existing instance of Excel. After all, the sheet object is below the application object in the hierarchy, right? Well yes, but there are two things about the **CreateObject** method that you need to understand.

- It always creates a brand new instance of the root OLE automation object. In our case, this is the Excel application, because that's the top of the object hierarchy.

- It "knows" how to go back up the object hierarchy from a certain level and find the root object.

So, in our case, when we told the **CreateObject** function that we wanted an **Excel.Sheet**, it went back up the object hierarchy and opened up a new instance of Excel.

It would therefore be logical to assume that there is some method that is internal to the **Excel.Application** object that will let us create a new worksheet. After all, we don't want to open a new instance of the application every time we want a new worksheet. There is, but to understand how it works, we need to first get a feeling for how to make things happen inside the new instance of our OLE automation server (in this case, Excel).

Before we leave the subject of declarations and instancing, I should mention that we have also uncovered a useful aspect of `CreateObject`. Because it knows its way up the object hierarchy, you don't always have to declare all the predecessors in order to create a new object. To create a new worksheet inside Excel, we just write:

```
Set MySheet = CreateObject("Excel.Sheet")
MySheet.Application.Visible = True
```

The OLE 2 system runs Excel out of sight, and says "Hey, this guy wants a sheet object. Got one of those?". Excel replies with a "Yes" and the object is created. Had we asked for `Excel.SnazzyVideoClip`, then the code would fail, since Excel doesn't have a clue what a `SnazzyVideoClip` object is and so can't service your request.

Controlling the Server App

1 Load up the `OLEType.VBP` project. This is a simple form with no code in it as yet.

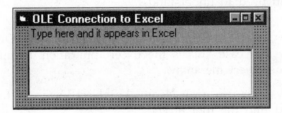

2 Add this code to the declarations section:

```
Dim MySheet As Object
```

3 Now add the code to load Excel into the load event again:

```
Private Sub Form_Load()

    Set MySheet = CreateObject("Excel.Sheet")
    MySheet.Application.Visible = True

End Sub
```

FYI

This is actually bad design. It takes a while for Excel to load up and we're leaving the user in the dark by loading up the form last. A `Form1.Show` command at the start would be more user-friendly.

4 Now add this code to make what you type into the text box appear in the first cell of the spreadsheet:

```
Private Sub Text1_Change()

    MySheet.Cells(1, 1).Value = Text1.Text

End Sub
```

5 Run the program. Position the windows so you can see both the form and Excel and then type away.

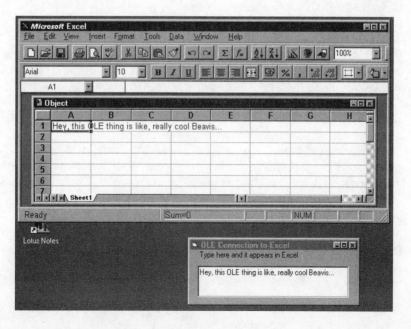

How It Works

In the text box change event, the program creates and declares an Excel worksheet object and makes it appear on the screen as before. To pass the text from the form to the first cell in the open spreadsheet, we pass it to the first element in the cells collection:

```
MySheet.Cells(1, 1).Value = Text1.Text
```

This needs some investigation. We have missed a level out of the object hierarchy here, namely the workbook. The map of the object hierarchy looks like this:

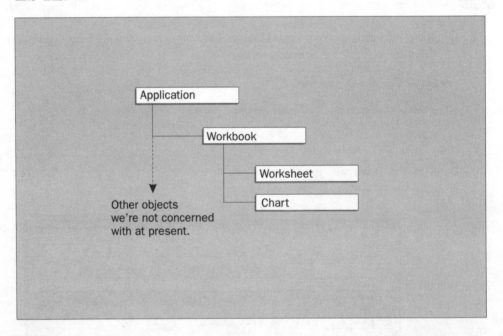

Each worksheet belongs to a workbook, and each workbook belongs to an instance of the application. However, you can have more than one workbook in Excel and more than one sheet in a workbook. This first diagram is oversimplified. We've just been working with the active sheet and active workbook in the collections of each of these objects. These collections are object arrays. The real diagram is more like this.

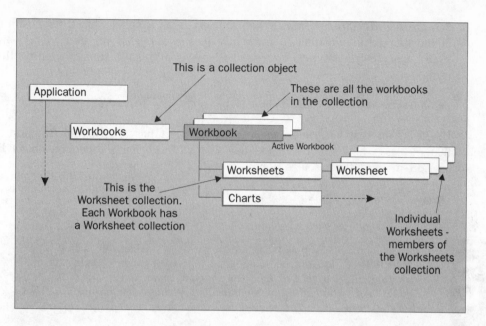

There is also a cells collection that is a property of each worksheet object. Like all arrays, we can address this using index numbers. As you might expect, this is a two dimensional array.

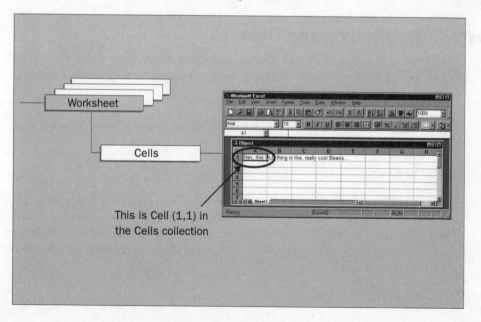

Because we declared **MySheet** and created it as a sheet object, its position in the hierarchy is contained internally in the object. If we had created an **Excel.Application** type object instead, we could have done the same thing using

```
MyExcel.Workbooks(1).Worksheets(1).Cells(1,1) = Text1.Text
```

I said earlier that an **Excel.Application** object has an internal function that creates a new sheet - this is the **Add** method. Each collection object has an **Add** method that creates a new member of the array.

```
MyExcel.Worksheets.Add
```

You can see already that we're being sucked into learning a hell of a lot about Excel in order to make OLE automation work. As I said at the beginning, the VB side of OLE automation is not hard - what is complex is understanding and controlling your server application. That's why you need lots of documentation about how your target servers work.

Let's take a step back now and look at a couple of other things we need to know before we look at an example program.

Working with Existing Objects

As its name suggests, **CreateObject** is great when you need to create a new object in your code. However, when you need to access a file that already exists, you need **GetObject** .

For example, let's say that we were going to work with a file called **TEST.XLS**. In that case, we could have said:

```
Set MyFile = GetObject("Test.XLS", "Excel.Sheet")
```

This would create an OLE automation link between your VB program and a specific file on the disk, using Excel to maintain it. You haven't created anything new because in an object-oriented view of the world, **TEXT.XLS** and the Excel app that created it and maintains it, are one and the same.

Closing Down an Object

If you've been running the example code so far, you may well have ended up with loads of instances of Excel drifting around on your system - really improving your system performance! This is because, unlike with a linked object, it's up to you to close down the instances of the server application when you have finished.

To do this, you use the **Application** object of the **MySheet** object and call its **Quit** method.

```
MySheet.Application.Quit
```

This uses an application level method for the application object that relates to the sheet we are using. Note that if you just say:

```
Set MySheet = Nothing
```

the sheet disappears but the application remains active. You can't use this method to close down the whole application.

If you set an object variable to nothing, you are basically destroying that object, telling the OLE server application that you no longer need its services in maintaining the file you either just created, or pulled off the hard disk. The net result of doing this is that the memory used by the OLE object is freed up, and the server application, in this case Excel, destroys the document you were working on. This is quite an important point - if you need to save any changes you make to the data, then make sure you call your OLE object's relevant save method, if it has one.

OLE objects, like all objects, cease to exist when they go out of scope. If you want to see this, move the **Dim MySheet as Object** declaration from the declarations section to the **Form_Load** event. This makes the sheet object local to that procedure, instead of to the form module. As you load the form, the sheet appears, but it then disappears as the event ends. It has gone out of scope. Excel, though, remains open. If you now create a new workbook inside Excel, this will have the default name Book2, indicating a ghostly predecessor.

It's now time to look at a larger application.

Excel Automation

Try It Out!

This is a fairly simple program that lets you enter eight numbers, and then, using option buttons, lets you choose whether to total them or work out their average. You can then click on a Perform The Calculation button and the program will carry out your request and display the result. Nothing special there, I hear you cry, and you'd be right. However, the application doesn't work out the calculation itself, it gets Excel to do it.

1 Load in the **EXCEL1.VBP** project and run it.

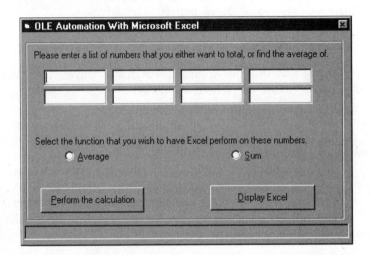

2 Put in some numbers and click the Perform button. Notice that the first time you do this, and when the program starts up, there are some quite hefty delays. This is because the program is running up Excel in the background. After you have performed the calculation once, though, doing it again, with the same or different numbers, is much faster.

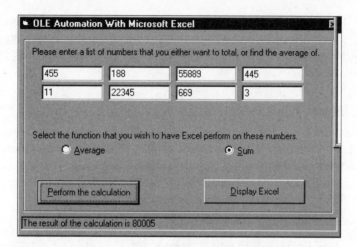

3 If you need some proof that it is Excel doing the legwork, not the VB app, then after doing the calculation, click on the Show Excel button. Providing you have Excel installed, of course, Excel will show itself, complete with a new worksheet created by the program, containing the numbers you entered.

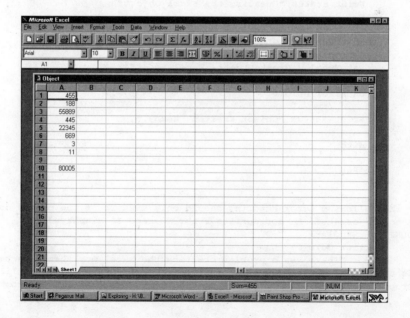

4 Once Excel is on display, stop the **EXCEL1.VBP** program. Notice how the Excel sheet disappears. Excel manages the data, but when no applications need to use it anymore, Excel is quite happy to ditch the sheet.

How It Works

Let's take a look at the code. With VB in design mode, double-click on the form to bring up the Code Window. We are going to take a look at the **Form_Load** event first.

```
Private Sub Form_Load()

    ' Centre the form on the screen
    With frmMain
        .Left = (Screen.Width - .Width) / 2
        .Top = (Screen.Height - .Height) / 2

        ' Display the form
        .Show
        DoEvents

        ' Tell the user that we are creating an object
        Print_Status "Creating the Excel Object"

        ' Create the object
        On Error GoTo OLE2ErrorHandler
        Screen.MousePointer = 11
        Set Excel = CreateObject("Excel.Sheet")
        Screen.MousePointer = 0
        On Error GoTo 0

        Print_Status "Object created. Ready."

    End With

    Exit Sub


' The following error handling should only kick in if the object could
' not be created. An appropriate error message is displayed.
OLE2ErrorHandler:
    On Error GoTo 0
    MsgBox "There was a problem creating the Excel worksheet. Perhaps Excel
is not installed, or it is not registered as an OLE 2 server application
properly. This program will now shut down.", vbExclamation, "Error"
    End

End Sub
```

The start of the event is really quite straightforward: some housekeeping code runs to center the form on the screen, and then the **Show** method is called to make the form visible.

After that, a call is made to a subprocedure elsewhere in the program to display a message in the status bar at the bottom of the main form.

```
' Tell the user that we are creating an object
Print_Status "Creating the Excel Object"
```

With the housekeeping out of the way, the OLE code itself can take over.

```
' Create the object
On Error GoTo OLE2ErrorHandler
Screen.MousePointer = 11
Set Excel = CreateObject("Excel.Sheet")
Screen.MousePointer = 0
On Error GoTo 0
```

First an error handler is started. In the event that something should go wrong, control jumps to the bottom of the **Form_Load** event, to a label called **OLE2ErrorHandler**. This should only really happen if you don't have Excel installed on your system.

The mouse pointer is then changed to an hourglass since, as you have seen already, creating an OLE object in code can take a little while.

Finally, an object variable called **Excel** is set using the **CreateObject** method. This **Excel** variable is declared earlier on in the module like this.

```
Dim Excel As Object
```

The remaining code in the **Form_Load** event code just changes the mouse pointer back to normal, and updates the status bar once again to tell the world that the new object now exists.

The real meat of the automation code lies in the **cmdPerform_Click** event.

```
Private Sub cmdPerform_Click()

    Dim nElement As Integer

    ' Use a For loop to copy all the numbers into the Excel worksheet
    Screen.MousePointer = 11
```

```
    Print_Status "Passing numbers to Excel"
    For nElement = 0 To 7

        Excel.Cells(1 + nElement, 1).Value = Val(txtNumber(nElement))

    Next

    ' Use the option buttons to determine which formula to use, then insert
    ' that in the sheet as well
    Print_Status "Passing formula to Excel"
    If optSum.Value = True Then
        Excel.Cells(10, 1).Formula = "=Sum(A1:A8)"
    Else
        Excel.Cells(10, 1).Formula = "=Average(A1:A8)"
    End If

    ' Get the result from Excel and display it in the picture box at the
    ' foot of the form.

    Print_Status "The result of the calculation is " & Excel.Cells(10,
⤷1).Value
    Screen.MousePointer = 0

End Sub
```

On the surface, the code looks quite complex. It isn't really, though. It consists mainly of a **For** loop which takes each of the values in the text boxes and copies them into the Excel sheet we created and have stored in **Excel**. The **Cells** object lets you access the values, formatting and general state of being of any cell in an Excel sheet. All you need to do is tell Excel which cell you want to deal with in (Row, Column) format, followed by the property you are interested in.

The example code looks complex only because the values are being set in a **For** loop, with the loop index being used to work out the coordinates on the sheet.

```
For nElement = 0 To 7

        Excel.Cells(1 + nElement, 1).Value = Val(txtNumber(nElement))

Next
```

All this does is set a cell value to the value of the data entered in each text box. The result, as you can see from the previous screen shot, is a single column of values in the sheet itself.

Another useful property of the **Cells** object is **Formula**. By setting the **Formula** of a cell to any valid Excel formula, you can harness the processing abilities of Excel from within your application. This is exactly what our example does.

```
If optSum.Value = True Then
        Excel.Cells(10, 1).Formula = "=Sum(A1:A8)"
Else
        Excel.Cells(10, 1).Formula = "=Average(A1:A8)"
End If
```

The code looks to see which option button you selected, and hence what kind of calculation you want to do. It then feeds the appropriate formula into a cell directly beneath the column of numbers the rest of the code created.

Having done that, all that remains is to get the results of the calculation from the **Value** property of the cell whose formula we just set.

```
Print_Status "The result of the calculation is " & Excel.Cells(10,
1).Value
```

Just to force the point home, though, remember that these are objects and properties that are specific to Excel. Always read up on what's available to you with the applications you try to control before embarking on a coding frenzy.

We have only dealt with some really easy high school type math here. But, what if we needed to work out variance on some figures, chart the figures, work out a bit of standard deviation, or analyze a trend? At that point, things would normally get quite complex. However, this example program would change very little.

Summary

This has been a very cursory tour of OLE and OLE automation. We have covered the general principles, though you must remember that the objects that each OLE server exposes and the methods and properties they support differ drastically.

When linking and embedding, you learnt that:

▶ Linking shells out to an application to work on the actual disk file version of the data, while embedding works on a local copy of the data, using the application as an object in your program.

▶ You can link or embed objects easily using the clipboard's Paste Special method.

▶ You can work with OLE objects in code or at design-time.

The basic template for OLE automation is:

▶ Define a variable as an object to hold the OLE object you are going to work with.

▶ Use `GetObject` or `CreateObject` to form a link to an existing or a new file.

▶ Use the sub-objects and properties of your newly created object to access the functionality of the server application.

Why Not Try.......

1 Replace the text box in the **WORKPAD** project with an embedded **WordPad** object and implement the same commands as before.

2 Create a database reporting module that uses Excel to import the data from the **ORDPRODB** database and then prints it out as a nice table. Quite often database users want to "slice and dice" data on their own: Excel is a great application for this.

3 Replace the bound grid control in the **INTSQL** project with an embedded Excel object.

4 If you have the Excel documentation, then create a chart of the numbers you enter into the grid.

15

Using DLLs and The API

Visual Basic does a good job of shielding developers from the nitty-gritty details of Windows. However, there comes a point where you can no longer hide behind the safe walls of Visual Basic. Windows is out there, waiting to talk to your program.

Windows provides a number of function calls, in the form of DLLs, that are useful to VB programmers. You can also co-opt DLLs from other programs to do work for you. We'll concentrate on using the Windows DLLs here, but what we learn is widely applicable.

In this chapter you'll learn:

▶ How to declare API and DLL functions in your programs and how to utilize the underlying power of Windows.

▶ How to use the API to harness the power of multimedia in your VB applications.

How VB and Windows Fit Together

In this chapter, we're going to look at how to use tools that lie outside what you might consider as Visual Basic itself, meaning functions and procedures that are actually part of Windows itself. These are pieces of code that Windows has at its disposal to do what it has to do: manage your systems and provide a consistent user interface and operating environment for your programs.

This sounds complicated, but it isn't. The first thing to note is that we've effectively used part of the Windows code already, without really knowing it, when we used the common dialog control. Let's consider for a while what's really happening when we do this.

DLLs the Easy Way - the Common Dialog

You remember the common dialog. It's that great little control that is a window onto a load of different dialogs. Here's the file open dialog:

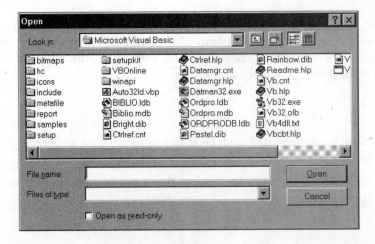

All of these dialogs not only save us time, but also give our programs the look and feel of a real Windows application. The reason they're called *common* dialogs is that they look the same in all Windows applications. So what's the story? It makes you wonder whether they aren't really part of Windows after all....

Well they are. If you load up Explorer and take a look in your **WINDOWS\SYSTEM** directory you'll see a file named **COMDLG32.DLL**.

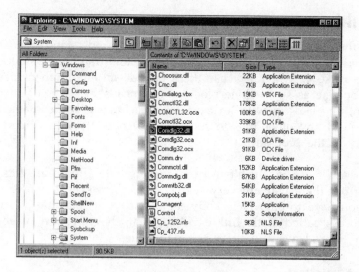

This file contains all the code needed to create the various common dialogs that Windows supports. Lumping all this code together in a common directory makes it accessible to all Windows programs, including Windows itself.

You can't look inside it - it's a compiled lump of C/C++ code and would look like gobbledygook. What interests us, of course, is how we can talk to this little monster and tell it what to do from our VB code. To understand that, we'll have to take a quick lesson in how Windows works.

Dynamic Linking

The **COMDLG32.DLL** file is what's known as a **dynamic link library**, hence the file extension. To you and me, this means that it's a block of code containing procedures and functions that are useful for more than one program; it is available to any program that wants to use it. The question, of course, is how.

Let's take a quick lesson in the history of programming. If this really is your first toe in the water of programming, then you don't need to bother to read this. Think yourself lucky you got into the game at the right time and skip this next bit.

Static Linking

This is the opposite of dynamic linking; if you understand how it works, you'll see why dynamic linking is a good plan. Traditional programming languages like C, when you use them outside an environment like Windows, like to operate as stand-alone blocks. This means that when you compile the program, you end up with an executable file that is self-contained, and doesn't need any other files to run. All the code it needs is hardwired into the body of the program.

This doesn't mean you can't use pre-written code - there are lots of C libraries out there that are very widely used. However, in order to use them, you have to effectively copy them into your final file at compile-time in a process called **static linking**. After that, they are part of your program, locked away in your executable file.

Dynamic Linking

In dynamic linking, the external library file never gets bound into the final executable file. It remains outside the program as a DLL, hopefully in a place where the executable file can find it and send it messages. At run-time, these messages are function or procedure calls, requesting that certain parts of the DLL code are executed.

To link your executable and the DLL it needs to run, you just tell your program where the DLL is and which bit of code you want to run from inside it. It's up to your program to make the connection when the big moment arrives. It is, as they say, dynamically linked.

The VB40032.DLL File

Probably the most graphic illustration of this in action is to look at how VB itself works. When you install VB, you are, in fact, installing two separate components.

VB32.EXE

This is the application file that creates and maintains the VB environment and provides all the tools you need to assemble your programs. Its output is an EXE file that, however, isn't a true Windows EXE file: it can't be run on its own. It's a program in a "language" called **p-code**, that just calls lots of functions and procedures from a DLL file that is the second half of VB

VB40032.DLL

This is the DLL than contains all the machinery that actually does the work in VB. It contains hundreds of functions and procedures that correspond to every control, command, method and property that you can throw at it from the p-code file you built using the VB front-end.

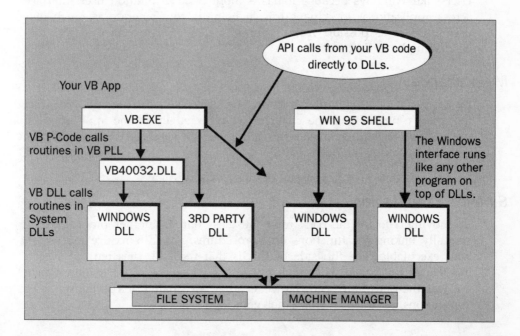

It could be that your version of the **VB40032.DLL** file has a slightly different name than mine. Microsoft may have amended VB after the release and issued a new DLL to maybe correct some mistakes. Incredible, but it happens.

The inevitable question is - what's the point? Why go to all the trouble of having all these files drifting around on the off chance that they meet up successfully at run-time?

The Advantages of Dynamic Linking

The main disadvantage of dynamic linking is the associated hassle of making sure that all the DLLs a program needs are present, in the right place and in the right version. While this is not a trivial problem, you are well taken care of by Windows and VB in this respect. However, the advantages of dynamic linking are real and important.

Consistency

Users like Windows because it has a more or less common user interface across applications. To achieve this, it helps if you generate as much of your user interface as possible from common code. The common dialog is the best example of this.

Maintenance

By having a lot of common code in one place, you can update and amend that code centrally, and the changes are reflected in all the applications that use it. That's why, when you run Windows 3.1 apps on Windows 95, they inherit some user interface features of the new system. This applies to VB as well.

Smaller Executables

By moving a lot of the back room business out to another file, rather than statically linking the functions and procedures, you can reduce the size of your executable. The flip side of this is that the DLL files tend to be massive as they need to contain every possible piece of code they support, not just the ones you need. However, they are shared across many applications, so there is still a net gain.

The Windows Architecture

Dynamic linking is fundamental to the design of Windows. Windows is really just a bag of DLLs that the various applications you run use to do their jobs. In fact, even things that you think of as being Windows itself, like the desktop and Explorer, are just applications that run like any other program, calling the procedures from the intrinsic Windows DLLs as you need them.

The great news is that they aren't the only ones that can tap into the Windows DLL goodie bag. All those DLLs are sitting there waiting to work, and they'll work for anyone who shows up with the right program code. If the mood takes you, you can even replace the Windows desktop with your own version, although I'd suggest we leave that one for a rainy day.

There a lot of DLLs that ship with Windows to give it all the functionality it needs. Inside each of these is anything from a handful to hundreds of available functions and procedures. Collectively, these 1000+ individual routines are called the Windows API.

The Windows API

The **Application Programmer's Interface (API)** is a collection of ready-made functions and procedures. These have traditionally been the domain of C and C++ programmers - the way that the connections to the API operate are more intuitive for C and C++ programmers, for whom arcane and incomprehensible syntax are a stock in trade.

Visual Basic was created to free us from the kind of drudgery that bedevils C/C++ Windows development, and that extends to the API as well. Most of the API calls are already implemented in Visual Basic in the form of Visual Basic commands, keywords, methods and properties. These are translated into the corresponding API calls inside VB. In a way, VB is a friendly wrapper around the Windows API.

However, there are still some API functions for which Visual Basic has no substitute. For example, standard Visual Basic has no way for the programmer to access the Windows multimedia system. With the API, however, life is simple. Well, relatively speaking. Although there is nothing to be frightened of, using API calls in VB is a little fiddly at times. However, armed with a clear understanding of what to do and why you're doing it, you can unlock the power of the API.

API Wrappers

An alternative to diving around in the API is to look for a custom control that does what you want to do. Many custom controls (OCXs) are themselves a wrapper around a particular bit of the API, that deliver that functionality to your program in a VB style, user-friendly manner.

Having said that, more and more OCXs go much further than this, like, for example, a mapping OCX. I can tell you there's no DrawAmerica function call in the API, no matter how hard you look.

Another approach is to enclose some API calls into a VB class module of your own, which brings the power of the API into a VB object. We will have a look at doing this ourselves later in the chapter.

Common API Calls

We said that Windows has a lot of DLLs in it - some large, some small. There's no point in trying to take all these in at one go, let alone all of the 1000+ calls they contain. The best strategy for working with the API is to get to know a few common API calls and then fan out your knowledge from there.

Let's start by looking at some of the more common API calls, and the DLLs in which they are contained.

Function	DLL	Description
SetParent	USER32	Moves controls in and out of container objects at run-time. Can even put a form inside a container object, such as a picture box.
SetClassLong	USER32	Allows you to modify the style of a form or window, for example removing the caption on MDI forms.
FlashWindow	USER32	Flashes the caption of a window. Good for grabbing the user's attention.
GetActiveWindow	USER32	Finds out which window the user is currently interacting with in any program.
RemoveMenu	USER32	Allows you to remove items from the control box menu on your forms.
MciSendString	WINMM	Plays sounds, music and video.

Common DLLs

If it helps, think of each API call as a subroutine. Given the number of API calls that make up Windows, Microsoft wisely decided to group them together into four main libraries.

Library	Description
KERNEL32	The main DLL, **Kernel32**, handles memory management, multi-tasking of the programs that are running, and most other functions which directly affect how Windows actually runs.
USER32	Windows management library. Contains functions which deal with menus, timers, communications, files and many other non-display areas of Windows.
GDI32	Graphics Device Interface. Provides the functions necessary to draw things on the screen, as well as checking which areas of forms need to be redrawn.
WINMM	Provides multimedia functions for dealing with sound, music, real-time video, sampling and more. This is a 32-bit only DLL. The 16-bit equivalent is called **MMSYSTEM**.

You can see these files in your **WINDOWS\SYSTEM** directory.

There are also many other smaller, less frequently used DLLs which provide specialist services to applications.

These are the 32-bit DLL names. To write a program in 16-bit Visual Basic using these DLLs, you need to remove the 32 from the end of the name. This is a fairly important point. You can't use 32-bit DLLs in 16-bit programs and vice versa.

The exception to the naming convention is **MMSYSTEM**. This a 16-bit DLL. The 32-bit version in not named **MMSYSTEM32,** as you might expect, but instead **WINMM**.

Having done our homework, now comes the fun part. We're going to check out some common API calls and, along the way, make sure we know everything we need to know about using the API in general. After that, it's up to you to explore away.

Using API Calls

Calling an API is really no different from calling a function or procedure that you have written yourself and added to a module in your project. For example, we used the following function in Chapter 12:

```
Public Sub FindText(objDataControl As Control, sFieldName As String)

' Code to implement function does here.

End Sub
```

To invoke the function, we used this code:

```
FindText datTitles, "Titles"
```

Let's apply the same logic to an API call, which is a procedure that is not only outside our current module, but also outside VB.

A Quick Look at Declaring an API Call

Before a DLL routine can be used, it needs to be declared. Visual Basic needs to be told:

▶ The name of the DLL.

▶ Which DLL file it can be found in.

▶ The parameters it expects to receive.

▶ The type of value that it can return if the routine is a function.

Instead of using the word **Sub** or **Function** to start the code off, you use the word **Declare**. Because we're calling an API function, the code isn't directly in our VB program after the declaration, it's off in the DLL we indicated. Apart from that, the declaration is the same as for a function that you wrote yourself.

Once the function is declared, calling it is straightforward. Let's take a look at how this works, using a quick example of an API call.

Flashing a Window with an API Call

1 Create a new project in Visual Basic.

2 Draw a timer control on the form and set the timer Interval property to 10. This will cause a timer event to occur every 10 milliseconds.

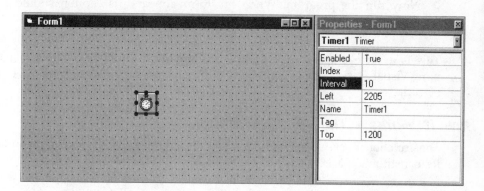

3 Double-click on the timer control to display its Code Window. Then type in code so that it looks like this:

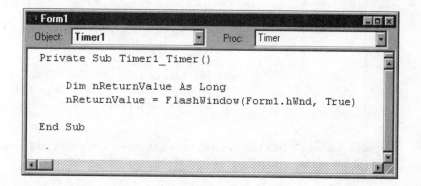

4 Now declare the **FlashWindow** function in the general declarations section as follows:

```
Private Declare Function FlashWindow Lib "user32" Alias
"FlashWindow" (ByVal hwnd As Long, ByVal bInvert As Long) As Long
```

FYI

When you type the declaration, make sure you put all the code onto a single line in the Code Window.

5 Now run the program. When the form appears, its caption should be flashing.

This is a very simple program, but flashing the caption of a window using pure Visual Basic code is extremely difficult and requires a number of lines of code.

How It Works - The API Declaration

The function declaration itself is fairly straightforward once you understand its constituent parts.

*The word **Declare** tells Visual Basic that we're declaring a DLL routine.*

*Immediately following **Declare** is the word **Sub** or **Function**, which declares either a subroutine or a function. Of course, you can't declare subprocedures and functions indiscriminately. It helps to have a Windows API reference manual handy to determine whether the API call you're about to use is a subprocedure or function, which DLL it's contained in, and what the parameters to be passed to it should be.*

*The **Lib** keyword tells Visual Basic the DLL in which the function we want is contained. In this case, it's the **User32** DLL file.*

```
Private Declare Function FlashWindow Lib "user32" Alias "FlashWindow"
↳(ByVal hwnd As Long, ByVal bInvert As Long) As Long
```

Finally the parameters which are to be passed to the function are declared, along with the type of value that the function will return.

The parameters we're passing here are:

```
(ByVal hWnd As Long, ByVal bInvert As Long) As Long
```

The first parameter, **hWnd**, is a **handle** that identifies the window we want to blink. It's important that you understand the concept of handles in Windows, so we'll come back to it later. The second parameter, **bInvert**, switches the flashing property on and off. If **bInvert** is set to true by the calling statement, then the bar flashes. To return it to its original state, you need to call the function again, with the value false.

How It Works - Calling the API

We called the function in this way:

```
nReturnValue = FlashWindow(Form1.hWnd, True)
```

Once you have declared an API call, it's used in almost exactly the same way as a normal call to a Visual Basic function or subprocedure. In the above example, the **FlashWindow** call is a call to a function held in a DLL. Just as with Visual Basic functions, API functions return values to us which must then be stored somewhere. We store the value that the **FlashWindow** function returns in a variable called **nReturnValue**.

Again, just as with Visual Basic functions, you don't have to do anything with the values returned by API functions. But you *do* need to store them somewhere, even if you intend to ignore the return value. Most API functions return numeric error codes which you can use to see if everything worked correctly.

Windows' Handles

Visual Basic provides you with a nice soft buffer between your code and the underlying Windows DLL calls. One of the areas where this is most evident is in a control's properties.

Take the form as an example. Windows uses something called a **structure** to hold information about a form. This information is almost identical to the information contained in the form's Properties Window. However, whereas you or I can easily check a window's properties - we just click on a form and press *F4* to bring up its Properties Window - Windows stores each window's structure in a large list of structures which relates to every window of every program actually running. To determine which structure relates to which window, it uses something called a **handle**. It can't use the name of the form to find it, because the name is just a property of that form. The handle is Windows' own shorthand ID for an object.

As you start to use API calls more and more, particularly those that deal directly with your Visual Basic forms, you'll find handles cropping up again and again. Conveniently, Visual Basic stores handles as read only properties, which you can use to pass to Windows functions when required.

The property is called **hWnd** (handle to a window) and can only be accessed at run-time. The property means nothing to your Visual Basic code, but can be read and passed to API calls as a parameter to those functions that need it.

Declaring Parameter Types

When you declare the type of parameter that a DLL subprocedure or function needs, it's important to make sure that the **ByVal** keyword is used whenever necessary.

With regular Visual Basic code, if you pass a parameter to a function **ByVal**, it tells Visual Basic that the function can only deal with a copy of the parameter you pass it. This is how you do it with a regular function:

```
Function Square (ByVal Number)
```

The alternative to passing **ByVal** is to pass by reference. Here, you pass the whole variable to the function, not just a copy of its contents. Therefore, if the function changes the parameter, those changes are also reflected in the original variable. If you don't specify **ByVal**, the variable will be passed by reference.

Once your internal Visual Basic function or subprocedure has been written, as long as you pass the correct number of parameters to the code, nothing serious will go wrong. Sure, you may get cases where variables passed as parameters are changed, causing your program to have weird results, but nothing *really* serious will happen. Windows won't crash, for example!

However, with DLLs, the situation is a little more serious. If you omit the **ByVal** keyword, Visual Basic actually passes a pointer to the variable. This is a long number, which tells the function being called where the variable is stored in memory. It's then up to the function to go to that memory location and retrieve the value itself. This is also what happens in Visual Basic-only situations, but since, in that case, the functions and subprocedures are all written in Visual Basic code, Visual Basic can cope. DLL code, written in a language like C, expects things to happen in a certain way, and can get quite upset when they don't.

If a DLL function expects a number, let's say between 0 and 3, and you pass it a variable by reference, the actual value passed could be something like 1,002,342, which would be the address in memory where your variable lives. The DLL function would then try to deal with the number 1,002,342 instead of a number between 0 and 3, the net result of which would be that your system crashes.

Using Classes With The API

It goes without saying that the API is a powerful weapon in the VB programmer's arsenal. However, if you were to put API calls throughout your VB apps, you would pretty soon end up with a garbled mass of code that makes no sense to anyone, except perhaps you.

The solution with VB4 is to turn the Windows API into easily reusable classes. Each API call can be categorized according to which part of Windows it deals with. These categories can, in turn, be translated quite effectively into VB classes.

For example, you could write a class that encapsulates all the functionality in the `INI` file handling API calls `GetPrivateProfileString` and `WritePrivateProfileString`. Even better, how about a multimedia class that encapsulates the functionality of the multimedia API calls and, thus, the entire Windows multimedia system? That's what we'll look at next.

We'll start off by seeing how the class that I've put together works, then delve inside and see what's really happening.

Using the Multimedia Class

On the examples disk, there's a class module called **MMEDIA.CLS**. This class turns a set of common multimedia calls into a stand-alone class. When substantiated into an object, this functions exactly the same as a control - it has properties you can set and examine, along with methods that actually make the object do something.

This fits in well with the way we think about controls, and makes using the API calls invisible.

The methods that the class supports are as follows:

Method	Description
mmOpen	Opens a file (video, sound, music etc) ready for playback.
mmClose	Closes the open file down, preventing any more playback.
mmPause	Pauses playback of the current file.
mmStop	Stops playback permanently.
mmSeek	Seeks a specific position within the file.
mmPlay	Take a guess; plays the open file, more often than not causing your speakers to burst into life.

These methods are all individual routines in **MMEDIA.CLS** and all make use of the multimedia API calls in some way. We'll take a look at some of them in a moment to give you a feel for how the code actually fits together.

The following properties are implemented as property procedures in the source file:

Properties	Description
Filename	The name of the currently open file.
Length	The length of the currently open file.
Position	The current position through the file - you can use this in conjunction with the **Length** property to give the user some visual feedback as to the status of playback.
Status	A text word indicating the status of the file (playing, paused, stopped etc).
Wait	Set this to true to make your code stop until playback has completed, or false to multi-task.

Before we take a look at how the class does its thing, let's take a look at how to use the class itself. Along the way, you'll also see how seamless incorporating API calls into an app can be if you wrap the calls up nicely in a VB class.

Using the Multimedia Class

1 Start a new project in Visual Basic, and add **MMEDIA.CLS** to it.

2 From the tools menu select Custom Controls and make sure that the Microsoft Common Dialog Control is selected - we are going to use the common dialog to get a file name to pass to the multimedia class.

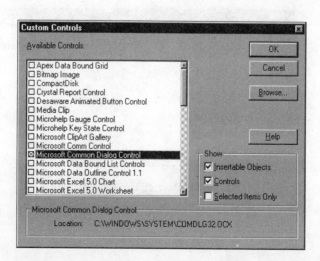

Try It Out!

3 Re-size the main form and draw a command button and common dialog control on it so that it looks like this:

4 We want to pop up the common dialog when the command button is pressed, so that the user is able to select a file name. Bring up the Code Window for the command button's click event, and type this little lot in:

```
Private Sub Command1_Click()

    With CommonDialog1
        .Filter = "WaveAudio (*.wav)|*.wav|Midi (*.mid)|*.mid|Video files
(*.avi)|*.avi"
        .FilterIndex = 0
        .ShowOpen
    End With

End Sub
```

If you run the program now and click on the command button, you will see the familiar file open dialog appear, asking you to select a multimedia file.

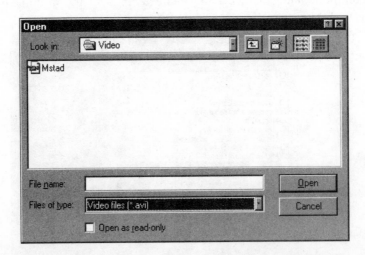

5 Quick and painless so far - all that remains is to bring the multimedia class into being as an object and actually make use of it. Bring up the command button click event again and change it so that it looks like this:

```
Private Sub Command1_Click()

    Dim Multimedia As New Mmedia

    With CommonDialog1
        .Filter = "WaveAudio (*.wav)|*.wav|Midi (*.mid)|*.mid|Video files
(*.avi)|*.avi"
        .FilterIndex = 0
        .ShowOpen
    End With

    If CommonDialog1.Filename <> "" Then
        Multimedia.mmOpen CommonDialog1.Filename
        Multimedia.mmPlay
    End If

End Sub
```

6 Run the program. Select the **ROCKCLIMB.AVI** that is on the examples disk and play it. The finished project is on the disk called **PLAY.VBP**.

You need a sound card to play WAV and MID files. That's why there's an AVI file on the disk. Everyone should be able to play that.

How It Works

In the first line of the command button click event code we create a multimedia object which is derived from the **MMEDIA** class. This turns a class (which at this point is something ethereal and theoretical) into an object (something that can be used).

```
Private Sub Command1_Click()

    Dim Multimedia As New Mmedia
```

The four lines of code we added at the bottom make use of our new multimedia object by opening the selected file using the class' **mmOpen** method and playing it using the class' **mmPlay** method.

```
If CommonDialog1.Filename <> "" Then
        Multimedia.mmOpen CommonDialog1.Filename
        Multimedia.mmPlay
End If
```

As you can hopefully see from this, wrapping API calls up in a nice class makes life a whole lot easier. If this class were used in a commercial organization, then the programmers using it wouldn't have to know anything about the underlying API calls - they would only need to be trained in how to use the multimedia class.

Understanding the Multimedia Class

You may think that a class which can handle video, sound, and music with no pain must be really quite complex. It's not. While Visual Basic is great at detaching a programmer from some of the underlying complexities of Windows itself, there are still certain areas in which the API just can't be beaten, multimedia being one of them.

For example, the multimedia class here uses just one API call, **mciSendString**. Before we take an in-depth look at the code itself, it's probably a good idea to look at this particular API call in a little detail.

The MCI

Windows itself actually consists of a number of subsystems: separate units within Windows that handle entire areas of functionality. One such area is something called the **MCI**. MCI stands for Media Control Interface and provides a device independent way to use the multimedia features of Windows through code.

Device independent? OK! In the bad old days of DOS, for example, a programmer writing a video game would have to cope with every possible type of sound card standard in order to satisfy the game's playing market. Device independence, and the device drivers that Windows provides, let you hit any sound card, video card and so on with the same code, just so long as it is supported by Windows.

The MCI provides this layer of independence, putting a neat bunch of functionality between you, the programmer, and the devices which would normally be used to handle multimedia data, namely the video and sound cards.

All this theory is great, but how exactly does the MCI work, and how does it provide this independence? The answer to both questions is that the MCI is responsible for talking to the Windows device drivers, and ultimately the multimedia hardware. You, the programmer, issue commands to the MCI using the API call **mciSendString**. These commands are then translated into calls to the appropriate Windows device driver, something that you no longer have to worry about.

To put it into VB terms then, the MCI is a built-in Windows class, which we have essentially super-classed in the earlier example.

Hang on a minute - programmers issue commands to the MCI. A little strange? Yes it is. Normally, when you deal with API calls, you are actually calling subroutines and functionality that is embedded in Windows in order to do something. The MCI really is an independent object, though. It can be programmed and has its own programming language. When you use **mciSendString** you are in fact programming the MCI just as easily as if you were firing VB commands out of the Debug Window.

Using mciSendString

The format of **mciSendString** is quite simple

```
<Result code> = mciSendString( " <command> ", <Return string>, < Return
length >, <Callback handle> )
```

This needs a bit of explanation. The **Result code** is a long integer, and varies depending on the command issued. The **command** part (notice it is in quotes, so it is passed as a string literal) is the command you are sending to the MCI, such as **Play** to play a file, **Open** to open one and so on. We'll look at exactly which commands the MCI understands later on, but for now let's cover the rest of the parameters.

Some MCI commands actually return a string value to your program. The MCI **status** command, for example, can return a string telling your code whether a file is **Stopped**, **Paused**, **Playing** and so on. The string variable you place here will contain that return string.

The API call needs to know just how much data it can put in this string variable, so the next parameter passed is a number that is the length of the string. For this reason, if you are issuing a command to the MCI which returns a string, you must pass a fixed length string variable to the call and tell the **mciSendString** just how long that string is.

```
Dim sReturnString As String * 255
Dim nReturn As Long

nReturn = mciSendString("status waveaudio mode", sReturnString, 255, 0)
```

Don't worry about what this specific command does at this point, but notice the use of the fixed length string. Adding the ***255** to the declaration of **sReturnString** tells VB to fix its length to 255 characters.

The final parameter, the **Callback Handle**, only applies to those writing code in C or some other low-level compiled language. Us VB types can ignore it.

Opening the Media File

Before you can tell the MCI what to do, you have to tell it which file you want to do it on. This is like using disk files. You must start by sending the **Open** command before you can do anything else.

The first part of this code should be self explanatory: you tell the **Open** command the name of the file that you want to open. This is a standard filename, like **C:\VIDEO.AVI.**

```
Open <filename> Type <Type string> Alias <A name>

   :

Issue a command to do something to the file

   :

Close <A name>
```

After the **Type** keyword, you need to tell Windows what kind of file you are dealing with. The standard Windows ones are **WaveAudio** for **WAV** files, **AVIVideo** for **AVI** files and **Sequencer** for **MID** files.

Finally, you can tell the MCI to give the file you just opened a name, an **Alias**, which you will use from now on to refer to the open file. It's rather like naming a variable, in that the name can be almost anything you want, For example:

```
"Open c:\video.avi Type AVIVideo Alias Peter"
```

If you sent this to the MCI with **MCISendString**, it would tell the MCI to open a file called **c:\video.avi** as a Microsoft video file and that, in future MCI commands, we will refer to this file using the name **Peter**.

Once opened, normal MCI commands can be issued using the alias to play the file, stop it, pause it, find out its status and so on. For example:

```
Play Peter
Pause Peter
Stop Peter
```

There are literally hundreds of combinations of MCI commands that you can use, and we'll take a look at the most common a little later.

Once you have done your stuff with a file, you need to close it down by sending the `Close` command, followed by the alias of the file you are dealing with.

```
nReturn = mciSendString("Close Peter", "",0,0)
```

Let's take a look at how the code does what it does now, in the context of a full application.

A Multimedia Viewer

Try It Out!

1 On the disk is a program called `CONTROL.VBP` that we've used a couple of times before. This make full use of the `MMEDIA` class. Load it up.

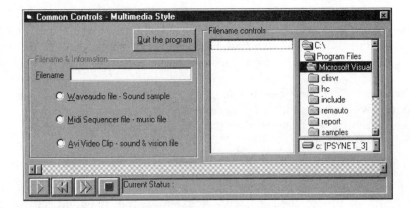

2 Select the `ROCKCLMB.AVI` - the filename and radio buttons on the left will indicate the type of multimedia file you selected. Now hit the green play button.

3 You can pause the player, and jump forwards and back using the control buttons. The bottom of the form contains a status bar that shows you what the file you just selected is doing.

How It Works - Getting the File Name

The first time that our multimedia class gets kicked into life is when the user selects a file by clicking it in the file list. When this happens, the file name gets copied across to the text box on the left-hand side of the display, triggering a change event which starts the multimedia ball rolling.

```
Private Sub txtFilename_Change()

    Select Case Right$(txtFilename, 3)
        Case "wav"
            optWaveaudio.Value = 1
        Case "mid"
            optMidi.Value = 1
        Case "avi"
            optVideo.Value = 1
        Case Else
            Exit Sub
    End Select

    Multimedia_Clip.Filename = txtFilename

    scrPosition.Min = 0
    scrPosition.Max = Multimedia_Clip.Length
    scrPosition.Value = 0

End Sub
```

The first thing to happen is that the right three letters of the file name are checked. We only want this program to deal with **WAV**, **MID** and **AVI** files, so checking the right three characters of the file name is a simple way to find out what kind of file it is we are dealing with.

A **Select Case** construct is used to look at these three letters and set the appropriate option button on the display, providing the user with instant feedback on what just happened.

After this, the code sets the **Filename** property of something called **Multimedia_Clip**. This is the name of an object that was created way back in the declarations section of the form as an instance of our **Mmedia** class.

```
Private Multimedia_Clip As New Mmedia
```

Since this is not a built-in VB object, there is code in the **Mmedia** class file saying what should happen when someone does go and poke something into the **Filename** property. That code looks like this:

```
Property Let Filename(ByVal sTheFile As String)

    mmOpen sTheFile

End Property
```

Pretty simple stuff. In order to set the property, you need to pass it a value, in this case a string that is the name of the file you want to deal with. The **Property Let** procedure then passes the buck to the **mmOpen** method in this class module.

How It Works - Opening the File

```
Public Sub mmOpen(ByVal sTheFile As String)


    Dim nReturn As Long
    Dim sType As String

    If sAlias <> "" Then
        mmClose
    End If

    Select Case UCase$(Right$(sTheFile, 3))

        Case "WAV"
            sType = "Waveaudio"

        Case "AVI"
            sType = "AviVideo"

        Case "MID"
            sType = "Sequencer"

        Case Else

            Exit Sub

    End Select

    sAlias = Right$(sTheFile, 3) & Minute(Now)

    nReturn = mciSendString("Open " & sTheFile & " ALIAS " & sAlias &
 " TYPE " & sType & " wait", "", 0, 0)

End Sub
```

First off, we declare a couple of local variables to hold temporary values. We'll see what these are for shortly. Then there's a lot of code devoted to building up the command string, before we send it to the MCI.

First the **mmOpen** routine checks a class level/module level variable called **sAlias**.

```
If sAlias <> "" Then
        mmClose
End If
```

Whenever you deal with the MCI, it is a good idea to assign aliases to each file you have open. Here, the **Mmedia** class works out a name for the alias for you and stores it in **sAlias**. When you next go to open a file with **mmOpen**, or by setting the file name property, the code can check this and call another routine which closes the first file down. Closing multimedia files down when they are no longer needed frees up memory and speeds up playback, so it is always a good idea.

A familiar **Select Case** construct is then used to figure out the file type. When you open a file with the MCI, you need to tell it what type of data the file holds. The **Select Case** construct here does that, storing the MCI type name in the **sType** variable declared at the start of the routine.

```
Select Case UCase$(Right$(sTheFile, 3))

        Case "WAV"
            sType = "Waveaudio"

        Case "AVI"
            sType = "AviVideo"

        Case "MID"
            sType = "Sequencer"

        Case Else

            Exit Sub

End Select
```

At this point, any previously opened file has been closed, and the type name of the new file has been stored in **sType**. All that remains is to decide on an alias for the file and then open it.

Aliases must be unique since the MCI can cope with having more than one file open, or even playing. Since we don't want to force unnecessary complexity on the user of the class, it makes sense if the class decides on its own alias.

```
sAlias = Right$(sTheFile, 3) & Minute(Now)
```

It does this by taking the right three characters of the file name and appending the minute segment of the current time. So if it was 16:15 when you opened **c:\video.avi**, then the alias the class would come up with would be **AVI15**. The newly calculated alias is then stored in the **sAlias** module level variable that we checked when the procedure first started. The value in **sAlias** is then used throughout the rest of the module whenever we need to do something to the open file, like play it.

So, armed with the file type in one variable, the alias in a second, and the file name in a third, we can finally send the **Open** command to the MCI.

```
nReturn = mciSendString("Open " & sTheFile & " ALIAS " & sAlias & " TYPE "
↳& sType & " wait", "", 0, 0)
```

The command sent is **Open**, followed by the file name, followed by **ALIAS** then the new alias (held in **sAlias**), followed by **TYPE** and the type, and finally, the word **wait**.

The **wait** statement on the end tells the API not to let our VB code continue running until it has finished. Without this, on a fast machine with a slow hard disk, problems can occur - you might try to play the file before it has loaded, simply because the code is running a lot faster than the hard disk.

So let's just recap what's happened. The file name text box activated the **txtFilename_Change()** procedure. This then assigned the name to the multimedia object file name. This invoked the **Property Let Filename** procedure. We took changing the file name to mean that we needed to open a new file, so the **Property Let** procedure called the **mmOpen** procedure. Having got to the end of this procedure and successfully opened the file, we drop back to the **txtFilename_Change()** procedure again.

```
Private Sub txtFilename_Change()

    Select Case Right$(txtFilename, 3)
        Case "wav"
            optWaveaudio.Value = 1
        Case "mid"
            optMidi.Value = 1
        Case "avi"
            optVideo.Value = 1
        Case Else
            Exit Sub
```

```
    End Select

    Multimedia_Clip.Filename = txtFilename

    scrPosition.Min = 0
    scrPosition.Max = Multimedia_Clip.Length
    scrPosition.Value = 0

End Sub
```

After the **Filename** property has been set, the scrollbar which tracks the current location in the file is set up

```
scrPosition.Min = 0
  scrPosition.Max = Multimedia_Clip.Length
  scrPosition.Value = 0
```

The scrollbar's minimum and current values are set to 0. The maximum value is set to the length of the newly opened file. Let's look at how we find the length of the file.

How It Works - Get Length

```
Property Get Length() As Single
    Dim nReturn As Long, nLength As Integer
    Dim sLength As String * 255

    If sAlias = "" Then
        Length = 0
        Exit Property
    End If

    nReturn = mciSendString("Status " & sAlias & " length", sLength, 255,
0)
    nLength = InStr(sLength, Chr$(0))
    Length = Val(Left$(sLength, nLength - 1))

End Property
```

First **sAlias** is checked to see if a file has been opened. If it hasn't, then the value returned from the property procedure is 0. If a file has been opened, then the MCI **status** command is used to find out how long it is.

You needn't worry about how the length of the file is measured, since any unit of measurement will be suitable for setting up the scrollbar. Just for your interest, though, you can set the unit of measurement to various values, ranging from frames in a video clip to milliseconds in a sound file. However, it's a little beyond the scope of what we are trying to achieve here to give you a complete rundown of the options.

The **Status** command is a rather special MCI command and can be used in conjunction with keywords like **Length** and **Mode** to find out a great deal of information about the current file. It returns this information in a fixed length string variable which is passed to **mciSendString** after the MCI command. In this example, the return string is called **sLength** and is declared to be 255 characters long.

Of course, you're not always going to get 255 characters back from the **Status** command, especially if you only want to know the length of the file. The unused space in the string is filled with the character 0, making it easy for us to use VB's **InStr** function to find out exactly how long the returned data is, and pull it out.

```
    nReturn = mciSendString("Status " & sAlias & " length", sLength, 255,
↳0)
    nLength = InStr(sLength, Chr$(0))
    Length = Val(Left$(sLength, nLength - 1))
```

Here, the position of the first 0 is stored in **nLength**, since **InStr** returns the character position at which the search data is located, or 0 if it can't find what you are looking for. This now gives us enough information to pull the number from the left side of the fixed length string, convert it to a number (rather than a string) and return that value ready to go into the scrollbar.

When the file is actually playing, the **Status** command can be used repeatedly to find out exactly where in the file playback has reached. Take a look at the code in the timer event:

```
scrPosition.Value = Int(Multimedia_Clip.Position)
```

The code to return the value of the **Mmedia** position property looks strangely familiar:

```
Property Get Position() As Single

    Dim nReturn As Integer, nLength As Integer
    Dim sPosition As String * 255
```

```
    If sAlias = "" Then Exit Property

    nReturn = mciSendString("Status " & sAlias & " position", sPosition,
255, 0)
    nLength = InStr(sPosition, Chr$(0))
    Position = Val(Left$(sPosition, nLength - 1))

End Property
```

The only real difference this time is that instead of sending `Status Length` to the MCI, we are sending `Status Position`. The result is fed out of the property procedure and back into the `Value` property of the scrollbar in the timer event on the form.

How It Works - Playback

Playback of the file is accomplished in the program by clicking the Play button on the form, which in turn calls the class' `mmPlay` method.

```
Public Sub mmPlay()

    Dim nReturn As Long

    If sAlias = "" Then Exit Sub

    If bWait Then
        nReturn = mciSendString("Play " & sAlias & " wait", "", 0, 0)
    Else
        nReturn = mciSendString("Play " & sAlias, "", 0, 0)
    End If

End Sub
```

The first thing this does is take a look at our old friend, the `sAlias` variable. If this is empty, then the user obviously hasn't tried to open a file yet, so the routine discreetly exits.

Providing there is something in `sAlias`, though, which in turn means that a file has been opened, the `Play` command is issued. Notice in the code how there are actually two play commands issued, each contained in its own branch of an `If` condition.

You can tell the `Play` MCI command to wait until it is done before control is returned to your program, just as you can with the `Open` MCI command. Telling the MCI to `Play` and `Wait` stops your code running until the file has finished playing. Removing the word `Wait` tells the MCI to play the file, and while it is playing, to let the calling application get on with its own thing. This is great for our application, where you need to update a scroll bar to show the position through the file that playback has reached.

I have put a property in the `mMedia` class to handle this thing called `Wait`. Setting this to true sets up the `bWait` variable to hold true. It is this `bWait` variable which is checked when you play a file, to see how you want the file played: synchronously or asynchronously.

The rest of the code in the module really should be self-explanatory by now, with the exception of the MCI commands used

Command	Description
Play	Plays a file.
Pause	Pauses playback, ready to start up again at any time.
Stop	Stops a file - you need to seek to a position to continue playback.
Seek	Followed by a number, seeks to that position in the file (check out the multimedia reference guide in the Enterprise and Pro editions for information on time formats).
Status Mode	Returns a string indicating what the file is doing (i.e. Stopped, Paused, Playing, Ready).
Status Position	Returns a number indicating the position through the file that playback has reached.
Status Length	Returns the length of the file and helps to put the number returned from **Status Position** into some meaningful context.
Close	Closes the file and frees up the memory it previously occupied.

The MCI supports a few more commands than this, and also a number of specialized ones for each file format. If you intend to do more multimedia that the `Mmedia` class can handle for you, then you really do need to get hold of my *Revolutionary Guide To Multimedia Programming in Visual Basic*, or the drier *Multimedia Reference Guide* from Microsoft.

Hopefully, though, I have shown you here how even seemingly complex topics such as multimedia really aren't that hard if you drop down to the API. Also, that the API itself is not the daunting mother of all nightmares that many VB programmers make it out to be.

Summary

This chapter should have provided you with a glimpse of the power that lies beyond the strict limits of Visual Basic, as defined in the language itself. This is a huge subject, so all we've done is to touch on the principles of using the Windows API.

With power comes responsibility, because once you choose to operate outside the confines of Visual Basic, you have to look after yourself. It pays to develop a deep understanding of all the components of Windows, so you can write Visual Basic programs that are truly well-behaved members of the Windows desktop community.

In our brief tour we covered:

- How Windows and Visual Basic fit together.
- The Windows API.
- How to use the Windows API to extend the power of Visual Basic.
- How to write well-behaved Windows applications.

Why Not Try.......

1 Make a combined image file and media file viewer by adding the ability to read image files to **CONTROL.VBP**. You could do this by loading up an embedded version of Paint at run-time, depending on the file type you load.

2 Replace all the file controls on the **CONTROL.VBP** project with a menu using the common dialog. Add a previous file list to the menu.

3 Add a method to the **MMedia** class that allows you to step through an **AVI** frame by frame.

4 Use the **GetCursorPos** API function to locate the position of the cursor on the screen. The declaration for this function is:

```
Declare Sub GetCursorPos Lib "User32" (lpPoint as POINTAPI)
```

The function returns a pointer to a type called **POINTAPI**. To use the function, you need to declare the type as well. Don't forget you have to declare this in a module, not in a form.

```
Type POINTAPI
    X As Integer
    Y As Integer
End Type
```

Then you have to declare an instance of this type:

```
Dim Current as POINTAPI
```

Then you can access the coordinates as **Current.X** and **Current.Y**. Write a program that locates the cursor, then cycles through the controls collection and identifies which control the cursor is currently over.

etail :

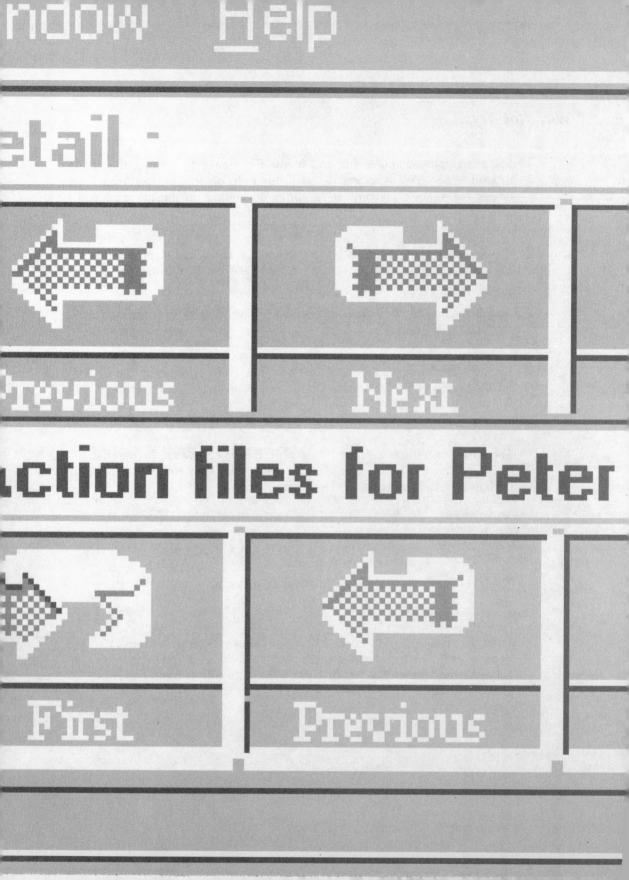

Previous

Next

ction files for Peter

First

Previous

16

Putting It All Together

By now you should have a pretty good grasp of the foundations of Visual Basic. So we are going to do things a little differently in this chapter.

In this chapter you are going to see a complete application, utilizing almost everything we have covered in the rest of the book, as well as one or two tricks that you haven't come across yet.

The sections in this chapter will look at the quirks, hassles and design issues surrounding the development of a full blown application in Visual Basic. More than that, it will also show you how to get the most out of VB's standard controls so that you can give your application the kind of look and feel that you would normally expect from a program written with hundreds of pounds worth of OCXs. We should know, since that is how this program started out - it's a VB4 conversion of a full contact manager, written by Psynet, utilizing lots of off-the-shelf add-in components.

In this chapter you will see:

▶ How to put a decent toolbar into your applications, using only two picture controls.

▶ How to implement graphical buttons - command buttons with text and graphics.

▶ How to print your application's data.

▶ How to make real use of OLE in your apps.

▶ The two methods available to you to display information from your database.

In addition, you should also see a great deal of code that you can pull out and use in your own applications, speeding up the development processes.

An Overview of PsyCON

PsyCON is a contact management system. In fact, the PsyCON you have here is a VB4 conversion of a shareware VB app written by Psynet, so it really is like a full application.

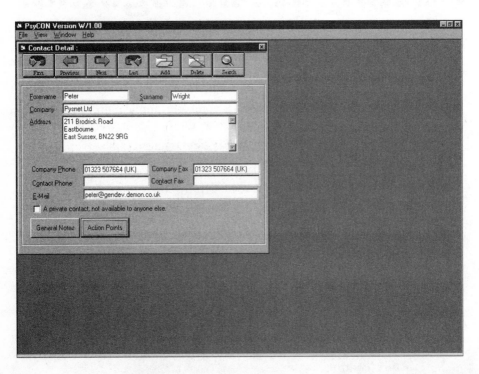

PsyCON

1 Take a look at the app in action; either run **PSYCON.EXE** from the examples provided, or load **PSYCON.VBP** into VB4 and run it from there.

The first thing you will see is the security screen. There is already a test user set up so just enter Test for the Username, followed by Password for the Password. Notice how, as soon as you move focus from the Username field, the full name of the user is displayed at the bottom of the form.

2 In the event that you get the username/password combination wrong, a messsage box pops up telling you how many retries you have left. Get it wrong three times and the application will end - you'll get kicked out.

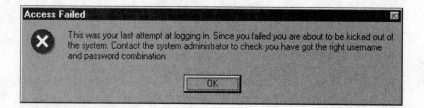

3 Next up is the MDI form. The menus on this form give you access to the features within the program.

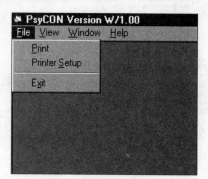

For example, to print, set up the printer or exit the application, you use the options on the File menu. If you want to view your contacts, edit their details or allow new users access to your system, then you use the View menu. The Window menu lets you re-arrange the windows on display, while the Help menu gives you access to the program's About screen.

If your toolbars look a bit funny, then you are probably running this in a screen mode other than 800x600. I created this program only to work in this mode. You can change your resolution in the Display dialog in the Win95 Setting folder.

4   To actually enter your contact information, you choose Contact Detail from the View menu.

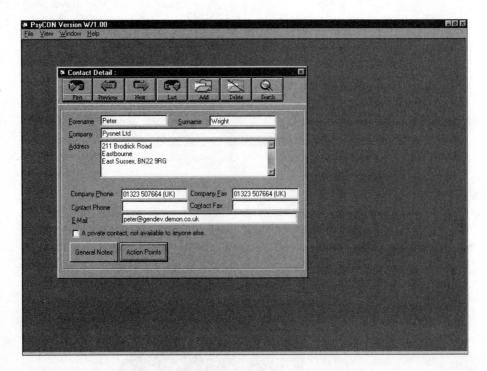

5 The toolbar across the top of the form lets you navigate around the database, adding records, deleting records, searching for information and so on. The actual contact information is displayed in the center of the form, with the General and Action buttons allowing you access to the general notes part of the program, or the Action files list

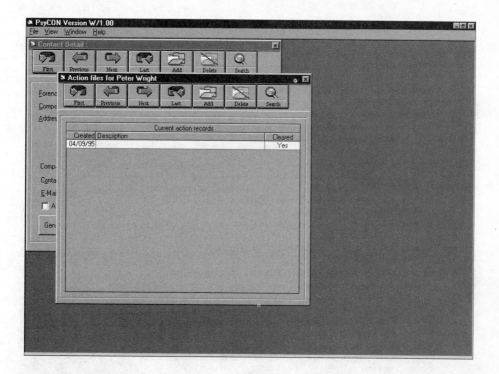

6 The Action list allows you to link files on your hard disk to the contact. These could be WordPad documents explaining things to do, graphic files, or any other file on your hard disk that can be used through OLE 2. Hit Add to get to the dialog to enter a new item.

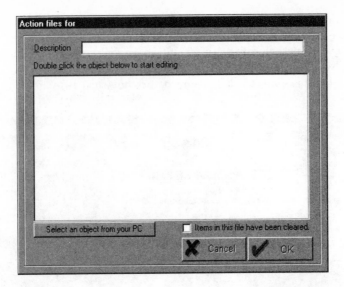

You can't actually create a document here at the moment, but you can create a link to an existing object, such as a fax or e-mail message.

7 The View menu also allows you to open a contact summary window. This is a listing of everyone in the database.

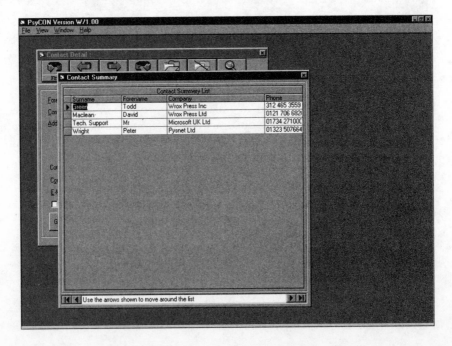

8 The same menu opens a list of authorized users.

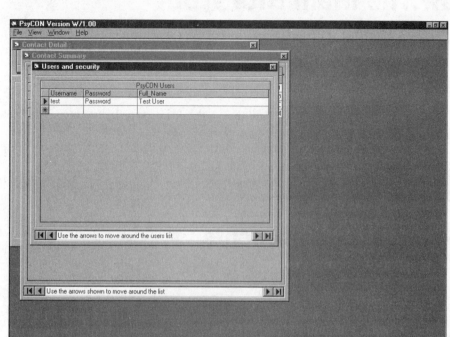

9 The Window menu lets you arrange the windows and select the top one.

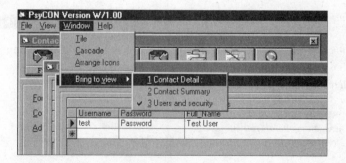

I have deliberately whizzed through this explanation, since what you really want to know is how it works. On the whole it is quite easy to work out how to use the program, but I suspect that you may already be wondering about the toolbars, graphical command buttons and so on.

How The Main Bits Work

Having said that, I'm not going to examine the program line by line, although there are some parts of the application that do need explaining. There are also some interesting parts that you can reuse in your own applications.

The main parts of the program that I think are worth looking at in detail are the funky graphical toolbar and the code that prints to the printer. These cover new ground and are definitely re-usable. The other techniques I've used are just extensions of things we've used before. What's interesting is how it all fits together. So, before we look at the toolbars and printing in gory detail, let's get an overview of the project.

The Project Components

Here's what the Project Window looks like for PsyCON.

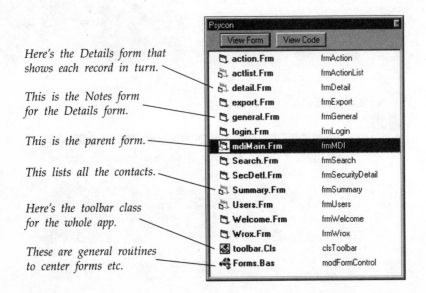

Here's the Details form that shows each record in turn.

This is the Notes form for the Details form.

This is the parent form.

This lists all the contacts.

Here's the toolbar class for the whole app.

These are general routines to center forms etc.

We are going to be taking a long look at the whole toolbar fest later on, so we'll leave that for now.

The Main Form

The main MDI form, frmMDI, has a data control and a common dialog on it.

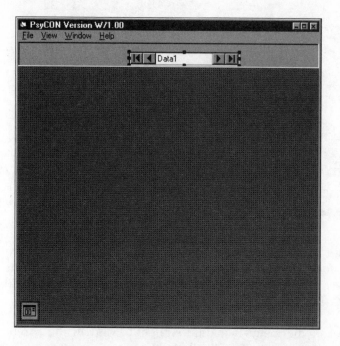

The data control datContacts is in a picture control at the top of the form. We need the data control here for the Print option in the File menu to enable us to print a contact summary without having a child form open. There are, in fact, identical data controls on the child forms that need them, namely the Detail and Summary forms.

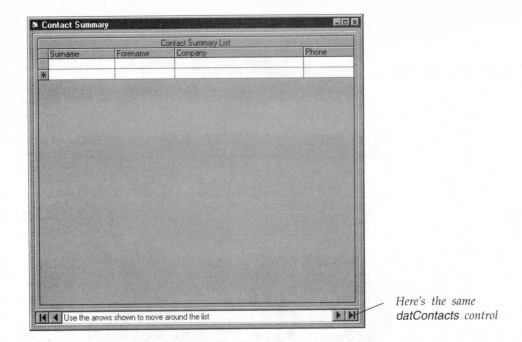

Here's the same
datContacts control

It would have been perfectly OK to have just the one control, say on the details form, and to reference that control by using the form name. However, for the sake of simplicity, I decided that we would have a control on each form.

The rest of the menu items are straightforward in the parent form, so let's turn our attention to the details form.

The Details Form

The details form has some interesting features.

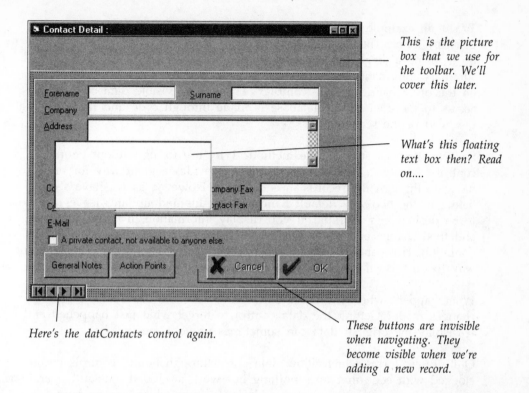

This is the picture box that we use for the toolbar. We'll cover this later.

What's this floating text box then? Read on....

Here's the datContacts control again.

These buttons are invisible when navigating. They become visible when we're adding a new record.

The floating text box is a neat trick that we use to create an event. This needs explanation but, before we can understand it, we need to look at how the database is handled overall.

To Bind or Not to Bind

There are two methods for getting at data in a database and displaying it on the screen - an easy one and a hard one. With the easy method, life is simple. You draw your controls onto a form and bind them all to a data control. With the hard method, you still have a data control on the form, but the data is put into the controls on the form manually, through code.

To see an example of each, take a look at the Contact Detail and Contact Summary forms. The Contact Summary form is an example of the easy way to do it, using a single grid control bound to a data control to display summary information on all the contacts in your database. The Detail form, on the other hand, is quite complex. There is no visible data control and access to the data in the database is made through code and the toolbar at the head of the screen.

So, why not just stick to one method? Why use forms without bound controls? The data control, when visible, provides a great way for users to navigate through the records in a database. However, as we have seen before in the book, its default handling of edits and updates leaves a little to be desired. For example, if you display information in bound controls and then change one of the controls through code, this triggers an **Edit** operation. How about canceling an operation? The data control provides no way to do this effectively, except through its validate event.

What happens when your user edits some data and decides to cancel the changes made? Getting the data control to forget what just happened and re-display the original data can sometimes prove a messy job.

Quite often, forms which allow data entry through bound controls become clogged with code that does nothing but work around the default operation of the data control. It's simpler to design a form which has no bound controls and where the data is put on display manually.

If the user then decides to cancel an update operation, you simply call your data display routine, overwriting the data currently on display and having no effect at all on the underlying database. If the user enters some data into the form and clicks OK, then we only need to lock the database for just a few seconds while the **Edit** method is sent and data is copied from the controls on the form to the record in the database. Let's look at how these procedures are implemented in the program.

Database Handling in PsyCON

First the **Clear_Display** procedure from the Details form. This is called by the **imgCancel** button whenever the user aborts the creation of a new record. It blanks out all the fields in the form.

```
Private Sub Clear_Display()

    bLoading = True
    txtForename = ""
    txtSurname = ""
    txtCompany = ""
    txtAddress = ""
    txtCompanyPhone = ""
    txtCompanyFax = ""
    txtContactPhone = ""
    txtContactFax = ""
    txtNotes = ""
    txtEmail = ""
    chkPrivate.Value = 0
    bLoading = False

End Sub
```

The code that copies the contents of the controls to the database to create a new record or amend a new one is called **Update_Display**. This is it:

```
Private Sub Update_Display()

    Dim nIndex As Integer

    Clear_Display

    With datContacts

        If .Recordset.EOF Or .Recordset.BOF Then

            Clear_Display
            Frame1.Enabled = False
            For nIndex = 0 To 6
                ToolBar.Disable nIndex
            Next

            ToolBar.Enable 4

        Else
            bLoading = True
            Frame1.Enabled = True
            txtForename = "" & .Recordset.Contact_Forename
            txtSurname = "" & .Recordset.Contact_Surname
            txtCompany = "" & .Recordset.Company_Name
            txtAddress = "" & .Recordset.Company_Address
            txtCompanyPhone = "" & .Recordset.Company_Phone
```

```
                txtCompanyFax = "" & .Recordset.Company_Fax
                txtContactPhone = "" & .Recordset.Contact_Phone
                txtContactFax = "" & .Recordset.Contact_Fax
                txtEmail = "" & .Recordset.Contact_EMail
                txtNotes = "" & .Recordset.Notes

                If .Recordset.Private Then chkPrivate.Value = 1 Else
   ⌙chkPrivate.Value = 0
                bLoading = False
                For nIndex = 0 To 6
                    ToolBar.Enable nIndex
                Next

            End If

        End With

        bChanging = False

    End Sub
```

The body of this procedure, where the contents of the text boxes on the form are copied to the database, is straightforward. However, before and after this, we meet the toolbar for the first time. While we'll explain it all in detail later, it won't have escaped your attention, both now and when looking at the Project Window, that there is a toolbar class in the project which we have instanced as **Toolbar**. The buttons have numbers from 0 to 6 across the form, and each can be enabled and disabled by using the **Enable** function accordingly.

In this particular procedure, if we are at either the start or the end of the recordset (i.e. if the record is empty), we disable all but the Add button (#4)

```
If .Recordset.EOF Or .Recordset.BOF Then

            Clear_Display
            Frame1.Enabled = False
            For nIndex = 0 To 6
                ToolBar.Disable nIndex
            Next

            ToolBar.Enable 4
```

We then enable all the controls at the end of the code that writes the changes to the database:

```
For nIndex = 0 To 6
            ToolBar.Enable nIndex
       Next
```

If you use your own toolbar to handle navigation around the database with an unbound form, you also benefit from not having to worry about canceling any updates the data control may feel the need to start as soon as the current record changes.

We got a bit side-tracked there in our discussion of how I've implemented the database handling parts of the code. Anyway, to summarize, the rule I tend to stick to is, if the form is to be used for editing, then I'll use it unbound. If, on the other hand, all I want to do is display read-only data, then bound controls set to read-only are fine.

The Mystery Text Box

Having got a picture of how the database access works, we can now look at what the floating text box is for. It's a mirror of the text box on the notes form called **frmGeneral**. The problem is this: whenever the user has made any changes to the database, we need to set the **bChanging** variable and disable the controls. Entering or changing text in **frmGeneral** counts as a change to the record; it's there to display the Notes field in the Contacts table. The action of clicking on the OK button on the **frmGeneral** form signals to the program that we expect to keep what's in the Notes field.

Instead of creating a nasty global variable to keep track of the changes, the OK button has this code attached to it:

```
Private Sub imgOK_Click()
    frmDetail.txtNotes = txtNotes
    Unload frmGeneral
End Sub
```

In copying back the contents of the text box to the invisible one on the Details form, we trigger a change event on that text box:

```
Private Sub txtNotes_Change()
    Start_Updating
End Sub
```

This then calls the **Start_Updating** procedure:

```
Private Sub Start_Updating()

    Dim nIndex As Integer

    If bChanging Or bLoading Then Exit Sub

    bChanging = True
    For nIndex = 0 To 6
        ToolBar.Disable nIndex
    Next

    imgOK.Visible = True
    imgCancel.Visible = True

End Sub
```

This sets **bChanging** to true and disables all the command buttons. Once the whole of the toolbar is disabled, all the user is left with is the choice of the OK and Cancel buttons that are now visible at the bottom of the form. It's decision time - stick or twist, put up or shut up, double or quits...

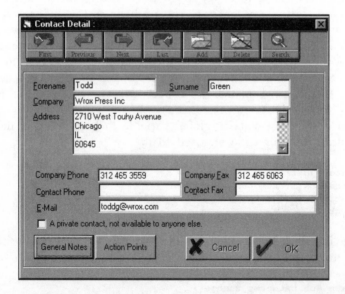

The reverse is also true, in that when each record is loaded into the Details form, the Notes field is copied into the invisible text box and then fired into the frmGeneral text box when it is loaded.

There's a lot more going on here, but it's all routine stuff. It's time to check out this magical toolbar doodah. Before we do that, however, we just need to take a look at how I've done the graphical buttons throughout the application.

The Graphical Buttons

You may have noticed by now that most of the command buttons used in PsyCON are not your average run-of-the-mill command buttons. For example, these can actually display graphics alongside the text. Have I found some useful quirk of VB that we can all make use of? Alas no, I have just written two routines which can draw command buttons in their up and down state using an image control. What is cool about it, though, is that all the work is done by one bit of code.

Take a look at the Login form for a second:

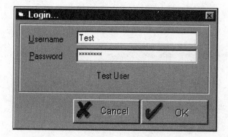

Look at the OK and Cancel buttons; on the surface they look like normal command buttons, but with a graphic drawn on them. However, if you select one and bring up the Properties Window, you will see that they are in fact image controls. That's obvious, but to see what isn't, take a look at the Tag property of each button.

The Cancel button's Tag property has the letters CAN in it, while the OK button's Tag property has the letters OK in it. At run-time, the public **Draw_Down** and **Draw_Up** methods use these Tag properties to figure out the file name of the new image to display.

For example, the down image of the Cancel button is **CANDN.BMP** while the up image of the same button is **CANUP.BMP**. The **Draw_Down** and **Draw_Up** methods simply put **DN.BMP** or **UP.BMP** on the end of whatever is in the Tag property and load the new file into the image control. The result is, of course, that these are image controls that you can push down and bring up, just like a normal command button.

```
Public Sub Draw_Down(imgButton As Image)

    On Error GoTo DownError

    imgButton.Picture = LoadPicture(App.Path & "\" & imgButton.Tag &
↳"dn.bmp")
    DoEvents
    On Error GoTo 0
    Exit Sub

DownError:
    On Error GoTo 0
    MsgBox "There was a problem locating " & App.Path & "\" & imgButton.Tag
↳& "dn.bmp. Please make sure that this is in the same directory as the
↳application itself", vbCritical, "Fatal Error"
    End

End Sub
```

```
Public Sub Draw_Up(imgButton As Image)

    On Error GoTo UpError

    imgButton.Picture = LoadPicture(App.Path & "\" & imgButton.Tag &
↳"up.bmp")
    DoEvents
    On Error GoTo 0
    Exit Sub

UpError:
    On Error GoTo 0
    MsgBox "There was a problem locating " & App.Path & "\" & imgButton.Tag
↳& "up.bmp. Please make sure that this is in the same directory as the
↳application itself", vbCritical, "Fatal Error"
    End

End Sub
```

Most of the code in these two routines is error handling - what action to take if the image file cannot be found in the same location as the application itself. The important line, though, is the load image one:

```
imgButton.Picture = LoadPicture(App.Path & "\" & imgButton.Tag & "up.bmp")
```

All this does is work out the full name of the file, prefixing the Tag letters with the application path, followed by a \, then appending either **UP.BMP** or **DN.BMP**. For example, if the application is running from **C:\BEGVB4** and the Tag property contains CAN, when you call **Draw_Down**, the file loaded into the image control is **C:\BEGVB4\CANDN.BMP**.

To include this in your own programs, just copy the **Draw_Down** and **Draw_Up** methods out of **FORMS.BAS** into your own code module. When you want to put a button onto a form, draw an image control, load one of the button bitmaps included with the samples into the image control and set up Tag with the start of the file name (**OKUP.BMP** becomes OK, **CANUP.BMP** becomes CAN).

All that remains is to add code to the image control's mousedown and mouseup events to call the **Draw_Down** and **Draw_Up** routines:

```
Private Sub Image1_MouseDown(..............)
    Draw_Down Image1
End Sub

Private Sub Image1_MouseUp(............)
    Draw_Down Image2
End Sub
```

The Toolbars

Some time back we took a look at one method of creating toolbars: the infamous control array. There are many ways to skin a cat, though, and while using a blunt knife does indeed get the job done, it's not the most elegant. A better way is the one I used in PsyCON.

Take a look at the Detail form.

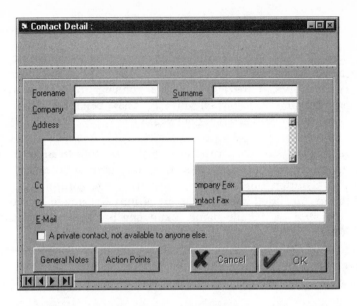

Here you can see only one picture box - there is another hiding behind the frame on the form. Dragging the frame down reveals it:

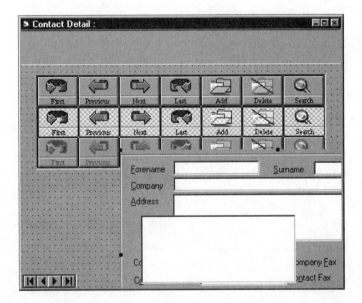

So, given that these toolbars don't make use of control arrays, how on earth can we create fully functioning works of art like those available when PsyCON is running? Here we have buttons going up and down, as well as being disabled and grayed out at will.

The theory is simple. The bitmap you don't see at run-time consists of three rows of buttons; the top holds images of the buttons in their up state, the next holds images of the buttons in their down state and the third holds images of the buttons in their disabled state. It's really an array, but it's not declared as an array and, as far as VB is concerned, it's one big bitmap. It's only because we know the height and width of each button that we can slice it up into individual bits.

What happens at run-time is that VB's `PaintPicture` method is used to copy the required sections of this larger graphic into the picture box you see at the top of the form. The required section is a complete image of the button we want. In order to find it and cut it out using `PaintPicture`, we need to know where in the grid the button is located and give this to the function in pixels.

The whole thing is controlled by a `Toolbar` class which we'll look at in a moment. First, let's see what happens. When the user triggers a `Mouse_Down` event on the top picture box by trying to click on an image, all we have to do is to pass the coordinates of the cursor to the `Draw_Down` method of the toolbar and voilà - the button sinks. Need to disable a button? Just call the `Disable` method and tell it which button to kill. It's really that simple and it's all thanks to the power of Visual Basic. Who said C egg-heads had all the fun?

Creating Toolbars

To use the `Toolbar.Cls` to create your own toolbars, first make sure the module is in your project. Then draw two picture boxes on the form and load your button image into one of them, setting its Visible property to false. Next, draw your main picture box onto the form, i.e. the picture box that will hold the buttons at run-time. The toolbar class also assumes that the ScaleMode of each picture control is set to Pixel, something best done at design-time to save time at run-time.

Now the code issue. Before you can do anything, you need to declare a toolbar object of some kind.

```
Dim Toolbar As New clsToolbar
```

In order for your new toolbar object to be accessible to all the code in your form, make sure you declare it in the declarations section of the form. Take a look at the declarations section of the detail form, for example:

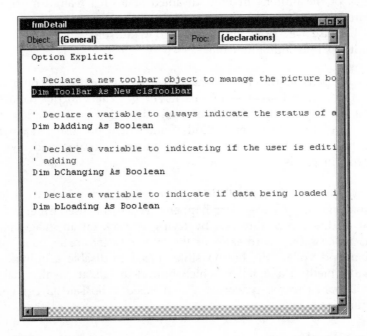

Setting Up the Toolbar

The class itself is totally reusable. For this reason it doesn't assume a particular number of buttons you want to use, nor does it need to know their dimensions. You specify all this at run-time. If you take a look at the **Form_Load** event in the Detail form, you'll see how this is done:

```
Private Sub Form_Load()

    Dim nIndex As Integer

    Screen.MousePointer = 11

    ToolBar.Setup picSource, picToolbar, 7, 3
```

It's the bottom line that we are interested in (as ever). Here we use the
Setup method of the **Toolbar** object. The parameters you pass are the name
of the picture box containing the single bitmap of all the buttons in all their
states, in our case **picSource**. Next is the name of the picture box that will
become your toolbar at run-time, here **picToolbar**. The final two parameters
declare the number of button images there are in your bitmap, in this case
7 across and **3** down.

These last two parameters are absolutely vital, since this is what allows the
toolbar object to figure out the width and height of each button. Without
this information, it couldn't use the **PaintPicture** method to draw the
buttons on screen. The object knows the dimensions of the **picSource**
container and it is a case of simple arithmetic to determine the size of each
button. We've effectively created a visual array, where each element is
referenced by its physical location in the grid, rather than by an index
number. However, the outcome is the same.

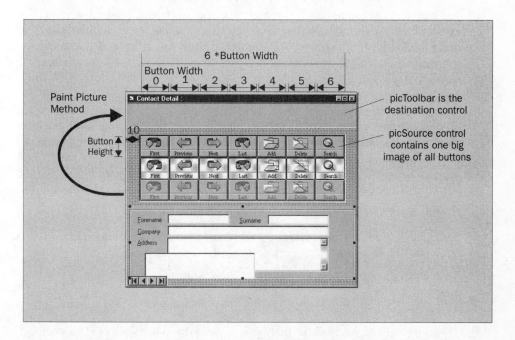

That is all there is to putting a graphical toolbar on your form. Making it
come to life is a little more complex, but not much.

Clicking on the Toolbar

In order to make the buttons on the toolbar go down when pressed, come up when released and respond to mouse clicks, you need to code the toolbar picture box's mousedown, mouseup and click events. Let's deal with mousedown first.

I'll assume that you've called the toolbar picture box something useful like **picToolbar**.

```
Private Sub picToolbar_MouseDown(Button As Integer, Shift As Integer, X As
⤷Single, Y As Single)

    ToolBar.Draw_Down X, Y

End Sub
```

The mousedown event comes ready equipped with some very useful parameters. As far as you're concerned, the user just pushed a mouse button down over the toolbar, but you don't know over which button and don't really want to know yet. You can throw the **x** and **y** parameters (the coordinates of the mouse when the button went down) to the toolbar object and let it do the work.

You do this by calling the **Draw_Down** method of the toolbar, using **x** and **y** as parameters. Based on the button width and heights, the toolbar object then uses these parameters to work out which button your user clicked. A down image of the button is then painted onto the toolbar. We will look at exactly how this is implemented shortly.

Handling the mouseup event works in exactly the same way.

```
Private Sub picToolbar_MouseUp(Button As Integer, Shift As Integer, X As
⤷Single, Y As Single)

    ToolBar.Draw_Up X, Y

End Sub
```

The only difference here is that, this time, you call the **Draw_Up** method, instead of **Draw_Down**. Now let's consider something more tricky - the click event.

The Toolbar Click Event

Click events are a lot more complex than they seem on the surface. Think about how you might interact with a normal command button. If you hold the mouse button down over a command button, then it sinks; in other words the mousedown event is triggered. If, while holding the mouse button down, you move the pointer somewhere else on the form and release it, then the button gets a mouseup event, but not a click. However, if you release the mouse button while still pointing at any part of the original button, then you do get a click event.

How does this affect us? If you hold down the mouse over a button on the toolbar, it sinks because there is code in the mousedown event to make it happen that way. If you then move the pointer to another button in the toolbar and release it, you would expect the button to come up, but no click event to be triggered. However, since the buttons in this case aren't real, and since you would still be pointing at the toolbar when the button comes up, the toolbar will get a click event. Bad news. How can we handle this?

The good news is you don't have to - there is code in the toolbar's **Draw_Up** method to determine if you released the mouse over the button you last pressed. If you did, then the toolbar figures that the "logical" button (for want of a better word) was pressed. The toolbar method has a property called **ClickButton** which you can examine to see which, if any, button on the toolbar was pressed.

Take a look at the toolbar click event in the Detail form to see what I mean:

```
Private Sub picToolbar_Click()

        Dim nIndex As Integer
        Dim nResponse As Integer

        Select Case ToolBar.ClickButton

            Case 0    ' Move to first record

                On Error Resume Next
                datContacts.Recordset.MoveFirst
                On Error GoTo 0
```

Since this toolbar has seven buttons on it, `ClickButton` will return a number between 0 and 6 to indicate which button was clicked. If the toolbar object decides that no button was clicked then it returns `-1`. A simple `Select` statement is all that is needed to add code to respond to clicks on any of the buttons on the toolbar.

What about disabling and enabling the buttons, something the Detail form does a lot? If you want to disable a button, you just call the `Disable` method and tell it which button to disable:

```
Toolbar.Disable 0
```

Remember that the button numbers start at 0. To enable a button, call the **Toolbar**'s `Enable` method:

```
Toolbar.Enable 0
```

So, to summarize, the methods of the `Toolbar` object are:

Method	Description
Setup	Pass it four parameters: the name of the picture control containing images of all the buttons, the name of the picture control that will become the toolbar, the number of buttons across and the number of states the source picture holds (up, down and disabled = 3).
Draw_Down	Pass it two parameters: the X and Y coordinates of the mouse on the toolbar when the mousedown event occurred.
Draw_Up	Pass it two parameters: the X and Y coordinates of the mouse on the toolbar when the mouseup event occurred.
Disable	Pass it the number of the button that you want to disable.
Enable	Pass it the number of the button that you want to enable.

The Toolbar Class Code

Let's first take a look at the code in the **Setup** method.

```
Public Sub Setup(picSource As Control, picDestination As Control, ByVal
⤷nButtonsAcross As Integer, ByVal nButtonsDown As Integer)

    Dim Element As Variant

    ReDim bDisabled(nButtonsAcross)
    For Each Element In bDisabled
        Element = False
    Next


    Set SourcePicture = picSource
    Set TargetPicture = picDestination

    ButtonsAcross = nButtonsAcross
    ButtonsDown = nButtonsDown


    ButtonWidth = SourcePicture.ScaleWidth \ ButtonsAcross
    ButtonHeight = SourcePicture.ScaleHeight \ ButtonsDown


    TargetPicture.ScaleHeight = ButtonHeight + 2


    TargetPicture.PaintPicture SourcePicture.Picture, 10, 0,
⤷SourcePicture.ScaleWidth, ButtonHeight, 0, 0, SourcePicture.ScaleWidth,
⤷ButtonHeight

    LastButtonDown = -1
    Clicked = False

End Sub
```

It looks a lot more complex than it really is, simply because there is a lot
to it. However, it's quite straightforward.

The first thing that happens is that an array in the module called
bDisabled is redimensioned, based on the number of buttons parameter, so
that it can hold a true or false value for each button on the toolbar. This is
used later on when deciding whether or not to respond to events like click
and mousedown.

As soon as the array has been redeclared as the correct size, a **For** loop moves through each element of the array, setting each element to false; by default all the buttons on the toolbar are enabled.

Next, two object variables, **SourcePicture** and **TargetPicture** are set up to hold the picture boxes used as the source and target.

The next two lines of code set up the **ButtonsAcross** and **ButtonsDown** variables to hold the number of buttons across and down the toolbar in the source bitmap. Armed with these, we can store the button width and height into yet two more variables.

```
ButtonWidth = SourcePicture.ScaleWidth \ ButtonsAcross
ButtonHeight = SourcePicture.ScaleHeight \ ButtonsDown
```

It should make sense to anyone who paid attention in school that the width of each button is the width of the source image divided by the number of buttons across the toolbar. Likewise, the height of the buttons is equal to the height of the toolbar divided by the number of buttons in each column in the source picture.

The next line looks a little obscure:

```
TargetPicture.ScaleHeight = ButtonHeight + 2
```

Personally, I feel that toolbar buttons look better with a nice gap between their top and bottom and the top and bottom of the toolbar itself. That's what this line does - re-size the target picture box to take into account the height of the buttons, plus 2 pixels.

Finally, the toolbar can be drawn in all its glory:

```
TargetPicture.PaintPicture SourcePicture.Picture, 10, 0,
↳SourcePicture.ScaleWidth, ButtonHeight, 0, 0, SourcePicture.ScaleWidth,
↳ButtonHeight
```

This line of code is a bit complex, so let's remind ourselves how the **PaintPicture** method works. This is the format:

```
object.PaintPicture picture, x1, y1, width1, height1, x2,
↳y2, width2, height2, opcode
```

The line in the program copies the top line of buttons from the hidden control into the toolbar. Let's look at each of the parameters for our code in turn:

Parameter	In Our Example	Explanation
object	TargetPicture	This is the picture box that is going to hold the toolbar image at run-time, in our case picToolbar.
picture	SourcePicture	This is the source control for the function, in our case the grid of button images that is hidden at run-time in picSource
x1	10	Top corner X coordinate of the destination. This is a number of pixels along the picToolbar box and marks the start position of the button image. In our case, it's 10, as we added the gap.
y1	0	Top corner Y coordinate of the destination. There is only one row of images in the toolbar, so they are up against the top of the control.
width1	SourcePicture. ScaleWidth	Width of the destination control, in our case it's the full width.
height1	ButtonHeight	Height of the destination control. We only want one row of buttons.
x2	0	Top left X coordinate of the source control.

Continued

Parameter	In Our Example	Explanation
y2	0	Top left Y coordinate of the required row in the source control. We want the top row.
width2	SourcePicture. ScaleWidth	Width of the source. Here, it's the whole row.
Height2	ButtonHeight	Height of the source, i.e. size of the button we're copying from.

The **PaintPicture** method is the reason we use this method of creating the toolbar. It's so fast. It's much faster than loading in all sorts of little button images at run-time.

The final two lines in the code set up **LastButtonDown** and **Clicked** (two more variables in the class) to indicate that no buttons have previously been pressed and that no click event has occurred.

While the **Setup** method handles the drawing of the entire top line of the toolbar, the **Draw_Down**, **Draw_Up**, **Disable** and **Enable** methods draw individual buttons.

The Draw Methods

Take a look at the code for **Draw_Down**

```
Public Sub Draw_Down(nX As Single, nY As Single)

    Dim nCurrentButton As Integer

    If nX < 10 Or nX > SourcePicture.ScaleWidth Or nY >
ꝏSourcePicture.ScaleHeight Then Exit Sub

    nX = nX - 10
    nCurrentButton = nX \ ButtonWidth
    If bDisabled(nCurrentButton) Then Exit Sub
```

```
    TargetPicture.PaintPicture SourcePicture.Picture, 10 + (nCurrentButton
 * ButtonWidth), 0, ButtonWidth, ButtonHeight, nCurrentButton *
 ButtonWidth, ButtonHeight, ButtonWidth, ButtonHeight

    LastButtonDown = nCurrentButton
    Clicked = False

End Sub
```

The main thrust here is to use the mouse coordinates passed to the
procedure to determine which button the mouse was over when the down
event occurred.

Before drawing anything, the mouse X and Y coordinates are checked to
make sure that the mouse pointer is actually over the toolbar area. You
have to bear in mind that the on screen toolbar picture box could be
substantially wider than the original toolbar image, so such checks are
necessary. In this case, we make sure that the X coordinate is greater than
10 (since the painted toolbar is offset from the left of the toolbar by ten
pixels), but less than the width of the source toolbar. The Y coordinate must
be less than the height of a single button (our painted toolbar is only one
button high).

Providing these checks are passed, control moves to a section of code that
calculates the number of the button clicked from the coordinates passed to
the routine. The current X coordinate is divided by **ButtonWidth**, which
gives us the number of the button across the toolbar.

Integer division (using \ instead of /) performs the calculation and
rounds the result down to a whole number, which is ideal since we
don't really need to know that the user clicked button 2.773.

```
TargetPicture.PaintPicture SourcePicture.Picture, 10 + (nCurrentButton *
 ButtonWidth), 0, ButtonWidth, ButtonHeight, nCurrentButton * ButtonWidth,
 ButtonHeight, ButtonWidth, ButtonHeight
```

Having calculated which button was clicked, it's easy to figure out the
coordinates of the button in the target toolbar and in the source picture.
The X coordinate in the target picture box is:

```
10 + (Button Number * Button Width)
```

The Y coordinate in the target picture box is 0. The X coordinate for the source is the button number multiplied by the button width. The Y coordinate is equal to the button height for the **Draw_Down** routine. (It's the button height times two for the **Disable** procedure).

The rest of the code in **Draw_Down** sets up the **LastButtonDown** variable so that the **Draw_Up** routine can determine if a button simply needs to travel up, or whether a button was actually clicked.

That about covers the toolbar. It's a good way of implementing this kind of device as its quick and relatively light on resources.

Implementing the PsyCON Printing Facility

A topic we haven't covered yet is, of course, printing. Why haven't we covered it yet? Because very few people still do it. The advent of OLE 2 means that you can now export data to OLE 2 enabled applications, like Word or Excel, and let them format and print your data for you. In the Professional and Enterprise editions of Visual Basic 4, you actually get a whole application dedicated to printing your reports for you: Crystal Reports.

Device Independence Makes It Easy

Handling printing from Visual Basic is really quite simple. Windows supports something known as **device independence**. What this means, in a nutshell, is that you should be able to write code to produce output on any output device connected to your system, be it the monitor, the printer, a plotter or whatever.

For this reason, many of the properties of a form which you use to display text and/or graphics also apply to Visual Basic's printer object. For example, if you wanted to change the font style, you could simply say:

```
Printer.Font.Size = 24
Printer.Font.Name = "Times New Roman"
Printer.Font.Bold = True
```

Likewise, any of the graphics methods you could apply to a form, you can also apply to a printer. For example:

```
Printer.Line (0,0)-(1000,1000)
```

Of course, for the purposes of printing reports, the most useful method available to us is the **Print** method. However, positioning the text in your report can be tricky unless you set the printer's ScaleMode property to 4 (character). This allows you to set the printer's **CurrentX** and **CurrentY** properties to the number of characters across or down to print.

Printer Methods and Properties

The printer object also comes fully equipped with a couple of new properties and methods specifically for dealing with printed data.

The **NewPage** method, for example, tells the printer to feed the current page and start a new one. The **EndDoc** method tells Windows that you have finished with the printer and that it can now go ahead and actually print. This is really quite important - you must use the **EndDoc** method at the end of your report or nothing will appear and your users may get quite upset.

In terms of properties, the most useful is **Page**. You can use **CurrentX** and **CurrentY** to find out where exactly you are on the printed page, but the **Page** property will tell you which page of the report you are on.

Printing in PsyCON

You can see all these methods and properties in action in the **mnuFPrint_Click** routine attached to the MDI form.

```
Private Sub mnuFPrint_Click()

    Dim sAddress As String
    Dim nIndex As Integer

    ' Display the print dialog
    Common.Flags = cdlPDPrintToFile + cdlPDNoSelection + cdlPDNoPageNums
    Common.CancelError = True
    On Error GoTo Print_Cancelled
    Common.ShowPrinter
    On Error GoTo 0
```

```
    ' Now we can start to print - it would be a good idea then
    ' to turn the cursor into an hourglass and set up the data control

    Screen.MousePointer = 11

    datContacts.DatabaseName = App.Path & "\psycon.mdb"
    datContacts.RecordSource = "Select * from Contacts where (Owner_ID = "
& gnOwnerID & " and Private) or not Private order by Contact_Surname"
    datContacts.Refresh

    ' Now we can start to loop through the records and print them out
    On Error GoTo Print_Cancelled
    datContacts.Recordset.MoveFirst
    On Error GoTo 0
    Print_Contact_Heading

    Do While Not datContacts.Recordset.EOF

        ' Print the record detail
        Printer.CurrentX = 3
        Printer.Print "Contact Name : " &
datContacts.Recordset.Contact_Forename & " " &
datContacts.Recordset.Contact_Surname
        Printer.CurrentX = 3
        Printer.Print "Company        : "; datContacts.Recordset.Company_Name

        sAddress = datContacts.Recordset.Company_Address
        Do While sAddress <> ""
            Printer.CurrentX = 21
            nIndex = InStr(sAddress, Chr$(13))
            If nIndex > 0 Then Printer.Print Left$(sAddress, nIndex - 1)
Else Printer.Print sAddress
            If nIndex > 0 Then sAddress = Mid$(sAddress, nIndex + 2) Else
sAddress = ""
        Loop

        Printer.Print
        Printer.CurrentX = 3
        Printer.Print "Company Phone: " &
datContacts.Recordset.Company_Phone;
        Printer.CurrentX = 45
        Printer.Print "Company Fax: " & datContacts.Recordset.Company_Fax
        Printer.CurrentX = 3
        Printer.Print "Contact Phone:" &
datContacts.Recordset.Contact_Phone;
        Printer.CurrentX = 45
        Printer.Print "Contact Fax: " & datContacts.Recordset.Contact_Fax
        Printer.Print
        Printer.CurrentX = 3
        Printer.Print "E-Mail       " & datContacts.Recordset.Contact_EMail
        Printer.Print
```

```
        Printer.Print
        Printer.Print

        ' If we are near the bottom of the page then start a new one and
↳re-print the
        ' headings.
        If Printer.CurrentY > 45 Then
            Printer.NewPage
            Print_Contact_Heading
        End If

        datContacts.Recordset.MoveNext

    Loop

    Printer.EndDoc

    MsgBox "Windows 95 is now taking care of your print request.",
↳vbInformation, "Print finished"

    Screen.MousePointer = 0

    Exit Sub

Print_Cancelled:
    On Error GoTo 0
    Exit Sub
End Sub
```

The code is big, but on the whole is quite self-explanatory. The first thing it does is run up the print common dialog in order to let the user set up the printer properties, choose which printer to use and so on.

The rest of the code just loops through the records in the contacts table and prints out the data it finds. Extensive use is made of the **CurrentX** property to ensure that all the data is positioned nicely on the printout.

The one area that may be a little confusing, though, is the bit that prints the address. The **Address** field in the Contacts table is actually a memo field and so it could easily contain carriage returns which mess up our report formatting. So that the address gets printed out properly, we need to write a little code to split the address into chunks and print those out.

```
        sAddress = datContacts.Recordset.Company_Address
        Do While sAddress <> ""
            Printer.CurrentX = 21
            nIndex = InStr(sAddress, Chr$(13))
```

```
            If nIndex > 0 Then Printer.Print Left$(sAddress, nIndex - 1)
    ↳Else Printer.Print sAddress
            If nIndex > 0 Then sAddress = Mid$(sAddress, nIndex + 2) Else
    ↳sAddress = ""
        Loop
```

The address field is first copied into the **sAddress** variable, then a loop is run for as long as there is data in the **sAddress** variable.

Inside the loop, the **Instr** method is used to search for carriage returns (character 13) in the **sAddress** variable. When one is found, the data to its left is printed, then removed from the string. As soon as the search for a carriage return fails, the remaining data in **sAddress** is printed and **sAddress** is set to **"",** causing the loop to end.

Another interesting point about this code is that it prevents data from being printed over a page break. It does this by looking at the **CurrentY** property. If, after printing the contact details, the printer is at line 45 or greater, then a new page is started and the headings reprinted.

```
        If Printer.CurrentY > 45 Then
            Printer.NewPage
            Print_Contact_Heading
        End If
```

Fine Tuning Your Application

Having created a real application, you now have to get it ready for prime-time. You may have noticed by now that this application is a little slow. By default, and I am sure Microsoft will agree, Visual Basic is a slow system. It is too easy to write verbose code, code that is duplicated throughout the program and other such nasties which all contribute to making a slow application.

Throughout the book I've tried to show you how VB and Windows fit together. If you write an application without any idea of how VB actually works, or how it interacts with Windows, then your resulting product will be slow.

The Need for Speed

In this version of PsyCON, I have broken every optimization rule I could find in order to make the code as easy to understand and as easy to explain as I possibly could. The result is a slow application. However, this provides a good foundation for you to experiment with in order to try out some optimization techniques.

Let's take a look at what to do and how to do it.

Optimize Last

The way I have written PsyCON as it stands makes it slow. However, there are good reasons for adopting this approach. I have tried to make all parts of the program, from naming conventions to code organization, as intuitive as possible for humans. This isn't just for your benefit, however. It makes sense to keep your code clear and organized in the development phase. Let's review why by back-tracking to some of the issues we discussed in Chapter 12 - Writing Programs that Work.

Writing decent, bug free code is difficult. An average application will contain thousands, if not hundreds of thousands, of lines of code. Understanding the execution of each line and its relationship to the rest of the code takes quite a bit of brainpower.

For this reason there are a number of tricks that programmers will employ to increase their understanding of an application and the way in which the application solves the problem it was written for.

Making Code Readable

Structured programming atomizes code into small building blocks which can be pieced together to form an app. If you can guarantee the reliability of a single building block in the program, then you can probably make certain assumptions about any part of the program that uses the block. In addition, where an average program might contain thousands of lines of code, it will only ever include tens of blocks. Understanding the relationships between these blocks is normally quite easy to do in your head, but it is even easier when drawn into some kind of flowchart or organizational chart.

Structured programming provides a method whereby developers can produce self-contained reusable blocks of both code and data. OOP techniques, when used properly, of course, also increase the chances that your code can be reused. Whereas a proven block of code in a structured program helps in understanding and testing that program, a proven object is even more widely applicable as it can modify its own data.

The downside, of course, is that a bug in such an object could screw up all the programs that use it. For example, there was a bug in the Windows calculator that was attributed to a library of code shipped with Microsoft's original C compiler. The same bug that appeared in calculator could also be found in hundreds of other applications produced with the same compiler.

There are other ways of working to reduce the risk of bugs - writing code that is easy to read, for example. Use variable names like **sEmployee_Name** instead of **sX**, use decent function and procedure names, lay your code out with simple logic. For example:

```
If chkLoadData.Value =1 then bLoaded = True else bLoaded = False
If bLoaded Then
   :
   :
End If
```

is a lot nicer to read than:

```
If (bloaded = (chkLoadData = 1)) = True Then
   :
   :
End If
```

All these techniques, together with the many others we have seen in the rest of the book, combine to give you a readable, easily maintainable application. However, for those times when you need outright speed in your app, they are bad news. In an interpreted environment like Visual Basic, short, concise code will always run faster than reams of verbose code, although the former will undoubtedly look nasty and be a nightmare to maintain unless your whole team are on the same wavelength as you.

When code is compiled and then run, as it is in environments like C++ and Delphi, the compiler strips out all the unnecessary verbiage. VB does this a little, but not as much.

For this reason, write code that you can read first. Use this easy code to remove the bugs and make sure that the application is as stable as it will ever be, then go back over the problem areas and convert small sections of code to faster, more confusing code. This way, if you make a change and the app stops, you don't have to wade through line after line of complex logic trying to guess where the problem may lie - it lies in the last few lines of code you changed.

So, the next obvious question is, "How can I optimize my code when I have got it running, but running slowly?". It really depends what you are trying to accomplish...

Turbo Injected Databases

The Standard Edition of Visual Basic, which this book covers, only allows you to access recordset objects through a data control. In the Pro and Enterprise editions, you can actually create a recordset through code without having to use a graphical control. So what, I hear you cry? What does it matter how you create the recordset? Well, it matters a lot.

Each time you load a form with a data control on, the data control needs to connect to a database. This involves finding the database file on the hard disk, sending calls to the Jet engine to open the database, finding out what objects are in the database, opening an object in the database and building the recordset. What if you could eliminate some of these steps?

The easiest way around this in the Standard Edition of VB is to draw an invisible container control (normally a picture box) onto your application's initial form. Then, in this picture box, create data controls for every type of recordset your application uses. This will dramatically slow down the load time for the first form (something your users probably won't mind if you put a welcome screen up, play some sound or generally do something to keep them amused while this is happening).

Once you have these data controls set up, you can code the load event of each form in the application to simply copy the recordset object from one of these data controls to the data control on the child form you are loading. For example:

```
Private Sub Form_Load()

    Set Data1.Recordset = frmMDI.datEmployees.Recordset

End Sub
```

Since the recordset has already been created, the new data control doesn't have to worry about opening the database, finding the objects and so on - it was all done when your first form loaded. The result, of course, is forms that appear almost instantly when loading and an application that will generally experience a 2-3 fold increase in loading and unloading any form with a data control on.

Don't Assume It Ain't Broke

Some of the more sceptical among you may now be questioning this - surely that can't be right, Microsoft would have spotted this optimization black hole and fixed it!? Wrong, they didn't spot it, they didn't fix it and life has been this way since Visual Basic 3. If you want to see it in action for yourself, follow these simple steps in the PsyCON project

Loading Databases at Start-up

Try It Out!

1 Run the PsyCON application, log in, then when the main form appears, choose Contact Detail from the View menu. Count how long it takes the form to load and write the time down.

2 Now quit the application, draw a picture box on the MDI form and set its Visible property to false.

3 Next draw a data control onto the picture box and, at design-time, set the **DatabaseName** property to point at **Psycon.MDB**, then set the RecordSource to Contacts.

4 Now bring up the load event code for frmDetail. Find these lines

```
datContacts.DatabaseName = App.Path & "\psycon.mdb"
datContacts.RecordsetType = vbRSTypeDynaset
datContacts.RecordSource = "Select * from Contacts where (Owner_ID = " &
↳gnOwnerID & " and Private) or not Private order by Contact_Surname"
datContacts.Refresh
```

... and change them to this one line:

```
Set datContacts.Recordset = frmMDI.Data1.Recordset
```

5 Now run the application again, log in and bring up the Contact Detail window as before. Don't forget to time it. You should notice at least a 200% increase in the speed - on the P90 I am using here, the time for the form to come into view and be usable dropped from 5 seconds to just 1.

Of course, coding all the forms in an app like PsyCON to work like this takes a lot of time and effort, and would generally result in an application that is difficult to understand. That is why I haven't done it. It is more important to me to be able to show you how code works and then how it can be made better, than it is to show you beautiful code that many of you just won't be able to follow without too many questions popping into your head.

Using Transactions

Another little trick for you, but one which unfortunately doesn't help PsyCON, is speeding up database updates. I often see messages on the Internet and Compuserve from programmers asking questions like this:

"I have a database and I need to change 1 field in 200 records in response to a change on a form. However, when I do this it takes almost 10 minutes to finish - I thought VB was supposed to be good for database development."

This is obviously a message from a guy who has spent time learning the language, but nothing about the environment it runs in or the Jet database engine. The answer is to use a feature of the Pro and Enterprise Editions called **transactions**. Although we're focusing on the Standard Edition here, it's worth just looking at transactions briefly.

Each time you make a change to a record, using **Edit** or **Addnew**, the Jet database engine either locks the current record, or moves to a new one. It then copies the contents of the record into a buffer in memory. Your code then changes the fields in the record and, when **Update** is called, Jet copies these values from the buffer to the database record, then unlocks it. This is a very simplistic view, but you get the picture.

However, if changes are made in transaction mode, then things are done differently. In transaction mode, there is very little disk access since Jet stores every change you make in a buffer in memory, rather than loading from then saving straight back to the hard disk. When you commit the transaction, the buffer is written out to the database in the background - leaving your app to get on with whatever it needs to do. The results are the same, a changed set of records, but far less disk access occurs. Again a simplistic view, but it demonstrates the point.

So, the guy above should change his code, which is probably like this:

```
Data1.Recordset.MoveFirst
Do While Not Data1.Recordset.EOF
   Data1.Recordset.Edit
   Data1.Recordset("FieldName") = "changed"
   Data1.Recordset.Update
   Data1.Recordset.MoveNext
Loop
```

... to something like this

```
Dim nRecordCount As Integer

nRecordCount = 100
Data1.Recordset.MoveFirst

BeginTrans
   Do While Not Data1.Recordset.EOF
      nRecordCount = nRecordCount - 1

      Data1.Recordset.Edit
      Data1.Recordset("FieldName") = "changed"
      Data1.Recordset.Update
      Data1.Recordset.MoveNext

      If nRecordCount = 0 then
         nRecordCount = 100
         CommitTrans
         BeginTrans
      End If
   Loop
CommitTrans
```

In this case, the code has grown dramatically, but the update will run a great deal faster, typically one and a half times to double the speed. What we are doing here is storing all the updates inside a transaction. Since transaction updates are held in memory, we don't want to store so much data in memory that the application runs out of space and crashes, so a variable is used to count how many edits have been done. Every 100 edits, the transaction is committed (the changes are written to the database) and a new transaction started.

When the loop ends, there will still be a transaction open, so that is committed too. This is one of the very rare examples of more verbose code actually benefiting the speed of the application.

Optimizing the Recordset

How else can we speed up a database app? Well, if you don't intend to make any changes to a recordset, then open it as **ReadOnly**. There is a great deal less overhead in opening a **ReadOnly** file, simply because Jet doesn't have to worry about allocating change buffers, locking records and such like. Better still, though, would be to open the recordset as a **Snapshot** type recordset.

Many users develop database applications for their own use, or for use on a single computer. It amazes me how many totally forget about the Exclusive property of the data control and leave it set at its default (false) value. This means Jet has to constantly manage your one user as if he or she were in a multi-user environment. If the app is for a single user, then set your data control's Exclusive property to true.

If you use just these few simple database tricks, you will find your database apps can compete with the best of them. I take great pleasure in demonstrating a decent VB database app to the new Delphi programmer who has just sent me a message saying how bad he thinks the speed of VB is compared to Delphi. With just these techniques, rigorously employed, you will be able to produce database apps with instantly loading forms, instant updates of information, incredibly fast searching and generally a much nicer app than your competitors.

The rule with database apps is this:

> *"Make the 386 owners love their machine and make the Pentium owners feel like gods"*

Unfortunately, too many developers use this one:

"Force the 386 owners to upgrade and make the Pentium owners consider it too".

This version of PsyCON falls into the latter category. It's a deliberate ploy, since I intend to leave you with something to think about at the end of this chapter, as you enter the world of the VB programmer, but with very little real experience.

Speeding Up Controls and the Display

The arrival of Windows way back in the mists of time brought with it a brand new phrase for us all to play with: **perceived speed**. What this means is that the user will be quite happy if he or she thinks the program is running nice and fast. How do you make them think it's fast? Show them something.

That's not as stupid as it sounds. How many times have you seen half a form come into view and then a few seconds later the rest of it with the controls on the display flashing about, as Windows struggles to re-draw them. You can increase the perception that the computer and system are fast with two simple commands: **Show** and **DoEvents**. Immediately after loading a form, call the **Show** method for it, followed by **DoEvents** to force the re-draw to take place now. The form will flash into view nice and quick, at which point you can leave an hourglass on the screen to keep the user amused.

Because the form comes up nice and fast, the user has something to do. There are usually a few subconcious moments spent by the user as he or she takes in the controls on the form and tries to figure out which control has focus and where the input cursor is. You can use this time to do the rest of the stuff, like set up any data controls, set properties on the rest of the controls on the form and so on.

Properties Are Slow

Which brings me to another point. Dealing with controls, or more precisely their properties, is slow. Take a look at this:

```
Do While Not Data1.Recordset.EOF

   :
   :
   Data1.Recordset.Field  = dlgOpen.Filename
   :
   :
Loop
```

This is quite a common scenario: a loop, probably massive, which deals with one or more properties of a control. The bogey man in this is the **Filename** property of **dlgOpen**. If it takes 1 millisecond to access a variable and 2 to access a property, then what's the problem?

The problem is that if you have a loop that runs 2000 times, then that's a two second wait the user has to put up with because you want to deal with properties, rather than a one second wait which you would get if the code had been written like this:

```
sFilename = dlgOpen.Filename
Do While No Data1.Recordset.EOF

   :
   :
   Data1.Recordset.Field = sFilename
   :
   :

Loop
```

This is another problem with programmers. When you sit in front of that monitor hacking away at your latest object or subroutine, a two second delay for the users doesn't seem that much. However, if you watched a cartoon on TV that only updated twice every second, you would turn it off - it's too slow. But hey, twice a second is less than a half second delay between each frame. Our theoretical two seconds is immense when you think of it in this light.

Now we have another problem. What if that loop runs 10-20,000 times? We would then have a serious problem, even if we do cache the properties in variables. In this case, use a **DoEvents** loop. As you have already seen, **DoEvents** passes control back over to Windows, no matter how much more time you have in your timeslice. If you are working in a loop which doesn't directly affect the user, such as writing audit records to a database, deleting records, etc., then try this:

```
Do While DoEvents() and ...........
    :
    :
Loop
```

Your loop will run slower, but the user can get on and use your program - perceived speed again.

Here's Looking at You Kid

Ok, now it's your turn. I have spent the last 16 chapters trying to get you on your feet with VB and in the frame of mind that you want to learn more. Well, now is your big chance. The problem with most new programmers is that they can't put their new knowledge into practice because they have nothing serious to do. I am going to solve that for you now.

PsyCON, the version you have here, of course, has some problems. The database forms load too slowly, you can't print a single contact's details out, the OLE stuff is slow, there is no support for Microsoft Office in there, you can't choose which contacts to export, you can't delete groups of contacts or action records at once and so on. If you fancy getting really down and dirty with VB, then choose a couple of refinements from the list below and try to implement them.

Above all, don't worry. You'll make a lot of silly mistakes, at times you may find yourself pulling your hair out, confronted with seemingly infeasible problems. At the end of it, though, you will have learnt a great deal. You will also start to develop your own coding style in VB. You will emerge a more seasoned VB programmer, with some experience, a lot more confidence and an application that you can call your own. Here's the wish list.

1 What about those toolbars - pretty neat, huh? But hang on, they don't even support standard stuff like pop-up hints. Add a method to the toolbar object that the programmer can call from the mousemove event to figure out which button the user is over and then display a hint.

2 Shame about the MDI form's status bar, isn't it! What status bar, I hear you cry? Exactly. Add a picture box to the MDI form to give the user some feedback on what they are doing, or should be doing, in the application. How about writing a global routine to update the status bar, pulling a message to display out of the Tag property of the `ActiveControl`? (Hint: Look up `ActiveControl` in the online help.)

3 Those database form load times are awful. Can we speed them up? (Hint: we discussed this earlier in the chapter.)

4 Those OLE load times are awful. Why not force the user to deal with text documents only and run up WordPad when the application starts? With WordPad already running before the link is made, the app should speed up greatly.

5 It's great that the program picks up the name of the database and its path at run-time. But what happens if you move the database away from the directory where PsyCON lives. The answer is the program crashes. Add code to stop this happening.

6 Implement multi-select code on the grids in the contact summary and action point lists. With this, you could loop through the selected records when the user selects Delete and take out a whole bunch.

7 How about adding code to look at the values returned from the Print dialog to print only a single contact, or even a range of contacts? How about adding a new dialog, so that the user can key in a customizable header for the report that gets printed out?

8 The OLE export is really weedy since it uses WordPad and WordPad does not support OLE automation. If you have Microsoft Office, then why not take a look at making an exported document in Word, on the fly, using OLE automation. Perhaps you could even expand on this and write mailshot code to automatically head up letters to some or all of your contacts.

9 With a lot of action points for a contact, it can be difficult to tell which points are still outstanding and which are not. Put a check box on the form to let the user choose to see all or only uncleared points. You'll need a little code, too!

10 Change the security form so that it double checks the password.

11 Add code to the toolbar to re-size both the Picture container controls and the toolbar image to take account of the different screen resolutions. You determine the screen resolution by counting the number of pixels across and down the screen.

All these improvements will turn the version you have into something close to the version we produce commercially, perhaps even better. If you want to take a look at the app in all its glory, then why not drop me a line, or e-mail me - you can find my e-mail address and Psynet's postal address in the PsyCON database, or in the ad at the back of the book.

Summary

I've tried to give you a feeling for what a complete VB application is like. In covering the PsyCON contacts manager we also covered:

▶ How to create a fast toolbar.

▶ How to create printed reports.

▶ What you can do to speed up your apps.

I hope you enjoy using VB as much as I do. I'll be back with another Wrox Press book soon, this time on developing Multimedia applications using VB, so I hope to see you then.

That's all for now, though. Good luck, and enjoy your time with the world's premier Windows development environment.

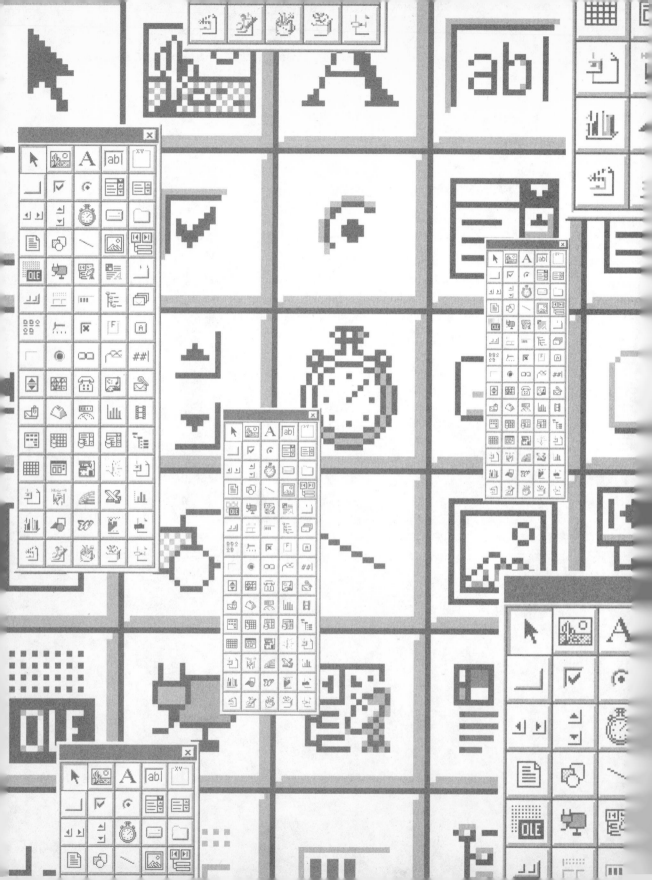

Where To Now?

By now you should have a pretty good idea of how to piece together a Visual Basic application. Well done, you've come a long way and deserve a pat on the back.

However, the learning curve does not end here. As many programmers and developers already know, simply learning the semantics of how to use a development environment is but a small step on the path to that most revered title of Programming Guru.

So, what you need to know now is

- What are the tools I need to empower my VB apps.....big time?
- What about the other versions of Visual Basic - will they help me?
- Where can I go for help?

In this small appendix, you will learn the answers to all these questions and more.

All About the VB Family

If you have followed the book all the way to this point then you should have got the hang of the Standard Edition of Visual Basic 4. However, the Standard Edition is only one in a growing family of four. The good news for you is that the skills you have acquired can be translated effortlessly to any of the other three versions - which you choose depends on the job you need to do.

VBA (Visual Basic: Applications Edition)

We all know the Microsoft goal: to put a computer running Microsoft software on every desk in every house and business. However, there are a number of clear subplots to this goal. One of them, it seems, is to put a version of Visual Basic inside every one of the above computers.

VBA is now shipped with every application in the Microsoft Office suite, giving users a standard way in which to control both the applications themselves (Excel, Access, Word, Powerpoint), as well as the OLE 2 objects that these applications can export.

VBA is basically a cut-down version of VB4. In fact, to put it the other way around, VB4 is a direct, more powerful descendant of VBA. Unlike its younger brother, VBA does not provide database tools, nor come in various different flavours (such as a 16-bit and 32-bit). However, it does include all the facilities you need to make effective use of OLE 2 - ideal since all the applications in Office are OLE 2 enabled.

So, who would use VBA? Basically, anyone who needs to breathe more life into the Office suite than is already there, as well as applications developers who need to supply apps that are native to any of the Office components.

For example, if you have been assigned the task of producing a complete order entry system, making use of Excel for the financial side, Access for the database side and Word for the reporting and documentation side, then VBA could well be the product for you. It's included in VB4's Professional and Enterprise Editions, as well as in the Office package itself.

Visual Basic: Professional Edition

In the bad old days of VB3, the Professional Edition was the only place a programmer could go from the Standard one when looking for a more powerful version of Visual Basic. With the advent of the Enterprise Edition, the Pro has really become an in-between step. However, that does not mean that it has lost any of its attractiveness as an upgrade from the Standard Edition. It simply means that the incredibly powerful Enterprise Edition has raised the bar even higher.

Aside from the convenience of having all the Visual Basic manuals supplied on CD-ROM, the Professional Edition also lets you take control of Data Access Objects (DAO) directly through code. This means that you can create database applications that essentially do away with the need for the somewhat clumsy data control. As a result, database applications run faster and, by taking direct control, you as developer are able to take even more measures to safeguard the data you deal with.

Also related to database development is Crystal Reports, a package not included with the Standard Edition. This handy utility and OCX takes all the pain out of creating reports for database applications, by letting you draw the report on screen in much the same way as you would draw components onto a Visual Basic form. The result is a saved report file which you simply tell the OCX to load at run-time in order to print out your reports.

The Professional Edition is also supplied with even more controls and components that the Standard one, giving you easy access to the serial communications systems in Windows, a powerful way to deal with multimedia files and various other neat controls.

The Pro Edition also comes with an extensive API reference that lets you paste those annoying API declarations and function calls directly into your code. It's hard to do any real API work without this.

On the OLE front, the Pro Edition lets you create your own OLE servers. This means you can create DLLs that talk to your code through OLE. You can then control these applications through OLE automation, as you would a component of, say, the Office suite.

Typically, if you need to create powerful, single user database systems, or have an urge to dabble in the wacky world of communications, then you need to be looking at the Professional Edition. Those of you with a need to do something more powerful - perhaps a multi-user, distributed client/server application - should take a look at what the Enterprise Edition has to offer.

Visual Basic: Enterprise Edition

The mother of all Visual Basics, the Enterprise Edition, has absolutely nothing to do with Kirk and friends, but is, instead, an incredibly powerful client/server application development tool.

In addition to everything included in the Standard and Professional Editions, the Enterprise Edition also comes with a whole host of new applications, including an Automation manager for monitoring connections to OLE objects, the Component manager for managing all your new controls and OLE objects, various client/server database and connection management tools, a multi-developer version control system known as SourceSafe, a resource editor and much more besides.

If you work in a large team of VB developers, and need to create supremely powerful and well-connected database apps, then you'd really better get the boss to get the check book out for this little beauty.

Help... I Feel So Alone

So goes the cry of many a lonely developer, particularly those learning or just starting out with a new development system. Fear not - there are thousands of people out there dying to help your solve your latest coding dilemma, and for free as well. Never be afraid of asking for help, no matter how trivial the problem may seem. There were even times when I had to resort to using the developer community to help me, rather than returning the favor.

The best place to start when you need help is, of course, cyberspace. If you have a modem, then make sure you are either a member of the Microsoft Network, Compuserve or the Internet. If you don't have a modem yet, then please put this book down and go and get one; it's not healthy to have your nose stuck in a book all day.

Compuserve is by far and away the best online service to be a member of if you have VB troubles. You can either go to the MSBASIC forum, or the VBPJ forum - both are populated by thousands of VB developers ranging from the complete novice to total guru (yes I use Compuserve too ;->), all providing valuable hints and tips, support code and some very interesting discussions on nothing more than coding technique, or the rashness of the latest Microsoft decision. Microsoft use Compuserve too, and frequently join in.

On the Internet, check out the comp.lang.visual.basic newsgroup. It's a little more easy going than Compuserve, but equally well populated.

If online services are really not your scene, then how about a user group. In the UK you can join the Visual Basic User Group (VBUG) which regularly holds local meetings as well as an annual conference. It also provides its members with a bi-monthly magazine providing some very handy hints and tips. In the US, pick up a copy of The Visual Basic Programmer's Journal - an excellent publication, again backed up by user group meetings and four yearly conferences of astounding quality and reputation called VBITS.

Both VBUG and VBPJ (415 833 7100) carry regular reviews of the latest add-in controls and applications to make your choice of these a lot more informed than it may have been previously. In the last edition of this book, I listed some of the best controls on the market - however, the market has grown so much since that book was released, that it is now proving impossible for even Psynet to keep up with everything that's out there.

If you are looking for a new add-in, or a new set of OCXs, then check out either VBUG or VBPJ to see what they think, post a few messages on the Internet to gauge public opinion, or simply pop down to your local newsagents and see what the magazines in there say.

Bedtime Reading

As you begin to move towards the more complex stuff (client/server databases, multimedia, communications etc.) you will need to read a fair amount more in order to get the results you want.

To get to grips with the advanced versions of Visual Basic, you may like to take a look at Wrox's *Revolutionary Guide to VB4 Pro*.

If you want to get down and get dirty with Windows itself, then there is no better book that the *Visual Basic Programmer's Reference to the Windows API* by Daniel Appleman.

Multimedia is all the rage at the moment, although the range of decent books covering it is not that great. Although a slightly biased opinion, you should check out the *Revolutionary Guide to Multimedia Programming in Visual Basic*.

To learn more about SQL, take a look at *Instant SQL* from Wrox.

Finally, although VB is a great language, it is useless unless your work in it is backed up by effective design and programming practices. The bible for this is *Code Complete*, written by Steve McConnell and published by Microsoft Press. It has no VB-specific information in it at all, but the background information and insight it provides into the entire development cycle is invaluable.

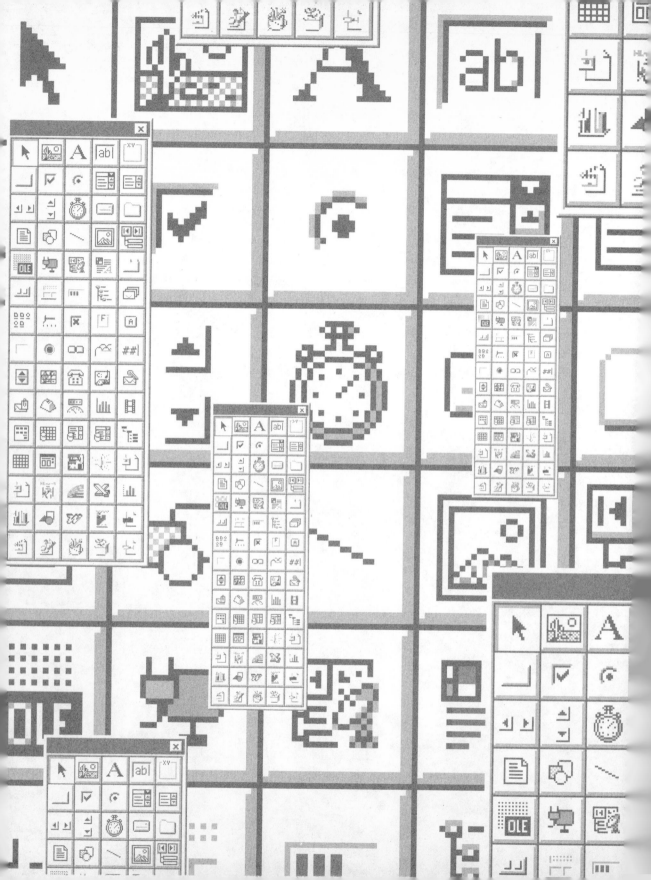

Visual Basic Naming Conventions

This appendix introduces a scheme for naming all the objects in Visual Basic in a way that increases the safety and readability of your code. Some parts of this are taken from standards published by Microsoft, and some are my own.

There are three kinds of object we need to have standard names for in our Visual Basic code:

▶ Controls

▶ Variables

▶ Functions and procedures

Before we come to each of these in turn, let's consider why it's necessary to have a naming scheme at all.

Why Have a Standard Naming Scheme?

Naming standards can help prevent costly and embarrassing mistakes. By adopting a set of standards and by sticking to them, you're guaranteeing that in x months time, when you return to debug or change some code, you'll understand what you were trying to say back when it was written.

Think about road signs. Imagine how confusing it would be if each town in the country had different designs and standards for their road signs. Each time you came to a new town, you'd waste valuable reaction time trying to understand unfamiliar drawings and symbols, time that is better spent on the job - driving.

The same applies to programming. With a decent set of programming standards, your code can, in many ways, becoming self-documenting; reading such code could be as easy as reading a book about it.

Take a look at this - it's a program that your boss has just given you which has a bug in it, and you have ten minutes to fix it.

```
For a = 1 To z

d(a) = d(a) - cv(d(a))
q(a) = q(a) + d(a)
v(a) = cv(d(a))

next a
```

Impossible! You can't make any sense of it. There's no indication of what the code does, or what the variables are that it deals with. As a contrast, look at the same piece of code, now with some standards applied:

```
For nInvNo = 1 to nTotalNumberOfInvoices

nPrice(nInvNo) = nPrice(nInvNo) - Vat(nPrice(nInvNo))
nBalance(nInvNo) = nBalance(nInvNo) + nPrice(nInvNo)
nVat(nInvNo) = Vat(nPrice(nInvNo))

Next
```

Here, the code is spaced out to make it easier to read, and the variables now have sensible names. It's obvious that the code is dealing with invoice totals, in particular the outstanding balance of an invoice, the amount payable and the VAT (sales tax).

From this it's easy to see that the bug is in the first line. `vat` should be added to the price, not subtracted.

Naming Controls

The objective, when naming a control, is to help anyone reading the text to understand two things about the control that the code refers to:

▶ What kind of control is it? Each control has a unique three letter **prefix** that tells you what kind of control it is.

▶ What does the control do? Does this command button exit the form, or print the data? This function is described by the **usage identifier**.

Each control name is, therefore, made up of a prefix followed by a usage identifier:

Prefix   *Usage identifier*

`cmdExit`

Control Prefixes

A three letter prefix is used to identify the type of control, and to make it clear which names in your code are variables and which are controls.

The control prefixes I use are as follows:

Prefix	Control
cbo	Combo box
cfrm	MDI Child Form
chk	Checkbox
cls	Class Module
dat	Data control
dir	Directory list box
dlg	Common dialogs
drv	Drive list box
fil	File list box
fra	Frame
frm	Form
gph	Graphic control (lines, boxes and circles)
grd	Grid
hsb	Horizontal Scroll Bar
img	Image control
lbl	Label
lst	List box
mdifrm	MDI Form
mnu	Menu
obj	A generic object, perhaps derived from a class
ole	OLE control
opt	Option/Radio buttons
pic	Picture Box
tim	Timer
txt	Text box
vsb	Vertical Scroll Bar

The lin and shp names that are in the Visual Basic manuals for Line and Shape have been ignored here. This is purely a question of personal taste; I rarely use the graphical controls so I use the same prefix for all of them, namely gph.

Naming Custom Controls

There's a temptation with custom controls that you add in to projects, to use the brand name of the product as the prefix. Don't do it! If you decide later on to switch to a control from another supplier, then you'll have to change all your code. The safe way to do it is to use a name that describes the function of the control. For example, if you're using the Image Knife control, don't use the prefix `knf`; instead, use something like `imp` (**im**age processing).

Choosing a Control Usage Identifier

When choosing the main part of the name for a control, your aim should be to convey a clear idea about what that control is used for in the code. You can use one or more English words that clearly define this usage. General rules that are worth following include:

> ▶ Use capital letters for parts of the name.

> ▶ Underscore characters can be used to separate the words of the name (this is left to your personal preference).

> ▶ You can make the name as long, or as short, as you like. If it's too short, though, it probably won't tell you anything, and if it's too long, you're giving yourself a lot of typing to do - a sensible limit is about 15 characters.

There are some limitations to the names you can use. For example, you can't create variables that have identical names to Visual Basic keywords. Equally, you can't start a variable name with a number, or with a special character, such as $,%,^,&,*.

Example Control Names

First the bad names. These are all too cryptic to be useful:

```
Text1     Combo     A_Form      txtDSADSXZ chkB
Alfred    Henry     God_Knows
```

Don't laugh! I've seen all these in Visual Basic programs!

These, on the other hand, are much nicer:

```
txtSurname        cboEmployees        frmMainForm
chkSex            txtEmpCode
```

Naming Variables

When naming a variable, there is a piece of information we need to include, in addition to its type and a description of its usage: its scope. Controls are all local to the form on which they are placed, but variables can be either local, global or static.

The format of a typical variable name is:

Scope Prefix Usage identifier

gsUserName

Variable Scope

The scope part of the name consists of a single letter prefix to the variable name.

Prefix	Variable Name
g	Global variables - variables defined with the `Public` keyword.
m	Module level variables -, defined with `Dim` or `Private` in the declarations section of a form (`.FRM`) or module (`.BAS`).
no prefix	All local variables, - those defined using `Dim`, `Private` or `Static` in a function or procedure -, have no prefix.

Variable Type

Just as with scope, a single alphabetic character can be used to define the type of a variable, such as string, integer, and so on. These **type** letters are as follows:

Character	Type of Variable
s	String
i	Integer
l	Long (a large integer)
f	Floating point number, both singles and doubles
c	Currency
var	Variant
b	Boolean
d	Date

Choosing a Variable Usage Identifier

The rules for naming variables are similar to those for controls. Never use quick names for variables, such as the traditional **X, Y, I, J, Z**. An experienced programmer knows that **I** means an Integer index in a **For** loop, but a beginner might not. Badly named variables can lead to you using them in the wrong place in your code, such as typing **I** where you meant to type **J**, and so on. If you've taken the time to declare a variable for a particular purpose, then take the time to give it a useful name!

Example Variable Names

To summarize, some examples of variable names are:

gsUserName	A global string holding a user name.
iCounter	An integer used as a counter of some kind.
bMale	A boolean value, true represents male.
mdDate	A module level date.

Declaring Variable Data Types

Although Visual Basic supports the use of type identifiers such as $ for string, and % for integer, they're really only a hang over from the original ANSI specification for BASIC. Type identifiers can easily be mistyped. Notice how $ is next to % on the keyboard. Also, they don't jump out at you when you re-read a buggy section of code for the 12th time, and they look cryptic if your code is handed to a beginner.

▶ When declaring data types, *always* use the data type name, such as **String** instead of **$** and so on.

▶ Remember never to leave the data type off a declaration, as this results in you defining a variant, which would probably mean your variable name is wrong.

Object Variables

Most object variables are controls, so you just go ahead and name them as you would a normal control. However, object variables relating to databases are named along the same lines as controls. The prefixes to use are:

Prefix	Variable
dyn	Dynaset type recordset
tbl	Table type recordset
snp	Snapshot type recordset
db	Database
rec	Recordset
que	Query type recordset

Naming Functions and Procedures

Function and procedure names should reflect the purpose of the procedure or function, using English words.

Naming Functions

Functions always return a value and, where possible, should be given a name that reflects the return value. A function that returns the square root of a number should simply be called `Square_Root`, or `Square_Root_Of`, rather than `Calculate_Square_Root`. You can tell if a function has been given a good name by seeing how the code reads:

```
fRoot = Square_Root_Of ( 36 )      ' This is good!
fRoot = ClcSqrRt( 36 )             ' This is bad, read aloud!
```

Naming Procedures

The same amount of thought should be given to procedure names. Procedures generally perform a task, such as clearing a list box, or changing a frame layout. The task the procedure performs should be reflected in the name.

```
Remove_Borders Frame1     ' Easy enough!
RBF1_V1 Frame1            ' No idea - bad name!
```

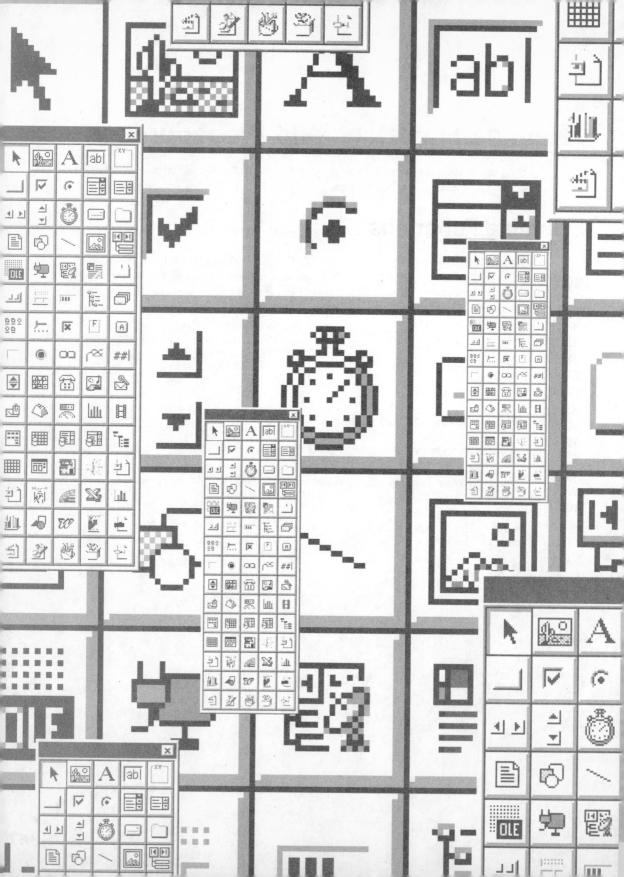

BEGINNER'S VB4

Index

Symbols

.AVI 150
.BAS 238
.BAT 150
.BMP 116
.EXE 60
.FRM 52
.ICO 67
.MDB 440
.MID 150
.TXT 150
.VBP 24
.WAV 150
.WMF 116
+ (plus) 198
- (minus) 198
* (multiply) 198
/ (divide) 198
\ (integer divide) 198
< (less than) 145
< = (less than or equal to) 145
< > (not equal to) 145
= (equals) 145
> (greater than) 145
> = (greater than or equal to) 145
| (Filter property) 327

A

About boxes
  graphics 383
Access database 436
  BIBLIO.MDB 440
Action parameter 513 - 514
Add 754
Add File... 14
  individual files within project 55
Add-Ins
  plug-in progams 12
Align property
  MDI parent forms 606
Alignment 109
  grid
    postioning controls 85
  property 444
ANIMATE.VBP
  changing images at run-time 381
API
  calls 772, 774
    declaring 774
    FlashWindow() function 772
    GetActiveWindow() function 772
    mciSendString() function 772
    RemoveMenu 772
    SetClassLong() function 772
    SetParent() function 772
  classes 779 - 780
    multimedia 780 - 784

Wrox Press Present
Their New *Bestselling* Author

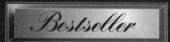

Could This Be You?

Have you ever thought to yourself "I could do better than that"?

Well here's your chance to prove it! Wrox Press are continually looking for

new authors and contributors. It doesn't matter if you've never been published before.

If you are a professional programmer, or simply a great developer,

we'd be very interested to hear from you.

Contact John Franklin at:

Wrox Press, Unit 16, 20 James Road, Birmingham, B11 2BA, UK

from US call: **800 814 3461**

or

e-mail: **johnf@wrox.com**

compuserve: **100063,2152**

WIN FREE BOOKS

TELL US WHAT YOU THINK!

Complete and return the bounce back card and you will:

- Help us create the books you want.
- Receive an update on all Wrox titles.
- Enter the draw for 5 Wrox titles of your choice.

FILL THIS OUT to enter the draw for free Wrox titles

Name _____

Address _____

_____

_____

Postcode/Zip _____

Occupation _____

How did you hear about this book?

- ☐ Book review (name) _____
- ☐ Advertisement (name) _____
- ☐ Recommendation
- ☐ Catalogue
- ☐ Other _____

Where did you buy this book?

- ☐ Bookstore (name) _____
- ☐ Computer Store (name) _____
- ☐ Mail Order
- ☐ Other _____

would be interested in receiving information about Wrox Press titles
y email in future. My email/Internet address is:

What influenced you in the purchase of this book?

- ☐ Cover Design
- ☐ Contents
- ☐ Other (please specify) _____

How did you rate the overall contents of this book?

- ☐ Excellent   ☐ Good
- ☐ Average   ☐ Poor

What did you find most useful about this book? _____

What did you find least useful about this book? _____

Please add any additional comments. _____

What other subjects will you buy a computer book on soon? _____

What is the best computer book you have used this year? _____

Note: This information will only be used to keep you updated about new Wrox Press titles and will not be used for any other purpose or passed to any other third party.

WROX

WROX PRESS INC.

Wrox writes books for you. Any suggestions, or ideas about how you want information given in your ideal book will be studied by our team. Your comments are always valued at WROX.

Free phone in USA 800 814 4527
Fax (312) 465 4063

Compuserve 100063,2152.
UK Tel: (44121) 706 6826   Fax   (44121) 706 2967

——— Computer Book Publishers ———

NB. If you post the bounce back card below in the UK, please send it to:
Wrox Press Ltd. Unit 16, Sapcote Industrial Estate, 20 James Road, Birmingham, B11 2BA